P9-CBD-803

Intimate Relationships

3478

The McGraw-Hill Social Psychology Series

This popular series of paperback titles is written by authors about their particular field of expertise and is meant to complement any social psychology course. The series includes:

Berkowitz, Leonard: *Aggression: Its Causes, Consequences, and Control*

Brehm, Sharon S., and Rowland S. Miller, Daniel Perlman and Susan M. Campbell: *Intimate Relationships, 3/e*

Brown, Jonathon: *The Self*

Burn, Shawn, M.: *The Social Psychology of Gender*

Brannigan, Gary G., and Matthew Merrens: *The Social Psychologists: Research Adventures*

Ellyson, Steve L. and Amy G. Halberstadt: *Explorations in Social Psychology: Readings and Research*

Fiske, Susan T. and Shelley E. Taylor: *Social Cognition, 2/e*

Schroeder, David, Louis Penner, John Dovidio, and Jane Piliavan: *The Psychology of Helping and Altruism: Problems and Puzzles*

Keough, Kelli A., and Julio Garcia: *Social Psychology of Gender, Race, and Ethnicity: Readings and Projects*

Milgram, Stanley: *The Individual in a Social World, 2/e*

Myers, David G.: *Exploring Social Psychology, 2/e*

Pines, Ayala M. and Christina Maslach: *Experiencing Social Psychology: Readings and Projects, 4/e*

Plous, Scott: *The Psychology of Judgment and Decision Making*

Ross, Lee and Richard E. Nisbett: *The Person and the Situation: Perspectives of Social Psychology*

Rubin, Jeffrey Z., Dean G. Pruitt, and Sung Hee Kim: *Social Conflict: Escalation, Stalemate, and Settlement, 2/e*

Triandis, Harry C.: *Culture and Social Behavior*

Zimbardo, Philip G. and Michael R. Leippe: *The Psychology of Attitude Change and Social Influence*

Intimate Relationships

THIRD EDITION

Sharon S. Brehm
Indiana University Bloomington

Rowland S. Miller
Sam Houston State University

Daniel Perlman
University of British Columbia

Susan M. Campbell
Middlebury College

Boston   Burr Ridge, IL   Dubuque, IA   Madison, WI   New York
San Francisco   St. Louis   Bangkok   Bogotá   Caracas   Kuala Lumpur
Lisbon   London   Madrid   Mexico City   Milan   Montreal   New Delhi
Santiago   Seoul   Singapore   Sydney   Taipei   Toronto

McGraw-Hill Higher Education

A Division of The **McGraw-Hill** Companies

INTIMATE RELATIONSHIPS, THIRD EDITION

Published by McGraw-Hill, a business unit of The McGraw-Hill Companies, Inc., 1221 Avenue of the Americas, New York, NY 10020. Copyright © 2002, 1992, 1985 by The McGraw-Hill Companies, Inc. All rights reserved. No part of this publication may be reproduced or distributed in any form or by any means, or stored in a database or retrieval system, without the prior written consent of The McGraw-Hill Companies, Inc., including, but not limited to, in any network or other electronic storage or transmission, or broadcast for distance learning.

Some ancillaries, including electronic and print components, may not be available to customers outside the United States.

This book is printed on acid-free paper.

5 6 7 8 9 0 DOC/DOC 0 9 8 7 6 5 4 3

ISBN 0–07–007452–6

Editorial director: *Jane E. Karpacz*
Senior sponsoring editor: *Rebecca H. Hope*
Developmental editor: *Rita Lombard*
Marketing manager: *Chris Hall*
Project manager: *Sheila M. Frank*
Production supervisor: *Enboge Chong*
Coordinators of freelance design: *Michelle M. Meerdink/Rick D. Noel*
Cover designer: *Michael Warrell, Design Solutions*
Cover image: *©SuperStock Inc., Picnic in May, 1873, Merse (no. 8621160)*
Senior photo research coordinator: *Carrie K. Burger*
Photo research: *Chris Hammond*
Supplement producer: *Tammy Juran*
Compositor: *Precision Graphics*
Typeface: *10/12 Palatino*
Printer: *R. R. Donnelley & Sons Company/Crawfordsville, IN*

The credits section for this book begins on page 531 and is considered an extension of the copyright page.

Library of Congress Cataloging-in-Publication Data

Intimate relationships / Sharon S. Brehm . . . [et al.].
    p. cm. — (McGraw-Hill series in social psychology)
  Rev. ed. of: Intimate relationships / Sharon S. Brehm. 2nd ed. 1992.
  Includes bibliographical references and index.
  ISBN 0–07–007452–6
  1. Family life education. 2. Interpersonal relations. I. Brehm, Sharon. II. Brehm,
Sharon. Intimate relationships. III. Series.

  HQ10 .I58   2002
  306.7'07—dc21   2001030345
                                                       CIP

www.mhhe.com

Contents

Part Two
GETTING TOGETHER AND BASIC PROCESSES IN INTIMATE RELATIONSHIPS

Part Three
FRIENDSHIP AND INTIMACY

Part Four
RELATIONSHIP ISSUES

Foreword

Intimate relationships are at the core of the human experience—forming the basic plot line in life's drama across all its stages. We are attracted to some people, come to like and love some, have romantic and sexual relationships with some, marry and give support and comfort to partners, and suffer when those relationships end sadly. Intimate relationships fulfill basic human needs for belonging and caring, they involve strong emotional attachments to others, and often interdependence with others as well. It is now well known that the single best protection anyone can have against the risks of many mental or physical illnesses is being part of a viable social support network. Intimate relationships provide meaningful, often enduring, networks of social support, of other people we can call upon when distressed, and in turn give aid and care to others when they are in need. When middle-aged successful business people are asked how their lives might be different if they had to do it all over again, none ever says they would work more; rather, they say they would love more and spend more time with family and friends.

Given the obvious centrality of intimate relationships in our lives, it is curious that the topic is relatively new in the history of social psychology. It has emerged as an exciting field of research and practice only in the past few decades. Previously, scholarly interest had been in dyads and small groups studied in structured relationships, often public ones, as people compete or cooperate, negotiate and bargain, conform, comply, or resist. But a hardy band of researchers, including the authors of this book, began to demonstrate that it was possible to investigate the subtle features of interpersonal dynamics, to understand some of the ingredients that go into liking, loving, and sexual relationships. As research unfolded, the net of interested investigators extended from social psychology to personality, to cognitive psychology, to developmental psychology, to evolutionary psychology, to sociology, to family studies, to communication studies, and home economics. Each perspective now contributes new insights and fresh ideas about the nature of intimate relationships.

I believe that one impetus to the growth of this field of study has been the first and second editions of Sharon Brehm's *Intimate Relationships* book in this McGraw-Hill Social Psychology Series. Hers were not only the most successful of any of our monographs in terms of sales, but their broad appeal to faculty and students alike also illustrated to researchers the significance of this area of investigation that Sharon's writing had conveyed so effectively. What she accomplished in her landmark books was to create an authoritative, scholarly text that could be respected by her colleagues, and an accessible, warm, and enjoyable to read book that could be embraced by her student readers.

So what is there left to do in this revision of such a successful book? The new team of Sharon Brehm, Rowland Miller, Daniel Perlman, and Susan Campbell worked hard to retain its core values and its friendly, lively "voice" that speaks so eloquently to the reader, while reflecting the current discipline's state-of-the-art. This third incarnation of *Intimate Relationships* is a thorough update, much more than a simple revision, as can be seen in the hundreds of new references, many to research, theory, and popular articles published in the past few years. Three entirely new chapters reflect current directions in this field, among them, chapter 4 on Social Cognition, chapter 7 on Friendship, and chapter 13 on Dissolution and Divorce. Structural changes also enhance the new presentation, such as introducing core concepts up front in the first chapter and then developing them more fully in subsequent chapters, among them, attachment styles, gender roles, and evolutionary social psychology. The "big ideas" that now organize the field of study are accorded privileged attention throughout, with key terms highlighted in bold font where they first appear.

Other pedagogical innovations include the use of boxed material in each chapter that illustrates the currency and relevance of this new book to this generation of students, such as chat room communication, or self-assessment of opening line skills, or dealing with betrayals. A similar focus on providing pragmatic advice to enhance intimate relationships shows up in new sections on improving communication to be more clear and kind and effective. Taken together, the updating and revising of content, the new structural platform for highlighting both basic and applied ideas, and practical advice to the reader all combine to make this a worthy successor to the previous editions. I anticipate that *Intimate Relationships Third Edition*, will be even more successful than its predecessors, thus stimulating further growth in this challenging field of social psychology.

And now a commercial break for our series. This innovative McGraw-Hill Series in Social Psychology has been designed as a celebration of the fundamental contributions being made by researchers, theorists, and practitioners of social psychology to improving our understanding of the nature of human nature and enriching the quality of our lives. It has become a showcase for presenting new theories, original syntheses, analyses, and current methodologies by distinguished scholars and promising young writer-researchers. Common to all of our authors is the commitment to sharing their vision with an audience that starts with their colleagues but extends out to graduate students, undergraduates, and all those with an interest in social psychology. Some of our titles convey ideas that are of sufficient general interest that their message needs to be carried out into the world of practical application to those who may translate some of them into public action and public policy. Although each text in our series is created to stand alone as the best representative of its area of scholarship, taken as a whole, they represent the core of social psychology. Many teachers have elected to use them as "in-depth" supplements to a basic, general textbook, while others organize their course entirely around a set of these monographs. Each of our authors has been guided by the goal of conveying the essential lessons and principles of her or his area of expertise in an interesting style, that informs without resorting to technical jargon, that inspires readers to share their excitement by joining in utilizing these ideas, or in participating in the research endeavor to create new and better ideas.

I welcome new co-authors, Rowland (Rody) Miller, Daniel Perlman and Susan Campbell, as the newest members of this special society of educators, along with my dear long-time friend, Sharon Brehm. And I welcome you, dear reader, to join the group of similarly situated students who will enjoy and benefit from the scholarship, wonderfully engaging writing style, and the obvious dedication of this team of authors to the science of social psychology as translated into this exciting literary form.

Philip G. Zimbardo
Series Consulting Editor

Preface

Is there anything more important to us than our relationships with others? Our health, perhaps, but think about it: Where would you be without close, meaningful attachments to other people? Would you have even been born? Would you have survived childhood? Probably not. Throughout our lives, our relationships are often sources of invaluable joy and support and, sometimes, stress and sorrow. Love 'em or hate 'em, win or lose, we find it extremely hard to do without them. People suffer without intimate connections to others.

Indeed, close relationships have always elicited curiosity and comment. Ancient philosophers analyzed them, and today, authors, songwriters, grandmothers—indeed, nearly all of us—have observations about relationships. In recent years, social scientists have been systematically studying them, too, adding their wisdom to the insights that abound in cultures around the world. This work has been enormously productive, and in this book, now in its third edition, we synthesize and share with you what social scientists have learned about intimate relationships.

The Broad Goals of Intimate Relationships, *Second and Third Editions*

In her preface to the second edition of *Intimate Relationships*, Sharon Brehm described her book as "a concise overview of developments in the field." She said:

> The primary audience for whom the book is intended consists of undergraduate students and their instructors. Written in clear, everyday language, the text provides numerous examples from everyday life. It does not, however, avoid complex issues involving research findings and theoretical interpretations. In short, the text sustains the personal appeal of the subject matter and maintains rigorous standards of scholarship.

The second edition of *Intimate Relationships* was published in 1992. Since then, relationship science has been much like "a boomtown during the gold rush days of the American West." Much has happened. Many of the details of the second edition needed updating, and a new team of authors has completely updated the book from start to finish. In many respects, this is a brand new text. But some things haven't changed. The core qualities that made the first and second editions of the book so successful are as cherished today as when the book first appeared. The third edition preserves the personal appeal of the subject matter, the rigorous standards of scholarship, and the reader-friendly tone that Brehm established and communicated so well.

Like the second edition, *Intimate Relationships, Third Edition,* provides a concise overview of the field aimed toward middle level undergraduate students. We convey to readers the key findings, the major theoretical perspectives, and some of the current questions in the field. The presentation demonstrates the relevance of relationship science to readers' everyday lives, encouraging thought and analysis but not prescribing action.

Intimate Relationships: The Field of Study

The modern study of close relationships is a multidisciplinary enterprise. The authors of the third edition are social psychologists, but volumes of work from other disciplines (e.g., family studies, communications, social gerontology, and sociology) are featured in the book. The new edition is as multidisciplinary as the science it reports. Furthermore, we sought to capture the leading edge of research in a thoroughgoing manner, but we also respect the importance of older work in the field. Thus, we honor classic contributions to relationship science at various points throughout the text.

Intimate partnerships involve behavioral interdependence, need fulfillment, and emotional attachment to friends or romantic partners. While there are unique features to various specific types of relationships, there are also generic relationship processes that occur in all intimate partnerships. Both are portrayed in this text.

Changes in Content

The third edition of this book retains the developmental backbone of the previous edition but some changes in organization have occurred.

Main Sections of Intimate Relationships, Second and Third Editions

Second Edition	Third Edition
Introduction	Introduction
Getting Together	Getting Together and Basic Processes
Progress and Fairness in the Relationship	Friendship and Intimacy
Relationship Issues	Relationship Issues
When a Relationship Ends	Losing and Enhancing Relationships
Improving Intimate Relationships	

Like the second edition, *Intimate Relationships, Third Edition,* has 15 chapters. Eight of its chapters are very similar to chapters in the second edition: Methods, Attraction, Love, Sexuality, Communication, Power, Loneliness, and the Promotion, Enhancement and Repair of Intimate Relationships. Other chapters combine or expand topics that appeared in individual chapters previously. A new interdependence chapter in the third edition combines the material on interdependence and equity (chapters 6 and 7) in the second edition. Jealousy is covered in the new edition as part of a stresses and strains chapter instead of appearing in a separate chapter of its own. Additionally, the third edition devotes entire chapters to conflict and the dissolution and loss of relationships instead of considering them in a single chapter as was previously done. Two chapters from the second edition have been dropped—Social Networks and Relationships Tomorrow—although vital material from those chapters is retained in other chapters of the third edition. Most importantly, this edition covers several *new* topics that have become important to the field. Brand new chapters on social cognition and friendship appear in the third edition. A variety of additional topics such as Internet friendships, deception, and betrayal are now included in the book. And several key topics—such as attachment styles, evolutionary social psychology, and nonverbal communication—now receive ample coverage that befits their importance to modern relationship science.

Recurrent Themes

Chapter 1 now introduces core influences on relationships—human nature, culture, experience, individual differences, and interaction between partners—and sets the stage for examining these influences as recurring themes throughout the book. In particular, gender and ethnic factors in relationships are repeatedly considered. In addition, two other themes recur throughout the book:

1. Theories provide frameworks for understanding many different aspects of relationships, and
2. Relationships are beneficial, yet problematic.

A life-span perspective has been used as one component of both the friendship and loneliness chapters, and life-span issues crop up elsewhere as well. Diverse theoretical formulations are covered in the third edition (i.e., cognitive consistency, developmental, dialectical, reinforcement, etc.), but three are featured: attachment, evolutionary, and interdependence. Besides explicitly developed themes, there are a few more implicit recurring foci and/or concerns. These include such matters as the affective, cognitive and behavioral elements of relationships; the question of the extent to which current vs. childhood factors determine the success of adult relationships; and our need for a balance between contact and solitude.

Student Orientation

Intimate Relationships is a book written to inform and benefit its readers. Several features of this edition are designed to help achieve that goal. A first step in connecting with readers is picking and framing questions in ways that have relevance to them. We try to present information in a down-to-earth, yet dynamic way that makes the flow of ideas intrinsically engaging. We strive to give students more systematic analyses, facts, figures, and even some questions that most wouldn't have had prior to reading the book. We think that if we can arouse responses like "That's interesting, I didn't know that," "Now I understand," or even "That's a crucial question I hadn't thought of," we will have achieved one measure of success.

We also take pride in writing in a clear, well-organized style, and have tried to package our information so it can be readily grasped. We carefully define terms and have continued the tradition of the second edition of having both abbreviated tables of contents at the beginning of each chapter and strong summaries at the end. We also realize that good scholarship need not lack a sense of humor—a touch of wit here and there helps us achieve our goal of informing and benefiting readers.

We seek to describe relationship science in an engaging, coherent, and straightforward way. But we also want readers to recognize that there are multiple schools of thinking that don't always agree with one another. Where we can, we give particular attention to comprehensive reviews of a literature, especially meta-analytic summaries. We also acknowledge differences among cultures. We also often provide descriptive information about research studies (e.g., the subject populations, the procedures employed, and the nature of the data) that helps readers put themselves in the place of the studies' participants to more critically evaluate the studies' results.

In addition, we seek to give readers cohesive, cumulative insights as they proceed through the volume. This has been fostered in two ways. First, the book explains key theoretical constructs early on, and then uses them whenever they are relevant to aid understanding of later issues. Second, each of the book's chapters covers a specific topic, but because relationship phenomena are not compartmentalized, connections to other elements of relationships are frequently mentioned.

Intimate Relationships, Third Edition, also continues the tradition of including personality inventories and other scales that students can use to enhance their understanding of themselves and their relationships. This edition also introduces new special focus boxes that address a variety of short topics that augment each chapter's main material.

For Instructors

A new Instructor's Manual and Test Bank is available for instructors. It contains standard test questions (e.g., multiple choice, completion, and essay). It also features some broader questions to help students integrate material from the whole course, selected popular films on personal relationships, and possible paper assignments. Dan Perlman d.Perlman@ubc.ca maintains a course website and does item analyses of questions from our test bank. He is happy to share these with you. Instructors may also wish to contact the International Society for the Study of Personal Relationships http://www.isspr.org/ and the

International Network on Personal Relationships http://www.inpr.org/; both offer teaching materials and/or tips. (As this volume goes to press, ISSPR and INPR are considering a merger, so the new organization may have a new name.)

A Partnership

This book is about relationships, and, as far as we're concerned, one very important partnership is the one that exists between us, its authors, and you, our reader. We've endeavored to make this edition the best we possibly can. But we realize that in reading it, you may want to throw bricks, send bouquets, or just tell us how you think we could do even better next time. Whichever your preference, we invite your feedback. Write either Rody Miller, Psy_RSM@Shsu.edu, or Dan Perlman, d.perlman@UBC.CA. Please let us know what works and what needs improvement. As Ralph Waldo Emerson said, "'Tis the good reader that makes the good book."

We wish you a good read. And feel free to share your experience with a friend or loved one. We hope the book will benefit you and your relationships, and to both you and your intimate partners, we wish a "bon voyage" in reading and, more importantly, in relating.

PART ONE

Introduction to the Study of Intimate Relationships

The Building Blocks of Relationships

THE NATURE AND IMPORTANCE OF INTIMACY ◆ The Nature of Intimacy ◆ The Need to Belong ◆ THE INFLUENCE OF CULTURE ◆ Sources of Change ◆ THE INFLUENCE OF EXPERIENCE ◆ THE INFLUENCE OF INDIVIDUAL DIFFERENCES ◆ Sex Differences ◆ Gender Differences ◆ Personality ◆ Self-Concepts and Self-Esteem ◆ THE INFLUENCE OF HUMAN NATURE ◆ THE INFLUENCE OF INTERACTION ◆ THE DARK SIDE OF RELATIONSHIPS ◆ CHAPTER SUMMARY

Talk to a friend. Listen to a song. Watch a movie. At some point, the conversation, the lyrics, or the plot will probably touch on the topic of relationships. We think about relationships so much because they are a central aspect of our lives: a source of great joy when things go well, but a cause of great sorrow when they go poorly. We're curious. Most of us want to understand how our relationships get started, how they grow, and how, sometimes, they end in a haze of anger and pain. When it comes to relationships, we are all on a lifelong voyage of discovery.

This book will promote your own process of discovery. Drawing on psychology, sociology, communication studies, and family studies, it describes what social scientists have learned about relationships through careful research. This is a different, more scientific view of relationships than you'll find in song lyrics or the movies; it's more reasoned, more cautious, and often less romantic. You'll also find that this book is not a how-to manual. Intimacy takes many forms, and there is no magic formula for a satisfying relationship. Instead, each of us must bring his or her beliefs, values, and personal experiences to bear on the information presented here. The purposes of this book are to guide you through the diverse foci of relationship science and to help you arrive at your own conclusions about relationships.

To set the stage for the discoveries to come, we'll first define our subject matter. What are intimate relationships? Why do they matter so much? Then, we'll consider the fundamental building blocks of close relationships: the cultures we inhabit, the experiences we encounter, the personalities we possess, the human origins we all share, and the interactions we conduct. In order to understand relationships, we must first comprehend who we are, *where* we are, and how we got there.

THE NATURE AND IMPORTANCE OF INTIMACY

People have all kinds of relationships with each other. They have parents and may have children; they have colleagues at work or school; they encounter grocery clerks, physicians, and office receptionists; they have friends; and they have lovers. This book concentrates on just the last two types of partnerships, which exemplify *intimate* relationships. Our primary focus is on intimate relationships between adults (although we do discuss childhood friendships in chapter 7).

The Nature of Intimacy

What, then, is intimacy? The answer can depend on whom you ask, because intimacy is a multifaceted concept with several different components (Perlman & Fehr, 1987; Prager, 1995). However, both researchers (Chelune, Robison, & Kommor, 1984; Walster, Walster, & Berscheid, 1978) and laypeople (Marston et al., 1998; Monsour, 1992; Parks & Floyd, 1996) agree that intimate relationships differ from more casual associations in at least six specific ways: **knowledge, caring, interdependence, mutuality, trust,** and **commitment.**

First, intimate partners have extensive personal, often confidential, *knowledge* about each other. They share information about their histories, preferences, feelings, and desires that they do not reveal to most of the other people they know. Intimate partners also *care* about each other, feeling more affection for one another than they do for most others.

Their lives are also intertwined: What each partner does affects what the other partner wants to do and can do. *Interdependence* between intimates—the extent to which they need and influence each other—is frequent (they often affect each other), strong (they have a meaningful impact on each other), diverse (they influence each other in many different ways), and enduring (they influence each other over long periods of time). When relationships are interdependent, one's behavior affects one's partner as well as oneself.

As a result of these close ties, people who are intimate also consider themselves to be a couple instead of two entirely separate individuals. They exhibit a high degree of *mutuality,* which means that they recognize the overlap between their lives and think themselves as "us" instead of "me" and "her" (or "him") (Levinger & Snoek, 1972). In fact, that change in outlook—from "I" to "us"—often signals the subtle but significant moment in a developing relationship when new partners first acknowledge their attachment to each other (Agnew, Van Lange, Rusbult, & Langston, 1998).

A quality that makes these close ties tolerable is *trust,* the expectation that an intimate partner will treat one fairly and honorably (Holmes, 1991). People expect that no undue harm will result from their intimate relationships, and when such trust is lost, they often become wary and reduce the openness and interdependence that characterize closeness (Jones, Crouch, & Scott, 1997).

Finally, intimate partners are ordinarily *committed* to their relationships. That is, they expect their partnerships to continue indefinitely, and they invest the time, effort, and resources that are needed to realize that goal. Without such commitment, people who were once very close may find themselves less and less interdependent and knowledgeable about each other as time goes by and they slowly drift apart.

None of these components is absolutely required for intimacy to occur, and each may exist when the others are absent. For instance, spouses in a stale, unhappy marriage may be very interdependent, closely coordinating the practical details of their daily lives, but still live in a psychological vacuum devoid of much affection, openness, or trust. Such partners would certainly be more intimate than mere acquaintances are, but they would undoubtedly feel less close to one another than they used to (for instance, when they decided to marry), when more of the components were present. In general, our most satisfying and meaningful intimate relationships include all six of these defining characteristics (Fletcher, Simpson, & Thomas, 2000). Still, intimacy can exist to a lesser degree when only some of them are in place. And as unhappy marriages demonstrate, intimacy can also vary enormously over the entire course of a relationship.

Thus, there is no one kind of intimate relationship (Haslam & Fiske, 1999). Indeed, perhaps the most fundamental lesson about relationships is a very simple one: They come in all shapes and sizes. This variety is a source of great complexity, but it can also be a source of endless fascination. (And that's why we wrote this book!)

The Need to Belong

Our focus on intimate relationships means that we will not consider a wide variety of the interactions that you have with others each day. For instance, we will not examine the relationships you have with most of your classmates. Should we be so particular? Is such a focus justified? The answers, of course, are yes. Although our casual interactions with strangers, acquaintances, and others can be very influential (Miller, 2001), there's something special about intimate relationships. In fact, a powerful and pervasive drive to establish intimacy with others may be a basic part of our human nature. According to theorists Roy Baumeister and Mark Leary (1995), we *need* frequent, pleasant interactions with intimate partners in lasting, caring relationships if we're to function normally. There is a human **need to belong** in close relationships, and if the need is not met, a variety of problems follow.

Our need to belong is presumed to necessitate "regular social contact with those to whom one feels connected" (Baumeister & Leary, 1995, p. 501). In order to fulfill the need, we need (no pun intended) to establish and maintain close relationships with other people; only interaction and communion with those who know and care for us will do. We don't need many close relationships, just a few; when the need to belong is satiated, our drive to form additional relationships is reduced. (Thus, when it comes to relationships, quality is more important than quantity.) It also doesn't matter much *who* our partners are; as long as they provide us stable affection and acceptance, our need can be satisfied. Thus, if their spouses die after a long marriage, people are often able to find replacement partners who—though they may be quite different from their previous partners—are nonetheless able to satisfy the widow's or widower's need to belong.

Some of the support for this theory comes from the ease with which we form relationships with others and from the tenacity with which we then resist the dissolution of our existing social ties. Indeed, when a valued relationship is in peril, we may find it hard to think about anything else—and the resulting preoccupation and strong emotion show how much our partnerships mean to us. Consider, too, that we use solitary confinement, the deprivation of social interaction, as *punishment* for those who misbehave. For most people, being entirely alone for a long period of time is a surprisingly stressful experience (Schachter, 1959).

In fact, some of the strongest evidence supporting a need to belong comes from studies of people who have lost their close ties to others (Ryff & Singer, 2000). Such losses impair one's health (Levin, 2000). Spouses whose marriages have turned angry and antagonistic (Kiecolt-Glaser et al., 1993) or who have actually been divorced (Kiecolt-Glaser et al., 1987) have higher blood pressure and weaker immune systems than those whose relationships are happier. And if such people continue to leave their social needs unfulfilled, they're likely to die younger than those who are happily attached to others. Across the life span, people who have few friends or lovers have much higher mortality rates than do those who are closely connected to caring partners (Berkman & Glass, 2000); in one extensive study, people who lacked close ties to others were two to three times more likely to die over a nine-year span (Berkman & Syme, 1979).

The quality of our relationships also affects our mental health (Berscheid & Reis, 1998). People with satisfying marriages, for instance, are generally happier a year later than are those whose marriages are less pleasant (Ruvolo, 1998). And a variety of problems such as depression, alcoholism, eating disorders, and schizophrenia are more likely to afflict those whose social needs are unfulfilled than those who have adequate ties to others (Segrin, 1998). On the surface (as we explain in detail in chapter 2), such patterns do not necessarily mean that bad relationships *cause* such problems; after all, people who are prone to schizophrenia may find it difficult to form loving relationships in the first place. Nevertheless, it does appear that a lack of intimacy can both cause such problems and/or make them worse (Assh & Byers, 1996; Segrin, 1998). In general, our well-being seems to depend on how well we satisfy the need to belong.

Why should we need intimacy so much? Why are we such a social species? One possibility is that the need to belong *evolved* over eons, gradually becoming a natural tendency in all human beings (Baumeister & Leary, 1995). That argument goes this way: Because early humans lived in small tribal groups surrounded by a difficult environment full of saber-toothed tigers, people who were loners were less likely than gregarious humans to have children who would grow to maturity and reproduce. In such a setting, a tendency to form stable, affectionate connections to others would have been evolutionarily *adap-*

tive, giving those who possessed it a reproductive advantage. As a result, our species slowly came to be characterized by people who cared deeply about what others thought of them and who sought acceptance and closeness from others. Admittedly, this view—which represents a provocative way of thinking about our modern behavior (and about which we'll have more to say later in this chapter)—is speculative. Nevertheless, whether or not this evolutionary account is entirely correct, there is little doubt that now, in the twenty-first century, almost all of us care deeply about the quality of our attachments to others. We are also at a loss, prone to illness and maladjustment, when we have insufficient intimacy in our lives. We know that food, water, and shelter are essential for life, but the need to belong suggests that intimacy with others is essential for a good, long life as well.

Now, let's examine the major influences that will determine what sort of relationships we construct when we seek to satisfy the need to belong. We'll start with a counterpoint to our innate need for intimacy: the changing cultures that provide the norms that govern our intimate relationships.

THE INFLUENCE OF CULTURE

We know it seems like ancient history—cell phones and VCRs and the Internet and AIDS didn't exist—but let's look back at 1960, which may have been around the time that your grandparents were deciding to marry. If they were a typical couple, they would have married in their early twenties, before she was 21 and before he was 23.[1] They probably would not have lived together, or "cohabited," without being married, because almost no one did at that time. And it's also unlikely that they would have had a baby without being married; 95 percent of the children born in the United States in 1960 had parents who were married to each other. Once they settled in, your grandmother probably did not work outside the home—most women didn't—and when her kids were preschoolers, it's quite likely that she stayed home with them all day; most women did. It's also likely that their children—in particular, your mom or dad—grew up in a household in which both of their parents were present at the end of the day.

Now, however, things are different. The last several decades have seen dramatic changes in the cultural context in which we conduct our close relationships. Indeed, you shouldn't be surprised if your grandparents are astonished and consternated by the cultural landscape that *you* face today in the United States:

- Fewer people are marrying than ever before. Almost everyone (94 percent) married at some point in their lives in 1960, but more people remain unmarried today. Demographers now predict that only 85 percent of young adults will ever marry (Fletcher, 1999).

[1]These and the following statistics were obtained from the U.S. Census Bureau at www.census.gov and the U.S. National Center for Health Statistics at www.cdc.gov/nchswwww, and from various other reports, including Curtin & Martin, 2000; "Data Reveal," 1999; and Fletcher, 1999.

Compared with marriages that took place a generation ago, today's newlyweds are older, more likely to
have children from a previous marriage, and more
likely to be committed to their careers as well as to
their families.

- People are waiting longer to marry. A woman is now 25 years old, on average, when she marries for the first time, and a man is 27 (Schmid, 1996).
  That's much older than your grandparents probably were when they got
  married (see Figure 1.1). More than a third of all Americans now remain
  unmarried into their middle thirties, and *most* African-Americans (53 percent) have never married when they reach age 34 (U.S. Census Bureau,
  1998).
- People routinely live together even when they're not married. Cohabitation
  was very rare in 1960—only 5 percent of all adults ever did it—but it is now
  ordinary. Half of your classmates will at some time live with a lover without being married. In fact, almost one-third of American households (32
  percent) are made up of an unmarried man and woman living together
  ("Data reveal," 1999).
- People often have babies even when they're not married. This was an un-
  common event in 1960; only 5 percent of the babies born in the United
  States that year had unmarried mothers. Some children were *conceived* out
  of wedlock, but their parents usually got married before they were born.
  Not so now. In 1999, *one-third* (33 percent) of the babies born in the U.S. had
  mothers who were not married (Curtin & Martin, 2000).
- Nearly half of all marriages end in divorce. The likelihood that a married
  couple would someday divorce skyrocketed from 1960 to 1980 (see Figure
  1.2). The divorce rate peaked in the early 1980s and has since dropped

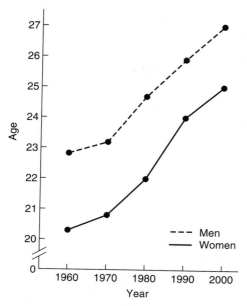

FIGURE 1.1. Average age of first marriage in the U.S. American men and women are waiting longer to get married than ever before.

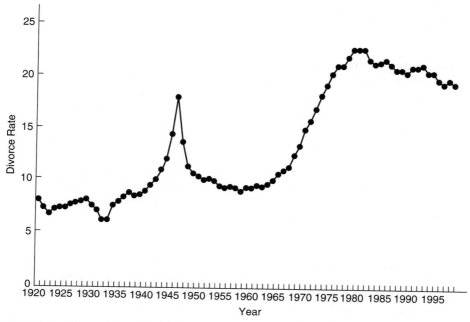

FIGURE 1.2. Divorce rates in the U.S. After an extraordinary increase from the mid-1960s to 1980, the American divorce rate has leveled off and even declined slightly in recent years. Note. The figure illustrates the divorce rate per 1,000 married women age 15 and older in the United States.

(Source: National Center for Health Statistics, 2000)

slightly, but divorces are still more than twice as common as they were when your grandparents married (Clarke, 1995; National Center for Health Statistics, 2000).

- Most children (about 60 percent) live in a single-parent home sometime during their childhoods (Eskey, 1992). As a result of the higher divorce and unmarried-birth rates, it's now *unlikely* that an American child will live with both parents throughout his or her entire youth. Indeed, at any one time, more than a quarter (28 percent) of the children in the U.S. are living with only one of their parents (U.S. Census Bureau, 1998).
- Most preschool children have mothers who work outside the home. In 1960, more than three-quarters of American mothers stayed home all day when their children were too young to go to school, but fewer than 40 percent of them do so now (Matthews & Rodin, 1989). Even if a child lives with both parents, neither of them is likely to be a full-time caregiver at home all day.

These remarkable changes suggest that some of our shared assumptions about the role that marriage and parenthood will play in our lives have changed substantially in recent years. Once upon a time, everybody got married, usually soon after they left college, and happy or sad, they were likely to stay with those partners. Pregnant people felt they *had* to get married, and cohabitation was known as "living in sin." But not so anymore. Marriage is now a *choice*, even if a baby is on the way, and increasing numbers of us are putting it off or not getting married at all. If we do marry, we're less likely to consider it a solemn, life-long commitment (Myers, 2000). In general, recent years have seen enormous change in the cultural norms that used to encourage people to get, and stay, married (Putnam, 2000; Stanfield & Stanfield, 1997).

Do these changes matter? Almost certainly they do. Cultural standards provide a foundation for our relationships (Huston, 2000); they shape our expectations and define what patterns are thought to be normal. In the view of some observers, Western cultures such as the United States have become "increasingly individualistic and hedonistic" since you were born (Glenn & Weaver, 1988, p. 323). As a result, we have come to expect more from our intimate partnerships—more pleasure and delight, and fewer hassles and sacrifices—even as cultural changes have made it easier to end a marriage or even avoid one altogether (Attridge & Berscheid, 1994). Consequently, fewer people get married and fewer marriages last.

Sources of Change

Thus, the patterns of your intimate relationships in the twenty-first century may differ from those experienced by prior generations, and there are undoubtedly several reasons why. One likely influence is our culture's increasing level of *socioeconomic development*. There is a general trend for a society to harbor more single people, tolerate more divorces, and support a later age of marriage the more industrialized and affluent it becomes (South, 1988). Education and financial resources allow people to travel more widely and be more independent. With more options, fewer of us may be motivated to tie ourselves to just one partner for our entire lives.

Western cultures also emphasize individual liberty, encouraging people to pursue personal fulfillment, and if anything, this *individualism* has become more pronounced in recent years (Myers, 2000). Eastern cultures promote a more collective sense of self in which people feel more closely tied to their families and social groups, and the divorce rates in such cultures (such as Japan) are much lower than they are in the United States (Triandis, McCusker, & Hui, 1990).

New *technology* matters, too. Modern reproductive technologies allow single women to bear children fathered by men picked from a catalog at a sperm bank whom the women have never met! In addition, more and more of our leisure time is absorbed by private, often solitary entertainments such as watching television or surfing the Web instead of socializing with friends or neighbors (Putnam, 2000). People who would have hosted parties in 1960 are now often sitting home alone watching video and computer screens.

However, an even more important—but more subtle—influence on the norms that govern relationships may be the relative numbers of young men and women in a given culture. Societies in which men are more numerous than women tend to have very different standards than those in which women outnumber men. We're describing a culture's **sex ratio,** a simple count of the number of men for every 100 women in a specific population. When the sex ratio is high, there are more men than women; when the sex ratio is low, there are fewer men than women. A sex ratio of 100 means that there are equal numbers of women and men. In the United States, women are usually in their twenties, marrying a man two years older (on average), when they marry for the first time; thus, relationship researchers usually compute sex ratios that compare the number of women to the number of men who are slightly older.

The baby boom that followed World War II caused the American sex ratio, which was very high in 1960, to plummet to low levels at the end of that decade. For a time after the war, more babies were born each year than in the preceding year; this meant that when the "boomers" entered adulthood, there were fewer older men than younger women, and the sex ratio dropped. However, when birthrates began to slow and fewer children entered the demographic pipeline, each new flock of women was smaller than the preceding flock of men, and the American sex ratio crept higher in the 1990s (see Figure 1.3). Since then, fairly stable birthrates among "boomer" parents have resulted in equal numbers of marriageable men and women today.

These changes may have been more important than most people realize. Cultures with high sex ratios (in which there aren't enough women) tend to support traditional, old-fashioned roles for men and women (Pedersen, 1991; Secord, 1983). The women stay home raising children while the men work outside the home. Such cultures also tend to be sexually conservative. The ideal newlywed is a virgin bride, unwed pregnancy is shameful, and open cohabitation is rare. Divorce is discouraged. In contrast, cultures with low sex ratios (in which there are too few men) tend to be less traditional and more permissive. Women are encouraged to work and support themselves, and they are allowed (if not encouraged) to have sexual relationships outside of marriage. If a pregnancy occurs, unmarried motherhood is an option.

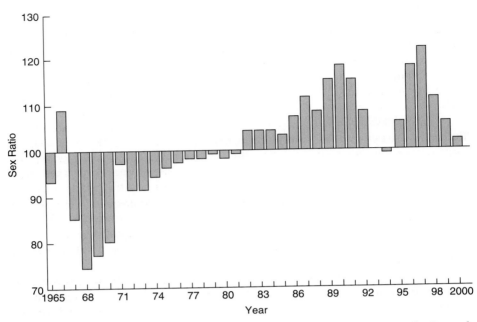

FIGURE 1.3. Sex ratios in the U.S. American sex ratios were very low during the "sexual revolution" of the late 1960s, but there were equal numbers of young men and women in the population as we entered the twenty-first century.

Women even wear shorter skirts (Barber, 1999). The specifics vary with each historical period, but this general pattern has occurred throughout history (Guttentag & Secord, 1983). Ancient Rome, which was renowned for its sybaritic behavior? A low sex ratio. Victorian England, famous for its prim and proper ways? A high sex ratio. The Roaring Twenties, a footloose and playful decade? A low sex ratio. And in more recent memory, the "sexual revolution" and the advent of "women's liberation" in the late 1960s? Take another look at Figure 1.3.

Theorists Marcia Guttentag and Paul Secord (1983) argued that such cultural changes are not accidental. In their view, a society's norms evolve to promote the interests of its most powerful members, those who hold economic, political, and legal power. In the cultures we just mentioned, those people have been men. As a result, the norms governing relationships usually change to favor the interests of men as the numbers of available men and women change.

This is a daring assertion. After all, recent decades have seen enormous improvement in the status of American women, and few of us would want to change that. But let's think it through. When sex ratios are high, there aren't enough women to go around. If a man is lucky enough to attract a woman, he'll want to keep her. And (a) encouraging women to be housewives who are financially dependent on their husbands, and (b) discouraging divorce, are ways to do just that (and that's the way things were in 1960). On the other hand, when sex ratios are low, there are plenty of women, and men may be less interested in being tied down to just one of them. Thus, women work and delay marriage, and couples divorce more readily if dissatisfaction sets in.

Thus, the remarkable changes in the norms for American relationships since 1960 may be due, in part, to dramatic fluctuations in American sex ratios. Indeed, we may already be seeing the effects of the higher sex ratios of the late 1990s. The U.S. divorce rate, which *doubled* from 1967 to 1980, has leveled off and has even dropped slightly. Politicians now care about "family values." Teenagers are being more sexually responsible; the U.S. birthrate for unmarried teen mothers (although still higher than in other industrialized countries) is now lower than it's been for thirty years (Curtin & Martin, 2000). And career women are rethinking their single-minded devotion to the workplace, pondering new ways of integrating motherhood with their professions (Benschop & Doorewaard, 1998). With roughly equal numbers of men and women now approaching marriageable age, it's likely that the cultural pendulum will swing back to sexual norms that are less permissive than those of the 1980s, but not as restrained as those of 1960.

We should note that Guttentag and Secord's (1983) explanation of the operation of sex ratios—that things work to the advantage of men—is speculative. However, there is a rough but real link between a culture's proportions of men and women and its relational norms, and it serves as a compelling example of the manner in which culture can affect our relationships. To a substantial degree, what we expect and what we accept in our dealings with others can spring from the standards of the time and place in which we live.

THE INFLUENCE OF EXPERIENCE

Our relationships are also affected by the histories and experiences we bring to them, and there may be no better example of this than the global orientations toward relationships known as **attachment styles.** Years ago, developmental researchers (e.g., Bowlby, 1969) realized that infants displayed various patterns of attachment to their major caregivers (usually their mothers). The prevailing assumption was that whenever they were hungry, wet, or scared, some children found responsive care and protection to be reliably available. A loving and nurturing caregiver always came when they called. Such youngsters came to rely on others comfortably, learning that other people were trustworthy sources of security and kindness. As a result, such children developed a **secure** style of attachment: They happily bonded with others, and they readily developed relationships characterized by relaxed trust.

Other children encountered different situations. For some, attentive care was unpredictable and inconsistent. Their caregivers were warm and interested on some occasions but distracted, anxious, or unavailable on others. These children thus developed fretful, mixed feelings about others known as **anxious-ambivalent** attachments. Being uncertain of when (or if) a departing caregiver would return, such children became nervous and clingy, displaying excessive neediness in their relationships with others.

Finally, for a third group of children, care was provided reluctantly by rejecting or hostile adults. Such children learned that little good came from depending on others, leading them to withdraw from others with an **avoidant** style of attachment. Avoidant children were often suspicious of and angry at others, and did not easily form trusting, close relationships.

Thus, early interpersonal experiences were presumed to shape the course of one's subsequent relationships. Indeed, attachment processes became a popular topic of research because the different styles were so obvious in many children. When they were faced with a strange, intimidating environment, for instance, secure children ran to their mothers, calmed down, and then set out to bravely explore the unfamiliar new setting (Ainsworth, Blehar, Waters, & Wall, 1978). Anxious-ambivalent children cried and clung to their mothers, ignoring the parents' reassurances that all was well. And avoidant children actually shunned their mothers, keeping their distance and evading close contact even when they were scared. As these examples suggest, the different styles of attachment could generally be linked to quite different patterns of friendship and play among young children (Koski & Shaver, 1997).

Still, attachment styles took on new relevance for relationship researchers when Cindy Hazan and Phillip Shaver (1987) demonstrated that similar orientations toward close relationships could also be observed among *adults*. In one of their studies, Hazan and Shaver invited readers of the *Rocky Mountain News* to participate in a "love quiz" by selecting the paragraph in Table 1.1 that fit them best; as you can see, each paragraph describes one of the attachment styles. Most people reported a secure style, but a substantial minority (about 40 percent) said they were *in*secure by picking either the avoidant or anxious-ambivalent self-description. In addition, the three groups of people reported childhood memories and current attitudes toward love and romance that fit their styles. Secure people generally held positive images of themselves and others and remembered their parents as loving and supportive. In contrast, insecure people viewed others with uncertainty or distrust and remembered their parents as inconsistent or cold.

With provocative results like these, attachment research quickly became one of the hottest fields in relationship science (see Cassidy & Shaver, 1999). Wide-ranging surveys have since shown that about 60 percent of us are secure, 25 percent avoidant, and 10 percent anxious-ambivalent (Mickelson, Kessler, & Shaver, 1997). And importantly, attachment tendencies seem to broadly influence our thoughts, feelings, and behavior in our relationships. People with secure styles tend to be more satisfied with their close partnerships than avoidant or anxious-ambivalent people are (Feeney, 1999). Avoidant people have a lack of faith in others that leads them to warily avoid interdependent intimacy, whereas anxious-ambivalent people seek such closeness but nervously fret that it won't last (Feeney, 1998). Both groups are less comfortable and relaxed in intimate relationships than secure people are.

Naturally, there have been several theoretical and methodological advances in studies of attachment; researchers now recognize *four* different styles instead of three, and assess them with more sophisticated measures than the

TABLE 1.1. Attachment Styles

Which of the following best describes your feelings? (Make your choice before reading the labels given at the end of this table.)

A. I find it relatively easy to get close to others and am comfortable depending on them and having them depend on me. I don't often worry about being abandoned or about someone getting too close to me.

B. I am somewhat uncomfortable being close to others; I find it difficult to trust them completely, difficult to allow myself to depend on them. I am nervous when anyone gets too close, and often, love partners want me to be more intimate than I feel comfortable being.

C. I find that others are reluctant to get as close as I would like. I often worry that my partner doesn't really love me or won't want to stay with me. I want to merge completely with another person, and this desire sometimes scares people away.

The first type of attachment style is described as "secure," the second as "avoidant," and the third as "anxious/ambivalent."

Source: From Shaver, Hazan, & Bradshaw, 1988.

simple paragraphs in Table 1.1. We'll bring you up to date on the latest thinking about attachment in chapter 8. For now, the important point is that attachment styles appear to be orientations toward relationships that are largely *learned* from our experiences with others. They are a prime example of the manner in which the proclivities and perspectives we bring to a new relationship emerge in part from our experiences in prior partnerships.

Let's examine this idea more closely. Any relationship is shaped by many different influences—that's the point of this chapter—and both babies and adults affect through their own behavior the treatment they receive from others. As any parent knows, for instance, babies are born with various temperaments and arousal levels. Some newborns have an easy, pleasant temperament, whereas others are fussy and excitable. Inborn differences in personality and emotionality make some children easier to parent than others, and caregivers may be especially attentive to bubbly, happy infants who are usually in good moods. Thus, the quality of parenting a baby receives can depend, in part, on the child's own personality and behavior; in this way, people's attachment style may be influenced by the traits with which they were born (Carver, 1997).

On the other hand, a child's temperament has only a moderate effect on the kind of parenting he or she receives (Vaughn & Bost, 1999), and people do not seem to be genetically predisposed to develop certain kinds of attachment styles (Waller & Shaver, 1994). Instead, just as developmental theorists originally assumed, our experiences seem to play a larger part in shaping the styles we bring to subsequent relationships. Mothers' behavior toward their infants when the babies are newborns predicts what styles of attachment the children will have when they are older (Isabella, 1998): Moms who are content with closeness and who enjoy intimacy tend to have children who share that style, whereas insecure mothers tend to have insecure children. In fact, it's possible to predict with 75 percent accuracy what attachment style a child will have by assessing the mother's style before her baby is even born (Fonagy, Steele, & Steele, 1991)! Thereafter, the parenting adolescents receive as seventh graders predicts how they will behave in their own romances when they are young adults (Conger, Cui, Bryant, & Elder, 2000). Youngsters apparently import the lessons they learn at home into their subsequent relationships with others.

We're not prisoners of our experiences as children, however, because our attachment styles continue to be shaped by the experiences we encounter as adults (Carnelley & Janoff-Bulman, 1992). Being learned, attachment styles can be *unlearned*, and over time, attachment styles can and do change (Baldwin & Fehr, 1995). A bad breakup can make a formerly secure person insecure, and a good relationship can make an avoidant person less so (Kirkpatrick & Hazan, 1994). As many as a third of us may encounter real change in our attachment styles over a two-year period (Fuller & Fincham, 1995), and the good news is that the avoidant and anxious-ambivalent styles are more likely to change than a secure style is (Davila, Burge, & Hammen, 1997).

Nevertheless, once they have been established, attachment styles can also be stable and long-lasting, as they lead people to create new relationships that reinforce their existing tendencies (Scharfe & Bartholomew, 1997). By remaining aloof and avoiding interdependency, for instance, avoidant people may never learn that some people can be trusted and closeness can be comforting—and that perpetuates their avoidant style. In the absence of dramatic new experiences, people's styles of attachment can persist for decades (Klohnen & Bera, 1998).

Thus, our global beliefs about the nature and worth of close relationships appear to be shaped by our experiences within them. By good luck or bad, our earliest notions about our own interpersonal worth and the trustworthiness of others emerge from our interactions with our major caregivers, and thus they start us down a path of trust or fear. But that journey never stops, and later obstacles or aid from fellow travelers may divert us and change our routes. Our learned styles of attachment to others may either change with time or persist indefinitely, all depending on our interpersonal experiences.

THE INFLUENCE OF INDIVIDUAL DIFFERENCES

Once they are formed, attachment styles also exemplify the idiosyncratic personal characteristics that people bring to their partnerships with others. We're all individuals with singular combinations of experiences and traits that shape our abilities and preferences, and the differences among us can influence our relationships. In romantic relationships, for instance, some pairings of attachment styles in the two partners are better—that is, more satisfying and stable—than others (Jones & Cunningham, 1996). Consider the mismatch that results when an anxious-ambivalent person falls in love with an avoidant partner; one of them may be unnerved by the other's emotional distance, while the other may be annoyed by the first's clingy intrusiveness. Both partners are likely to be less at ease than they would be with lovers who had more secure attachment styles.

Of course, the possibility that we can get along better with some people than with others is no surprise; we all know that. In this section of the chapter, we'll move beyond that simple truth in two ways. First, we'll explore the nature of individual differences, which are often gradual and subtle instead of abrupt. Then, we'll show that individual differences not only influence our behavior in close relationships, they may direct our choice of partners in the first place. We'll consider four different types of individual variation: sex differences, gender differences, personalities, and self-concepts.

Sex Differences

At this moment, you're doing something rare. You're reading an academic textbook about relationship science, and that's something most people will never do. This is probably the *first* serious text you've ever read about relationships, too, and that means that we need to confront—and hopefully correct—some of the simple stereotypes you may hold about the differences between men and women in intimate relationships.

This may not be easy. Many of us are used to thinking that men and women have very different approaches to intimacy—that, for instance, "men are from Mars, women are from Venus." In a well-known book with that title, the author asserted that:

> men and women differ in all areas of their lives. Not only do men and women communicate differently but they think, feel, perceive, react, respond, love, need, and appreciate differently. They almost seem to be from different planets, speaking different languages and needing different nourishment. (Gray, 1992, p. 5)

Wow. Men and women sound like they're members of different species. No wonder heterosexual relationships are sometimes problematic!

But the truth is more subtle. Human traits obviously vary across a wide range, and (in most cases) if we graph the number of people who possess a certain talent or ability, we'll get a distinctive chart known as a *normal curve.* Such curves describe the frequencies with which particular levels of some trait can be found in people, and they demonstrate that (a) most people have talents or abilities that are only slightly better or worse than average, and (b) extreme levels of most traits, high or low, are very rare. Consider height, for example: A few people are very short or very tall, but the vast majority of us are only an inch or two shorter or taller than the average for our sex.

Why should we care about this? Because many lay stereotypes about men and women portray the sexes as having very different ranges of interests, styles, and abilities. As one example, men are often portrayed as being more interested in sex than women are (see Box 1.1), and the images of the sexes that people hold often seem to resemble the situation pictured in Figure 1.4: The difference between the average man and the average woman is large, and there is almost no overlap between the sexes at all. But this is *not* the way things really are.

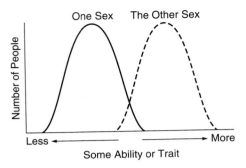

FIGURE 1.4. An imaginary sex difference. Popular stereotypes portray the sexes as being very different, with almost no overlap between the styles and preferences of the two sexes. This is *not* the way things really are.

BOX 1.1

Combating Simplistic Stereotypes

Here's a joke that showed up in our e-mail one day:

How to Impress a Woman:

Compliment her. Cuddle her. Kiss her. Caress her. Love her. Comfort her. Protect her. Hug her. Hold her. Spend money on her. Wine and dine her. Listen to her. Care for her. Stand by her. Support her. Go to the ends of the earth for her.

How to Impress a Man:

Show up naked. Bring beer.

It's a cute joke. But it may not be harmless. It reinforces the stereotypes that women seek warmth and tenderness in their relationships, whereas men simply seek unemotional sex. In truth, men and women differ little in their desires in close relationships; they're not "opposite" sexes at all (Schwartz & Rutter, 1998). Although individuals of both sexes may differ substantially from each other, the differences between the average man and the average woman are

rather small. Both women *and* men generally want their intimate partners to provide them lots of affection and warmth (Canary & Emmers-Sommer, 1997).

But so what? What are the consequences of wrongly believing that men are all alike, having little in common with women? Pessimism and hopelessness, for two (Metts & Cupach, 1990). People who really believe that the sexes are very different are less likely to try to repair their heterosexual relationships when conflicts occur (as they inevitably do). Thinking of the other sex as a bunch of aliens from another world is not only inaccurate, it can be damaging, forestalling efforts to understand a partner's point of view and preventing collaborative problem-solving. For that reason, we'll try to do our part to avoid perpetuating wrongful impressions by comparing men and women to the *other* sex, not the *opposite* sex, for the remainder of this book.

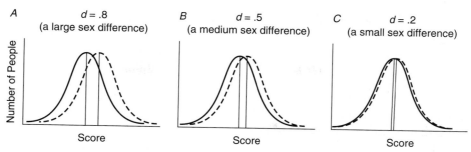

FIGURE 1.5. Actual sex differences take the form of overlapping normal curves. The three graphs depict large, medium, and small sex differences, respectively. (To keep them simple, they portray the ranges of attitudes or behavior as being the same for both sexes. This isn't always the case in real life.)

Actual sex differences take the form of the graphs shown in Figure 1.5, which depict normal curves that *overlap* to a substantial extent (Schwartz & Rutter, 1998).

The three graphs in Figure 1.5 illustrate sex differences that are considered by researchers to be large, medium, and small, respectively. Formally, they differ with respect to a *d* statistic that specifies the size of a difference between groups.[2] In the realm of sexual attitudes and behavior, graph A depicts the general size of the difference between men and women in incidence of masturbation (men masturbate more frequently), graph B illustrates the sex difference in sexual permissiveness (men approve of a wider range of behavior), and graph C depicts the difference in number of sexual partners (men have more) (Oliver & Hyde, 1993). Obviously, these real-life examples look nothing like the stereotype pictured in Figure 1.4. More specifically, these examples make three vital points about psychological sex differences:

- Some differences are real, but quite small. (Don't be confused by researchers' terminology; when they talk about a "significant" sex difference, they're usually referring to a "*statistically* significant"—that is, numerically reliable—difference, and it may not be large at all.)
- The range of behavior and opinions among members of a given sex is always *huge* compared to the average difference between the sexes. Some men may be very permissive, but other men are not permissive at all, and the two groups of men resemble each other much less than the average man and the average woman do. Another way to put this is that despite the sex difference in sexual permissiveness, a highly permissive man has more in common with the average *woman* on this trait than he does with a low-scoring *man*.

[2]To get a *d* score in these cases, you compute the difference between the average man and the average woman, and divide it by the average difference of the scores *within* each sex (which is the standard deviation of those scores). The resulting *d* value tells you how large the sex difference is compared to the usual amount by which men and women differ among themselves.

- The overlap in behavior and opinions is so large that many members of one sex will always score higher than the average member of the other sex. With a sex difference of medium size (with men higher and a *d* value of .5), one-third of all women will still score higher than the average man. What this means is that if you're looking for folks with permissive attitudes, you shouldn't just look for *men* because you heard that "men are more permissive than women"; you should look for permissive *people,* many of whom will be women despite the difference between the sexes.

The bottom line is that men and women usually overlap so thoroughly that they are much more similar than different on most of the dimensions and topics of interest to relationship science (Burn, 1996; Schwartz & Rutter, 1998). Indeed, the label "sex *differences*" is actually misleading, because it emphasizes dissimilarities more than likenesses and gives the wrong impression. And it's really misleading to suggest that men and women come from different planets, because it simply isn't true. "Research does *not* support the view that men and women come from different cultures, let alone separate worlds" (Canary & Emmers-Sommer, 1997, p. vi). According to the careful science of relationships you'll study in this book, it's more accurate to say that "men are from North Dakota, women are from South Dakota" (Wood & Dindia, 1998, p. 32).

Thus, sex differences in intimate relationships tend to be much less noteworthy and influential than laypeople often think. Common sense tends to glorify and exaggerate sex differences, perhaps because it's easy to classify individuals as either men or women and convenient to apply simple stereotypes to them. But now that you're reading a serious text on intimate relationships, you need to think more carefully about sex differences and interpret them more reasonably. There are interesting and occasionally important sex differences that are meaningful parts of the fabric of relationships. But they occur in the context of even broader similarities between the sexes, and the differences are always modest when they are compared to the full range of human variation. It's more work, but also more sophisticated and accurate, to think of individual differences, not sex differences, as the more important influences on interpersonal interaction. People differ among themselves whether they are male or female (as in the case of attachment styles), and these variations are usually much more consequential than sex differences are.

Gender Differences

We need to complicate things further by distinguishing between sex differences and *gender* differences in close relationships. When people use the terms carefully, sex differences refer to biological distinctions between men and women that spring naturally from their physical natures. In contrast, gender differences refer to social and psychological distinctions that are created by our cultures and upbringing (Burn, 1996; Canary & Emmers-Sommer, 1997). For instance, when they are parents, women are mothers and men are fathers—that's a sex difference—but the common belief that women are more loving, more nurturant parents than men reflects a gender difference. Many men are capable of just as much tenderness and compassion toward the young as any woman is, but if we expect and encourage women to be the primary caregivers of our children, we can create cultural gender differences in parenting styles that are not natural or inborn at all.

Distinguishing sex and gender differences is often tricky, because the social expectations and training we apply to men and women are often confounded with their biological sex (Eagly & Wood, 1999). For instance, because women lactate and men do not, people often assume that predawn feedings of a newborn baby are the mother's job and that women are better than men at such things—even when the baby is being fed formula from a bottle that was warmed in a microwave! It's not always easy to disentangle the effects of biology and culture in shaping our interests and abilities. Nevertheless, the distinction between sex and gender differences is important, because some influential differences between men and women in relationships—gender differences— are largely *taught* to us as we grow up.

The best examples of this are our **gender roles,** the patterns of behavior that are culturally expected of "normal" men and women. Men, of course, are supposed to be "masculine," which means that they are expected to be assertive, self-reliant, decisive, competent, and competitive. Women are expected to be "feminine," or warm, sensitive, emotionally expressive, and kind. They're the "opposite" sexes to most people, and to varying degrees men and women are expected to specialize in different kinds of social behavior all over the world (Williams & Best, 1990). However, people inherit only a small portion of their tendencies to be assertive or kind; most of these behaviors are learned (Lippa & Hershberger, 1999). In thoroughgoing and pervasive ways, cultural processes of socialization and modeling (rather than biological sex differences) lead us to expect that all men should be tough and all women should be tender (Burn, 1996).

Nevertheless, those stereotypes don't describe real people as well as you might think; only *half* of us have attributes that fit these gender role expectations cleanly (Bem, 1993). Instead of being just "masculine" or "feminine," a sizable minority of people—about 35 percent—are both assertive *and* warm, sensitive *and* self-reliant. Such people possess both sets of the competencies that are stereotypically associated with being male and with being female, and are said to be **androgynous.** If androgyny seems odd to you, you're probably just using a stereotyped vocabulary: On the surface, being "masculine" sounds incompatible with also being "feminine." In fact, because those terms are confusing, relationship researchers often use alternatives, referring to the "masculine" task-oriented talents as **instrumental** traits and to the "feminine" social and emotional skills as **expressive** traits (Spence & Helmreich, 1981). And it's not all that remarkable to find both sets of traits in the same individual. An androgynous person would be one who could effectively, emphatically stand up for himself or herself in a heated salary negotiation, but who could then go home and sensitively, compassionately comfort a preschool child whose pet parakeet had died. A lot of people, those who specialize in either instrumental *or* expressive skills, would feel at home in one of those situations, but not both. Androgynous people would be comfortable and capable in both domains.

In fact, the best way to think of instrumentality and expressiveness is as two separate sets of skills that may range from low to high in either men or women. Men who fulfill our traditional expectations are high in instrumentality but low in expressiveness, and are stoic, "macho" men. Traditional women are high in expressiveness but low in instrumentality; they're warm and friendly, but not assertive or dominant. Androgynous people are both instrumental and expressive. The rest of us—about 15 percent—are either high in the skills typically associated with the other sex (and are said to be "cross-typed") or low in both sets of skills (and are said to be "undifferentiated"). Equal proportions of men and women fall into all these categories, so, as with sex differences, it's simplistic and inaccurate to think of men and women as wholly distinct groups of people with separate, different traits (Bem, 1993).

In any case, gender differences are of particular interest to relationship researchers because, instead of making men and women more compatible, they "may actually be responsible for much of the *incompatibility*" that causes relationships to fail (Ickes, 1985, p. 188). From the moment they meet, for instance, traditional men and women enjoy and like each other less than androgynous people do. In a classic experiment, Ickes and Barnes (1978) paired men and women in couples in which (a) both partners fit the traditional gender roles, or (b) one or both partners were androgynous. The two people were introduced to each other and then simply left alone for five minutes in a waiting room while the researchers covertly videotaped their interaction. The results were striking. The traditional couples talked less, looked at each other less, laughed and smiled less, and afterward reported that they liked each other less than did the other couples. (Think about it: Stylistically, what do a masculine man and a feminine woman have in common?) When an androgynous man met a traditional woman, an androgynous woman met a traditional man, or two androgynous people got together, they got along much better than traditional men and women did.

More importantly, the disadvantage faced by traditional couples does not disappear as time goes by. Surveys of marital satisfaction demonstrate that such couples—who have marriages in which both spouses adhere to stereotyped gender roles—are generally *less* happy with their marriages than nontraditional couples are (Antill, 1983; Zammichieli, Gilroy, & Sherman, 1988). With their different styles and different domains of expertise, masculine men and feminine women simply do not find as much pleasure in each other as less traditional, less stereotyped people do.

Perhaps this should be no surprise. When human beings devote themselves to intimate partnerships, they want affection, warmth, and understanding (Reis et al., 2000). People who are low in expressiveness—who are not very warm, tender, sensitive people—do not readily provide such warmth and tenderness. As a result, men or women who are married to spouses with low expressiveness are chronically less satisfied than are those whose partners are more sensitive, understanding, and kind (Miller, Huston, & Caughlin, 2000). For this reason, traditional gender roles do men a disservice, depriving them of skills that would make them more rewarding husbands.

On the other hand, people who are low in instrumentality—who are low in assertiveness and personal strength—tend to have low self-esteem and to be less well-adjusted than those who have better task-oriented skills (Aube, Norcliffe, Craig, & Koestner, 1995). People feel better about themselves when they are competent and effective at "taking care of business" (Reis et al., 2000), so traditional gender roles also do women a disservice, depriving them of skills that would facilitate more accomplishments and achievements.

The upshot of all this is that both instrumentality and expressiveness are valuable traits, and the happiest, best-adjusted, most effective people possess both sets of skills (Helgeson & Fritz, 1999). In particular, the most desirable spouses, those who are most likely to have contented, satisfied partners, are people who are both instrumental and expressive (Bradbury, Campbell, & Fincham, 1995). And in fact, when they're given a choice, most people say that they'd prefer androgynous dating partners or spouses to those who are merely masculine or feminine (Green & Kenrick, 1994).

So, it's ironic that we still tend to put pressure on those who do not rigidly adhere to their "proper" gender roles. Women who display as much competitiveness and assertiveness as men risk being perceived as pushy, impolite, and "unladylike" (Rudman, 1998), and as actually unsuited for some jobs (Rudman & Glick, 1999). If anything, however, gender expectations are stricter for men than for women; girls can be tomboys and nobody frets too much, but if a boy is too feminine, people really worry (Sandnabba & Ahlberg, 1999). American gender roles may be changing slowly but surely; in particular, American women are becoming more instrumental with each new generation (Twenge, 1997). Nonetheless, even if they limit our individual potentials and are right only half the time, gender stereotypes persist. Today we still expect and encourage men to be instrumental and women to be expressive (Prentice & Carranza, 2000), and such expectations are important complications for many of our close relationships.

Personality

Some consequential differences among people (such as attachment styles and gender differences) are affected by experience and may change over a few years' time, but other individual differences are more stable and lasting. Personality traits may influence people's behavior in their relationships across their entire lifetimes (Soldz & Vaillant, 1999), and in general, personalities affect people's relationships, but not vice versa (Asendorpf & Wilpers, 1998).

Personality researchers have identified a handful of central traits that characterize people all over the world (McCrae & Costa, 1997), and several of them seem to affect the quality of the relationships people have (see Box 1.2). Extraverted, agreeable, and conscientious people have more, and more pleasant, relationships than do those who score lower on those traits (Bouchard, Lussier, & Sabourin, 1999; Watson, Hubbard, & Wiese, 2000), but neuroticism has the opposite effect; highly neurotic people are chronically less satisfied with their partnerships than are those of lower neuroticism (Karney & Bradbury, 1997). In

---

BOX 1.2

The Big Five Personality Traits

A small cluster of fundamental traits does a good job of describing the broad themes in behavior, thoughts, and emotions that distinguish one person from another (Wiggins, 1996). These key characteristics are called the Big Five traits by personality researchers, and most—but not all—of them appear to be very influential in intimate relationships. Which one of these would you assume does not matter much?

Extraversion—the extent to which people are outgoing, gregarious, talkative, and sociable versus cautious, reclusive, and shy.

Agreeableness—the degree to which people are good-natured, cooperative, and trusting versus irritable, cranky, and hostile.

Conscientiousness—the extent to which people are responsible, dutiful, and dependable versus unreliable and careless.

Neuroticism—the degree to which people are impulsive and prone to worry, anxiety, and anger.

Openness to experience—the degree to which people are imaginative, unconventional, and artistic versus conforming, uncreative, and stodgy.

The five traits are not listed in order of importance, but it is the last one, openness, that seems to have little to do with success and satisfaction in close relationships. The other four all make a difference.

---

fact, a remarkable study that tracked 300 couples over a span of forty-five years found that a full 10 percent of the satisfaction and contentment spouses would experience in their marriages could be predicted from measures of his and her neuroticism when they were still engaged (Kelly & Conley, 1987). The less neurotic the partners were, the happier their marriages turned out to be.

One reason why these traits are influential is that they affect the moods and emotional outlook with which people approach others. Optimistic, enthusiastic, and cheerful moods are experienced most often by extraverted and agreeable people (DeNeve & Cooper, 1998), and people in such happy moods tend to have fun and rewarding interactions with others (Vittengl & Holt, 1998). Over time, they also have marriages that are more satisfying (Watson et al., 2000). On the other hand, neurotic people tend to feel nervous, fearful, and guilty, and those unhappy moods result in unpleasant, argumentative, negative interactions (Furr & Funder, 1998; Vittengl & Holt, 1998). Everyone has good days and bad days, but some of us have more good days (and fewer bad ones) than other people—and those lucky folks are especially likely to have happy, enjoyable relationships.

Working alongside the global influences of the Big Five traits are other more specific personality variables that regulate our relationships, and we'll mention several in later chapters. For now, let's consider one last individual difference of note, the self-concepts we bring to our transactions with others.

Self-Concepts and Self-Esteem

Most of us like ourselves, but some of us do not. Such judgments are part of our **self-concepts,** which encompass all of the beliefs and feelings we have about ourselves. Our self-concepts include both straightforward, factual knowledge—"I am a man" or "I am a woman"—and evaluations of ourselves in the form of **self-esteem.** Both aspects of the self-concept are intimately tied to our relationships with others.

During social interaction, our self-concepts try to fulfill two different functions (Sedikides & Strube, 1997). On the one hand, people seek feedback from others that will *enhance* their self-concepts and allow them to think of themselves as desirable, attractive, competent people. We like to hear good things about ourselves, and we try to associate with others who will help us support positive self-images.

On the other hand, because it's unsettling to encounter information that contradicts our beliefs, we also want feedback that supports our existing self-concepts (Swann, 1997). For better or worse, our self-concepts play vital roles in organizing our views of the world; they make life predictable and sustain coherent expectations about what each day will bring. Without a stable, steady self-concept, social life would be a confusing, chaotic jumble, and being constantly confronted with information that contradicts our self-images would be unnerving. For that reason, people also seek feedback from others that is *consistent* with what they already think about themselves.

These two motives, **self-enhancement** and **self-consistency**, go hand-in-hand for people who like themselves and have positive self-concepts. When such people associate with others who compliment and praise them, they receive feedback that is simultaneously self-enhancing and self-consistent. But life is more complex for people who genuinely do not like themselves very much. Positive evaluations from others make them feel good, but threaten their negative self-images; negative feedback and criticism affirm their self-concepts, but feel bad.

How do both motives coexist in people with negative self-concepts? The answer is that the self-enhancement motive appears to be an automatic, relatively nonconscious response that is primarily emotional, whereas self-consistency emerges from deliberate and conscious cognition. What this means is that people with poor self-concepts *like* praise and compliments from others, but once they get a chance to *think* about them, they don't believe or trust such feedback (Swann, Hixon, Stein-Seroussi, & Gilbert, 1990).

Okay, so what? The relevance of these phenomena to the study of relationships lies in the fact that if people are choosing relationship partners carefully, they'll seek intimate partners who *support their existing self-concepts,* good or bad (Katz, Anderson, & Beach, 1997). Here's an example: Imagine that after a semester of sharing a double room in a college dorm, you're asked if you want to change roommates. You have a positive self-concept, and your roommate likes you and tells you so. Do you want to leave? Probably not. But if your roommate *dis*liked you and constantly disparaged you, you'd probably want out. You'd not want to live with someone who disagreed with you about who you are because it would be wearying and unpleasant to have to face such a contrary point of view all the time.

Now imagine that you have a lousy self-concept and you're paired with a roommate who compliments you all the time. Such praise is self-enhancing and feels great, and you want more, right? Wrong. The motive to protect and maintain our existing self-concepts is so strong that people with negative self-concepts want to *escape* roommates who like and approve of them; they'd rather have roommates who dislike them (Swann & Pelham, 1999). Such disapproval is unpleasant, but at least it reassures the recipients that the world is a predictable place.

Things get more complicated in romantic relationships. When people choose dating partners, self-enhancement seems to be the preeminent motive, and everybody prefers partners who like and accept them. Thus, even people with poor self-concepts pursue casual partners who provide positive feedback. However, in more interdependent, committed relationships such as marriage, self-consistency rises to the fore—a phenomenon called the *marriage shift*—and people want feedback that supports their self-concepts (Swann, De La Ronde, & Hixon, 1994). If people with negative self-images find themselves married to spouses who praise and appreciate them, they'll gradually find ways to avoid their spouses as much as possible:

> Imagine a man who receives what he construes to be undeserved praise from his wife. Although such praise may make him feel optimistic and happy at first, the positive glow will recede if he concludes that his wife could not possibly believe what she said . . . . [or] he may decide that she is a fool. In either case, overly favorable evaluations from someone who knows one well may foster a sense of uneasiness, inauthenticity, and distrust of the person who delivered them. (Swann, 1996, p. 118)

On the other hand, if their spouses belittle them, people with negative self-concepts will stay close at hand. (And of course, it's the other way around for those who have positive self-concepts.)

Overall, then, our self-concepts help direct our choices of intimate partners. Approval and acceptance from others is always pleasant, and, at least for brief periods, we tend to like those who like us. But in meaningful relationships over the long haul, people prefer reactions from others that confirm what they think of themselves. And that means that although most of us will be most content with spouses who uplift us, people with negative self-concepts will not.[3]

Where do these influential self-evaluations come from? A leading theory argues that self-esteem is a subjective gauge, a *sociometer*, that measures the quality of our relationships with others (Leary & Baumeister, 2000). When other

---

[3]Of course, self-concepts can change, and the ease with which they do depends on the certainty with which they are held (Swann & Ely, 1984). The good news is that if you suspect you're a nincompoop but aren't really sure, positive feedback from an adoring lover may change your self-image rather quickly as you enjoy, and come to believe, what your partner says. The bad news is that if you're quite sure you're unworthy, you'll feel more at home around those who know you well enough to take you as you are—that is, those who *agree* that you're unworthy.

BOX 1.3

An Individual Difference that's Not Much of a Difference: Homosexuality

---

We haven't said anything about gays or lesbians until now, and that's because there hasn't been much to say. There are no differences of any note between heterosexuals and homosexuals on any of the topics we've covered so far. For instance, gay men and lesbians exhibit the same attachment styles in the same proportions as heterosexual men and women do (Ridge & Feeney, 1998). They display similar gender roles (Storms, 1980), and they, too, are happier with partners of high (rather than low) expressivity (Kurdek & Schmitt, 1986a).

Indeed, the big difference between homosexual and heterosexual relationships is that a gay couple is comprised of two men and a lesbian couple of two women. To the extent that there are meaningful sex and gender differences in the way people conduct their relationships, they will show up in homosexual couples—not because of their sexual orientation but because of the sex of the people involved. Otherwise, there are scant differences between homosexual and heterosexual relationships. They operate in very similar manners (Peplau & Spalding, 2000). Homosexuals fall in love the same way, for instance, and they feel the same passions, experience the same doubts, and feel the same commitments as heterosexuals do (Kurdek, 1994, 1998; Kurdek & Schmitt, 1986b). Except for the sex of the partner, homosexual romances and partnerships are very much like heterosexual relationships (Baeccman, Folkesson, & Norlander, 1999).

So, we don't have to write two different books on intimate relationships; the same patterns exist in both heterosexual and homosexual partnerships. We'll certainly mention homosexuality where it's appropriate, but it won't be a major theme in this book because we'd typically just be reiterating what we've said in this box: The processes of close relationships are very similar in heterosexual and homosexual couples—and there's often not much else to say.

---

people regard us positively and value their relationships with us, self-esteem is high. However, if we judge that we are not attractive to others—if others seem not to care whether or not we are part of their lives—self-esteem is low. This view of self-esteem casts it as an evolved mechanism that serves our need to belong. Events that make us less desirable to others damage our self-esteem and motivate actions designed to increase our interpersonal worth. If we're unable to improve our relationships—if the need to belong goes unmet for too long—then we may become convinced of our lack of desirability and develop genuinely low self-esteem.

Thus, our self-concepts both result from, and then subsequently influence, our interpersonal relationships. What we think of ourselves seems to be dependent, at least in part, on the quality of our connections to others. And those self-images affect our ensuing searches for new partners, who provide us further evidence of our interpersonal worth. In fundamental ways, what we know of ourselves emerges from our partnerships with others, and matters thereafter.

THE INFLUENCE OF HUMAN NATURE

Now that we have surveyed several types of differences that distinguish people from one another, we can address the possibility that our relationships display some underlying themes that reflect the animal nature shared by all humankind. Our concern here is with evolutionary influences that have shaped close relationships over thousands of generations, instilling in us certain tendencies that are found in everyone (Kenrick & Trost, 2000).

Evolutionary psychology starts with three fundamental assumptions. First, *natural selection* has helped make us the species we are today. Motives such as the need to belong have presumably come to characterize human beings because they were *adaptive,* conferring some sort of reproductive advantage to those who possessed them. Thus, as we suggested earlier, the early humans who sought cooperative closeness with others were probably more likely than asocial loners to have children who grew up to have children of their own. Over time, then, natural selection would have made the need to belong more prevalent, with fewer and fewer people being born without it. In keeping with this example, evolutionary principles assert that any universal psychological mechanism exists in its present form because it consistently solved some problem of survival or reproduction in the past (Buss, 1999).

Second, evolutionary psychology suggests that men and women should differ from one another only to the extent that they have historically faced different reproductive dilemmas (Buss, 1995; Geary, 1998). Thus, men and women should behave similarly in close relationships except in those instances in which different, specialized styles of behavior would allow better access to mates or promote superior survival of one's offspring. Are there such situations? Let's answer that question by posing two hypothetical queries:

> If, during one year, a man has sex with 100 different women, how many children can he father? (The answer, of course, is "lots, perhaps as many as 100.")

> If, during one year, a woman has sex with 100 different men, how many children can she have? (Probably just one.)

Obviously, there's a big difference in the minimum time and effort that men and women have to invest in each child they produce. For a man, the minimum requirement is a single ejaculation; given access to receptive mates, a man might father hundreds of children during his lifetime. But a woman can have children only until her menopause, and each child she has requires an enormous investment of time and energy. These biological differences in men's and women's **parental investment** in their children may have supported the evolution of different strategies for selecting mates (Geary, 2000). Conceivably, given their more limited reproductive potential, women in our ancestral past who chose their mates carefully reproduced more successfully (with their children surviving to have children of their own) than did women who were less thoughtful and deliberate in their choices of partners. In contrast, men who promiscuously pursued every available sexual opportunity probably reproduced more successfully. If they flitted from partner to partner, their children may have been less likely to survive, but what they didn't offer in quality (of parenting) they could make up for in quantity (of children). Thus, today—as this evolutionary account predicts—women do choose their sexual partners more carefully than men do. They insist on smarter, friendlier, more prestigious, and more emotionally stable partners than men will tolerate (Kenrick, Sadalla, Groth & Trost, 1990), and are less accepting of casual, uncommitted sex than men are (Gangestad & Simpson, 1993). Perhaps this sex difference evolved over time.

Another reproductive difference between the sexes is that a woman always knows for sure whether or not a particular child is hers. By comparison, a man suffers **paternity uncertainty;** unless he is completely confident that his mate has been faithful to him, he cannot be absolutely certain that her child is his (Buss & Schmitt, 1993). Perhaps for that reason, the same men who consider promiscuous women to be desirable partners in casual relationships often prefer chaste women as partners when they wed (Buss, 2000). Men are also especially vigilant toward the threat of marital infidelity, and they generally feel less certain that their mates have been faithful to them than women do (Paul, Foss, & Galloway, 1993). This difference, too, may have evolved over time.

A third basic assumption of evolutionary psychology is that cultural influences determine whether evolved patterns of behavior are adaptive—and cultural change occurs faster than evolution does (Crawford, 1998). Thus, our species displays patterns of behavior that *were* adaptive eons ago, but not all of those inherited tendencies may fit the modern environments we inhabit now (Gaulin & McBurney, 2001). For instance, cavemen may have reproduced successfully if they mated with every possible partner, but modern men may not: In just the last two generations, we have seen (1) the creation of reproductive technologies—such as birth control pills—that allow women complete control of their fertility, and (2) the spread of a lethal virus that is transmitted through sexual contact (the human immunodeficiency virus that causes AIDS). These days, an interest in sexual variety and an openness to multiple partners are probably less adaptive for men than they were millions of years ago. The human race is still evolving, and natural selection will ultimately favor styles of behavior that fit this new environment, but it will take several thousand generations for such adaptations to occur. (And how will our cultures have changed by then?)

Thus, an evolutionary perspective provides a fascinating explanation for common patterns in modern relationships. Certain themes and some sex differences exist because they spring from evolved psychological mechanisms that were useful long ago. We are not robots who are mindlessly enacting genetic directives, but we do have inherited habits that are triggered by the situations we encounter (Buss & Kenrick, 1998). Moreover, our habits may fit our modern situations to varying degrees. Behavior results from the interplay of both personal and situational influences, but some common reactions in people result from evolved human nature itself.

This is a provocative point of view that has attracted both acclaim and criticism. On the one hand, the evolutionary perspective has prompted intriguing new discoveries, most of which are consistent with the ideas it asserts (Buss, 2000; Gaulin & McBurney, 2001). On the other hand, assumptions about the primeval social environments from which human nature emerged are necessarily speculative (Eagly, 1997). In addition, an evolutionary model is not the only reasonable explanation for many of the patterns at issue. For instance, women may have to pick their mates more carefully than men do because cultures routinely allow women control over fewer financial resources (Eagly & Wood, 1999); if women had social status as high as men's, they could conceivably afford to be less cautious, too.

In any case, there *are* notable patterns in human relationships that appear everywhere, regardless of culture, and we'll describe several of them in later chapters. Whether it evolved or was a social creation (or both), there is a human nature, and it affects our intimate relationships.

THE INFLUENCE OF INTERACTION

The final building block of relationships is the interaction that the two partners share. So far, we have had much to say about the idiosyncratic experiences and personalities that individuals bring to a relationship, but it's time to acknowledge that relationships are often much more than the sum of their parts. Relationships emerge from the *combination* of their participants' histories and talents (Robins, Caspi, & Moffitt, 2000), and those amalgamations may be quite different from the simple sum of the individuals who create them. Chemists are used to thinking this way; when they mix two elements (such as hydrogen and oxygen) they often get a compound (such as water) that doesn't resemble either of its constituent parts. In a similar fashion, the relationship two people create results from contributions from each of them but may only faintly resemble the relationships they share with other people.

Moreover, a relationship emanates from the dynamic give-and-take of its participants day by day; it's a fluid *process* rather than a static, changeless thing (Berscheid, 1999). Individually, two partners inevitably encounter fluctuating moods and variable health and energy; then, when they interact, their mutual influence on one another may produce a constantly changing variety of outcomes. Over time, of course, unmistakable patterns of interaction may distinguish one relationship from another. Still, at any given moment, a relationship may be an inconstant entity, the product of shifting transactions of complex people.

Overall, then, relationships are constructed of diverse influences that may range from the fads and fashions of current culture to the basic nature of the human race. Working alongside those generic influences are a variety of idiosyncratic factors such as personality and experience, some of them learned and some of them inherited. And ultimately, two people who hail from the same planet but who may otherwise be different—to a degree—in every other respect, begin to interact. The result may be frustrating or fulfilling, but the possibilities are always fascinating—and that's what relationships are made of.

THE DARK SIDE OF RELATIONSHIPS

We began this chapter by asserting the value of intimacy to human beings, so, to be fair, we should finish it by admitting that intimacy has potential costs as well. We need intimacy—we suffer without it—but distress and displeasure sometimes result from our dealings with others. Indeed, relationships can be disappointing in so many ways that whole books can, and have been, written about them (Kowalski, 1997, 2001; Spitzberg & Cupach, 1998)! When they're close to others, people may fear that their sensitive secrets will be revealed or turned against them. They may dread the loss of autonomy and personal control that comes with interdependency, and they may worry about being abandoned by those on whom they rely (Hatfield, 1984). They recognize that there is dishonesty in relationships and that people sometimes confuse sex with love (Firestone & Catlett, 1999). And in fact, most of us (56 percent) have had a very troublesome relationship in the last five years (Levitt, Silver, & Franco, 1996), so these are not empty fears.

As you might expect after our discussion of attachment styles, some people fear intimacy more than others (Greenfield & Thelen, 1997). Indeed, some of us anxiously expect that others will reject us, and we live on edge waiting for the relational axe to fall (Downey, Feldman, & Ayduk, 2000). But whether our fears are overstated or merely realistic, we're all likely to experience unexpected, frustrating costs in our relationships on occasion (Miller, 1997b).

So why take the risk? Because we are a social species. We need each other. We prematurely wither and die without intimate connections to other people. Relationships can be complex, but they are essential parts of our lives, so they are worth understanding as thoroughly as possible. We're glad you're reading this book, and we'll try to facilitate your understanding in the chapters that follow.

CHAPTER SUMMARY

The Nature and Importance of Intimacy

This book focuses on adult friendships and romantic relationships, topics that most of us find endlessly fascinating.

The Nature of Intimacy. Intimate relationships differ from more casual associations in at least six specific ways: *knowledge, caring, interdependence, mutuality, trust,* and *commitment.* None of these components is required for intimacy to occur, and relationships come in all shapes and sizes, but our most meaningful relationships include all six components.

The Need to Belong. Humans display a need to belong, a drive to maintain regular interaction with affectionate, intimate partners. When the need is not met for short periods, people become distressed and distracted. More severe consequences, such as poor physical and mental health, may follow if the need remains unfulfilled over time. The need to belong probably evolved over eons, favoring those early humans who sought stable, affectionate connections to others. We are a very social species.

The Influence of Culture

Cultural norms regarding relationships in the United States have changed dramatically over the last forty years. Fewer people are marrying than ever before, and those who do wait longer to marry. Then, nearly half of all new marriages end in divorce. People routinely live together and often have babies even when they're not married. As a result of these trends, most American youths will live in a single-parent home before they're 18.

Sources of Change. High levels of socioeconomic development, increasing individualism, and new technology contribute to cultural change. So does the *sex ratio*, the number of men who are available for every 100 women in a population. Cultures with high sex ratios are characterized by traditional roles for men and women, and sexually conservative behavior. In contrast, low sex ratios are correlated with permissive, less traditional behavior. This pattern may promote the interests of a society's most powerful members—men.

The Influence of Experience

Children's interactions with their major caregivers produce three different styles of attachment. *Secure* children bond happily with others and trust them; *anxious-ambivalent* children are nervous and clingy; and *avoidant* children are suspicious of others and do not trust them readily. Remarkably, similar orientations toward close relationships can also be observed among adults. Most of us (60 percent) are secure, but a quarter of us are avoidant, and 10 percent are anxious-ambivalent.

These orientations appear to be learned. Attachment styles can change, and a third of us—mostly those with avoidant or anxious-ambivalent styles—may encounter meaningful change in our styles over a two-year period. Thus, our global beliefs about the nature and worth of close relationships appear to be shaped by our experiences within them.

The Influence of Individual Differences

There's wide variation in people's abilities and preferences, but individual differences are more often gradual and subtle instead of abrupt. Nevertheless, such differences influence our behavior in close relationships and may even direct our choice of partners in the first place.

Sex Differences. Despite lay beliefs that men and women are quite different, the distributions of their behavior and interests in intimate relationships take the form of *overlapping normal curves*. Careful analysis indicates that some sex differences, although real, are quite small. The range of variation among members of a given sex is always large compared to the average difference between the sexes, and the overlap of the sexes is so substantial that many members of one sex will always score higher than the average member of the other sex. Thus, the sexes are much more similar than different on most of the topics and dimensions of interest to relationship science. Men and women are not from Mars and Venus, they're from North Dakota and South Dakota.

Gender Differences. *Sex* differences refer to biological distinctions between men and women that spring naturally from their physical natures, whereas *gender* differences refer to social and psychological distinctions that are taught to people by their cultures. Classifying a distinction between men and women as a sex or gender difference isn't always easy, but gender roles—the patterns of behavior that are culturally expected of normal men and women—are unquestionably gender differences. Men are expected to be dominant and assertive, women to be warm and emotionally expressive. These expectations only fit half of us, however. A third of us are *androgynous* and possess both *instrumental,* task-oriented skills and *expressive,* social and emotional talents. In fact, people can be high or low in either instrumentality or expressiveness, but traditional gender roles encourage us to specialize in one and not the other.

Such specialization is disadvantageous in close relationships. Men and women who adhere to traditional gender roles do not like each other, either at first meeting or later during a marriage, as much as less stereotyped, androgynous people do. This may be because expressiveness makes one a rewarding partner in intimate relationships, and instrumentality fosters personal adjustment, and only androgynous people enjoy both assets.

Personality. Personality traits are stable tendencies that characterize people's thoughts, feelings, and behavior across their whole lives. Extraversion, agreeableness, and conscientiousness help produce pleasant relationships, but neurotic people are less satisfied with their partnerships than are those with less neuroticism. These traits may be influential because they affect the chronic moods with which people approach others. Extraverted and agreeable people tend to be cheerful and enthusiastic, whereas neurotic people tend to feel fearful and guilty.

Self-Concepts and Self-Esteem. Our self-concepts encompass all of the beliefs and feelings we have about ourselves. During interaction, we seek reactions from others that are self-enhancing and complimentary *and* that are consistent with what we already think of ourselves. *Self-enhancement* is an automatic, emotional motive, whereas *self-consistency* is deliberate and cognitive—and these different spheres of operation explain how both motives coexist in people with negative self-concepts, who like praise but don't believe it.

People ordinarily seek intimate partners who support their existing self-concepts. Although people with negative self-concepts often date and appreciate casual partners who compliment and praise them, they prefer spouses who tell them that they are undesirable, deficient people. Such self-evaluations stem, in part, from our interactions with others. The *sociometer* theory argues that self-esteem is a subjective gauge of the quality of our relationships; if others regard us positively, self-esteem is high, but if others don't want to associate with us, self-esteem is low. Thus, our self-concepts both derive from, and then subsequently influence, our close relationships.

The Influence of Human Nature

An evolutionary perspective on modern relationships starts with three assumptions. First, natural selection shapes humankind, and any universal psychological mechanism exists because it was adaptive in the past. Second, men and women should differ only to the extent that they routinely faced historically different reproductive dilemmas. Such differences probably occurred; men and women make different *parental investments* in their offspring, and men suffer *paternity uncertainty* that does not plague women. Perhaps as a result, women choose their mates more carefully than men do, but men are especially vigilant toward the threat of marital infidelity. Finally, the evolutionary perspective assumes that cultural influences determine whether inherited habits are still adaptive—and some of them may not be. Altogether, this point of view has attracted both adherents and critics. Still, whatever its source, there is a human nature, and it directs our intimate relationships.

The Influence of Interaction

Relationships result from the combinations of their participants' histories and talents, and thus are often more than the sum of their parts. The shifting, changeable interactions that two partners share are the result of their fluctuating moods and variable energy, and they demonstrate that relationships are fluid processes rather than static entities.

The Dark Side of Relationships

There are potential costs, as well as rewards, to intimacy. People may fear exposure, a loss of control, or abandonment. Such fears afflict some people more than others, but we all experience unexpected costs on occasion. So why take the risk? Because we are a social species, and we need each other.

CHAPTER 2

Research Methods

A Brief History of Relationship Science ◆ Developing a Question ◆ Obtaining Participants ◆ Choosing a Design ◆ Correlational Designs ◆ Experimental Designs ◆ Developmental Designs ◆ Selecting a Setting ◆ The Nature of Our Data ◆ Self-Reports ◆ Observations ◆ Physiological Measures ◆ Archival Materials ◆ Couples' Reports ◆ The Ethics of Such Endeavors ◆ Interpreting and Integrating Results ◆ A Final Note ◆ Chapter Summary

Students often dread chapters on research methods, regarding them as distractions to be endured before getting to "the good stuff." You're probably interested in topics like love, sex, and jealousy, for instance, but do not have a burning desire to understand research designs and procedures. Chapters like this one often seem irrelevant to what students really want to know.

However, for several reasons, some basic knowledge of the methods of inquiry is especially valuable for consumers of relationship science. For one thing, there are more charlatans and imposters competing for your attention in this field than in most others (Stanovich, 1998). Bookstores and websites are full of ideas offered by people who don't really study relationships at all, but who (a) base suggestions and advice on their own idiosyncratic experiences, or (b) simply make them up (Honeycutt, 1996). Appreciating the difference between trustworthy, reliable information and simple gossip can save you money and disappointment. Furthermore, misinformation about relationships is more likely to cause people real inconvenience than are misunderstandings in most other sciences. People who misunderstand the nature of astronomical black holes, for instance, are much less likely to take action that will be disadvantageous to them than are people who are misinformed about the effects of divorce on children. Studies of relationships often have real human impact in everyday life.

Indeed, this book speaks more directly to topics that affect you personally than most other texts you'll ever read. Because of this, you have a special responsibility to be an informed consumer who can distinguish flimsy whimsy from solid truths.

This isn't always easy. As we'll see in this chapter, there may be various ways to address a research question, and each may have its own advantages and disadvantages. Reputable scientists gather and evaluate information systematically and carefully, but no single technique may provide the indisputable answers they seek. A thoughtful understanding of relationships often requires us to combine information from many studies, evaluating diverse facts with judicious discernment. This chapter provides the overview of research methods and the history of the field that you need to make such judgments.

Only basic principles are described here, but they should help you decide what evidence to accept and what to question. Hopefully, when we're done, you'll be better equipped to distinguish useful research evidence from useless anecdotes or speculation. For even more information, don't hesitate to consult other sources such as Acitelli, 1997, and Duck, 1997.

A BRIEF HISTORY OF RELATIONSHIP SCIENCE

Isaac Newton identified some of the basic laws of physics in 1687. Biology, chemistry, and physics have been vital fields of inquiry for several centuries. The systematic study of human relationships, on the other hand, is a recent invention. In fact, it is so new and so recent that most of the scientists who have ever studied human intimacy are still alive! This is no small matter. Because relationship science has a short history, it is less well-known than most other sciences, and for that reason it is less well understood. Very few people outside of colleges and universities appreciate the extraordinary strides this new discipline has made in the last forty years.

It's remarkable that it took scientists so long to begin studying relationships, because philosophers have always been keenly interested in the nature of friendship and intimacy. As an example, Table 2.1 provides a sampling of observations about relationships made by ancient philosophers; they pondered faithfulness, shyness, beauty, marital satisfaction, jealousy, and bereavement, among other issues. (But be forewarned: They were not always correct!)

Of all these ancient authors, Aristotle, who lived more than 2,300 years ago (circa 384–322 B.C.), may have analyzed close relationships most insightfully (see Books VIII and IX of his *Nicomachean Ethics*). He believed that "Man is by nature a social animal," and thought that there were three different kinds of friendships. In relationships based on utility, Aristotle argued, we are attracted to others because of the help they provide. In relationships based on pleasure, we are attracted to others because we find them pleasant and engaging. And in relationships based on virtue, we are attracted to others because of their virtuous character. Relationships of virtue were the highest form, Aristotle believed, because they were the only type in which partners were liked for themselves rather than as merely means to an end. They were also the longest lasting; Aristotle felt that a relationship of utility or pleasure would evaporate if the benefits provided by one's partner stopped, but a friendship based on virtue would endure as long as the partner remained pure.

TABLE 2.1. A Sample of Interpersonal Comments in the Writings of Early Philosophers

Friendship makes prosperity more brilliant, and lightens adversity by dividing and sharing it. (Cicero)

It goes far toward making a man faithful to let him understand that you think him so, and he that does but suspect I will deceive him, gives me a sort of right to do it. (Seneca)

Shyness is in fact an excess of modesty. (Plutarch)

What is beautiful is good. (Sappho)

Love must be fostered with soft words. (Ovid)

He that is not jealous, is not in love. (St. Augustine)

By all means marry; if you get a good wife, you'll be happy. If you get a bad one, you'll become a philosopher. (Socrates)

If you marry wisely, marry your equal. (Ovid)

There is no grief that time does not lessen and soften. (Cicero)

Friendship was just one of the relational matters that occupied Aristotle, and he gave them considerable attention, as you can see. He was also right some of the time; remember Aristotle when you read about the modern reward theory of attraction in chapter 3. However, Aristotle only contemplated relationships; he did not engage in systematic efforts to determine whether his musings were correct. Neither did the many poets and philosophers such as Aquinas, Montaigne, Kant, and Emerson (see Pakaluk, 1991), who wrote on love and friendship between Aristotle's era and the end of the nineteenth century.

When modern psychology and sociology began to emerge in the late 1800s, theorists often incorporated relationships into their seminal formulations. Freud felt that parent-child relationships were crucial in human development. Durkheim believed that *anomie* (or being socially disconnected) is associated with suicide. Simmel wrote about dyads, partnerships that involve just two people. These intellectuals sought support for their beliefs—for instance, Freud had his patients and Durkheim examined social statistics—but their primary contributions were conceptual.

Relationship science may have begun when Will S. Monroe (1898) asked 2,336 children in western Massachusetts to identify the traits and habits they considered to be important in selecting friends. (They mentioned such attributes as kindness, cheerfulness, and honesty.) This simple procedure marked a significant shift in the study of relationships—a change from analyses that were primarily philosophical to those that were grounded in data and empirical evidence.

In the years immediately after Monroe's pioneering project, very few similar studies were done. A trickle of historically important studies of children's friendships (e.g., Moreno, 1934), courtship (e.g., Waller, 1937) and marriages and families (see Broderick, 1988) began in the 1930s, but relatively few relationship studies were done before World War II. After the war, several important field studies, such as Whyte's (1955) *Street Corner Society* and Festinger, Schachter, and Back's (1950) study of student friendships in campus housing, attracted attention and respect. Still, relationships did not become a broad focus of research until an explosion of studies put the field on the scientific map in the 1960s and 1970s.

One of the most influential developments during that period was the new emphasis on laboratory experiments in social psychology. In a quest for precision that yielded unambiguous results, researchers began studying specific influences on relationships that they were able to control and manipulate. For instance, in a prominent line of research on the role of attitude similarity in liking, Donn Byrne and his colleagues (e.g., Byrne & Nelson, 1965) gave people an attitude survey that had supposedly been completed by a stranger in another room; participants inspected the survey and reported how much they liked the stranger. What they didn't know was that the researchers had prepared the survey either to agree or disagree with the participants' own attitudes, which had been assessed earlier. This manipulation of attitude similarity had clear effects: Apparent agreement caused people to like the stranger more than disagreement did.

Experiments like these demonstrated that the sources of liking could be understood through careful study, and with their methodological rigor they satisfied researchers' desires for clarity and concision. They legitimized and popularized the study of interpersonal attraction, making it an indispensable part of social psychology textbooks for the first time. In retrospect, however, these investigations often did a poor job of representing the natural complexity of real relationships. The participants in many of Byrne's experiments never actually met that other person or interacted with him or her in any way. Indeed, in the procedure we have been discussing, a meeting couldn't occur because the stranger didn't actually exist! In this "phantom stranger" technique, people were merely reacting to check marks on a piece of paper and were the only real participants in the study. The researchers were measuring attraction to someone who wasn't even there. Byrne and his colleagues chose this method, limiting their investigation to one carefully controlled aspect of relationship development, in order to study it conclusively. However, they also created a rather sterile situation that lacked the immediacy and drama of chatting with someone face-to-face on a blind date.

But don't underestimate the importance of studies like these: They showed that studies of relationships had enormous promise. And in the decades since, through the combined efforts of family scholars, psychologists, sociologists, and communication researchers, relationship science has grown and evolved to encompass new methods of considerable complexity and sophistication. At the start of the twenty-first century, the field now (Felmlee & Sprecher, 2000; Hoobler, 1999; Perlman, 1999):

- often uses diverse samples of people drawn from all walks of life,
- examines varied types of family, friendship, and romantic relationships,

TABLE 2.2. A Typical Rochester Interaction Record

Date:_____　Time:_____ A.M./P.M.　Length:_____ hours _____ minutes

List the initials, and sex of up to 3 main participants:_____

If there were more than 3 people, how many: Males _____　Females _____

Now rate the interaction on the following dimensions:

How **intimate** was it	superficial	1 2 3 4 5 6 7	meaningful
Did **you disclose:**	very little	1 2 3 4 5 6 7	a great deal
Did **others disclose:**	very little	1 2 3 4 5 6 7	a great deal
The **quality** was?	unpleasant	1 2 3 4 5 6 7	very pleasant
How **satisfied** were you?	less than expected	1 2 3 4 5 6 7	more than expected

- frequently studies those relationships over long periods of time,
- studies both the pleasant and unpleasant aspects of relationships, and
- often follows relationships in their natural settings.

Here are some examples of how the field currently operates:

- At the University of Rochester, Ladd Wheeler, John Nezlek, and Harry Reis have developed the Rochester Interaction Record (or RIR), a short form with which research participants record important details about their ordinary dealings with others soon after they occur each day. (See Table 2.2.) The RIR captures information about authentic, natural interactions; studies typically compile these reports over a week or more, allowing the patterns in people's interactions to stand out.
- At the University of Texas at Arlington, William Ickes and his colleagues study spontaneous, unscripted interactions between people who have just met by leaving them alone on a comfortable couch for a few minutes while their conversation is covertly videotaped (Ickes, 1997). The camera is actually hidden in another room across the hall and can't be seen even if you're looking directly at it, so there's no clue that anyone is watching. (See Figure 2.1.) Afterwards, participants can review the tapes of their interaction in private cubicles where they are invited to report what they were thinking at each point in the interaction. The method thus provides an objective videotaped record of the interaction, and participants' thoughts and feelings can be obtained, too. (Visit this lab at http://www.uta.edu/psychology/faculty/ickes/social_lab/.)
- At the University of Washington (http://depts.washington.edu/famlylab/), John Gottman and his colleagues invite married couples to a pleasant, furnished apartment with a picture window overlooking Lake Washington (Gottman, 1999). In this homey setting, a couple may take several hours

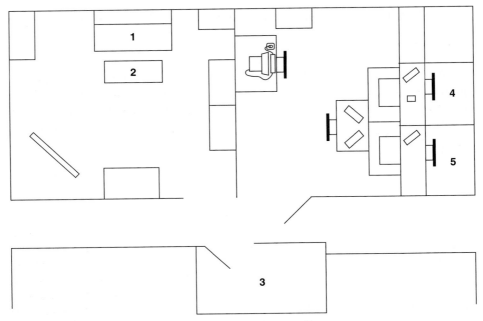

FIGURE 2.1. Schematic Diagram of William Ickes's Lab at the University of Texas at Arlington. Participants in a typical study will be left alone on a couch (1)—the only place to sit—in a spacious room. A microphone hidden under a coffee table (2) and a video camera completely out of sight in another room (3) record their conversation. Afterwards, the participants may offer insights into what they were thinking during their interaction when they watch their videotape in individual viewing rooms (4 and 5).

revisiting the disagreement that caused their last argument. They know that they are being videotaped, but after a while they typically become so absorbed in the interaction that the cameras are forgotten. The researchers may even take physiological measurements such as heart rate and electrodermal responses from the participants. Painstaking second-by-second analysis of the biological, emotional, and behavioral reactions he observes allows Gottman to predict with 94 percent accuracy which of the couples will, and which will not, divorce years later (Gottman & Silver, 1999).

• At the University of Texas at Austin (http://www.utexas.edu/research/pair/), Ted Huston and his colleagues (e.g., Huston & Houts, 1998) continue to monitor the outcomes experienced by 161 couples who joined a marital research project, the Processes of Adaptation in Intimate Relationships (or PAIR) project, years ago. In 1981, newlywed couples in Pennsylvania were invited to participate in the PAIR investigation by providing extensive reports about the nature and status of their relationships. Since then, although many of them are now divorced and others have moved elsewhere, researchers have conducted brief follow-up interviews with these people every two years. Entire marriages are being carefully tracked from start to finish as time goes by.

We hope that you're impressed by the creativity and resourcefulness embodied in these methods of research. (We are!) They barely scratch the surface in illustrating the current state of relationship science. Although still young, the field is now supported by hundreds of scholars around the world who hail from diverse scientific disciplines and whose work appears in several different professional journals devoted entirely to personal relationships. Look in your campus library for issues of the *Journal of Marriage and the Family*, the *Journal of Social and Personal Relationships*, and the journal simply entitled *Personal Relationships*.

DEVELOPING A QUESTION

How do these scholars study relationships? The first step in any scientific endeavor is to ask a question. In a field like this one, some questions emerge from personal experience. There has been a considerable amount of recent research on divorce, for example, as the divorce rate has increased among social scientists (and everyone else; see chapter 13). Questions also come from previous research: Studies that answer one question may delineate a whole new set of complexities. In addition, questions come from theories. If a theory says that certain things should happen under given conditions, scientists will usually want to see if those predictions are correct. Research on intimate relationships involves questions that spring from all three sources; scientists will put together their personal observations, their knowledge of previous research, and their theoretical perspectives to create the questions they ask.

The questions themselves are usually of two broad types. First, researchers may seek to *describe* some event or series of events as it naturally occurs. In this case, their goal is to delineate the nature of events as fully and accurately as they can. Alternatively, researchers can focus on *causal connections* between events to determine which events have meaningful effects on subsequent outcomes and which do not. This distinction has many ramifications, both for the scientists who conduct research and for those who consume it. For the researchers, the specific question often determines the design of the investigation. In turn, the design limits the conclusions that consumers can draw from the results. Most social science research contains at least a hint of both types of questions, although one type may receive more emphasis than the other. For instance, John Gottman's marital research at the University of Washington generally began with the descriptive goal of identifying the behaviors that differentiated happy spouses from those who were discontented. As that goal was met, Gottman began to determine whether such behavior could predict the fate of a marriage as time went by, and if so, why. Like this program of research, most of the issues that we consider in this book should be examined with regard to both goals: trying to get a picture of what naturally occurs *and* trying to see if our ideas about causal factors are correct.

OBTAINING PARTICIPANTS

Relationship science may study the behavior and feelings of people who are currently in relationships, those who have been in relationships in the past, or those who want to be in relationships in the future. One or both partners may participate. Scientists may study specific types of relationships (e.g., cohabitation versus marriage), or people who are happy in their relationships may be compared to those who are not. But whatever aspect of relationships we study, we need people to participate in our research.

Studies of intimate relationships usually recruit participants in one of two ways. The first approach involves the use of a **convenience sample,** which uses whatever potential participants are readily and conveniently available. University professors who study intimate relationships often work with college students who are required to be research participants as part of their course work. Clinical psychologists may study distressed couples who come to their clinics seeking help. Researchers may also advertise for volunteers through the mass media or local community organizations. Although some specific characteristics must sometimes be met (for instance, dating partners who have known each other for less than two months), researchers who use convenience samples are usually glad to get the help of everyone they can.

In contrast, projects that use a **representative sample** strive to ensure that their participants resemble the entire population of people who are relevant to the research question. A study of marriage, for example, would need, in theory, a sample that is representative of all married people—all ages, all nationalities, and all socioeconomic levels. No such study has ever been conducted, and it probably never will be. If nothing else, the people who voluntarily consent to participate in a research study may be somewhat different from those who choose not to participate (see Box 2.1). Still, some studies have tried to obtain samples that are representative of the adult population of individual countries or other delimited groups.

There is no question that if we seek general principles that apply to most people, representative samples are better than convenience samples (Sears, 1986). With convenience samples, there is always the danger that the results we obtain apply only to people who are just like our participants—students at a certain university, clients in a certain clinic, volunteers from a certain area of the country, and so on. Attitudes, in particular, can vary considerably from one group to the next. On the other hand, many processes studied by relationship researchers are basic enough that they don't differ substantially across demographic groups; people all over the world, for instance, share similar standards about the nature of physical beauty (see chapter 3). To the extent that research examines fundamental aspects of the ways humans react to each other, there's little disadvantage to convenience samples, because little variability is expected from group to group. (About half of all relationship research is conducted with convenience samples comprised of college students [de Jong Giervald, 1995]. Do *your* relationships operate differently from those of other people?) Still, with convenience samples we can't be certain that our findings pertain to people we haven't studied. Representative samples offer reassurance that scientific results can be widely applied.

The people in a representative sample reflect the demographic characteristics (sex, age, race, etc.) of the entire population of people that the researchers wish to study.

BOX 2.1

The Challenge of Volunteer Bias in Relationship Research

Regardless of whether investigators use convenience or representative sampling, they still face the problem of **volunteer bias:** Of the people invited to participate, those who do may differ from those who don't. In one illustration of this problem, Karney et al. (1995) simply asked 3,606 couples who had applied for marriage licenses in Los Angeles County whether they would participate in a longitudinal study of their relationships. Only 18 percent of the couples contacted agreed to participate, a typical rate in procedures of this sort. But their marriage licenses, which were open to the public, provided several bits of information about the spouses (e.g., their addresses, their ages, and their jobs). The volunteers differed from those who refused to participate in several ways; they were better educated, employed in higher-status jobs, and more likely to have cohabited. If the researchers had carried out a complete study with these people, would these characteristics have affected their results?

The answer may depend on what questions are asked, but volunteer bias can color the images that emerge from relationship research. People who volunteer for studies dealing with sexual behavior, for instance, tend to be more sexually experienced and active than nonvolunteers (Wiederman, 1999). This is a subtle form of sampling bias that can limit the extent to which research results apply to those who did not participate in a particular study.

The problem with representative samples, however, is that they are difficult and expensive to obtain (Acitelli, 1997); many researchers have neither the money nor the personnel to contact people dispersed across a large geographic area. Even if they can contact a representative group of people, they may not be able to afford the payment and other expenses required to ask more than just a few questions of their participants.

Thus, when it comes to sampling, researchers usually face a difficult choice. They can work with convenience samples, getting detailed information that may or may not apply to the larger population of interest. Or they can go to the trouble and expense of obtaining a representative sample but find themselves restricted to limited information from each participant. Each choice has advantages and disadvantages. Our job, when we evaluate research using either type of sample, is to be aware that each, by itself, may be imperfect.

Indeed, relationship science often presents dilemmas like these: Choices must be made but no flawless option is available. In such cases, our confidence in our collective understanding of relationships rests on a gradual accumulation of knowledge with varied methods. Here, diversity is an asset. Different investigators study a given topic in different ways (Houts, Cook, & Shadish, 1986). Any single study may have some imperfections, but those weaknesses may be answered by another study's strengths. With a series of investigations, each approaching a problem from a different angle, we gradually delineate the truth. As a thoughtful consumer of relationship science, you should try to think the way the scientists do: No one study is perfect. Be cautious. Diverse methods are valuable. Wisdom takes time. But the truth is out there, and we're getting closer all the time.

CHOOSING A DESIGN

Once we have a research question and a means of obtaining participants, we need to arrange our observations in a way that will answer our question. This section describes several different research strategies that are commonly used in relationship science.

Correlational Designs

A **correlation** allows us to answer the questions, "Do two events, x and y, go together? That is, are the changes in x and y related in some way?" Correlations are numbers that can range from -1.00 to $+1.00$. The larger (the absolute value of) a correlation is, the more highly related two events are. If x and y are perfectly *positively* correlated (which means they go up and down together—as x goes up, so does y; as y goes down, so does x), we will obtain a correlation of $+1.00$. If x and y are perfectly *negatively* correlated (so that as x goes up, y goes down; as x goes down, y goes up), we will obtain a correlation of -1.00. When x and y have no relationship at all, their correlation is 0. Some examples of these patterns are shown in Figure 2.2.

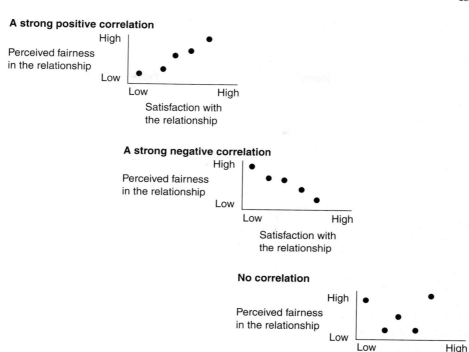

FIGURE 2.2. Correlational patterns.

The question of whether two events go together is enormously important, and very common. Consider a question we'll answer in chapter 6: Do people who feel fairly treated in a relationship also tend to feel satisfied with that relationship? Reliable correlations between satisfaction and fairness may help us understand the nature of contentment in close relationships, and we could find out if those two events are linked by simply measuring them in a large number of relationship partners.

On the other hand, if there is a correlation between fairness and satisfaction, we may not be sure what it means. Indeed, unsophisticated consumers often misinterpret the results of correlational designs. A correlation tells us that an association exists between two things, but it does *not* tell us *how* or *why* those things are related. Correlations do not tell us about the causal connections between events. Be careful not to assume too much when you encounter a correlation; many different plausible causal connections may all be possible when a correlation exists. Here are three straightforward possibilities:

- *x* may cause *y*—in the example of fairness and satisfaction, it could be that being fairly treated causes people to feel satisfied. *Or,*
- *y* may cause *x*—it could be that being satisfied causes people to feel fairly treated. *Or,*
- some other influence, a third variable, may cause both *x* and *y*. The two events *x* and *y* may not affect each other at all; some other event, such as

being in a good mood, may cause people to feel both satisfied and fairly treated.

Any of these three, along with many other more complex chains of events, may be possible when x and y are correlated. If all we have is a correlation, all we know is that two events are related. We don't know what causal connections are involved.

Sometimes, however, we have more than a simple correlation. If our design includes measures of several different variables, or if we have taken our measurements on several different occasions over time, a number of sophisticated statistical analyses (e.g., partial correlations, path analysis, structural equation modeling) can help rule out some of the possible causal connections that make correlational findings ambiguous. If you're interested, consult an advanced statistics text for details (e.g., Grimm & Yarnold, 1995). For now, the important point is that these procedures enable us to get close to making defensible causal statements based on correlational data. Although we should be very careful not to turn a simple correlation into a causal connection, we should also realize that, using the appropriate statistical techniques, it is possible to draw some reasonable conclusions about cause and effect within a correlational design.

Experimental Designs

When it's possible, a simpler way to investigate ideas about causation is to use an experimental design. **Experiments** allow researchers to identify causal connections, because experimenters create and control the conditions they study. In a true experiment, researchers will intentionally manipulate one or more variables and randomly assign participants to the different conditions they have created to see how those changes affect people. Thus, instead of just asking "Do x and y go together?" experimenters ask "If we change x, what happens to y?"

Let's illustrate the difference between an experiment and a correlational study by reconsidering Donn Byrne's classic work on attitude similarity and attraction (e.g., Byrne & Nelson, 1965). Had Byrne wished to test his belief that similarity and liking were related, he could have simply measured partners' attitudes and their liking for each other. He would have obtained a positive correlation between similarity and liking, but he wouldn't have been sure what it meant. Similarity could lead to liking. On the other hand, liking someone could lead people to share that person's attitudes and gradually cause similarity. And so on. Simple correlations are informative, but they're also ambiguous.

What Byrne did instead was an experiment. Once his participants arrived at his lab, Byrne flipped a coin to determine randomly who would encounter a similar stranger and who would encounter one who didn't agree with them at all. He *controlled* that apparent agreement or disagreement, and it was the only difference between the two situations in which participants found themselves. With this procedure, when Byrne observed higher liking for the similar stranger, he could reasonably conclude that the greater agreement had *caused* the higher liking. How? Because the participants were randomly assigned to the two situations, he couldn't attribute the different liking to differences in the people who encountered each situation; on average, the two groups of participants were identical. Moreover, they all had identical experiences in the experiment except for the apparent similarity of the stranger. The only reasonable explanation for the different behavior Byrne observed was that similarity leads to liking. His experiment clearly showed that the manipulated cause, attitude similarity, had a noticeable effect, higher liking.

Experiments provide clearer, more definitive tests of our causal ideas than other designs do. Done well, they clearly delineate cause and effect. Why, then, do researchers ever do anything else? The answer lies in the fact that experimenters must be able to control and manipulate the events they wish to study. Byrne could control the information that his participants received about someone they had never met, but he couldn't manipulate other important factors in intimate relationships. We still can't. (How do you create full-fledged experiences of romantic love in a laboratory?) You can't do experiments on events you cannot control.

Comparing correlational and experimental designs, we can see that each has an advantage that the other lacks. With a correlational design, we can study compelling events in the real world—commitment to a relationship, passionate love, unsafe sex—and see what events go together. But correlational designs are limited in what they can tell us about the causal relationships among events. With an experimental design, we can examine causal connections, but we are limited in the events we can study. Once again, there is no perfect solution—another reason for studying the same topic in different ways, from different perspectives.

Developmental Designs

Developmental designs study the manner in which behavior or events change over time. There are three major types of such designs.

Cross-Sectional Designs

The most common type of developmental design, a **cross-sectional design,** compares different people at different stages or ages in a developmental process. If we wished to examine risk factors for divorce at different stages of marriage, for instance, we could ask divorced couples who had been married for various lengths of time about the chief complaints that caused their divorces. We might find an association between the duration of marriages and the reasons they fail.

As this example suggests, cross-sectional designs are correlational designs, so we should be careful about the conclusions we draw from them. What if we found that marital infidelity was the leading cause of divorce after thirty years of marriage but that arguments over money were the primary complaints after only three years? Should we assume that infidelity is more common after years and years of the same old thing? Do spouses become more threatened by infidelity as they age? Not necessarily. We need to remember

In a cross-sectional design, researchers obtain responses from people from different age groups. To see if musical preferences differ with age, for example, we could ask 20-year-olds and 60-year-olds to evaluate various entertainers.

that our cross-sectional design is comparing people who married around 1975 to others who married in 2000. We're not only comparing people who were married for different lengths of time, we're comparing people who grew up in different circumstances. For all we know, their complaints about marriage haven't changed with the years and simply reflect the different eras from which they emerged.

As you can see, the correlations that result from cross-sectional designs are always open to a specific kind of ambiguity: the different social, cultural, and political events our participants have experienced. Whenever we find a correlation between age and any other variable, we must carefully question whether it is really age that is involved or a difference in the backgrounds of our different age groups.

Longitudinal Designs

Cross-sectional designs confuse age with history. However, if we recruit participants who are all the same age and follow them over time as they get older, we have a study in which people's history is the same but their age changes. This is a **longitudinal design,** in which the same people are followed with repeated measurements over a period of time. If we repeatedly monitor the complaints of married couples who joined our study as newlyweds and who continue to participate as they grow older—as Ted Huston and his colleagues (e.g., Huston & Houts, 1998) are doing with the PAIR project—we will be using a longitudinal design. If these people fought over money in their twenties but became increasingly concerned about marital infidelity in their fifties, we might assume that their worries had changed and that age and marital maturity were the causes of it.

But are the participants' ages the only things that might have changed over those thirty years? Probably not. Longitudinal designs do a better job of disentangling history and age than cross-sectional designs do, but they're still not perfect. Dramatic changes in the surrounding culture can still be mistaken for the effects of age and experience. What if some epidemic that affected women more than men changed the sex ratio so that 50-year-old men were gradually more numerous than 50-year-old women? Based on our discussion of sex ratios in chapter 1, we'd expect that people would adopt more conservative sexual attitudes and be more concerned about marital infidelity. What appears to be a normal developmental change in marital concerns in our study may really be a temporary cultural shift that doesn't affect most marriages at all! Even though we tried to control for historical effects by ensuring that all our participants had the same general histories, we may still end up studying history rather than age.

If we are very persistent and clever, we could generally rule out historical influences by combining longitudinal and cross-sectional designs. We could start out with two groups, people who are 20 and another group of people who are 40, and follow both groups until they reach their middle fifties. If, at age 55, members of both groups developed a distinct concern about marital infidelity, then we might really begin to believe that, regardless of their idiosyncratic historical experiences, older people fear infidelity.

Of course, a study like this wouldn't be easy. In fact, there would be enormous logistical difficulties involved in conducting a single investigation that takes thirty years! One of the bigger problems facing longitudinal designs is **participant attrition,** the loss of participants over time. People move away and cannot be located, or they get busy or bored and just don't want to continue participating in the study. And the longer the study goes on, the greater these problems become. Long-term longitudinal studies sometimes end up with a small and select group of people who have stayed with the study from start to finish. Indeed, even if the study started with a representative sample, it may not have one when it's done. In particular, those who stay with the study may have some particular interest in, or even some particular problems with, intimate relationships. If so, whatever results we obtain may apply only to people who have this specific interest or problem.

Retrospective Designs

Given the difficulties of staying in touch with our participants over the course of a longitudinal study, maybe we should go backward rather than forward in time. Why don't we just ask people about their past experiences rather than trying to follow them through the future? We can, of course, and many studies of intimate relationships use such a **retrospective design.** Sometimes, long periods of time are involved ("What major arguments did you have before you got married?"); sometimes very short periods are studied ("How pleasant were your interactions with your spouse over the last twenty-four hours?").

Retrospective designs are very flexible. If we are worried about historical influences, we can ask people of different ages to think back to the same younger age, and see if they recall similar experiences. Indeed, if people had perfect memories, retrospective designs would be extremely useful. Unfortunately, of course, no one has perfect recall (e.g., Neyer, 1997). As we will see later in this chapter (and again in chapter 4), there are difficulties with asking people about their lives, and these problems increase dramatically if we ask people about events that took place long ago. Whenever we rely on retrospective reports, we cannot know whether we are getting a clear picture of the past or one that has been contaminated by more recent events.

Overall, then, this review of developmental designs points to the same conclusion we reached earlier. Each type of design has its imperfections, but each type can also contribute important information—a critical angle—on our research question. The focus on change over time provided by developmental designs is particularly valuable in research on intimate relationships. Our significant relationships with others are often long-term events, and if we want to understand them, we need to understand how they may change as time goes by.

SELECTING A SETTING

Now that we've developed our research question, recruited our participants, and chosen our design, we still have to select a setting in which to conduct our investigation. The usual choices include (a) a laboratory or (b) a natural, everyday environment, such as a couple's home. Either choice has advantages and disadvantages. (But you're getting used to that now, aren't you?) The lab offers the advantage of greater control over extraneous, unwanted influences. Researchers can regulate the exact experiences their participants will have and arrange the physical environment itself to fit the purposes of the study. Natural settings offer the advantage of obtaining more typical behavior, as people will usually feel more comfortable and relaxed in their ordinary surroundings.

The disadvantages of these two settings are mirror images of their benefits. A laboratory may elicit artificial behavior that tells us little about what people usually do. On the other hand, natural settings may be full of distractions that are quite irrelevant to the research question but that heavily influence participants' behavior. People do behave differently in different environments, so we need to be sensitive to the possible impact of our setting on the results we obtain (O'Rourke, 1963).

In addition to its physical location, another aspect of the setting is the assignment that participants are given. Our procedure may entail specific directions and a limited choice of activities—this would be a *structured* situation—or it may allow people to do whatever they want, an *unstructured* assignment. Laboratory investigations often involve more structure than studies in naturalistic settings, but this isn't always the case. William Ickes's studies at the University of Texas at Arlington are often very unstructured (i.e., couples are just left alone for a few minutes to do whatever they please), whereas an interview that takes place in a couple's home may be quite structured (telling the couple exactly what we want them to do).

The pros and cons of these two approaches resemble those of the physical settings we've already mentioned. Structured assignments give researchers more command over the behaviors they observe but can evoke reactions that are more contrived. Unstructured tasks elicit more realistic, more ordinary behavior but run the risk that the desired behaviors will not occur. The exact amount of structure varies widely in studies of intimate relationships, but most investigations require at least some structure. If, like John Gottman at the University of Washington, we were interested in studying disagreements between spouses, just watching and waiting for a fight would be a very frustrating way to proceed. It might never happen! Thus, Gottman straightforwardly asks his participants to revisit the topic of their last argument, but then leaves them alone and lets them proceed without further interference.

A final consideration is relevant only for studies that take a fairly structured approach. Within such a strategy, the investigator has to decide whether to study "real" or "as if" behavior. If we wanted to capture examples of "real" jealousy, for instance, we would have to do something to get people jealous. Not only might this be hard to do, it might also be unethical (a point we'll discuss at the end of this chapter). In fact, some real behaviors are difficult to study. They may be fairly rare. They may be unpleasant and/or very intimate, so arranging for them to happen is inappropriate. Does this mean we cannot study sensitive topics such as jealousy, or conflict, or sexual interaction? Not really. We *can* study such topics, but only with certain techniques. One method is to ask people to tell us what has happened to them. Such self-reports can be very informative, but (as we will see in the next section) self-report data have a number of drawbacks (stop us if you've heard that before). Another approach is to have subjects **role-play** the behavior we're studying—to act "as if" they were jealous, or were having an argument, or were getting involved sexually with someone.

Role-play studies vary a great deal in how realistic they are. At one extreme, participants may be asked to read a story involving the relevant behavior and imagine those events happening to them. Such *scenarios* lack the vivid impact of reality and allow people to respond in a cool, collected fashion that may be quite different from the impulsive and emotional reactions they display when such events really take place. At the other extreme, studies known as *simulations* ask people to act out a particular role in a hypothetical situation. For example, an investigator might ask a couple to pretend that they are angry with each other and then observe how they behave. This strategy is more engrossing, but participants still know that they are only pretending. As you can see, participants' knowledge that they are playing a role, instead of having a real experience, detracts from the value of such procedures. Role-play studies are an ethically defensible way of studying emotionally charged topics, but people may do what they think they *should* do in these situations rather than what they really *would* do if the events actually occurred. Once again, there are both advantages and disadvantages to consider.

THE NATURE OF OUR DATA

We now need to consider just what data we're actually collecting. Are we recording others' judgments and perceptions of a relationship, or are we inspecting specific interactions ourselves? Two major types of research measures are described here: (a) people's own reports about their thoughts, feelings, and behaviors and (b) observations of people's behavior. We'll also examine three other kinds of data that are variations on self-reports and observations: couples' reports in which self-report and observation are combined, physiological measures, and archival evidence. No matter what data we use, our measures of behavior should have psychometric **validity** and **reliability.** That is, we should really be measuring the events we're trying to measure (that's validity), and, if those events aren't changing, we should get the same scores time after time (that's reliability).

Self-Reports

The most common means of studying intimate relationships is to ask people about their experiences. Such responses are **self-reports,** and they can be obtained in a variety of formats: through written questionnaires, verbal interviews, or even unstructured diaries in which participants write about whatever comes to mind (Harvey, Hendrick, & Tucker, 1988). The common theme linking such techniques is that people are telling us about their experiences—we're not watching them ourselves. Otherwise, the exact nature of participants' self-reports may vary in several ways. Self-reports may be:

- *Retrospective versus concurrent.*   Are people telling us about past events or are they keeping track of something happening now?
- *Global versus specific.*   Do the self-reports summarize feelings or behaviors in broad, general terms (e.g., "How active is your sex life?"), or do they describe specific, concrete events (e.g., "How many times did you have sexual intercourse in the past week?")?
- *Subjective versus objective.*   Does the self-report call for a subjective, feeling-based judgment (e.g., "How satisfying is your relationship?") or an objective, fact-based response (e.g., "Did your partner give you a present for your birthday?")?

Self-report data have important benefits. For one thing, they can tell us about the meaning that relational events have for those who experience them, and those meanings may be much richer and more important than an outside observer may know (Bruess & Pearson, 1993). Consider, for example, all those "little things that mean a lot." An observer who sees Margaret bring ice cream home for Kathy may regard Margaret's behavior as kind and thoughtful, but nothing more. However, if Kathy knows that Margaret went to lots of trouble to find the special kind of ice cream that Kathy really loves, Margaret's gift may mean much more to Kathy than anyone else can readily appreciate. To the extent that self-reports allow us to "get inside people's heads" and understand their personal points of view, we obtain invaluable information that can help us understand the workings of relationships.

Self-report data are also inexpensive and easy to obtain. Investigators do not need elaborate equipment, research assistants, or an expansive laboratory. All they need is paper, some pencils, and willing participants. However (and this probably isn't a surprise!), self-reports offer potential problems. Following are three major concerns.

Participants' Interpretations of the Questions

Self-reports always occur in response to a researcher's instructions or questions. If the participants misinterpret what the researcher means or intends, their subsequent self-reports can be misleading. For instance, what do you think virginity means? Berger and Wenger (1973) found that 41 percent of their participants (who were both men and women) accepted "she brings herself to climax" as a possible way for a woman to lose her virginity! Thus, even an apparently simple question such as "Are you a virgin?" could be misunderstood, generating false conclusions. In fact, undetected problems with people's comprehension of terms referring to sexual behavior have been cited as a major problem in research on AIDS (Catania, Gibson, Chitwood, & Coates, 1990).

Difficulties in Recall or Awareness

There is considerable controversy about how accurately people can remember and report on things that have happened to them (Davis, 1999; Kruglanski, 1996). Nevertheless, there is general agreement that people are most accurate when they describe specific, objective events that have occurred recently. People are more likely to be inaccurate, and to fill in their memory gaps with their present beliefs and opinions, when we ask them to make global, subjective reports about things that happened long ago. In particular, if a passionate romance ends in pain and discontent, the disappointed lovers are likely to have a very hard time remembering how happy and enthusiastic they felt months earlier when they had just fallen in love (Grote & Frieze, 1998).

Bias in Participants' Reports

A final major worry about self-report data involves the possibility of systematic bias or distortion in people's reports. Even when they want to be helpful, people may not necessarily tell the truth. This may occur for two reasons. First, they may not know what the truth is. That is, the participants' own perceptions may be distorted so that, although they are being honest, their reports aren't accurate. One example of this (which we'll mention again in chapter 4) is the **self-serving bias** that leads people to overestimate their responsibility for positive events in their relationships and to underestimate their blame for the bad times. People like to think of themselves in a positive light, so they tend to take the credit for their successes but duck the fault for their failures. If nothing else, domestic partners think they do a larger share of the housework than they really do (Ross & Sicoly, 1979)! Mistakes like this are interesting in their own right, and they are not dishonest attempts to mislead anyone, because they reflect people's genuine, if erroneous, views. Nevertheless, researchers need to be aware that they are sometimes obtaining participants' *perceptions* of the truth, which may differ somewhat from the whole, unvarnished truth.

A more serious problem occurs when people are reluctant to tell the truth as they see it. The best known example of this is the **social desirability bias,** which refers to distortion that results from people's wishes to make good impressions on others. Participants will be reluctant to admit anything that makes them look bad or that portrays them in an undesirable light. For instance, concerns about

TABLE 2.3. The Marriage Conventionalization Scale

Each of the following questions is answered by indicating whether it is *true* or *false* in regard to your marriage (or other type of relationship).

1. There are times when my mate does things that make me unhappy.
2. My marriage is not a perfect success.
3. My mate has all of the qualities I've always wanted in a mate.
4. If my mate has any faults I'm not aware of them.
5. My mate and I understand each other perfectly.
6. We are as well adjusted as any two persons in this world can be.
7. I have some needs that are not being met by my marriage.
8. Every new thing I have learned about my mate has pleased me.
9. There are times when I do not feel a great deal of love and affection for my mate.
10. I don't think anyone could possibly be happier than my mate and I were and are with each other.
11. My marriage could be happier than it is.
12. I don't think any couple could live together in greater harmony than my mate and I.
13. My mate completely understands and sympathizes with my every mood.
14. I have never regretted my marriage, not even for a moment.
15. If every person in the world of the opposite sex had been available and willing to marry me, I could not have made a better choice.

To determine your score on this scale, give yourself 1 point when you have responded *false* to questions 1, 2, 7, 9, and 11, and 1 point when you have responded *true* to any of the other questions. The maximum high score is, thus, 15. Such a score would mean either that you have an extraordinarily happy relationship, or that you are concerned to present your relationship in a very positive way even if it is not quite as perfect as your answers would indicate.

Source: Adapted from Edmonds, 1967.

social acceptance may make some homosexuals hesitate to honestly report their sexual preferences to researchers; as a result, there is continuing argument about the real prevalence of homosexuality (Cameron & Cameron, 1998; Michaels, 1996). Procedures that guarantee participants' anonymity help reduce social desirability problems, but bias can still creep into various self-reports.

Consider something as innocuous as a rating of the quality of your marriage: The social desirability bias may make you reluctant to report that things aren't so great. In fact, Edmonds (1967) fretted that people often say they're more happily married than they really are, and to measure this tendency he developed a "marriage conventionalization" scale (see Table 2.3). Edmonds assumed that there is no such thing as a marriage that had no faults or problems, and people who said their marriages were perfect were misrepresenting the truth. (Just take a look at his scale.) In fact, there is a high positive correlation between responses to Edmonds's scale and reports of marital satisfaction (Edmonds, Withers, & Dibatista, 1972). Either there really are a lot of perfect, problem-free marriages out there (and Edmonds is wrong), or the same people who say that they are very happy are also likely to describe their marriages in unrealistic, overglorified terms. Which do you think it is?

Observations

Another way to collect information about intimate relationships is to rely on the reports of observers. In **participant observation,** the observer typically engages in the activities of the group he or she is studying. The observer becomes a member of the group. In **systematic observation,** the observer typically takes an outsider's role, watching others' behavior without interacting with them in any way.

Systematic observers are often trained investigators who are members of a research team. Indeed, most studies that use observers go to great lengths to ensure that there will be high *interrater reliability* (or good agreement among the observers). Researchers often develop written manuals to teach their observers what to observe; they also conduct extensive practice sessions and often check on interrater congruity throughout the course of the study. Even with these elaborate precautions, however, interrater reliability may be difficult to obtain. Careful observation is hard work. Reliability may be high at the beginning of a study but decline over time as the observers become tired or bored. Reliability can also be affected by the observers' motivation. For instance, agreement between observers tends to be better when they know they are being supervised than when observations are checked without their knowledge. And even reliable observations can be misleading. Pairs of observers who work together over long periods of time may develop their own, idiosyncratic styles. Left to themselves, their observations may be highly reliable, but they may not agree with those made by newly trained observers who are going by the book. In short, capturing "objective reality"—that is, a reality that everyone sees in the same way—is harder than it may seem.

There are several different methods of observation. Some studies involve direct observations of ongoing behavior, whereas others use audio or video recordings from which observations are made at a later time. The amount of time that is analyzed also varies widely. Observations may continue over long periods of time (days or even weeks) or occur for only short periods of time (just minutes). One method of observation, called **time-sampling,** uses intermittent, short periods of observation to capture samples of behavior that actually occur over longer periods of time. In time-sampling, investigators first specify those times at which the target behaviors can occur. For example, a study of married life might designate mornings (before the couple goes to work), evenings (when they're home again), and weekends as observation periods. Then, they randomly sample short episodes from these relevant times, perhaps observing only fifteen minute periods but scattering these observations at different times on different days. (Time-sampling can also be used with self-reports; for instance, participants can be given beepers that signal them to record who they're talking to or what they're doing at random intervals during the day.)

Time-sampling helps avoid the disadvantages of both long and short periods of observation. With long observation periods, we need a number of observers; otherwise, observer fatigue becomes a problem. With short observations, we run the risk of either missing the behaviors of interest or catching unusual moments and not realizing that they are atypical. Still, even time-sampling faces a fundamental problem if we are interested in relatively rare events (such as arguments, episodes of jealousy, or consoling a partner after a misfortune): The event may not occur while the observations are being made.

Regardless of the method used, most observations involve one or more of the following techniques:

- *Notes.* Here, observers record in writing everything they notice. Notes tend to be rich in interesting detail, but they also tend to have low interrater reliability. Field notes are especially important in participant observation, often being the primary form of data the investigator assembles.
- *Ratings.* When observers make ratings, they try to characterize what they have seen in relatively global (and usually subjective) terms. For example, if they're watching a couple arguing, they might rate the extent to which the interaction is "constructive and problem-solving" or "argumentative and hostile." With carefully developed rating scales and extensive training of observers, it's usually possible to obtain ratings that are reasonably reliable.
- *Coding.* Coding procedures focus on very specific behaviors such as the amount of time people speak during an interaction, the number of smiles they display, or the number of times they touch each other. Because coding is typically more objective than either narratives or ratings, it is usually quite reliable; nevertheless, complex schemes that require the coding of several different behaviors will require extensive training of observers.
- *Sequential observations.* More complex observations may focus on the *sequence* of interaction between two or more individuals (e.g., Bakeman & Gottman, 1997). Here, investigators examine the effects one person's behavior has on the subsequent behavior of others. When Susan smiles during a conversation, for example, is John more likely to smile back at her later on? Sequential observations are complicated and are usually limited to relatively short periods of time. Nevertheless, they can represent the back-and-forth flow of interaction with a high level of sophistication.

Observations like these generally avoid the disadvantages of self-reports. Trained observers are usually immune to misinterpretations of the researchers' intent, faulty memories, or self-serving biases. On the other hand, as we've already noted, we need self-reports if we're to understand people's personal perceptions of their experiences. Observational studies are also expensive; they often consume hours and hours of observers' time and require expensive videotaping equipment.

Observational research can also suffer from the problem of **reactivity:** People may change their behavior when they know they are being observed (Webb et al., 1981). Participants may be just as concerned with creating a good impression when they know others are watching as they are when they fill out a questionnaire or answer an interviewer's questions. Sometimes, they deliberately alter their actions. Cromwell and Olson (1975) described an incident in which an experimenter working with couples had to leave the room for a moment; she did not intend to record what happened in her absence, but she forgot to turn off the recorder, and the couple was unaware that their conversation was still being taped. The experimenter later found (probably to her dismay) that the couple had engaged in an animated conversation that ended with one partner saying, "She's coming back; we'll have to be more careful."

But even when people don't try to act in socially desirable ways, the presence of an observer may subtly influence their behavior. In order to avoid such problems of reactivity, some investigators have devised elaborate, creative methods of observation. For example, Christensen (1979) got families to allow hidden microphones into a room where family conversations often occurred. The microphones were hooked to a timer that selected a random fifteen-minute period for recording when the family was home each day. Thus, the families knew that their interactions were being recorded, but they never knew when. Presumably, it was such a nuisance trying to create good impressions for hours each day—when most of the time it didn't matter—that the participants soon began to act naturally in spite of being observed.

Physiological Measures

Of course, we can avoid the potential problem of reactivity if we observe behavior that people cannot consciously control, and physiological measures of people's autonomic and biochemical reactions often do just that. Physiological measures assess such responses as heart rate, blood pressure, genital arousal, and hormone production to determine how interactions with others affect people physically. For instance, studies of loneliness (Cacioppo et al., 1999) have examined brain waves during sleep and levels of cortisol (a stress hormone) in saliva to determine that lonely people sleep poorly (e.g., they take a long time to get to sleep and wake up often during the night) and are rather anxious. Other investigations have found that people who have unhappy marriages exhibit poor immune system responses, making them more prone to various infections (Kiecolt-Glaser, 1999). Physiological measures are obviously impartial and objective, and they allow relationship researchers to explore the important ties between our interactions and our health. With the right instruments, it is even possible for researchers to take continuous measures of physiological responses while participants are engaged in various activities.

Archival Materials

Historical **archives** also avoid the problem of reactivity. Personal documents such as photographs and diaries, public media such as newspapers and magazines, and governmental records such as marriage licenses and census information can all be valuable sources of data about relationships (see Webb et al., 1981), and when these get dated, they become "archival" information. The use of marriage licenses in the study of volunteer bias we discussed in Box 2.1 is one example of the use of archival materials. In another study that examined the correlation between past physical attractiveness and current earning capacity, researchers rated people's attractiveness in old university yearbook photos (Frieze, Olson, & Russell, 1991). (What did they find? See chapter 3!)

Archival materials allow researchers to study past eras, and they are typically inexpensive to use. Obviously, they are also "nonreactive," because inspection of archival data does not change the behaviors being studied. Archival data can be limited, however. In particular, the material that has been saved from some previous era may not contain all the information a researcher would really like to have.

Couples' Reports

A final type of data involves self-reports in which each member of a couple provides reports of his or her own behavior but also acts as an observer of his or her partner's behavior. Thus, when the partners' perspectives are compared, couples' reports provide both a self-report and an observation of the same event. This is often fascinating, in part because there is sometimes little agreement between the partners' reports (Christensen, Sullaway, & King 1983; Elwood & Jacobson, 1982). A husband may report showing affection to his wife, for example, when she doesn't perceive his actions to be affectionate at all. Couples' reports agree more when they get a chance to practice making their ratings and when they are asked to describe objective, specific events instead of making global, subjective judgments. However, the couple's disagreement about the general nature of their interactions is not necessarily a bad thing; it can be interesting in its own right. What does it mean when Betty and Barney do not agree on what Betty did? It may be useful to find out.

THE ETHICS OF SUCH ENDEAVORS

Obviously, research on relationships occasionally requires investigators to ask questions about sensitive topics or to observe private behavior. Should we pry into people's personal affairs?

This really isn't an issue we pose lightly. Although it's enormously valuable and sorely needed, relationship science presents important ethical dilemmas. Just asking people to fill out questionnaires describing their relationships may have subtle but lasting effects on those partnerships (McGregor & Holmes, 1999). When we ask people to specify what they get out of a relationship or to rate their love for their partners, for instance, we focus their attention on delicate matters they may not have thought much about. We encourage them to evaluate their relationships, and stimulate their thinking. Moreover, we arouse their natural curiosity about what their partners may be saying in response to the same questions. In general, a researcher's innocent inquiries run the risk of alerting people to relationship problems or frustrations they didn't know they had (Rubin & Mitchell, 1976).

Simulations and other observational studies may have even more impact. Consider John Gottman's (1994) method of asking spouses to revisit the issue that caused their last argument: He doesn't encourage people to quarrel and bicker, but some of them do. Spouses that disagree sourly and bitterly are at much greater risk for divorce than are spouses who disagree with grace and humor, and Gottman's work has illuminated the specific styles of behavior that forecast trouble ahead. This work is extremely important. But does it do damage? Should we actually invite couples to return to a disagreement that may erode their satisfaction even further?

The answer to that question isn't simple. Relationship scientists ordinarily are very careful to safeguard the welfare of their participants. Detailed information is provided to potential participants before a study begins so that they can make an informed decision about whether or not to participate. Their consent to participate is voluntary and can be withdrawn at any time. After the data are collected, the researchers provide prompt feedback that explains any experimental manipulations and describes the larger purposes of the investigation. Final reports regarding the outcomes of the study are often made available when the study is complete. In addition, when ticklish matters are being investigated, researchers may provide information about where participants can obtain couples' counseling should they wish to do so; psychological services may even be offered for free.

As you can see, relationship science is based on compassionate concern for the well-being of its participants. People are treated with respect, thanked warmly for their efforts, and may even be paid for their time. They may also enjoy their experiences and benefit from them. For instance, newlyweds who were asked about their reactions to one laboratory study (Bradbury, 1994) were much more likely to have positive feelings about their experience than mixed or negative feelings (72 percent versus 3 percent). In a longitudinal study of marriages, participants who made frequent self-reports felt more competent as spouses than did those in a control condition who provided only minimal data (Veroff, Hatchett, & Douvan, 1992). At least some of the time, participation in relationship studies can be interesting and enlightening (Hughes & Surra, 2000). Still, should we be trying to study such private and intimate matters as close relationships?

The answer from here is absolutely yes. There's another side to the issue of ethics we haven't yet mentioned: science's ethical imperative to gain knowledge that can benefit humanity. In a culture in which more marriages are failures than successes (Martin & Bumpass, 1989), it would be unethical *not* to try to understand how relationships work. Intimate relationships can be a source of the grandest, most glorious pleasure human beings experience, but they can also be a source of terrible suffering and appalling destructiveness. It is inherently ethical, we believe, to try to learn how the joy might be increased and the misery reduced.

INTERPRETING AND INTEGRATING RESULTS

This isn't a statistics text (and we know you're pleased by that), but there are some aspects of the way relationship scientists do business that the thoughtful consumer of the field should understand. Most relationship studies subject the data they obtain to statistical analysis in order to determine whether their results are statistically "significant." This is a calculation of how likely it is that the results (i.e., the observed correlations or the effects of the manipulated variables in an experiment) could have occurred by chance. If it's rather unlikely that the results could be due to chance—the standard convention is that the risk must be 5 percent or less—we have a "significant" result. All of the research results reported in this book are significant results. You can also be confident that the studies that have obtained these results have passed critical inspection by other scientists. This does not mean, however, that every single specific result we may mention is unequivocally, positively true: Some of them might have occurred by chance, reflecting the influence of odd samples of people or unwanted mistakes of various sorts. When scientific results in psychology, sociology, or communication studies are significant, it means that chance occurrence is unlikely, not that chance occurrence is impossible.

The data obtained in relationship studies can also present unique challenges and complexities. Here are three examples:

Paired, interdependent data. Most statistical procedures assume that the scores of different participants are independent and do not influence each other, and when there's no apparent connection between one participant and the next, this is typically true. If researchers study the correlation between marital satisfaction and personal health in 100 different wives, for example, one woman's responses have no effect on the data obtained from other women, and the data are independent. However, if the women's husbands are included, there probably *will* be a connection between the spouses' responses. A wife's contentment with her marriage may be influenced by both her husband's satisfaction and his health—indeed, the researchers may be studying these very patterns—and her answers are *not* independent of his.

The point here is that data obtained from relationship partners are often interdependent and can't be analyzed with the same techniques that are used in simpler investigations. Relationship researchers recognize that special statistical procedures are advisable for analyzing data collected from couples (e.g., Gonzalez & Griffin, 2000).

Different levels of analysis. Relationship researchers must also choose between two entirely different levels of analysis, one focusing on the individuals who make up couples, and the other focusing on the couples themselves (Bulcroft & White, 1997). For instance, researchers may examine how an individual's attachment style affects the interactive outcomes he or she obtains, or they may examine how the styles of two different partners combine to affect the quality of their relationship. The first of these questions analyzes individuals, but the second analyzes dyads, and relationship scholars must be careful to ensure that their procedures fit the level of analysis of interest to them.

Three sources of influence. Furthermore, even if we ignore situational and cultural influences, relationships are routinely shaped by influences from three different sources (of both individual and dyadic types). Specifically, relationships emerge from the individual contributions of the separate partners *and* from the unique effects of how they combine as a pair. For example, imagine that Fred and Wilma have a happy marriage. One reason for this may be the fact that Fred is an especially pleasant fellow who gets along well with everyone, including Wilma. Alternatively (or, perhaps, in addition), Wilma may be the one who's easy to live with. However, Fred and Wilma may also have a better relationship with each other than they could have with anyone else because of the unique way their individual traits combine; the whole may be more than the sum of its parts. Relationship researchers often encounter phenomena that result from the combination of all three of these influences, the two individual partners and the idiosyncratic partnership they share. Sophisticated statistical analyses are required to study all of these components at once (see Kenny, 1994), another indication of the complexity of relationship science.

So what's our point here? We've noted that studies of close relationships tackle intricate matters and that statistical significance testing involves probabilities, not certainties. Should you take everything we say with a grain of salt, doubting us at every turn? Well, yes and no. We want you to be more thoughtful and less gullible, and we want you to appreciate the complexities underlying the things you're about to learn. Remember to think like a scientist: No study is perfect, but the truth is out there. We put more faith in patterns of results that are obtained by different investigators working with different samples of participants. We are also more confident when results are replicated with diverse methods.

For these reasons, scientists now do frequent **meta-analyses,** which are studies that statistically combine the results from several prior studies. In a meta-analysis, an investigator compiles all existing studies of a particular phenomenon and combines their results to identify the themes they contain. If the prior studies all produce basically the same result, the meta-analysis makes that plain; if there are discrepancies, the meta-analysis may reveal why.

With tools like this at its disposal, relationship science has made enormous strides despite its short history and the complexity of its subject matter. And despite our earlier cautions, most of the things we have to tell you in this text are dependable facts, reliable results you can see for yourself if you do what the researchers did. Even more impressively, most of them are facts that had not been discovered when your parents were born.

A FINAL NOTE

In our desire to help you be more discerning, we've spent most of this chapter noting various pros and cons of diverse procedures, usually concluding that no single option is the best one in all cases. In closing, let us reassure you that relationship science is in better shape than all of these uncertainties may make it seem. The variety of methods with which researchers study relationships is a *strength,* not a weakness (Ickes, 2000). And the field's judicious ability to differentiate what it does and does not yet know is a mark of its honesty and its developing maturity and wisdom.

People like easy answers. They like their information cut-and-dried. Many people actually prefer simple nonsense—like the idea that men come from Mars and women come from Venus—to the scientific truth, if the truth is harder to grasp. However, as a new consumer of the science of relationships, you have an obligation to prefer facts to gossip, even if you have to work a little harder to make sense of their complexities. Don't mistake scientific caution for a lack of quality. To the contrary, we want to leave you with the thought that it demonstrates scientific respectability to be forthright about the strengths and weaknesses of one's discipline. It's more often the frauds and imposters who claim they are always correct than the cautious scientists, who are really trying to get it right.

CHAPTER SUMMARY

A Brief History of Relationship Science

Philosophers such as Aristotle have been concerned with the analysis of close relationships for over 2,000 years. However, the scientific study of relationships is a recent endeavor that has come of age in the last thirty years. Since its blossoming in contrived lab experiments during the 1960s, the field has grown to include the longitudinal study of all types of relationships in their natural settings around the world.

Developing a Question

Research questions come from a number of sources, including personal experience, the results of prior research, and theoretical predictions. The questions themselves are usually of two types: They seek either to describe events or to delineate causal connections among variables. A given research program will often involve both approaches.

Obtaining Participants

Convenience samples are composed of participants who are easily available to the researcher. Findings based on such samples may not apply readily to other people, although this is rarely a problem when basic processes of behavior are involved. *Representative samples* are selected to reflect the demographic characteristics of the population of interest. They are expensive to select and maintain, so the time available with each participant is often limited. Both types of samples can suffer from volunteer bias.

Choosing a Design

Correlational Designs. A correlation describes the strength and direction of an association between two variables. Correlations are inherently ambiguous, because events can be related for a variety of reasons. By themselves, correlations do not necessarily indicate the presence of any causal connection between events.

Experimental Designs. In experiments, researchers control and manipulate the conditions they study, allowing them to examine cause-and-effect relationships among events. Experiments are very informative, but many events cannot be studied experimentally for practical or ethical reasons.

Developmental Designs. Developmental designs study changes in behavior or events over time. There are three kinds of developmental designs. *Cross-sectional designs* compare participants from different age groups or time periods; however, because these people have different histories, the source of any differences obtained in cross-sectional research is often ambiguous. *Longitudinal* research follows the same group of participants across time. Such studies often suffer from *participant attrition,* the loss of participants as time goes by. *Retrospective designs* rely on participants' recall of past events, but people's memories can be inaccurate.

Selecting a Setting

Research can be conducted in laboratories or in real-world settings such as a couple's home. Laboratory research emphasizes control but pays the price of artificiality. Real-world settings can promote more natural behavior, but control over extraneous variables is reduced. The participants' duties may be highly structured, entailing specific directions, or relatively unstructured, allowing them to do whatever they want. *Role-play* studies allow researchers to examine highly emotional events in an ethical manner but may fail to indicate what people really do in such situations.

The Nature of Our Data

Self-Reports. Relationship research often asks participants directly about their thoughts, feelings, and behavior. Self-reports are convenient and provide information about participants' personal perceptions. However, participants may misunderstand the researchers' questions, have faulty memories, and be subject to *self-serving* and *social desirability biases.* Overall, self-reports are more accurate when they focus on recent, specific, and objective events instead of global, subjective impressions of events long past.

Observations. When we observe people's behavior, reliability is a crucial concern. When interrater reliability is high, different observers agree on their observations. *Time-sampling* is often used in observational research: A set of different, usually brief, observations are made at times randomly selected from a longer period of interest. Observations may take the form of detailed narratives, global ratings, the coding of specific behaviors, and sequential observations. They avoid the problems of self-reports, but pose their own problems: Observations are expensive to conduct, and participants' behavior may change when they know they are being observed.

Physiological Measures. Measurements of people's autonomic and hormonal changes indicate how social interaction affects people's physical well-being.

Archival Material. Historical records are nonreactive and allow researchers to compare the present with the past.

Couples' Reports. Couples' reports combine self-reports and observations—each partner is asked to report his or her own thoughts, feelings, and behavior, and each also acts as an observer of the other partner's behavior. Couples' reports often disagree, a fact that intrigues, rather than distresses, researchers.

The Ethics of Such Endeavors

Participation in relationship research may change people's relationships by encouraging them to think carefully about the situations they face. As a result, researchers take pains to protect the welfare of their participants. Information about the study is provided in advance, and participation is voluntary. Counseling is sometimes offered. Properly conducted, research on relationships can contribute to more enduring and satisfying relationships. Participants may even benefit from participating in couples' studies.

Interpreting and Integrating Results

Statistical analysis determines the likelihood that results could have occurred by chance. When this likelihood is very low, the results are said to be significant. Some such results may still be due to chance, however, so the thoughtful consumer does not put undue faith in any one study. Results that occur repeatedly with different samples of participants and with a variety of methods inspire greater confidence. *Meta-analysis* can lend confidence to conclusions by statistically combining results from several studies. Nevertheless, relationship researchers face several unique statistical and interpretative problems such as (a) paired interdependent data, (b) different levels of analysis, and (c) influences from both the individual partners and their mutual interactions.

A Final Note

Scientific caution is appropriate, but it should not be mistaken for weakness or imprecision. Relationship science is in great shape.

PART TWO

Getting Together and Basic Processes in Intimate Relationships

CHAPTER 3

Attraction

How do intimate relationships get started? What sets the wheels of friendship or romance in motion? Obviously, the specifics vary widely. Relationships can begin under all kinds of circumstances—in the classroom, on a blind date, at work, in a grocery store, or on the Web. But psychologically, the first big step toward a relationship is always the same: interpersonal attraction, the desire to approach someone. Feelings of attraction are not the same as love, nor do they guarantee that love will develop. Attraction does, however, open the door to the possibility.

Perhaps because attraction plays such a crucial role in so many different kinds of relationships, there has been an enormous amount of research on it (Berscheid & Reis, 1998). We won't try to examine all of this material in this chapter. Instead, we will focus here on several major factors that appear to be particularly important in the beginning of an intimate relationship. But first, let's consider a basic principle about how attraction works.

THE FUNDAMENTAL BASIS OF ATTRACTION: A MATTER OF REWARDS

The most fundamental assumption about interpersonal attraction is that we are attracted to others whose presence is rewarding to us (Clore & Byrne, 1974; Lott & Lott, 1974). Two different types of rewards influence attraction: direct rewards we receive from our interaction with others, and indirect rewards that are merely associated with another's presence. Direct rewards refer to all the positive consequences we obtain from being with someone. When a person showers us with attention, interest, and approval, we enjoy these rewarding behaviors. When a person is witty and beautiful, we take pleasure in these rewarding characteristics. And when a person gives us access to desired goods such as money or status, we are pleased with the opportunities presented. The more of these rewards that a person provides for us, the more we should be attracted to that person.

But what about just being in someone's company under pleasant circumstances? What happens when your team scores the winning touchdown in a close game, and Chris is right there with you? Will you be attracted to Chris even though Chris did not cause the happy event? Such things happen (Byrne & Murnen, 1988). In attraction by association, our feelings about another person result from the emotional tone of the surrounding situation. If Chris is present during a pleasant event, we may experience a positive emotional response the next time we interact with Chris.

These two kinds of rewards—direct and indirect-by-association—highlight the interactive nature of attraction (Gifford & Gallagher, 1985; Wright, Ingraham, & Blackmer, 1985). Most people simply think that they are attracted to someone if he or she is an appealing person, but it's really more complex than that. Attraction does involve the perceived characteristics of the person who seems attractive, but it also depends on the needs, preferences, and desires of the person who becomes attracted, and on the situation in which the two people find themselves. Our own needs and personalities can affect how we perceive others and react to the situation, and the situation itself can modify our preferences and our perceptions. Attraction is based on rewarding experiences with another person, but those rewarding experiences can come about in a variety of ways that depend on the time, place, and people involved. We consider a number of possible routes to attraction in this chapter, starting with a basic prerequisite—being there.

PROXIMITY: LIKING THE ONES WE'RE NEAR

We might get to know someone in a chat room online, but isn't conversation more rewarding when we can hear others' voices, see their smiles, and actually hold their hands? Most of the time, relationships are more rewarding when they involve people who are near one another (who are physically, as well as psychologically, close). Indeed, our physical **proximity** to others often deter-

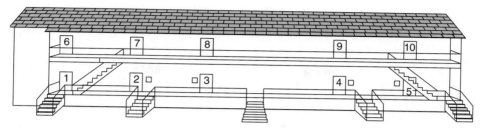

FIGURE 3.1. Schematic diagram of a student apartment building at MIT.

TABLE 3.1. Friendship Choices in Campus Housing at MIT

Two hundred seventy people living in buildings like that pictured in Figure 3.1 were asked to list their three closest companions. Among those living on the same floor of a given building, here's how often the residents named someone living:

1 door away	41% of the time
2 doors away	22%
3 doors away	16%
4 doors away	10%

Only 88 feet separated residents living four doors apart, at opposite ends of the same floor, but they were only one-quarter as likely to become friends as were people living in adjacent apartments. Evidently, small distances played a large part in determining who would and who would not be friends.

mines whether or not we ever meet them in the first place. More often than not, our friendships and romances grow out of interactions with those who are nearby. To meet people is not necessarily to love them, but to love them we must first meet them!

In fact, there is a clear connection between physical proximity and interpersonal attraction, and a few feet can make a big difference. Think about your Relationships classroom: Who have you gotten to know since the semester started? Who is a new friend? It's likely that the people you know and like best sit near you in class. In one study in which strangers were assigned seats in a classroom, students were much more likely to become friends with those sitting near them than with those sitting across the room, even though the room was reasonably small (Segal, 1974).

A similar phenomenon occurs in student apartment complexes. In a classic study, Festinger, Schachter, and Back (1950) examined the friendships among students living in campus housing at the Massachusetts Institute of Technology. Residents were randomly assigned to apartments in 17 different buildings that were all like the one pictured in Figure 3.1. People who lived close to each other were much more likely to become friends than were those whose apartments were further apart. Indeed, the chances that residents would become friends were closely related to the distances between their apartments, as Table 3.1 shows. Remarkably, the same result was also obtained from one building to the next: People were more likely to know and like residents of other buildings that were close to their own. Obviously, even small distances have a much larger influence on our relationships than most people realize. Whenever we choose the exact place where we will live or work or go to school, we also take a major step toward determining who the significant others in our lives will be. We know we are choosing a location; we may not fully realize we are also choosing the people we will meet.

Convenience: Proximity Is Rewarding, Distance Is Costly

Why does proximity have such influence? One answer is that when others are nearby, it's easy to enjoy whatever rewards they offer. Everything else being equal, a partner who is nearby has a big advantage over one who is far away (Gilbertson, Dindia, & Allen, 1998): The expense and effort of interacting with a distant partner—such as long-distance phone bills and hours on the road—make a distant relationship more costly overall than one that is closer to home. Distant relationships are less rewarding, too; an expression of love in an e-mail message is less pleasant than an actual kiss on the cheek. Thus, long-distance romantic relationships are generally less satisfying than romances with partners who are nearby (Van Horn et al., 1997).

The only notable thing about this result is that anyone should find it surprising. However, lovers who have to endure a period of separation may blithely believe, because their relationship has been so rewarding up to that point, that some time apart will not affect their romance. If so, they may be surprised by the difference distance makes. When a relationship that enjoys the convenience of proximity becomes inconvenient due to distance, it may suffer more than anyone suspected. Even those who are already married are more likely to get divorced when they live apart than when they live together (Rindfuss & Stephen, 1990). Absence does *not* seem to make the heart grow fonder.

Familiarity: Repeated Contact

Proximity also makes it more likely that two people will cross paths often and become more familiar with each other. Folk wisdom suggests that "familiarity breeds contempt," but research evidence disagrees. Instead of being irritating, repeated contact with—or **mere exposure** to—someone usually increases our liking for him or her (Bornstein, 1989). Even if we have never talked to them, we tend to like people whose faces we recognize more than those whose faces are unfamiliar to us.

Moreland and Beach (1992) provided an interesting example of the mere exposure effect when they had college women attend certain classes either fifteen times, ten times, or five times during a semester. The women never talked to anyone and simply sat there, but they were present in the room frequently, sometimes, or rarely. Then, at the end of the semester, the real students were given pictures of the women and asked for their reactions. The results were very clear: The more familiar the women were, the more attracted to them the

students were. And they were all liked better t
never seen at all.

Thus, because proximity often leads to fami
liking, frequent contact with someone not only m
ient, it may make that person seem more attracti
not be surprising, then, that heterosexual peopl
or lesbians have more positive attitudes towar
who have no contact with gays or lesbians (Here

72

TABLE 3.2. Wh
Both male an
more likel

The Power of Proximity

Of course, there are limits to the power of proximity to increase attraction. Constant exposure to anything—a favorite food or song, or perhaps even a lover—can be boring when saturation sets in (Bornstein, 1989). Familiarity enhances attraction, but overexposure does not. And close proximity to obnoxious, disagreeable people does not necessarily get us to like them better (Ebbesen, Kjos, & Konecni, 1976). The best conclusion to make about proximity is that it accentuates our feelings about others. If we're able to get along with people, we like them better when they're nearby. However, if they annoy us, proximity may only make things worse.

Indeed, a study in a condominium complex in California found that although most of the residents' friends lived nearby, most of their enemies did, too (Ebbesen et al., 1976)! Only rarely did people report that they really disliked someone who lived several buildings away from them. Instead, they despised fellow residents who were close enough to annoy them often—by playing music too loudly, letting pets run wild, and so on. Evidently, proximity makes interaction more likely, but it cannot guarantee that what follows will be desirable. We tend to be attracted to those who are near us, but if our contact with them becomes unpleasant, we may like them even less, not more.

PHYSICAL ATTRACTIVENESS: TO SEE YOU IS TO LIKE YOU

After proximity brings people together, what's the first thing we're likely to notice about those we meet? Their looks, of course. And, although we all know that there is much more to people than their external appearance, looks count. Physical attractiveness has a substantial influence on the first impressions that people form of one another. In general, right or wrong, we tend to assume that good-looking people are more likable, better people than those who are unattractive (Etcoff, 1999).

The Bias for Beauty: "What Is Beautiful Is Good"

Imagine that you are given a photograph of a stranger's face and, using only that information, are asked to guess at the personality and prospects the person possesses. Studies of judgments like these routinely find that physically attractive

What Is Beautiful Is Good

Male and female research participants judged that physically attractive people were more likely than physically unattractive people to have the following characteristics:

Kind	Interesting
Strong	Poised
Outgoing	Sociable
Nurturant	Exciting dates
Sensitive	Better character
Sexually warm and responsive	

These same judges also believed that the futures for physically attractive people would differ in the following ways from the futures of physically unattractive people:

More prestige	Be more competent in marriage
Have a happier marriage	Have more fulfilling lives
Have more social and professional success	

Source: Findings from Dion, Berscheid, & Walster, 1972.

people are presumed to be interesting, sociable people who are likely to encounter personal and professional success in life and love (see Table 3.2). In general, we seem to use the crude stereotype that what is beautiful is good; we assume that attractive people have desirable traits that complement their desirable appearances (Langlois et al., 2000).

We don't expect good-looking strangers to be wonderful in every respect. The attractiveness stereotype leads us to assume that beautiful people are vivacious and socially skilled, reasonably intelligent and well-adjusted, but it does not affect our judgments of their integrity or compassion (Eagly, Ashmore, Makhijani, & Longo, 1991). There is even a downside to beauty; gorgeous people are assumed to be more likely to be vain and promiscuous (Dermer & Theil, 1975). Still, there's no question that attractive people make better overall impressions on strangers than less attractive people do.

The bias for beauty exists in Eastern as well as Western cultures, but the specific advantages attributed to attractive people vary somewhat from place to place. In Korea, for instance, pretty people are presumed to be sociable, intelligent, and socially skilled, just as they are in the United States. However, in keeping with Korea's collectivist culture (which emphasizes group harmony), attractive people are also presumed to be concerned with the well-being of others, a result that is not obtained in the West (Wheeler & Kim, 1997). The physical attractiveness stereotype may be pervasive, but its specific content seems to depend on the specific values of a culture.

The bias for beauty may also lead people to confuse beauty with talent. In the workplace, physically attractive people are more likely to be hired after a job interview and to receive higher rates of pay (Hamermesh & Biddle, 1994). If you rate the looks of people with MBA degrees from the University of Pittsburgh on a 1 to 5 scale, each one-point increase in physical attractiveness is worth $2,600 in average annual salary for men and $2,150 for women (Frieze,

Olson, & Russell, 1991). Attractive people even make better impressions in court; good-looking culprits convicted of misdemeanors in Texas get lower fines than they would have received had they been less attractive (Downs & Lyons, 1991).

But are the interactions and relationships of beautiful people any different from those of people who are less pretty? We'll address that question shortly. First, though, we need to assess whether we all tend to agree on who is pretty and who is not.

Who's Pretty?

The first research study ever conducted by one of your current authors (Rowland Miller) involved physical attractiveness. When I was an undergraduate at Cornell University, I needed photographs depicting attractive and unattractive women, so I got a school yearbook from another campus and carefully selected pictures of the people I thought were the most and least desirable of the bunch. I was startled to find, when I solicited the opinions of friends and classmates, that some of the women I thought were gorgeous got low ratings from some men, and some women I considered quite unattractive were appealing to other fellows. I did get a subset of photos on which there was unanimous agreement, but I've never forgotten that surprising idiosyncrasy in judgments of attractiveness.

Now, (too many!) years later, several studies have shown that, to a limited extent, beauty is indeed in the "eye of the beholder" (e.g., Diener, Wolsic, & Fujita, 1995). If you ask several men and several women to sit down, take a close look at each other, and rate everyone else's physical attractiveness, you'll get some mild disagreement among the observers as each one sees things, to some degree, his or her own way (Marcus & Miller, 2001).

However, diverse observers still agree in their perceptions of beauty much more than they disagree. Despite some variability from person to person, people generally share the same notions of who is and who isn't pretty (Marcus & Miller, 2001). Moreover, this consensus exists across ethnic groups; Asians, Hispanics, and black and white Americans all tend to agree with each other about the attractiveness of women from all four groups (Cunningham, Roberts, Barbee, Druen, & Wu, 1995). Even more striking is the finding that three-month-old infants exhibit preferences for faces like those that adults find attractive, too (Langlois, Ritter, Roggman, & Vaughn, 1991); when they are much too young to be affected by social norms, babies spend more time gazing at attractive than unattractive faces.

What faces are those? There's little doubt that women are more attractive if they have "baby-faced" features such as large eyes, a small nose, a small chin, and full lips (Jones, 1995). The point is not to look childish, however, but to appear feminine and youthful (Cunningham, Druen, & Barbee, 1997); beautiful women combine those baby-faced features with signs of maturity such as prominent cheekbones, narrow cheeks, and a broad smile (Cunningham, 1986). Women who present all these features are thought to be attractive all over the world (Jones, 1995).

Male attractiveness may be more complex. Men who have strong jaws and broad foreheads—who look strong and dominant—are usually thought to be handsome (Cunningham, Barbee, & Pike, 1990). (Envision George Clooney.) On the other hand, one study has shown that when average male faces are made slightly more feminine and baby-faced through computer imaging, the "feminized" faces—which look warm and friendly—are more attractive (Perrett et al., 1998). (Envision Leonardo DiCaprio.) More remarkably, there may be cyclical variations in women's preferences for these two types of looks; they may find rugged, manly features more appealing when they are ovulating and fertile, but be more attracted to youthful boyishness the rest of the month (Penton-Voak et al., 1999).

In any case, good-looking faces in both sexes have features that are neither too large nor too small. Indeed, they are quite average. If you use a computer to create composite images that combine the features of individual faces, the "average" faces that result are more attractive than nearly all of the faces that make up the composite (Langlois & Roggman, 1990; Rhodes & Trememwan, 1996). This is true not only in the United States but in China, Nigeria, and India as well (Pollard, 1995).

However, this doesn't mean that gorgeous people have bland, ordinary looks. The images that result from this averaging process are actually rather unusual. Their features are all proportional to one another; no nose is too big. Averaged faces are also *symmetrical*, with the two sides of the face being mirror images of one another; the eyes are the same size, the cheeks are the same width, and so on. Facial symmetry is attractive in its own right, whether or not a face is "average" (Grammer & Thornhill, 1994). In fact, if you take a close look at identical twins, whose faces are very similar, you'll probably think that the twin with the more symmetric face is the more attractive of the two (Mealey, Bridgstock, & Townsend, 1999). Apparently, symmetry and "averageness" each make their own contribution to facial beauty; even in a group of symmetrical images, faces are more appealing the more average they become (Rhodes, Sumich, & Byatt, 1999). Thus, beautiful faces seem to combine the best features of individual faces in a balanced, well-proportioned whole (Perrett, May, & Yoshikawa, 1994).

Of course, some bodies are more attractive than others, too. Men find women's shapes most alluring when they are of normal weight, neither too heavy nor too slender, and their waists are noticeably narrower than their hips (Singh, 1993). The most attractive **waist-to-hip ratio,** or WHR, is a curvy 0.7 in which the waist is 30 percent smaller than the hips; this shape seems to appeal to men in diverse cultures (Singh & Luis, 1995). In the United States, women make better impressions when they're underweight rather than overweight, but skinny women are *not* as attractive to men as they would be if they put on a few pounds. Normal weight is clearly the most attractive of all (Singh, 1993). Men also like larger, as opposed to smaller, breasts, but only if a woman has a low WHR; larger breasts don't enhance a woman's appeal if they are paired with a stocky body (Furnham, Dias, & McClelland, 1998).

Once again, male attractiveness is more complex. Men's bodies are most attractive when their waists are only slightly narrower than their hips, with a

WHR of 0.9. However, a nice shape doesn't attract a woman to a man unless he has other resources as well; a man's WHR only affects women's evaluations of him when he earns a healthy salary (Singh, 1995). A man is not all that attractive to women if he is handsome but poor.

An Evolutionary Perspective on Physical Attractiveness

Have you noticed that people's preferences for prettiness generally fit the assumptions of evolutionary psychology? Consider these patterns:

- Despite striking cultural differences, people all over the world tend to agree on who is and who is not attractive (Cunningham et al., 1995; Jones, 1995; Pollard, 1995).
- Babies appear to be born with preferences for the same faces that adults find attractive (Langlois et al., 1991). Some reactions to good looks may be inherited.
- People with symmetrical faces that we find attractive tend to enjoy better mental and physical health—and therefore make better mates—than do people with asymmetrical faces (Shackelford & Larsen, 1997).
- Hormones influence waist-to-hip ratios by affecting the distribution of fat on people's bodies. Women with WHRs near the attractive norm of 0.7 get pregnant more easily and tend to enjoy better physical health than do women with fewer curves (Singh, 1994). A man with an attractive WHR of 0.9 is likely to be in better health than another man with a plump belly (Singh, 1995). Both sexes are most attracted to the physical shapes that signal the highest likelihood of good health in the other sex.
- Finally, although everybody likes good looks, physical attractiveness matters most to people who live in equatorial regions of the world where there are many parasites and pathogens that can endanger good health (Gangestad & Buss, 1993). In such areas, unblemished beauty may be an especially good sign that someone is in better health—and will make a better mate—than someone whose face is in some way imperfect.

These patterns convince some theorists that standards of physical beauty have an evolutionary basis (e.g., Buss, 1999). Presumably, early humans who successfully sought fertile, healthy mates were more likely to reproduce successfully than were those who simply mated at random. As a result, the common preference of modern men for symmetrical, baby-faced, low-WHR women may be an evolved inclination that is rooted more in their human nature than in their particular cultural heritage.

Culture Matters, Too

On the other hand, there's no doubt that standards of attractiveness are also affected by changing economic and cultural conditions. Have you seen those Renaissance paintings of women who look fat by modern standards? During hard times, when a culture's food supply is unreliable, slender women are actually *less* desirable than heavy women are (Anderson, Crawford, Nadeau, &

Lindberg, 1992). Only during times of plenty are slender women considered to be attractive. Indeed, as economic prosperity spread through the United States during the twentieth century, women were expected to be slimmer and slimmer (Barber, 1998), so that *Playboy* Playmates and Miss America contestants are now skinnier, on average, than they were when you were born (Spitzer, Henderson, & Zivian, 1999).

Norms can differ across ethnic groups as well (influenced in part, perhaps, by different patterns of economic well-being). Black women in America are much more likely to be obese than white women are (Kuczmarski, Flegal, Campbell, & Johnson, 1994), but they are actually much more likely to be satisfied with their weight (Stevens, Kumanyika, & Keil, 1994). White women consider obesity to be unattractive, but black women do not (Hebl & Heatherton, 1998). (But watch out: Black *men* prefer the same curvaceous 0.7 WHR that white men do [Singh & Luis, 1995]).

These findings suggest the possibility that human nature and environmental conditions work together to shape our collective judgments of who is and who isn't pretty. Nothing is certain; although we expect people with attractive faces to be especially healthy, it doesn't always turn out that way (Kalick, Zebrowitz, Langlois, & Johnson, 1998). Still, beauty is not just in the eye of the beholder. There is remarkable agreement about who's gorgeous and who's ugly around the world.

Who Has a Bias for Beauty?

Still, we should note that some people do care more about physical attractiveness than others do. How important are others' looks to you? Your answer may depend on whether you are a man or a woman. All over the world, men report higher interest in having a physically attractive romantic partner than women do (see Figure 3.2). If they run a personal ad seeking a partner, for instance, men are more likely than women to come right out and specify that they're looking for an attractive mate (Feingold, 1990).

But don't get the wrong impression: Women do care about men's looks. When college students meet each other, physical attractiveness is one of the most powerful—if not *the* most potent—influences on how much the two sexes will initially like each other (Sprecher, 1989). In one compelling example of this effect, researchers at the University of Minnesota created 376 blind dates when they invited freshmen students to a "computer dance" at which the students expected to meet a compatible partner who had been selected for them by computer (Walster, Aronson, Abrahams, & Rottman, 1966). The students had filled out a variety of scales that assessed their personalities and attitudes, but the researchers paired them off at random to see what would happen. Two hours later, after these young adults had gotten a chance to know one another, what do you think determined how much they liked each other? Similar backgrounds? Shared interests? Compatible personalities? Of all the variables measured by the researchers, there was only one influence that mattered: physical attractiveness. The better-looking the students were, the more their partners liked them.

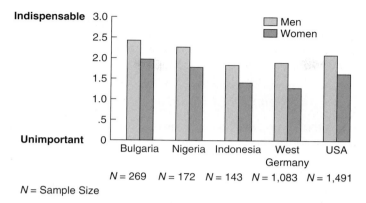

FIGURE 3.2. Desire for physical attractiveness in a romantic partner.
From Buss, D. M., & Schmitt, D. P. (1993). Sexual strategies theory:
An evolutionary perspective on human mating. *Psychological
Review, 100,* 204–232. Copyright © 1993 by the American
Psychological Association. Adapted with permission.

Overall, a partner's physical attractiveness is more important to men than
to women. That may be why 91 percent of the cosmetic surgery performed in
the United States in 1998 was done on women (Kalb, 1999); women know that
men are judging them by their looks. However, women are also attracted to a
handsome man, and physical attractiveness may be the single most important
influence on early attraction among both men and women.

Nevertheless, the bias for beauty is stronger in some people than others, as
research on the personality trait of **self-monitoring** shows. Self-monitoring
refers to people's tendency to regulate their social behavior to meet the demands of different social situations (Snyder, 1974; Snyder & Gangestad, 1986).
High self-monitors are ready, willing, and able to tailor their behavior to make
a good impression on others. In contrast, low self-monitors strive to be true to
their private beliefs and desires and are more consistent across situations. (You
can assess yourself on the Self-Monitoring Scale; it's reprinted in chapter 4.)

Men who are high self-monitors—who are sensitive to the impressions
they make on others—are especially interested in having good-looking dating
partners. In fact, if they have to choose between (a) a date with an attractive
woman who has an ugly personality and (b) a date with an unattractive woman
who has a lovely personality, they'll pick the gorgeous shrew (Snyder,
Berscheid, & Glick, 1985). Even more remarkably, if they're asked to pick a new
employee, high self-monitoring men hire women who are beautiful but incompetent over women who are talented but plain (Snyder, Berscheid, &
Matwychuk, 1988). Appearance is obviously very important to such men. In
contrast, men who are low self-monitors are more attracted to substance than
style. They select dates with desirable personalities and employees with talent
over better-looking competitors who are less friendly or skilled.

So personalities matter, too. The studies just mentioned required men to
make difficult choices, and the preferences of high and low self-monitoring

men are not so starkly different when you allow them to rate many different partners (Shaffer & Bazzini, 1997). Nevertheless, both men and women may find appearance more appealing than substance if they are high self-monitors (Snyder & DeBono, 1985).

The Interactive Costs and Benefits of Beauty

People obviously notice the physical attractiveness of those they meet, and some of us are consistently considered to be more attractive than others. What effects do our looks have on our interactions with others? To adequately answer that question, we need to examine various interactions with diverse partners on varied occasions, and several studies have done just that. Physical attractiveness *is* influential.

As you might expect, beautiful women get more dates than plain women do (Reis, Nezlek, & Wheeler, 1980). Moreover, people tend to enjoy their interactions with attractive women; they talk more and are more involved, and they feel that the interactions are of higher quality (Garcia, Stinson, Ickes, Bissonnette, & Briggs, 1991). Handsome men fare well, too, receiving more smiles, talk, and positive feelings from others than unattractive men do (Garcia et al., 1991; Stiles, Walz, Schroeder, Williams, & Ickes, 1996).

However, men's attractiveness may play an even larger part in influencing their access to the other sex than women's looks do (Reis et al., 1982). There is actually no correlation overall between a woman's beauty and the amount of time she spends interacting with men. Attractive women get more dates, as we noted, but plain women spend plenty of time interacting with men in group settings where others are present. In contrast, men's looks *are* correlated with the number and length of the interactions they have with women. Unattractive men have fewer interactions of any sort with fewer women than good-looking guys do. In this sense, then, physical attractiveness has a bigger effect on the social lives of men than it does on women.

Being more popular, attractive people tend to be less lonely, more socially skilled, and a little happier than the rest of us (Diener, Wolsic, & Fujita, 1995; Feingold, 1992b). One study even suggested that physical attractiveness accounts for about 10 percent of the variability in people's adjustment and well-being over their lifetimes (Burns & Farina, 1992). The lives of beautiful people aren't as rosy as the "beautiful is good" stereotype would suggest, however, because there are disadvantages to being attractive as well. For one thing, others lie to pretty people more often. People are more willing to misrepresent their interests, personalities, and incomes to get a date with an attractive person than they are to fabricate an image for a plain partner (Rowatt, Cunningham, & Druen, 1999). As a result, realizing that others are often "brown-nosing," or trying to ingratiate themselves, gorgeous people may cautiously begin mistrusting or discounting some of the praise they receive from others.

Consider this clever study: Attractive or unattractive people receive a written evaluation of their work from a person of the other sex who either does or does not know what they look like (Major, Carrington, & Carnevale, 1984). In every case, each participant receives a flattering, complimentary evaluation. (Indeed, everyone gets exactly the same praise.) How did the recipients react to this good news? Attractive men and women trusted the praise more and assumed that it was more sincere when it came from someone who didn't know they were good-looking. They were evidently used to getting insincere compliments from people who were impressed by their looks. On the other hand, unattractive people found the praise more compelling when the evaluator did know they were plain; sadly, they probably weren't used to compliments from people who were aware of their unappealing appearances.

So, gorgeous people are used to pleasant interactions with others, but they may not trust other people as much as less attractive people do (Reis et al., 1982). In particular, others' praise may be ambiguous. If you're very attractive, you may never be sure whether others are complimenting you because they respect your abilities or because they like your looks. Over time, this may not be good for your self-confidence (Satterfield & Muehlenhard, 1997).

There even seem to be various costs and benefits for those of us who merely associate with other very attractive people. On the plus side, for most of us, it feels good to gaze at handsome or lovely people of the other sex; simply looking at them puts us in a good mood (Kenrick, Montello, Gutierres, & Trost, 1993). On the other hand, when we encounter gorgeous people of the same sex, we often feel worse, probably because we suffer by comparison. People create different—and poorer—evaluations of their own looks when they compare themselves to attractive others than when they compare themselves to ordinary folks (Thornton & Moore, 1993). This is an example of a **contrast effect,** a perceptual phenomenon in which a given object is perceived differently depending on the other objects to which it is compared. If we compare ourselves to supermodels, for instance, we can seem quite frumpy, although we may actually be rather appealing compared to most people.

A similar contrast effect can influence our perceptions of other people, too. If people examine very attractive models from *Playboy* or *Penthouse* magazines, they then give lower ratings to pictures of nude women of average attractiveness (Kenrick & Gutierres, 1989). Worse, men who view such models feel less sexual attraction and love for their own lovers (Kenrick & Gutierres, 1989)! Women's ratings of their lovers are not affected in this manner. Nevertheless, both men and women tend to underestimate the attractiveness of average people when they use unusually attractive people as a standard of comparison. These findings raise the disturbing possibility that our popular culture leaves us ill-equipped to appreciate the beauty of the real people we're likely to meet. Stop a moment and consider the media you consume each day; the TV you watch, the magazines you read, and the websites you visit probably all present an endless parade of very attractive people, most of whom are prettier than the people who sit next to you in class. The danger is that you may be doing your classmates a disservice, thinking that they're not especially attractive, because you're using an unrealistic, artificially high standard of attractiveness based on a select group of people that you'll never actually meet!

Still, despite these various pros and cons, the bottom line is that good looks make someone attractive to others. Beauty is aesthetically pleasing and puts us in a good mood, and we usually assume that beautiful people possess a variety of other desirable traits as well. Thus, the effects of physical attractiveness, like proximity, are consistent with the reward model of interpersonal attraction.

Matching in Physical Attractiveness

We've spent several pages discussing physical attractiveness—which is an indication of its importance in relationship research—but there is one last point to make about its influence at the beginning of a relationship. People may want gorgeous partners, but they're likely to end up paired off with others who are only about as attractive as they are (Feingold, 1988). Partners in established relationships tend to have similar levels of physical attractiveness; that is, their looks are well-matched. This phenomenon is known as **matching.**

Matching helps determine whether partners ever get together in the first place. For instance, when customers pay a fee to a professional dating service to gain access to videos and background information about potential partners, what data do they use to select a desirable date? Physical attractiveness, of course (Folkes, 1982). But in these situations, if a client indicates interest in someone, the dating service notifies that person and gives him or her a chance to see the first client's tapes. Only when both people are interested does the service give each of them the other's phone number. Then, after they talk on the phone, one or more dates sometimes follow. The point here is that clients often record interest in potential partners who are more attractive than they are, but nothing happens because those other people aren't interested in return. The relationships that get started typically involve two people who are a reasonably good match in physical attractiveness, and the more similar their looks, the further their relationship is likely to progress (Folkes, 1982).

Indeed, the more serious and committed a relationship becomes, the more obvious matching usually is. People sometimes share casual dates with others who are not as good-looking as they, but they are unlikely to go steady with, or become engaged to, someone who is "out of their league" (White, 1980b). What this means is that, even if everybody wants a physically attractive partner, only those who are also good-looking are likely to get them. None of the really good-looking people want to pair off with us folks of average looks, and we, in turn, don't want partners who are "beneath us," either (Carli, Ganley, & Pierce-Otay, 1991).

Thus, it's not very romantic, but similarity in physical attractiveness may operate as a screening device. If people generally value good looks, matching will occur as they settle for the best-looking partner who will have them in return (Kalick & Hamilton, 1986). As a result, husbands and wives tend to be noticeably similar in physical attractiveness (Price & Vandenberg, 1979). And trouble may loom if that match fades away. A leading cause of sexual difficulty among married men is the perception that—although *they* still "look good"— their wives have "let themselves go" and are less attractive than they used to be (Margolin & White, 1987).

RECIPROCITY: LIKING THOSE WHO LIKE US

The matching phenomenon suggests that, to enjoy the most success in the relationship marketplace, we should pursue partners who are likely to return our interest. In fact, most people do just that. When we ponder possible partners, most of us rate our realistic interest in others—and the likelihood that we will approach them and try to start a relationship—using a formula like this (Shanteau & Nagy, 1979):

$$\text{Desirability} = \text{Physical Attractiveness} \times \text{Probability of Acceptance}$$

Everything else being equal, the better-looking people are, the more desirable they are. However, this formula suggests that physical attractiveness is multiplied by our judgments of how likely it is that someone will like us in return to determine a particular person's overall appeal. Do the math. If someone likes us a lot but is rather ugly, that person probably won't be our first choice for a date. If someone else is gorgeous but doesn't like us back, we won't waste our time. The most appealing potential partner is often someone who is moderately attractive and who seems to offer a reasonably good chance of accepting us (perhaps *because* he or she isn't gorgeous [Huston, 1973]).

Not everyone follows this formula—some people just think desirability equals physical attractiveness (Shanteau & Nagy, 1979)—but a high likelihood of acceptance from others appears to be an important consideration for most of us. For instance, surveys of men at the University of Wisconsin and Texas A&M University found that, if they found a woman attractive, very few of them— only 3 percent—would offer her a date if they had no idea what she would say in response (Muehlenhard & Miller, 1988). Almost all of the men reported that they would either bide their time and look for signs of reciprocal interest or simply give up and do nothing at all if they weren't confident, before they even asked, that a potential date would say yes.

Obviously, people are usually reluctant to risk rejection. Another demonstration of this point emerged from a clever study in which college men had to choose where to sit to watch a movie (Bernstein, Stephenson, Snyder, & Wicklund, 1983). They had two choices: squeeze into a small cubicle next to a very attractive woman, or sit in an adjacent cubicle—alone—where there was plenty of room. The key point is that some of the men believed that the *same* movie was playing on both monitors, whereas other men believed that *different* movies were showing on the two screens. Let's consider the guys' dilemma. Presumably, most of them wanted to become acquainted with the beautiful woman. However, when only one movie was available, squeezing in next to her entailed some risk of rejection; their intentions would be obvious, and there was some chance that the woman would tell them to "back off." However, when two different movies were available, they were on safer ground. Sitting next to the woman could mean that they just wanted to see that particular movie, not that they were attracted to her, and a rebuff from her would be rude. In fact, only 25 percent of the men dared to sit next to the woman when the same movie was on both monitors, but 75 percent did so when two movies were available and their intentions were more ambiguous. Moreover, we can be sure that the men were taking advantage of the uncertain situation to move in on the woman—instead of really wanting to see that particular movie—because the experimenters kept changing which movie played on which screen. Three-fourths of the men squeezed in with the gorgeous woman no matter which movie was playing there!

In general, then, people seem to take heed of the likelihood that they will be accepted and liked by others, and they are more likely to approach those who offer acceptance than rejection. Indeed, everything else being equal, it's hard *not* to like those who like us (Curtis & Miller, 1986). Imagine that the first thing you hear about a new transfer student is that he or she has noticed you and really likes you; don't you feel positively toward him or her in return?

Obviously, this tendency to like those who like us is consistent with the reward model of attraction. It also fits another perspective known as **balance theory** that suggests that people desire consistency among their thoughts, feelings, and social relationships (Heider, 1958). When two people like each other, their feelings fit together well and can be said to be "balanced." This is also true when two people dislike each other, but not when a person likes someone else but is disliked in return. But what happens when there are three people involved? In a study that addressed this question, college students encountered an experimenter who was either pleasant or rude to them (Aronson & Cope, 1968). After that, the experimenter's supervisor walked in and was pleasant or rude to the experimenter! The students then had an opportunity to do a favor for the supervisor. How did they react? The students were more generous toward the supervisor when he or she had been either nice to the pleasant experimenter or mean to the unpleasant experimenter—that is, when the two interactions seemed balanced. This study and the rest of the research evidence generally support the notion that we prefer balance among our relationships. For that reason, then, before we ever meet them, we often expect that our enemies' enemies will be our friends.

SIMILARITY: LIKING PEOPLE WHO ARE JUST LIKE US

It's rewarding to meet people who like us. It's also enjoyable to find others who are *just* like us and who share the same background, interests, and tastes. Indeed, one of the most basic principles of interpersonal attraction is the rule of similarity: Like attracts like. The old cliché that "birds of a feather flock together" is absolutely correct. Few other aspects of attraction have been as thoroughly and extensively documented. Consider these examples:

- At the University of Michigan, male transfer students were given free rooms in a boardinghouse in exchange for their participation in a study of developing friendships among the previously unacquainted men (Newcomb, 1961). At the end of the semester, the men's closest friendships were with those housemates with whom they had the most in common.

BOX 3.1

What's a Good Opening Line?

You're shopping for groceries, and you keep crossing paths with an attractive person you've seen somewhere on campus who smiles at you warmly when your eyes meet. You'd like to meet him or her. What should you say? You need to do more than just say, "Hi," and wait for a response, don't you? Perhaps some clever food-related witticism is the way to go: "Is your dad a baker? You've sure got a nice set of buns."

Common sense suggests that such attempts at humor are good opening lines. Indeed, various books invite you to use their funny pickup lines to increase your chances of getting a date (e.g., Allen & Ferrari, 1997; Dweck & Ivey, 1998). Be careful with such purchases, however; they may lead you astray. Careful research has compared the effectiveness of three different types of opening lines, and a cute or flippant remark may be the *worst* thing to say.

Let's distinguish cute lines from "innocuous" openers (such as just saying, "Hi" or "How're you doing?") and "direct" lines that honestly communicate your interest (such as "Hi, I'm a lit-

tle embarrassed about this, but I'd like to get to know you"). When women evaluate lines like these by watching videotapes of men who use them, they like the cute lines much less than the other two types (Kleinke & Dean, 1990). More importantly, when a guy actually uses one of these lines on a woman in a singles bar, the innocuous and direct openers get a favorable response 70 percent of the time, compared to a success rate of only 24 percent for the cute lines (Cunningham, 1989). There's no comparison: Simply saying hello is a much smarter strategy than trying to be cute.

Why, then, do people write books full of flippant pickup lines? Because they're men. When a *woman* uses a cute line on a *man* in a singles bar, she gets a favorable response 90 percent of the time. In fact, any opening line from a woman works well with a man; in Cunningham's (1989) study, saying "Hi" succeeded every time. Men don't seem to care much what opening lines women use, and this may lead them to overestimate women's liking for cute openers in return.

- At Purdue University, researchers intentionally created blind dates between men and women who held either similar social and political attitudes or dissimilar views (Byrne, Ervin, & Lamberth, 1970). Each couple spent 45 minutes at the student union getting to know each other over soft drinks. After the "dates," similar couples liked each other more than dissimilar couples did.
- At Kansas State University, 13 men spent 10 days jammed together in a simulated fallout shelter (Griffit & Veitch, 1974). Their feelings about each other were assessed along the way. The men got along fine with those with whom they had a lot in common, but would have thrown out of the shelter, if they could, those who were the least similar to themselves.

As these examples suggest, similarity is attractive.

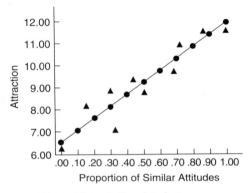

FIGURE 3.3. The relationship between attitude similarity and attraction.

Attraction is strongly influenced by similarity. People who are similar in background characteristics, personality, physical attractiveness, and attitudes are more likely to be attracted to each other than are those who are dissimilar.

What Kind of Similarity?

But what kinds of similarities are we talking about? Well, almost any kind. Whether they are lovers or friends, happy relationship partners resemble each other more than random strangers do on almost any measure. First, there's *demographic* similarity in age, sex, race, education, religion, and social class (Warren, 1966). Remember your best friends from high school? Most of them were probably of the same age, sex, and race (Kandel, 1978). Then there's similarity in *attitudes and values*. As Figure 3.3 shows, there is a straightforward link between the proportion of the attitudes two people share and their attraction to each other: the more agreement, the more liking (Byrne & Nelson, 1965). Take note of this pattern. Attraction doesn't level off after a certain amount of similarity is reached, and there's no danger in having "too much in common." Instead, where attitudes are concerned, the more similar two people are, the more they like each other. Think again about your high school friends: Your alcohol and drug use was probably similar to that of your friends (Kandel, 1978), and if you were a virgin, your best friend probably was, too (Billy & Udry, 1985).

Finally, partners may have similar *personalities*. People with similar styles and traits like each other better, especially as time goes by (Botwin, Buss, & Schackelford, 1997; Tesser et al., 1998). In particular, husbands and wives with similar personalities have happier marriages than do spouses with different styles (Caspi & Herbener, 1990). Moreover, the effects of personality similarity on attraction can be observed in both cognitive and emotional domains. People who think in similar ways—who resemble each other in "cognitive complexity," the way that they structure and organize their thoughts and perceptions—are more attracted to each other than are those who differ in cognitive complexity (Neimeyer, 1984). Similar emotional styles also enhance attraction. Happy people like to associate with other happy people, of course, but gloomy people are actually more attracted to other gloomy people than to those with brighter moods (Locke & Horowitz, 1990). Given these findings, you probably won't be surprised to learn that people are most attracted to others with similar attachment styles, too (Frazier et al., 1996); secure people prefer other secure people, whereas anxious people actually prefer others who are also anxious.

Do Opposites Attract?

The more similar two people are to one another, the more they like each other. Why, then, do many people believe "opposites attract?" Are there instances in which people become more attracted to each other the less they have in common? In general, the answer is no. With perhaps just one exception (which we'll mention later), there is no evidence that people are routinely more content with dissimilar, rather than similar, partners. However, there are several important subtleties in the way similarity operates that may mislead people into thinking that opposites do sometimes attract.

Matching Is a Broad Process

We've already seen that people tend to pair off with others who are similar to them in physical attractiveness. On the other hand, notable mismatches in looks sometimes occur—as in 1993, when Anna Nicole Smith, a 26-year-old *Playboy* Playmate of the Year, married J. Howard Marshall II, an 89-year-old billionaire. In such cases, the partners are dissimilar in specific ways, and "opposites" may seem to attract. That's an unsophisticated view, however, because such partners are really just matching in a broader sense, trading looks for money and vice versa (Elder, 1969). They may have different assets, but such partners are still seeking good matches with others who have similar standing overall in the interpersonal marketplace.

This sort of thing goes on all the time. Among heterosexuals, high-income men who advertise for romantic partners (in personal ads or at dating services) are likely to stipulate that they are seeking an attractive woman, whereas attractive women are likely to announce that they want a well-to-do man (Green, Buchanan, & Heuer, 1984; Koestner & Wheeler, 1988). Among homosexuals,

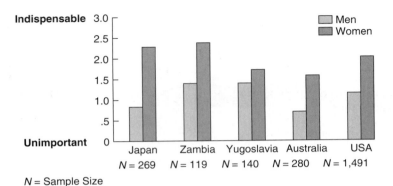

FIGURE 3.4. Desire for good financial prospects in a romantic partner.
From Buss, D. M., & Schmitt, D. P. (1993). Sexual strategies theory:
An evolutionary perspective on human mating. *Psychological Review,
100*, 204–232. Copyright © 1993 by the American Psychological
Association. Adapted with permission.

men who are not infected with HIV (the virus that causes AIDS) are picky, re-
questing higher status, more attractive partners in their personal ads than do
men who are infected with HIV (Hatala, Baack, & Parmenter, 1998). It doesn't
seem very romantic, but fame, wealth, health, talent, and looks all appear to be
commodities that people use to attract more desirable partners than they might
otherwise entice. If we think of matching as a broad process that involves both
physical attractiveness and various other assets and traits, it's evident that people usually pair off with others of similar status, and like attracts like.

    In fact, trade-offs like these are central ideas in evolutionary psychology.
Because men are more likely to reproduce successfully when they mate with
healthy, fertile women, natural selection has presumably promoted men's interest in youthful and beautiful partners (Buss, 1999). Youth is important because
women are no longer fertile after they reach menopause in middle age. Beauty
is meaningful because it is roughly correlated with some aspects of good health
(Gangestad & Buss, 1993; Singh, 1994). Thus, men especially value good looks
in women (see Figure 3.2), and, as they age, they marry women who are increasingly younger than themselves (Kenrick & Keefe, 1992): Men who marry
in their twenties pair off with women who are two years younger than they are,
on average, but if a man marries in his fifties, his wife is likely to be 15 years
younger than he.

    Women don't need to be as concerned about their partners' youth because
men normally retain their capacity for reproduction as long as they live. Instead, according to the parental investment model, women should seek mates
who can shelter and protect them during the long period of pregnancy and
nursing (Feingold, 1992a); they should prefer powerful, high-status men with
resources that can contribute to the well-being of mother and child. In fact, as
Figure 3.4 illustrates, women *do* care more about their partners' financial
prospects than men do (Buss & Schmitt, 1993). Furthermore, women's

---

BOX 3.2

Interethnic Relationships

Most of our intimate relationships are likely to be with others of the same race. Nevertheless, marriages between spouses from different ethnic groups are much more common than they used to be (Saluter, 1996), and they raise an interesting question: If similarity attracts, what's going on? The answer is actually straightforward: Nothing special. If you ignore the fact of their dissimilar ethnicity, interethnic couples appear to be influenced by the same motives that guide everyone else. The partners tend to be similar in age, education, and attractiveness (Kouri & Lasswell,

1993; Lewis, Yancey, & Bletzer, 1997), and their relationships, like most, are based on common interests and personal compatibility (Shibazaki & Brennan, 1998). Circumstances may matter; compared to other people, those in interethnic relationships report that they had a larger number of potential partners of other ethnicities available to them (Shibazaki & Brennan, 1998). In general, however, interethnic couples are just like any others: Two people who are more alike than different decide to stay together because they fall in love (Porterfield, 1982).

---

preferences for the age of their mates do not change as they age; women prefer to marry men who are a few years older throughout their entire lives (Kenrick & Keefe, 1992).

Thus, matching based on the exchange of feminine youth and beauty for masculine status and resources is commonplace. Indeed, it occurs around the world (Buss, 1989). Still, is it the result of evolutionary pressures? Homosexual men and women have age preferences for their partners that are like those of heterosexual men and women, which is a bit difficult for an evolutionary model to explain (Kenrick et al., 1995). In addition, advocates of the cultural perspective argue that women pursue desirable resources through their partners because they have been denied direct access to political and economic power on their own (Eagly & Wood, 1999; Howard, Blumstein, & Schwartz, 1987). Different possibilities exist. In any case, the bottom line here is that matching is a broad process that involves multiple resources and traits. When "opposites" seem to attract, people may be trading one asset for another in order to obtain partners of similar social status.

Discovering Similarities Takes Time

Another source of confusion lies in the fact that it takes a while for two people to get to know each other well enough to understand fully what they do and do not have in common. For one thing, various misplaced hopes and expectations can get in the way. Even when they know nothing else about her, for instance, men assume they have more in common with an attractive woman than with one who is plain (Marks & Miller, 1982). Initial attraction for any reason, such as physical attractiveness or demographic similarity, can lead us to

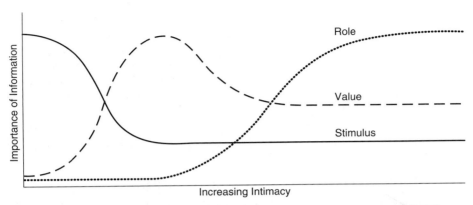

FIGURE 3.5. Three different phases of relationship development. Murstein's (1987) Stimulus-Value-Role theory suggests that developing relationships are influenced by three different types of information as time goes by and the partners learn more about each other.
Source: Murstein, 1987.

expect that someone has attitudes and values similar to ours. If we're mistaken, correcting such misperceptions can take time.

This process was evident in Newcomb's (1961) study of developing friendships among transfer students sharing a boardinghouse. Soon after they met, the men liked best the housemates who they thought were most like them; at first, their friendships were influenced mostly by **perceived similarity.** As the semester progressed, however, the actual similarities the men shared with each other played a larger and larger role in their friendships. When they got to know each other better, the men clearly preferred those who really were similar to them, although this was not always the case at first.

Even when we feel we know our partners well, there may be surprises ahead. According to Bernard Murstein's (1987) **stimulus-value-role** theory, there are three different types of information we gain about a new partner that influence developing relationships. When partners first meet, their attraction to each other is primarily based on "stimulus" information involving obvious attributes such as age, sex, and physical appearance. Thereafter, during the "value" stage, attraction depends on similarity in attitudes and beliefs, as people learn whether they like the same kinds of pizzas, movies, and vacations (see Figure 3.5). Only later does "role" compatibility become important as partners finally find out if they agree on the basics of parenting, careers, and housecleaning, among other life tasks. The point is that partners can be perfectly content with each other's tastes in politics and entertainment without ever realizing that they disagree fundamentally about where they'd like to live and how many kids—if any!—they want to have. Important dissimilarities sometimes become apparent only after couples have married; such spouses may stay together despite their differences, but it's not because opposites attract.

The influence of time and experience is also apparent in **fatal attractions** (Felmlee, 1995, 1998). These occur when a quality that initially attracts one person to another gradually becomes one of the most obnoxious, irritating things about that partner. For instance, partners who initially seem spontaneous and fun may later seem irresponsible and foolish, and those who appear strong may later seem domineering. In such cases, the annoying trait is no secret, but people fail to appreciate how their judgments of it will change with time. Importantly, such fatal qualities are often different from one's own; they may seem admirable and desirable at first, but over time people realize that such opposites aren't attractive (Felmlee, 1998).

Perceived Versus Real Similarity: Misperception Lingers

A third subtlety lies in the fact that we rarely get to know our partners as well as we think we do. The real similarities people share exert considerable influence on their relationships as time goes by. Even after years of marriage, however, spouses usually think they have more in common with each other than they really do. They overestimate the similarity that really exists. What makes this provocative is that there is a higher correlation between perceived similarity and marital satisfaction than there is between real similarity and marital bliss (Byrne & Blaylock, 1963; Levinger & Breedlove, 1966). To some degree, people seem to be married to illusory images of their partners that portray them as similar soulmates, and they might be disappointed to learn the true extent of their disagreements about various issues.

This tendency to form pleasant images of our partners can help maintain relationships, as we'll see in chapter 4. On the other hand, to the extent that it involves any misperception, it can also help explain why opposites sometimes seem to attract. If they try hard enough, people may perceive similarity where it does not exist and be attracted to others who are actually quite different from them. Perceived similarity can bring people together, at least for a while, even when their dissimilarity is apparent to everyone else.

Maybe It's Dissimilarity, Not Similarity, that Matters

Not all researchers agree that similarity is attractive; instead, some argue that *dis*similarity is *un*attractive and leads us to avoid others (Rosenbaum, 1986). In this view, we keep our distance from others who seem different from us, but we do not like others better the more similar they become. Such a process would mean that once we screen out those who are clearly unlike us, similarity has little effect on our choices of partners. As a result, people may pair off with others who are only somewhat like them, and opposites may seem to attract.

Indeed, romantic partners may not assess the similarity of their lovers as carefully as friends do. People may feel romantic infatuation for a wide variety of other people, including some with whom they have little in common (Lykken & Tellegen, 1993). On the other hand, real similarity improves romantic relationships (Hendrick, 1981), and it is plainly at work in most friendships (e.g., Carli, Ganley, & Pierce-Otay, 1991). The best conclusion appears to be that both similarity and dissimilarity are influential (Tan & Singh, 1995); people first avoid dissimilar others, and then are more attracted to everyone else the more similar they seem to be (Byrne, Clore, & Smeaton, 1986).

One Way "Opposites" May Attract: Complementarity

Finally, there may be one particular way in which different types of behavior can fit together well. We like responses from others that help us reach our goals. Such behavior is said to *complement* our own, and **complementarity**—reactions that provide a good fit to our own—can be attractive. Most complementary behaviors are actually similar actions; people who are warm and agreeable, for instance, are happiest when they are met with warmth and good humor in return. However, one reliable form of complementarity involves different behaviors from two partners: dominance and submission. When people feel very sure of themselves, they want their partners to heed their advice; on other occasions, when people need help and advice, they want their partners to give it (Dryer & Horowitz, 1997). In this manner, "opposites" may occasionally attract.

We shouldn't overstate this case. People like others who have similar personalities much more than they like those who are different (Richard, Wakefield, & Lewak, 1990), and even dominant people like other assertive folks more than they like those who are chronically servile and submissive (Dryer & Horowitz, 1997). On the other hand, when you really want something, it's nice when your partner lets you have your way. (And if you're both generous, understanding, and self-confident enough, you can take turns rewarding each other in this fashion.) The important thing to remember is that similar partners probably supply us what we want more often than anyone else can.

Why Is Similarity Attractive?

It's usually reassuring to meet others who are just like us. Encountering similarity in others can be comforting, reminding us that we're okay the way we are (Byrne & Clore, 1970). Similar others are also more likely to like us, so we anticipate pleasant, friendly interaction with such people (Condon & Crano, 1988). Then, when we give it a try, we usually do have smooth, relatively effortless interactions with those who are a lot like us (Davis, 1981); there are fewer points of disagreement and conflict, and more things we can happily do together. As we've seen, there are several reasons why opposites may seem to attract, but in fact birds of a feather do flock together. Similarity is rewarding; opposition is not.

BARRIERS: LIKING THE ONES WE CANNOT HAVE

A final influence on attraction involves the common tendency for people to struggle to overcome barriers that keep them from what they want. The theory of psychological **reactance** states that when people lose their freedom of action or choice, they strive to regain that freedom (Brehm & Brehm, 1981). As a result, we may want something more if we are threatened with losing it.

This principle can apparently affect our feelings about our partners in relationships. Among unmarried couples, researchers sometimes observe an interesting pattern called the **Romeo and Juliet effect:** The more their parents interfere with their romances, the more love people feel for their partners (Driscoll, Davis, & Lipetz, 1972). This may be more than just a simple correlation; over time, parental interference may play an active role in increasing the ardor young lovers feel for each other (Driscoll et al., 1972). This pattern doesn't occur all the time (Leslie, Huston, & Johnson, 1986), but it does suggest that parents should think twice before they forbid their teenagers to see certain partners. If they create a state of reactance, the parents may unintentionally make the forbidden partners seem more attractive than they are. The best course of action in such cases may be for the parents to express their displeasure mildly or even to do nothing at all.

Another kind of barrier occurs every night when bars close and everybody has to go home. If you're looking for a late-night date, you may find that the potential partners in a bar seem more and more attractive as closing time approaches and you face the prospect of leaving alone. In fact, when time is running out, unattached bar patrons consider the available members of the other sex to be better-looking than they seemed to be earlier in the evening (Pennebaker et al., 1979). This phenomenon doesn't involve "beer goggles," or intoxication; it occurs even if people haven't been drinking (Gladue & Delaney, 1990). However, it only occurs among those who are seeking company they don't yet have; those who are already committed to close relationships don't exhibit this pattern (Madey et al., 1996). Thus, the "closing time effect" appears to be another case of desired-but-forbidden fruit seeming especially sweet.

SO, WHAT DO MEN AND WOMEN WANT?

We are nearly at the end of our survey of major influences on attraction, but one important point remains. As we mentioned, men and women differ in the value they place on a partner's physical attractiveness and income. We don't want those results to leave you with the wrong impression, however, because despite those differences, the sexes generally seek the same qualities in their relational partners. Both men and women rate warmth and kindness, a desirable personality, and being liked in return as the three most important attributes they want in a friend or lover (Buss & Barnes, 1986; Sprecher, 1998). So, attraction isn't so mysterious after all. Everybody seems to want partners who are amiable, agreeable, and accepting, and men and women do not differ in this regard. To the extent there is any surprise here, it's in the news that women don't simply want strong, dominant men; they want their fellows to be warm and kind, too (Jensen-Campbell, Graziano, & West, 1995). If you're an unemotional, macho male, take note: Women will be more impressed if you develop some affectionate warmth to go with your strength and power.

CHAPTER SUMMARY

The Fundamental Basis of Attraction: A Matter of Rewards

According to most theories, we are attracted to people whose presence is rewarding to us. Two major types of reward influence attraction: direct rewards produced by someone (rewarding behaviors, rewarding characteristics, access to external rewards) and rewarding associations in which we connect the presence of another person with other positive experiences. Attraction is an interactive process involving personal needs, another's perceived characteristics, and the situation.

Proximity: Liking the Ones We're Near

Proximity provides the opportunity for social interactions but does not determine the quality of these interactions. We select our friends, and our enemies, from those around us.

Convenience: Proximity Is Rewarding, Distance Is Costly. Relationships with distant partners are ordinarily less satisfying than they would be if the partners were nearby, because long-distance interaction offers fewer rewards but requires more costs.

Familiarity: Repeated Contact. In general, familiarity breeds attraction. Even brief, *mere exposure* to others usually increases our liking for them.

The Power of Proximity. Close proximity accentuates our feelings about others. We like most people better when they're nearby, but repeated contact with someone we do not like can increase hostility instead.

Physical Attractiveness: To See You Is to Like You

In general, people are attracted to others who are physically attractive.

The Bias for Beauty: "What Is Beautiful Is Good". Widespread stereotypes lead us to assume that attractive people have other desirable personal characteristics, but the specific beliefs about good-looking people vary from one culture to the next.

Who's Pretty? People all over the world have similar standards of physical beauty. Symmetrical faces with features that approximate the mathematical average of individual faces are especially beautiful. *Waist-to-hip ratios* of 0.7 are very appealing in women, whereas a WHR of 0.9 is attractive in a man, if he has money.

An Evolutionary Perspective on Physical Attractiveness. The cross-cultural agreement about beauty, the increased importance of attractiveness in areas prone to parasites, and the link between attractive waist-to-hip ratios and good health are all consistent with the assumptions of evolutionary psychology.

Culture Matters, Too. On the other hand, standards of beauty fluctuate with changing economic and cultural conditions. Modern norms require women to be more slender than they used to be.

Who Has a Bias for Beauty? Men care about the physical attractiveness of a potential partner more than women do, but looks are one of the most important influences on initial attraction for both men and women. People who are high in the personality trait of *self-monitoring* place particular emphasis on the physical attractiveness of others.

The Interactive Costs and Benefits of Beauty. Physical attractiveness has a larger influence on men's interactions than on women's; unattractive men have less contact with women than attractive men do. However, there are disadvantages to being beautiful; attractive people doubt the praise they receive from others, and are lied to more often. Still, attractive people tend to have pleasant interactions with others, and are generally a little happier than unattractive people are.

Comparing ourselves and others to exceptionally attractive models can lead us to underestimate our own and others' attractiveness. The media may do us a disservice by creating artificially high standards of beauty.

Matching in Physical Attractiveness. People tend to pair off with others of similar beauty. Physical attractiveness may operate as a filter with which people seek the most attractive partners who will have them in return.

Reciprocity: Liking Those Who Like Us

People are reluctant to risk rejection. We like those who offer a high probability of accepting us in return, and rarely offer dates to people whose acceptance is uncertain. Indeed, most people seem to calculate others' global desirability by multiplying their physical attractiveness by their probability of reciprocal liking.

These findings are consistent with balance theory, which holds that people desire consistency among their thoughts, feelings, and relationships. A preference for balance encourages us to like our friends' friends and our enemies' enemies.

Similarity: Liking People Who Are Just Like Us

Birds of a feather flock together. People like those who are similar to them.

What Kind of Similarity? Happy relationship partners resemble each other on almost any measure. They come from similar demographic groups, share similar attitudes and values, and have similar cognitive and emotional traits.

Do Opposites Attract? Differences among people generally do not increase their attraction to each other. However, the belief that "opposites attract" may persist for several reasons. First, matching is a broad process in which people of similar social status sometimes offer each other different assets; fame, wealth, health, talent, and looks are all commodities people use to attract others. In particular, matching based on the exchange of women's youth and beauty for men's status and resources is commonplace.

Second, it takes time for *perceived similarity* to be replaced by a more accurate understanding of the attributes we share with others. The *stimulus-value-role* model suggests that there are three different types of information that influence developing relationships as time goes by. And time and experience can change people's perceptions of *fatal attractions*, characteristics of a new partner that are initially appealing but later aggravating. Still, misperception can linger. Even long-term partners usually think they have more in common than they really do.

Finally, even though we may avoid those who seem dissimilar to us, we may occasionally appreciate behavior from a partner that differs from our own but that complements our actions and helps us to reach our goals. Submissive responses to our attempts at dominance are an example of this.

Why Is Similarity Attractive? Similarity in others is reassuring. We also assume similar others will like us, and we usually enjoy pleasant interaction with those who are a lot like us.

Barriers: Liking the Ones We Cannot Have

The theory of psychological *reactance* suggests that people strive to restore lost freedom. The theory provides an explanation for the *Romeo and Juliet effect,* which occurs when parental interference increases the intensity of teenage romance. It may also influence the tendency for potential partners to get more attractive at closing time.

So, What Do Men and Women Want?

Men and women seek similar qualities in their partners, preferring those who offer warmth and kindness, desirable personalities, and acceptance. People generally desire amiable affection from their friends and lovers.

CHAPTER 4

Social Cognition

Imagine that you're home in bed, sick with a killer flu, and your lover doesn't call you during the day to see how you're doing. You're disappointed. Why didn't your partner call? Does he or she not love you enough? Is this just another frustrating example of his or her self-centered lack of compassion? Or is it more likely that your loving, considerate partner didn't want to risk waking you from a nap? There are several possible explanations, and you can choose a forgiving rationale, a blaming one, or something in between. And importantly, the choice may really be up to you; the facts of the case may allow several different interpretations. But whatever you decide, your judgments are likely to be consequential. At the end of the day, your perceptions will have either sustained or undermined the happiness of your relationship.

We'll focus on judgments like these in this chapter on **social cognition,** a term that refers generally to the processes of perception and judgment with which we make sense of our social worlds (Kunda, 1999). Our primary concern will be with the way we *think* about our relationships. We'll explore how our judgments of our partners and their behavior set the stage for the events that follow. We'll consider our own efforts to influence and control what our partners think of us. And we'll ponder just how well two people are likely to know each other, even in an intimate relationship. Throughout the chapter, we'll emphasize the fact that our perceptions and interpretations of our partnerships are of enormous importance: What we think helps to determine what we *feel,* and then how we *act*. This wouldn't be a problem if our judgments were always correct. However, there are usually a variety of reasonable ways to interpret an event (as our opening example suggests), and we can make mistakes, even when we're confident that we have arrived at the truth. Indeed, some of those mistakes may begin the moment we meet someone, as studies of first impressions reveal.

FIRST IMPRESSIONS (AND BEYOND)

Whether or not we realize it, we start judging people from the moment we meet them. Everyone we meet, for instance, fits some category of people about whom we already hold stereotyped first impressions. This may sound like a daring assertion, but it really isn't. Think about it: Everyone is either male or female, and (as we saw in chapter 1), gender-role stereotypes lead us to expect different behavior from men and women. Further, at a glance, we can tell if someone is beautiful or plain, and (as we saw in chapter 3), we assume that pretty people are likeable people. There are dozens of other distinctions that may come into play—young/old, black/white, pierced/unpierced, country/urban, and many more. The specifics of these stereotypes may vary from one perceiver to the next, but they operate similarly in anyone: Stereotypes supply us with preconceptions about what people are like. Moreover, we don't decide to use stereotypes; they influence us automatically, even when we are unaware of using them (Kunda, 1999).

Then, if we do interact with someone, we form preliminary impressions of them rapidly. Please take a moment to form a quick judgment of someone who is:

envious, stubborn, critical, impulsive, industrious, and intelligent.

Would you want this person as a coworker? Probably not much. Now, please take another moment to size up someone else who is:

intelligent, industrious, impulsive, critical, stubborn, and envious.

More impressive, yes? This person isn't perfect, but he or she seems competent and ambitious. The point, of course, is that the two descriptions offer the same information in a different *order,* and that's enough to engender two different impressions (Asch, 1946). Our judgments of others are influenced by a **primacy effect,** a tendency for the first information we receive about others to carry special weight, along with our stereotypes, in shaping our overall impressions of them.

There are several important reasons why first impressions matter and primacy effects occur. One is that, regardless of their source, our initial judgments of others influence our interpretations of the later information we encounter. Once a judgment forms, it affects how we use the data that follows—often in subtle ways that are difficult to detect. John Darley and Paget Gross (1983) demonstrated this when they showed Princeton students a videotape that established the social class of a young girl named "Hannah." Two different

When we meet others for the first time, we rarely form impressions of them in an unbiased, even-handed manner. Instead, various stereotypes and primacy effects influence our interpretations of the behavior we observe.

videos were prepared, and some people learned that Hannah was rather poor, whereas others found that she was pretty rich; she either played in a deteriorating, paved schoolyard and returned home to a dingy, small duplex, or played on expansive, grassy fields and went home to a large, lovely house. The good news is that when Darley and Gross asked the participants to guess how well Hannah was doing in school, they did not assume the rich kid was smarter than the poor kid; the two groups both assumed she was getting average grades. After that, however, the researchers showed the participants a tape of Hannah taking an aptitude test and doing an inconsistent job, answering some difficult questions correctly but blowing some easy ones. Everyone saw the same tape, but—and here's the bad news—they interpreted it very differently depending on their impressions of her social class. People who thought that Hannah was poor cited her mistakes and judged her as performing *below* average, whereas those who thought she was rich noted her successes and rated her as considerably *better* than average. Perceivers equipped with different preconceptions about Hannah's social class interpreted the *same* sample of her behavior in very different ways and came to very different conclusions. And note how subtle this process was: They didn't leap to biased assumptions about Hannah simply by knowing her social class, making a mistake that might easily be noticed, but their knowledge of her social class clearly lingered in their minds and contaminated their interpretations of her later actions. And they probably made their biased judgments with confidence, feeling fair and impartial. Both groups

could point to a portion of her test performance—the part that fit their preconceptions—and feel perfectly justified in making the judgments they did, never
realizing that people with other first impressions were watching the same
videotape and reaching contradictory conclusions.

Thus, first impressions affect our interpretations of the information we encounter about others. They also affect our choices of the new information we
seek. When we want to test a first impression about someone, we're more likely
to pursue information that will confirm that belief than to inquire after data
that could prove it wrong. That is, people ordinarily display a **confirmatory
bias:** They seek information that will prove them right more often than they
look for examples that would prove them wrong (Snyder, 1981). For instance,
imagine that you're instructed to interview a fellow student to find out if he or
she is a sociable extravert, and you're handed a list of possible questions to ask.
Some of the questions are neutral (e.g., "What are the good and bad points of
acting friendly and open?") but others are slanted toward eliciting introverted
responses (e.g., "What do you dislike about loud parties?"), while still others
are likely to get extraverted answers (e.g., "What do you do when you want to
liven things up at a party?"). How would you conduct the interview? If you're
like most people, you'd select questions that probe for evidence that your expectation is correct.

That's just what happened when researchers asked some people to find out
if a stranger was extraverted, but asked others to find out if the person was introverted (Snyder & Swann, 1978b). The two groups of interviewers adopted
two very different lines of investigation, asking questions that made it likely
that they'd get examples of the behaviors they expected to find. In fact, the interviews were so biased that audiences listening to them on tape actually believed that the strangers really were rather extraverted or introverted,
depending on the interviewers' preconceptions. Moreover, participants in this
study continued to display confirmatory biases even when they were given a
$25 incentive to be as accurate as possible.

The problem with confirmatory strategies is that they elicit one-sided information about others that fits our preconceptions—and as a result, we rarely
confront unequivocal evidence that our first impressions are wrong. Thus, not
only may we cling to snap judgments that are incorrect, we may think we're
right about others more often than we are. Indeed, most people are **overconfident** in their beliefs about others, making more mistakes than they realize.
Here's an example. After you begin dating a new romantic partner, you're
likely to become confident that you understand his or her sexual history as time
goes by. You'll probably feel increasingly certain, for instance, that you know
how many other lovers your partner has had, or whether or not he or she has a
sexually transmitted disease. Remarkably, however, you're not likely to be as
well-informed as you think. Studies at the University of Texas at Austin found
that people could not estimate the risk that a new acquaintance was HIV-
positive as well as they thought they could (Swann, Silvera, & Proske, 1995).
They were overconfident when a new relationship began, and they only got
worse (Swann & Gill, 1997). With greater familiarity, they became more certain

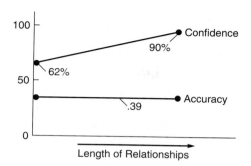

FIGURE 4.1. Accuracy and (over)confidence in developing relationships. At the beginning of their relationships, people felt that they knew more about the sexual histories of their new partners than they really did. Then, as time went by, they became quite certain that they were familiar with all the facts, when in truth, their actual accuracy did not improve.
(Data from Swann & Gill, 1997.)

that they understood their new partners well, but their accuracy did not change (see Figure 4.1).

Altogether, then, primacy effects occur when we form impressions of others, because the first things we learn (a) direct our attention to certain types of new information, and (b) influence our interpretations of the new facts we get. The net result is that we do not process information about others in an unbiased, evenhanded manner. Instead, our existing notions, whether they're simple stereotypes or quick first impressions, affect how we access and use the new data we encounter. (Thus, our beliefs about others are much like our beliefs about *ourselves* in this regard; remember that our existing self-concepts influence what we want to hear and what we are willing to believe about ourselves, too.) We are usually unaware of how readily we overlook evidence that we could be wrong. We're not tentative. Armed with only some of the facts—those that tend to support our case—we put misplaced faith in our judgments of others, being wrong more often than we realize.

Now, of course, we come to know our partners better with time and experience. One of the hallmarks of intimacy is personal knowledge about a partner, and first impressions certainly change as people gain familiarity with each other. However—and this is the fundamental point we wish to make—*existing beliefs are influential* at every stage of a relationship. Even flimsy first impressions typically change less easily than they logically should, because of the manner in which they influence subsequent thinking. And what happens when a relationship develops and you have a lot of information about an intimate partner? These patterns continue. People may see what they want to see and hold confident judgments that aren't always right.

Indeed, existing beliefs about lovers and friends are undoubtedly even more powerful than first impressions about new acquaintances. The stakes are higher, because interdependent intimacy means that emotions will be involved (Berscheid, 1983), and that makes things complex. In a close relationship, each partner may be the other's "most knowledgeable *and* least objective observer" (Sillars, 1985, p. 280). Despite knowing more about each other than outsiders do, intimate partners' hopes and dreams may sometimes make it hard for them to admit the truth.

For instance, who are the better judges of how long your current romantic relationship will last, you or your parents? Remarkably, when university students, their roommates, and their parents were all asked to forecast the future of the students' dating relationships, the parents made better predictions than the students themselves, and the roommates did better still (MacDonald & Ross, 1999). You'd think that people would be the best judges of their own relationships, but the students focused on the strengths of their relationships and ignored the weaknesses; as a result, they confidently and optimistically predicted that the relationships would last longer than they usually did. Parents and roommates were more dispassionate and evenhanded, and although they were less confident in their predictions, they were more accurate in predicting what the future would hold.

Thus, the same overconfidence, confirmatory biases, and preconceptions that complicate our perceptions of new acquaintances operate in established relationships as well. Obviously, we're not clueless about our relationships. When we thoughtfully evaluate our partnerships with a deliberate, cautious frame of mind, we make more accurate predictions about their futures than we do when we're in a romantic mood (Gagné & Lydon, 2000). Nevertheless, our perceptions of our relationships are often less detached and straightforwardly accurate than we think they are. (See Box 4.1). And, for better or for worse, they have considerable impact on our subsequent feelings and behavior in our relationships, as we'll see in the section that follows.

THE POWER OF PERCEPTIONS

Our judgments of our relationships and our partners seem to come to us naturally, as if there were only one reasonable way to view the situations we encounter. Little do we realize that we're often *choosing* to adopt the perspectives we use, and we facilitate or inhibit our satisfaction with our relationships by the choices we make.

Idealizing Our Partners

What are you looking for in an ideal romantic relationship? Most of us would like to have a partner who is warm and trustworthy, loyal and passionate, attractive and exciting, and rich and powerful, and our satisfaction with a lover depends on how well he or she approaches those ideals (Fletcher, Simpson,

---

BOX 4.1

Haste Makes Waste in Social Cognition

An important characteristic of social cognition in relationships is that a lot of it is done in a hurry, while we're engaged in interaction with others. People are at their best, making their most accurate judgments of others, when they can stop and think and analyze the available data in a deliberate, cautious way (Gilbert & Osborne, 1989). We make more mistakes when we hastily form snap judgments and then—because we are busy or distracted—we fail to double-check our reasoning (Gilbert, Krull, & Pelham, 1988). Unfortunately, social interaction is just the sort of task that can prevent people from carefully critiquing, and correcting, their erro-

neous impressions of others. When we're thinking of what to say next, we're not wondering just how accurate our perceptions are, and mistakes in judgment can go unnoticed (Osborne & Gilbert, 1992). There's a big difference between being caught up in the middle of the action and standing off to the side, thoughtfully analyzing what's going on, and those in the middle of things may make more hurried errors. Thus, another reason why roommates are likely to be astute critics of your current relationship is because they may be pondering the interactions they witness between you and your partner more carefully than you do much of the time.

Thomas, & Giles, 1999). What we usually get, however, is something less. How, then, do we ever stay happy with the real people we attract?

One way is to construct charitable, generous perceptions of our partners that emphasize their virtues and minimize their faults. People often judge their lovers with **positive illusions** that portray their partners in the best possible light (Murray, 1999). Such "illusions" are a mix of realistic knowledge about a partner and an idealized vision of who a perfect partner should be. They do not ignore a partner's real liabilities; they just consider such faults to be less significant than other people perceive them to be (Murray & Holmes, 1999). Thus, positive illusions idealize the partner, so that people usually judge their partners more positively than the partners judge themselves (Murray, Holmes, & Griffin, 1996a).

Isn't it a little dangerous to hold a lover in such high esteem? Won't people inevitably be disappointed when their partners fail to fulfill such positive perceptions? The answers may depend on just how unrealistic our positive illusions are. If we're genuinely fooling ourselves, imagining desirable qualities in a partner that he or she does not possess, we may be dooming ourselves to disillusionment (Miller, 1997b). Newlyweds do grow dissatisfied if they become aware that their new spouses fall too far short of their standards for an ideal spouse (Ruvolo & Veroff, 1997). On the other hand, if we're aware of all the facts but are merely interpreting them in a kind, benevolent fashion, such "illusions" can be very beneficial. When we idealize our partners, we're predisposed to judge their behavior in positive ways, and we are more willing to commit ourselves to maintaining the relationship (Murray, Holmes, & Griffin,

1996b). It bolsters our self-esteem to be loved by others who we perceive to be so desirable (Murray, Holmes, & Griffin, 2000). And we can slowly convince our partners that they actually are the wonderful people we believe them to be, as our high regard improves their self-concepts, too (Murray et al., 1996b). Add it all up, and idealized images of romantic partners are associated with greater satisfaction, love, and trust, and longer-lasting relationships as time goes by (Murray & Holmes, 1997).

In addition, there's a clever way in which we protect ourselves from disillusionment: Over time, as we come to know our partners well, we tend to revise our opinions of what we want in an ideal partner so that they fit the partners we've got (Fletcher, Simpson, & Thomas, 2001). To a degree, we conveniently decide that the qualities our partners have are the ones we want.

Thus, by choosing to look on the bright side—perceiving our partners as the best they can be—and by editing our ideals and hopes so that they fit what we've got, we can increase the chances that we'll be happy with our present partners. Our delight or distress is also affected by the manner in which we choose to explain the things our partners do, as we'll see next.

Attributional Processes

The explanations we generate for why things happen—and in particular why a person did or did not do something—are called **attributions.** Studies of attributions are important, because there are usually several possible explanations for most events in our lives, and they can differ in meaningful ways. We can emphasize influences that are either *internal* to someone, such as the person's personality, ability, or effort, or *external*, implicating the situation or circumstances the person faces. For instance (as you've probably noticed), students who do well on exams typically attribute their success to internal causes (such as their preparation and talent), whereas those who do poorly blame their grades more on external factors (such as a tricky, unfair test) (Forsyth & Schlenker, 1977). The causes of events may also be rather *stable* and lasting, as our abilities are, or *unstable* and transient, such as moods that come and go. Even further, causes can be said to be *global*, affecting many situations in our lives, or *specific*, affecting only a few. With all of these distinctions in play, diverse explanations for a given event may be plausible. And in a close relationship, in which interdependent partners may *both* be partly responsible for much of what occurs, judgments of cause and effect can be especially complicated.

Nevertheless, three broad patterns routinely emerge from studies of attributions in relationships. First, despite their intimate knowledge of each other, partners are affected by robust **actor/observer effects:** They generate different explanations for their own behavior than they do for the similar actions they observe in their partners (Orvis, Kelley, & Butler, 1976). This is a common phenomenon in social life (Krueger, Ham, & Linford, 1996). People are often acutely aware of the external pressures that have shaped their own behavior, so they make external attributions for themselves, but then they overlook how the same circumstances affect others, attributing others' behavior to internal sources such as their intentions and personality. What makes this phenomenon provocative in close relationships is that it leads the partners to overlook how *they* often personally provoke the behavior they observe in each other. During an argument, if one partner thinks, "she infuriates me so when she does that," the other is likely to be thinking, "he's so temperamental. He needs to learn to control himself." To complicate things further, the two partners are unlikely to be aware of the discrepancies in their attributions; each person is likely to believe that the other sees things his or her way (Harvey, Wells, & Alvarez, 1978). When partners make a conscious effort to try to understand the other's point of view, the actor/observer discrepancy gets smaller (Arriaga & Rusbult, 1998), but it rarely vanishes completely. The safest strategy is to assume that even your closest partners seldom comprehend all your reasons for doing what you do.

Second, despite genuine affection for each other, partners are also likely to display **self-serving biases** in which they try to take credit for their successes but avoid the blame for their failures. People like to feel responsible for the good things that happen to them, but they prefer external excuses when things go wrong. Thus, although they may not admit it to each other (Miller & Schlenker, 1985), partners are likely to believe that they personally deserve much of the credit when their relationships are going well, but they're not much to blame if a partnership is faltering (Thompson & Kelley, 1981). One quality that makes this phenomenon interesting is that people expect others to be self-serving, but they don't feel that they are themselves (Kruger & Gilovich, 1999). And in fact, when they consider themselves a close couple, loving partners are less self-serving toward each other than they are with other people (Sedikides, Campbell, Reeder, & Elliot, 1998). Nevertheless, self-serving biases exist even in contented relationships. In particular, when they fight with each other, spouses tend to believe that the argument is mostly their partner's fault (Schutz, 1999). And if they have extramarital affairs, people usually consider their own affairs to be innocuous dalliances, but they consider their spouse's affairs to be grievously hurtful (Buunk, 1987).

Thus, partners' idiosyncratic perspectives allow them to feel that they have better excuses for their mistakes than their friends and lovers do. They also tend to believe that their partners are the source of most disagreements and conflict. Most of us feel that *we're* pretty easy to live with, but *they're* hard to put up with sometimes. Such perceptions are undoubtedly influential, and, indeed, a third important pattern is that the general pattern of a couple's attributions helps determine how satisfied they will be with their relationship (Bradbury & Fincham, 1990). Happy people make attributions for their partners' behavior that are *relationship-enhancing*. Positive actions by the partner are judged to be intentional, habitual, and indicative of the partner's behavior in other situations; that is, happy couples make internal, stable, and global attributions for each other's positive behavior. They also tend to discount one another's transgressions, seeing them as accidental, unusual, and delimited; thus, negative behavior is excused with external, unstable, and specific attributions.

Through such attributions, satisfied partners magnify their partner's kindnesses and minimize their cruelties. In contrast, dissatisfied partners do just the

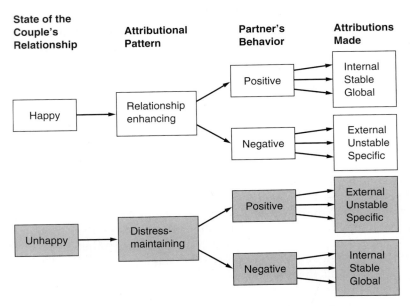

FIGURE 4.2. Attributions made by happy and unhappy couples.
(Brehm & Kassin, 1990.)

opposite, exaggerating the bad and minimizing the good. Unhappy people make *distress-maintaining* attributions that regard a partner's negative actions as deliberate and routine, and positive behavior as unintended and accidental. (See Figure 4.2.) Thus, whereas satisfied partners judge each other in benevolent ways that are likely to keep them happy, distressed couples perceive each other in ways that may keep them dissatisfied no matter how each behaves. When distressed partners *are* nice to one another, each is likely to write off the other's thoughtfulness as a temporary, uncharacteristic lull in the negative routine (Holtzworth-Munroe & Jacobson, 1985). When kindnesses seem accidental and hurts seem deliberate, satisfaction is hard to come by.

Where does such a self-defeating pattern come from? People who are high in neuroticism are more likely than others to make distress-maintaining attributions, but disappointments of various sorts may cause anyone to gradually adopt a pessimistic perspective (Karney & Bradbury, 2000). One thing is clear: Maladaptive attributions can lead to cantankerous behavior and ineffective problem-solving (Bradbury & Fincham, 1992), and they can cause dissatisfaction that would not have occurred otherwise (Fincham & Bradbury, 1993; Horneffer & Fincham, 1996). With various points of view at their disposal, people can choose to explain a partner's behavior in ways that are endearing and forgiving, or pessimistic and pejorative—and the success of their relationship may ultimately hang in the balance.

BOX 4.2
"You Must Remember This . . . "

Our perceptions of the current events in our relationships are obviously influential. So are our memories of the things that have happened in the past.

One of the intriguing aspects of relationship memories is that partners in close relationships typically *work together* to construct vivid stories about their shared past that are richer and more detailed than the memories of either of them alone (Wegner, Erber, & Raymond, 1991). Each of them may be entrusted with the details of certain events, and their shared recollections may be quite extensive. Like other beliefs and perceptions, such memories may be closely interwoven with the partners' satisfaction with their relationship (Karney & Coombs, 2000).

For one thing, partners' current feelings about each other influence what they remember about their past (McFarland & Ross, 1987). If they're happy, people tend to forget past disappointments; but if they're unhappy and their relationship is failing, they underestimate how happy and loving they used to be. These tricks of memory help us to adjust to the situations we encounter, but they often leave us feeling that our relationships have always been more stable and predictable than they really were—and that can promote damaging overconfidence.

Our memories also set the stage for our reactions to new events. The stories partners tell about their history as a couple influence their interpretations of their subsequent real-life interactions (McGregor & Holmes, 1999). Remarkably, for instance, close inspection of partners' memories of their past together allowed researchers in one study to accurately predict who would be divorced three years later (Buehlman, Gottman, & Katz, 1992)! Those whose partnerships were in peril remembered the early years of their relationships less fondly than did those who were likely to stay together; they recalled more tumultuous courtships, less mutuality, and bigger letdowns when they finally married. Such memories probably reflected pasts that really were more difficult and less rewarding. Nevertheless, by rehearsing such memories *now*, those couples were clearly setting themselves up for further frustration in the future (McGregor & Holmes, 1999). Like other perceptions, the stories we recount and the memories we rehearse influence subsequent interpretations, emotions, and behavior in close relationships.

Relationship Beliefs

People also enter their partnerships with established beliefs about what relationships are like. These are organized in mental structures called *schemas* that provide a filing system for our knowledge about relationships and, importantly, provide us with coherent assumptions about how they work (Baldwin, 1995). One set of interrelated beliefs that is often influential in our relationship schemas is **romanticism,** the view that love should be the most important basis for choosing a mate. Romanticism has several facets, and four of them can be

TABLE 4.1. The Romantic Beliefs Scale

How romantic are you? Rate how much you agree or disagree with each of these statements by using this scale:

1   2   3   4   5   6   7

Strongly disagree   *Strongly agree*

1. I need to know someone for a period of time before I fall in love with him or her.
2. If I were in love with someone, I would commit myself to him or her even if my parents and friends disapproved of the relationship.
3. Once I experience "true love," I could never experience it again, to the same degree, with another person.
4. I believe that to be truly in love is to be in love forever.
5. If I love someone, I know I can make the relationship work, despite any obstacles.
6. When I find my "true love" I will probably know it soon after we meet.
7. I'm sure that every new thing I learn about the person I choose for a long-term commitment will please me.
8. The relationship I will have with my "true love" will be nearly perfect.
9. If I love someone, I will find a way for us to be together regardless of any opposition to the relationship, physical distance between us, or any other barrier.
10. There will be only one real love for me.
11. If a relationship I have was meant to be, any obstacle (such as lack of money, physical distance, or career conflicts) can be overcome.
12. I am likely to fall in love almost immediately if I meet the right person.
13. I expect that in my relationship, romantic love will really last; it won't fade with time.
14. The person I love will make a perfect romantic partner; for example, he/she will be completely accepting, loving, and understanding.
15. I believe if another person and I love each other we can overcome any differences and problems that may arise.

To get your score, *reverse* the rating you gave to Question 1. If you chose 2, change it to a 6; if you chose 3, make it a 5, and so on. (4 stays the same.) Then determine the *average* of your responses by adding them up and dividing by 15. The mean score for men (4.8) is higher than the mean for women (4.6), but typical scores range a point above and below those averages for each sex. If you're a man and your average rating is 5.8 or higher, you have a very romantic outlook; if your average is 3.8 or lower, you're less romantic than the average guy. For women, the similar scores are 5.6 and 3.6, respectively. (From Sprecher & Metts, 1989.)

found on a Romantic Beliefs Scale created by Susan Sprecher and Sandra Metts (1989): People high in romanticism believe that (a) their loves will be perfect; (b) each of us has only one perfect, "true" love; (c) true love will find a way to overcome any obstacle; and (d) love is possible at first sight (see Table 4.1).

High scorers on the Romantic Beliefs Scale tend to experience more love, satisfaction, and commitment in their romantic relationships than low scorers do, but romanticism does not predict which relationships are likely to last over a four-year span (Sprecher & Metts, 1999). That's probably a good thing, because romanticism declines as the years go by, even in couples that stay together—and it drops a lot in partners who break up (Sprecher & Metts, 1999). Romantic beliefs apparently provide a rosy glow that makes a partnership seem special, but they do not play a significant role in affecting the partners' behavior in their relationship.

The same cannot be said for some other beliefs that are clearly disadvantageous. Certain beliefs that people have about the nature of relationships are *dysfunctional*; that is, they appear to have adverse effects on the quality of relationships, making it less likely that the partners will be satisfied. What ideas could people have that could have such deleterious effects? Here are six:

- Disagreements Are Destructive—Disagreements mean that my partner doesn't love me enough. If we loved each other sufficiently, we would never fight about anything.
- "Mindreading" Is Essential—People who really care about each other ought to be able to intuit each other's needs and preferences without being told what they are. My partner doesn't love me enough if I have to tell him or her what I want or need.
- Partners Cannot Change—Once things go wrong, they'll stay that way. If a lover hurts you once, he or she will hurt you again.
- Sex Should Be Perfect Every Time—Sex should always be wonderful and fulfilling if our love is pure. We should always want, and be ready for, sex.
- Men and Women Are Different—The personalities and needs of men and women are so dissimilar, you really can't understand someone of the other sex.
- Great Relationships Just Happen—You don't need to work at maintaining a good relationship. People are either compatible with each other and destined to be happy together or they're not.

Most of these beliefs were identified by Roy Eidelson and Norman Epstein (1982; Epstein & Eidelson, 1981) years ago, and since then several studies have shown that they put people at risk for distress and dissatisfaction in close relationships (Crohan, 1992; Fitzpatrick & Sollie, 1999; Knee, 1998). They're unrealistic. They may even be "immature" (Noller, 1996). When disagreements do occur—as they always do—they seem momentous to people who hold these views. Any dispute implies that their love is imperfect. Worse, people with these perspectives do not behave constructively when problems arise. Believing that people can't change and that true loves just happen, they don't try to solve problems, they just avoid them (Metts & Cupach, 1990), and they report more interest in ending the relationship than in making an effort to repair it (Knee, 1998). The net result is that their relationships are more costly, and they are less committed to their partners, than are people with more adaptive beliefs (Fitzpatrick & Sollie, 1999).

The good news is that such beliefs can change (Sharp & Ganong, 2000). Indeed, if you recognize any of your own views in the preceding list, we hope that these data are enlightening. Unrealistic assumptions can be so idealistic and starry-eyed that no relationship measures up to them, and distress and disappointment are certain to follow.

Expectations

Relationship beliefs are global assumptions about the nature of intimate part-nerships, and when they're false (as dysfunctional relationship beliefs are), they *stay* false. In contrast, people can also have more specific expectations about the behavior of others that are initially false but that become true (Rosenthal, 1994). We're referring here to **self-fulfilling prophecies,** which are false predictions that become true because they lead people to behave in ways that make the er-roneous expectations come true. Self-fulfilling prophecies are extraordinary ex-amples of the power of perceptions, because the events that result from them occur only because people expect them to, and then act as if they will.

Let's examine Figure 4.3 together to detail how this process works. In a first step in a self-fulfilling prophecy, a person who we'll call the *perceiver forms an expectancy* about someone else—the *target*—that predicts how the target will be-have. Various information about the target, such as his or her age, sex, race, physical attractiveness, or social class may affect the perceiver's judgments in ways of which the perceiver is unaware.

Then, in an important second step, the *perceiver acts,* usually in a fashion that is in accord with his or her expectations. Indeed, it may be hard for the per-ceiver to avoid subtly communicating what he or she really thinks about the target. Perceivers with favorable expectations, for instance, interact longer and more often with their targets, sharing more eye contact, sitting closer, smiling more, asking more questions, and encouraging more responses than do per-ceivers who have less positive expectations (Harris & Rosenthal, 1985).

The recipient of the perceiver's behavior is likely to notice all of this, and the *target's interpretation* will influence his or her response. In most cases, how-ever, when the *target responds* in the fourth step, it will be in a manner that is similar to the perceiver's behavior toward him or her. Enthusiasm is usually met with interest (Snyder, Tanke, & Berscheid, 1977), hostility with counterat-tacks (Snyder & Swann, 1978a). Thus, the perceiver usually elicits from the tar-get the behavior he or she expected, and that may be nothing like the way the target would have behaved if the perceiver hadn't gone looking for it.

But such is the nature of a self-fulfilling prophecy that, as the *perceiver inter-prets* the target's response in the last step in the process, the perceiver is un-likely to recognize the role that he or she played in producing it. The actor-observer effect will lead the perceiver to attribute the target's behavior to the target's personality or mood. And after all, the perceiver found in the target the behavior he or she expected; what better evidence is there that the per-ceiver's expectations were correct? (This is another reason why we tend to be overconfident in our judgments of others; when we make our false expectations come true, we never realize that we were ever wrong.)

Here, then, is another fundamental reason why our perceptions of others are so influential. They not only influence our interpretations of the information we gain, they guide our behavior toward others, too. We often get what we ex-pect from others, and that is sometimes behavior that would not have occurred without our prompting—but we're rarely aware of how our expectations have created their own realities.

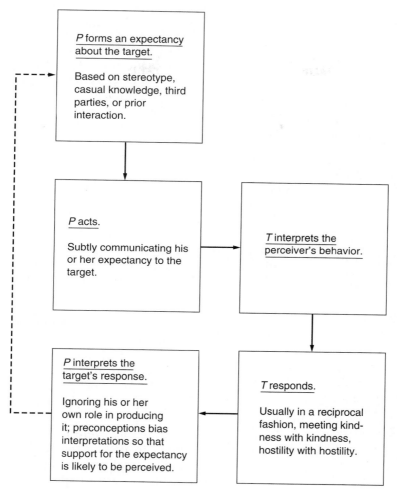

FIGURE 4.3. A self-fulfilling prophecy. Originally false expectations in a perceiver (*P*) can seem to come true when he or she interacts with the target (*T*).
(*Source: Leary & Miller, 1986.*)

Mark Snyder and his colleagues (1977) provided an elegant example of this when they led men at the University of Minnesota to believe that they were chatting on the phone with women who were either very attractive or quite unattractive. The experimenters gave each man a fake photograph of the woman with whom he'd be getting acquainted, and then recorded the ensuing conversations to see what happened. The men had higher expectations when they thought they'd be talking to gorgeous women than they did when they anticipated a conversation with a plain partner, and they were much more eager and interested when the interactions began; listeners rated them, for instance, as more sociable, warm, outgoing, bold, and socially adept. The men's (often erroneous) judgments of the women were clearly reflected in their behavior toward them. How did the women respond to such treatment? They had no knowledge of having been labeled as gorgeous or homely, but they did know that they were talking to a man who sounded either enthusiastic or aloof. As a result, the men got what they expected: The women who were presumed to be attractive really did sound more alluring, reacting to their obviously interested partners with warmth and appeal of their own. By comparison, the women who talked with the relatively detached men who thought they were unattractive sounded pretty drab. In both cases, the men got out of the women the behavior they expected, whether or not their expectations were accurate.

Because they guide our actions toward others, our expectations are not inert. Another fascinating example of this was obtained when researchers sent people to chat with strangers after leading them to expect that the strangers would probably either like or dislike them (Curtis & Miller, 1986). Participants in the study were told that, in order to study different types of interactions, the researchers had given a stranger bogus advance information about them, and they could anticipate either a friendly or unfriendly reaction from the stranger when they met. In truth, however, none of the strangers had been told anything at all about the participants, and the false expectations that the interaction would go well or poorly existed only in the minds of the participants themselves. (Imagine yourself in this intriguing position: You *think* someone you're about to meet already likes or dislikes you, but the other person really doesn't know anything about you at all.) What happened? People got what they expected. Expecting to be liked, people greeted others in an engaging, open, positive way—they behaved in a likeable manner—and really *were* liked by the strangers they met. However, those who expected to be disliked were cautious and defensive and were much less forthcoming, and they actually got their partners to dislike them. Once again, false expectations created their own behavioral reality—and positive expectations were beneficial and advantageous, but negative expectations were not.

Indeed, over time, people who chronically hold different sorts of expectations about others may create different sorts of social worlds for themselves. For instance, people who have high self-esteem are usually confident that their friendly overtures toward others will be met with warmth in return, but people with low self-esteem are less certain that they can get others to like them (Baldwin & Keelan, 1999). Consequently, people who doubt themselves tend to doubt their intimate partners, and are typically more insecure in their relationships than are people with higher self-esteem (Murray, Holmes, MacDonald, & Ellsworth, 1998). Moreover, people who tend to worry about rejection from others often behave in ways that make such rejection more likely; they behave more negatively when conflict occurs, and tend to perceive snubs from others when none are intended (Downey, Freitas, Michaelis, & Khouri, 1998). As a result, they (and their partners) tend to be dissatisfied with their close relationships (Downey & Feldman, 1996). (See Box 4.3.)

BOX 4.3

Attachment Styles and Perceptions of Partners

Another individual difference that's closely tied to the way people think about their partners is attachment style (Whisman & Allan, 1996). People with different attachment styles are thought to have different "mental models" of relationships; they hold different beliefs about what relationships are like, expect different behavior from their partners, and form different judgments of what their partners do. In particular, people with secure styles are more likely than avoidant or anxious/ambivalent people to make relationship-enhancing attributions (Collins, 1996). Secure people trust their partners more (Mikulincer, 1998) and are more likely than insecure people to remember positive past events (Miller & Noirot, 1999). Moreover, secure people are more likely than those with insecure styles to remain open to new information when they judge their partners (Green-Hennessy & Reis, 1998; Mikulincer, 1997); avoidant and anxious people rely on their existing beliefs and assumptions about their partners to a greater extent.

Attachment styles *can* change, as we noted in chapter 1, but no matter what style people have, they tend to remember their past perspectives on relationships as being consistent with what they're thinking *now* (Scharfe & Bartholomew, 1998). Happily, if positive experiences in a rewarding relationship help us to gradually develop a more relaxed and trusting outlook on intimacy with others, we may slowly forget that we ever felt any other way.

Misplaced expectations can even prevent relationships from ever getting started. When people want to initiate a romantic relationship but are shyly reluctant to make the first move, they're usually painfully aware of their own fear of rejection that keeps them from acting. However, if their potential partners behave in exactly the same way and wait for them to act, they assume that the others' passivity indicates a lack of interest in developing a relationship with them (Vorauer & Ratner, 1996). The occasional result is that nobody makes the first move, although both potential partners secretly wish the other would. Evidently, false expectations that others won't like us are especially likely to come true.

With time and experience, we undoubtedly learn the truth about some of our false expectations about others. In particular, some prophecies that initially fulfill themselves can dissipate over time as people become more familiar with each other (Smith, Jussim, & Eccles, 1999). On the other hand, some self-fulfilling prophecies can persist for years if people continue to act in accord with their early expectations (Smith et al., 1999). Altogether, then, our perceptions of our partners, the attributions we make, and the beliefs and expectations we bring to our relationships may exert a powerful influence on the events that follow. Our judgments of each other matter. And those of us who expect others to be trustworthy, generous, and loving may find that others actually *are* good to us more often than those with more pessimistic perspectives find others being kind to them.

IMPRESSION MANAGEMENT

Because others' impressions of us are so important, we often try to control the information that others receive about us. We sometimes try to make deliberate impressions on others, choosing our words, our apparel, our settings, and even our associates carefully to present a certain public image. On other occasions, when we're not consciously pursuing a particular impression, we often fall into habitual patterns of behavior that portray us in ways that have elicited desirable responses from others in the past (Schlenker & Pontari, 2000). So, whether or not we're thinking about it, we're often engaging in **impression management,** trying to influence the impressions of us that others form.

This is a significant idea for at least two reasons. First, nearly anything we do in the presence of others may be strategically regulated in the service of impression management. People are much more likely to wash their hands in a public restroom when others are present than they are when they believe they are completely alone (Munger & Harris, 1989). Women will eat less on a date with an attractive man than they would have eaten had they been out with their girlfriends (Pliner & Chaiken, 1990). Both men (Morier & Seroy, 1994) and women (Zanna & Pack, 1975) will edit what they say about themselves to appear compatible with an attractive member of the other sex, but they won't go to such trouble for undesirable people who they're not trying to impress. And because people like to advertise their association with winners, college students often wear school insignia to class on Mondays if their football team wins its game on the previous Saturday—but those clothes stay at home if the team loses (Cialdini et al., 1976).

A second reason why impression management is an important concept is that it is a pervasive influence on social life. Others' evaluations of us are eventful, and when we are in the presence of others, we are rarely unconcerned about what they may be thinking of us (Miller, 1996). By providing a means with which we can influence others' judgments, impression management increases our chances of accomplishing our interpersonal objectives. And there's rarely anything dishonest going on; impression management is seldom deceitful or duplicitous. To the contrary, although people do occasionally misrepresent themselves through lying and pretense, most impression management involves revealing— perhaps in a selective fashion—one's real attributes to others (Leary, 1995). By announcing some of their attitudes but not mentioning others, for example, people may appear to have something in common with almost anyone they meet; this simple tactic of impression management facilitates graceful and rewarding social interaction, and does not involve untruthfulness at all. Because frauds and cheats are rejected by others, people seldom pretend to be things they are not.

Strategies of Impression Management

Nevertheless, because most of us have diverse interests and talents, there may be many distinct impressions we can honestly attempt to create, and we may seek different images in different situations. Indeed, there are four different strategies of impression management people routinely use (Jones & Pittman, 1982). We use **ingratiation** when we seek acceptance and liking from others; we do favors, pay compliments, mention areas of agreement, describe ourselves in desirable ways, and are generally charming in order to get others to like us. Ingratiation is a common form of impression management in developing romances (Honeycutt, Cantrill, Kelly, & Lambkin, 1998), and as long as such efforts are not transparently manipulative or "slimy" (Vonk, 1998), they usually do elicit favorable reactions from others (Gordon, 1996).

On other occasions, when we wish our abilities to be recognized and respected by others, we may engage in **self-promotion,** recounting our accomplishments or strategically arranging public demonstrations of our skills. Self-promotion is a preferred strategy of impression management during job interviews (Stevens & Kristof, 1995), but even in settings like those, vigorous self-promotion can be risky for women because it makes them seem "unladylike" (Rudman, 1998). Indeed, men boast about their accomplishments to their friends more than women do (Dolgin & Minowa, 1997), but both men and women tend to be more modest among friends than they are toward strangers (Tice, Butler, Muraven, & Stillwell, 1995).

Both ingratiation and self-promotion create socially desirable impressions, but other strategies create *un*desirable images. Through **intimidation,** people portray themselves as ruthless, dangerous, and menacing so that others will do their bidding. Such behavior is obnoxious and tends to drive others away, but if it's used only occasionally—or if the recipients are children or impoverished spouses with no place else to go—intimidation may get people what they want. Finally, using the strategy of **supplication,** people sometimes present themselves as inept or infirm in order to avoid obligations and elicit help and support from others. People who claim that they're "just too tired" to do the dishes after a "hard day at work" are engaging in supplication. Most people avoid using intimidation and supplication if the other strategies work for them, because most of us prefer to be liked and respected rather than feared or pitied. But almost everyone uses intimidation and supplication occasionally. If you've ever made a point of showing a partner that you were angry about something, or sad about something else, in order to get your way, you were using intimidation and supplication, respectively (Clark, Pataki, & Carver, 1996).

Impression Management in Close Relationships

There are three specific features of impression management with intimate partners that are worthy of mention. First, although the impressions we make on our friends and lovers are much more influential than the images we create for acquaintances or strangers, we usually go to *less* trouble to maintain favorable images for our intimate partners than we do for others. We worry less about how we're coming across, and try less hard to appear likeable and competent all the time (Guerrero, 1997; Leary et al., 1994). For instance, the longer people have known their partners, the less time they spend preening and grooming themselves in the restroom during a dinner date (Daly, Hogg, Sacks, Smith, & Zimring, 1983). In general, we tend to the images we present to intimate partners less attentively than we do to the impressions we make on others, and there may be several reasons why (Leary & Miller, 2000). For one thing, we know our friends and lovers like us, so there's less motivation to be charming to win their approval. Also, because they know us well, there's less we can do to have much effect on what they think. However, it's also likely that people simply get lazy. Being on one's best behavior requires concentration and effort. Polite behavior usually involves some form of self-restraint. We can relax around those who already know and love us, but that means that people are often much cruder with intimate partners than they are with anyone else they know (Miller, 1997b). People who are very decorous early in a relationship— who would never show up for breakfast without being showered and dressed—often become spouses who sit at the table in their underwear, unwashed, scratching and picking, pilfering the last doughnut. This is ironic. Having behaved beautifully to win the love of a romantic partner, some of us never work at being so charming to that lover ever again. (And this may be a big problem in many relationships, as we'll see in chapter 6.)

A second interesting aspect of impression management, once a relationship develops, is that people often take pains to create desired public images of their *partners*. For instance, imagine that you are describing a friend to someone of the other sex who your friend finds very attractive, and you know this person's preferences for what he or she is looking for in an ideal date. What would you say about your friend? Faced with this situation, most people describe their friends in a way that fits the preferences of the attractive listener (Schlenker & Britt, 1999). On the other hand, if the listener is *un*attractive, people helpfully describe a friend as being *in*compatible with the listener, implicitly suggesting that the friend is "not your type." In general, the closer a relationship, the more people treat their partners' images as if they were their own, taking the time to make their partners look good whenever possible (Ault, Cunningham, & Bettler, 1999).

People may also go to some lengths to present a particular image of their relationships to others. Early on, the big decision is often whether or not to admit that a relationship even exists; college students are especially likely to conceal a relationship from their parents, usually because they wish to avoid comments and criticism (Baxter & Widenmann, 1993). Thereafter, once their partnership is established and acknowledged, the partners may collaborate to construct a particular public image of their relationship. One common example is the effort to hide spats and squabbles from others; couples who have bickered all the way to a party may "put on a happy face" and pretend to be perfectly happy once they arrive. People seem generally aware that the public images of their partners and their relationships do reflect on their own personal images to some extent.

Finally, there are individual differences in the extent of people's impression management that may have meaningful effects on the patterns of their relationships. As we saw in chapter 3, people who are high in the trait of

self-monitoring are adept at adjusting their behavior to fit the varying norms of different situations (Gangestad & Snyder, 2000). By comparison, low self-monitors seem less attentive to social norms and are less flexible, making the same stable impressions even when they're not appropriate to the situation. Thus, high self-monitors are more changeable and energetic impression managers.

These different styles lead to different networks of friends. Because they can deftly switch images from one audience to the next, high self-monitors tend to have more friends than low self-monitors do, but they have less in common with each of them.[1] High self-monitors often surround themselves with "activity specialists," partners who are great companions for some particular pleasure—such as a "tennis buddy" or "ballet friend"—but with whom they are not compatible in other respects (Snyder, Gangestad, & Simpson, 1983). High self-monitors are skilled at steering clear of the topics that would cause dispute, and the specialist friends allow them to really enjoy those activities—but if they threw a party and invited all those friends, very different people who have little in common with each other would show up. By comparison, low self-monitors must search harder for partners with whom they are more similar across the board. If low self-monitors had all their friends over, relatively few people would come, but they'd all be a lot alike.

These differences in style appear to be consequential as time goes by. When they first meet others, high self-monitors enjoy interactions of higher intimacy than low self-monitors do; they're skilled at finding common ground for a conversation, and are good at small talk (Snyder & Simpson, 1984). They can also feign interest in other people better than low self-monitors can (Leck & Simpson, 1999). Being able impression managers seems to help them to interact comfortably with a wide variety of people. On the other hand, they invest less of their time in each of their friends, so that they tend to have shorter, somewhat less committed relationships than low self-monitors do (Snyder & Simpson, 1987). The interactive advantage enjoyed by high self-monitors when a relationship is just beginning may become a small liability once the relationship is well established.

Altogether, then, the greater attentiveness to social images shown by high self-monitors seems to influence the partners they choose (see chapter 3) and the relationships they form. Would you rather be high or low on this trait? You can determine your own self-monitoring score using the scale in Table 4.2. Just remember that only very high and very low scorers closely fit the portraits we've drawn here.

---

[1]We should note that this and the following distinctions between high and low self-monitors are based on comparisons of the *highest* self-monitors, the 25% of us with the very highest scores, to the *lowest* self-monitors, the 25% of us with the lowest scores. Researchers sometimes do this to study the possible effects of a personality trait as plainly as possible, but you should recognize that half of us, those with scores ranging from somewhat below average to somewhat above, fall in between the examples being described here.

TABLE 4.2. The Self-Monitoring Scale
Is each of the following statements true or false?

1. I find it hard to imitate the behavior of other people.
2. At parties or social gatherings, I do not attempt to say or do things that others will like.
3. I can only argue for ideas that I already believe.
4. I can make impromptu speeches even on topics about which I have almost no information.
5. I guess I put on a show to impress or entertain others.
6. I would probably make a good actor.
7. In a group I am rarely the center of attention.
8. In different situations and with different people I often act like very different persons.
9. I am not particularly good at making other people like me.
10. I'm not always the person I appear to be.
11. I would not change my opinions (or the way I do things) in order to please someone.
12. I have considered being an entertainer.
13. I have never been good at games like charades or improvisational acting.
14. I have trouble changing my behavior to suit different people and different situations.
15. At a party I let others keep the jokes and stories going.
16. I feel a bit awkward in public and do not show up quite as well as I should.
17. I can look anyone in the eye and tell a lie (if for a right end).
18. I may deceive people by being friendly when I really dislike them.

Give yourself a point for each of these statements that were *true* of you: 4, 5, 6, 8, 10, 12, 17, 18.

Then give yourself a point for each of these statements that were *false*: 1, 2, 3, 7, 9, 11, 13, 14, 15, 16.

What's your total score? If it's 13 or higher, you're a relatively high self-monitor. If it's 7 or lower, you're a relatively low self-monitor (Snyder, 1987). Scores between 7 and 13 are average.

Source for scale: Snyder, M., & Gangestad, S. (1986). On the nature of self-monitoring: Matters of assessment, matters of validity. *Journal of Personality and Social Psychology, 51*, 125–139.

SO, JUST HOW WELL DO WE KNOW OUR PARTNERS?

Let's add up the elements of social cognition we've encountered in this chapter. In a close relationship, partners may hold idealized but overconfident perceptions of each other, and when they act in accord with those judgments, they may elicit behavior from each other that fits their expectations but which would not have otherwise occurred. Moreover, right or wrong, they are likely to interpret one another's actions in ways that fit their existing preconceptions. Combined with all this are the partners' efforts to adjust their behavior so that they make the impressions on each other that they want to make. Evidently, there are various processes at work in intimate partnerships that cause us to see in our partners those attributes and motives that we expect or want (or that *they* want us) to see. How accurate, then, are our perceptions of our partners? How well do we know them?

The simple answer is, "not as well as we think we do" (Sillars, 1998). As we saw in chapter 3, we routinely perceive our partners to be more like us than they really are. We believe that they agree with us more often than they really do (Acitelli, Douvan, & Veroff, 1993; Sillars et al., 1994), and we overestimate how similar their personality traits are to our own (Murray et al., 2000; Watson, 2000). As a result, we feel that we understand them, and they understand us, more than is actually the case. Such misperceptions are not disadvantageous. Indeed, the more similarity and understanding we perceive in our partners, the more satisfying our relationships with them tend to be (Murray et al., 2000). Still, we misunderstand our partners more than we realize. To a degree, our perceptions of our partners are fictions that portray our partners as people they are not.

There are several factors that determine just how (in)accurate our judgments are. Interpersonal perception depends both on the people involved and on the situation they face.

Knowledge

The conclusion that we don't know our partners as well as we think we do isn't inconsistent with the fact that intimate partners have a great deal of factual knowledge about one another. As their relationship develops and they spend more time together, two people do come to understand each other better (Colvin, Vogt, & Ickes, 1997; Thomas, 2000). Married people perceive each other more accurately than dating couples or friends do (Watson, Hubbard, & Wiese, 2000), and acquaintances judge each other more accurately than strangers do (Funder, Kolar, & Blackman, 1995). Intimate partners interact often and have detailed knowledge about each other—and, as we saw in chapter 3, they really are likely to have a lot in common—and all of these influences may contribute to accuracy (Stinson & Ickes, 1992).

Motivation

However, our perceptions of others don't necessarily become more accurate as time goes by (Park, Kraus, & Ryan, 1997). One study found that the length of time two people had known each other didn't predict how accurate they would be, but the length of time they had been living together did (Bernieri, Zuckerman, Koestner, & Rosenthal, 1994). Furthermore, another study found that spouses who had been married for *shorter* lengths of time did better at inferring what their partners were thinking than more experienced spouses did (Thomas, Fletcher, & Lange, 1997). Evidently, the interest and motivation with which we try to figure each other out help determine how insightful and accurate we will be (Graham & Ickes, 1997; Thomas & Fletcher, 1997), and people who have recently moved in with each other (who are presumably highly motivated to understand each other) may understand each other as well as they ever will.

Along these lines, no matter how long people have known each other, their judgments and evaluations of each other may depend in part on the moods they're in. Transient frames of mind affect people's perceptions of their partners and their relationships; when they're in a good mood, both are perceived more positively than when more surly, irascible moods prevail (Forgas, Levinger, & Moylan, 1994).

There is also evidence that women spend more time thinking carefully about their relationships than men do (Acitelli & Young, 1996). Both men and women often ponder their new partnerships, but women tend to analyze their relationships more thoughtfully once they are established.

Partner Legibility

Some of the traits people have are more visible than others—that is, they impel behavior that is observable and obvious—and the more evident a trait is, the more accurately it will be perceived (Watson, 2000). People who are sociable and extraverted, for instance, are likely to be accurately perceived as gregarious and affable, but high neuroticism is harder to detect (Ambady, Hallahan, & Rosenthal, 1995). Moreover, some people are generally easier to judge correctly than others are. People who are taciturn and reserved can be very hard to figure out, simply because they don't give observers many clues about what they're feeling; even the friends and lovers of such people may not often be able to tell what they're thinking (Hancock & Ickes, 1996).

Perceiver Ability

Some people may be hard to judge, but some judges are better than others. People who are intelligent and open-minded tend to perceive others more accurately than dogmatic, narrow-minded people do (Thomas, 2000). To judge others well, perceivers have to note, weigh, and combine diverse and often conflicting sources of information (such as a partner's behavior, facial expression, tone of voice, and vocabulary), and integrating all these pieces can be a complicated task. People who are flexible, complex thinkers seem to do this more capably than more rigid, less sophisticated people can (Davis & Kraus, 1997).

Attachment styles also appear to be important in this regard. Perceivers who have a secure style understand their partners better than insecure people do (Mikulincer, Orbach, & Iavnieli, 1998; Tucker & Anders, 1999). In particular, anxious-ambivalent people are especially likely to overestimate how much they have in common with their romantic partners (Mikulincer et al., 1998).

However, training and practice can improve people's abilities to understand their partners. In one study, participants in a 10-hour empathy training program were able to understand their partners' thoughts and feelings more accurately six months later. Their partners were also more satisfied with their relationship (Long et al., 1999).

Threatening Perceptions

Intimate partners typically understand each other much better than they understand mere acquaintances, but they may not want to on those occasions when a partner's feelings or behavior are distressing or ominous. When accurate perceptions would be worrisome, intimate partners may actually be motivated to be *in*accurate in order to fend off doubts about their relationship (Ickes & Simpson, 1997). Imagine this situation: You and your romantic partner are asked to examine and discuss several pictures of very attractive people your partner may be meeting later. Afterwards, while watching a videotape of the two of you discussing the pictures, you try to discern exactly what your partner was thinking when he was inspecting the pictures of gorgeous women (or she was inspecting the pictures of handsome men) that could be potential rivals for you. How astute would you be? Would you really want to know that your partner found one of the pictures to be especially compelling and was really looking forward to meeting that person? Not if you're like most people. The more attractive (and thereby threatening) the photos were, and the closer their relationship was, the *less* accurately dating partners perceived each other's thoughts and feelings in this situation (Simpson, Ickes, & Blackstone, 1995). Most people understood a partner's reactions to unattractive photos reasonably well, but they somehow remained relatively clueless about a partner's reactions to attractive pictures. They were inattentive to news they did not want to hear.

But not everyone managed threatening perceptions in this manner. People with an anxious-ambivalent attachment style were actually *more* accurate in judging their partners when the partners inspected the attractive photos (Simpson, Ickes, & Grich, 1999). They were unsettled by their perceptions, however, and they evaluated their relationships less favorably as a result. Anxious-ambivalent people were like moths drawn to a flame; they were especially good at intuiting their partners' feelings in just those situations in which accuracy was disconcerting and costly. Such sensitivity may be one reason why such people *are* chronically anxious and ambivalent about their relationships.

Perceiver Influence

Finally, we should remember that people are not passive judges of others. In a close relationship, they are engaged in continual interaction with their partners, behaving in accord with their expectations and reacting to the perceptions they construct. If they come to realize that their partners are not the people they wish they were, they may try to *change* their partners by encouraging some behaviors and impeding others. In a sense, people are sometimes like sculptors who try to construct the partners they want from the raw material a real partner provides (Drigotas, Rusbult, Wieselquist, & Whitton, 1999). If our partners seem dispirited, we may try to cheer them up. Or, if they're too pompous and pretentious, we may try to bring them back to earth (De La Ronde & Swann, 1998). Because intimate partners are continually shaping and molding each other's behavior, perceptions that are initially inaccurate may become more correct as we induce our partners to become the people we want them to be.

Summary

With all these influences at work, our perceptions of our partners can range from outright fantasy to pinpoint correctness. We certainly know our partners better as a relationship develops, but motivation and attentiveness can come and go, and some people are easier to read than others. Some of us are more astute perceivers than others, too. In addition, even if you know your partner well, there may be occasions for which *in*attention is profitable, helping you avoid doubt and distress. And partners influence each other, so perceptions can become either more or less accurate as time goes by. In general, we usually understand our partners less than we think we do, but our accuracy may vary with necessity, our moods, and the stage of our relationship.

Our important closing point is that our perceptions of our partners are clearly influential. Right or wrong, our judgments of our lovers and friends can either support or undermine our contentment in our relationships. Some of us look on the bright side, thinking well of our partners, using relationship-enhancing attributions, and expecting kindness and generosity—and that's what we get. Others of us, however, doubt our partners and expect the worst—and thereby make it more likely that our relationships will fail.

CHAPTER SUMMARY

Social cognition includes all the processes of perception and thought with which we make sense of our social worlds. This chapter focuses on the way we think about our relationships.

First Impressions (And Beyond)

When we first meet others, stereotypes and *primacy effects* (which cause us to attach particular importance to the first information we acquire about others) are especially influential in shaping our overall impressions. Early impressions matter, because any existing judgment is likely to influence our interpretations of the later information we encounter. People with different preconceptions may draw very different conclusions about others from the same information.

First impressions also affect our selection of subsequent data. People ordinarily display a *confirmatory bias,* seeking information that will confirm their beliefs with more interest and energy than they look for examples that will prove them wrong. As a result, we rarely confront unequivocal evidence that our impressions of others are incorrect. This leads to *overconfidence* that leads people to put unwarranted faith in their judgments. Most people make more mistakes in judging others than they realize.

Overconfidence, confirmatory biases, and preconceptions operate in established relationships as well. As a result, outsiders such as parents and friends who are not personally involved in a relationship can sometimes judge it more accurately than the participants can.

The Power of Perceptions

There are often a variety of ways to interpret a given event in a close relationship, and the partners' perspectives can be very consequential.

Idealizing Our Partners. Happy partners construct charitable, generous perceptions known as *positive illusions* that emphasize their partners' virtues and minimize their faults. Although highly unrealistic positive illusions may be risky, we tend to revise our opinions of what we want in a partner so that they fit the real partners we have. The resulting idealized perspectives—which perceive our partners as the best they can be—usually lead to good feelings and positive interpretations of a partner's behavior that result in greater satisfaction with a relationship.

Attributional Processes. The explanations we generate for why things happen are called *attributions.* We can emphasize influences that are internal or external to a person, stable or unstable, or global or specific, but such judgments may be especially complex in close relationships, where both partners may be partly responsible for a given event.

Despite their intimate knowledge of each other, partners are affected by *actor/observer effects:* They generate different explanations for their own behavior than they do for actions they observe in their partners. Whereas people are typically aware of the external pressures that have influenced their own behavior, they attribute their partners' behavior to internal sources in similar situations. This leads people to overlook how they have personally provoked the behavior they observe in each other, a problem that persists because partners are rarely aware of the discrepancies in their perspectives.

People also tend to be *self-serving;* they gladly take personal credit for their successes but try to avoid blame for their failures. In relationships, this leads partners to perceive problems as typically being the other person's fault. Most of us feel that we're pretty easy to live with, but our partners are hard to put up with sometimes.

Patterns of attribution can be either relationship-enhancing, giving a partner credit for his or her positive actions and excusing the partner's transgressions, or distress-maintaining, regarding a partner's negative actions as deliberate and routine. Relationship-enhancing attributions promote relationship satisfaction, but distress-maintaining attributions may keep people dissatisfied no matter what their partners do.

Partners may also work together to construct vivid stories about their shared past that set the stage for their reactions to new events. The partners' current feelings about each other influence what they are likely to remember, and if their memories are predominantly negative, their relationship may be at risk.

Relationship Beliefs. People enter their partnerships with established beliefs about what relationships are like. One such set of beliefs is *romanticism,* the view that love should be the most important basis for choosing a mate. People high in romanticism believe that (a) their loves will be perfect, (b) each of us has only one perfect, "true" love, (c) true love will find a way to overcome any obstacle, and (d) love is possible at first sight. Such beliefs apparently provide a rosy glow that makes a partnership seem special.

By comparison, *dysfunctional relationship beliefs* are clearly disadvantageous. People who believe that "disagreements are destructive," "mindreading is essential," "partners cannot change," "sex should be perfect every time," "men and women are different," or that "great relationships just happen" don't try to solve problems, they just avoid them. As a result, their relationships are more costly, and they are less committed to their partners than are people with more adaptive beliefs.

Expectations. Our expectations about others can become *self-fulfilling prophecies*, false predictions that make themselves come true. This happens because expectations guide our behavior toward others; people typically act in ways that fit their expectations, and they can elicit reactions from others that would not have occurred had the perceivers not created them. When this occurs, people are very unlikely to recognize their role in producing the reactions they obtained. Thus, men who think they are conversing with attractive women are likely to find that their partners actually sound quite appealing, and people who expect that others will dislike them typically *are* disliked. Some self-fulfilling prophecies dissipate over time, but others do not; they may persist for years if people continue to act in accord with their initial expectations.

Impression Management

Because others' impressions are so important, people often engage in *impression management*, trying to influence the impressions of them that others form. Nearly anything we do in the presence of others may be strategically regulated in the service of impression management, and the motive to control the information that others receive about us is a pervasive influence on social life.

Strategies of Impression Management. Four different strategies of impression management are commonplace. With *ingratiation*, people seek acceptance and liking from others, and with *self-promotion*, they seek respect. In contrast, people portray themselves as dangerous and menacing through *intimidation*, or as helpless and needy through *supplication*.

Impression Management in Close Relationships. Although our intimate partners mean much more to us than other people do, we work less hard to present favorable images to them than to others. We worry less about how we're coming across, and we try less hard to appear likable and competent all the time. Simple laziness may be involved, because being on our best behavior requires concentration and effort, and both may wane over time.

People often take pains to create desirable images for their partners as well as for themselves. They also go to great lengths to present particular images of their relationships to others. When a relationship is new, this often involves denying that it exists, especially to one's parents.

Individual differences in *self-monitoring* are influential because high self-monitors surround themselves with activity specialists, friends who are good companions for a particular pleasure but little else. Low self-monitors have fewer friends, but have more in common with each of them. Low self-monitors also are more committed to their romantic partners but do not enjoy as much intimacy with others at the beginning of their relationships as high self-monitors do.

So, Just How Well Do We Know Our Partners?

We generally do not understand our partners as well as we think we do, but there are several influences that determine just how accurate (or inaccurate) our perceptions of our partners will be.

Knowledge. As a relationship develops and partners spend more time together, they acquire detailed knowledge about each other and typically do understand each other better.

Motivation. The interest and motivation with which people try to figure each other out help determine how insightful and accurate they will be. Women tend to spend more time thinking about their relationships than men do. Moods are also influential; when people are in good moods, they perceive their partners more positively than they do when they're grumpy.

Partner Legibility. Some personality traits, such as extraversion, are more visible than others. In addition, some people are chronically easier to judge than others are.

Perceiver Ability. Some judges are better than others, too. People who are intelligent and open-minded tend to perceive others more accurately than dogmatic, narrow-minded people do. In addition, perceivers who have a secure style understand their partners better than insecure people do.

Threatening Perceptions. However, when accurate perceptions would be worrisome, intimate partners may actually be motivated to be inaccurate in order to fend off doubts about their relationship. Research participants who watched their romantic partners evaluate attractive photos of potential rivals intuited their partners' thoughts less accurately than did those who watched their partners evaluate less threatening photographs—unless the perceivers had an anxious-ambivalent attachment style. Anxious-ambivalent people could tell what their partners were thinking, but were disconcerted as a result.

Perceiver Influence. People are sometimes like sculptors who try to construct the partners they want from the raw material a real partner provides.

Because intimate partners are continually shaping and molding each other's behavior, perceptions that are initially inaccurate may become more correct as we induce our partners to become the people we want them to be.

Summary. Our perceptions of our partners are clearly influential. Right or wrong, our judgments of our lovers and friends can either support or undermine our contentment in our relationships.

CHAPTER 5

Communication

Imagine that you and your romantic partner are seated alone in a comfortable room, discussing the topic of your last disagreement. Your conversation is more structured than most, because before you say anything to your partner you record a quick rating of what you intend to say next. You rate the intended impact of your message by pushing one of five buttons with labels ranging from *super negative* through *neutral* to *super positive*. Then, after you speak, your partner quickly rates his or her perception of your message in the same way before replying to you. This process continues as you take turns voicing your views and listening to what your partner says in return. You're engaging in a procedure called the *talk table* that allows researchers to get a record of both your private thoughts and your public actions. The notable point is that if you're dissatisfied with your relationship, you may not *intend* to annoy or belittle your lover, but you're likely to do so, anyway. Unhappy couples don't differ on average from happy, contented couples in what they are trying to say to each other, but the impact of their messages—what their partners think they hear— is more critical and disrespectful nonetheless (Gottman, Notarius, Gonso, & Markman, 1976). And this is consequential, because this single afternoon at the talk table predicts how happy the two of you will be later on; regardless of how satisfied they were originally, couples whose communications were frustrating were less happily married five years later (Markman, 1981).

Communication is incredibly important in intimate relationships. And it's more complex than we usually realize. Let's consider the simple model of

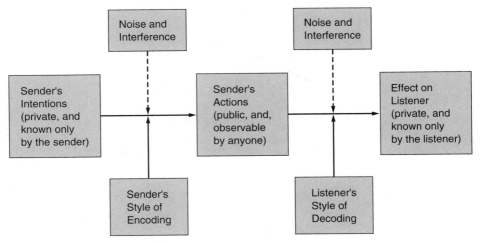

FIGURE 5.1. A simple model of interpersonal communication.
(Adapted from Gottman, Notarius, Gonso, & Markman, 1976.)

communication shown in Figure 5.1. Communication begins with the sender's intentions, the message that the sender wishes to convey. The problem is that the sender's intentions are private and known only to him or her. In order for them to be communicated to the listener, they must be encoded into verbal and nonverbal actions that are public and observable. A variety of factors, such as the sender's mood or social skill, or noisy distractions in the surrounding environment, can influence or interfere with this process. Then, the receiver must decode the speaker's actions, and interference can occur here as well. The final result is an effect on the receiver that is again private and known only to him or her.

The point here is that getting from one person's intentions to the impact of that person's message on a listener involves several steps at which error and misunderstanding may occur. We usually assume that our messages have the impact that we intended, but we rarely *know* that they do (Sillars et al., 1994). More often than we realize, we face an **interpersonal gap** in which the sender's intentions differ from the effect on the receiver (Gottman et al., 1976). And, as studies with the talk table show, such gaps are related to present and future dissatisfaction in close relationships.

This chapter examines communication in relationships, and we'll do what we can to help you close your own interpersonal gaps. But we'll start not with what people say in interaction but with what they do. Accompanying the spoken word in communication is a remarkable range of nonverbal actions that also carry many messages, whether you intend them or not.

NONVERBAL COMMUNICATION

Imagine that as part of a research study, you put on a cap that identifies you as a member of either an admired or disliked group, and you walk around town with it on, shopping, eating lunch, and applying for some jobs. You've put on the cap without looking at it, and you *don't know* what you're wearing. Would you be able to tell what sort of cap you have on by watching others' reactions to you? You might (Hebl, Foster, Mannix, & Dovidio, 2000). If you're wearing an obnoxious cap, your waitress may not be as warm and cheerful as usual. People you pass at the mall may glance at you and display a quick expression of distaste or disgust. Even if no one mentions your cap, others' behavior may clearly indicate that they do not like what they see. In fact, because you'd be curious and alert to how others responded, their sentiments might be unmistakably plain.

In such a situation, you'd probably notice the remarkable amount of information carried by nonverbal behavior, which includes all of the things people do in interaction except for their spoken words and syntax. Indeed, although we don't always notice, nonverbal behavior can serve several functions in our transactions with others. Table 5.1 lists seven such functions that have been identified by Miles Patterson (1988, 1990). We'll take particular note of four of them.

First, nonverbal behavior **provides information** about people's moods or about what they really mean by what they say. If you playfully tease someone, for instance, your facial expression and the sound of your voice may be the only way listeners can tell that you don't intend to be antagonistic. This function is so important that we have had to invent emoticons, the imitation facial expressions people put in e-mail messages, so that readers can correctly interpret our written messages.

Nonverbal behavior also plays a vital part in **regulating interaction.** Nonverbal displays of interest often determine whether or not interaction ever begins, and, thereafter, subtle nonverbal cues allow people to take turns in a conversation seamlessly and gracefully.

Finally, by expressing intimacy and carrying signals of power and status (the "social control" function), nonverbal behavior helps **define the relationships** we share with others. (Note that, for the sake of convenience, we're combining two specific functions from Table 5.1, "expressing intimacy" and "social control," into one broader category, "defining relationships.") People who are intimate with each other act differently toward one another than acquaintances do, and dominant, high-status people act differently than subordinates do. Without a word being spoken, observers may be able to tell who likes whom and who's the boss.

How are these functions carried out? The answer involves all of the diverse components of nonverbal communication, so we'll survey them next.

Components of Nonverbal Communication

One clue to the enormous power of nonverbal communication is the number of different channels through which information can be transmitted. We'll describe six.

TABLE 5.1. **Functions of Nonverbal Behavior in Relationships**

Category	Description	Example
Providing information	Actor's behavior patterns permit an observer to make inferences about the actor's states, traits, or reactions to people or to the environment.	A subtle change in a husband's facial expression may lead his wife to judge that he is upset, but the same cues would not be useful to a stranger.
Regulating interaction	Changes in nonverbal behavior serve as cues to regulate the efficient give-and-take of interactions.	Close friends and family members are more likely than mere acquaintances to anticipate when a partner will start or stop speaking by knowing the partner's idiosyncratic pattern of gaze changes or postural adjustments.
Expressing intimacy	Increased intimacy between partners is indicated by higher levels of nonverbal involvement.	Lovers are more likely to stand close, touch, and gaze towards one another more than do mere acquaintances.
Social control	Social control involves goal-oriented behavior designed to influence another person.	As a person requests a favor from his close friend, he leans forward, touches him on the arm, and gazes intently.
Presentational function	A behavior pattern is managed by an individual, or a couple, to create or enhance an image.	When a quarreling couple arrive at a party, they may cover their conflict by holding hands and smiling at one another.
Affect management	The experience of affect, especially strong emotion, leads to changing patterns of nonverbal involvement.	Unexpected good fortune (winning the lottery) leads to sharing the news with family and friends. Hugs, kisses, and other forms of touching are likely in celebrating the good fortune with others.
Service-task function	Patterns of nonverbal involvement are determined primarily by service or task goals in an interaction.	The close approach, touch, and gaze initiated by a physician towards a patient does *not* reflect interpersonal affect.

Source: From Patterson, 1988.

Facial Expression

People's facial expressions signal their moods and emotions in a manner that's similar anywhere you go (Ekman et al., 1987). Even if you don't speak the language in a foreign country, for example, you'll be able to tell if others are happy: If they are, the muscles in their cheeks will pull up the corners of their mouths, and the skin alongside their eyes will crinkle into folds. Obviously, they're *smiling*, and happiness, like several other emotions—sadness, fear, anger, disgust, and surprise—engenders a unique facial expression that's the same all over the world. Other emotions, such as embarrassment, involve sequences of facial actions and expressions that are also unmistakable (Keltner, 1995). In fact, the universality of these expressions suggests that they are hard-wired into our species. People don't *learn* to smile when they're happy—they're born to do it. People who have been blind all their lives, for instance, display the same facial expressions all the rest of us do (Galati, Scherer, & Ricci-Bitti, 1997).

The universal meanings of facial expressions make them extremely informative—when they're authentic. Unfortunately, because facial expressions do figure so prominently in nonverbal communication, people sometimes try to deliberately manage them to disguise their true emotions (DePaulo, 1992). On occasion, this occurs due to **display rules,** cultural norms that dictate what emotions are appropriate in particular situations (Andersen & Guerrero, 1998). There are at least four ways we may try to modify our expressions of emotion to follow these rules. First, we may *intensify* our expressions, exaggerating them so that we appear to be experiencing stronger feelings than we really are. If you're only mildly pleased by a gift you've just opened, for example, you should try to appear happier than you feel if the donor is present. Second, we sometimes *minimize* our expressions, trying to seem less emotional than we really are. Because our culture assumes that "big boys don't cry," a man may stoically try not to seem too affected by a sad movie. Third, we may *neutralize* our expressions, trying to withhold our true feelings altogether. Good poker players try to do this so that they give no hint of what their cards may be. Finally, we can *mask* our real feelings by replacing them with an entirely different apparent emotion. A first runner-up in a beauty pageant who looks so thrilled when the other contestant actually wins the pageant is almost certainly masking her true feelings.

However, even when people try to control their expressions, the truth may leak out. First, feigned expressions often differ in subtle ways from authentic expressions. For instance, people can easily pull up the corners of their mouths when they want to fake a smile, but they have a harder time voluntarily crinkling the skin around their eyes; as a result, the difference between a real and fake smile is often apparent to an attentive viewer (Ekman, Friesen, & O'Sullivan, 1988). Second, despite our efforts, authentic flashes of real emotion, or *microexpressions*, can be visible during momentary lapses of control. If you watched the network television news anchors carefully during the 1976 and 1984 U.S. presidential campaigns, for example, it was apparent which candidate each one secretly supported; despite their posed professional detachment, they all revealed their preferences through favorable or unfavorable brief expressions during their reports about each candidate (Friedman, DiMatteo, & Mertz, 1980; Mullen et al., 1986).

Gazing Behavior

Obviously, facial expressions provide meaningful information about a partner's feelings. Gazing, the direction and amount of a person's eye contact, is also influential. For one thing, looking at someone communicates interest, and that can determine whether or not two strangers begin talking with each other (Cary, 1978). If you find someone glancing at you in a singles bar and you don't want to talk to him or her, look away and don't look back.

Gazing also helps define the relationship two people share once interaction begins. Lovers really do spend more time looking at each other than friends do, and friends look more than acquaintances do (Kleinke, 1986). Moreover, when strangers spend time gazing into each other's eyes, they end up liking each other more than they would have if they'd spent the time together looking someplace else (Kellerman, Lewis, & Laird, 1989). A lot of looking can evidently communicate affection as well as simple interest.

But it can communicate dominance, too. In ordinary interaction, people usually look at their conversational partners more when they're listening (gazing at the speaker about 60 percent of the time, on average) than when they're speaking (looking at the listener about 40 percent of the time). However, powerful, high-status people tend to depart from these norms—they look more while speaking but less while listening than the average person does (Ellyson, Dovidio, & Brown, 1992). Researchers summarize these patterns in a **visual dominance ratio** (VDR) that compares "look-speak" (the percentage of time a speaker gazes at a listener) to "look-listen." A high-power pattern of gazing turns the typical ratio of 40/60 on its head, producing a high VDR of 60/40 (Dovidio et al., 1988). Dominant partners in an interaction can insist, "Look at me when I'm talking to you!" but they often do not offer as much visual attention in return.

Body Language

So far, we've only been describing nonverbal communication from the neck up, but the whole body is involved. Body movements routinely accompany and support our verbal communication, making it easier for us to convey what we mean—try describing the size of a fish you caught without using your hands (Rauscher, Krauss, & Chen, 1996)—but they can also replace spoken words entirely, in the form of gestures that are widely understood. (A good example, for better or worse, is a gesture in which one holds up one's hand with one's middle finger extended. The recipient of the gesture will probably know what it means.) The problem with gestures is that, unlike facial expressions, they vary widely from culture to culture (Axtell, 1991). For instance, in the United States, touching your thumb to your index finger and extending the other fingers is a gesture that means "okay," or "good." However, in France it means "zero," in Japan it means "money," and in the Middle East it's an obscene insult (just like the American middle finger). The language of the face needs no interpreter, but that's not true of the language of gestures.

Less specific, but still useful information can be conveyed by the posture or motion of the body. For instance, the impressions observers get from brief (10-second) silent videotapes allow them to predict the teaching evaluations college professors will get from their students (Ambady & Rosenthal, 1993), and, even more remarkably, the sexual orientation of total strangers (Ambady, Hallahan, & Conner, 1999) at levels noticeably better than chance. One reason why body language is informative is that it's harder to control than facial expressions are; it's "leakier," which means that it's more likely to indicate what our true feelings are (Babad, Bernieri, & Rosenthal, 1989). United States customs inspectors, for example, use bodily signs of restlessness and anxiety, not facial expressions, to decide whether or not to search travelers' luggage for contraband (Kraut & Poe, 1980).

Body postures can also signal status. High-status people tend to adopt open, asymmetric postures in which the two halves of the body assume different positions (Leffler, Gillespie, & Conaty, 1982). They take up a lot of space. In contrast, low-status people use closed, symmetric postures that are relatively compact. If a powerful boss is talking with a subordinate seated across from him or her, you can usually tell who's who just by watching them.

Touch

Physical contact with another person can also have various meanings. On the one hand, two people tend to touch each other more as their relationship becomes more intimate (Emmers & Dindia, 1995). Touch clearly conveys closeness and affection. On the other hand, uninvited touch can be an implicit signal of dominance that establishes one's place in a status hierarchy (Major & Heslin, 1982). In fact, when two people differ in status, touch tends to be a one-way street; high-status people are more likely to touch those of lower status than vice versa. Think about it: If you ask a question of your instructor during an exam, it would not be bizarre for him or her to rest a hand on your shoulder as he or she bends over your seat to talk to you. However, if you go to the front of the room to ask your question, it would be quite odd for you to touch your instructor in the same way.

The potential mixed message of touch may be the reason why men and women tend to respond differently to touches from strangers. When they are touched briefly by others on the hand or arm, women usually respond positively, but most men do not. Sheryl Whitcher and Jeffrey Fisher (1979) provided a compelling demonstration of this in a study in which a nurse touched some hospital patients, but not others, when she was giving them instructions the night before their surgery. The nurse rested her hand on the patient's arm for about a minute, an action that could be construed as comforting. That's how women reacted; the touch calmed them and lowered their blood pressure. In contrast, the touch made men *more* anxious and actually made their blood pressure go up.

Perhaps because of this sex difference, men tend to touch women more than women touch men (Major, Schmidlin, & Williams, 1990), particularly among younger couples (Hall & Veccia, 1990). In fact, women who touch men during casual interaction are not evaluated favorably by observers unless the women are clearly of higher status than their male counterparts (Storrs & Kleinke, 1990).

Interpersonal Distance

One aspect of touching that makes it momentous is that people have to be located very close to each other for touching to occur. That means that the two partners are typically in a region of interpersonal distance—the physical space that separates two people—that is usually reserved for relatively intimate interactions. The **intimate zone** of interpersonal distance extends out from the front of our chests about a foot-and-a-half (Hall, 1966). If two people are standing face-to-face that close to each other, their interaction is probably quite loving or quite hostile. More interactions occur at greater distances, in a **personal zone** that ranges from $1^1/_2$ to 4 feet away from us. Within this range, friends are likely to interact at smaller distances, acquaintances at larger ones, so distancing behavior helps to define the relationships people share. Even further away, in a **social zone** (4 to 12 feet), interactions tend to be more businesslike. When you sit across a desk from an interviewer or a professor, you're in the social zone, and the distance seems appropriate; however, it would seem quite odd to stand five feet away from a good friend to hold a personal conversation. Beyond 12 feet, interactions tend to be quite formal. This is the **public zone,** which is used for structured interaction like that between an instructor and his or her students in a lecture class.

These distances describe the general patterns of interactions among North Americans, but they tend to be larger than those used by many other peoples of the world (Burgoon, Buller, & Woodall, 1989). French, Latin, and Arabic cultures prefer distances smaller than these. A person's sex and status also affect distancing behavior. Men tend to use somewhat larger distances than women do, and people usually stand further away from high-status partners than from those of lower power and prestige. Whatever one's preferences, however, spacing behavior is a subtle way to calibrate the desired intimacy of an interaction, and it may even be an indirect measure of the quality of a relationship: Spouses who are unhappy choose to maintain larger distances between each other than do spouses who are currently content (Crane, Dollahite, Griffin, & Taylor, 1987).

Paralanguage

The final component of nonverbal communication isn't silent like the others can be. Paralanguage includes all the variations in a person's voice other than the actual words he or she uses, such as rhythm, pitch, loudness, and rate. Thus, paralanguage doesn't involve *what* people say, but *how* they say it. A good example of distinctive paralanguage is "baby talk," the vocal style that is marked by variable intonation, high pitch, and unique rhythms. On the one hand, baby talk communicates affection; people use it with their lovers (Bombar & Littig, 1996), babies, and pets (DePaulo & Friedman, 1998). On the other hand, it can also mean that the speaker believes that the listener is incapable or infirm; people sometimes use baby talk to address people who are mentally retarded or institutionalized in nursing homes. Interestingly, if the elderly residents of nursing homes *are* ailing or feeble, they like being addressed this way, but the more competent they are, the less they like it (Caporael, Lukaszewski, & Culbertson, 1983).

    Paralanguage helps define relationships, because lovers tend to talk to each other with different rhythms than friends use. Lovers tolerate longer delays in responding, are silent more often, and say less overall (Guerrero, 1997). The sound of a woman's voice can also tell eavesdropping strangers whether she's talking to an intimate or casual male friend; women sound more submissive and scatterbrained when they're conversing with their boyfriends than they do when they're talking to other men (Montepare & Vega, 1988). In fact, women often use more submissive paralanguage in mixed-sex interactions than men do (Berger, 1994).

Combining the Components

    We have introduced the components of nonverbal communication as if they are independent, discrete sources of information, and, in one sense, they are: Each of them can have its own effects on interaction. Usually, however, they reinforce each other, working together to convey consistent information about a person's sentiments and intentions. When you're face-to-face with someone, all of these components are in play, and together, they often tell you what people really mean by what they say. Consider sarcasm, for instance, when people say one thing but mean another: Their true intent is conveyed not in their words but in their actions and paralanguage. Most of the time, our nonverbal behavior communicates the same message as our words. But when there *is* a discrepancy between people's words and actions, the truth behind their words usually lies in their nonverbal, not their verbal, communication (Burgoon, 1994).

    These various nonverbal actions also allow us to fine-tune the intimacy of our interactions to establish a comfortable level of closeness (Patterson, 1990). Imagine that you're seated next to an acquaintance on a two-person couch when the conversation takes a serious turn and your acquaintance mentions an intimate personal problem. If this development makes you uncomfortable—if that's more than you needed to hear—you can adjust the perceived intimacy of your interaction by nonverbally "backing off." You can turn away and lean back to get more distance. You can avert your gaze. And you can signal your discomfort through your paralanguage and facial expression, all without saying a word. Nonverbal communication serves several important functions in interaction and is the source of useful subtlety in social life.

Nonverbal Sensitivity

Given all this, you might expect that it's advantageous for couples to do well at nonverbal communication, and you'd be right. The sensitivity and accuracy with which couples communicate nonverbally predict how happy their relationship will be (Carton, Kessler, & Pape, 1999). In particular, husbands and wives who do poorly at nonverbal communication tend to be dissatisfied with their marriages. Moreover, when such problems occur, it's usually the husband's fault (Noller, 1987).

    What? How can researchers arrive at such a conclusion? Well, when nonverbal exchanges fail, there may be errors in encoding or decoding, or both: The sender may enact a confusing message that is difficult to read (that's encoding), or the receiver may fail to correctly interpret a message that is clear to anyone else (decoding). Women typically start with an advantage at both tasks because, if no deception is involved, women are both better encoders and more astute decoders than men are on average (Hall, 1998). (There's no difference in men's and women's abilities to detect deception, as we'll see in chapter 10.) Thus, the old stereotype about "women's intuition" actually has a basis in fact; women tend to be better than men at using subtle but real nonverbal cues to discern what's really going on.

Furthermore, researchers can assess husbands' and wives' encoding and decoding skills by asking them to send specific nonverbal messages that are then decoded by the other spouse. The messages are statements that can have several different meanings, depending on how they are nonverbally enacted; for instance, the phrase, "I'm cold, aren't you?" could be an affectionate invitation ("Come snuggle with me, you cute thing"), a spiteful complaint ("Turn up the damn heat, you cheapskate!"), or something else. In research on nonverbal sensitivity, a spouse is assigned a particular meaning to convey and is videotaped sending the message. Then, impartial strangers are used as a control group. If they can't figure out what the spouse is trying to communicate, the spouse's encoding is assumed to be faulty. On the other hand, if they *can* read the message but the other spouse *can't*, the partner's decoding skill is implicated.

In the first ingenious study of this sort, Patricia Noller (1980) found that husbands in unhappy marriages sent more confusing messages and made more decoding errors than happy husbands did. There were no such differences among the wives, so the poorer communication Noller observed in the distressed marriages appeared to be the husbands' fault. Men in troubled marriages were misinterpreting communications from their wives that were clearly legible to total strangers. Other researchers observed this pattern, too (Gottman & Porterfield, 1981). Even worse, such husbands were completely clueless about their mistakes; they assumed that they were doing a fine job communicating with their wives, and were confident that they understood their wives and that their wives understood them (Noller & Venardos, 1986). The men were doing a poor job communicating and didn't know it, and that's why they seemed to be at fault.

On the other hand, to be fair, marital miscommunication in the nonverbal domain is not entirely due to husbands' shortcomings. In another study, Noller (1981) compared spouses' accuracy in decoding the other's messages to their accuracy in decoding communications from strangers. In unhappy marriages, *both* the husbands and wives understood strangers better than they understood each other. Moreover, the greater their dissatisfaction, the greater the disparity between their inaccuracy with each other and their accuracy with strangers. Evidently, distressed husbands and wives were both miscommunicating despite being capable of adequate nonverbal communication with others.

This is a key point because, based on Noller's findings, there are at least two possible ways nonverbal communication and relationship satisfaction could affect each other:

1. Nonverbal skills may determine how satisfying relationships are. Poor skills may lead to poor relationships, and good skills may lead to good relationships. Alternatively,
2. Relationship satisfaction may determine how hard people work to communicate well. Poor relationships may engender poor communication, and good relationships may foster good communication.

Actually, both of these propositions are probably correct. It's likely that nonverbal insensitivity makes someone a less rewarding partner than he or she otherwise would be. But once partners grow dissatisfied for any reason, they may start tuning each other out and communicate less adeptly than they could if they really tried (Sabatelli, Buck & Dreyer, 1980, 1982). In this fashion, nonverbal insensitivity and dissatisfaction can become a vicious cycle, with each exacerbating the other.

In any case, people's problems with communication may stem from either skill deficits or performance deficits, and the distinction is an important one. If miscommunication results from a skill deficit—a person does not know how to communicate clearly—then we can improve that person's relationships by teaching the skill. If, on the other hand, the problem is a performance deficit—the person knows how to communicate clearly but doesn't do so with a particular partner—then efforts to improve the skill will probably have no effect on that relationship.

Some people do appear to have nonverbal skill deficits, and they are provocative (and a little eerie). For instance, convicted rapists are especially poor at identifying negative feelings such as distaste and displeasure when they are expressed by women (Lipton, McDonel, & McFall, 1987). Abusive mothers have trouble identifying signs of distress in infants; they even tend to see negative emotions as positive ones (Kropp & Haynes, 1987). Both of these results suggest the possibility that skill deficits can give people blind spots that make them insensitive to nonverbal reactions from others that would inhibit unlawful behavior in all the rest of us (although, because these were correlational studies, we don't know that for sure).

For most of us, however, the likely cause of any nonverbal insensitivity will be a performance deficit born of a lack of attention and a lack of effort. Most of us are reasonably skilled and can interpret others' nonverbal messages accurately when we look and listen and put our minds to it. But inattention and laziness can lead us to frustrate our partners by sending mixed messages and misunderstanding their moods and meanings. And there lies an almost certain path to less happiness and relationship satisfaction than we otherwise could have had (Noller, 1987).

Sex Differences in Nonverbal Communication

We just noted that women tend to be more adept at nonverbal communication than men are (Hall, 1998), and we mentioned in passing that there are specific differences between the sexes in paralanguage (Berger, 1994), interpersonal distancing (Burgoon et al., 1989), and touching (Major et al., 1990), as well. What

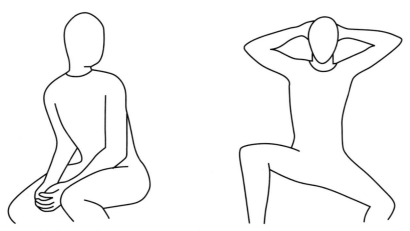

FIGURE 5.2. These silhouettes portray a man and a woman. Which is which?
(Adapted from Frieze et al., 1978, p. 330.)

we haven't yet mentioned is that there are sex differences in all of the other components of nonverbal communication, too. Women smile more than men do, even when they're not particularly happy (Hecht & LaFrance, 1998), and they display lower visual dominance ratios when they're interacting with men than men display toward them in return (Ellyson et al., 1992). They also tend to adopt postures that are less open and more symmetrical than those used by men (Cashdan, 1998). Take a look at Figure 5.2 and you'll see what we mean.

Individually, these sex differences aren't remarkable, and each is open to various interpretations. A simple explanation for the difference in body language, for instance, is the different apparel men and women often wear; if men were wearing dresses (or kilts), they probably wouldn't adopt postures like the one in Figure 5.2! Collectively, however, these sex differences are rather striking: In each instance, the behavior of women who are interacting with men mirrors the behavior of low-status people who are interacting with their superiors. This pattern, which is documented in Table 5.2, was first noticed by Nancy Henley (1977), who argued that one reason people often consider women to be less powerful than men is that women constantly communicate that they are less forceful and decisive through their nonverbal behavior. In fact, as Table 5.2 shows, women often do interact with men using a style that is less assertive and powerful than that displayed by the men in return.

However, the question of why this occurs has many possible answers. Sex is merely correlated with nonverbal behavior, and that leaves things ambiguous. One fact is clear: When women occupy positions of power and interact with their subordinates, these sex differences disappear. Moreover, anyone, male or female, is likely to behave in the relatively deferential manner described in Table 5.2 when he or she interacts with others of higher status (Snodgrass, 1985, 1992).

TABLE 5.2. Sex and Status Differences in Nonverbal Behavior

Nonverbal Behavior	Women	Men	Low-Status Person	High-Status Person
Smiling	more	less	more	less
Gazing	low VDR	high VDR	low VDR	high VDR
Posture	closed, symmetric	open, asymmetric	closed, symmetric	open, asymmetric
Touch	less	more	less	more
Distance	less	more	less	more
Paralanguage	submissive	assertive	submissive	assertive
Nonverbal Sensitivity	more	less	more	less

Note: The table lists patterns in the behavior of men and women in mixed-sex, but not same-sex interactions. When women are interacting with other women, they do not display all of the styles listed here. Similarly, the table lists patterns that distinguish high- and low-status people in interactions where status differentials exist. People generally do not display these styles with others of equal status.

Thus, nonverbal behavior tends to change as people play different roles in different settings. Nevertheless, the pattern remains: Around men of similar status, women often act as if they were of lower status than their male partners. And because cultural expectations are involved, such habits may be surprisingly resistant to change. If you're a woman, try using the male style of behavior listed in Table 5.2, and see what people think; you'll probably come across as "pushy" or "brazen." Our nonverbal behavior may be influential in perpetuating unspoken and unwanted stereotypes about what it means to be a man or woman.

VERBAL COMMUNICATION

If nonverbal communication is so important, what about the things we actually say to each other? They are probably even more consequential, of course (Dindia & Fitzpatrick, 1985). Verbal communication is a vital part of close relationships, and it is extensively involved in the development of intimacy in the first place (Sprecher & Duck, 1994).

Self-Disclosure

Imagine that as part of a psychology experiment you meet a stranger and engage in tasks that lead you to gradually reveal more and more personal information about yourself. For instance, you describe your relationship with your mother, an embarrassing moment, or a deep regret. The stranger does the same thing, and 45 minutes later, you know a lot of personal details about each other.

What would happen? Would you like the stranger more than you would have if the two of you had just shared small talk for the same amount of time? In most cases, the answer is definitely yes. An experience like this usually generates immediate closeness between the participants. People who open up to each other, even when they're just following researchers' instructions, like each other more than do couples who do not reveal as much (Aron, Melinat, Aron, Vallone, & Bator, 1997).

The process of revealing personal information to someone else is called **self-disclosure.** It is one of the defining characteristics of intimacy: Two people cannot be said to be intimate with each other if they do not share some personal, relatively confidential information with one another (Laurenceau, Barrett, & Pietromonaco, 1998; Parks & Floyd, 1996). Self-disclosure also feels good; it improves the moods of those who do it (Vittengl & Holt, 2000).

The Theory of Social Penetration

Of course, in real life, meaningful self-disclosure takes longer than 45 minutes. Most relationships begin with the exchange of superficial information—"small talk"—and only gradually move to more meaningful revelations. The manner in which this occurs is the subject of **social penetration theory,** which holds that the development of a relationship is closely tied to systematic changes in communication (Altman & Taylor, 1973). People who have just met may feel free to talk with each other about only a few, impersonal topics: "Where are you from?" "What's your major?" But if this superficial conversation is rewarding, they're likely to move closer to each other by increasing two aspects of their communication:

1. Its *breadth:* the variety of topics they discuss, and
2. Its *depth:* the personal significance of the topics they discuss.

According to the theory, if we diagram all the things there are to know about someone, interaction with a new relationship partner is likely to take the form of a wedge that's both narrow (only a few different topics are being discussed) and shallow (only impersonal information is being revealed). (See Figure 5.3.) As the relationship develops, however, the wedge should become broader (with more topics being discussed) and deeper (with more topics of personal significance being revealed).

In general, that is what happens. Ordinarily, however, breadth and depth don't change at the same rate. As you can see in Figure 5.4, breadth usually increases faster than depth at the beginning of a relationship. People talk about a wide variety of superficial topics before they get to the real personal stuff, and the wedge becomes broader before it becomes deeper. Then, intimate self-disclosure grows faster: The wedge becomes deeper without much change in breadth (Hornstein & Truesdell, 1988).

In addition, early encounters between acquaintances usually involve obvious *reciprocity* in self-disclosure. New partners tend to match each other's level of openness, disclosing more as the other person does, and disclosing less if the other person's self-disclosure declines (Dindia, 2000). Just how

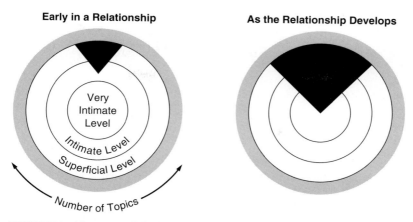

Early in a Relationship   **As the Relationship Develops**

Very
Intimate
Level

Intimate Level

Superficial Level

Number of Topics

FIGURE 5.3. Altman and Taylor's wedge of social penetration.

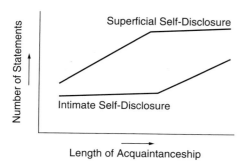

Number of Statements

Superficial Self-Disclosure

Intimate Self-Disclosure

Length of Acquaintanceship

FIGURE 5.4. Changes in the rate of
self-disclosure over time.

much people reveal about themselves, then, tends to depend on the specific partner and may vary considerably from relationship to relationship (Dindia, Fitzpatrick, & Kenny, 1997).

Once a relationship is well established, however, obvious reciprocity occurs less often (Altman, 1973; Derlega, Wilson, & Chaikin, 1976). A partner who discloses some rather personal information may not receive a similar disclosure in return for some time. Instead of reciprocity, sustained intimacy seems to hinge on *responsiveness* from a partner (Reis & Patrick, 1996); that is, people want their self-disclosures to be met with apparent understanding, caring, support, and respect (Laurenceau et al., 1998; see Box 5.1). When we reveal some private confidence to a close friend or lover, we don't need a similar secret in exchange, but we do want our honesty to engender sympathy, tolerance, and acceptance (Sprecher et al., 1995).

BOX 5.1

Communicating Sympathy and Concern

Few of us know what to say when we encounter bereaved others who are suffering from the loss of a loved one. We want to express sympathy and support, but our words often seem inadequate to the task. However, grief, and others' reactions to it, have been studied by relationship researchers (Lehman, Ellard, & Wortman, 1986), and we can offer some advice about this important kind of communication. First, you *should* mention the person's loss (Okonski, 1996). The death of a beloved is a huge loss, something that the person will never forget. Assuming that the person's pain has ended or is no longer salient to him or her, even months later, is simply insensitive (Martin, 1997). Talking about the lost partner acknowledges the person's distress and communicates caring and concern.

What should you say? Something simple. Try "I'm so sorry," or "I feel so sad for you" and then *stop.* Do not try to comfort the person with optimistic projections about the future. Do not imply that the loss is not the most tragic, awful thing that has ever happened. And do not offer advice about how the person can put his or her life back together. Such efforts may spring from kind intentions, but each of them ultimately demeans the person's current suffering. Offer heartfelt sympathy and nothing more. Just nod your head and be a good listener and be nonjudgmental.

Thus, offering welcome comfort to others is more straightforward than you may have thought, as long as you avoid the pitfalls of saying too much. With this in mind, can you see what's wrong with the following dumb remarks? Each is a quote from someone who was probably trying—and failing—to be kind (Landers, 1997; Martin, 1997; Lehman et al., 1986):

> "The sooner you let go, the better."
>
> "You'll get over it."
>
> "He should have been wearing a seat belt."
>
> "She's with God now."
>
> "You're young, you can have other children."
>
> "You have many good years left."

It's also likely that, even in the closest partnerships, we'll keep some things to ourselves. Social penetration is almost never total, and it probably shouldn't be, because partners like their privacy, too (Altman, Vinsel, & Brown, 1981). No relationship is likely to be able to sustain total openness and intimacy over long periods of time, and it may be a mistake to even try: Both intimate self-disclosure and selective secrecy contribute to marital satisfaction (Finkenauer & Hazam, 2000). Some privacy is desirable even in a close, intimate relationship. (We're reminded of a recent cover story in *Cosmopolitan* magazine that asked, if you've had an affair, "Should You Ever Tell?" Their answer, after much discussion, was "probably not.") In the long run, it may be a healthy balance between self-disclosure and respect for privacy that sustains an intimate attachment (Baxter & Montgomery, 1997).

There are also important issues that many close partners simply don't want to talk about. Explicitly or implicitly, partners may agree to steer clear of **taboo topics,** sensitive matters that, in the opinion of the partners, may threaten the quality of their relationship. Curiously, the most common taboo topic is the state of the relationship itself; in one survey, 68 percent of the respondents acknowledged that the current or future state of their romantic relationships was a subject that was better off not being mentioned (Baxter & Wilmot, 1985). (Other common taboos involved current relationships with *other* partners, avoided by 31 percent of the respondents, and past relationships [25 percent].) People are often keenly interested in the likely future of their partnerships and are eager to learn their partners' expectations and intentions, but they don't ask. Instead, romantic partners may create *secret tests* of their lovers' fidelity and devotion (Baxter & Wilmot, 1984). They watch closely to see how their lovers respond to other attractive people (that's a "triangle test"); they contrive difficulties that the lover must overcome in order to demonstrate his or her devotion (an "endurance test"); and they find reasons to be apart to see how enthusiastically their lovers welcome their return (a "separation test"). This all seems like a lot of trouble when they could simply ask the partner what he or she is thinking—and they *do* often ask the partner's *friends*—but in many relationships, such matters seem too delicate to be discussed openly. In general, the more taboo topics there are in a relationship, the less satisfied the partners are, unless they are highly committed to each other; taboo topics are not related to adverse outcomes when people feel that they're in their relationships to stay (Roloff & Ifert, 1998).

Finally, let's note that two different patterns of social *depenetration* often occur when relationships are in trouble. For some couples, both breadth and depth decrease as partners gradually withdraw from their relationship and their interaction returns to a superficial level (Baxter, 1987). For others, breadth contracts as satisfaction declines, but the depth of self-disclosure actually increases, stimulated by the barrage of negative feelings that the unhappy partners express to each other (Tolstedt & Stokes, 1984). In this case, self-disclosure in a distressed relationship does not resemble the sliver of a superficial relationship or the wedge of a satisfying intimate relationship, but rather a long, thin dagger of words designed to hurt.

Is It Always Gradual?

The theory of social penetration describes a gradual process of communication change and relationship development. But not all relationships develop gradually. Sometimes, people meet each other and quickly bare their souls and tell all. There seem to be two major types of these "quick revelation encounters." The first is the legendary stranger-on-the-plane phenomenon. Settling down next to a stranger while embarking on a long journey, you may find yourself telling the stranger things you have never mentioned to very good friends. Does this phenomenon contradict social penetration theory? The authors of the theory, Irwin Altman and Dalmas Taylor, think not. They believe that this kind of "intimacy" only occurs because you know you will never see the other person again. The stranger doesn't know any of your friends and can't reveal your secrets, so such circumstances let you talk over your concerns without having to worry about any long-term consequences (Derlega & Chaiken, 1977). And, because thinking through your problems and confiding in others improves people's psychological and physical health (Pennebaker, 1997), the stranger-on-the-plane phenomenon offers an opportunity to obtain a real benefit at virtually no cost.

But then there's love, and self-revelation, at first sight. In this case, people who quickly self-disclose a great deal may have every intention of creating a long-lasting relationship. However, Altman and Taylor caution against such premature self-disclosure. When two partners have not established a base of trust, instant openness can be exhilarating, but conflict often follows. In essence, Altman and Taylor view immediate intimacy experiences as "boom-and-bust" encounters. At first, everything goes right, and instant intimacy is gratifying, but there is an increased chance that everything will later go wrong. College roommates who participated in a study by Berg (1984) appear to have experienced this boom-and-bust cycle. Those who indicated high levels of self-disclosure after living together for only two weeks reported *less* liking for each other six months later.

If there is some risk that high levels of early self-disclosure can be a case of "too much, too soon," should we conclude that relationship development should be gradual, for safety's sake? Not necessarily. Lasting friendships are sometimes created quickly (Hays, 1985). On occasion, intimate self-disclosure takes place very rapidly without becoming excessive. In general, as long as you stay within your comfort zone, the best strategy may be to play it by ear, judging the appropriateness of self-disclosure by taking the context and the partner into account (Miller, 1990).

Self-Disclosure and Relationship Satisfaction

The bottom line is that self-disclosure that fits the situation breeds liking and contentment in close relationships. The more spouses self-disclose to each other, for instance, the more happily married they tend to be (Hendrick, 1981; Meeks, Hendrick, & Hendrick, 1998). Indeed, happy spouses talk to each other differently than less intimate partners do. For one thing, they are likely to have their own idiosyncratic codes and figures of speech that allow them to communicate in a manner that is not transparent to others. They use pet phrases and specialized vocabulary, or **idioms,** whose meaning is known only to them, and the more idioms they use, the happier their marriages tend to be (Bell, Buerkel-Rothfuss, & Gore, 1987; Bruess & Pearson, 1993). The resulting interactions are so distinctive that strangers who listen to the conversations of couples in research studies can usually tell whether the speakers are close friends or just acquaintances (Planalp & Benson, 1992). The conversations of intimate partners are marked by more obvious knowledge of the other person, more personal self-disclosure, and greater relaxation than occurs in the interactions of people who are not intimate.

There are several reasons why self-disclosure is linked to liking (Collins & Miller, 1994). First, we tend to reveal more personal information to those we like.

BOX 5.2

Are You a High "Opener?"

Some people are especially good at eliciting self-disclosure from others. Lynn Miller, John Berg, and Rick Archer (1983) developed the Opener Scale to assess this ability, and people who get high scores really do draw out more intimate information from others than do people who receive low scores on the scale. They do this through both verbal and nonverbal channels: High openers appear more attentive during conversation—gazing and nodding more, and looking comfortable and interested—and they verbally express more interest in what others are saying (Purvis, Dabbs, & Hopper, 1984).

They seem to enjoy their conversations and to be absorbed by what others have to say (Pegalis, Shaffer, Bazzini, & Greenier, 1994). As a result, they tend to be very good interviewers (Shaffer, Ruammake, & Pegalis, 1990).

Women tend to be better openers than men (Miller et al., 1983). The average score for women on the Opener Scale is 31, whereas 28 is typical for men. If your own score is 5 points higher than average, you're a fairly high opener, but if it's 5 points lower, your score is rather low. You can figure your score by rating yourself on each item using this scale:

0	1	2	3	4
Strongly disagree	Disagree	Neither agree nor disagree	Agree	Strongly disagree

The Opener Scale

1. People frequently tell me about themselves.
2. I've been told that I'm a very good listener.
3. I'm very accepting of others.
4. People trust me with their secrets.
5. I easily get people to "open up."
6. People feel relaxed around me.
7. I enjoy listening to people.
8. I'm sympathetic to people's problems.
9. I encourage people to tell me how they are feeling.
10. I can keep people talking about themselves.

If we're attracted to others, we tend to be more open with them. However, we also tend to like others more *because* we have self-disclosed to them. Everything else being equal, opening up to others causes us to like them more. Finally, and perhaps most importantly, it's rewarding to be entrusted with self-disclosures from others. People who engage in intimate disclosures are liked more by others than are those who say less about themselves (Sprecher, 1987). Thus, it feels good to give and to receive self-disclosures, and this aspect of verbal communication is an essential building block of close relationships. Try it yourself for 45 minutes, and you'll probably make a new friend (Aron et al., 1997).

Gender Differences in Verbal Communication

People have made a lot of money writing books that describe men and women as different species that come from different planets and speak different languages. We've tried to combat that simple-minded way of thinking throughout this book, because the sexes really are more similar than they are different. However, men and women do tend to use different styles of nonverbal communication when they interact with each other, as we saw in Table 5.2. What about verbal communication? Some differences exist there, too. As we'll see, men and women don't speak different languages, but they tend to talk about different things.

Topics of Conversation

If you read a transcript of a conversation between two friends, would you be able to tell if the participants were men or women? You might. Among themselves, women are more likely than men to discuss their feelings about their close relationships and other personal aspects of their lives (Clark, 1998). They're also more likely to gossip, critiquing other people and coming to more negative conclusions than positive ones (Leaper & Holliday, 1995). Feelings and people figure prominently in the conversations of women. In contrast, men tend to stick to more impersonal matters, discussing objects and actions such as cars and sports, and seeking a few laughs instead of support and counsel (Clark, 1998; Martin, 1997). As a result, the conversations men have with each other tend to be less intimate and personal than the conversations women share (Reis, 1998).

Styles of Conversation

Women also tend to speak with less forcefulness than men do (Berger, 1994). Their style of speech is more indirect and tentative. For instance, women use more hedges that soften their assertions—"We're kind of interested"—and employ more verbs that express uncertainty—"It seems to be that way" (Mulac, 1998). More often than men, they ask questions in conversation and make statements in a questioning tone with a rising inflection at the end (Lakoff, 1975). This manner of speech—"I skipped class, um, on Thursday?"—is much less commanding than men's usual style, which seems more certain and knowledgeable. Women are also less profane (Martin, 1997).

Moreover, in conversations with women, men do most of the talking (Haas, 1979), and despite hackneyed stereotypes about women being more talkative than men, we're apparently used to this pattern. When people listen to recordings of conversations, they think it's more disrespectful and assertive for a woman to interrupt a man than vice versa (LaFrance, 1992).

Self-Disclosure

In established relationships, women are more self-disclosing than men are, and in keeping with their higher scores on the "Opener" scale (see Box 5.2), they elicit more self-disclosure as well (Dindia & Allen, 1992). However, men and women do not differ in their self-disclosures to acquaintances and strangers, so it's clear that gender differences in self-disclosure depend on the nature of a relationship and the sex of one's partner (Miller, 1990). In particular, men offer less intimate self-disclosures to their male partners (such as their best friends) than to their female partners in close relationships. As we noted above, topics of conversation among men tend to be relatively impersonal, so they say less about their personal feelings and private thoughts to other men than they do to women. As a result, interactions that involve a woman tend to be more intimate and meaningful than are interactions that involve only men (Reis, 1998). Men open up to women, and women are open among themselves, but men disclose less to other men.

An important consequence of all this is that men are often more dependent on women for emotional warmth and intimacy than women are on them in return (Wheeler, Reis, & Nezlek, 1983): Whereas women may have intimate, open, supportive connections with partners of both sexes, men are likely to share their most meaningful intimacy only with women. Consequently, a man may need a woman in his life to keep him from being lonely, but women don't usually need men in this way (see chapter 14).

This pattern of lower intimacy among men in the United States is almost certainly the result of sociocultural influences, because it does not occur in countries with different traditions (Reis, 1998). For instance, in Jordan, a country that encourages same-sex bonding among men, there's no difference at all in the meaningfulness of the interactions men share with women or other men. Moreover, even in the U.S., men can have very intimate conversations with their male best friends when they are following researchers' instructions to do so (Reis, Senchak, & Solomon, 1985). Thus, the communicative styles of men and women appear to have more to do with learned habits and preferences than with any actual differences in ability.

Instrumentality Versus Expressivity

Indeed, the differences between men and women we have described in this section are *gender* differences that are more closely associated with their gender roles than with their biological sex. Women engage in intimate verbal communication with trusted partners because they tend to be high in expressivity and are comfortable talking about their feelings. However, this also comes naturally to men who are high in expressivity, as androgynous men are, and such men tend to have meaningful, intimate interactions with both sexes just like women do (Aube, Norcliffe, Craig, & Koestner, 1995). So, to refine the point we made previously, it's really just traditional, macho men who have superficial conversations with their best friends and who need relationships with women to keep from being lonely. More than other men, macho guys shut out their male friends (Shaffer, Pegalis, & Bazzini, 1996) and tend to be sad and lonely when they do not have a female romantic partner (Wheeler et al., 1983). In contrast, androgynous men (who are both assertive *and* warm) self-disclose readily to both sexes and enjoy meaningful interactions with all their friends; as a result, they tend to not be lonely, and they spend more time interacting with women than less expressive, traditional men do (Reis, 1986).

Given this, it's silly to think that men and women speak different languages and come from different planets. Many men *are* more taciturn than the average woman, but there are also men who are more open and self-disclosing than most women are. The typical intimacy of a person's interactions is tied to his or her level of expressivity, and once you take that into account, it doesn't much matter whether the person is a man or woman. Moreover, expressivity is a trait that ranges from low to high in both women and men, so it makes more sense to take note of individual differences in communicative style than to lump all men together and treat them as a group distinct from women.

Nevertheless, it's true that about half of all men are sex-typed, which means that they're high in instrumentality and low in expressivity, and such macho men are much less expressive than most women are. Thus, they are likely to display a style of emotional communication that is rather different from that of most women. Whereas women tend to be open with their feelings, such men are likely to be comparatively close-mouthed. As a result, many wives get into the habit of thinking that if their husbands don't complain about anything, then everything's okay; the wives interpret a lack of hostility as an indication of continued love. In contrast, most husbands seem to think that if their wives don't express obvious affection for them, then everything's not okay; the husbands interpret a lack of overt love as a sign of hostility (Gaelick, Bodenhausen, & Wyer, 1985). This means that men and women tend to differ in their reactions to neutral interactions that are devoid of either affection or animosity: A woman is likely to think things are fine, but a man may start worrying that she doesn't love him anymore. In this manner, gender differences in communication can be problematic.

A closing note: Men value instrumental communication skills such as the ability to give clear instructions and directions more than women do. And women value affective communication skills such as expressing affection and feelings more than men do. But both men and women consider affective skills to be more important in close relationships than instrumental skills are (Burleson, Kunkel, Samter, & Werking, 1996). Although they are sometimes caricatured as speaking different languages, men and women agree that the ability to adequately communicate one's love, respect, and regard for one's partner is indispensable in close relationships.

DYSFUNCTIONAL COMMUNICATION AND WHAT TO DO ABOUT IT

As we've seen, the more open and self-disclosing spouses are to one another, the more happily married they tend to be (Meeks et al., 1998). But not all our efforts to speak our minds and communicate with our partners have positive results. More often than we realize, we face an interpersonal gap that causes misunderstanding or confusion in those who hear what we have to say. And the nature and consequences of miscommunication are very apparent in

---

BOX 5.3

Communication and the Internet

This may be hard to believe, but back in a more primitive time, your parents often had to use a phone and talk to only one person at a time when they wanted to chat with friends! Now, of course, you can communicate with several people at once in an Internet chat room and/or conduct simultaneous one-on-one interactions with a variety of people who may either be next door or in another hemisphere. If you remember the old days, this is remarkable, and this new technology is undoubtedly changing how we communicate with others and with whom we interact (McKenna & Bargh, 2000).

The nature and pace of interactions on the Net is quite different than talking on the phone, and that's one reason people like them. We can take our time to consider what we want to say, and because no "leaky" paralan-guage is involved, we have more control over the messages we send. Typing those messages takes work, however, so we often develop idioms, acronyms (such as BRB for "be right back"), and code words that constitute a unique language and that may distinguish special online relationships from more casual interactions (Ruane, 1999). Internet chat is also much more anonymous than other conversation, so influences such as physical attractiveness that have enormous impact on other forms of social interaction are much less important online. Coupled with the worldwide reach of the Web, these characteristics make the Internet a unique platform for the development of close relationships, a fact that is drawing increasing attention from relationship researchers (e.g., McCown, 2000; Merkle & Richardson, 2000).

---

relationships in which the partners are distressed and dissatisfied. The verbal communications of unhappy partners often just perpetuate their discontent and make things worse instead of better.

Miscommunication

Indeed, we can gain valuable insights about what we shouldn't do when we talk with others by carefully comparing the communicative behaviors of happy lovers to those of unhappy partners. John Gottman and his colleagues at the University of Washington have been doing this for over 25 years, and they have observed several important patterns. First, unhappy people do a poor job of *saying what they mean* (Gottman, 1994). When they have a complaint, they are rarely precise; instead, they're prone to **kitchen-sinking,** in which they tend to address several topics at once (so that everything but the "kitchen sink" gets dragged into the conversation). This usually causes their primary concern to get lost in the barrage of frustrations that are announced at the same time. If they're annoyed by late fees at the video store, for instance, they may say, "It's not just your carelessness, it's those friends you hang out with, and your lousy attitude about helping out around the house." As a result, their conversations frequently drift **off-beam,** wandering from topic to topic so that the conversation never stays on one problem long enough to resolve it: "You never do what I ask. You're just as hard-headed as your mother, and you always take her side." Flitting from problem to problem on a long list of concerns makes it almost certain that none of them will be fixed.

Second, unhappy partners do a poor job of *hearing each other.* They rarely try to patiently double-check their understanding of their partners' messages. Instead, they jump to conclusions (often assuming the worst) and head off on tangents based on what they presume their partners really mean. One aspect of this is **mindreading,** which occurs when people assume that they understand their partners' thoughts, feelings, and opinions without asking. All intimate couples mindread to some extent, but distressed couples do so in critical and hostile ways; they tend to perceive unpleasant motives where neutral or positive ones actually exist: "You just said that to make me mad, to get back at me for yesterday." Unhappy partners also **interrupt** each other in negative ways more than contented couples do. Not all interruptions are obnoxious. People who interrupt their partners to express agreement or ask for clarification may actually be communicating happily and well. But people who interrupt to express disagreement or to change the topic are likely to leave their partners feeling disregarded and unappreciated (Daigen & Holmes, 2000).

Distressed couples also listen poorly by finding something wrong or unworkable with anything their partners say. This is **yes-butting,** and it communicates constant criticism of the others' points of view: "Yeah, we could try that, but it won't work because . . ." Unhappy partners also engage in **cross-complaining** that fails to acknowledge others' concerns; instead of expressing interest in what their partners have to say, they just respond to a complaint with one of their own:

> "I hate the way you let the dishes pile up in the sink."
> "Well, I hate the way *you* leave your clothes lying around on the floor."

Finally, unhappy partners too often display *negative affect* when they talk with each other (Gottman & Levenson, 1992). They often react to their partner's complaints with sarcastic disregard that is demeaning and scornful, and instead of mending their problems, they often make them worse. Damaging interactions like these typically begin with **criticism** that attacks a partner's personality or character instead of identifying a specific behavior that is causing concern. For instance, instead of delineating a particular frustration ("I get annoyed when you leave your wet towels on the floor"), a critic may inflame the interaction by making a global accusation of a character flaw ("You are such a slob!"). **Contempt** in the form of insults, mockery, or hostile humor is often involved as well. The partners' common response to such attacks is **defensiveness;** instead of treating the clumsy complaint as legitimate and reasonable, the partners seek to protect themselves from the perceived attack by making excuses or by cross-complaining, hurling counterattacks of their own. **Stonewalling** may follow, particularly in men, as a partner "clams up" and reacts to the messy situation by withdrawing into a stony silence (Heavy, Layne, & Christensen, 1993). People may believe they're helping the situation by refusing to argue further, but their lack of responsiveness can be infuriating (Zadro & Williams, 2000). Instead of demonstrating appropriate acknowledgement and concern for a partner's complaints, stonewalling typically communicates "disapproval, icy distance, and smugness" (Gottman, 1994, p. 94). Ultimately, destructive **belligerence** may occur, with one partner aggressively rejecting the other altogether ("So what? What are you gonna do about it?").

When communication routinely degenerates into these contentious patterns, the outlook for the relationship is grim (Gottman, Coan, Carrère, & Swanson, 1998). In fact, videotapes of just the first three minutes of a marital conflict enable researchers to predict with 83 percent accuracy who will be divorced six years later (Carrère & Gottman, 1999). Couples whose marriages are doomed display noticeably more contempt, defensiveness, and belligerence than do those who will stay together. And among those who stay together, spouses who communicate well are happier and more content than those who suffer frequent misunderstanding (Feeney, 1994).

The challenge, of course, is that it's not always easy to avoid these problems. When we're angry, resentful, or anxious, we may find ourselves cross-complaining, kitchen-sinking, and all the rest. How can we avoid these traps? Depending on the situation, we may need to send clearer, less inflammatory messages, listen better, or stay polite and calm, and sometimes we need to do all three.

Saying What We Mean

Complaints that criticize a partner's personality or character disparage the partner and often make mountains out of molehills, portraying problems as huge, intractable dilemmas that cannot be easily solved. (Given some of the broad complaints we throw at our partners, it's no wonder that they sometimes get defensive.) It's much more sensible—and accurate—to identify as plainly and concretely as possible a specific behavior that annoyed us. This is **behavior description,** and it not only tells our partners what's on our minds, it focuses the conversation on discrete, manageable behaviors that, unlike personalities, can often be readily changed. A good behavior description specifies a particular event and does not involve generalities; thus, words such as *always* or *never* should never be used. This is *not* a good behavior description: "You're always interrupting me! You never let me finish!"

We should also use **I-statements** that specify our feelings. I-statements start with "I" and then describe a distinct emotional reaction. They force us to identify our feelings, which can be useful both to us and our partners. They also help us to "own" our feelings and acknowledge them instead of keeping the entire focus on the partner. Thus, instead of saying, "You really piss me off," one should say, "I feel pretty angry right now."

A handy way to use both behavior descriptions and I-statements to communicate more clearly and accurately is to integrate them into **XYZ statements.** Such statements follow the form of "When you do **X** in situation **Y**" (that's a good behavior description), "I feel **Z**" (an I-statement). Listen to yourself next time you complain to your partner. Are you saying something like this:

"You're so inconsiderate! You never let me finish what I'm saying!"

Or, are you being precise and accurate and saying what you mean:

"When you interrupted me just now, I felt annoyed."

There's a big difference. One of those statements is likely to get a thoughtful, apologetic response from a loving partner, but the other probably won't.

Active Listening

We have two vital tasks when we're on the receiving end of others' messages. The first is to accurately understand what our partners are trying to say, and the second is to communicate that attention and comprehension to our partners so that they know we care about what they've said. Both tasks can be accomplished by **paraphrasing** a message, repeating it in our own words and giving the sender a chance to agree that that's what he or she actually meant. When people use paraphrasing, they don't assume that they understood their partners and issue an immediate reply. Instead, they take a moment to check their comprehension by rephrasing the message and repeating it back. This sounds awkward, but it is a terrific way to avoid arguments and conflict that would otherwise result from misunderstanding and mistakes. Whenever a conversation begins to get heated, paraphrasing can keep it from getting out of hand. Look what's wrong here:

WILMA: (sighing) I'm so glad your mother decided not to come visit us next week.
FRED: (irate) What's wrong with my mother? You've always been on her case, and I think you're an ungrateful witch.

Perhaps before Fred flew off the handle, some paraphrasing would have been helpful:

WILMA: (sighing) I'm so glad your mother decided not to come visit us next week.
FRED: (irate) Are you saying you don't like her to be here?
WILMA: (surprised) No, she's always welcome. I just have my paper due in my relationships class and won't have much time then.
FRED: (mollified) Oh.

Another valuable listening skill is **perception checking,** which is the opposite of mindreading. In perception checking, people assess the accuracy of their inferences about a partner's feelings by asking the partner for clarification. This communicates one's attentiveness and interest, and it encourages the partner to be more open: "You seem pretty upset by what I said, is that right?"

Listeners who paraphrase and check their perceptions make an *active* effort to understand their partners, and that care and consideration is usually much appreciated. Active listening is also likely to help smooth the inevitable rough spots any relationship encounters. Indeed, people who practice these techniques typically report happier marriages than do those who simply assume that they understand what their partners mean by what they say (Markman, Stanley, & Blumberg, 1994).

Being Polite and Staying Cool

Still, even the most accurate sending and receiving may not do much good if our conversations are too often surly and antagonistic. It's hard to remain mild and relaxed when we encounter contempt and belligerence from others, and people who deride or disdain their partners often get irascible, irritated reactions in return. Indeed, dissatisfied spouses spend more time than contented lovers do locked into patterns of *negative affect reciprocity* in which they're contemptuous of each other, with each being scornful of what the other has to say (Levenson, Carstensen, & Gottman, 1994). Happy couples behave this way, too—there are probably periods of acrimonious disregard in most relationships—but they break out of these ugly cycles more quickly than unhappy partners do (Burman, Margolin, & John, 1993).

In fact, defusing cycles of increasing cantankerousness when they begin may be very beneficial, but it may not be easy. Although XYZ statements and active listening skills can help prevent surly interactions altogether, Gottman and his colleagues argue that people rarely have the presence of mind to use them once they get angry (Gottman, Carrère, Swanson, & Coan, 2000). It can be

Unhappy partners often have difficulty saying what they mean, hearing each other, and staying polite and calm when disagreements arise.

difficult or even "impossible to make 'I-statements' when you are in the 'hating-my-partner, wanting revenge, feeling-stung-and-needing-to-sting-back' state of mind" (Wile, 1995, p. 2).

Thus, being able to stay cool when you're provoked by a partner, and being able to calm down when you begin to get angry, are very valuable skills. You'll be better able to do this if you construe anger as just one way of thinking about a problem. Anger results from the perception that others are causing us illegitimate, unfair, avoidable grief. Use a different point of view and anger is reduced or prevented altogether (Tavris, 1989; Zillman, 1993). Instead of thinking, "S/he has no right to say that to me!," it's more adaptive to think, "Hmm. Contrary statements from someone who loves me. I wonder why?"

Of course, it can be hard to maintain such a placid stream of thought when one is provoked. So it's also a good idea to (try to) reduce the number of provocations you encounter by agreeing in advance to be polite to each other whenever possible (Gottman, 1994). You may wish to schedule regular meetings at which you and your partner (politely) air your grievances; knowing that a problem will be addressed makes it easier to be pleasant to your partner the rest of the week (Markman et al., 1994). And under no circumstances should the two of you continue an interaction in which you're just hurling insults and sarcasm back and forth at each other. If you find yourself in such a pattern of negative affect reciprocity, take a temporary *time out* to stop the cycle. Ask for a short break—"Honey, I'm too angry to think straight. Let me take 10 minutes to calm down"—and then return to the issue when you're less aroused (Markman et al., 1994). Get off by yourself and take no more than six long, slow, deep breaths per minute, and you will calm down, faster than you think (Tavris, 1989).

The Power of Respect and Validation

The central ingredients in all of these components of good communication—our conscious efforts to send clear, straightforward messages, to listen carefully and well, and to be polite and nonaggressive even when disagreements occur—are the indications we provide that we care about and respect our partners' points of view. We expect such concern and regard from our intimate partners, and distress and resentment build when we think we're disrespected (Reis & Patrick, 1996). Thus, **validation** of our partners that acknowledges the legitimacy of their opinions and communicates respect for their positions is always a desirable goal in intimate interaction.

Validation does not mean that you agree with someone. You can communicate appropriate respect and recognition of a partner's point of view without agreeing with it. Consider the following three responses to Barney's complaint:

BARNEY: I hate it when you act that way.

Cross-complaining	BETTY: And I hate it when you get drunk with Fred.
Agreement	BETTY: Yeah, I agree. It's not a nice way to act, and I'll try to change.
Validation	BETTY: Yeah, I can understand that, and I don't blame you. But I'd like you to try to understand what I'm feeling, too.

Only the last response, which concedes the legitimacy of Barney's point of view but allows Betty her own feelings, invites an open, honest dialogue. We need not be inauthentic or nonassertive to respect our partners' opinions, even when we disagree with them.

Indeed, validating our partners will often make disagreement much more tolerable. All of the skills we have mentioned here support an atmosphere of responsive care and concern that can reduce the intensity and impact of disputes with our partners (Huston & Chorost, 1994). You may even be able to set a troubled relationship on a more promising path by rehearsing these skills and pledging to be polite and respectful to one another when difficulties arise (Stanley, Bradbury, & Markman, 2000).

CHAPTER SUMMARY

Communication is an important factor in the development and quality of relationships. Research using the "talk table" demonstrates that unhappy partners frustrate and annoy each other through miscommunication more often than happy partners do. When a sender's intentions differ from the impact that a message has on the recipient, a couple faces an *interpersonal gap*.

Nonverbal Communication

Nonverbal communication serves vital functions, *providing information, regulating interaction,* and *defining the nature of the relationship* two people share.

Components of Nonverbal Communication.

Facial expression. Several basic facial expressions, such as happiness, sadness, fear, anger, disgust, and surprise, appear to be inborn; people all over the world display the same expressions when they experience those emotions. As a result, facial expressions are good guides to others' moods. Following *display rules,* people often try to control their expressions, but subtle indications of their real feelings often leak out.

Gazing behavior. The direction and amount of a person's looking is important in defining relationships and in regulating interaction. In particular, high-status people use a higher *visual dominance ratio* than low-status people do.

Body language. Small elements of body language such as gestures vary widely across cultures, but the posture and motion of the entire body is informative as well. Customs agents use body language to decide whether or not to search a traveler's luggage.

Touch. Men and women tend to respond differently to touches from strangers, with women responding positively, men negatively. As a result, men touch women more than women touch men.

Interpersonal distance. We use different zones of personal space for different kinds of interactions. Preferred distances vary with culture, sex, and status.

Paralanguage. Paralanguage involves all the variations in a person's voice other than the words he or she uses. A good example is baby talk, which is often used to address lovers, elderly people, and pets, as well as babies.

Combining the components. Together, these nonverbal actions are very informative. When there is a discrepancy between people's words and actions, the truth usually lies in their nonverbal, not their verbal, communication. Nonverbal actions also allow us to fine-tune the intimacy of our interactions in subtle but real ways.

Nonverbal Sensitivity. Nonverbal accuracy predicts relationship satisfaction. Unhappy spouses, especially husbands, do a poor job at nonverbal communication. Either skill or performance deficits may be involved in such problems, but no matter why it occurs, nonverbal insensitivity probably makes one an unrewarding partner.

Sex Differences in Nonverbal Communication. When they interact with men, women display deferential patterns of nonverbal behavior that resemble those of low-status people interacting with those of higher status. The reason why is unclear, but such behavior may be influential in perpetuating unwanted stereotypes.

Verbal Communication

Self-Disclosure. Two people cannot be said to be intimate with one another unless they have revealed personal information about themselves to their partners.

The theory of social penetration. As a relationship develops, both the breadth and depth of self-disclosure increase. Participants discuss more topics and reveal more personally meaningful information. However, breadth increases faster than depth does at first. Reciprocity in self-disclosure is also more common between strangers than between intimates.

Both self-disclosure and selective secrecy contribute to relationship satisfaction. Partners try to avoid talking about *taboo topics* such as the state of their relationship, but they may resort to a variety of secret tests to assess their partners' commitment. When their relationships are failing, some couples decrease the breadth but increase the depth of their self-disclosure, reflecting the intense negative emotions expressed during conflict.

Is it always gradual? Sometimes people disclose highly personal information soon after they first meet. In the "stranger-on-the-plane" phenomenon, quick self-disclosure is usually safe because people don't expect to meet again. But where an enduring relationship is possible, premature self-disclosure may damage the long-term prospects of the relationship. The best strategy is to judge the appropriateness of self-disclosure by taking both the context and the partner into account.

Self-disclosure and relationship satisfaction. Appropriate self-disclosure breeds liking and contentment, because we reveal more personal information to those we like, like others more because we have self-disclosed to them, and like to be entrusted with self-disclosures from others.

Gender Differences in Verbal Communication. Men and women are more similar to each other than different, but there are some gender differences in communicative style.

Topics of conversation. Among themselves, women are more likely than men to discuss feelings and people, whereas men are more likely to seek a few laughs and talk about more impersonal matters.

Styles of conversation. When they are conversing with men, women also tend to speak less often and with less forcefulness than men do. Men are more profane.

Self-disclosure. On average, women self-disclose more than men in close relationships, but there are no such differences in more casual relationships. Men self-disclose relatively little to other men even when they are friends, and thus they are likely to share their most meaningful intimacy only with women. This is not true in some other countries, so this pattern appears to be a learned preference that is influenced by cultural norms.

Instrumentality versus expressivity. Intimate self-disclosure is linked to expressivity, so traditional, macho men (who are low in expressivity) need relationships with women to keep from being lonely. In contrast, androgynous men, who are more expressive, enjoy more meaningful interactions with all their friends.

However, because so many men are sex-typed and are close-mouthed about their feelings, wives often interpret a lack of hostility from their husbands as a sign of love. Men, on the other hand, tend to interpret a lack of overt love as a sign of hostility. In this manner, gender differences in communication can be problematic. In any case, both men and women agree that affective communication is indispensable in close relationships.

Dysfunctional Communication and What to Do About It

The impact of miscommunication is obvious in unhappy relationships, where conversation often makes things worse instead of better.

Miscommunication. Distressed couples have trouble saying what they mean. They're prone to *kitchen-sinking*, and their conversations frequently drift *off-beam*. They also do a poor job of hearing each other. They engage in *mind-reading* and *interrupt* each other disagreeably, finding fault with what the other says. Worst of all, they display negative affect and say things that are *critical, contemptuous,* and *defensive*; they may also *stonewall* each other and become *belligerent*. Such behavior is very destructive, and too much of it may doom spouses to divorce.

Saying What We Mean. When they are complaining about something, skillful senders focus on specific, concrete actions instead of personalities. They also make their feelings clear with *I-statements*, often integrating them into *XYZ statements* that identify discrete events they found annoying.

Active Listening. Good listeners make an effort to understand their partners, often *paraphrasing* a sender's message to double-check its meaning. They also assess the accuracy of their inferences by asking whether their judgments are correct.

Being Polite and Staying Cool. Happy couples also avoid extended periods of negative affect reciprocity, but this is sometimes hard to do. Anger can be defused with adaptive mental scripts and slow breathing, but it's a good idea for couples to agree in advance to be polite to each other whenever possible. Regular meetings that address problems can be helpful in this regard.

The Power of Respect and Validation. Finally, even when they disagree, partners should strive to *validate* each other by communicating respect and recognition of the other's point of view. Such actions reduce the impact of disputes, and may even save troubled relationships.

CHAPTER 6

Interdependency

If you've been in a relationship for a while, why are you staying in that relationship? Are you obligated to continue it for some reason? Do you consider it your duty? Or are you simply waiting for something better to come along? Hopefully, all of your current relationships have been so rewarding that none of these questions will apply. However, all of them provide the focus for this chapter, which will take an *economic* view of our dealings with others.

Our subject will be interdependency, our reliance on others, and they on us, for valuable interpersonal rewards. We'll examine why we stay in some relationships and leave others, and we will ponder the nature of lasting relationships. We'll say nothing about love, which is the topic of another chapter. Instead, here we will ponder the balance sheets with which we tally the profits and losses of our interactions with others. You may not yet have thought of yourself as an interpersonal accountant, but doing so provides powerful insights into the workings of close relationships.

SOCIAL EXCHANGE

Interdependency theories assume that people are like shoppers who are browsing at an interpersonal shopping mall. We're all looking for good buys. We seek interactions with others that provide maximum reward at minimum cost, and we only stay with those partners who provide sufficient profit (Rusbult & Arriaga, 1997). However, because everybody behaves this way, both partners in a relationship must be profiting to their satisfaction or the relationship is unlikely to continue.

From this perspective, social life entails the mutual exchange of desirable rewards with others, a process called **social exchange** (Blau, 1964; Homans, 1961). There are several different social exchange theories, but the ideas introduced by John Thibaut and Harold Kelley (1959; Kelley, 1979; Kelley & Thibaut, 1978)—now known as *interdependence theory*—are most often used by relationship scientists, so we'll feature them here. Let's first consider the central elements of social exchange.

Rewards and Costs

The rewards of interactions are the gratifying experiences and commodities we obtain through our contact with others. They come in very different forms, ranging from impersonal benefits, such as the directions you can get from strangers when you're lost, to personal intimacies, such as acceptance and support from someone you love. We'll use the term *reward* to refer to anything within an interaction that is desirable and welcome and that brings enjoyment or fulfillment to the recipient.

In contrast, *costs* are punishing, undesirable experiences. They can involve financial expenditures, such as buying dinner for your date, or actual injuries, such as split lips and blackened eyes. However, some of the most important costs of intimate interaction are psychological burdens: uncertainty about where a relationship is headed, frustration over your partner's imperfections, and regret about all the things you don't get to do because you're in that relationship (Sedikides, Oliver, & Campbell, 1994). All of the diverse consequences of interaction that are frustrating or distressing are costs.

We'll summarize the rewards and costs associated with a particular interaction with the term **outcome,** which describes the net profit or loss a person encounters, all things considered. Adding up all the rewards and costs involved:

Outcome = Rewards − Costs

Obviously, if an interaction is more rewarding than punishing, a positive outcome results. But remember, the social exchange perspective asserts that people want the *best possible* outcomes. The simple fact that your interactions are profitable doesn't mean that they are good enough to keep you coming back to that partner. Indeed, one of the major insights of interdependence theory is its suggestion that whether your outcomes are positive or negative isn't nearly as important as where they stand compared to two criteria with which we evaluate the outcomes we receive. The first criterion involves our expectations, and the second involves our perceptions of how well we could manage without our current partner.

What Do We Expect from Our Relationships?

Interdependence theory assumes that each of us has an idiosyncratic **comparison level** (which we'll abbreviate as **CL**), which describes the value of the outcomes that we believe we deserve in our dealings with others. Our CLs are based on our past experiences. People who have a history of highly rewarding partnerships are likely to have high CLs, meaning that they expect, and feel they deserve, very good outcomes now. In contrast, people who have had troublesome relationships in the past are likely to expect less and have lower CLs.

A person's comparison level represents his or her neutral point on a continuum that ranges all the way from abject misery to ecstatic delight. Our CLs are the standards by which our *satisfaction* with a relationship is measured. If the outcomes you receive exceed your CL, you're happy; you're getting more than the minimum payoff you expect from interaction with others. Just how happy you are depends on the extent to which your outcomes surpass your expectations; if your outcomes are considerably higher than your CL, you'll be very satisfied. On the other hand, if your outcomes fall below your CL, you're dissatisfied, even if your outcomes are still pretty good and you're doing better than most people. This is a significant point: Even if you are still making a profit on your transactions with others, you may not be happy if the profit isn't big enough to meet your expectations. If you're a rich, spoiled celebrity, for instance, you may have an unusually high CL and be rather dissatisfied with a fabulous partner who would bedazzle the rest of us.

So, satisfaction in close relationships doesn't depend simply on how good in an absolute sense our outcomes are; instead, satisfaction derives from how our outcomes compare to our comparison levels, like this:

Outcomes − CL = Satisfaction/Dissatisfaction

How Well Could We Do Elsewhere?

However, another important assumption of interdependence theory is that satisfaction is not the only, or even the major, influence that determines how long relationships last. Whether or not we're happy, we use a second criterion, a **comparison level for alternatives** (or CL_{alt}), to determine if we could be doing even better somewhere else. Our CL_{alt}s describe the outcomes we can receive by leaving our current relationships and moving to the best alternative partnerships or situations we have available. And if you're a good accountant, you can see that our CL_{alt}s are also the lowest levels of outcome we will tolerate from our present partners. Here's why: If other relationships promise better profits than we currently receive, we're likely to leave our present partners and pursue those bigger payoffs even if we're satisfied with what we already have. (Remember, we want the best possible deal we can get.) On the other hand, even if we are dissatisfied with our current relationships, we are unlikely to leave them unless a better alternative presents itself. This is a very important point, which helps explain why people stay in relationships that make them miserable: even though they're unhappy where they are, they think they'd be worse off if they left. If they thought a better situation awaited them elsewhere, they'd go (Choice & Lamke, 1999; Heaton & Albrecht, 1991). This idea—that our contentment with a relationship is not the major determinant of whether we stay in it or leave—is one of interdependence theory's most interesting insights.

Thus, our CL_{alt}s determine our *dependence* on our relationships. Whether or not we're satisfied, if we believe that we're already doing as well as we possibly can, we are dependent upon our present partners and are unlikely to leave them. Moreover, the greater the gap between our current outcomes and our poorer alternatives, the more dependent we are. If our current outcomes are only a little better than those that await us elsewhere, we don't need our current partners very much and may leave if our alternatives improve.

But would people really leave relationships in which they're already happy? Presumably, they would, if their CL_{alt}s are genuinely better than what they're getting now. To keep things simple when you consider this, think of a CL_{alt} as the global outcome, the net profit or loss, that a person believes will result from switching partners, all things considered (Kelley, 1983). If the whole process of ending a present partnership and moving to an alternative promises better outcomes, a person should move. It's just economic good sense.

A problem, of course, is that these are difficult calculations to make. There's a lot to consider. On the one hand, there are the new external attractions that can lure us away from our present partners. We need to assess the desirability and availability of alternative partners, and solitude—being alone—is also an option to ponder. When other partners or simple solitude seem attractive, our CL_{alt}s go up. However, there may also be a variety of costs that we will incur by leaving an existing relationship, and they can dramatically affect the net profit to be gained by moving elsewhere (Levinger, 1999). For instance, social psychologist Caryl Rusbult has demonstrated that one's **investments** in a present relationship, the things one would lose if the relationship were to end, are also important influences on one's decision to stay or go (e.g., Rusbult, Drigotas, & Verette, 1994). The investments a person leaves behind can either be tangible goods, such as furniture and dishes you have to split with an ex-spouse, or psychological benefits, such as love and respect from in-laws and friends. An unhappy spouse may refrain from filing for divorce, for example, not because she has no other options but because she doesn't want to accept the potential costs of confused children, a bitter ex-spouse, disappointed parents, and befuddled friends. All of these would reduce the global desirability of leaving, and thus reduce one's CL_{alt}.

Another complication is that a person's CL_{alt} is what he or she *thinks* it is, and a variety of factors can influence people's perceptions of their alternatives. Self-esteem, for one. When people don't like themselves, they're unlikely to think that others will find them desirable (Kiesler & Baral, 1970), and they may underestimate their prospects with other partners. Learned helplessness may also be influential (Strube, 1988). If people get stuck in a bad relationship for too long, they may lose hope and glumly underestimate their chances of doing better elsewhere. And access to information may affect one's CL_{alt}, too. If you become a stay-at-home parent who doesn't work, you'll probably have much more limited information about potential alternatives than you would have if you went to work in a large city every day (Rusbult & Martz, 1995); as a result, you'll probably have a lower CL_{alt} than you would have if you got out and looked around.

Indeed, desirable alternatives will only enhance your CL_{alt} if you are aware of them, and if you're content with your current partners you may not pay much attention to people who could be compelling rivals to your existing relationships. In fact, people who are satisfied with their existing relationships do report less interest in looking around to see how they could be doing elsewhere; as a result, they also think they have lower CL_{alt}s than do those who pay more attention to their alternatives (Miller, 1997a). This may be important. College students who keep track of their options and monitor their alternatives with care switch romantic partners more often than do those who pay their alternatives less heed (Miller, 1997a).

These results mean that although interdependence theory treats satisfaction and dependence as relatively independent components of relationships, they are actually correlated. As an old cliché suggests, the grass may be greener in other relationships, but if you're happy with your current partner, you're less likely to notice. Still, there's wisdom in remembering that satisfaction with a relationship has only a limited role in a person's decision to stay in it or go. Consider the usual trajectory of a divorce: Spouses who divorce have usually been unhappy for quite some time before they decide to separate. What finally prompts them to act? Something changes: Their CL_{alt}s finally come to exceed their current outcomes (Albrecht & Kunz, 1980). Things may get so bad that their outcomes in the marriage slip below those that are available in alternative options that used to seem inadequate. Or, the apparent costs of ending the marriage decrease (which raises one's CL_{alt}); because the spouses have been unhappy for so long, for instance, their kids, parents, and pastor may change their minds and support a divorce for the first time. Or, the apparent rewards of leaving increase, perhaps because they have saved some money or found an alternative partner. (This also raises one's CL_{alt}.) The bottom line is that people don't divorce when they get unhappy; they divorce when, one way or the other, their prospects finally seem brighter elsewhere.

So, if we remember that CL_{alt} is a multifaceted judgment encompassing both the costs of leaving—such as lost investments—and the enticements offered by others, we get:

Outcomes – CL_{alt} = Dependence/Independence

Four Types of Relationships

Now that we understand CLs and CL_{alt}s, let's see how they work together to define the types of relationships people encounter. CLs, CL_{alt}s, and the outcomes people experience can all range from low to high along a continuum of outcome quality. Interdependence theory suggests that when we consider all three of these factors simultaneously, four different broad types of relationships result.

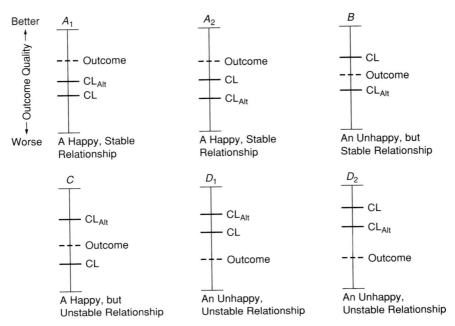

FIGURE 6.1 Types of relationships in interdependence theory.

Consider what happens when people's outcomes exceed both their CLs and their CL_{alt}s. They're getting more from their partners than they feel they must have *and* they believe they're doing better than they could anywhere else. So, they're happy and (as far as they're concerned) their relationships are stable. They're not going anywhere. This pleasant situation is depicted in Figure 6.1 in two different ways. In one case, a person's CL is higher than his or her CL_{alt}, whereas in the other case the reverse is true. In these and all the other examples we'll explain, the specific amount of satisfaction or dependence a person feels depends on the extent to which CL and CL_{alt} differ from the person's current outcomes. So, in graph A_1, the person is more satisfied than dependent, whereas in graph A_2, the person is more dependent than satisfied. However, in both cases—and this is the point we wish to make—the person is in a happy, stable relationship. We showed you both graphs A_1 and A_2 to demonstrate that, in terms of the simple classifications illustrated in Figure 6.1, it doesn't matter whether CL is higher than CL_{alt} or vice versa. Even if they're exactly the same, the same broad category will apply; if the person's current outcomes surpass both CL and CL_{alt}, that person will be content and unlikely to leave.

Contrast that situation with what happens when people's outcomes fall below their CLs but are still higher than their CL_{alt}s (in graph B). These folks are dissatisfied. They're getting less than they expect and feel they deserve, but they're still doing better than they think they can elsewhere. They're in an unhappy but stable relationship that they will not leave. Hopefully, you've never

---

BOX 6.1

Power and (In)Dependence

Figure 6.1 portrays the situations that may face one member of a couple, but a relationship involves two people. How might their CL_{alt}s influence their interactions with each other? Let's assume a romantic couple, Betty and Barney, receive similar outcomes from their relationship and each is dependent on the other, but Barney's CL_{alt} is lower than Betty's is. That would mean that Barney needs Betty more than she needs him; if the relationship ended, he would lose more by moving to his next best option than she would. Because neither of them wants to leave their partnership, this might seem like a trivial matter, but, in fact, this disparity in dependence gives her more *power* than he has.

As we'll see in chapter 11, power is the ability to influence another person's behavior. A nuance of social exchange, the **principle of lesser interest,** suggests that the partner who is less dependent on a relationship has more power in that relationship (Waller & Hill, 1951). Or, the person with less to lose by ending a desired partnership gets to call the shots. In fact, when it comes to winning

arguments and getting one's way, the principle seems to be accurate; the more independent member of a romantic relationship is usually acknowledged by both partners to be the more dominant of the two (Berman & Bennett, 1982). Betty's higher CL_{alt} is likely to mean that she's the boss.

FIGURE 6.1A
In this situation, Betty and Barney are dependent on each other, and neither is likely to leave. Nevertheless, Betty's alternatives are better than Barney's, and that gives her more power in their relationship.

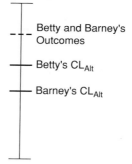

Betty and Barney's Outcomes

Betty's CL_{Alt}

Barney's CL_{Alt}

---

encountered such a situation yourself, but if you've ever had a lousy, low-paying job that you disliked but couldn't leave because it was the best job available at the time, you know what we're talking about. That's the sort of fix these folks are in.

By comparison, if people's CL_{alt}s are higher than their outcomes but their CLs are lower, they're in a much more favorable situation (graph C). They're satisfied with their present partners but believe that they have even more attractive outcomes, all things considered, awaiting them somewhere else. Their current relationships are happy but unstable because they're not likely to stay where they are. In an analogous situation in the workplace, you'd face this situation if you liked your existing job but you got an even better offer from another employer. If you added it all up—including the friends you'd leave behind, the costs of relocating, and the uncertainties of your new position—and thought you'd be better off by leaving, you would leave, wouldn't you?

Finally, people's outcomes may be lower than both their CLs and CL_{alt}s. Again, at this level of analysis, it wouldn't matter whether their CLs were lower than their CL_{alt}s (graph D_1) or vice versa (graph D_2); as long as their present outcomes were lower than both of them, they'd be in an unhappy and unstable relationship that probably wouldn't last much longer.

In real relationships, of course, a huge variety of configurations are possible as people's CLs, CL_{alt}s, and outcomes all range from excellent to poor. These four types of relationships are only meant to be general guides to diverse possibilities. CLs, CL_{alt}s, and outcomes may all change over time as well. In fact, changes in these variables lead to further interesting nuances of interdependence theory.

CL and CL_{alt} as Time Goes By

Imagine you find the perfect relationship. Your partner is loving, gorgeous, smart, rich, generous, and tireless, and is an award-winning chef, accomplished masseuse, and expert auto mechanic and computer programmer. He or she provides you outcomes that exceed your wildest dreams. When you get home each night, your partner has something exquisite for you to eat after you get your welcome-home massage and pedicure. Would you be satisfied? Of course you would. But what's likely to happen after you've enjoyed several straight months of this bliss?

You might get home one evening to find no massage and no supper because your partner has been delayed by traffic. "Hey," you might think, "where's my gourmet meal? Where's my backrub?" You've come to expect such marvelous treatment, which means your comparison level has risen. But if your CL goes up and your outcomes remain the same, satisfaction goes down (see Box 6.2). Once you get used to your perfect partner, you may find that you derive less pleasure from his or her pampering than you used to.

Indeed, interdependence theory predicts such a pattern. Because they are based on our experiences, our CLs tend to fluctuate along with the outcomes we receive. When we first encounter excellent outcomes, we're delighted, but our pleasure may slowly dwindle as we come to take such benefits for granted and our CLs rise. In this manner, rewarding relationships can gradually become less and less satisfying even though nothing (but our expectations) has changed.

That's a problem. Worse, since you were born, sociocultural influences may have caused our expectations to creep up and up. Blessed with economic prosperity, Americans have more disposable income than ever before, and they now expect a standard of living that used to be thought luxurious (Myers, 2000). In the view of some observers, a similar sense of entitlement has crept into our expectations for our relationships (Attridge & Berscheid, 1994). We expect our romances to be magical rather than merely pleasant, and it's hard to be happy when we expect so much (see Box 6.2 again). In fact, on average, American marriages are less happy than they were 30 years ago, and our higher CLs may be partly responsible (Glenn, 1996).

Cultural changes may also have caused widespread increases in our CL_{alt}s. The sex ratio has been climbing in recent years, so women have had more men

---

BOX 6.2
Comparison Levels in Lottery Winners

Most people think that they'd be pretty happy if they just had a few thousand dollars more than they have now, so they think that they'd be *really* happy if they won a big lottery and became rich (Myers & Diener, 1995). Are they correct? You may find this surprising, but the answer is "not really." For a time, lottery winners are often delighted with their improved standard of living. Getting rich can be a lot of fun at first. But remarkably soon after they win, they begin to get used to their newfound riches. They adapt to their changed circumstances, start to take them for granted, and feel less and less delighted as their expectations change (Diener, 2000). They may live better, but they tend to be just as frustrated as you and I. Whereas we get frustrated when the video store is sold out of the new release we wanted to rent, the rich get frustrated at their crummy seats at the Cannes Film

Festival, and they're just as frustrated as we are. Typical lottery winners end up a year later no happier, on average, than they were before they won.

In the terms of interdependence theory, their global comparison levels, what they expect out of life, have gone up. Satisfaction results from the *discrepancy* between people's CLs and the outcomes they receive, and if their expectations are almost as high as their outcomes, they won't be very happy no matter how high those outcomes are. Rich people may have very high outcomes, but if they expect them and take them for granted, they may derive little satisfaction from them (Houston, 1981). So, in fact, the usual trajectory for lottery winners is initial delight that gradually fades as they adjust to their new lives and their CLs rise. Is finding a wonderful relationship partner anything like winning a lottery?

---

to pick from (see chapter 1). Women's increased participation in the workforce has also provided them more financial freedom (South & Lloyd, 1995). People are more mobile than ever before, changing residences and traveling at unprecedented rates (Putnam, 2000). And legal, religious, and social barriers against divorce have gradually eroded (Berscheid & Lopes, 1997). No-fault divorce legislation that has made it easier for spouses to get divorces, for example, may be directly responsible for thousands of divorces that might not have otherwise occurred (Rodgers, Nakonezny, & Shull, 1999). Altogether, the costs of departing a marriage have declined even as, in many cases, people have found more options and more partners available to them. We may even have entered an era of "permanent availability," in which people remain on the marriage market—continuing to size up the people they meet as potential future mates—even after they're married (Farber, 1987)! If you add up these influences and look back at Figure 6.1, maybe we shouldn't be surprised that the American divorce rate has risen sharply since 1960; when CLs and CL$_{alt}$s are both high, people are more likely to find themselves in unhappy and unstable relationships (White & Booth, 1991).

THE ECONOMIES OF RELATIONSHIPS

As you can see, interdependence theory and its cousins take an unromantic view of close relationships. We even likened a happy, stable relationship to a desirable job with good benefits in describing some of the nuances of this approach. But can the success or failure of close relationships really be reduced to nothing more than the profits or losses on an interaction spreadsheet? Are rewards and costs, or the size of your "salary," everything that matter? The answer, of course, is no. Too specific a focus on the rewards and costs of a couple's interactions can lead us to overlook important influences that can make or break a partnership. For instance, your ultimate success in an important relationship may someday depend on how well you adapt to external stresses that you cannot control (Karney & Bradbury, 1995).

On the other hand, interdependence theory's businesslike emphasis on the outcomes people derive from interaction is enormously important. Counting up the rewards and costs of a relationship provides extraordinary information about its current state and likely future (see Bradbury, 1998). And the picture of normal intimacy that emerges from studies of this sort is a bit surprising. The stereotype of intimate relations is that they are generous and loving, and, sure enough, couples who are nice to each other are more likely to stay together over time than are those who provide each other fewer rewards (e.g., Bui, Peplau, & Hill, 1996; Fitzpatrick & Sollie, 1999). In one study, for instance, measures of generosity, affection, and self-disclosure administered at the very beginning of a dating relationship were quite accurate at predicting whether the couples would still be together four months later (Berg & McQuinn, 1986).

But costs are informative, too, and the surprise is that a lot of unpleasantness actually occurs in many relationships. On any given day, 44 percent of us are likely to be annoyed by a lover or friend (Averill, 1982). Each week, college students report an average of 8.7 aggravating hassles in their romantic relationships, a rate of more than one frustrating nuisance per day (Perlman, 1989). Most young adults complain that their lovers were overly critical, stubborn, selfish, *and* unreliable at least once during the past week (Perlman, 1989). Typical spouses report one or two unpleasant disagreements in their marriages each month (McGonagle, Kessler, & Schilling, 1992). Long-term intimacy with another person apparently involves more irritation and exasperation than some of us may expect. Indeed, during their lives together, married people are likely to be meaner to each other than to anyone else they know (Miller, 1997b). This does *not* mean that close relationships are more punishing than rewarding overall; that's not true (in many cases) at all. However, on those (hopefully rare) occasions when intimates are at their worst, they're likely to be more tactless, impolite, sullen, selfish, and insensitive with each other than they would be with total strangers.

In fact, research has compared the manners in which people interact with their spouses and with total strangers on a problem-solving task (Vincent, Weiss, & Birchler, 1975). When they were discussing issues with others they did not know well, people were polite and congenial; they withheld criticism, swallowed any disapproval, and suppressed signs of frustration. In contrast, with their spouses, people were much more obnoxious. They interrupted their lovers, disparaged their points of view, and openly disagreed. Intimacy and interdependence seemed to give people permission to be impolite instead of courteous and considerate.

Does this matter? You bet it does. Over time, irritating or moody behavior from a spouse puts a marriage at risk (Caughlin, Huston, & Houts, 2000; Karney & Bradbury, 1997). Outright hostility is even worse (Matthews, Wickrama, & Conger, 1996). When people seek a divorce, they usually have a list of several recurring aggravations that have caused them grief (Amato & Rogers, 1997). And even a few frustrations may be influential, because negative behaviors in a close relationship seem to carry more psychological weight than similar amounts of positive behavior do (e.g., Pasch & Bradbury, 1998). That is, "bad is stronger than good" (Baumeister, Frankenauer, & Bratslavsky, 1999).

Here's an example of what we mean. Imagine that you're walking down a sidewalk when a $20 bill blows into your path. There's no one else around, and it's obviously yours to keep. Does finding the money feel good? Of course it does. But now imagine that on another occasion you reach into a pocket where you put a $20 bill and find nothing but a hole. That's a disappointment. But which has the stronger effect on your mood, finding the new money or losing the money you already had? The answer is that losses usually affect us more than equivalent gains do; we hate losses but we merely like gains (Kahneman & Tversky, 1982).

In a similar fashion, undesirable events in close relationships are more noticeable and influential than logically equivalent desirable events are (Baumeister et al., 1999). If you get one compliment and one criticism from your lover during an evening at home, for instance, they probably won't cancel each other out; the compliment will help soften the blow of the criticism, but the combination will leave you somewhat distressed. Bad is stronger than good.

In fact, in order to stay satisfied with a close relationship, we may need to maintain a rewards-to-costs ratio of at least 5-to-1. That figure comes from research by John Gottman and Robert Levenson (1992), who observed married couples who were revisiting the topic of their last argument. They carefully coded the partners' behavior during their discussion, giving each spouse a point for each attempt at warmth, collaboration, or compromise, and subtracting a point for each display of anger, defensiveness, criticism, or contempt. Some of the couples were able to disagree with each other in a manner that communicated respect and regard for each other, and the longer their conversations went on, the more positive their scores became. These couples, who were said to be "well-regulated" by Gottman and Levenson, were maintaining a ratio of positive to negative exchanges of 5:1 or better. (See Figure 6.2.) However, other couples disagreed with sarcasm and disdain, and in those cases, the longer they talked, the worse their scores got. When the researchers compared the two groups at the time of the study, the well-regulated couples were more satisfied with their marriages than the other couples were. No surprise there. More impressively, however, more than half (56 percent) of the poorly regulated couples were divorced or separated only four years later, whereas just under a quarter (24 percent) of the well-regulated couples had split up. A short discussion on a single afternoon clearly provided meaningful information about the chances that a marriage

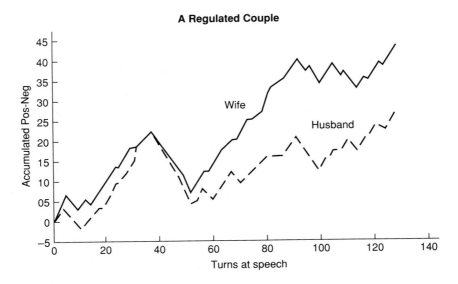

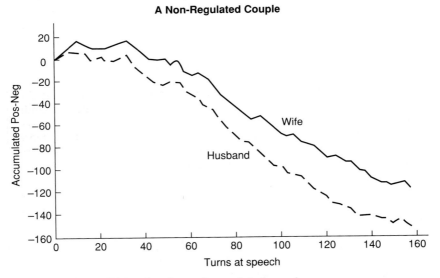

FIGURE 6.2 Well-regulated and poorly regulated couples.
(Pos-Neg = number of positive vs. negative exchanges.)
(Adapted from Gottman & Levenson, 1972.)

would last. And couples who did not maintain a substantial surfeit of positive exchanges faced twice the risk that their marriages would fail.

So, both rewards and costs are important influences on relationship satisfaction and stability, and there may need to be many more of the former than the latter if a relationship is to thrive. On the surface, this is a pretty obvious conclusion; we'd expect happy relationships to be more rewarding than punishing. In

---

BOX 6.3

"To Show You I Love You, I Washed Your Car":
Sex Differences in the Evaluation of Relationship Rewards

There are no price tags on the various commodities and rewards people exchange in their relationships, and partners sometimes disagree about what an exchange is worth. In a study by Wills, Weiss, and Patterson (1974), seven married couples kept track of their behavioral exchanges for two weeks. The rewards they exchanged either involved tasks and responsibilities (such as taking out the garbage) or emotion and affection (such as saying, "I love you"). When the spouses rated their pleasure with their partners' behavior, wives particularly appreciated their husbands' affectionate behavior, whereas husbands liked their wives' task-oriented help. The sexes apparently attached different values to such actions as doing the dishes and expressing warmth and love. The consequences of this sex difference were revealed when, toward the end of the study, the husbands were asked to increase their affectionate behavior toward their wives. Most did, but they also engaged in more task-oriented helping, which suggests that they were confusing the two. One husband was no more affectionate than usual but was annoyed when he was asked why; he had washed his wife's car, and he thought that was a perfectly good way

to communicate his affection for her. She didn't see it that way.

This study used a very small sample, so we shouldn't make too much of it. However, there are some differences in the rewards men and women extract from intimate relationships; for instance, men are more likely than women to describe sexual gratification as a substantial benefit, whereas women are more likely to say that a relationship has increased their self-onfidence and self-esteem (Sedikides et al., 1994). Men also think that their partners' sexual faithfulness is more valuable and important than their own, whereas women attach equal value to their own and their partners' fidelity (Regan & Sprecher, 1995). These results offer the useful lesson that although the language of social exchange sounds straightforward—rewards and costs, gains and losses—the reality is more complex. Exchanges with others involve a *psychological* arithmetic in which people's motives, beliefs, and emotions affect their perceptions of the outcomes they receive. What matters to me may not matter as much to you, and those differing perceptions add complexity to our quest for mutually satisfying interaction.

---

another study, for instance, 93 percent of the happily married couples reported making love more often than they argued, whereas none of the unhappily married couples did (Howard & Dawes, 1976). But if it's so obvious, why are there so many unhappy relationships? One possibility is that the partners disagree about the meaning and the value of the rewards they try to provide one another (see Box 6.3). Another answer is that those couples began their relationships when their interactions were more rewarding, but things changed with time. Let's take a look at how rewards and costs change as relationships develop.

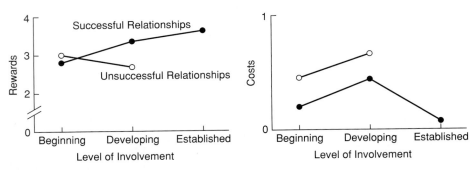

FIGURE 6.3 Rewards and costs in beginning relationships.
(Adapted from Eidelson, 1981.)

Rewards and Costs as Time Goes By

Here's the situation: You've just started dating a new partner with many appealing qualities, and your initial interactions have been reasonably rewarding. Can you predict at this point what the future holds? Will the relationship prosper or will it ultimately fail? Every partnership may have its unique qualities, but there are still some common patterns in situations like this. Roy Eidelson (1981) studied these questions by asking young adults to keep track of the specific rewards and costs they encountered in new relationships, and he found *no difference* between the number of rewards offered by relationships that would thrive and by those that would founder. When they began, relationships that would succeed were no more rewarding than those that would not (see Figure 6.3). However, there *was* a difference in the number of costs people encountered in the two types of relationships. Doomed partnerships were more costly from the moment they started. People reported more frustrations and annoyances in relationships that would fail than in those that would succeed.

   This is interesting. Evidently, there's a lot to like in partnerships that will not work out. The only difference between successful and unsuccessful relationships at the start is in the number of costs they exact. But what happens next is intriguing, too. Even in relationships that will ultimately succeed, costs typically *rise* as the partners spend more time together. Eidelson explained this by suggesting that there are pros and cons to investing time and effort in a new relationship. On the one hand, intimate partners exchange more valuable rewards, but on the other, they lose some independence and freedom. Instead of waiting to be asked out on a date, for instance, a new partner may start *assuming* that you'll get together this weekend, and your loss of autonomy can be disconcerting. In prosperous relationships, rewards rise, too, but the increasing costs can cause a lull in the amount of satisfaction people feel. Take a look at Figure 6.4; Eidelson (1980) found that as successful relationships developed, people routinely experienced a sharp increase in satisfaction that was followed by a lull—perhaps a period of reflection and reevaluation as they came to grips

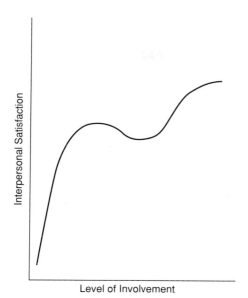

FIGURE 6.4 Satisfaction in beginning
relationships.
(Adapted from Eidelson, 1980.)

with the costs of increased interdependency. After that, however, costs decreased as people adjusted to the limitations imposed by the new partner. This
resulted in a new but more gradual increase in satisfaction as the relationship
continued to develop.

What happened in those relationships that did not continue? Eidelson
found that their costs also increased but their rewards did not (Figure 6.3). As a
result, the partner's outcomes fell and the relationships ended. This took time
to unfold, however, so the only way to distinguish successful and unsuccessful
relationships at the start was by a careful accounting of their costs.

There may be some valuable lessons here. First, thoughtful consumers of
relationships should pay heed to their doubts about new partners. There are
more such doubts and irritations in relationships that will fail, and they will
only get worse. On the other hand, we shouldn't be surprised when our increasing delight with a budding relationship suddenly levels off for a time;
that's not unusual, and it doesn't mean that there's not a happy future ahead.

Still, Eidelson (1980, 1981) only studied relationships that were just beginning. Do rewards and costs change with time in established relationships as
well? They do. Ted Huston and his colleagues have been following the fortunes
of a large group of spouses who married in 1981 (Huston & Houts, 1998).
They've been especially interested in the couples that divorced (and 13 years
later, 35 percent of them had; Huston, 1999). In general, the problems the couples faced did not change over time; the complaints the spouses had were

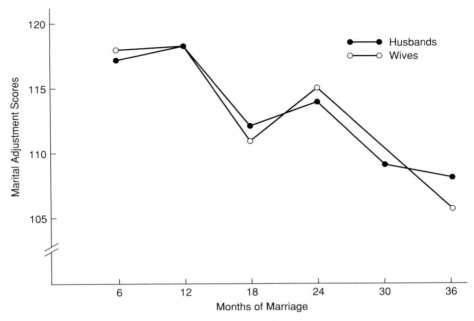

FIGURE 6.5 The average trajectory of marital satisfaction.
(Data from Karney & Bradbury, 1997.)

known to them when they decided to get married in the first place. But marriage did not make those costs seem more manageable; to the contrary, existing problems became more obnoxious once people were wed. Worse, the rewards of their relationships fell once they married and moved in with each other. In particular, acts of kindness and expressions of affection dropped by half within their first two years as husband and wife. As a result, with the spouses' costs rising and rewards dropping, Huston observed a pattern that is also a routine result in other studies (e.g., Karney & Bradbury, 1997; Kurdek, 1998; Leonard & Roberts, 1997): Relationship satisfaction declines in the first few years after people are married, as Figure 6.5 illustrates.

This is bad news. Interdependence theory suggests that satisfaction can wane as people's CLs rise, but the research data actually reveal that outcomes fall, too. Why does this occur? We can suggest several reasons (Miller, 1997b). First, we all know how to be polite and thoughtful, and we can behave that way when we want to (Vincent et al., 1975), but it takes work. Once a courtship is over and a partner is won, for instance, people may stop trying so hard to be consistently charming. The same people who would never fart noisily on a blind date may become spouses who fart at will at the dinner table, perhaps dismissing their lack of propriety by saying, "Sorry, I couldn't help it." The point is that they *could* help it if they wanted to—they just didn't go to the trouble to do so (Miller, 2001).

Second, interdependency magnifies conflict and friction. We spend lots of time with our intimate partners and depend on them for unique, especially valuable rewards, and that means that they are certain to cause us more frustration—even inadvertently—than anyone else can. For instance, we're more affected by the moods (Caughlin et al., 2000) or work stress (Chan & Margolin, 1994) of intimate partners than by the similar difficulties of others. Frequent interaction also means that trivial annoyances may gradually cause real grief through sheer repetition, in the same way that the light tapping of a slowly dripping faucet can drive you mad when you're trying to sleep at night (Cunningham, Barbee, & Druen, 1997).

Third, intimacy means that others know your secrets, foibles, and weaknesses. That gives them ammunition with which to wound and tease us when conflict occurs. But even when they have no wish to do us harm, their access to sensitive information practically guarantees that they will accidentally reveal some secret (Petronio, Olson, & Dollar, 1989), hurt our feelings (Kowalski, 2000), or embarrass us (Miller, 1996) sometime or other. They can unintentionally hurt us in ways others can't.

Fourth, even if people are usually aware of most of their incompatibilities and problems before they marry, there will almost always be some surprises ahead. These tend to be of two general types. First, there's learning the truth about things we thought we knew. A good example of this are the "fatal attractions" we mentioned in chapter 3. You may know and even like the fact that your lover is fun-loving and spontaneous, but you may not appreciate how irresponsible, flighty, and unreliable that same behavior may seem after a few years of marriage when you have a mortgage and babies to contend with. Speaking of babies, the other type of unwelcome surprise is learning undesired things that you didn't know at all, and the real facts of parenthood are often good examples. If you don't have kids, you might assume that parenthood will be fun, your kids will be invariably adorable, and raising children will bring you and your partner closer together. The reality, however (as you know if you do have kids), is that "after the birth of a child the prognosis for the course of the marital relationship is unequivocally grim" (Stafford & Dainton, 1994, p. 270). We can safely say that parenthood is an extraordinary and often marvelous adventure, but it is unquestionably hard on the relationship between the parents; children are endless work, and most parents experience a steep and unexpected decline in the time they spend having fun together (Kurdek, 1993). When babies arrive, conflict increases, and satisfaction with the marriage (and love for one's partner) decrease, especially among women (Belsky, 1990). If the parents don't expect such difficulties, they're going to be surprised.

Finally, all of this means that close relationships are often much different from the blissful, intimate idylls we want them to be, and the difference between what we expected and what we get can leave us feeling cheated and disappointed, sometimes unnecessarily so (Attridge & Berscheid, 1994). To the extent that great relationships still involve hard work and sacrifice, people with misplaced, glorified expectations about relationships may end up disappointed in their outcomes even when they're doing better than everyone else. (Remember, satisfaction derives from the difference between the outcomes we receive and our CLs—our expectations.)

So, through (a) **lack of effort;** because (b) **interdependency is a magnifying glass;** and through (c) **access to weaponry;** (d) **unwelcome surprises;** and (e) **unrealistic expectations,** people usually fail to maintain the outcomes that lead them to marry (Miller, 1997b), and satisfaction actually declines during the first years of marriage. There are certainly some valuable lessons here, too. Ted Huston's (1999) work demonstrates that existing problems and incompatibilities do not gradually disappear after people marry; to the contrary, if anything, they are accentuated. We should not naively hope that our problems will just fade away. And marriage does not increase the spouses' delight with one another; if anything, their contentment is likely to decrease somewhat. There may be several reasons why, but we suspect that the impact of all of them can be minimized if people are better informed and know what to expect about the usual trajectories of marital intimacy. Indeed, we don't want this analysis to seem pessimistic at all! To the contrary, we suspect that a thorough understanding of these issues can help people to avoid needless disappointment, and it may even help them to forestall or avoid the creeping decline in outcomes that would otherwise occur. We think there's more danger in naïve optimism than in informed caution.

And importantly, if nothing else, this perspective reminds us of our constant responsibility to be as pleasant as possible to those whose company we value. We want great outcomes, but so do they, and even if they like us, they'll go elsewhere if we don't give them enough reward. This is a consequential idea, and it leads to some subtleties of the social exchange perspective that we have not yet considered.

ARE WE REALLY THIS GREEDY?

So far in this chapter, we have portrayed people as greedy hedonists who are only concerned with their own outcomes. That's not a complimentary portrayal, but it is useful because rewards and costs matter enormously in close relations. The research data support the basic precepts of interdependence theory quite well. Nevertheless, at this point, our portrait is incomplete. There are good reasons why people will usually want their partners to prosper as well.

The Nature of Interdependency

Okay, you've got the idea: According to interdependence theory, people want maximum reward at minimum cost, and always want the best interpersonal deals they can get. Everybody behaves this way. But what happens when they get a good deal? Then they're dependent on their partners and don't want to leave them. That's significant, because it means that they have an important stake in *keeping their partners happy,* so that their partners will continue providing those desired rewards. If you want to keep valued relationships going, it's to your advantage to ensure that your partners are just as dependent on you as you are on them, and a straightforward way to do that is to provide them high outcomes that make them want to stay.

Pursuing this strategy can influence the value of many transactions with a desired partner. Actions that would be costly if enacted with a stranger can actually be rewarding in a close relationship, because they give pleasure to one's partner and increase the likelihood that one will receive valuable rewards in return (Kelley, 1979). Providing good outcomes to one's partner, even when it involves effort and sacrifice, can ultimately be self-serving if it causes a desirable relationship to continue. Indeed, even greedy people should be generous to others if it increases their own profits!

So, interdependence theory suggests that in the quest for high outcomes, individuals will often be magnanimous to those on whom they depend because it is reasonable (and valuable) to do so. And if both partners in a relationship want it to continue, both of them should thoughtfully protect and maintain the other's well-being. If people need each other, it can be advantageous to be positively philanthropic to each other, increasing the partner's profits to keep him or her around. Thus, even if people are greedy, there is likely to be plenty of compassionate thoughtfulness and magnanimity in interdependent relationships.

Exchange versus Communal Relationships

Indeed, when people seek closeness with others, they are often generous from the moment they meet those new partners (Berg & Clark, 1986). We seem to realize that rewarding interdependency is more likely to develop when we're *not* greedily pursuing instant profit. With this in mind, Margaret Clark and Judson Mills (1979, 1993) proposed a distinction between partnerships that are clearly governed by explicit norms of even exchange and other, more generous, relationships that are characterized by obvious concern for the partner's welfare. **Exchange** relationships are governed by the desire for and expectation of immediate repayment for benefits given. Thus, any costs should be quickly offset by compensating rewards, and the overall balance should remain at zero. As Table 6.1 shows, people in exchange relationships don't like to be in one another's debt; they track each other's contributions to joint endeavors; they monitor the other person's needs only when they think there's a chance for personal gain; and they don't feel badly if they refuse to help the other person. As you might expect, exchange relationships are typified by superficial, often brief, relatively task-oriented encounters between strangers or acquaintances.

In contrast, **communal** relationships are governed by the desire for and expectation of mutual responsiveness to the other's needs. People who seek a communal relationship avoid strict cost accounting. They do not prefer to have their favors quickly repaid; they do not make a clear distinction between their work and that of their partners; they monitor their partners' needs even when they see no opportunity for personal gain; and they feel better about themselves when they help their partners. People often make small sacrifices on behalf of their partners in communal relationships, such as going to a movie they

TABLE 6.1. Differences Between Exchange and Communal Relationships

Situation	Exchange Relationships	Communal Relationships
When we do others a favor	We prefer those who pay us back immediately.	We don't prefer those who repay us immediately.
When others do us a favor	We prefer those who ask for immediate repayment.	We prefer those who do not ask for immediate repayment.
When we are working with others on a joint task	We try to ensure that our contributions are distinguished from those of others.	We don't make any clear distinction between others' work and our own.
When others may need help	We keep track of the others' needs only when they can return any favors.	We keep track of the others' needs even when they will be unable to return any favors.
When we help others	Our moods and self-evaluations change only slightly.	Our moods brighten and our self-evaluations improve.
When we don't help others	Our moods do not change.	Our moods get worse.

Source: Clark, 1984; Clark & Mills, 1979; Clark, Mills, & Corcoran, 1989; Clark, Mills, & Powell, 1986; Clark & Waddell, 1985; Williamson & Clark, 1989; and Williamson, Clark, Pegalis, & Behan, 1996.

don't want to see, just to please their partners, but they enjoy higher quality relationships as a result (Clark & Grote, 1998). Meaningful romantic attachments are typically communal relationships, but communal and exchange norms are about equally likely to apply to friendships, which may be of either type (Clark & Mills, 1993).

But does the lack of apparent greed in communal relationships indicate that the principles of exchange we've been discussing do not apply there? Not at all. One possibility is that tit-for-tat exchanges are also taking place in communal partnerships, but in a manner that involves more diverse rewards across a longer span of time (Clark, 1981). In more businesslike relationships, exchanges are expected to occur quickly, so that debts are rapidly repaid. They should also be comparable, so that you pay for what you get. In more intimate relationships, there's more versatility. What we do to meet a partner's needs may involve very different actions from what the partner did to meet our own needs. We can also wait longer to be repaid because we trust our partners and expect the relationship to continue. In this sense, both exchange and communal partnerships are "exchange" relationships in which people expect to receive benefits that fit those they provide, but the exchanges take different forms and are less obvious in communal relationships.

In addition, the exchange perspective may not seem to describe intimate relationships because, when they are healthy, the partners enjoy an "economy of surplus" and seem unconcerned with how well they're doing (Levinger, 1979). Both partners are prospering, and there seems to be little need to "sweat the small stuff" by explicitly quantifying their respective rewards and costs. People in happy and stable relationships, for instance, probably haven't been wondering "what has my partner done for me lately?" both because the partner has done plenty and because they're happy enough not to care. However, if their outcomes start falling and their heady profits evaporate, even intimate partners in (what were) communal relationships may begin paying close attention to the processes of exchange. Indeed, when dissatisfaction sets in, people in (what were) communal relationships often become very sensitive to minute injustices in the outcomes they receive (Jacobson, Follette, & McDonald, 1982). In a sense, they start balancing their "checkbooks" and counting every "penny."

So, a distinction between exchange and communal relationships isn't incompatible with interdependency theory at all. However, the workings of communal relationships do demonstrate how readily people provide benefits to those with whom they wish to develop close relationships, and how quickly people begin to take others' welfare under consideration once interaction begins (Berg & Clark, 1986). Most people seem to recognize, as interdependency theory suggests, that if you want others to be nice to you, you've got to be nice to them.

Equitable Relationships

Another point of view argues that you not only have to be nice, you have to be *fair.* **Equity** theorists extend the framework of social exchange to assert that people are most satisfied in relationships in which there is *proportional justice,* which means that each partner gains benefits from the relationship that are proportional to his or her contributions to it (Hatfield, 1983; Sprecher & Schwartz, 1994). A relationship is equitable when the ratio of your outcomes to your contributions is similar to that of your partner, or when:

$$\frac{\text{Your outcomes}}{\text{Your contributions}} = \frac{\text{Your partner's outcomes}}{\text{Your partner's contributions}}$$

Note that equity does not require that two partners gain equal rewards from their interaction; in fact, if their contributions are different, equality would be inequitable. A relationship is fair, according to equity theory, only when a partner who is contributing more is receiving more as well.

Let's look at some examples. Here are three equitable relationships, with outcomes and contributions rated on a 0-to-100-point scale:

	Partner X		Partner Y
(a)	80/50	=	80/50
(b)	20/100	=	20/100
(c)	50/25	=	100/50

In relationships (a) and (b) both partners are receiving equal outcomes and making equal contributions, but the quality of outcomes is much higher for the partners in relationship (a) than for those in relationship (b). Equity theory emphasizes fairness, not the overall amount of rewards people receive, and because both (a) and (b) are fair, they should both be satisfying to the partners. (Do you think they would be? We'll return to this point later.) Relationship (c) is also equitable, even though the partners do not make equal contributions or derive equal outcomes. Partner Y is working harder to maintain the relationship than partner X is, but both of them are receiving outcomes that are proportional to their contributions—each is getting two units of benefit for every unit he or she contributes, so Y's higher outcomes are fair.

In contrast, in inequitable relationships, the two ratios of outcomes to contributions are not equal. Consider these examples:

Partner X		Partner Y
(d) 80/50	≠	60/50
(e) 80/50	≠	80/30

In relationship (d), the partners are working equally hard to maintain the relationship, but one of them is receiving better outcomes than the other. In (e), their outcomes are the same, but their contributions are different. In either case, the partners are likely to be distressed—even if they're getting good outcomes—because the relationship isn't fair. In such situations, one partner is **"overbenefited,"** receiving better outcomes than he or she deserves, and the other is **"underbenefited,"** receiving less than he or she should. Does that matter? Interdependence theory says it shouldn't, much, as long as both partners are prospering, but equity theory says it does.

The Distress of Inequity

One of the most interesting aspects of equity theory is its assertion that everybody is nervous in inequitable relationships. It's easy to see why underbenefited partners would be unhappy; they're being cheated and deprived, and they may feel angry and resentful. On the other hand, overbenefited partners are doing too well, and they may feel somewhat guilty. It's better to be over- than underbenefited, of course, but equity theory proposes that everybody is most content when both partners receive fair outcomes. Any departure from an equitable relationship is thought to cause some discomfort, if only because such situations are inherently unstable: People are presumed to dislike unfairness and will want to change or escape it, especially if they're underbenefited. So, according to this perspective, the most satisfactory situation is an equitable division of outcomes; equity theory predicts that overbenefited people will be somewhat less content than those who have equitable relationships, and underbenefited people will be *much* less satisfied (Hatfield, 1983).

Ways to Restore Equity

If you're underbenefited, what can you do? First, you can try to restore *actual equity* by changing your (or your partner's) contributions or outcomes. You can request better treatment so that your outcomes will improve—"it's your turn to cook dinner while I relax"—or you can reduce your contributions, hoping that your outcomes stay about the same. You could even sabotage your partner, reducing his or her outcomes so that they're no longer out of line (Hammock, Rosen, Richardson, & Bernstein, 1989).

If these efforts fail, you can try to restore *psychological equity,* changing your perceptions of the relationship and convincing yourself it really is equitable after all. You could talk yourself into thinking that your partner is someone special who deserves the better deal (McDonald, 1981). Or, you could start doubting yourself and decide that you deserve your lousy outcomes.

Finally, as a last resort, you could *abandon the relationship* to seek fairness elsewhere. You could actually leave your partner, or perhaps just have an affair (Prins, Buunk, & VanYperen, 1993).

In any case, as all these examples suggest, equity theory argues that people are motivated to redress inequity when it occurs. That certainly makes sense if you're underbenefited. But would you really want to change things if you're overbenefited? Let's see what the data have to say.

How Much Is Enough? Equity versus Overbenefit

Several studies that have assessed the satisfaction of spouses and other romantic couples have obtained results that fit the predictions of equity theory very nicely (e.g., Davidson, 1984; Sprecher, 1986, 1992; Walster, Walster, & Traupmann, 1978): Partners who were overbenefited were less relaxed and content than were those whose outcomes were equitable, and people who were underbenefited were less happy still. However, most of these studies used cross-sectional designs that compared people who were overbenefited to those in equitable situations at one point in time. In addition, few of them assessed the participants' comparison levels or otherwise took note of just how good their outcomes were. (Remember, you can be overbenefited relative to how your partner is doing and still be getting crummy outcomes that could cause some dissatisfaction.) A different picture could emerge when equity is compared to the overall quality of outcomes people receive; fairness may not matter much if everybody's prospering.

Indeed, some more recent investigations have tracked couples over long periods of time (often for several years) using a broader array of measures, and they provide less support for the particulars of equity theory (e.g., Sprecher, 1998, 1999). Nobody likes being underbenefited—all studies agree on that—but being overbenefited is not always associated with reduced satisfaction. In fact, some people who are overbenefited like it just fine (Sprecher, 1998), especially when they have been underbenefited in the past (Buunk & Mutsaers, 1999). Moreover, several studies that assessed the quality of partners' outcomes found that—just as interdependence theory asserts—the overall amount of reward that people receive is a better predictor of their satisfaction than is the level of equity they encounter (Cate, Lloyd, & Henton, 1985; Cate, Lloyd, Henton, & Larson, 1982; Cate, Lloyd, & Long, 1988). In these studies, it didn't matter what one's partner gave or got as long as one's own benefits were high enough, and the more rewards people said they received from a relationship, the better they felt about it.

There's complexity here. Some studies suggest that fairness is an important factor in the workings of intimate relationships, and some do not. One reason for these conflicting results may be that some people are more concerned with fairness in interpersonal relations than other people are. Across relationships, some people consistently value equity more than others do, and they, unlike other people, are more satisfied when equity exists than when it does not (Buunk & VanYperen, 1991). Curiously, however, such people tend to be less satisfied overall with their relationships than are people who are less concerned with equity (Buunk & VanYperen, 1991). They may be paying too much attention to a careful accounting of their rewards and costs!

Nevertheless, no matter who we are, equity may be more important in some domains than in others. Two sensitive areas in which equity appears to be advisable are in the allocation of household tasks and child care: When these chores are divided fairly, spouses are more satisfied with their marriages (Benin & Agostinelli, 1988; Grote, Frieze, & Stone, 1996). Unfortunately, equitable allocation of these duties is often difficult for women to obtain. Even when they have similar job responsibilities outside the home, working mothers tend to do twice as many household chores as their husbands do (Huppe & Cyr, 1997), and this inequity can produce considerable strain on the relationship. Indeed, one general admonition offered by marriage researchers to modern couples is for men "to do more housework, child care, and affectional maintenance if they wish to have a happy wife" (Gottman & Carrère, 1994, p. 225). Equity in these conspicuous domains may be much more influential than similar fairness applied to other areas of a couple's interactions.

A third possible reason why research results are mixed may be that equity is a salient issue when people are dissatisfied, but it's only a minor issue when people are content (Holmes & Levinger, 1994). When rewards are in good supply, equity may not matter. People who are prospering in their relationships may spend little time monitoring their exchanges and may casually dismiss any imbalances they do notice. (They might also tend to report that their partnerships are "fair" when researchers ask.) But if costs rise and rewards fall, people may begin tracking their exchanges much more carefully, displaying concern about who deserves to get what. And no matter what the truth is, people who are very dissatisfied are likely to perceive that they are being underbenefited by their partners. In this sense, then, inequity may not cause people to become dissatisfied; instead, being dissatisfied could lead people to think they're being treated unfairly.

Finally, it's also likely that people apply different rules for allocating outcomes to different situations or to different relationships (Clark & Chrisman, 1994). Whereas a business relationship had better be equitable at all times, for instance, communal relationships often seem to involve episodes of compassionate sacrifice and generosity. As we noted earlier, people may only make investments like this when they expect the partnership to provide substantial benefits in the long run, so such behavior may not be altruistic at all. Nevertheless, some close relationships may be inequitable for long periods without causing much distress.

Overall, the best conclusion appears to be that both the global quality of outcomes people receive *and* underbenefit, when it occurs, play important roles in predicting how satisfactory and enduring a relationship will be (Feeney, Peterson, & Noller, 1994; Sprecher, 1999). Overbenefit doesn't seem to bother people much, and equity doesn't seem to improve a relationship if it is already highly rewarding. In contrast, the inequity that accompanies deprivation and exploitation—underbenefit—is indicative of distress. Still, the bottom line is that outcome level is probably a more important factor than inequity is; if our outcomes are poor and unsatisfactory, it isn't much consolation if they're fair, and if our outcomes are wonderful, inequity isn't a major concern.

Summing Up

So, what's the final answer? Is simple greed a good description of people's behavior in intimate relationships? The answer offered by relationship science is a qualified yes. People are happiest when their rewards are high and their costs (and expectations) are low. But because we are dependent on others for the rewards we seek in intimate relationships, we have a stake in satisfying them, too. We readily protect the well-being of our intimate partners and rarely exploit them if we want those relationships to continue. Such behavior may be encouraged by selfish motives, but it is still thoughtful, generous, and often loving. So, even if it is ultimately greedy behavior, it's not undesirable or exploitative.

THE NATURE OF COMMITMENT

The good news is that happy dependence on an intimate partner leads to **commitment,** the intention to continue the relationship. People who both need their partners and are content associate the concept of commitment with positive qualities such as sharing, supportiveness, honesty, faithfulness, and trust (Fehr, 1999). (You can see why these people are staying put.) The bad news is that unhappy people can be committed to their relationships, too, not because they want to stay where they are but because they feel they *must.* For these people, commitment is probably experienced more as burdensome entrapment than as a positive feeling.

Indeed, commitment seems to be a multifaceted decision that can result from both positive and negative influences. For instance, Caryl Rusbult and her colleagues have developed a well-known conceptualization of commitment known as the *investment model* that explicitly ties commitment to all of the elements of social exchange that are associated with people's CLs and $CL_{alt}s$ (e.g., Rusbult et al., 1994; Rusbult, Wieselquist, Foster, & Witcher, 1999). First, the investment model suggests that satisfaction increases commitment. People generally wish to continue the partnerships that make them happy. However, alternatives of high quality are also influential, and they *decrease* commitment. People who have enticing alternatives luring them away from their present partners are less likely to stay in their existing relationships. But people don't

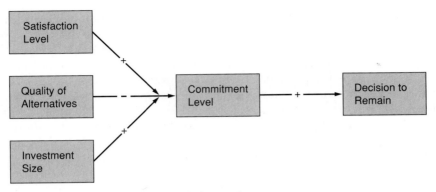

FIGURE 6.6 The investment model of commitment.
(From Rusbult, Drigotas, & Verette, 1994.)

always pursue such alternatives even when they're available, if the costs of leaving their current relationships are too high. Thus, a third determinant of commitment is the size of one's investments in the existing relationship. High investments increase commitment, regardless of the quality of one's alternatives and whether or not one is happy.

Altogether, then, the investment model suggests that people will wish to remain with their present partners when they're happy, or when there's no other desirable place for them to go, or when they won't leave because it would cost too much (see Figure 6.6). These influences are presumed to be equally important, and commitment emerges from the complex combination of all three. Thus, as people's circumstances change, relationships often survive periods in which one or both partners are dissatisfied, tempted by alluring alternatives, or free to walk out at any time. Episodes like these may stress the relationship and weaken the partners' commitment, but the partnership may persist if the other components of commitment are holding it together.

In general, research results support the investment model quite well (Rusbult et al., 1999). Satisfaction, the quality of one's alternatives, and the size of one's investments each tell us something useful about how committed a person is likely to be, and the model applies equally well to men and women (Bui et al., 1996), heterosexuals and homosexuals (Kurdek, 1992), and people in both the Netherlands (Van Lange et al., 1997) and Taiwan (Lin & Rusbult, 1995), as well as the United States. Moreover, the usefulness of the investment model provides general support for an exchange perspective on intimate relationships. The economic assessments involved in the investment model do a very good job of predicting how long relationships will last (Drigotas & Rusbult, 1992), whether or not the partners will be faithful to each other (Drigotas, Safstrom, & Gentilia, 1999), and even if battered wives will try to escape their abusive husbands (Rusbult & Martz, 1995).

However, the investment model treats commitment as a unitary concept—that is, there's really only one kind of commitment—and other theorists argue that commitment not only springs from different sources, it comes in different forms. For instance, sociologist Michael Johnson (1999) asserts that there are actually three types of commitment. The first, **personal commitment,** occurs when people *want* to continue a relationship because they are attracted to their partners and the relationship is satisfying. In contrast, the second type, **constraint commitment,** occurs when people feel they *have* to continue a relationship because it would be too costly for them to leave. In constraint commitment, people fear the social and financial consequences of ending their partnerships, and they continue them even when they wish they could depart. Finally, the third type of commitment, **moral commitment,** derives from a sense of moral obligation to one's partner or one's relationship. Here, people feel they *ought* to continue the relationship because it would be improper to end it and break their promises or vows. Spouses who are morally committed tend to believe in the sanctity of marriage and may feel a solemn social or religious responsibility to stay married no matter what.

Research using this scheme demonstrates that the three types of commitment do feel different to people, and there is value in distinguishing them in studies of relationships (Adams & Jones, 1997, 1999; Johnson, Caughlin, & Huston, 1999). When people embark on a long-distance romantic relationship, for example, moral commitment does a better job of predicting whether or not the partnership will survive the period of separation than personal commitment does (Lydon, Pierce, & O'Regan, 1997). Evidently, moral commitment can keep a relationship going even when one's enthusiasm for the relationship wanes.

The Consequences of Commitment

Nevertheless, whatever its origins or nature, commitment substantially affects the relationships in which it occurs (Rusbult et al., 1999). People who are committed to a partnership tend to adopt a long-term orientation that reduces the pain that would otherwise accompany rough spots in the relationship. When people feel that they're in a relationship for the long haul, they may be better able to tolerate episodes of high cost and low reward in much the same way that investors with a long-range outlook will hold on to shares of stock during periods of low earnings. In addition, commitment can lead people to think of themselves and their partners as a single entity, as "us" instead of "him" and "me" (Agnew, Van Lange, Rusbult, & Langston, 1997). This may substantially reduce the costs of sacrifices that benefit the partner, as events that please one's partner produce indirect benefits for oneself as well.

Perhaps the most important consequence of commitment, however, is that it leads people to take action to protect and maintain a relationship, even when it is costly for them to do so. Committed people engage in a variety of behavioral and cognitive maneuvers that both preserve and enhance the relationship and reinforce their commitment to it (Rusbult et al., 1999). These *relationship maintenance mechanisms* will be described in detail in chapter 15. However, to close this chapter, we'll give you a brief preview of that material.

As one example, commitment promotes **accommodative behavior** in which people refrain from responding to provocation from their partners with similar ire of their own (Rusbult, Bissonnette, Arriaga, & Cox, 1998; Rusbult, Verette, Whitney, Slovik, & Lipkus, 1991). Accommodating people tolerate destructive behavior from their partners without fighting back; they swallow insults, sarcasm, or selfishness without retaliating. By so doing, they avoid quarrels and altercations and help dispel, rather than perpetuate, their partners' bad moods. That's usually good for the relationship. Such behavior may involve considerable self-restraint, but it is not motivated by weakness; instead, accommodation often involves a conscious effort to protect the partnership from harm.

Committed people also display greater **willingness to sacrifice** their own self-interests for the good of the relationship (Van Lange et al., 1997). They do things they wouldn't do if they were on their own, and they do not do things they would have liked to do, in order to benefit their partners and enhance their relationships.

As a final example, commitment changes people's perceptions of their partnerships. Committed people exhibit **perceived superiority**—they think their relationships are better than those of other people (Buunk & van der Eijnden, 1997; Van Lange & Rusbult, 1995). In particular, they think that they enjoy more rewards and suffer fewer costs than other people encounter with their partners.

There are other mechanisms with which people maintain their relationships, but these three sufficiently illustrate the manner in which commitment motivates thoughts and actions that preserve partnerships. People seek maximum reward at minimum cost in their interactions with others, but dependency on a partner leads them to behave in ways that take the partner's well-being into account. As a result, committed partners often make sacrifices and accommodate their partners, doing things that are not in their immediate self-interest, to promote their relationships.

If people did these things indiscriminately, they would often be self-defeating. However, when they occur in interdependent relationships, and when both partners behave this way, such actions provide powerful means of protecting and enhancing desired connections to others (Drigotas, Rusbult, & Verette, 1999). In this manner, even if we are basically greedy at heart, we are often unselfish, considerate, and caring to those we befriend and love.

CHAPTER SUMMARY

Social Exchange

The economic view of social interaction offered by interdependence theory suggests that people seek relationships that provide maximum reward at minimum cost.

Rewards and Costs. Rewards are gratifying and costs are punishing. The net profit or loss from an interaction is its *"outcome."*

What Do We Expect from Our Relationships? People have *comparison levels* (CLs) that reflect their expectations for their interactions with others. When the outcomes they receive exceed their CLs, they're satisfied, but if their outcomes fall below their CLs, they're discontented.

How Well Could We Do Elsewhere? People also compare their outcomes to those available elsewhere using a *comparison level for alternatives* (CL$_{alt}$). When the outcomes they receive exceed their CL$_{alt}$s, they're dependent on their current partners. Both the external rewards awaiting us outside our current relationships and the *investments* we would lose by leaving influence the calculation of our CL$_{alt}$s. However, these are complicated judgments, and they depend on whether we're paying attention to our alternatives or are relatively heedless of them.

Four Types of Relationships. Comparing people's CLs and CL$_{alt}$s with their outcomes yields four different relationship states: happy and stable; happy and unstable; unhappy and stable; and unhappy and unstable.

CL and CL$_{alt}$ as Time Goes By. People adapt to the outcomes they receive, and relationships can become less satisfying as the partners' CLs rise. Cultural influences shape both our expectations and our CL$_{alt}$s, and may have put more pressure on relationships in recent years than in years past.

The Economies of Relationships

Counting up the rewards and costs of a relationship provides extraordinary information about its current state and likely future. A lot of unpleasantness occurs in many relationships. This is influential, because negative events carry more psychological impact than similar positive events do. As a result, a ratio of at least five rewards to every one cost may be needed to maintain a satisfactory partnership.

Rewards and Costs as Time Goes By. When they begin, relationships that will succeed are no more rewarding than those that will quickly fail. Their rewards increase over time, but so do their costs, leading to a lull in increasing satisfaction as they develop. Costs also rise in unsuccessful relationships, but their rewards drop, and the unpleasant combination brings the faltering relationships to an end.

Marital satisfaction actually decreases over the first years of marriage. This may be due to the partners' *lack of effort* and to the manner in which interdependence magnifies small irritations, and to other routine influences such as *unwelcome surprises* and *unrealistic expectations*. Insight may forestall or prevent these problems.

Are We Really This Greedy?

The Nature of Interdependency. Interdependent partners have a stake in keeping each other happy. As a result, generosity toward one's partner is often beneficial to oneself.

Exchange versus Communal Relationships. *Exchange* relationships are governed by the desire for immediate repayment of favors, whereas *communal* relationships are governed by the expectation of mutual responsiveness to another's needs. Communal partners do not seem to keep track of their rewards and costs, but they usually resume careful accounting if they become dissatisfied.

Equitable Relationships. *Equity* occurs when both partners gain benefits from a relationship that are proportional to their contributions to it. People are overbenefited if they receive better outcomes than they deserve, and underbenefited if they get less than they should.

The distress of inequity. According to equity theory, people dislike inequity and are motivated to change or escape it.

Ways to restore equity. Manipulation of one's outcomes or effort can sometimes restore equity. If not, people may change their perceptions of the relationship in order to convince themselves that it is equitable anyway. If all these efforts fail, people may abandon the relationship.

How much is enough? Equity versus overbenefit. Recent studies suggest that overbenefit is not always associated with reduced satisfaction with a relationship, although underbenefit is. Variable research results may be due to differences among people in their desire for equity and the possibility that equity doesn't matter much when one's outcomes are good. People probably apply different rules for the allocation of rewards to different types of relationships as well.

Summing Up. Altogether, both the quality of outcomes one receives and underbenefit, when it occurs, appear to play meaningful roles in determining how happy and stable a relationship will be.

The Nature of Commitment

Commitment is the intention to continue a relationship. The investment model of commitment asserts that satisfaction, the quality of one's alternatives, and the size of one's investments determine how committed one will be. However, there may be three different kinds of commitment that are based on attraction to a relationship, the costs of leaving it, and moral obligation to the relationship.

The Consequences of Commitment. Committed people tend to adopt a long-term orientation to their relationships and think of themselves and their partners as a collective whole. They also take action to protect and maintain their relationships, being accommodating, making sacrifices willingly, and considering their relationships to be better than those of other people. When both partners behave this way, commitment exerts a powerful influence on the stability of relationships.

PART THREE

Friendship and Intimacy

CHAPTER 7

Friendships Across the Life Cycle

THE NATURE OF FRIENDSHIP ◆ Attributes of Friendships ◆ The Rules
of Friendship ◆ FRIENDSHIP ACROSS THE LIFE CYCLE ◆ Infancy ◆
Childhood ◆ Adolescence ◆ Young Adulthood ◆ Midlife ◆
Old Age ◆ DIFFERENCES IN FRIENDSHIP ◆ Gender Differences
in Same-Sex Friendships ◆ Individual Differences
in Friendship ◆ CHAPTER SUMMARY

Without friendship life is not worth living. *Cicero*
Friendship is the only cement that will ever hold the world together.
Woodrow Wilson
Each friend represents a world in us, a world possibly not born until they
arrive, and it is only by this meeting that a new world is born. *Anais Nin*
I get by with a little help from my friends. *John Lennon*
A friend in need is a friend to be avoided. *Anonymous*
I don't trust him. We're friends. *Bertolt Brecht*

As you begin reading this chapter, pause for a few seconds to identify your
best friends. Mentally list two or three of their names. We bet you can do it. In-
tuitively, you know who your friends are and the importance of friendship to
you. Now define what friendship means to you. Jot down the three or four
main characteristics of friendship.

Did listing the defining qualities of friendship prove to be a bit harder than
simply listing your friends' names? Some social scientists have seen it that way
(e.g., Adams & Blieszner, 1996, p. 340). And if you were to ask each of your
friends to give their views of friendship, they might offer different definitions.

The French poet Jacques Delille (1738–1813) wrote, "Fate chooses your relations, you choose your friends." His distinction is one that is often still given in
describing friendship. Beverley Fehr summed up the various definitions social
scientists have given by saying that **friendship** is a "voluntary, personal relationship, typically providing intimacy and assistance, in which the two parties

189

like one another and seek each other's company" (1996, p. 7). In this chapter we are going to consider friendship. We will first amplify the nuances of what friendship is by looking at the characteristics people associate with friendship, by comparing it with love, and by discussing the rules of friendship. Then we will delve into how friendship varies across the life cycle. Finally, we will consider how friendships vary as a function of gender and individual differences, such as need for intimacy and depression.

THE NATURE OF FRIENDSHIP

Attributes of Friendships

A number of researchers have tried to illuminate the essential properties of friendships. Some of these researchers have posed simple, opened-ended questions similar to the one we used in our opening paragraph. Others have built on these endeavors and added theoretical formulations to develop structured questionnaires to assess key friendship dimensions.

Illustrative of the first approach, Sapadin (1988) asked 156 professional men and women living in Boston, New York, and Los Angeles to complete the sentence "A friend is someone . . . ." Responses were coded into eight categories (listed from most to least frequent), indicating that a friend is someone:

With whom we are intimate,

Whom we trust,

On whom we can depend,

Who shares,

Who is accepting,

Who is caring,

With whom we are close, and

Whom we enjoy.

The more structured approaches, such as the early work of Davis and Todd (1985), have identified as many 15 to 20 prototypical features. Clearly, friendship is a multidimensional phenomenon. In recently reflecting on these dimensions, deVries (1996) suggested that they can be distilled into three broad aspects: friendship's *affective*, shared or *communal*, and *sociable* elements. The affective component refers to

> The sharing of personal thoughts and feelings (i.e., self-disclosure) and other related expressions of intimacy, appreciation, and affection (including respect and feelings of warmth, care and love). Additionally, friends are described as providing encouragement, emotional support, empathy, and bolstering one's self-concept, all of which are made possible by an underlying sense of trust, loyalty, and commitment. (p. 252)

The shared or communal aspect of friendship refers to participating in common activities, similarity, and giving and receiving assistance of a nonaffective nature. The sociability theme presents friends as "sources of amusement, fun, and recreation" (p. 253).

Friendship can be distinguished from other types of relationships, such as romantic partnerships. As we'll see in chapter 8 when we consider love in detail, loving involves more complex feelings than liking does. Both liking and loving involve positive evaluations of one's partner (Rubin, 1973), but liking and loving feel different. Love relationships are more likely to be characterized by fascination with one's partner and by a desire for exclusiveness than friendships are. Love relationships also involve more stringent standards of conduct; we're supposed to be more loyal to, and more willing to help, our lovers than our friends (Davis & Todd, 1985). The social norms that regulate friendship are less confining than those that govern romantic relationships, and friendships are easier to dissolve (Fehr, 1996). In addition, friendships are less likely to involve overt expressions of positive emotion, and friends, as a general rule, spend less of their free time together than romantic partners do.

Of course, because most romantic relationships involve partners of different sexes while most friendships do not, we could wonder if the difference between friendship and romantic relationships partially reflects the difference between same-sex and other-sex relationships. Connolly, Craig, Goldberg, and Pepler (1999) shed light on this by asking 1,755 junior-high school students living in Toronto, Ontario, to describe other-sex friendships and romantic relationships. The adolescents reported that their friendships with members of the other sex were less passionate and less committed than their romantic relationships were. So, differences between friendships and love don't appear to be due solely to the sexes of the people involved.

All in all, it's clear that friendships entail fewer obligations and are usually less emotionally intense and less exclusive than romantic relationships are. And friendships typically do not involve sexual intimacy, whereas romantic relationships often do (see chapter 9).

The Rules of Friendship

Related to the attributes that delineate what friendships are, we have **rules of relationships.** These rules are the shared beliefs among members of a culture about what behaviors friends should (or should not) perform. We learn such rules as children through our interactions with others, and one of the things we learn is that when the rules are broken, disapproval and turmoil often result. But because such rules are cognitive representations of how to behave, children's understanding and expression of friendship rules change as they mature cognitively (Bigelow, Tesson, & Lewko, 1996).

By the time we reach adulthood, we have a well-established set of rules for relationships. For instance, in a seminal study, two British researchers, Argyle and Henderson (1984), generated a set of 43 possible friendship rules. They then had adults in Britain, Italy, Hong Kong, and Japan indicate which of the rules they would endorse. Overall, Japanese participants had the fewest number of highly endorsed rules, Hong Kong and British participants the most. The most important friendship rules that Argyle and Henderson identified are shown in

TABLE 7.1. The Rules of Friendship

Volunteer help in time of need.

Respect the friend's privacy.

Keep confidences.

Trust and confide in each other.

Stand up for the other person in their absence.

Don't criticize each other in public.

Show emotional support.

Look him/her in the eye during conversation.

Strive to make him/her happy while in each other's company.

Don't be jealous or critical of each other's relationships.

Be tolerant of each other's friends.

Share news of success with the other.

Ask for personal advice.

Don't nag.

Engage in joking or teasing with the friend.

Seek to repay debts and favors and compliments.

Disclose personal feelings or problems to the friend.

Source: Argyle & Henderson, 1985.

Table 7.1. These rules pertain to such things as giving help, disclosure and privacy, third parties, and things to avoid (e.g., publicly criticizing or nagging).

Rules are dictates about what we should and shouldn't do. Naturally, we don't always adhere to the rules of friendship. When asked the proportion of people who follow various rules (25 percent or less, 50 percent, or 75 percent or more), students at two San Francisco universities most commonly estimated 50 percent (Gambrill, Florian, & Thomas, 1999). But that doesn't mean the rules are unimportant. When people compare their current friendships to those that have lapsed, they remember following the rules of friendship less regularly in their lapsed friendships (Argyle & Henderson, 1984). Furthermore, these participants believed that failure to keep various rules had been moderately or very important in the decline of these friendships. Thus, whether or not we consciously think about them, there appear to be standards of behavior in friendships—the social rules of relationships—that can make or break our friendships.

FRIENDSHIP ACROSS THE LIFE CYCLE

There are various types of friendships. They differ in terms of the social context in which they are maintained (for instance, whether your friends are colleagues at work or neighbors at home), the degree of closeness or intimacy involved, and the age and sex of the participants (Fehr, 1996). We will now examine some of the ways friendships change and are intermingled with other types of relationships across the life cycle.

Infancy

From virtually the moment they are born, babies have a particular interest in the human face as compared to other stimuli (Mondloch et al., 1999). By about two months of age, babies will smile spontaneously at any human face, and if the recipient responds, they will usually make happy noises. So, although children may later begin to show anxiety in the presence of strangers (around seven months), humans appear to be social animals virtually from birth.

Of course, at first, children's peer relationships are very limited. Social psychologist Zick Rubin paid close attention to the early years of his son, Elihu. When Elihu was eight months old, four mothers brought their children together to get to know each other. Here is Rubin's description of what happened:

> The babies ignored one another. They would occasionally look at one another with what seemed to be mild interest. But the interest was never sustained for more than a few seconds. Instead, the babies divided most of their time between two sorts of activities—boldly exploring the room, furniture, and available toys, and cautiously retreating to their mothers as a base of security. Even at the earliest sessions, however, there were isolated instances in which one baby approached and made physical contact with another. For example (from my original notes): "Vanessa takes Elihu by surprise by crawling to him, screaming, and pulling his hair. Elihu looks bewildered. Then he starts to cry and crawls to his mother to be comforted." (Rubin, 1980, p. 15).

Rubin did not believe such episodes reflected hostile intent; rather, he interpreted them as indicating infants' interest in exploring one another as physical objects.

Just before Elihu turned one, Rubin saw his son look at a playmate, Sarah, as if he wanted to give her a block. By 15 months, Elihu "quite regularly and unambiguously offered objects to other toddlers" (Rubin, 1980, p. 17). At this stage, Elihu's generosity was probably often ignored. If it wasn't, his playmate may have been more concerned with the offered object than with interacting with Elihu.

Around the age of two, parallel play becomes quite common among children: that is, they do not interact with the other child in their play, but they play by themselves alongside the other child (Barnes, 1971). For instance, two children might sit side by side, each building with blocks but not talking to one another or working on each other's structures. As children go through the preschool years, their play becomes more associative and cooperative. As they get older, preschoolers' play involves more interaction, following another child's lead, and trying to achieve a common goal. Returning to our earlier example, older preschoolers are more likely to be found working together with blocks, talking about which block should go where and trying to have a structure such as a castle that they build jointly.

When do friendships first emerge? Children who are often together are capable of simple complimentary and reciprocal interactions as early as 13 to 15 months (see Howes, 1996, p. 69). Before their second birthdays, Rubin (1980) believes that pairs of children sometimes gravitate toward one another and take pleasure in each other's company. In one study of two-year-olds, mothers thought that their children had attachments to particular peers who would be missed if these relationships were ended (see Howes, 1996, p. 80). Evidence such as this leads some observers to conclude that, rudimentary as they may be, friendships can emerge during the toddler period. In the preschool years (ages 3 to 5), Rubin found children labeling playmates as friends. As three-year-old Tony put it: "We're friends now because we know each other's names."

Childhood

There is substantial literature on friendships in childhood and adolescence (e.g., Bukowski, Newcomb, & Hartup, 1996; Hartup, 1993; Berndt, 1996). Our approach to children's friendships will be to focus on two theoretical models: a cognitive approach and a social needs perspective.

Selman's Cognitive Model

Selman and his associates (e.g., Selman & Jaquette, 1977; Selman, 1981) were interested in how children understand friendships. He believes this understanding is related to children's cognitive development. By talking to children about how they see friendships and getting their reactions to friendship conflicts, Selman has identified five successive stages (see Table 7.2) in children's views of friendship. These evolve to form an increasingly comprehensive set of insights. As children move from one stage to another, they build upon the understanding gained from the earlier levels of development, and their advances in awareness about friendship are related to advances in their perspective-taking ability. As children get older, their conceptions of friendship become less egocentric and more complex.

In the initial stage of development, **Momentary Playmate** (Level 0, ages 3 to 7), friends are defined by their proximity, and they are valued for their possessions and physical attributes. Young children have difficulty differentiating other children's viewpoints from their own; they don't appreciate the need to consider the other person's wishes or will in relationships. "Friendships" are likely to exist with anyone with whom the child is playing at the moment. Typical of this stage, a preschooler might explain why he liked a friend by saying: "He lives close by" or "Andy's got red hair and toy cars." If they have a conflict, children at this level tend to believe it is over once you are no longer with the other child.

The next developmental stage is **One-Way Assistance** (Level 1, ages 4 to 9). Children in this stage are able to distinguish another's viewpoint and wishes from their own. They are becoming concerned with their peers' likes and dislikes; knowing the other child relatively well in this sense is a key factor in thinking of them as a close friend. But at this stage, youngsters have not fully recognized the necessity of give-and-take in a relationship. Friends are valued

TABLE 7.2 A Cognitive View of Children's Friendships

Stage (Age)	Friendship Awareness	Perspective Taking
0 (3–7)	Momentary physical playmate	Undifferentiated, egocentric
1 (4–9)	One-way assistance	Subjective, differentiated
2 (6–12)	Fairweather cooperation	Reciprocal, self-reflective
3 (9–15)	Intimate-mutual sharing	Mutual, third person
4 (12+)	Autonomous interdependence	In-depth, societal

Source: Adapted from Selman & Jaquette (1977).

for what they will do for oneself. When children are caught taking something from a peer, they are likely to recognize an obligation to return it and perhaps do something to make him or her feel better. Yet in resolving conflicts at this stage, children's criteria for a successful resolution are likely to be whether their own needs are satisfied, not whether both parties' interests are served. During this stage many children engage in make-believe activities, and imaginary friends are common (see Box 7.1).

Fairweather Cooperation (Level 2, ages 6 to 12) comes next. Children are beginning to have a self-reflective or reciprocal perspective; that is, they are starting to fathom how their friends see them. At this stage, children realize that reciprocal cooperation is important for interpersonal relationships. They do consider outcomes and conflict resolution in terms of whether both parties' interests are served, but they see the basic purpose of the friendship as serving self-interests rather than mutual interests. In Fairweather Cooperation, two children playing darts might take turns, but if one child's dart totally misses the dartboard, that child might say, "That throw doesn't count, I get another turn." If conflict erupts, the children at this stage believe that offering an apology means not only saying you are sorry, but also meaning it. At this stage, however, the child's temporal perspective is limited, so if conflicts aren't solved when they occur, the child is likely to feel the relationship is over.

At the next stage, **Intimate-Mutual Sharing** (Level 3, ages 9 to 15), children have advanced to the point that they can take an objective, third-person perspective of the friendship: friendship is seen as a collaboration with others for mutual and common interests, but it is also seen as an exclusive and possessive relationship. At this stage, children would be hurt and offended if their invitation for a friend to play at their house was rejected because their friend had already agreed to play at that time with someone else. But these children see continuity in their relationships that can transcend relationship turbulence. The concepts of loyalty and commitment emerge in children's friendship expectations. Trust assumes significance. Talking things through is considered a key way of resolving conflicts. Moreover, children at this stage judge others not only in terms of the consequences of their actions but also in terms of their intentions and dispositions. Thus research complementing Selman's model has shown that the psychological qualities of the other person, such as their extroversion or kindness, become more important (Barenboim, 1981).

BOX 7.1

Imaginary Companions and Other Extraordinary Relationships

In the movie Bogus, seven-year-old Albert is the son of a Las Vegas circus performer whose single mom assists the magician, Mr. Antoine. Early in the film, his mother is killed in a traffic accident. Albert wants to stay with his circus friends, but his mother has provided in her will that he is to live with someone he never knew about: his mother's foster sister, Harriet Franklin (Whoopi Goldberg). Harriet is a slightly harried woman struggling to run a restaurant supply business in New Jersey. Neither Albert nor Harriet are thrilled with their new family arrangement. Soon, Bogus, played by Gerard Depardieu, comes springing out of the pages of Albert's coloring book. In the rest of the film, Albert and then eventually Harriet take refuge in the company of this flamboyant, gentle, loving, and altogether imaginary Frenchman. Bogus becomes Albert's best friend. Bystanders find it a bit odd, but Albert has conversations with Bogus, and they duel in the park. Bogus encourages Albert and Harriet to accept one another, he protects Albert from passing traffic, and he even eats the food Albert doesn't want. By the end of the movie, Albert and Harriet have formed a mother-child bond, and Albert's world is bright again. Bogus leaves, reflecting, "Sometimes they remember us, maybe not."

Imaginary friends in childhood are common. Estimates of the exact proportion of children who have such friends vary, but in a carefully done longitudinal study, 63 percent of children Albert's age, seven, currently or previously had imaginary companions of some sort (humans, animals, snowmen, etc.). Forty-three percent had imaginary people as friends whom they could both identify and describe (Taylor, 1999). Although in this investigation it was more true among preschool children than among seven-year-olds, several other studies have found that girls are more likely to have imaginary friends than boys (see Seiffge-Krenke, 1997, p. 138). Imaginary friends are more common in

Albert in the tub with his imaginary friend, Bogus.

childhood than later in life, but even teenagers and adults have such companions. For instance, in working out her own thoughts, Senator Hillary Rodham Clinton has reputedly engaged in imagined conversations with Eleanor Roosevelt.

Children such as Albert may create an imaginary companion as a way of dealing with trauma, fear, and loneliness. But it would be incorrect to believe that these are the only or even the main reasons why children have imaginary companions. In her work, Taylor identified several other functions that such companions serve. For instance, for many children they are simply fun. Imaginary friends provide companionship, someone with whom to communicate. Children can use them as an excuse in their own efforts to avoid blame. Sometimes via their companions children vicariously get to be highly competent or to do things that they can't in their own lives (e.g., stay up however late they want).

Some parents may worry about their children having imaginary companions, suspecting that it is because they lack peer relationships or have adjustment problems. Taylor challenges this view, citing evidence that in daycare settings, children with imaginary companions are less fearful and less anxious in playing with other children. Similarly, college students who remembered having had imaginary companions scored lower on introversion and neuroticism scales. Instead, Taylor argues for the importance such fantasies usually have in healthy children's cognitive and emotional development. She notes that children who have pretend friends tend to score above average on intelligence tests and seem to be able to better focus their attention than other children. There is some, albeit not strong, evidence that they are more creative.

Besides imaginary companions, many people have relationships with pets or with God. A growing body of evidence shows that at least in some circumstances, companion animals can enhance the psychological, physical, social, and behavioral well-being of their human partners (Garrity & Stallones, 1998). For instance, during a one-year longitudinal study of 995 noninstitutionalized Canadians aged 65 and over, the capacity to perform activities of daily living (e.g., dressing oneself) deteriorated less on average for pet owners than for seniors who did not have a pet (Raina, Waltner-Toews, Bonnett, Woodward, & Abernathy, 1999).

Lee Kirkpatrick (1999) argues that God and other deities often serve people as attachment figures. In his newspaper surveys and college student studies, Kirkpatrick has found that over two-thirds of respondents believe they "have a personal relationship with Jesus Christ and/or God." Just as there are different attachment styles in human relationships (e.g., secure, avoidant, and ambivalent), so too do people's relationships with God vary. Relationships with God aren't reciprocal or sexual in the way other adult attachment relationships tend to be. Yet, Kirkpatrick maintains that relationships with God involve many of the same key processes as other attachment relationships (e.g., people seek out God, feel comforted by God during difficult times, and gain from their relationship with God a sense of security for exploring their environment). As the 23rd Psalm states, "Yea, though I walk through the valley of the shadow of death, I will fear no evil: for thou art with me; thy rod and thy staff, they comfort me." Kirkpatrick marshals evidence to support his claim that belief in God as an attachment figure confers psychological benefits.

BOX 7.2

At What Level of Friendship Understanding Are Joey and Marvin?

Joey and Marvin are having lunch together in a cafeteria. Marvin is playing with a new spaceship toy; Joey is interested in it. Read Selman's notes on their interaction and then decide which of his levels of friendship Joey and Marvin are manifesting.

JOEY: Marvin, let me play with your rocket and I'll do anything you want.

MARVIN: Get me another dessert.

JOEY: (returning with a second orange) Now can I play with your rocket?

MARVIN: Nope.

JOEY: If you let me use your rocket, I'll be your . . . Let me use it because I *am* your friend.

MARVIN: (Matter of factly) You're not my friend.

JOEY: (Losing control, screaming until red in the face) Yes, I am! I *am* your friend! Yes, I *am*!

Selman classified these children as being at the One-Way Assistance stage of friendship. Joey does realize what Marvin wants, but characteristic of Level 1, Marvin does not recognize the need for give and take in the relationship. Marvin is happy to simply get his second dessert; he's not concerned whether the outcomes of this interaction are satisfactory to both himself and Joey.

Source: Selman, 1981, p. 242.

The final level of development (age 12+), **Autonomous Interdependence,** is characterized by complex relationships: the adolescent or adult realizes that one friendship cannot fulfill all emotional and psychological needs. Therefore, friends are allowed to develop independent relationships, and there is respect for both dependence and autonomy in friendships. Apropos of dependence, adolescents realize they rely on their friends for psychological support and gain a sense of identity via identification with others. Yet, in this stage, adolescents understand that we have networks of relationships; the reasons for refusing a social invitation because of prior social commitment or other interpersonal obligations would be better appreciated. More subtle aspects of conflict are understood (e.g., that another person's internal turmoil may contribute to their interpersonal conflicts, or that subtle, unspoken vibrations can signal the end of a fight). Adolescents believe that relationships are dynamic rather than fixed; as the people involved change, so too does their friendship.

In Box 7.2 you will find a note on the interaction between two boys, Joey and Marvin, who were having lunch together. At which of Selman's levels would you classify them?

Selman and Jaquette (1977) tested their model by interviewing a cross-section of people ranging in age from 4 to 32 years old about their responses to hypothetical stories of interpersonal conflict. An additional sample of 48 males (6 to 12 years old) was interviewed and then re-interviewed two year later. Data from both the cross-sectional and longitudinal samples supported Selman's hierarchical levels of friendship development. There was evidence of increasing friendship awareness in children between 6 and 15 years of age in that, in this age range, the average increase was approximately two stages, from Stage 1 to Stage 3. There was large variability in ages at each level of awareness; some children reached a given stage sooner than others. Nonetheless, the children's movements through the stages weren't random; they typically moved through the stages in the manner Selman suggested.

Buhrmester and Furman's Socioemotional Model of Friendship Development

As you can see, Selman's model of the development of friendship emphasizes children's increasingly elaborate cognitive skills. An alternative approach focuses on the different interpersonal needs children develop as they grow older; at different stages of development, different needs are preeminent. According to Buhrmester and Furman (1986), these key needs are *tenderness* in infancy, *companionship* in the preschool period, *acceptance* in the early elementary years, *intimacy* in preadolescence, and *sexuality* in early adolescence. At each stage, the predominant need intensifies particular emotions. New needs are added on top of old ones, so that older children have more needs to satisfy than younger children do. And the successful resolution of each stage requires the development of specific competencies that affect the way a child handles later stages; if those skills aren't acquired, problems occur.

We'll start our discussion of Buhrmester and Furman's model at the **Juvenile Era** (ages 6 to 9), when children enter elementary school and the companionship of, and acceptance by, other children becomes increasingly important (see Table 7.3). Friendships at this stage are equalitarian relationships in which the child learns about cooperation and compromise, as opposed to competition and greed. The early elementary student learns about differences among his or her peers and about the status hierarchies that exist among people. Children who are not accepted by their peers feel ostracized and excluded. This may leave them with reduced self-esteem that leads them to denigrate and disparage others.

Later, in the **Preadolescent Stage** (ages 9 to 12), children acquire a need for intimate exchange. Through this process, preadolescents learn that their hopes, fears, preferences, and interests are worthy and shared by others. This social validation gives them a sense that their views are "right." Preadolescent relationships can have therapeutic value, helping children who have had trouble at prior stages to overcome their sense of isolation or rejection. Preadolescents typically focus their need for intimacy on a friend who is similar to them in age, background, and interests. These partnerships are characterized by intense closeness fostered via extensive self-disclosure. This is when full-blown friendships first emerge, and, arguably, only after experiencing such friendships can a child miss them when they're gone. Consequently, according to the needs perspective, this is the first period in which children experience true loneliness (see chapter 14 for other viewpoints on this issue). During this period, children

TABLE 7.3 Buhrmester and Furman's Model of Socioemotional Development

Developmental Stage	Emerging Needs/ Key Relationship	Interpersonal Competencies	Developmental Arrests	Focal Emotion
Infancy (0–2 yrs.)	Tenderness/ Parents	Coordinated responding	Insecure attachment	Distress and fear/security
Childhood (2–6 yrs.)	Companionship/ Parents	Compliance and assertion	Isolation (reclusive self-play and boredom)	Isolation, boredom/ enjoyment, and amusement
Juvenile era (6–9 yrs.)	Acceptance/ Peer society	Cooperation, compromise, and competition	Peer group ostacism and disparagement of others	Ostracism and rejection/Social pride and self-worth
Preadolescent (9–12 yrs.)	Intimacy/ Same-sex friend	Collaboration: Perspective-taking, empathy, and altruism	Loneliness, isolation	Loneliness/love
Early adolescence (12–16 yrs.)	Sexuality/ Opposite-sex partner	Balancing intimacy, sexuality, and anxiety	Confused sexuality	Sexual frustration/love

Source: Buhrmester and Furman, 1986.

develop the skills of perspective taking, empathy, and altruism that are the foundation for close adult relationships, and children who encounter difficulty at this stage are likely to be susceptible to loneliness later in life.

Thereafter, during the **Early Adolescent** phase, sexuality erupts. The child develops a sense of lust that promotes an interest in the opposite sex and extends the need for intimacy. Unfortunately, it is usually difficult for the early adolescent to establish relationships with others that will satisfy these needs. Their lustful feelings can become intense, pushing them into real or fantasized sexual encounters that are accompanied by anxiety, shame, or guilt. If these feelings occur, they can make it more difficult for the early adolescent to form sensitive, caring, and open relationships. In late adolescence, the individual typically begins a characteristic pattern of fulfilling intimacy and sexual needs (see chapter 9). Developmental arrest in early adolescence leads to a confused sexual identity, and difficulties in this period produce feelings of lust and frustration.

Summary

Overall, Selman's (1981) and Buhrmester and Furman's (1986) models of the development of friendship focus on different perspectives. Selman's model emphasizes the cognitive capacity and perspective-taking ability of a growing child, whereas Buhrmester and Furman concentrate on the primary needs that characterize a certain age. Nevertheless, the two models have points of similarity. For instance, both suggest that children learn cooperative skills during the early elementary years. Both agree that children develop new forms of intimacy in their relationships as they approach puberty. Perhaps most fundamentally, both models assume that our relationships change as we grow older. Thus the complex, sophisticated ways adults connect are years in the making.

Childhood Peer Status and Later Well-Being

As we've seen, Buhrmester and Furman (1986) asserted that a central need during the early elementary years is acceptance by one's peer group. Psychologists have been studying the sociometric patterns of children in school classes for nearly 70 years (see Asher & Coie, 1990; Bukowski & Cillessen, 1998). In these studies, children have been asked questions about which of their classmates they like or dislike and with whom they would or wouldn't want to do things such as have lunch. Initially, researchers focused on children's popularity. But since the mid-1980s, researchers have found it useful to distinguish among at least three categories of children: those who are popular (i.e., liked by a large number of their peers), those who are neglected (i.e., those who are neither liked nor disliked by their classmates), and those who are rejected (i.e., disliked by others). Neglected children tend to be shy; rejected children tend to be aggressive (Parker & Asher, 1987, p. 360).

Many researchers who have measured young children's patterns of friendship in this manner have also examined what became of them several years later (e.g., at the end of high school) (see Parker & Asher, 1987; Kupersmidt, Coie, & Dodge, 1990). Parker and Asher (1987) identified over 120 studies of this type. Most of the studies in their review were earlier ones that had used a unidimensional sociometric measure rather than dividing nonpopular participants into the neglected versus rejected subgroups. Some of the studies did, however, have ratings of the children's interpersonal style (aggressive versus shy). The most common follow-up measures in these studies assessed whether students completed or dropped out of high school, engaged in criminal-type behavior, and/or encountered difficulty with psychological adjustment.

After a careful review of these studies, Parker and Asher concluded that there is

> general support for the hypothesis that children with poor peer adjustment are at risk for later life difficulties. Support is clearest for the outcomes of dropping out and criminality. It is also clearest for low acceptance and aggressiveness as predictors, whereas a link between shyness/withdrawal and later maladjustment has not yet been adequately tested. (Parker & Asher, 1987, p. 360)

In a later examination of this literature, Kupersmidt et al. reached a similar overall conclusion about the negative later life correlates of early peer rejection. They did find evidence of low sociometric status being associated with poor mental health and added that the risks of peer rejection generally seemed greater for males than for females.

As an example of the studies included in Parker and Asher's analysis (1987, p. 365), one examined high school dropout rates in the 1950s (Gronlund &

Holmlund, 1958). In that investigation, more than half (54 percent) of the boys who were not accepted by their peers in sixth grade dropped out of high school before graduating; in contrast, only 19 percent of the boys who were well liked dropped out. For girls, the respective percentages were 35 and 4 percent. And importantly, these differences were not due to intelligence; the researchers matched the groups of high- and low-acceptance children so that they had similar academic skills.

We can't tell from correlational studies like these whether peer rejection *causes* poor adjustment later in life or is simply a symptom of other influences that are responsible for such problems (Kupersmidt et al., 1990). Regardless, it is good to know that psychologists are developing interventions to help youths to enhance their peer acceptance and are showing in treatment outcome studies that these strategies work (see Coie & Koeppl, 1990; Waas & Graczyk, 1998).

Adolescence

The Growing Importance of Peers

One of the central features of the period between the middle elementary school years and young adulthood is the shift of relationships from family to peers. Two lines of research support this view: experience sampling (or pager) studies and attachment research. In a beeper study of predominantly white, working- and middle-class Chicago youths, the amount of time they spent with family was found to decrease from 35 percent in grade 5 to 14 percent in grade 12 (Larson, Richards, Moneta, Holmbeck, & Duckett, 1996). Time just with peers (i.e., no family members also present) increased for both boys and girls, especially for girls (i.e., from 18 percent in grade 5 for girls to 34 percent in grade 9) (Larson & Richards, 1991). Time alone increased, too, so the ratio of time with family to the time with peers dropped appreciably. Of course, some of the time adolescents spend with peers is with romantic partners. A common pattern as adolescents get older is for time with romantic partners to increase, encroaching on time with friends (Zimmer-Gembeck, 1999).

Adolescents also turn to their friends more often for the satisfaction of important attachment needs (Fraley & Davis, 1997). Attachment theorists identify four components or functions of attachment (Hazan & Zeifman, 1994): (a) *proximity seeking*, which involves approaching, staying near, or making contact with an attachment figure; (b) *safe haven*, turning to an attachment figure as a source of comfort and support in times of stress; (c) *separation protest*, in which people resist being separated from a partner and are distressed by separation from him or her; and (d) *secure base*, using a partner as a foundation for exploration of novel environments and other daring exploits. A survey of more than 100 youths aged 6 to 17 demonstrated that all of these components of attachment can be found in the relationships young children have with their parents, but, as they grow older, adolescents gradually shift their primary attachments from their parents to their peers in a component-by-component fashion (Hazan & Zeifman, 1994).

This sequence of changes begins with proximity seeking around the age of 7, and continues with a shift in the location of one's safe haven in the 11 to 14 age group. Adolescents who are 15 to 17 years old still mention their parents most often as their secure base, and they continue to feel some distress when they are separated from their parents, but peers are increasingly used for these functions, too. Indeed, a number of these older teens (41 percent) identified a peer, rather than a parent, as their primary attachment figure. (Most of the time, however, that person was a romantic partner rather than a friend.)

Peers gradually replace parents in the lives of older adolescents, but even young adults may still rely on their parents for some components of attachment. A study of 237 college students found that they were quite likely to seek proximity with their friends, and willing to turn to them as a safe haven, but least likely to rely on them as a secure base (Fraley & Davis, 1997). That was a role still often reserved for Mom or Dad, although a long, caring relationship with a trustworthy peer and a secure attachment style made it more likely that a young adult would have a high level of attachment to his or her peers.

Friendships within Cliques and Crowds

Friendships involve just two participants, but they often operate within cliques and crowds. *Cliques* are small networks of individuals who hang around with one another. In some activities, such as large parties, cliques link together to form *crowds*. Crowds can also be created by a collection of peers who share a particular reputation or identity (such as jocks, brains, loners, or druggies) who may or may not spend time together (Brown, 1989; Stone & Brown, 1999).

As adolescents age, their peer groups usually become more complex, moving through five different stages (Dunphy, 1963). Think back to sixth or seventh grade: That's Stage 1, where interaction occurs in same-sex cliques. At Stage 2, occasional group-level interaction between boy and girl cliques occurs, but any interaction on an individual basis is still rare and is perceived as rather daring. At Stage 3, upper-status members of same-sex cliques initiate heterosexual interactions that lead to the formation of crowds that subsume male, female, and mixed-sex cliques. (Remember ninth grade?) During the next stage, the intersecting same-sex and cross-sex cliques re-form to comprise separate mixed-sex cliques that associate in a crowd. And finally, in the final stage, the crowd begins to disintegrate into loosely associated groups of couples. Thus, as adolescents go from the middle school years to the end of high school, their peer groups are constantly evolving, and the number of friendships they share with the other sex are gradually increasing (Hartup, 1993).

Support, Conflict, and Peer Influence in Adolescent Relationships

Berndt (1996) identified three key functions of relationships in adolescence: support, conflict, and peer pressure. Intimacy is a key component of support; during intimate conversations, friends provide practical advice and emotional support for each other. Supportive friendships also tend to involve generosity and loyalty, and they enhance adolescents' self-esteem, improving their ability to cope with stressful events.

However, adolescent friendships can also involve arguments, teasing, competition, and other forms of conflict. Discord and conflict (which will be discussed more fully in chapter 12) are prevalent in adolescence; on average, adolescents report seven disagreements with others each day (Laursen & Collins, 1994). Some of this conflict is with their parents. The negativity and acrimony of parent-child conflict reaches a peak in mid-adolescence, but the frequency of such disputes actually declines during the teen years (Laursen, Coy, & Collins, 1998). Thus, much of the conflict adolescents encounter is with their peers. Negative affect usually does not run as high in conflicts with friends as it does with family members (Laursen & Collins, 1994). Nonetheless, Way, Cowal, Gingold, Bissessar, and Pahl (2001) found that roughly a fifth of ethnically diverse, low-income adolescents' relationships with their best friends were simultaneously characterized by both positive feelings and high conflict. These friendships were apparently desirable because the participants typically enjoyed better self-esteem and family relations and lower depression than did "disengaged" youths whose closest friendships manifested neither intimacy nor strong conflict. For some adolescents, conflict with friends is undoubtedly a source of tension, but for many teens, conflict may simply be a part of direct, honest relating.

Finally, adolescent friendships involve peer pressure that reaches a peak around the age of 15 (Berndt, 1996), influencing a person's choice of clothing, academic performance, drinking behavior, smoking, sexual standards, and more. Friends often behave similarly because they naturally have a lot in common (remember chapter 3?), but peer influence matters, too. On occasion, friends may coerce a partner to do what they want, but most peer pressure is probably more innocuous than that (Berndt, 1996). Friends often discuss issues freely until they reach a consensus. They use reasoning, offers of rewards, or teasing to persuade each other. These influences can be either negative or positive, but they are probably only rarely coercive and obnoxious.

Young Adulthood

During their late teens and twenties, people enter young adulthood. Intimacy is an important aspect of social support in adolescent relationships (Berndt, 1996), but many developmental researchers believe that intimacy is even more consequential in young adulthood. For instance, Erik Erikson (1950), a historically prominent theorist, believed that the central task of a person's late teen years and early twenties was working through the developmental stage of "intimacy versus isolation." From this vantage point, intimacy does not necessarily involve sexuality, but it does involve sensitivity to the aspirations, needs, and wishes of one's partner. Erikson believed that intimacy sprang in part from mutual trust and was more likely for individuals who had already achieved a sense of identity.

This search for intimacy is often undertaken in a novel environment—when many North Americans leave home to attend college. When people move away from home, new friends help compensate for any old friends that are lost, but in general, "the transition to university has deleterious effects on friendships" (Fehr, 1999b, p. 269). Shaver, Furman, and Buhrmester (1985) provide one illustration of this phenomenon. They examined the changing social networks of 166 students in the University of Denver's freshman class of 1980. Shaver et al. surveyed students during the summer before they arrived at the University of Denver, and again in the autumn, the winter, and the spring of the students' first year. Not surprisingly, the friendships students had at home tended to erode and be replaced by new relationships. However, this didn't happen immediately, and the students' satisfaction with their friendship networks was lowest in the fall and winter after they arrived at college. Almost all (97 percent) of the incoming students quickly found a new "close" friend, but few of these relationships retained their prominence for long; only about a third of them were still designated as best friendships in the spring. The students were evidently shuffling and reshuffling their social networks, and those who were outgoing and self-disclosing had an easier time of it; during this freshman year, socially skilled students were more satisfied with their relationships than were those who were less socially skilled. By the close of the study in the spring, the students had generally regained their satisfaction with their social networks, but they did so by relying less on their families and forming new friendships; as the year went on, family relationships had less and less to do with how satisfied people were.

How do things change after college? In one study, Reis, Lin, Bennett, and Nezlek (1993) had 113 young adults keep daily diaries of their social interactions for one to two weeks on two separate occasions, once when they were freshman or seniors in college and again six to seven years after graduation. (Interactions mandated by participants' work were not counted in this study). Overall, these people spent less time interacting with others after they graduated than they did when they were in college. In particular, the amount of interaction with same-sex friends and groups of over three people declined after graduation. Time with opposite-sex partners increased, although the number of opposite-sex partners with whom participants spent that time decreased, especially for men. Just as developmental theorists would suggest, the average intimacy levels of the participants' interactions increased during their twenties. For women, the shift occurred between the first and last year of college, while for men it occurred after they graduated from college. Participants were not, however, necessarily more satisfied with their interactions. These trends occurred for both married and single participants. One possible interpretation of the pattern of results in this study is that after college more of our interactions occur with people with whom we have deeper, more interdependent relationships. That interactions in this study increased in intimacy but were not more satisfying may reflect that in our late twenties we more often have to come to grips with responsibilities and daily problems in our close relationships.

Midlife

The Dearth of Information about Midlife Friendships

The first thing to note about friendships in middle age is that we don't know as much as we'd like to (or perhaps as much as we should). In reflecting on the state of knowledge about adult friendships, Adams and Blieszner (1996, p. 340) lament

> Unfortunately, most studies of midlife friendship have not been very sophisti-
> cated . . . Researchers usually have not studied midlife friendship in terms of
> differences across the life course (by comparing friendships of people of differ-
> ent ages concurrently) or in terms of changes over time (by comparing people's
> friendships at one age to their friendships when they are older, in a longitudi-
> nal design). Because of these shortcomings, knowledge about midlife friend-
> ship is suggestive rather than conclusive.

Even when age comparisons *are* made, the results are sometimes rather bland,
suggesting that adults in midlife don't differ much from other age groups. For
instance, Adams and Blieszner consider evidence on the way adults describe
their actual friends and the density (i.e., the interconnectedness) among their
network members. They conclude that neither of these two aspects of adults'
friendships differ much from those of other age groups. Similarly, they cite evidence that self-disclosure doesn't differ much with age, once duration of
friendships is taken into consideration (Adams & Blieszner, 1996, p. 352).

So, is there anything unique about friendship in midlife? Two avenues to
approaching this question are (a) to look at age differences that have been
found, and (b) to examine the associations between adult-related roles or life
events and friendships. We will briefly consider each approach.

Age Group Comparisons with Midlife Friendships

Blieszner and Adams (1992, see also Adams & Blieszner, 1996) analyzed
three broad aspects of friendship: structure, process and phases. Under *structure,* they include how much power or status each partner has, how similar the
partners are, how much the partners like each other, and the interweaving of
friendships with networks of relationships. *Process* refers to the interactive aspects of friendships, including how partners behave toward one another and
their thoughts and feelings during those interactions. The *phases* of friendship
include establishing, maintaining, and dissolving friendships. In general, they
were not able to find many age differences, and those they did find were often
obtained in single studies.

In the structural domain, there is some evidence that the difference between the ages of midlife friends is likely to be further apart than it is for young
adults (cf. Dickens & Perlman, 1981, p. 112). Nonetheless, the difference between the attributes desired in a friend and the qualities one's friends actually
possess has been found to be smaller in midlife than at younger or older ages.
In the process domain, middle-aged people, along with older adults, have been
found to make more effort than young adults to reduce disagreements with
friends. Perhaps in midlife this is in part due to the fact that their friends possess the attributes people are seeking.

In the phases domain, Wall, Pickert, and Paradise's (1984) study of 58 col-
lege-educated, 25- to 50-year-old men showed that the older the participants
were, the more difficulty they reported in forming friendships. Younger men
were more concerned about personality factors as an inhibitor of friendship formation; men approaching 50 were concerned with a lack of time. It is not too
surprising that other studies have shown that midlife friends, on average, have

known each other a little longer than young adult friends. Argyle and Henderson (1984), whose work we considered earlier, looked at people's views of how rule violations contributed to the ending of their friendships. Comparing between teens (aged 17 to 19) and young adults (aged 20 to 35), the teens attributed more importance to public criticism as leading to the demise of their friendships. The young adults focused on lack of respect for privacy and requests for personal advice.

Life Event and Role Influences on Midlife Friendships

In addition to leaving one's childhood home for school or work, several other major life events are likely to occur in adulthood—new jobs or careers, marriage, parenthood, the departure from home of one's own children, and perhaps a divorce. Events such as these and the new roles they create for us are entwined with the stability of our friendships and our other relationships with members of our social networks (see Fehr, 1999b). To illustrate these interconnections here, we will focus on relational life events such as courtship, marriage, and parenthood. (Divorce is covered in detail in chapter 13.)

The connection between people's friendships and their romances is clear: When people become more involved with a romantic partner, they typically spend less time with their families and friends. A pattern of **dyadic withdrawal** occurs as intimacy grows in a blossoming romantic relationship; as people see more and more of a lover, they become less involved with their larger network, especially their friends (Fehr, 1999b). One study found that people usually spent two hours per day with good friends when they were casually dating someone, whereas people who were engaged saw their friends for less than 30 minutes per day (Milardo, Johnson, & Huston, 1983). Romantic couples do tend to increase their contact with friends they have in common, but this doesn't offset declines in the total number of friends they have and the amount of time they spend with them. Moreover, because heterosexual couples in the United States tend to socialize more often with *his* friends than with *her* friends, women's friendships with other women are especially likely to be affected by dyadic withdrawal (Fehr, 1999b).

The erosion of people's friendships doesn't stop once they get married. Both marriage and parenthood are "associated with the deterioration and dissolution of friendships" (Fehr, 1999, p. 265). Fehr adds that parenthood has similar effects. For marriage, cross-sex friendships are especially affected; people tend to see much less of friends who could be construed by a spouse to be a potential romantic rival. Some of the support for these conclusions comes from pager studies that examine how adults spend their time. Additional support comes from surveys. For instance, Fischer and Oliker (1983) interviewed 1,050 northern Californians about the people with whom they engaged in social exchanges (e.g., help with chores, advice, socializing, lending money). Table 7.4 shows their results. The total network size increased with marriage in this study, but the ratio of friends to kin dropped. Younger, single participants had the highest ratio of friends to kin. In the under-36 age group, women with young children had relatively few friends.

TABLE 7.4 Mean Number of Friends and Kin Relations Across the Family Life Cycle

	Life Cycle Stage of Respondent						
	Young Adults (< 36)			Midlife Adults (36–64)		Older Adults (65+)	Row Mean
	Unmarried	Married, No Child	Married, Child	Married, Child	Married, No Child[a]		
Friends[b]							
Men	12.6	15.3	14.7	10.4	9.1	5.6	11.3
Women	12.7	14.7	10.4	9.9	10.5	8.2	10.3
Kin							
Men	4.6	8.0	10.4	8.2	8.5	6.8	7.2
Women	6.5	8.6	10.2	10.0	9.6	7.3	8.2
Friend/Kin Ratio							
Men	2.74	1.91	1.41	1.27	1.07	.82	1.56
Women	1.95	1.71	1.02	.99	1.09	1.12	1.26

Source: Fischer & Oliker, 1983.
[a]Most of the married individuals 36 to 64 without children were in the post-parental stages of the family life cycle with their children having left home.
[b]*Friends* refers to all associates the respondents considered friends.

But a decline in friendships following marriage and parenthood is not the whole story. For both of these transitions, the drop in friendships is offset by increases in kin relationships. In the transition to parenthood, friendships with other parents may prosper. There also appears to be a rebound in the number of close friends people have when children leave home (deVries, 1991). Finally, among married individuals, those who have intimate marital relationships also tend to have intimate friendships (see Mayseless, Sharabany, & Sagi, 1997). In sum, people's social lives don't necessarily wither away when they commit themselves to a spouse and kids, but the focus of their socializing does shift from their personal friends to family and friends they share with their husbands or wives.

Old Age

The Extent of Sociability among the Elderly

There is a good deal of evidence that sociability declines in old age. For example, in Larson's (1990) beeper studies, the percentage of time that people spent in the presence of others declined steadily over the life course: It started at 83 percent of the time for children ages 9 to 12 and then dropped to 74 percent of the time for high-school-aged adolescents, 71 percent of the time for adults, and 48 percent of the time for older, retired individuals. Complementing this finding, "Longitudinal and cross-sectional studies reveal far smaller social networks among old as compared with younger people" (Carstensen, Isaacowitz, & Charles, 1999, p. 173). Illustrative of this, Table 7.4 shows that the number of friends and even the number of kin are lower for older adults than for most adults under age 65 (Fischer & Oliker, 1983). Turning from networks to specific types of relationships, Connidis and Davies (1992) found that among Canadians aged 65 to 92, increasing age was associated with a reduced probability of having a friend who serves as a confidant. Approaching declining social participation from yet a slightly different perspective, Adams and Blieszner (1995, p. 213) conclude that "longitudinal studies show that contacts with friends tend to decline as people grow older, . . . with older women appearing better able to make and keep friends than older men."

Of course, not all older adults face the same situation, and circumstances matter. For example, Adams and Blieszner (1995) review evidence that employed older women have more friends than nonemployed older women and that community residents have more friends than seniors living in nursing homes. Some older adults have more friends than they did during their midlives. Friendships certainly persist. In a study of elders who were 85 or older, Johnson and Troll (1994) found that most of the participants had at least one close friend, three-fourths were in at least weekly contact with a friend, and 45 percent reported having made a new friend since their 85th birthday. In this study, having friends and making contact with them was fostered by the social environment (e.g., easy access to similar others, being in a neighborhood with friends of long standing), better health, and a gregarious personality.

Perspectives on Levels of Sociability

A variety of explanations have been offered to account for the usual drop in sociability in old age. One possibility is that older people want the same social contact as anyone else, but their social participation is impeded by a variety of **barriers** younger people don't have to overcome (Havighurst, 1961). Such barriers might include mandatory retirement, poor transportation, the death of friends, and subtle discrimination against the elderly. In fact, practical matters of mobility and health sometimes do complicate seniors' social lives. However, older adults often bypass opportunities for social participation even when they are freely available (Lansford, Sherman, & Antonucci, 1998). In addition, if older people were blocked from having relationships they desired, you'd expect them to be dissatisfied with their social networks; however, "older people express great satisfaction with their social relationships" (Lang & Carstensen, 1994, p. 315), a fact that makes the "barrier" perspective on seniors' sociability suspect.

According to the **disengagement perspective,** people do not need to be active to be well adjusted (Cumming & Henry, 1961). Instead, proponents of this view see decreases in activity levels and the seeking of more passive roles as a normal, inevitable part of aging, which may be started either by the individuals themselves or by society. They believe disengagement has benefits for both the individual (e.g., being released from expectations of being productive in a competitive environment) and for society as a whole (e.g., by fostering an orderly transfer of power and responsibility to the next generation).

Sharing the view that older adults themselves play a role in the decline in their social contacts is a third, more recent perspective: **socioemotional selectivity theory** (SST, Carstensen et al., 1999). This model is concerned with how time influences people's goals. According to socioemotional selectivity theory, our goals can be classified into intellectual and emotional categories. When we are more future-oriented, we pursue knowledge-oriented goals; we seek information that may be useful to us later in life. (That's presumably what you're doing now that you're in college.) When we are more present- than future-time oriented (as these theorists assume happens in old age), we are involved with emotional goals. From this theory, Carstensen and her associates believe that younger adults seek relatively larger, more diverse social networks that include a high proportion of novel social partners. As one's future time perspective shrinks, advocates of this position expect that "people will systematically hone their social networks such that available social partners satisfy emotional needs" (Carstensen et al., 1999, p. 173). In other words, as adults get older they should retain close relationships with friends and family members but let casual relationships lapse. Compared with a disengagement explanation, this viewpoint focuses more attention on the specific types of declines that occur. Consistent with socioemotional selectivity theory, Lang and Carstensen (1994) demonstrate a differential decline pattern: while seniors do drop less-close friends as they advance in years, the number of close family members and long-time friends in their networks remains about the same. Related predictions derived from this theory have been supported cross-culturally in Hong Kong and by using other ways of operationalizating time perspective (HIV status among young adults, Carstensen et al., 1999). Given its conceptual sophistication and varied forms of empirical support, socioemotional selectivity theory currently fares well as a framework for interpreting declines in sociability.

Friendship and Well-Being in Old Age

In chapter 2 we discussed Aristotle's three types of relationships: those of pleasure, utility, and virtue. Aristotle conjectured that young people seek friendships of pleasure; old people seek friendships of utility. Contemporary social scientists believe that family members are generally more likely than friends to provide instrumental assistance to older adults (Adams & Blieszner, 1995). But friends do help under some circumstances (e.g., when the need for help is unpredictable, when assistance is short-term, when the elderly person has no family). Furthermore, even though the friendships of older adults can be problematic (see Box 7.3), based on the evidence of the past two decades, researchers think friends are more crucial to the psychological well-being of older adults than are family members (Adams & Blieszner, 1995).

Friends can even contribute to our physical well-being. In a 10-year longitudinal study of 2,812 New Haven seniors, Mendes de Leon et al. (1999) examined disabilities in daily living (e.g., not being able to dress oneself, bathe oneself, or walk across a room). Having frequent interactions with friends re-

---

BOX 7.3

Problematic Aspects of Older Adults' Friendships

After years of being a widow and living her own life, she married a jerk. He listens to her conversations when she talks on the phone. He meddles in our relationship and tells her he doesn't want her doing things.

Way back when, we went to college together. Bob gets drunk—he's been doing it for 40 years. I'll talk to him at reunions, but it's a bummer. I never call him.

She grew up in a family of four girls; she was the big sister. She's never stopped acting that way; she still wants to be the boss of everything.

After we retired things changed. I have some money of my own and a good pension plan. She relies a lot on her social security, for what that's worth. I think it is a little hard when we get together because she knows I thought she should have saved more. Now she's a bit jealous because I can travel and do things I want but she can't.

These remarks are similar to ones Blieszner and Adams (1998) obtained in interviews with 53 older adults (55+) living in Greensboro, North Carolina.

Among this sample, 79 percent discussed negative aspects of their friendships. A few mentioned having friends who were too close, but having difficult relationships and the phenomenon of relationships fading were more common. Blieszner and Adams classify the problems into four different categories: the internal structure of the relationship (e.g., differences in power), interactive processes (e.g., the other person's actions hurt my feelings, my attributing relationship problems to my friend's personality), external factors (e.g., spousal interference, one partner's declining health, one partner's work obligations), and that the friends no longer intersected due to their living far apart or changing daily routines. Probably these problems undermined the closeness of these relationships but only a small percentage of the relationships involving problems had ended. So despite problems, most friendships continue.

---

duced the risk of developing disabilities and increased the odds of recovering from them. Other research shows that social ties, including contacts with friends, reduce mortality rates—those who have friends are likely to live longer (see Sabin, 1993).

In sum, sociability does decline in old age, especially with the more distant members of our networks. Yet, the existence of friendships contributes to the health and morale of older adults.

DIFFERENCES IN FRIENDSHIP

So far in this chapter, we have been examining the nature of friendships and how they differ across the life cycle. They also fluctuate as a function of other factors. For instance, in chapter 4 we gleaned insight into the ways people high and low in self-monitoring relate to their friends. In the next sections, we want to look at how the nature of friendships is intertwined with gender, motivational, and personality differences.

Gender Differences in Same-Sex Friendships

Consider the following two descriptions of some same-sex friendships:

Sarah and Janet are very close friends. Often, they stay up half the night talking about love and life and how they feel about everything and everyone. In times of trouble, each is always there for the other to lean on. When they experience problems in their romantic relationships, they immediately get on the phone with each other, asking for, and getting, all the advice and consolation they need. Sarah and Janet feel that they know everything about each other.

Larry and Bob are very close friends. Often, they stay up half the night playing cards or tinkering with Bob's old car, which is constantly breaking down. In times of trouble, they always help each other out. Bob will loan Larry money whenever he runs short; Larry will give Bob a ride home from work whenever their best efforts have failed to revive Bob's beloved 1980 Chevy. They go everywhere together—to the bars, to play basketball, on double dates. Larry and Bob feel they are the best of buddies.

Do these two descriptions seem reasonable to you? Based on your own experience and your observations of others, do you believe that women's friendships tend to be like Sarah and Janet's, while men's friendships tend to be like Larry and Bob's? If so, you are in agreement with a good deal of research on gender differences in friendship that shows that women's friendships are usually characterized by **emotional sharing,** whereas men's friendships revolve around **common activities** (Fehr, 1996; Winstead, Derlega, & Rose, 1997; Wright, 1998).

In focusing on gender differences in friendships, Fehr and others have found additional generalizations about how men and women's friendships differ. These include:

- young girls tend to interact in pairs, while boys are more likely to play in groups;
- women have "holistic" (all-purpose) friendships with one another covering many areas of experience, while men have "circumscribed" relationships with different partners for different things (Wright, 1998, pp. 43, 53);
- women spend more time talking to friends on the phone;
- men and women talk about different topics; for instance, men are more likely to talk about sports, whereas women are more likely to talk about relationships and personal issues;
- women's self-disclosure to women is higher than men's self-disclosure to men;
- women's friendships involve more social support, especially emotional support, than men's;
- women are more likely to express feelings of love and affection in their friendships than are men; and
- women's same-sex friendships tend to be closer than men's.

Terms used roughly 20 years ago by Wright (1982) seem to remain pithy and accurate descriptors of two different, gender-related approaches: Women's friendships are "face-to-face," whereas men's are "side-by-side."

While developing a portrait of the differences in men and women's friend-ships, we should recognize that there are exceptions to the rule, and all close friendships involve some of the same key elements. In the discussion of gender differences in friendship, the caveats are more than mere minor qualifications to the general principles. Canary and Dindia (1998) divided researchers con-cerned with gender differences in interaction into two camps: those with what they called "alpha biases" and those with "beta biases." Those with an alpha bias observe that gender differences are pervasive, and they accentuate the dif-ferences between men's and women's friendships. Illustrative of this camp, Berscheid and Reis (1998) stress that "gender differences, in fact, are ubiquitous in relationship findings" (p. 198). Those with a beta bias note that the magni-tudes of any differences are small and may be due to other factors than gender. For them, men and women's friendships are similar in more ways and to a greater degree than they are dissimilar (Wright, 1998). In this vein, Winstead and her associates conclude that "In sum, research indicates that women's and men's best and close same-sex friendships probably are more similar than they are different" (Winstead et al., 1997, p. 123).

Both camps may have a point. In an integrative reconciliation of these two perspectives, Wright (1998) distinguished the themes of agency (e.g., activi-ties) and communion (e.g., intimacy, expressiveness, and self-disclosure) in friendships. Wright suggested that any gender differences on the first dimen-sion are relatively small, whereas the differences on the second dimension are larger.

Why, then, are men's same-sex friendships less intimate than women's? It's not a matter of how they define intimacy, because men and women think of intimacy in much the same way (Reis, 1998). Is it a matter of capacity or choice? That is, are men less capable of forming intimate friendships with each other or just less willing? In most cases, the answer seems to be "less willing." When it is considered socially appropriate, men self-disclose *more* than women do (Derlega, Winstead, Wong, & Hunter, 1985). Indeed, Reis, Senchak, and Solomon (1985) maintained that men are fully capable of forming intimate friendships with other men when the circumstances support such closeness—but they generally choose not to do so because such intimacy is typically less socially acceptable than female-to-female intimacy. Support for this view can be found in cross-cultural studies like those we mentioned briefly in chapter 5: The magnitude of gender differences in the intimacy of interactions with same-sex friends varies as a function of culture (Reis, 1998). In cultures where expressions of affection and intimacy between men are discouraged (such as the United States and Germany), gender differences are marked. In contrast, in societies where cross-sex friendships are discouraged and same-sex intimacy is fostered, the sex difference in intimacy disappears. So, why don't North American norms support more intimacy in men's friendships? Three factors probably play a part (Bank & Hansford, 2000): homophobia (generalized dis-like of homosexuals), gender roles that support a stoic masculine identity, and emotional constraint (a prevailing reluctance to express worries and emotions to others). In general, the lower intimacy of men's friendships isn't due to a lack of ability; it's a choice supported by cultural pressures that play "an important role in shaping men's reluctance to engage in intimate interactions with one another" (Reis, 1998, p. 225).

Individual Differences in Friendship

Need for Intimacy

Besides the effects of gender, people also take different approaches to friendship on the basis of their personal needs. Consider, for example, the **need for intimacy**, N_{int}. "The intimacy motive," according to Dan McAdams (1985, p. 87), "is a recurrent preference or readiness for warm, close and communicative exchange with others—an interpersonal interaction perceived as an end in itself rather than as a means to an another end." The need for intimacy is associated with less controlling social behavior that emphasizes the depth and quality of social relations. Those with a high N_{int} experience a greater sense of personal well-being and are more trusting and confiding in their relationships than are those who have lower needs for intimacy (McAdams & Bryant, 1987; McAdams, Healy, & Krause, 1984).

A need for intimacy may play a particularly important role in close friendships. The friendships of individuals high in the need for intimacy involve high levels of self-disclosure, the desire to avoid separation, and a belief in the importance of loyalty between friends. McAdams and his collaborators have documented these differences in several studies that involved participants of various ages (see McAdams, 1985). For instance, in an investigation with fourth and sixth graders, McAdams asked children about their friendships in both October and May. Compared to children low in intimacy motivation, those high in N_{int} were less likely to be disliked or rejected by their peers. They also knew more about their friends and were more likely to keep the same friends from fall to spring.

In a complementary study of 105 college students, McAdams collected reports of interactions that had occurred between friends during the past two weeks (see McAdams, 1985). He particularly focused upon episodes that strengthened or weakened their relationships. In situations that strengthened relationships, students high in need for intimacy disclosed more and listened more. In low points in their relationships, those high in need for intimacy blamed their partner less and were more likely to achieve a reconciliation.

There is also some evidence that the need for intimacy may contribute to long-term positive life outcomes. In a longitudinal study, McAdams and Vaillant (1982) related the social motives of a group of male college graduates at age 30 to their psychosocial adjustment almost two decades later. Those who had been high in N_{int} when young were better adjusted when older. These findings complement the evidence on the role of friends in old age in suggesting that, in the long run, the quality of one's friendships matter to one's well-being.

Depression

If N_{int} has a salutary role in friendships, are there personality attributes that can have a detrimental role? The answer is yes, and one candidate is depression. In general, when people experience the gloomy, dour moods of depression, others don't like them much. Studies of interactions that involve depressed people demonstrate that "rejection of depressed persons is consistent across studies and methodologies" (Gurtman, 1986, p. 99). For example, Coyne (1976) had female undergraduates engage in telephone conversations with depressed and nondepressed female psychiatric outpatients. Those who interacted with a depressed patient were more rejecting of their partner. Using a different methodology, Hammen and Peters (1978) had undergraduates interact with a confederate who did or did not portray a depressed role. Those undergraduates getting to know a "depressed" confederate manifested greater interpersonal rejection and less interest in further interaction than did those getting to know a "nondepressed" confederate.

Complementing the results on specific interactions, Gotlib and Whiffen (1991, p. 182) conclude "the results of a considerable number of studies converge to suggest that, compared to nondepressed persons, depressed individuals report having smaller and less supportive social networks." They also cite studies showing that depressed women are less likely to have an intimate confidant, that depressed people consider a higher proportion of their interactions to be unpleasant, and that depressed people report fewer close friends.

Why is it that depressed people tend to have impoverished friendships? One explanation starts with the proposition that they put others in a bad mood, and this then generalizes to their friends' judgments of them (see Coyne, 1976; Joiner & Metalsky, 1995; Joiner, Metalsky, Katz, & Beach, 1999). Advocates of this position also argue that depressed people seek reassurances that they are liked, but when reassurances are offered, depressed people tend to question their sincerity. Going one step further, Joiner and Metalsky maintain that receiving positive feedback is inconsistent with depressed people's self-concepts. Thus, in addition to seeking reassurances, depressed people are likely to seek negative feedback, too. Joiner and Metalsky (1995) believe that the contradictory nature of the depressed person's reassurance and negativistic self-confirmation seeking may alienate others.

To test their view, they conducted a study of college roommates who had been unacquainted before they began sharing a dorm room together. As expected, depressed roommates were both less positively evaluated and more likely to be avoided. Consistent with their explanation of this basic phenomenon, this rejection of depressed individuals was especially strong when the depressed roommate engaged in high reassurance and negative feedback seeking.

Another possible factor in the rejection and smaller social networks of depressed people are their social skills. Gotlib and Whiffen (1991) have reviewed studies showing that depressed people behave differently in social interactions than do nondepressed people. For example, in comparison to nondepressed participants in these studies, depressed individuals:

were less skillful at solving interpersonal problems,

spoke more slowly and more monotonously,

took longer to respond to others' verbalizations,

maintained less eye contact,

made less appropriately timed verbal responses, and

were more self-focused and negatively toned in their conversations.

As Gotlib and Whiffen note, depressed people themselves feel they are less so-cially competent than do nondepressed people. Presumably this contributes to their having difficulty establishing and maintaining friendships.

We have been focusing on the role that depression plays in relationships. We should note, however, that this is probably a two-way street. Dating back to seminal studies in the 1970s (e.g., Brown & Harris, 1978), psychologists have been sensitive to how the lack of intimate friendships and social support con-tributes to people becoming depressed.

CHAPTER SUMMARY

The Nature of Friendship

Attributes of Friendships. This chapter has considered friendships, de-scribing their nature, tracing their course over the life cycle and examining how they differ for different types of people. Fehr (1996, p. 7) has defined *friendship* as a "voluntary, personal relationship, typically providing intimacy and assis-tance, in which the two parties like one another and seek each other's com-pany" (1996, p. 7). Friendships involve affective, shared or communal, and sociable elements.

The Rules of Friendship. Friendships also have rules, the shared beliefs among members of a culture about what behaviors friends should (or should not) perform. Although not always followed, rules help relationships go more smoothly.

Friendship Across the Life Cycle

Infancy. Infants attend to the human face. Toddlers engage in parallel play and may form rudimentary friendships.

Childhood. Both a cognitive and a social needs model have been offered to describe the changing nature of children's friendships. According to Selman's cognitive model, there are five levels of children's understanding of friendships:

- Momentary Playmates, in which young children ages 3 to 7 consider those with whom they are playing at the moment to be their friends,
- One-Way Assistance, in which children ages 4 to 9 are aware of their friends' likes and dislikes but primarily value their friends for what they will do for oneself,
- Fairweather Cooperation, in which elementary school children ages 6 to 12 see friendships as following rules and serving both parties' interests—so long as everything is going well,

- Intimate-Mutual Sharing (ages 9 to 15), in which friendships are seen as exclusive relationships and children become concerned with their friends' interests and internal attributes, and
- Autonomous Interdependence (age 12+), in which adolescents understand that we have networks of relationships, that relationships involve both dependence and autonomy, and subtleties are better understood.

According to Buhrmester and Furman's model of emerging needs, peer group acceptance is crucial in the juvenile era (ages 6 to 9), intimate exchange becomes central in the preadolescent period, and sexuality erupts in adolescence.

Research shows that children often have imaginary friends, and these characters can serve a positive function in children's development. Meta-analyses show that isolated, rejected children are at risk for dropping out of school before high school graduation, engaging in criminal behavior, and exhibiting poor psychological adjustment.

Adolescence. As children go from the elementary school years to young adulthood, their relationships shift from family to peers. At the beginning of this period, children's friendships tend to be organized in terms of same-sex cliques. These lead to larger crowds and dating, and finally pair-based relationships. In terms of changing aspects of attachment during this phase of life, proximity seeking changes first, followed by the safe haven and finally the secure base functions. In adolescence, peer relations are characterized by support, conflict, and peer pressure.

Young Adulthood. Going away to university can disrupt friendships, especially for less socially skilled students. But by the end of their first year, most students have satisfying social networks. Erikson and others consider intimacy a key developmental task of young adulthood. Consistent with this viewpoint, in Reis et al.'s (1993) diary study, the average intimacy level of the participants' interactions was higher six to seven years after college than it was while they were undergraduates. But increased intimacy was not accompanied by increased satisfaction.

Midlife. Knowledge about midlife friendships has been called "suggestive rather than conclusive." Age differences in friendships are not as well mapped or as dramatic as they might be. Nonetheless, fairly solid evidence links life events and role influences to midlife friendships: courtship, marriage, and parenthood each generally are associated with declines in friendships, but they may be accompanied by increases in kin relations.

Old Age. In old age, sociability generally drops. Of the three explanations of this (in terms of barriers to activities, disengagement, or socioemotional selectivity), we favor the socioemotional selectivity perspective. This view predicts that restricted time frames shift people toward more emotionally close relationships and permit distant relationships to atrophy. Friendships in old age are associated with morale and well-being.

Differences in Friendship

Gender Differences in Same-Sex Friendships. In general, women's friendships are based on emotional sharing (face-to-face) and men's on engaging in common activities (side-by-side). Women also regard their same-sex friendships more favorably than men regard theirs. It is likely that male friendships are less intimate because, at least in the United States and Canada, such intimacy is less socially acceptable.

Individual Differences in Friendship. The need for intimacy is a social motive that prompts individuals to seek out social contact. N_{int} involves the desire to maintain many rewarding interpersonal relationships; it is associated with more passive, less controlling social behavior that emphasizes depth and quality of social relations. The need for intimacy may play a particularly important role in the development of close friendships and may contribute to long-term adjustment.

Depression, on the other hand, is associated with social rejection and having smaller social networks. Depressed people lack social skills. They may also put others in a negative mood that influences others' evaluations of them. According to Joiner and his associates, depressed people paradoxically seek both reassurances and confirmation of their negativistic self-concepts in a way that may alienate others.

Love

Here's an interesting question: If someone had all the other qualities you desired in a spouse, would you marry that person if you were not in love with him or her? Most people reading this text would say no. At the end of the twentieth century, huge majorities of American men and women considered romantic love to be necessary for marriage (Simpson, Campbell, & Berscheid, 1986). Along with all the other characteristics people want in a spouse—such as warmth, physical attractiveness, and dependability—young adults in Western cultures insist on romance and passion as a condition for marriage. What makes this remarkable is that it's such a new thing. Throughout history, the choice of a spouse has usually had little to do with romantic love (de Rougemont, 1956); people married each other for political, economic, practical, and family reasons, but they did not marry because they were in love with each other. Even in North America, people have only recently begun to feel that marriage requires love. In 1967, 76 percent of women and 35 percent of men *would* have married an otherwise perfect partner whom they did not love (Kephart, 1967). Now, most people would refuse such a marriage.

In a sense, then, we have embarked on a bold experiment. Never before has a culture considered love to be an essential reason to marry. People experience romantic passion all over the world (Jankowiak & Fischer, 1992), but most cultures still do not consider it a precondition for marriage (Dion & Dion, 1996). North Americans use romance as a reason to marry to an unprecedented degree (Sprecher et al., 1994). Is this a good idea? If there are various, overlapping types of "love" and different types of lovers—and worse, if passion and romance decline over time—marriages based on love may often be prone to confusion and, perhaps, disappointment.

In this chapter, we will examine these possibilities and try to avoid those problems by examining what social scientists have to say about love. We'll start with a brief history of love and then ponder different varieties of love and different types of lovers. Then, we'll finish with a question of substantial interest: Does love last? By the time you're done with this chapter, you'll have a much better understanding of the complexities of love.

A BRIEF HISTORY OF LOVE

Our modern belief that spouses should love one another is just one of many perspectives with which different cultures have viewed the experience of love (de Rougemont, 1956; Hunt, 1959). Over the ages, attitudes toward love have varied on at least four dimensions:

- Cultural value: Is love a desirable or undesirable state?
- Sexuality: Should love be sexual or nonsexual?
- Sexual orientation: Should love involve homosexual or heterosexual partners?
- Marital status: Should we love our spouses or is love reserved for others?

Different societies have drawn upon these dimensions to create some strikingly different patterns of what love is, or should be.

In ancient Greece, for instance, passionate attraction to another person was considered a form of madness that had nothing to do with marriage or family life. Instead, the Greeks admired platonic love, the nonsexual adoration of a beloved person that was epitomized by love between two men.

Heterosexual love took on more positive connotations in the concept of "courtly love" in the twelfth century. Courtly love required knights to seek love as a noble quest, diligently devoting themselves to an aristocratic lady love. It was very idealistic, very elegant, and—at least in theory—nonsexual. It was also explicitly adulterous. In courtly love, the male partner was expected to be unmarried and the female partner married—to someone else! In the Middle Ages, marriage was not expected to be romantic; in contrast, it was a deadly serious matter of politics and property.

Over the next 500 years, people came to believe that passionate love could be desirable and ennobling, but that it was usually doomed. Either the lovers would be prevented from being with each other (often because they were married to other people), or death would overtake one or the other (or both) before their love could be fulfilled. It was not until the seventeenth and eighteenth centuries that Europeans, especially the English, began to believe that romantic passion could occasionally result in a "happy ending." Still, the notion that one *ought* to feel passion and romance for one's husband or wife was not a widespread idea.

Even now, the assumption that romantic love should be linked to marriage is the exception rather than the rule (Xiaohe & Whyte, 1990). Nevertheless, as a reader of this book, you probably do think love and marriage go together. Why should your beliefs be different from those of most people throughout history? Why has the acceptance of and enthusiasm for marrying for love been most complete in North America? Probably because of America's individualism and economic prosperity (which allow most young adults to live away from home and choose their own marital partners) and its lack of a caste system or ruling class. The notion that individuals (instead of families) should choose marriage partners because of emotional attachments (not economic concerns) makes more sense to Americans than it does to many other peoples of the world.

In any case, let's consider all the different views of love we just encountered:

- Love is madness.
- Love has little to do with marriage.
- The best love occurs among people of the same sex.
- Love need not involve sexual contact.
- Love is a noble quest.
- Love is doomed.
- Love can be happy and fulfilling.
- Love and marriage go together.

Some of these distinctions simply reflect ordinary cultural and historical variations (Sternberg, 1998). However, these different views may also reflect an important fact: There may be diverse forms of love. In the next section, we consider the various types of love that have been explored in recent theory and research.

TYPES OF LOVE

Advice columnist Ann Landers was once contacted by a woman who was perplexed because her consuming passion for her lover fizzled soon after they were married. Ms. Landers suggested that what the woman had called "the love affair of the century" was "not love at all. It was one set of glands calling to another" (Landers, 1982, p. 2). There was a big distinction, Ms. Landers asserted, between horny infatuation and real love, which was deeper and richer than mere passion. Love was based in tolerance, care, and communication, Landers argued; it was "friendship that has caught fire" (p. 12).

Does that phrase characterize your experiences with romantic love? Is there a difference between romantic love and infatuation? According to a leading theory of love experiences, the answer to both questions is probably yes.

The Triangular Theory of Love

Robert Sternberg (1986, 1987) proposed that three different building blocks combine to form different types of love. The first component of love is **intimacy.** It includes the feelings of warmth, understanding, communication, support,

and sharing that often characterize loving relationships. The second component is **passion,** which is characterized by physical arousal and desire. Passion
often takes the form of sexual longing, but any strong emotional need that is
satisfied by one's partner fits this category. The final ingredient of love is **commitment,** which includes the decisions to devote oneself to a relationship and
to work to maintain it. Commitment is mainly cognitive in nature, whereas intimacy is emotional and passion is a motive, or drive. The "heat" in loving relationships is assumed to come from passion, and the warmth from intimacy; in
contrast, commitment reflects a decision that may not be emotional or temperamental at all.

In Sternberg's theory, each of these three components is said to be one side
of a triangle that describes the love two people share. Each component can vary
in intensity from low to high so that triangles of various sizes and shapes are
possible. In fact, countless numbers of shapes can occur, so to keep things simple, we'll consider the relatively pure categories of love that result when one or
more of the three ingredients is plentiful but the others are very low. As we proceed, you should remember that pure experiences that are this clearly defined
may not be routine in real life.

Nonlove. If intimacy, passion, and commitment are all absent, love does not
exist. Instead, you have a casual, superficial, uncommitted relationship between people who are probably just acquaintances, not friends.

Liking. Liking occurs when intimacy is high but passion and commitment
are very low. Liking occurs in friendships with real closeness and warmth
that do not arouse passion or the expectation that you will spend the rest of
your life with that person. If a friend *does* arouse passion or is missed terribly when he or she is gone, the relationship has gone beyond liking and has
become something else.

Infatuation. Strong passion in the absence of intimacy or commitment is infatuation, which is what people experience when they are aroused by others they barely know. Sternberg (1987) admits that he was painfully
preoccupied with a girl in his tenth-grade biology class whom he rarely
talked to; he pined away for her but never got up the courage to get to
know her. This, he now acknowledges, was nothing but passion. He was
infatuated with her.

Empty love. Commitment without intimacy or passion is empty love. In
Western cultures, this type of love can be seen in burned-out relationships
in which the warmth and passion have died, and the decision to stay is the
only thing that remains. However, in other cultures in which marriages are
arranged, empty love may be the first, rather than final, stage in the
spouses' lives together.

None of the categories mentioned so far may seem much like love to you.
That's probably because each is missing some important ingredient that we associate with being in love—and that is precisely Sternberg's point. Love is a
multifaceted experience, and that becomes clear when we combine the three
components of love to create more complex states.

Love can last a lifetime. But companionate love seems
to endure longer than passionate love for most
people.

Romantic love. When high intimacy and passion occur together, people experience romantic love. Thus, one way to think about romantic love is as a
combination of liking and infatuation. People often become committed to
their romances, but Sternberg argues that commitment is not a defining
characteristic of romantic love. A summer love affair can be very romantic,
for instance, even when both lovers know that it is going to end when the
summer is over.

Companionate love. Intimacy and commitment combine to form love for a
close companion, or companionate love. Here, closeness, communication,
and sharing are coupled with substantial investment in the relationship as
the partners work to maintain a deep, long-term friendship. This type of
love is epitomized by a long, happy marriage in which the couple's youthful passion has gradually died down.

TABLE 8.1. The Triangular Theory of Love: Types of Relationships

	Intimacy	Passion	Commitment
Nonlove	Low	Low	Low
Liking	High	Low	Low
Infatuated love	Low	High	Low
Empty love	Low	Low	High
Romantic love	High	High	Low
Companionate love	High	Low	High
Fatuous love	Low	High	High
Consummate love	High	High	High

Source: Based on Sternberg, 1986.

Fatuous love. Passion and commitment in the absence of intimacy create a foolish experience called fatuous love. This type of love can occur in whirlwind courtships in which two partners marry quickly on the basis of overwhelming passion, but don't know (or necessarily like) each other very well. In a sense, such lovers invest a lot in an infatuation—a risky business.

Consummate love. Finally, when intimacy, passion, and commitment are all present to a substantial degree, people experience "complete," or consummate, love. This is the type of love many people seek, but Sternberg (1987) suggests that it's a lot like losing weight: easy to do for a while, but hard to maintain over time.

Thus, according to the triangular theory of love, diverse experiences can underlie the simple expression, "I love you." (The different types of love are summarized in Table 8.1.) Another complication that makes love tricky is that the three components can change over time, so that people may encounter various types of love in a given relationship (Sternberg, 1986). Of the three, however, passion is assumed to be the most variable by far. It is also the least controllable, so that we may find our desire for others soaring and then evaporating rapidly in changes we cannot consciously control.

Is the theory right? Are these assertions accurate? Consider that, if the triangular theory's characterization of romantic love is correct, one of its major ingredients is a high level of passion that simply may not last. There's much to consider in wondering whether love lasts, however, so we'll put that off until the end of the chapter. For now, let's note that the three components of intimacy, passion, and commitment do all appear to be important aspects of loving relationships (Acker & Davis, 1992; Aron & Westbay, 1996), but they seem to be more highly interrelated than the triangular theory may imply (Whitley, 1993). As Sternberg (1987) admits, for instance, it is probably easier to feel long-lived passion for someone with whom you also share substantial intimacy.

As a result, as we warned you earlier, the clearly defined categories offered by the triangular theory may not seem so distinct in real life. People's actual experiences of love appear to be complex. For instance, a sister's love for her brother is likely to revolve around the central feature of intimacy, as the theory suggests, but it is also likely to include a variety of other mixed feelings (Fehr & Russell, 1991). A father's love for his son is likely to resemble his love for his own father, but the two feelings are also likely to differ in subtle, idiosyncratic ways that the triangular theory does not readily explain. Different types of love probably overlap in a messier, more confusing way than the theory implies (Fehr, 1994).

Nevertheless, the theory offers a very useful framework for addressing different types of love, and whether or not it is entirely correct it identifies two types of love that may be especially likely to occur in many marriages. Let's examine each of them more closely.

Romantic, Passionate Love

Has anyone ever told you, "I love you, but I'm not *in* love with you"? If so, it was probably bad news. As you probably knew, they were trying to say that, "I like you, I care about you, I think you're a marvelous person with wonderful qualities and so forth, but I don't find you sexually desirable" (Myers & Berscheid, 1997, p. 360). Just as the triangular theory of love proposes, sexual attraction (or "passion") appears to be one of the defining characteristics of romantic love (Regan, Kocan, & Whitlock, 1998). So, it's disappointing if your romantic partner says, "I just want us to be friends."

The fact that romantic love involves passion is important. Remarkably, *any* form of strong emotion, good or bad, can influence our feelings of romantic love.

Arousal

A provocative analysis of romantic love by Elaine Hatfield and Ellen Berscheid proposed that passionate attraction is rooted in (1) physiological arousal that is coupled with (2) the belief that another person is the cause of your arousal (Berscheid & Walster, 1974). (This is an idea that you may recognize as an application of Schachter's [1964] two-factor theory of emotion.) Sometimes, the connection between arousal and love is obvious. It's no surprise, for example, that when men become sexually aroused by inspecting sexually explicit material, they report more love for their romantic partners than they do when they're not "turned on" (Dermer & Pyszczynski, 1978; Stephan, Berscheid, & Walster, 1971). But the two-factor theory of passionate love allows for an unexpected twist. Arousal can be attributed to the wrong source—that is, we can make mistakes, or **misattributions,** in interpreting our feelings—and we can thereby create all kinds of interesting complications.

According to the two-factor perspective, romantic love is produced, or at least intensified, when feelings of arousal are attributed to the presence of another attractive person. This can be a *mis*attribution if other influences that are also exciting us are overlooked. One example of this is called **excitation transfer** (Zillmann, 1978, 1984); this occurs when arousal caused by one stimulus combines with additional arousal elicited by a second stimulus, but the first stimulus is ignored. The combined arousal is then thought to be caused only by the second stimulus, which seems more influential than it really is.

Suppose for example, that Fred is afraid of flying, but his fear is not extreme and he doesn't like to admit it to himself. Flying does, however, cause him to be nervous and aroused. Suppose further that Fred takes a flight and finds himself sitting next to Wilma on the plane. With his heart racing and palms sweating, Fred chats with Wilma as the plane takes off. Fred begins to find Wilma terribly attractive, and he starts pondering ways to see her after the flight is over. What accounts for Fred's sudden surge of interest in Wilma? Is she really that appealing to him, or has he taken the real physical arousal of fear and mislabeled it as attraction?

The possibility that fear can fuel sexual attraction was first examined by Dutton and Aron (1974), who conducted a famous experiment on two bridges in a park in Vancouver. One bridge was made of wooden planks that were suspended by wire hanging hundreds of feet over a deep gorge; the bridge had a low railing and bounced and swayed from side to side when people walked on it, and crossing it made most people quite nervous. The other bridge was made of wide, stable logs and was just a few feet off the ground, and most people were perfectly comfortable walking across it. As unaccompanied young men (between 19 and 35 years of age) walked across each bridge, they were met by a research assistant, who was either male or female. The research assistant asked each fellow to answer a few questions and write a brief story in response to a picture he was shown. After that, each man was thanked and invited to give the assistant a call at home if he wanted more information about the study.

The picture that the men wrote a story about was from the Thematic Apperception Test, and it was possible to score each story in terms of sexual imagery. Dutton and Aron found that the men who met a woman on the spooky suspension bridge used more sexual imagery than did any of the other men. In addition, those men were more likely to call the assistant later at her home. Fear had apparently fueled attraction.

Or had it? Some critics responded that it wasn't necessary to rely on complicated processes like misattribution and excitation transfer to explain why romance blossoms in the midst of fear (Kenrick & Cialdini, 1977; Riordan & Tedeschi, 1983). Fondness for those who are with us in a time of distress could simply come from the comfort we take from their presence. If it is reassuring to have others present in a frightening situation, the link between fear and love could be just another example of how social rewards influence attraction (Epley, 1974).

However, further research has indicated that a reward-based explanation does not provide an adequate explanation for the link between arousal and romance. Consider this procedure: You're a young man who runs in place for either 2 minutes or 15 seconds; as a result, either your pulse rate is high and you're breathing hard, or you're just a little more aroused than normal. Then you move to another room and see a videotape of a young woman whom you expect to meet later on. Through the wonders of makeup, the woman is either quite attractive or rather unattractive. What do you think of her? When real research participants reported their reactions, it was clear that that high arousal intensified the men's ordinary responses to the woman (White, Fishbein, & Rutstein, 1981). The attractive version of the woman was always preferred to the unattractive version, of course, but the men liked the attractive model even more—and liked the unattractive model even less—when they were aroused than when they were calm.

Another study demonstrated that the effects of arousal on attraction did not depend on the type of arousal that is produced. In this investigation (White et al., 1981), men listened to one of three tapes:

- *Negatively arousing.* A description of the brutal mutilation and killing of a missionary while his family watched.
- *Positively arousing.* Selections from Steve Martin's comedy album, *A Wild and Crazy Guy.*
- *Neutral.* A boring description of the circulatory system of a frog.

Thereafter, as before, the men viewed a videotape of an attractive or unattractive woman and provided their impressions of her. Arousal again fueled attraction, and it didn't matter what type of arousal it was. When the men had experienced strong emotion—whether by laughing hard at the funny material or by being disgusted by the gory material—they were more attracted to the appealing woman and less attracted to the unappealing woman than they were when they had listened to the boring biology tape.

Taken together, these two studies demonstrate that the association between arousal and romance is not a simple matter of rewards. In both studies, the same principle applied: Arousal intensified subjects' initial emotional reactions, positive or negative, to a member of the other sex. Adrenaline fueled love.

The implications of this research are startling. Is love totally at the mercy of airplanes, bridges, exercise, and comedy routines? Fortunately, the answer is no. Misattribution and excitation transfer have their limits (Marshall & Zimbardo, 1979; Reisenzein, 1983). One limit is imposed by the passing of time. A long delay between initial arousal and subsequent emotional response wipes out the possibility of excitation transfer. Initial arousal dissipates, and no leftover excitation is available to be misattributed (Cantor, Zillmann, & Bryant, 1975).

Another limit may be set by attributional clarity (White & Kight, 1984). If excitation transfer depends on misattribution, then knowing the real reason for any initial arousal may short-circuit the process. If Fred thinks, "Oh boy, here I go again, afraid of flying," he might not be likely to mistake his fear as sexual attraction to Wilma. Some researchers even question whether misattribution is necessary for arousal from one source to fuel some unrelated emotional response (Allen, Kenrick, Linder, & McCall, 1989). Instead, they propose that a simple process of **response facilitation** is involved. Whenever arousal is present, no matter where it comes from or how we interpret it, our predominant response to the situation will be energized. According to this perspective, it doesn't matter whether Fred knows that his initial arousal was elicited by his fear of flying. His heart is still pounding, and in Wilma's presence, his dominant response is sexual attraction; as a result, that response is automatically strengthened by any arousal that accompanies it. In essence, then, the debate between the misattribution and response-facilitation explanations of arousal carryover effects centers on the issue of cognitive control: Does our interpretation of our arousal really make a difference? At the moment, the best answer appears to be "yes, but only to a limited extent." On the one hand, arousal increases attraction even when the source of the arousal is unambiguous (Foster, Witcher, Campbell, & Green, 1998); that is, even if Fred does realize that he's anxious about his plane flight, his nervous arousal is likely to increase his attraction to Wilma. On the other hand, arousal has a stronger effect on attraction when we *don't* know why we're keyed up (Foster et al., 1998). So, both the misattribution and response-facilitation explanations of arousal effects are correct, but neither one tells the whole story.

In any case, there's little doubt that arousal from an unrelated source can intensify our emotional reactions. Think about the implications of this for your own life. Have you ever had a screaming argument with a lover and then found that it was especially sweet to "kiss and make up" a few minutes later? Might your anger have fueled your subsequent passion? Is that what being "in love" is like?

To some degree, it is. One useful measure of the passion component of romantic love is the Passionate Love Scale (Hatfield & Rapson, 1987). The short form of the scale is reprinted in Table 8.2; as you can see, the scale assesses fascination and preoccupation with, high desire for, and strong emotions about the object of one's love. Scores on the Passionate Love Scale increase as someone falls deeper and deeper into love with someone else, only leveling off when the partners become engaged or start living together (Hatfield & Sprecher, 1986). (Note that—as we mentioned earlier—American couples decide to marry or live together when their passion is at a peak.) Interestingly, although there are no differences between men's and women's average passion later on, men report higher passion than women do when they first start dating. As we saw in chapter 4, men tend to be more romantic than women are, and they also tend to "fall in love" more easily than women do (Hatfield & Sprecher, 1986).

In any case, the vision of romantic love that emerges from the Passionate Love Scale is one of need and desire—ecstasy when one is loved in return and agony when one is rejected—and these are clearly responses that burn brighter when one is aroused than when one is calm and relaxed. One researcher has even argued that there is a chemical basis for the elation and excitement of romantic passion (Liebowitz, 1983): We feel passion when our bodies produce increased quantities of phenylethylamine (or PEA), a substance that is chemically related to amphetamines and has similar effects on our moods and energy. From this perspective, romantic passion *is* a form of physical activation and arousal, so arousal and love are closely connected. Moreover, the emotional crash that can follow the end of a romantic love affair is thought to be much like the lethargy and despondency that accompanies withdrawal from amphetamines.

So, one aspect of romantic love is the exhilaration and euphoria of high arousal, and various events that excite us may increase our feelings of love for our partners. Romance is more than just passion, however. It also involves our thoughts.

TABLE 8.2. The Passionate Love Scale (Short Form)

This questionnaire asks you to describe how you feel when you are passionately in love. Some common terms for this feeling are: passionate love, infatuation, love sickness, or obsessive love. Please think of the person whom you love most passionately *right now*. If you are not in love right now, please think of the last person you loved passionately. If you have never been in love, think of the person whom you came closest to caring for in that way. Keep this person in mind as you complete this questionnaire. (The person you choose should be of the opposite sex if you are heterosexual or of the same sex if you are homosexual.) Try to tell us how you felt at the time when your feelings were the most intense.

Answer each item using this scale:

1	2	3	4	5	6	7	8	9
Not at all true			Moderately true			Definitely true		

1. I would feel deep despair if _____ left me.
2. Sometimes I feel I can't control my thoughts; they are obsessively on _____.
3. I feel happy when I am doing something to make _____ happy.
4. I would rather be with _____ than anyone else.
5. I'd get jealous if I thought _____ were falling in love with someone else.
6. I yearn to know all about _____.
7. I want _____—physically, emotionally, mentally.
8. I have an endless appetite for affection from _____.
9. For me, _____ is the perfect romantic partner.
10. I sense my body responding when _____ touches me.
11. _____ always seems to be on my mind.
12. I want _____ to know me—my thoughts, my fears, and my hopes.
13. I eagerly look for signs indicating _____'s desire for me.
14. I possess a powerful attraction for _____.
15. I get extremely depressed when things don't go right in my relationship with _____.

Higher scores on the PLS indicate greater passionate love. Across all 15 items, the average rating per item—add up all your ratings and divide by 15—for both men and women is 7.15.

Source: Hatfield & Sprecher, 1986.

Thought

The two-factor theory of passionate love emphasizes the role of our thoughts and beliefs in accounting for arousal. Thoughts may also be linked to romance in other ways. In particular, romantic lovers are likely to think about each other in ways that differ from the ways they think about their friends. Some of these distinctions are apparent in the contents of a Love Scale and a Liking Scale created by Zick Rubin in 1973. Years before Hatfield and Sprecher created the Passionate Love Scale, Rubin created dozens of statements that reflected a wide range of interpersonal attitudes and asked people to use them to

TABLE 8.3. Rubin's (1973) Love and Liking Scales: Some Example Items

Rubin's Love Scale

1. I feel that I can confide in my partner about virtually anything.
2. If I could never be with my partner, I would be miserable.
3. I would do almost anything for my partner.

Rubin's Liking Scale

1. My partner is one of the most likable people I know.
2. My partner is the sort of person that I would like to be.
3. I think that my partner is unusually well-adjusted.

describe both a lover and a friend. The handful of items that epitomized people's romances ended up on a Love Scale that gives a partial indication of what lovers are thinking.

One theme in the items on the Love Scale is *intimacy,* just as the triangular theory of love defines it. Romance is characterized by openness, communication, and trust (see item 1 in Table 8.3). A second theme, in Rubin's (1973) terminology, is needy *attachment* (see item 2 in Table 8.3). The attachment items describe longing for contact with one's partner that has much in common with the passion we discussed. A last theme on the Love Scale, however, describes feelings that are not mentioned by the triangular theory: *caring.* Romantic lovers report concern for the welfare and well-being of their partners (see item 3). They want to take care of their partners and keep them happy.

Thus, like other efforts to characterize love (e.g., Fehr, 1994; Regan et al., 1998), the Love Scale portrays romantic love as a multifaceted experience that involves both giving (i.e., caring) and taking (i.e., attachment). If you're in love with someone, it's probably partly selfish—you love your partner because of how that person makes you feel—and partly generous; you genuinely care for your partner and will work to satisfy and protect him or her. In addition, these diverse sentiments are experienced with relative intensity and urgency: You'd do *anything* for your partner and be *miserable* without him or her.

Compare those thoughts and feelings to the sorts of things people say about their friends. As you can see in Table 8.3, the Liking Scale seems bland by comparison. People say they like their friends because their friends are nice, well-adjusted, likable people. But they love their lovers because they need them and would do anything the lover asks. There's a fervor to the thoughts that characterize romantic love that is lacking when we just like someone.

Indeed, preoccupation and obsessive thinking about one's partner is part of the passion component of romantic love (Hatfield & Rapson, 1987). Interestingly, however, the connection between love and thought seems to work both ways; if we spend a lot of time thinking about our partners, we may come to feel we love them more than we would have if we hadn't thought about them so much. For instance, on two occasions two weeks apart, researchers asked unmarried young adults how much they thought about and loved their dating

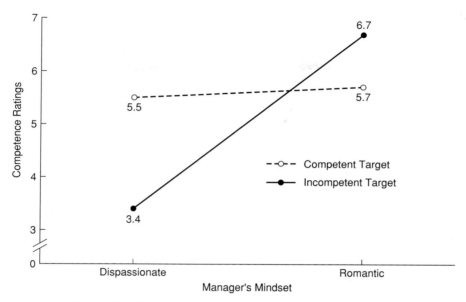

FIGURE 8.1. Love is blind. When men expected to date a woman, they thought her lousy work was much better than it really was.

partners (Tesser & Paulus, 1976). The study showed that the more people loved their partners, the more they thought about them. That's no surprise, but the reverse was true, too: The more people thought about their partners, the more they came to love them later on.

The specific judgments people make of their partners are important, too. As we saw in chapter 4, people tend to hold rosy views of their relationship partners, and their tendency to idealize and glorify their lovers is probably at a peak when they are most in love. In fact, the moment romance enters the picture, people start ignoring or reinterpreting undesirable information about potential partners. Imagine that you're a male college student who is asked to play the role of a supervisor who is evaluating the work of a female subordinate (Goodwin, Fiske, Rosen, & Rosenthal, 1997). You're given a sample of her work that is either coherent and well-written or clumsy and inept. Would you be able to tell the difference between the competent and incompetent work? Of course you would. But what if you knew that you'd be going out on a date with the woman on Friday? Would the possibility of a romance influence your judgment? You may not think so, but when men really participated in a procedure like this, a romantic orientation had a big effect, as Figure 8.1 illustrates. The upcoming date obviously contaminated the men's judgment, magically transforming lousy work into material of much higher quality. The poor work was not perceived to be better than the competent work—that difference was not statistically significant—but any distinction between the good and bad work disappeared entirely when the possibility of romance was in play.

The results of this and other studies (e.g., Gold, Ryckman, & Mosley, 1984) suggest that, in a real way, "love is blind": People underestimate or ignore their lovers' faults. They hold idealized images of their lovers that may differ in meaningful ways from the concrete realities they face. In fact, a major difference between love and friendship may be our imaginations—our lovers are fascinating, mysterious, and appealing in ways our friends are not (Aron, Dutton, Aron, & Iverson, 1989).

Finally, even our thoughts about ourselves can change when we fall in love. Arthur and Elaine Aron, a husband-wife team of social psychologists, suggest that love causes our self-concepts to expand and change (Aron & Aron, 2000). Romantic partners bring us new experiences and new roles, and we gradually learn things about ourselves that we didn't know before. One of the things we usually learn is that a desirable person likes us in return, and that's both rewarding and exciting (Aron et al., 1989). As a result, our self-concepts become more diversified and our self-esteem goes up (Aron, Paris, & Aron, 1995).

All of this is potent stuff. The arousal and cognition that characterize romantic, passionate love involve surging emotion, imagination and idealization, and occasional obsession (Lamm & Wiesmann, 1997; Shaver, Morgan, & Wu, 1996). And it is the presence of this complex, hectic state that leads most North Americans to consider marriage. However, romantic passion may not be the reason they stay married in the years that follow. The longevity of a relationship may have more to do with companionate love.

Companionate Love

Because it does not depend on passion, companionate love is a more settled state than romantic love is. The triangular theory suggests that it is a combination of intimacy and commitment, but we can characterize it more fully as a "comfortable, affectionate, trusting love for a likable partner, based on a deep sense of friendship and involving companionship and the enjoyment of common activities, mutual interests, and shared laughter" (Grote & Frieze, 1994, p. 275). It takes the form of a rich, committed friendship with someone with whom our lives are intertwined (Walster & Walster, 1978).

Sounds pleasant, but isn't it a bit bland compared to the ecstasies of romantic passion? Perhaps so, but you may want to get used to it. When hundreds of couples who had been married at least 15 years were asked why their marriages had lasted, they *didn't* say that they'd do anything for their spouses or be miserable without them, like romantic lovers do (Lauer & Lauer, 1985). Instead, for both men and women, the two most frequent reasons were (1) "My spouse is my best friend," and (2) "I like my spouse as a person." Long-lasting marriages seem to include a lot of companionate love.

Of course, deep friendships also occur often in the context of romantic love. In one study, 44 percent of the young adults in premarital relationships reported that their romantic partner was also their closest friend (Hendrick & Hendrick, 1993). However, when they are a part of romantic love, friendships

---

BOX 8.1

A Type of Love You May Not Want to Experience
Unrequited Love

Have you ever loved someone who did not love you back? You probably have. Depending on the sample, 80 percent (Aron, Aron, & Allen, 1998) to 90 percent of young adults (Baumeister, Wotman, & Stillwell, 1993) report that they have experienced unrequited love: romantic, passionate attraction to someone who did not return that love. It's a common experience that seems to be most frequent in one's late teens, between the ages of 16 and 20 (Hill, Blakemore, & Drumm, 1997). Still, it doesn't strike everybody; it happens to more men than women (Hill et al., 1997), and is more likely to befall people with an anxious/ambivalent attachment style than those with secure or avoidant styles (Aron et al., 1998).

Why do we experience such loves? Several factors may be involved. First, would-be lovers are very attracted to their unwilling targets, and they assume that relationships with them are worth working and waiting for. Second, they optimistically overestimate how much

they are liked in return (Aron et al., 1998). And third, perhaps most importantly, as painful as it is, unrequited love has its rewards. Along with their frustration, would-be lovers experience the real thrill, elation, and excitement of being in love (Baumeister et al., 1993).

It's actually worse to be the target of someone's unwanted adoration. Sure, it's nice to be wanted, but those on the receiving end of unrequited love often find their pursuers' persistence to be intrusive and annoying, and they usually feel guilty when they turn their ardent pursuers down. They are usually nice, "well-meaning people who find themselves caught up in another person's emotional whirlwind and who themselves often suffer acutely as a result" (Baumeister & Wotman, 1992, p. 203). As distressing as it was to gradually realize that the objects of our affection would not become our steady partners, we may have made it harder on them when we fell into unrequited love.

---

are combined (and sometimes confused) with sexual arousal and passion. The predominant importance of friendship in creating the experience is easier to detect in companionate love, when intimacy is paired with commitment, than in romantic love, when intimacy is paired with passion.

Still, as we noted earlier, we may only rarely encounter pure categories of these experiences that are comprised of just two of the components of love and none of the third. Companionate lovers can and do experience passion, and romantic lovers can and do feel commitment. As we experience them, the distinctions between romantic and companionate love are much fuzzier than this discussion may have implied (Fehr, 1988). Nevertheless, if we're willing to tolerate some ambiguity, we can conclude that there appear to be two major types of love that frequently occur in American marriages: a love that's full of passion that leads people to marry, and a love that's full of friendship that underlies marriages that last. We'll return to this point at the end of the chapter.

TABLE 8.4. Styles of Loving

Eros	The erotic lover searches for a person with the right physical appearance, and is eager for an intense relationship.
Ludus	The ludic lover is playful in love and likes to play the field.
Storge	The storgic lover prefers slowly developing attachments that lead to lasting commitment.
Mania	The manic lover is demanding and possessive toward the beloved, and has a feeling of being "out of control."
Agape	The agapic lover is altruistic, loving without concern for receiving anything in return.
Pragma	The pragmatic lover searches for a person with the proper vital statistics: job, age, religion, etc.

Source: Based on Lee, 1977, 1988. Reprinted from Brehm & Kassin, 1990.

Styles of Loving

Another scheme for distinguishing different types of love experiences was offered by sociologist John Alan Lee (1977, 1988), who used Greek and Latin words to describe six styles of love that differ in the intensity of the loving experience, commitment to the beloved, desired characteristics of the beloved, and expectations about being loved in return. (See Table 8.4.) A first style is **eros,** from which the word *erotic* comes. Eros has a strong physical component, and erotic lovers are likely to be heavily influenced by physical appearance and to believe in love at first sight.

The second style, **ludus** (pronounced loo-dus), treats love as an uncommitted game. Ludic lovers are often fickle and (try to) have several different partners at once. In contrast, the third style, **storge,** (store-gay) leads people to de-emphasize strong emotion and seek genuine friendships that gradually lead to real commitment.

The fourth style, **mania,** is demanding and possessive and full of vivid fantasy and obsession. The fifth style, **agape** (ah-gaa-pay), is giving, altruistic, and selfless, and treats love as a duty. Finally, the last style, **pragma,** is practical and pragmatic. Pragma leads people to dispassionately seek partners who will logically be a good match for them.

How useful are these distinctions? Instead of thinking of them as six additional types of love, it may make more sense to consider them as six themes in love experiences that overlap and are differentially related to the types of love identified by Sternberg's triangular theory (Woll, 1989). For instance, romantic love appears to be positively related to eros and agape (remember, it's love as giving *and* love as taking), and negatively related to ludus (which means it's serious business) (Levy & Davis, 1988). Clyde and Susan Hendrick, another husband-wife research team, have developed a Love Attitudes Scale to measure people's endorsement of the six styles, and they have found that men score higher on ludus than women do, whereas women are more storgic and pragmatic than men (Hendrick & Hendrick, 1995; Hendrick, Hendrick, & Dicke, 1998). Other researchers have detected a tendency for people to pair off with others who share similar attitudes toward love (Davis & Latty-Mann, 1987; Morrow, Clark, & Brock, 1995). In general, the love styles remind us of meaningful influences on love (such as practicality) that are sometimes overlooked. Also, differentiating the styles allows researchers to fine-tune their analyses of the diverse experiences people have with love.

INDIVIDUAL DIFFERENCES IN LOVE

Obviously, there are a variety of different feelings people may be experiencing when they say, "I love you." To make things even more complicated, certain people may be more likely than others to experience certain types of love. In this section, we consider relatively enduring differences among individuals that are linked to love. We'll begin by revisiting an idea we introduced in chapter 1: People have global orientations toward close relationships that result from, and subsequently influence, their intimate partnerships.

Attachment Styles

When relationship scientists (e.g., Hazan & Shaver, 1987) began to study attachment styles, they used the same three categories of attachment that had been identified in children by developmental researchers. Thus, as you may remember from chapter 1, early studies distinguished among **secure, avoidant,** and **anxious/ambivalent** orientations to close relationships. Secure people were said to be comfortable with emotional intimacy and interdependency, whereas avoidant people disliked dependency and closeness. Anxious/ambivalent people were said to be clingy, possessive folks who sought more intimacy and reassurance than others were generally willing to provide.

As a wave of studies quickly showed, attachment researchers were on to something. People who had a secure style tended to be more trusting, committed, and satisfied in their romantic relationships than avoidant or anxious people were. They also experienced more positive and fewer negative emotions in their relationships than insecure (i.e., avoidant or anxious/ambivalent) people. On the whole, secure people tended to have more contented, more interdependent, and more intimate romantic relationships than people with insecure styles did (Simpson, 1990).

In particular, it became clear that attachment styles were associated with the manner in which people tried to handle unpleasant emotions (Fuendeling, 1998). When something distressed them, secure people turned to others for comfort and support, and they remained relatively calm. In contrast, avoidant people withdrew from their partners and became hostile, and anxious people (as the name implies) became excessively anxious and fretful (Kobak & Sceery, 1988; Simpson, Rholes, & Nelligan, 1992).

When it came to love, researchers found that a secure style was positively correlated with all three of the components of love; secure people tended to experience high intimacy, passion, and commitment. Secure attachment was also linked to higher levels of the love styles of eros and agape, and lower levels of ludus (Levy & Davis, 1988). Altogether, then, secure attachment was associated with richer experiences of both romantic and companionate love. By comparison, insecure people experienced lower intimacy, passion, and commitment. Avoidant attachment was positively correlated with ludus, reflecting the lower commitment and interdependency of avoidant people, and anxious ambivalence was positively associated with the emotional extremes of mania (Levy & Davis, 1988; Shaver & Hazan, 1988).

A New Conceptualization of Attachment

As you can see, early studies of adults' attachment styles demonstrated that there were meaningful differences among people in the types of love they were likely to have. Results like these attracted attention, and attachment research soon became one of the most active areas of relationship science (see Cassidy & Shaver, 1999). But there were problems: Researchers began to worry that a usual means of assessing attachment styles—asking people which of three paragraphs described them best (look back at Table 1.1)—was a little simplistic. In addition, attachment expert Kim Bartholomew (1990; Bartholomew & Horowitz, 1991) thought that avoidant attachment was more complex than most researchers realized. Bartholomew suggested that there were two ways that people could seem to be avoidant. In one case, people could want relationships with others but be wary of them, fearing rejection and mistrusting others. In the other case, people could be independent and self-reliant, genuinely preferring autonomy and freedom to closeness with others.

Thus, Bartholomew (1990) proposed four general categories of attachment style (see Table 8.5). The first, a **secure** style, remained the same as the secure

TABLE 8.5. Examples of Bartholomew's (1990) Four Categories of Attachment Style

Secure	It is easy for me to become emotionally close to others. I am comfortable depending on others and having others depend on me. I don't worry about being alone or having others not accept me.
Preoccupied	I want to be completely emotionally intimate with others, but I often find that others are reluctant to get as close as I would like. I am uncomfortable being without close relationships, but I sometimes worry that others don't value me as much as I value them.
Fearful	I am uncomfortable getting close to others. I want emotionally close relationships, but I find it difficult to trust others completely, or to depend on them. I worry that I will be hurt if I allow myself to become too close to others.
Dismissing	I am comfortable without close emotional relationships. It is very important to me to feel independent and self-sufficient, and I prefer not to depend on others or have others depend on me.

Source: Bartholomew, 1990.

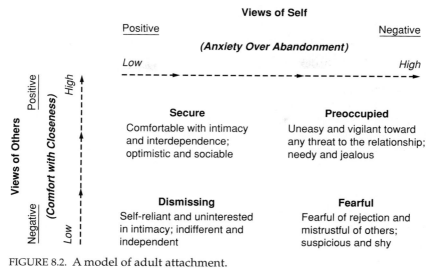

Views of Self

Positive   Negative

(Anxiety Over Abandonment)

Low   High

Secure
Comfortable with intimacy
and interdependence;
optimistic and sociable

Preoccupied
Uneasy and vigilant toward
any threat to the relationship;
needy and jealous

Dismissing
Self-reliant and uninterested
in intimacy; indifferent and
independent

Fearful
Fearful of rejection and
mistrustful of others;
suspicious and shy

Views of Others — Positive / Negative
(Comfort with Closeness) — High / Low

FIGURE 8.2. A model of adult attachment.
(Adapted from Bartholomew, 1990, and Brennan et al., 1998.)

style in the original three categories of attachment. The second, a **preoccupied** style, was a new name for anxious/ambivalence. Bartholomew renamed the category to reflect the fact that, because they nervously depended on others' approval to feel good about themselves, such people greedily sought acceptance and were preoccupied with relationships.

The third and fourth styles emerged from the old avoidant category, with one of them, a **fearful** style, retaining much of the flavor of that old category. Fearful people avoided intimacy with others because of their fears of rejection. Although they wanted others to like them, they worried about the risks of relying on others. In contrast, people with the last style, a **dismissing** style, felt that intimacy with others just wasn't worth the trouble. Dismissing people felt self-sufficient, and they rejected interdependency with others, not really caring much whether others liked them or not.

Bartholomew (1990) described these four revised styles as separate categories of attachment (just as the original three had been), but, in an important theoretical insight, she suggested that they could be arranged along two dimensions that differentiated them. As Figure 8.2 shows, Bartholomew proposed that people's global judgments of themselves and of others could both be relatively positive or rather negative, and the combination of the two created the four different categories. Secure people were thought to hold favorable opinions of both themselves and others; as a result, they happily pursued intimacy with other people. In contrast, fearful people held negative views of themselves and others, leading them to expect the worst from their relationships. Preoccupied people liked others but doubted themselves, causing them to be overly dependent on others, whereas dismissing people liked themselves but didn't respect others very much.

Researchers have determined that Bartholomew's predictions about the links between attachment styles and self-esteem are generally correct (e.g., Brennan & Morris, 1997; Diehl, Elnick, Bourbeau, & Labouvie-Vief, 1998). In addition, it's now widely accepted (see Brennan, Clark, & Shaver, 1998; Sanford, 1997) that it's useful to think about the "self" and "other" dimensions in terms of their interpersonal effects. People's judgments of others describe their *comfort with closeness,* the ease and trust with which a person can accept interdependent intimacy with others, whereas their judgments of themselves influence *anxiety over abandonment,* people's dread that others will find them unworthy and leave them. Secure people take great comfort in closeness with others and do not worry that others will mistreat them; as a result they gladly seek closeness with others. In contrast, with all three of the other styles, people are burdened with anxiety or discomfort that leaves them less at ease in close relationships. Preoccupied people want closeness but anxiously fear rejection. Dismissing people don't worry about rejection but don't like closeness. And fearful people get it from both sides, being uncomfortable with intimacy *and* worrying it won't last.

Importantly, the two themes of comfort with closeness and anxiety over abandonment are *continuous* dimensions that range from low to high. This means that, although it's convenient to talk about the four styles as if they were discrete, pure categories that do not overlap, it's not really accurate to do so (Fraley & Waller, 1998). This is the same subtlety we encountered when we discussed Sternberg's (1987) triangular theory of love; different types of love were easy to distinguish when intimacy, passion, and commitment were all very high or very low, but real emotions are more complex than that. Sternberg's classification scheme gets muddy, and some different types of love overlap, when the three components of love are all present to a moderate degree. So it is with attachment style. When they are simply asked to pick which one of the four paragraphs in Table 8.5 fits them best, most people, usually around 60 percent, describe themselves as being securely attached (Mickelson, Kessler, & Shaver, 1997). However, if someone has moderate anxiety over abandonment and middling comfort with closeness, which category fits him or her best? The use of any of the four categories is rather arbitrary in the middle range of anxiety and comfort, where the boundaries of the categories meet (Bartholomew & Shaver, 1998).

So don't treat the neat classifications in Figure 8.2 too seriously. The better, more sophisticated way to think about attachment is that there seem to be two important themes that shape people's global orientations toward relationships with others. Each is important, and if you compare high scorers on either dimension to low scorers on that dimension, you're likely to see meaningful differences in the manner in which those people conduct their relationships. On the other hand, small differences on either dimension may not be important, even if they would lead you, for instance, to label some people as secure and others as dismissing. Indeed, some recent studies of attachment have deemphasized the use of the four distinct style names, describing people with regard to their relative standing on the two dimensions of anxiety and comfort instead of labeling them as secure, preoccupied, fearful, or dismissing (e.g., Feeney, 1999).

Nevertheless, the four labels are so concise that they are still widely used, so keep your wits about you. Before 1990, researchers spoke of only three attachment styles: secure, avoidant, and anxious/ambivalent. Now they routinely speak of four styles, but they treat them as convenient labels for sets of anxiety and comfort scores, not as distinctly different categories that have nothing in common. The biggest distinction may be between people who are "secure" and those who are not (who have high anxiety over abandonment or low comfort with closeness, or both).

And attachment styles are worth studying. If either partner in a romantic relationship is insecure, both partners tend to be dissatisfied (Jones & Cunningham, 1996). Perhaps this should not be surprising: Secure people have more self-confidence and tend to be better adjusted than insecure people are (Diehl et al., 1998), so they may be easier to love. In general, comfort with closeness appears to be associated with the extent to which people self-disclose to and support their partners, and the extent to which they feel dependent on and committed to their relationships. By comparison, anxiety over abandonment is correlated with jealousy, high levels of conflict, low levels of compromise, and a lack of trust (Feeney, 1999). Higher anxiety over abandonment also seems to make married men more likely to have extramarital affairs (Lokey & Schmidt, 2000). Add it all up, and, as we noted above, secure people experience more intense romantic and companionate love than insecure people do (Levy & Davis, 1988).

People typically have several different partners, such as lovers, parents, and friends, who are important attachment figures at any one time, and they may be relatively secure in some of those relationships and somewhat insecure in others (Trinke & Bartholomew, 1997). A person's attachment quality can vary from partner to partner (Cook, 2000). Still, the global attitudes people have about relationships are important. The attachment styles we have described here occur all over the world, and they are clearly associated with the loves people experience (Ijsendoorn & Sagi, 1999). Not only are there different types of love, there are different types of lovers.

Age

Another slowly changing personal characteristic that may affect love is one's age. As we suggested in chapter 2, age can be a tricky variable to study because it's usually confounded with experience and history. As people age, they may have (a) relationships of longer duration and (b) more relationships overall. So if love does seem to change with age, it may be hard to tell whether it is really people's age that makes the difference or if it is the length of their present relationships, the extent of their previous romantic experience, or some combination of all three.

With these cautions in mind, we can note that there is evidence that some older people may actually hold more romantic attitudes about love than younger married people do. One study found that grandparents were simply less romantic than young adults (Hieger & Troll, 1973). However, Knox (1970) found that (a) people who had been married for five years were less romantic than high school seniors, but that (b) people who had been married for 20 years or more were the most romantic of all. Similarly, Munro and Adams (1978)

240   PART THREE: Friendship and Intimacy

found that married couples whose children had left home expressed stronger beliefs in the power of love than did people who were at an earlier stage in life (i.e., high school students, young marrieds without children, and married couples with children). It's conceivable that the link between romance and age is a curve in the shape of a shallow, wide-mouthed U: People may be especially romantic when they decide to marry as young adults, less romantic when some of the magic fades and they get mortgages and children, and more romantic again when they're older and the kids finally leave the nest. Or, at least this pattern may pertain to those who have successfully managed to keep their marriages going for 20 years! Other people may find themselves getting old with attitudes that are not romantic at all.

One thing seems clear about age: Most people mellow. When researchers compared spouses in their sixties to those in their forties, they found that the older couples interacted with more good cheer, but less physical arousal. Their emotions were less intense, but more positive on the whole, even in marriages that were not particularly happy at the time (Levenson, Carstensen, & Gottman, 1994). Some of the burning, urgent, emotional intensity that leads young people to marry seems to dwindle with time, to be replaced with a more genial and more mature outlook on love.

Men and Women

A potentially important individual difference that does not change with time is one's sex. However, on the whole, men and women are more similar than different when it comes to love (Canary & Emmers-Sommer, 1997; Hendrick & Hendrick, 1995). They experience the various types of love similarly, and there are no differences in the proportions of men and women who have each attachment style (Feeney & Noller, 1990; Fehr, 1994). Women do tend to experience stronger emotions than men do; on average, women's emotions are more intense and more volatile than men's (Brody & Hall, 1993). Nevertheless, studies rarely find any differences between men and women on measures of romantic feelings such as the Love Scale (Rubin, 1973) and the Passionate Love Scale (Hatfield & Sprecher, 1986). Evidently, as we have noted before, it's just plain silly to think that men come from one planet and women come from another.

On the other hand, as we saw in chapter 4, men tend to possess more romantic attitudes than women do. Men are more likely than women to think that if you just love someone enough, nothing else matters (Sprecher & Metts, 1989). They're also more likely to believe that it's possible to experience "love at first sight," and that may be why they tend to fall in love faster than women do (Hatfield & Sprecher, 1986). In fact, if you combine these trends with the sex differences in love styles we mentioned—remember, women are more pragmatic than men are, and men are more likely to treat love as a game (Hendrick et al., 1998)—you may find, as researchers have, that women tend to be more cautious than men when it comes to love (Kenrick, Sadalla, Groth, & Trost, 1990). Once they're in love, the experiences of men and women are very similar. However, women tend to be more selective about *whom* they love, feeling passion more slowly and limiting their affection to partners of relatively higher intelligence, status, and other desirable qualities (Kenrick et al., 1990). Men tend to be less discriminating, a fact that is reflected by their greater acceptance, on average, of casual sex (Hendrick et al., 1998). (All of these patterns, we should remind you, are consistent with the evolutionary model, which predicts that women *should* be cautious about whom they love because their parental investments in any offspring are so much greater than men's [Buss, 1999]. In contrast, the sociocultural model attributes women's greater selectivity to their traditionally lower status in many societies; according to this perspective, careful selection of a high-status mate is one of the few means available to women to obtain resources that are more accessible to men [Eagly & Wood, 1999]. Which explanation do you find more convincing?)

In any case, a person's gender may have more influence on love experiences than his or her sex does. Compared to the macho men and feminine women in traditional couples, nontraditional, androgynous men and women appear to share greater intimacy but less attachment, or romantic dependency, on Rubin's Love Scale (Critelli, Myers, & Loos, 1986). (However, traditional and nontraditional couples do not differ in their specific reports of sexual arousal and passion.) As a result, even if traditional and nontraditional couples get similar scores on the Love Scale, they may do so for different reasons. And over time, because of their greater intimacy, nontraditional couples may end up feeling greater companionate love for each other.

DOES LOVE LAST?

So, how does the passage of time affect love? Does love last? This is a difficult question to answer conclusively because, as we've seen, there are different types of loves and idiosyncratic types of lovers. Your experiences with love through the years may differ from those of another person reading this book. Nevertheless, the prototypical North American marriage occurs when people in their twenties who are flushed with romantic passion pledge to spend the rest of their lives together, probably expecting their passion to last. Will it? Despite the couples' good intentions, the best answer relationship science can provide is, probably not, at least not to the extent the partners expect.

The simple truth is that romantic love decreases after people marry (Sprecher & Regan, 1998). Scores on romantic and passionate love scales go down as the years go by (Acker & Davis, 1992; Tucker & Aron, 1993), and that's among couples who manage to stay married! After several years, husbands and wives are no longer claiming to the same degree that they'd do anything for each other or that they melt when they look into each other's eyes. Figure 8.3 provides an interesting example of this in a study conducted in India that compared couples who chose to marry for love—like most North Americans do—to couples whose marriages were arranged for them by their families (Gupta & Singh, 1982). Romantic couples who were still married after ten years reported much lower scores on Rubin's (1973) Love Scale than did those who had only been married for a year or two. (Couples who divorced and were not married that long were not included in the data you see in Figure 8.3. What do you think their love scores would be?)

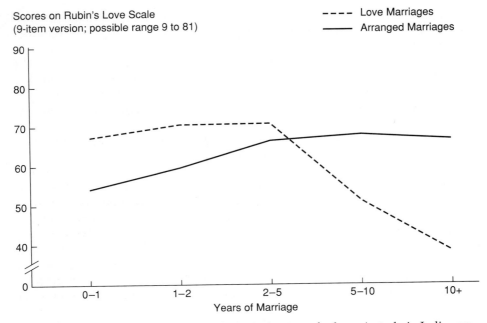

FIGURE 8.3. Romantic love decreases after people marry for love. A study in India compared arranged marriages to those in which the spouses married because they were in love. Just as the average American marriage, romantic love decreased substantially as the years went by after people married for love.

What's more, the decrease in a couple's romantic love may sometimes be quite rapid. After only two years of marriage, average spouses express affection for each other only half as often as they did when they were newlyweds (Huston & Chorost, 1994). Worldwide, divorces occur more frequently in the fourth year of marriage than at any other time (Fisher, 1995). Many, if not most, couples fail to maintain the urgent longing for each other that leads them to marry in the first place.

Why Doesn't Romantic Love Last?

In fact, if we consider it carefully, there may be several reasons why we should expect romantic love to decline over time (Walster & Walster, 1978). First, **fantasy** enhances romance. As we noted earlier, love is blind to some degree. Flushed with passion, lovers tend to idealize their partners and minimize or ignore information that should give them pause. In one study, men who learned that they had little in common with a woman were not attracted to her before they actually met her; however, if they did share a brief interaction, the men shrugged off their knowledge that they were incompatible and found her desirable anyway (Gold et al., 1984). Imagination, hope, and flights of fancy can make people who are quite different from us seem appealing, at least temporarily. The problem, of course, is that fantasy erodes with time and experience. To the extent that romance is enhanced by idealized glorification of one's partner, we should expect it to decline when people begin living together and reality slowly intrudes.

In addition, sheer **novelty** adds excitement and energy to new loves. A first kiss is often much more thrilling than most of the thousands that follow, and when people are invigorated and fascinated by a new partner, they may be unable to appreciate how familiar and routine that same lover may seem 30 years later. Indeed, novelty causes sexual arousal in other species. For instance, if a male rat is caged with a female in estrus, he'll mate with her repeatedly until he appears to be sexually exhausted; however, if the first female is then replaced with another receptive female, the male will mount her with renewed interest and vigor. By continuing to replace an old partner with a new one, researchers can elicit two to three times as many ejaculations from the male as would have occurred with only the single female (Dewsbury, 1981). Researchers call this effect of novelty on arousal the *Coolidge effect*, referring to an old story that may or may not be true. Supposedly, President Calvin Coolidge and his wife were once touring a chicken farm when Mrs. Coolidge noticed a rooster covering one hen after another. Impressed with the rooster's prowess, she asked the guide to mention the rooster to the president. When he heard about the rooster's stamina, Coolidge is said to have reflected a moment and then replied, "Please tell Mrs. Coolidge that there is more than one hen" (Walster & Walster, 1978).

Does novelty have similar effects on people? It might. Engaging in novel, arousing activities together gets romantic couples to feel more in love with each other (Aron, Norman, Aron, McKenna, & Heyman, 2000). Further, Roy Baumeister and Ellen Bratslavsky (1999) have suggested that romantic passion is directly related to changes in our relationships. When we're falling in love, everything is new and intimacy is increasing, and passion is likely to be very high. However, once a relationship is established, and novelty is lost, passion slowly subsides. Some support for this view is found in the results of a broad survey of American sexuality that showed that an average couple's frequency of intercourse (one measure of their passion for each other) declines continually over the course of their marriage (Call, Sprecher, & Schwartz, 1995). This decline is obviously confounded with age, as Figure 8.4 shows. However, people who remarry and change partners increase their frequency of sex, at least for a while, so aging does not seem to be wholly responsible for the decline of passion with time.

Finally, as Figure 8.4 also implies, **arousal** fades as time goes by. As we've seen, there's no question that physical arousal—such as a rapid pulse rate and fast, shallow breathing—fuels passion (Foster et al., 1998). But it's impossible to stay keyed up forever! In the case of romantic love, the brain may gradually habituate to high levels of PEA, the natural stimulant that is associated with romantic passion, so that even if your partner arouses you as much as ever, which is unlikely, you don't feel it as intensely (Liebowitz, 1983). In any case, for whatever reason, the passion component of love changes more rapidly than either intimacy or commitment (Acker & Davis, 1992), and that means that romantic love will change as well.

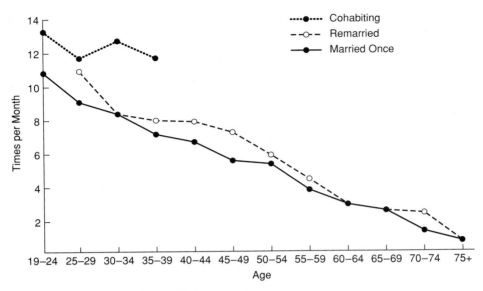

FIGURE 8.4. Frequency of sexual intercourse by age.
(Data from Call, Sprecher, & Schwartz, 1992.)

So, What Does the Future Hold?

Because three important influences on romantic passion—fantasy, novelty, and arousal—tend to dwindle over the years, romantic love decreases, too (Walster & Walster, 1978). In many relationships, it doesn't vanish entirely, of course, but it does tend to drop well below the levels that got a couple to marry in the first place. This is obviously a surprise for many couples, and it helps explain why the American divorce rate is so high: A common complaint is that the "magic" has died (see chapter 13).

However, we really don't want this news to be depressing! To the contrary, we think it offers important advice about how marriages can succeed. Often, the love that encourages people to marry is not the love that keeps them together decades later. Intimacy is more stable than passion. Thus, companionate love is more stable than romantic love is (Sprecher & Regan, 1998). And, as we noted earlier, people who have been happily married for a long time typically express a lot of companionate love for their spouses (Lauer & Lauer, 1985). Such people are often genuinely happy, too: Although it does not rely on passion, companionate love is very satisfying to those who experience it (Hecht, Marston, & Larkey, 1994). And because intimacy and passion are correlated (Whitley, 1993), being good friends may help to keep your passion alive.

Perhaps, then, we can distill some suggestions from all this. Enjoy passion, but don't make it the foundation of the relationships that you hope will last. Nurture a friendship with your lover. Try to stay fresh; grab every opportunity to enjoy novel adventures with your spouse (Aron et al., 2000). And don't be surprised or disappointed if your urgent desires gradually resolve into placid but deep affection for your beloved. That happy result is likely to make you a lucky lover.

CHAPTER SUMMARY

A Brief History of Love

Different societies have taken very different perspectives on love. Four dimensions on which views of love differ are cultural value, sexuality, sexual orientation, and marital status. The ancient Greeks took a negative view of love, seeing it as a kind of madness that had nothing to do with marriage. In medieval times, courtly love between an unmarried knight and a married lady was viewed as an idealistic, nonsexual quest. Modern ideas about love and marriage began to emerge in the seventeenth century, when, for the first time, love and marriage were viewed as compatible. Today, the belief that people should marry for love is widely accepted in North America, where most young adults say that they would not marry an otherwise perfect partner if they were not in love with him or her.

Types of Love

The Triangular Theory of Love. The triangular theory of love suggests that *intimacy, passion,* and *commitment* combine to produce eight different types of love. Of the three components, passion is thought to be the most variable and the least controllable.

Romantic, Passionate Love. Intimacy and passion combine to form romantic love, the experience people have in mind when they say they are "in love" with someone. A two-factor theory of passionate love holds that it occurs when physical arousal is attributed to the presence of a beloved person. In some circumstances, arousal can be *misattributed* to the wrong source, intensifying unrelated emotions through a process of excitation transfer. In excitation transfer, arousal caused by one stimulus is added to that caused by a second stimulus, making the second influence seem more powerful than it really is. Excitation transfer accounts for the fact that impersonal sources of arousal (such as fear of heights, or exercise) can enhance romantic attraction. An alternative explanation, the *response facilitation* account, argues that arousal merely strengthens a person's predominant reaction to a situation whether or not misattribution occurs. However, both misattribution and response facilitation seem to influence passion, which increases when a person becomes aroused for any reason. There may even be a chemical basis for these effects; our bodies may produce greater quantities of an amphetamine-like substance when we're in love.

Romantic love is also characterized by idealized evaluations of one's partner. In a sense, love is "blind"; objectivity and dispassion seem to decrease when romance enters the picture. Romantic love also tends to influence people's self-evaluations, leading them to develop more diversified self-concepts and increased self-esteem.

Companionate Love. Intimacy and commitment combine to form companionate love, a deep friendship with someone with whom one's life is intertwined. Spouses who have stayed married for more than 15 years describe friendship as the primary reason their marriages have lasted.

Styles of Loving. Six themes in love experiences that are differentially correlated with the various types of love have also been identified. People tend to pair off with others who share their attitudes toward love.

Individual Differences in Love

Individual differences are relatively enduring characteristics of people that exert an influence across different situations.

Attachment Styles. The *secure, avoidant,* and *anxious/ambivalent* styles of attachment originally described by developmental researchers have been revised and expanded in studies of adult relationships. Four styles—*secure, preoccupied, fearful,* and *dismissing*—are now recognized. They differ from each other along continuous dimensions that describe a person's comfort with closeness and anxiety over abandonment. People with a secure style, who relish closeness with others and who are not anxious about interdependency, enjoy stronger experiences of romantic and companionate love than insecure people do.

Age. People mellow with age, experiencing less intense love as time goes by. Nevertheless, some older adults feel more romantic after they have been married for many years than they did when they were younger.

Men and Women. Men and women are more similar than different when it comes to love. However, women are more selective than men are; they pick their lovers more carefully and fall in love less quickly than men do. One's gender may be more important than one's sex, because nontraditional couples share greater intimacy with each other than traditional couples do.

Does Love Last?

In general, romantic love decreases after people marry, sometimes quite rapidly.

Why Doesn't Romantic Love Last? Romance and passion involve *fantasy, novelty,* and *arousal,* and each fades with time. Novelty causes sexual arousal in other species—a phenomenon called the Coolidge effect—and it may fuel human passion as well. One theory links passion to changes in our relationships, so that a developing relationship often causes considerable passion that gradually evaporates after the relationship is established.

So, What Does the Future Hold? Companionate love is very satisfying and is more stable than romantic love is. If lovers are good friends and understand the usual course of romance, they may improve their chances for a long, contented relationship.

CHAPTER 9

Sexuality

In the last several years, we have seen a firestorm of media attention around the development of a little blue pill called Viagra. The pill was developed as a treatment for sexual impotence resulting from a physical disorder, such as diabetes or heart disease. Since its development, however, many men and women, some of whom are perfectly healthy, have come to see Viagra as the key to great sex. But is it? Is great sex defined as "successful" intercourse? Or more specifically, a great orgasm? Perhaps we are moving toward a world like the one portrayed in Woody Allen's movie, *Sleeper,* in which a man wakes up in a future world where "sex" consists of entering a machine (alone!) called an "orgasmatron." A pill or machine might promise reliable, consistent orgasms, but is there more to sex than that?

The social scientists who study sexuality in relationships would argue that the answer to that question is clearly yes. Sex is an important component of many romantic relationships, and the nature and status of our relationships have important consequences for our sexual attitudes, feelings, and behaviors. This chapter will consider a variety of questions: What kinds of attitudes do we have about sexuality in and out of relationships? How is sexual behavior affected by one's relationship status? What relationship factors influence feelings of sexual satisfaction? How do partners communicate with one another about sex? You will see that the answers to all these questions highlight the importance of the reciprocal association between sexuality and relationships.

SEXUAL ATTITUDES

Attitudes about Casual Sex

Our attitudes about sexual relationships have undergone a substantial shift over time. One focus of sexual attitudes research has been the degree to which we approve of premarital sexual intercourse. (Some have criticized the term *premarital sex,* because it suggests that all sex that isn't between spouses is just a precursor to heterosexual marriage. However, we will use this term throughout the chapter, because alternatives such as *nonmarital sex* don't distinguish among different kinds of sex outside of marriage.) In the first half of the twentieth century, very few people approved of sex outside of marriage (Hunt, 1974). Even as recently as 1972, when survey respondents were asked to describe their attitudes about sex between a man and a woman "before marriage," 46 percent felt it was "always or almost always wrong." That number has continued to drop, however; when asked the same question in 1996, 32 percent of those surveyed felt that premarital sex was always or almost always wrong (National Opinion Research Center, 1996 as cited in Hyde & DeLamater, 2000). So while for some people, marriage is seen as the most acceptable context for sex, the majority of people today have less restrictive attitudes than in the past. (See Box 9.1.)

Although the majority of people today feel that sex outside of marriage may be acceptable, this does not mean that most people endorse sex with strangers! In fact, there is good evidence that most people generally disapprove of sexual intercourse between people in an uncommitted relationship (Sprecher, McKinney, & Orbuch, 1987) and of sex with multiple partners (Gentry, 1998). People who are sexually active are viewed more positively when described as being in a "serious" rather than a "casual" relationship (Bettor, Hendrick, & Hendrick, 1995), and most people also prefer their own marriage or dating partners to have had limited sexual experience (Jacoby & Williams, 1985; Sprecher, Regan, McKinney, & Maxwell, 1997). These findings suggest that we endorse a "permissiveness-with-affection" standard (Reiss, 1967); we believe that some sexual activity among people who are not married is acceptable, as long as it is in the context of a committed relationship. So while people may no longer be expected to "save themselves for marriage," there is clearly an accepted prerequisite of relational attachment and affection as the most appropriate context for sexual activity.

While reading the last paragraph, you may have wondered whether gender plays a role in a person's attitudes about sex. Do men and women differ in their sexual opinions? On average, men are more permissive in their sexual values and attitudes than are women (Hendrick & Hendrick, 1987; Oliver & Hyde, 1993; Snyder, Simpson, & Gangestad, 1986), although how big the difference is depends on the attitude being measured. One of the largest sex differences is in attitudes toward casual premarital sex (Oliver & Hyde, 1993). Men are more likely than women to enjoy sex without intimacy, whereas women prefer sexual activities to be part of a psychologically intimate relationship (DeLamater, 1987; Whitley, 1988). While this is the area in which men's and women's sexual attitudes may differ most, the difference is not as big as it once was; research shows that the size of this difference has decreased over time (Oliver & Hyde, 1993).

BOX 9.1

Love and Lust

Rob and Nancy are college students who have been dating for about six months. Nancy is a psychology major with undetermined plans for her future career; Rob has not yet declared his major, but expects to go into business after graduation. They spend quite a bit of time together, and both enjoy rollerblading and going to the movies. Rob and Nancy feel a strong sexual desire for one another, and in fact, they have sex approximately three to four times a week. If you had to guess about the nature of Rob and Nancy's relationship, how happy would you say they are with each other? How much in love? How committed? And would you guess differently if you had been told instead that Rob and Nancy didn't have much sexual desire for one another?

If you are like most people, your answer to the last question would be yes. Pamela Regan (1998) conducted a study in which she gave college students the preceding description of Rob

and Nancy; the descriptions differed in how much sexual desire Rob and Nancy were described as having for one another. In the "high desire" condition, Rob and Nancy were perceived as being more in love, more committed, happier, and more satisfied than in the "no desire" condition. Interestingly, the presence or absence of desire played an important role in determining participants' perceptions of the relationship, but whether or not Rob and Nancy were actually engaging in sexual activity did not. In other studies, she found that the reverse was also true: couples described as being in love were seen as more likely to desire each other sexually (Regan, 1998). Regan's results highlight just how closely we view the association between love and desire. They may also suggest one reason why a lack of sexual desire by one partner in a couple can be a source of conflict: If love and lust go together, partners may view the absence of lust as a sign of waning love.

Somewhat smaller differences have been found for other kinds of sexual attitudes. For example, while most Americans strongly disapprove of a married person having sex with someone beside his or her spouse (Smith, 1994), men have been found to have somewhat more permissive attitudes toward extramarital sex than women (Glass & Wright, 1992; Oliver & Hyde, 1993).

Gender might influence sexual attitudes in another way as well. Traditionally, women and men have been evaluated differently for their sexual behavior, with women being judged more harshly than men for being sexually experienced or permissive. This idea is referred to as the sexual double standard, and it has been studied extensively. While it may seem intuitive that women who have multiple sexual partners are viewed as "sluts," whereas men who have multiple partners are "studs," the research findings suggest that the reality is somewhat more complicated. For example, one study found that while women who were described as sexually active were not evaluated more negatively than women who were not sexually active, sexually active women were seen as more liberal and assertive (Gentry, 1998). Another study examined people's preferences for dating and marriage partners, and found that men preferred potential spouses to be less sexually permissive, but favored greater permissiveness among potential dating partners. Women, on the other hand, preferred both dating and marriage partners to be less sexually permissive (Oliver & Sedikides, 1992). Yet another study found that Canadian university women believed that their culture judges sexually experienced women more harshly than sexually experienced men, but the women themselves did not endorse this belief (Milhausen & Herold, 1999). None of these found strong support for the existence of a traditional sexual double standard, but the results of these and other studies (e.g., Sprecher et al., 1987) do suggest that gender is still relevant to people's evaluations of men's and women's sexual experiences.

Attitudes about Homosexuality

Our discussion of sexual attitudes thus far has focused exclusively on people's attitudes about heterosexual sex. Attitudes about homosexuality, however, are decidedly more negative than attitudes toward premarital sex. A well-sampled survey by the National Opinion Research Center in 1996 showed that 62 percent of adult Americans believed that "sexual relations between adults of the same sex" are always or almost always wrong. Like other sexual attitudes we've discussed, attitudes toward homosexuality have become somewhat more accepting over time (Oliver & Hyde, 1993). In 1973, 81 percent of Americans believed that homosexual sex was always or almost always wrong. Despite the general trend toward decreasing disapproval, however, many experts have described the attitudes of Americans as homophobic (Fyfe, 1983).

Whether disapproval of homosexuality rises to the level of a true phobia or not, it is interesting to note that people's attitudes about homosexuality often extend beyond beliefs about the sexual act itself. For example, more than half of Americans object to what they consider to be the "homosexual lifestyle" (Turque, 1992). Gay and lesbian relationships (not just the sex itself) are assumed by many to be dysfunctional and unhappy (Testa, Kinder, & Ironson, 1987), although research evidence suggests that homosexual relationships are more similar to than different from heterosexual relationships (Peplau, Veniegas, & Campbell, 1996). Negative stereotypes and hate crimes against gays and lesbians are still an all-too-common occurrence.

On the other hand, there is some reason to believe that heterosexuals' attitudes about gays and lesbians will continue to become more positive. There are many more high-visibility gay and lesbian characters in the media now than in the past, as we've seen on television shows like "Ellen" and "Will and Grace." We have also witnessed recent political reforms such as the passage of a civil unions bill in Vermont, extending many of the rights of marriage to same-sex couples. Changes such as these may make it more acceptable for some people to declare themselves gay or lesbian. And there is evidence that knowing someone who is gay or lesbian may promote more positive attitudes toward homosexuality. One study found that heterosexuals who reported having some kind of personal contact with a lesbian or gay person had significantly more positive attitudes toward gay men (Herek & Glunt, 1993). The researchers in this study

TABLE 9.1. Attitudes toward Nonmarital Sex by Country

Numbers represent the percentage of respondents who felt this type of sex was always wrong.

Countries	Sex Before Marriage	Sex Before Age 16	Extramarital Sex	Homosexual Sex
Australia	13[a]	61	59	55
Bulgaria	23	71	51	81
Canada	12	55	68	39
Germany (West)	5	34	55	42
Great Britain	12	67	67	58
Ireland	35	84	80	71
Israel	19	67	73	57
Japan	19	60	58	65
Netherlands	7	45	63	19
Northern Ireland	31	81	81	80
Poland	18	77	74	77
Russia	13	45	36	57
Spain	20	59	76	45
Sweden	4	32	68	56
USA	29	71	80	70

Source: Adapted from Widmer, Treas, & Newcomb (1998).

point out that this result is probably due to two forms of reciprocal influence: Contact most likely results in more positive attitudes, and gay and lesbian people may also be more likely to disclose their sexuality to a heterosexual friend with generally positive attitudes. These findings, and the changes we have observed in popular culture and public policy, may foreshadow increasingly positive attitudes toward homosexuality over time.

Cultural Differences in Sexual Attitudes

We have seen that many sexual attitudes have become more permissive over time. If we think about all the sexual references and images in popular culture today, we may be tempted to think of Western cultures, particularly the United States, as being more permissive than most. But we'd be wrong. In fact, the sexual attitudes of Americans look surprisingly conservative when compared to the opinions expressed by people in other countries. Researchers compared sexual attitudes among 24 different countries and found that the United States (along with Ireland, Northern Ireland, and Poland) could be characterized as a sexually conservative culture (Widmer, Treas, & Newcomb, 1998). Table 9.1 shows the percentages of people in some of the countries surveyed who felt that different forms of nonmarital sex were "always wrong." While there is some evidence of agreement across cultures (all countries, to some degree, disapproved of extramarital sex), you can see that the United States is consistently among the most conservative countries in terms of beliefs about sex before marriage, sex before age 16, extramarital sex, and homosexual sex. Canada, on the other hand, is more permissive than the U.S. on all measures, particularly on attitudes about homosexual sex. These differences are not simply regional, then; countries that are close neighbors do not necessarily share the same sexual attitudes. There are a variety of possible explanations for the differences observed in Table 9.1, including cultural, historical, religious, and political factors, but there is clear evidence that despite a trend over time toward more permissive sexual attitudes, the United States is still sexually conservative, at least with respect to attitudes.

SEXUAL BEHAVIOR

As interested as people are in learning about the general public's attitudes and opinions about sexual matters, they are even more interested in patterns of sexual behavior. One reason for this fascination may be a desire to put one's own sexual behavior in context: How many people are still virgins by the time they are 20? How many times a week does the average couple have sex, and how does that compare to my own sexual frequency? How common is it for a person to cheat on his or her relationship partner? Knowing about general trends in sexual behavior allows us to think about whether our own behavior is "normal." Remember, however, as you read about these trends that the broad descriptions of sexual behavior patterns reported in this section mask the enormous variability in people's experiences. And behavior that is common is not necessarily more desirable or appropriate than sexual behavior that is less typical. As you will see, what is perhaps most important about sexual behavior in relationships is that it is desired by and satisfying for both partners.

Premarital Sex

When do most people engage in sex for the first time? Assuming that we are talking about heterosexual intercourse, the average age of first intercourse is approximately age 16 for males and 17 for females, with blacks experiencing sex somewhat earlier than whites or Latinos (Day, 1992). The general trend for many years was toward earlier first sexual experiences; however, during the 1990s, the rates of adolescent intercourse seem to have dropped off, with the number of adolescents who have never had sex rising 11 percent from 1991 to 1997 (cited in Christopher & Sprecher, 2000).

This rise in rates of adolescent virginity deserves some comment. Research suggests that young adults have a variety of reasons for not engaging in sexual intercourse (Sprecher & Regan, 1996). Some report that fear of the consequences of sex, including pregnancy, AIDS, and other sexually transmitted diseases, keeps them from having sex. Others cite moral beliefs about the value of virginity as their reason for abstaining from sex. Some feel that they have not yet experienced sufficient love with a relationship partner to justify engaging in sex. More women than men cite these reasons for maintaining their virginity. Men, on the other hand, are more likely than women to point to feelings of insecurity or inadequacy as a barrier to engaging in sex (Sprecher & Regan, 1996).

The reasons provided by adolescents who do not have sex are to some degree complemented by the reasons provided by those who do (Sprecher & McKinney, 1993). Some young adults have sex because they want to express their love or affection for their partner (e.g., Hill & Preston, 1996). Others are curious and want to experience the physical pleasure of sex. Other reasons focus on external factors, such as succumbing to peer pressure or wanting to please their relationship partner. It is worth noting that many of the reasons offered by young adults for engaging in their first sexual intercourse are similar to the sexual motives reported by people more generally. Browning and colleagues found that love, pleasure, conformity, and social recognition were all motives offered by college students for having sex (Browning, Hatfield, Kessler, & Levine, 2000). Thus, many key motives for engaging in sex are relational, highlighting the importance of relationships in most people's sexual experiences.

We have identified reasons that adolescents give for having sex, but what factors predict *when* a person will engage in sex for the first time? In general, a person's values and attitudes are the best predictors of premarital sexual behavior. Some of these values are tied to relationships. Premarital sexual activity is more likely among teenagers who view dating as important in their lives and express strong desires for a partner (Newcomb, Huba, & Bentler, 1986). In this study by Newcomb et al., the importance of dating was associated with (1) confidence about being popular with and attractive to the opposite sex, (2) a positive and accepting view of oneself, and (3) more experiences involving stressful physical or family-related events. Thus, the importance of dating, a predictor of premarital sexual activity, was correlated with both positive factors (social and personal confidence) and negative experiences (stress). Similar findings were obtained in research on pregnancies among adolescents (Robbins, Kaplan, & Martin, 1985). The likelihood of becoming a parent outside of marriage increased for those whose parents had a lower socioeconomic status, who had more difficulties in school, and who were more popular among their peers. It appears, then, that socially successful teenagers who face stressful life circumstances may be more likely than others to become sexually active and to run the risk of an unplanned pregnancy.

Another set of predictors of premarital sexual activity revolve around a desire for achieving adult status. Teenagers who engage in sex at an early age place greater value on independence (Jessor, Costa, Jessor, & Donovan, 1983) and early autonomy (Rosenthal, Smith, & de Visser, 1999). Rosenthal and colleagues reported that adolescent males who engaged in earlier sexual activity were more physically mature and were more likely to use drugs than those who engaged in sex at a later age. Lack of self-restraint (i.e., agreeing with statements like, "People who get me angry need to watch out") was also a predictor of early sexual activity for girls. The researchers argued that "the desire to achieve the transition to adulthood at an earlier age than their peers...constitutes a powerful incentive for young people to become sexually active" (Rosenthal et al., 1999, p. 332).

Family structure is also related to premarital sexual activity. Research by Newcomer and Udry (1987) indicated, however, that the influence of family structure may differ for girls and boys. These investigators found that white adolescent girls growing up in homes without a father present were more likely to engage in premarital sex than were girls living with a father. But the boys who reported the highest level of premarital sexual activity were those who had experienced a change from an intact family, with both mother and father present, to a home without a father. Newcomer and Udry suggest that males become sexually active in response to parental loss of control during the breakup of a family, while paternal absence per se (regardless of when it occurred) appears to prompt female premarital sexual activity. Not all researchers, however, regard the connection between father absence and female premarital sex as particularly strong. When Miller and Bingham (1989) surveyed a national sample of 15- to 19-year-old females, they found that many other factors were better predictors of the level of premarital sexual activity reported by their subjects. Regardless of family structure, younger teenagers and those who were highly religious were less likely to have engaged in premarital sex.

Sex in Committed Relationships

How often do people in relationships typically have sex? The answer to this question is surprisingly complicated. Sexual frequency depends on a number of factors. First, frequency varies depending on the status of the relationship. Couples who are living together, but not married, have sex about three times per week, on average, whereas those who are married have sex an average of about two times per week (Call, Sprecher, & Schwartz, 1995; Laumann, Gagnon, Michael, & Michaels, 1994). Couples in both kinds of relationships, however, have sex more often than those who are single (Laumann et al., 1994), which is probably due to the fact that singles are less likely to have consistent access to a sexual partner.

A second factor influencing sexual frequency is a person's age (Blumstein & Schwartz, 1983; Call et al., 1995). People who are older generally have sex less frequently than do younger people, and researchers have offered at least two explanations for this pattern. One has to do with physical changes associated with aging: Decreased hormone levels in older women may result in less vaginal lubrication, and decreased circulation in men may affect the ability to maintain an erection. So normal aging and declines in physical health may affect sexual frequency. In couples that have been together for a long time, however, there is an additional possibility. Call and colleagues have suggested

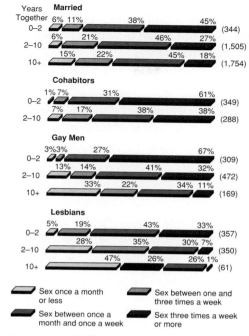

FIGURE 9.1. Differences in sexual frequency by relationship type and length of relationship.

Source: Blumstein & Schwartz, 1993.

that as people become more familiar with their sexual partner, their interest in sex decreases, a kind of sexual "habituation" (Call et al., 1995). This explanation is supported by the general drop in sexual frequency after the first year of marriage.

Another factor associated with differences in sexual frequency is sexual orientation. Interestingly, this association is tied to the drop in sexual frequency with increased duration of the relationship that we just discussed. Figure 9.1 shows the results of a large-scale survey of gay, lesbian, married, and cohabiting heterosexual couples. The researchers categorized couples in each type of relationship by how long the partners had been together. They found that early in their relationships, gay men have more frequent sex than either lesbian women or heterosexual couples (married or cohabiting). After ten years together, however, gay male partners have sex less frequently than do heterosexual couples. On the other hand, regardless of the duration of the relationship, lesbians have sex less frequently than any other relationship group (Blumstein & Schwartz, 1983). So although a question like "How often do people have sex?" may sound simple, the answer depends on a variety of characteristics related to the individual and the relationship.

Monogamy

A central issue for many sexual relationships is the extent to which couples are monogamous. As we have seen, the vast majority of people in most countries have a decidedly negative view of someone in a committed relationship engaging in sex with someone other than his or her partner (Widmer et al., 1998). Given these negative attitudes, we might expect that sexual infidelity would be relatively rare. How common is sexual infidelity? Most studies have focused on the incidence of extramarital sex. In a large-scale survey of sexual behavior, 25 percent of married men and 15 percent of married women reported having engaged in extramarital sex at least once during their marriage, and fewer than 4 percent of spouses reported having had an extramarital affair in the last year (Laumann et al., 1994).

What factors predict who will be most likely to have sex with someone who is not their relationship partner? Gender is one important predictor: Research has consistently shown that men are more likely than women to engage in extramarital affairs and are more accepting of nonmonogamy than are women (Glass & Wright, 1985; Seal, Agostinelli, & Hannett, 1994; Thompson, 1984). Moreover, of those spouses who engage in extramarital sex, men are more likely than women to have a greater number of outside sexual partners (Blumstein & Schwartz, 1983).

Gay and lesbian couples provide an interesting opportunity to observe this gender difference in the context of same-sex relationships. Given the general difference between women and men in the rates and acceptance of nonmonogamy, it is perhaps not surprising that gay male couples are much more likely to engage in nonmonogamous sex, sometimes with the consent of their partners (Blasband & Peplau, 1985; Kurdek, 1991; Lever, 1994), than are heterosexual married and lesbian couples. Blumstein and Schwartz (1983) reported the frequency of nonmonogamy in a variety of different relationship types; their data are depicted in Figure 9.2. You can see that many more gay men than married or cohabiting men in their sample reported having extradyadic sex. Lesbian women, on the other hand, look similar in their rates of nonmonogamy to female cohabitors, with rates for married women being somewhat lower. The same pattern holds for the number of outside sex partners reported by people in different types of relationships. Among those who have had sex outside their relationship, men in general, and gay men in particular, are more likely to have had a larger number of partners (Blumstein & Schwartz, 1983). While we don't know exactly why this difference occurs, some have speculated that the higher rates of nonmonogamy in gay men's relationships may be a function of men's greater tendency toward permissive sexual attitudes, unchecked by the greater sexual conservatism of a female partner (Blumstein & Schwartz, 1983).

Researchers have tried to identify a set of beliefs and characteristics common to those who are likely to engage in sex outside their committed relationships. Simpson and Gangestad (1991) have argued that some people endorse a set of beliefs that lead them to be more comfortable having nonmonogamous sexual experiences; the extent to which a person holds these beliefs is called his

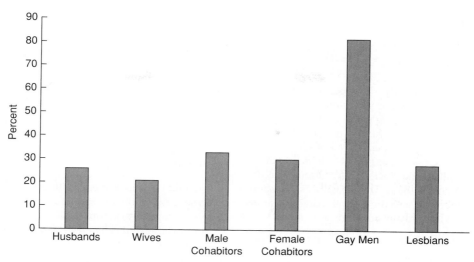

FIGURE 9.2 Percentage of individuals reporting any instance(s) of nonmonogamy since the beginning of their relationship.
(From Blumstein & Schwartz, 1983.)

or her sociosexual orientation. Those who have a restricted sociosexual orientation are generally willing to have sex only in the context of a committed and affectionate relationship. Those with an unrestricted sociosexual orientation, on the other hand, don't need the same degree of closeness and commitment before engaging in sexual behavior. These people are more likely to agree with a statement such as "Sex without love is OK." (See Box 9.2 for the measure of sociosexuality used by Simpson and Gangestad.) Given these definitions, it is probably not surprising that restricted people report greater commitment, dependency, and love in their sexual relationships than do those with an unrestricted orientation.

Sociosexuality, then, reflects a general orientation toward sex as either requiring commitment or not. So we might expect that sociosexual orientation would predict the likelihood that people will have sex outside their own committed relationship, and studies have confirmed this expectation (Simpson & Gangestad, 1991; Seal et al., 1994). Seal and colleagues demonstrated this association in a clever study involving heterosexual college students who were currently in a dating relationship. For this study, participants were recruited from a large group of students who had previously filled out a survey assessing their sociosexual orientation. Those who volunteered were asked to evaluate a computer dating video in which an attractive member of the other sex described him- or herself. After viewing and evaluating the tape, participants were told they could enter a drawing to win a free date with the person in the video by filling out a card with their name and phone number. After collecting the cards from those who chose to enter the drawing, the researchers then

---

BOX 9.2

Measuring Sociosexuality

Sociosexuality describes the degree to which a person is comfortable with the idea of having sex without relational commitment. Simpson and Gangestad (1991) developed a way of measuring a person's sociosexuality, using a survey called the Sociosexual Orientation Inventory (SOI). The measure asks respondents to answer the following questions as honestly as possible:

1. With how many different partners have you had sex (sexual intercourse) within the past year?

    _____

2. How many different partners do you foresee yourself having sex with during the next five years? (Please give a *specific, realistic* estimate.) _____

3. With how many different partners have you had sex on *one and only one* occasion? _____

4. How often do you fantasize about having sex with someone other than your current dating partner? (Circle one.)
    1. never
    2. once every two or three months
    3. once a month
    4. once every two weeks
    5. once a week
    6. a few times each week
    7. nearly every day
    8. at least once a day

5. Sex without love is OK.
    1 2 3 4 5 6 7 8 9
    I strongly   I strongly
    disagree   agree

6. I can imagine myself being comfortable and enjoying "casual" sex with different partners.
    1 2 3 4 5 6 7 8 9
    I strongly   I strongly
    disagree   agree

7. I would have to be closely attached to someone (both emotionally and psychologically) before I could feel comfortable and fully enjoy having sex with him or her.
    1 2 3 4 5 6 7 8 9
    I strongly   I strongly
    disagree   agree

Responses to the last item (7) are reverse scored, and a total score is computed by weighing the scores of some items more heavily than others. In general, higher numbers on each question (and for the total score) reflect an "unrestricted" sexual orientation, and lower numbers reflected a "restricted" orientation. Compared to those with a restricted orientation, people with an unrestricted orientation "typically engage in sex earlier in their romantic relationships, are more likely to engage in sex with more than one partner at a time, and tend to be involved in sexual relationships characterized by less expressed investment, less commitment, and weaker affectional ties" (Simpson & Gangestad, 1991, p. 879). Research on sociosexuality is a good example of how personal characteristics have a powerful impact on the nature of sexual interactions.

asked participants to imagine that they had actually won the free date, that they had gone on the date, and that they had had a good time. Participants then indicated how willing they would be to engage in a series of physically intimate behaviors, including sexual intercourse, with the date.

Seal and his associates reported a number of interesting findings (Seal et al., 1995). First, 36 percent of those who were unrestricted in their sociosexuality entered the drawing for a free date, whereas only 4 percent of those who were restricted did. (Remember that all the participants were currently involved in another relationship!) Second, unrestricted people were more likely to say they would be willing to engage in physical intimacy with their date than restricted people were. Third, commitment to their own relationship didn't make much difference in the responses of unrestricted people—they were fairly willing to become involved with the date—whereas restricted people did take their current relationship commitments into account. Thus, sociosexual orientation is useful for identifying people who are likely to become involved with someone other than their own relationship partners, and more specifically, those who are likely to have extradyadic sex (Seal et al., 1995).

Other attempts to predict patterns of extradyadic sex have focused on the qualities of a person's relationship. Levels of relationship satisfaction and commitment are both important in ways that probably won't surprise you: In general, those who are unhappy with their relationship are more likely to have engaged in recent acts of sexual infidelity (Brown, 1991; Treas & Giesen, 2000), and those who are cohabiting are more likely to have sex outside of their primary relationship than are those who are married (Forste & Tanfer, 1996; Treas & Giesen, 2000).

The principles of equity theory have proven useful for identifying relationship factors that are associated with sexual infidelity. Recall from chapter 6 that equity theory emphasizes that what we get out of a relationship (outcomes) and what we put into it (inputs) are both important in influencing how we feel about the relationship. The theory also assumes that we pay attention to our own inputs and outcomes and to those of our partner in an attempt to assess how fair the exchange is. Thus, an equitable relationship is one in which both partners get about the same amount of benefit from the relationship compared to what they put into maintaining it. Those whose benefits exceed their contributions are *overbenefited*. On the other hand, those whose contributions exceed their benefits are *underbenefited*.

With these concepts in mind, let us look at the association between equity and extramarital sex. Walster, Traupmann, and Walster (1978) recount their use of a *Psychology Today* questionnaire that was completed and mailed in by 62,000 people! From this huge number of replies, Walster and colleagues selected a smaller sample of 2,000 males and females, representing all age groups and a variety of intimate relationships. Their examination of extramarital sexuality was based on the replies of respondents who were married or living together. Two questions from the questionnaire were most relevant to extramarital sex: (1) How many, if any, extramarital affairs did the respondents report? and (2) if

260   PART THREE: Friendship and Intimacy

they had had such a relationship, when did they have it? Answers to both questions revealed an association between feeling underbenefited and engaging in extramarital relationships. On the average, underbenefited people reported having a greater number of extramarital relationships than did either overbenefited people or those who felt their marriage was equitable. Moreover, among respondents who had had extramarital affairs, underbenefited people had their first affair earlier in their marriages (after an average of 9 to 11 years) than people who felt themselves to be overbenefited or in an equitable relationship (12 to 15 years). In light of these results, Walster et al. (1978) suggested that lack of equity in the relationship may be one prominent reason why people have extramarital affairs. More recent research has supported this claim for wives, but not for husbands (Prins, Buunk, & VanYperen, 1993). In general, then, people who feel they are not getting the benefits to which they feel entitled are the ones most likely to turn, and to turn earlier, to other relationships.

Preventing Pregnancy and Sexually Transmitted Diseases

Social scientists have focused much attention in the last decade on the issues of pregnancy and sexually transmitted disease prevention. The social and personal costs of teen pregnancy, combined with the frightening incidence of sexually transmitted diseases, such as AIDS and chlamydia, point to a pressing need for more responsible sexual behavior. Although pregnancy and disease can and do occur outside the context of relationships, they are nonetheless relationship issues; both the prevention and, if prevention efforts fail, the consequences of pregnancy and sexually transmitted disease raise questions for relationship partners past, present, and future.

We know from the experience of the gay male community that sexual behavior can be modified. Among older gay and bisexual males, "AIDS education and prevention campaigns have resulted in the most profound modification of personal health-related behaviors ever recorded" (Stall, Coates, & Hoff, 1988, p. 878). On the other hand, efforts to promote the safe-sex use of condoms among intravenous drug users appear to have met with little success, and there is growing concern that younger gay males may be engaging in risky sexual practices (Griggs, 1990; Lemp et al., 1994). A survey of gay and bisexual men in the San Francisco Bay area reported that, in the last six months, one-third of those surveyed had engaged in unprotected anal intercourse, a behavior that puts them at very high risk of HIV infection (Lemp et al., 1994).

These concerns are not limited to gay men: Among a sample of largely heterosexual college students, Carroll (1988) found that there was more talk than action in response to the fear of AIDS. Although more than 40 percent of sexually active subjects said that they had modified their sexual behavior because of concerns about AIDS, their reports of actual sexual behavior failed to confirm these claims. In another study of heterosexual young people, Campbell and colleagues (1992) found that only 30 percent had used a condom the last time they had had sexual intercourse. Worse yet, those who had more sexual partners were less likely to say they would use a condom in the future than were those who had sex with fewer different partners! So those most at risk may be least likely to engage in risk-reducing behaviors. Other studies have reported essentially the same pattern: at best, heterosexuals have changed their behavior only minimally in the face of the AIDS threat (Catania et al., 1993; DeBuono et al., 1990).

This is frightening, given that casual sex among young adults is alive and well. Paul and colleagues have studied the phenomenon of "hookups." They defined a hookup as "a sexual encounter, usually lasting only one night, between two people who are strangers or brief acquaintances" (Paul, McManus, & Hayes, 2000, p. 76). The encounter may or may not include sexual intercourse. Their research showed that the vast majority of students in their study (78 percent) had had at least one hookup; of these students, 47 percent of the men and 33 percent of the women had had sexual intercourse when they hooked up. In another study, researchers questioned college students about their sexual experiences while on spring break. They found that 15 percent of men and 13 percent of women said they had engaged in sex with a new partner while on spring break (Maticka-Tyndale, Herold, & Mewhinney, 1998), and many more said they intended to! So rates of casual sex are relatively high, and rates of condom use are relatively low.

These studies, and many others that demonstrate the same patterns of sexual behavior, raise a crucial question: Why is it that among well-educated, young Americans, considerable high-risk sex still occurs? There is, of course, no easy answer. But research has suggested some possibilities. First, if condoms are the method of choice for preventing the transmission of sexually transmitted diseases (and for preventing pregnancy, as well), then it stands to reason that people who don't like condoms may not use them, even if they "know better." And research supports this notion; many people don't use condoms because they have a negative attitude about them: they may find condoms unpleasant or uncomfortable, for example (Campbell et al., 1992; Catania et al., 1989; Pleck, Sonenstein, & Ku, 1991).

This simple statement belies the complexity of people's attitudes about condoms, however. Research has identified a number of different components to these attitudes, not all of which are equally important for understanding who is likely to practice safer sex and who isn't. Campbell and colleagues (1992) developed a measure that assessed four aspects of condom attitudes: the comfort and convenience of condoms, the effectiveness of condoms for birth control and disease prevention, the interpersonal aspects of condom use, and the effects of condoms on sexual sensation. They found that the heterosexual college students in their sample were already convinced that condoms were effective for the prevention of pregnancy and disease; rates of agreement with statements in this subscale were quite high. Knowing that condoms were effective was not, however, associated with using condoms reliably. Instead, it was the interpersonal dimension that predicted college students' willingness to use a condom. If a student believed that using a condom would be embarrassing or would somehow "spoil the mood," he or she was less likely to intend to use condoms in the future (Campbell et al., 1992). Other research has also highlighted the predictive value of these interpersonal issues for understanding condom use (Catania et al., 1989; Pleck et al., 1991). So yet again, we see evidence of the link between sexuality and relationship issues and characteristics. For this reason, experts have argued that condoms need to be viewed as more than a "necessary evil" of sexual relations, and that attempts should be made to incorporate communication about condoms into the script for sexual interaction (Kyes, 1990; Kyes, Brown, & Pollack, 1991; Tanner & Pollack, 1988).

A second reason why people often don't use condoms when they should revolves around the potent mixture of sex and alcohol, commonplace on college campuses and in bars. There is good research evidence to suggest that when a person gets drunk, he or she is much more likely to have sex without a condom (Leigh & Stall, 1993). More specifically, these studies show that being intoxicated actually changes people's attitudes about having sex without a condom (MacDonald, Zanna, & Fong, 1996, 1998). Steele and colleagues (Steele, Critchlow, & Liu, 1985; Steele & Josephs, 1990) have referred to this phenomenon as evidence of "alcohol myopia," which involves the reduction of a person's ability to think about and process all of the information available to them when they are drunk. This limited capacity means that they are likely to focus only on the most immediate and salient environmental cues. An attractive partner, then, becomes a cue that elicits sexual arousal, and a person who is drunk may not be able to focus on anything but their own arousal, including their own usually good intentions to use a condom (MacDonald, MacDonald, Zanna, & Fong, 2000). For a person who wants to avoid high-risk sexual behavior, then, the best advice is to avoid mixing sex with alcohol.

A third factor is the illusion of unique vulnerability—believing that bad things happen to others, but not to you (Lehman & Taylor, 1987; Perloff, 1987). This illusion interferes with taking appropriate measures to prevent foreseeable dangers. In one study of sexually active female undergraduates, those who perceived themselves as less likely than other women to get pregnant were also less likely to use effective contraception (Burger & Burns, 1988). Similarly, gay males who underestimated the risk of getting AIDS from unsafe sex were more likely to engage in high-risk sex (Bauman & Siegel, 1987). If you think you are invulnerable, you may not bother to take precautions.

A fourth factor contributing to the practice of safe or unsafe sex is a person's general attitude toward sex. In research on contraceptive use by heterosexuals, it has been found that sexual attitudes and feelings have a strong influence on that behavior (Gerrard, 1987a). Negative reactions to sex—such as guilt, anxiety, and negative evaluations of sexual situations—are associated with failure to use contraceptives (Andres, Gold, Berger, Kinch, & Gillett, 1983; Byrne & Fisher, 1983). Note the irony of these findings. People with negative attitudes about sex are less likely to engage in sex. But if they do engage in sex, they are more likely to engage in unsafe sex (Fisher, 1986). Why? One possible reason is that people who are uncomfortable about sex know less about safe-sex practices (Goldfarb, Gerrard, Gibbons, & Plante, 1988). The lack of information among those with negative sexual attitudes does not reflect an inability to learn this information; rather, it appears to reflect active avoidance of such material. It also is possible that the tendency for men to rely on women to use contracep-

The quilt memorializing AIDS victims on display in Washington, DC. AIDS has had profound effects on the relationships of those touched by the disease.

tion (Geis & Gerrard, 1984) creates an impression-management problem for women. Women, especially those with negative attitudes and feelings toward sex, may fear that if they practice contraception or ask a man to use a condom, they will appear overly experienced and eager (Marecek, 1987). Unfortunately, for some people the need to appear sexually naive may take precedence over the determination to avoid an unwanted pregnancy or a deadly disease.

SEXUAL SATISFACTION

As interesting as it is to consider all the things people *do* in their sexual relationships, it is arguably more important to consider how people *feel* about their sexual relationships. After all, a wife who is having frequent sex with her husband is not likely to be very happy about her sex life if she still feels that her own sexual needs are not being met. How do we assess whether a person is satisfied with his or her sexual relationship? One way is simply to ask people how much physical pleasure they experience with their partners. When asked whether they were *"extremely* physically satisfied with their sexual relationship," nearly half of both the male and female respondents of the National Health and Social Life Survey said they were (Michael, Gagnon, Laumann, & Kolata, 1994). Interestingly, these numbers were somewhat higher for married respondents, particularly married men, than for unmarried men and women. If we include those who reported their sex lives to be at least *"very* physically satisfying," the numbers rise to almost 90 percent (Michael et al., 1994). Other studies have also found married couples to be quite satisfied with the sexual aspects of their relationships (e.g., Lawrance & Byers, 1995; Oggins, Loeber, & Veroff, 1993). This certainly suggests that the stereotype of boring, routine married sex may not be terribly accurate! Married couples do not have the market cornered on sexual pleasure, however. Byers, Demmons, and Lawrance (1998) reported very high levels of sexual satisfaction among heterosexual dating couples, and Kurdek (1991) found that the sexual satisfaction of gay, lesbian, and heterosexual cohabiting couples did not differ from that of married couples.

Sexual Frequency and Satisfaction

While average ratings of sexual satisfaction in relationships are high, some people are clearly more satisfied than others. What distinguishes those people who have fulfilling sexual relationships from those who don't? You might guess that people who have sex more often are happier with their sex lives, and in general, you'd be right. Blumstein and Schwartz (1983) showed that sexual satisfaction is closely tied to sexual frequency. Respondents to their survey were consistently happier about their sex lives when they were having sex more often. Eighty-nine percent of husbands and wives who had sex three times a week or more, for example, reported that they were satisfied with the quality of their sex life, whereas only 32 percent of spouses having sex once a month or less felt the same sexual satisfaction. The same pattern of results was found for cohabiting heterosexuals, gays, and lesbians. More recent studies have confirmed the general association between sexual frequency and sexual satisfaction (Greeley, 1991; Laumann et al., 1994).

Of course, establishing a relationship between frequent sex and sexual satisfaction does not allow us to conclude that having more frequent sex *causes* people to be more satisfied. The data collected by Blumstein and Schwartz are correlational, as are the data in the other studies mentioned, and this means that we cannot infer a causal relationship between frequency and satisfaction. We cannot rule out other explanations—perhaps those who are happier with their sex lives choose to have sex more often (a reasonable-sounding statement!). Or perhaps people who have a strong sex drive or who are sexually permissive in their attitudes are more likely *both* to have more frequent sex and to be happy with their sex lives.

Thus, for most couples, the quality of their sexual interactions is an important feature of the relationship. And while frequent sex is a likely contributor to sexual satisfaction, it is clear that contentment comes from more than the sexual act itself. This view was echoed by a lesbian woman describing the value of sexual intimacy for herself and her partner:

> "It is very important because it is one way of keeping in touch, feeling affectionate, keeping close, staying close....It is not so much the orgasm itself, although I feel this is a wonderful experience. It is the actual being close to each other and touching each other, feeling taken care of and taking care of someone else." (Blumstein & Schwartz, 1983, p. 490)

Sex and Relationship Satisfaction

This woman's comment on the importance of sex as a "relational" experience is echoed by research evidence. Many studies have demonstrated that couples who are happy with their sex lives tend also to be happy with their relationships, in general. Sexual satisfaction is strongly associated with measures of relationship satisfaction among married couples (Cupach & Comstock, 1990; Greeley, 1991; Haavio-Mannila & Kontula, 1997; Kurdek, 1991; Lawrance & Byers, 1995) and among gay, lesbian, and cohabiting heterosexual couples (Kurdek, 1991).

Not all studies have demonstrated a direct relationship between sexual frequency and relational satisfaction. In their pioneering study of marital relationships, Terman, Buttenweiser, Ferguson, Johnson, and Wilson (1938) found that frequency of sexual intercourse did not correlate with marital happiness. However, a close correspondence between desired and actual frequency of intercourse was associated with marital satisfaction. People who stated that their actual frequency of sexual intercourse was very close to the level of sexual activity they preferred were more likely to report that they were happy in their marriages.

More recent research also suggests that the relationship between sex and relational satisfaction can be a complicated one. For instance, Howard and Dawes (1976) reported that although neither sexual activity nor number of arguments was in itself associated with the marital happiness reported by couples in their study, a combination of sex and arguments (specifically, the rate of sexual interaction minus the rate of arguments) did predict marital contentment. Thus, it seems that those couples who had a positive balance in what Gottman et al. (1976b) call the "marital bank account" (more positive/sexual deposits than argumentative withdrawals) tended to be happier with each other. The importance of the relative balance is further demonstrated by the fact that in the Howard and Dawes study, sexual activity and arguing were positively correlated. Those couples who had more sex also had more arguments. It appears, then, that couples who argue a lot can be very happy with each other, providing they have more positive interactions (sexual and otherwise) more often.

A third study on the relationship between sex and marital satisfaction examined two groups of married couples: (1) happily married couples who volunteered to participate in the study and (2) unhappily married couples who had come to a mental health clinic for marital counseling (Birchler & Webb, 1977). The happily married couples in this study did have a greater frequency of sexual interaction than the unhappily married couples. They also were more

Happy couples enjoy spending time together—in bed and out of it.

likely to report joint participation in leisure-time activities, such as sports, hobbies, and social events. This suggests the somewhat surprising notion that having sex may have a lot in common with liking to play golf with each other. People who enjoy doing things together (including having sex!) are likely to be happier than those who don't.

Exchange Theories and Sexual Satisfaction

Perhaps it should not surprise us that sexual and relationship satisfaction are inextricably linked, given the relational nature of sexual activity. (Although even solitary sexual activity has been argued to have a relational component: Woody Allen once referred to masturbation as "sex with someone I love.") Social exchange theories, like the ones described in chapter 6, have been used to identify the relationship factors that might best explain a person's feelings of sexual contentment (Sprecher, 1998). The Interpersonal Exchange Model of Sexual Satisfaction (IEMSS, Lawrance & Byers, 1995) highlights the role of social exchange variables such as rewards, costs, and comparison levels, and research evidence has supported the model (see Box 9.3 for a description of some of the sexual rewards and costs identified by women and men). Experiencing more sexual rewards, fewer sexual costs, and having one's expectations about the rewards and costs in a sexual relationship favorably met or exceeded are all likely to result in feelings of sexual satisfaction among married and cohabiting heterosexual couples (Lawrance & Byers, 1995) and short-term dating couples

---

BOX 9.3

Sexual Costs and Rewards

Exchange theorists emphasize the importance of costs and rewards for understanding how satisfied people are in their relationships, and the principle applies to sexual satisfaction as well (Lawrance & Byers, 1995). Lawrance and Byers (1995) asked men and women in long-term heterosexual relationships to consider a variety of possible rewards and costs in sexual interactions and to indicate which they had experienced with their sexual partner.

What were the most commonly identified sexual rewards? More than 90 percent of both men and women reported that the degree of comfort they felt with their partner was a sexual reward. Other commonly reported rewards were the following: "how you feel about yourself during/after sex," "the physical sensations from caressing and hugging," and "the extent to which sexual interactions make you feel secure about the total relationship with your partner" (Lawrance & Byers, 1995). These rewards are interesting because they highlight the multifaceted nature of sexual experiences, involving a person's own psychological and physical sensations, as well as the nature of the relationship.

What constitutes a sexual cost? Having sex when either you or your partner is not in the mood is a frequently mentioned cost for both women and men. The amount of spontaneity (or

lack of it) in sexual activity is another common cost. The frequency of sexual activity and the amount of time spent in sexual activities were costs reported by many women and men, although it is unclear whether the cost for most involves less frequent activity for less time, or vice versa! Regardless, the theme of these costs seems to be mismatched sexual desire and availability (Lawrance & Byers, 1995).

Men and women were equally likely to report experiencing all of the rewards and costs described thus far. However, the researchers did report some significant gender differences. Women were more likely than men to say that the following constituted sexual rewards for them: "how your partner treats you during sex," "being with the same partner each time you have sex," "how your partner responds to your sexual advances," and "oral sex: your partner stimulates you." Women were also more likely to report experiencing sexual costs such as "how easily you reach orgasm" and "engaging in sexual activities that you dislike, but your partner enjoys" (Lawrance & Byers, 1995). Many of these findings are probably not surprising; these gender differences reflect general differences in the sexual attitudes and behaviors of women and men that we have already discussed.

(Byers, Demmons, & Lawrance, 1998). Moreover, sexual satisfaction was related to more general assessments of relationship satisfaction in all relationship types (Byers, Demmons, & Lawrance, 1998; Lawrance & Byers, 1995).

Like social exchange theory, the principles of equity theory have also been applied to sexual behavior and satisfaction. In a study by Walster, Walster, and Traupmann (1978), it was found that people in dating relationships who described their relationships as equitable also said that they were more content in the relationship than did people who felt they were underbenefited or overbenefited. In addition, the equitable relationships were more likely to last longer. When asked about their sexual experiences, partners in equitable relationships reported "going further" sexually and were more likely to indicate that they had had intercourse because both of them wanted to. It seems, then, that couples who feel they have an equitable relationship also feel they have a more satisfying, stable, and mutually responsive relationship; this total context of security and trust is associated with increased sexual expression.

Another study examined the relationship between feeling equitably treated and being sexually satisfied (Traupmann, Hatfield, & Wexler, 1983). Among the college students who took part in this research, those who perceived their relationships as equitable reported more sexual satisfaction across a variety of measures (e.g., overall sexual satisfaction, satisfaction after sex, perception of partner's satisfaction after sex). However, on all these measures, the difference between those who characterized their relationship as "equitable" and those who felt overbenefited was extremely small. Indeed, male subjects who felt overbenefited often reported somewhat greater satisfaction than equitably treated males. Among both males and females, feeling underbenefited was associated with the lowest level of sexual satisfaction. A similar pattern has been found with newlywed couples. Partners who felt equitably treated or overbenefited expressed considerably more sexual satisfaction than did those who regarded themselves as underbenefited (Hatfield, Greenberger, Traupmann, & Lambert, 1982).

The results of all the studies of sexual satisfaction point out that while sex is an important feature of many relationships, we cannot assume that frequent sexual activity is some kind of magical ingredient in the recipe for relational happiness. Moreover, having frequent sex is not necessarily the same thing as having good sex. Having good sex would seem to depend on:

- Each person having his or her needs met by a partner who respects the other's specific sexual desires.
- Having the proper balance of positive and negative interactions (sexual and nonsexual) in the relationship, so that there are more positives than negatives.
- Enjoying being with each other, in bed and out of it.

SEXUAL COMMUNICATION

All of the research evidence presented thus far demonstrates the two-way relationship between sex and relationship functioning. And like other relationship issues, sex that is satisfying and meaningful for both partners requires honest and trusting communication. But sexual communication presents couples with a special set of problems. Most of us are not very comfortable talking about sex. Most children are taught that sexual language and terminology is "dirty," and many adults avoid extensive or detailed sexual discussions with children. So we often grow up without a comfortable vocabulary for talking openly about sex. And things are made even more complicated by our concern about how a partner will respond to sexual talk. Will he or she be offended by an attempt at sexual communication? If a couple hasn't yet had sex, bringing up the issue of sex risks the embarrassment of discovering that one's partner isn't even interested.

Communicating Desire

Perhaps the most basic aspect of sexual communication involves conveying sexual desire to one's partner. Because sexual desire can be communicated effectively without words (e.g., by initiating a kiss or unbuttoning a partner's clothes), it may be the most common form of sexual communication (Metts, Sprecher, & Regan, 2000). Sprecher and Sedikides (1993) found that people in a variety of different types of relationships (i.e., dating, cohabiting, and married) all reported expressing their sexual desire to their relationship partners often in the past month, both verbally and nonverbally. The meaning of some nonverbal strategies is fairly clear, while others may be ambiguous. One study found that 60 percent of couples reported using fairly direct nonverbal techniques such as kissing or touching to communicate their desire for sex (Brown & Auerback, 1981). Another study asked college students to describe how they communicate sexual intent and interest to a partner, and responses included much less direct nonverbal strategies, such as good grooming and dressing attractively (Greer & Buss, 1994). The disadvantage of such strategies is obvious: what may be intended to convey sexual interest may be interpreted as neatness and an eye for fashion!

Of course, being direct about our sexual feelings requires that we *know* how we feel—sometimes we may not be sure of our own desire, or we may not have strong feelings one way or the other. O'Sullivan & Gaines (1998) investigated college students' ambivalence about engaging in sexual activity. They found that most had experienced such ambivalence, but not everyone dealt with it in the same way. Some communicated directly to their partner that they weren't sure they wanted to have sex. It was more common, however, for students to either feign interest in sex or reject their partner's advances, despite being uncertain of their own feelings. The fact that we often use such indirect strategies is probably a measure of how vulnerable we are in sexual situations: we opt for indirect communication because we don't want to risk rejection ourselves or risk hurting our partner's feelings.

Vulnerable or not, men are more likely than women to initiate sexual activity (Sprecher & McKinney, 1993). This is true in a variety of relationship types. For example, in the majority of married couples, husbands are more likely to initiate sex than wives (Blumstein & Schwartz, 1983); studies have found the same pattern among cohabiting couples as well (Blumstein & Schwartz, 1983; Byers & Heinlein, 1989). Interestingly, Blumstein and Schwartz argued that this sex difference in sexual initiation is reflected in sexual frequency differences between gay and lesbian couples; gay male couples may have sex more frequently than lesbian couples because both male partners are comfortable communicating their sexual desire, whereas female partners may be less at ease initiating sexual activity.

Once one partner has communicated a desire to initiate sex, it is up to the other partner to indicate his or her consent (or lack of consent). How is consent communicated? Surely this type of sexual communication is a simple matter—all that's required is a straightforward "Yes, I'd like to have sex," right? While it may sound easy, research suggests that conveying a willingness to engage in sex is often more complicated than this (Hickman & Muehlenhard, 1999). In a recent study, young heterosexual adults reported using a wide variety of strategies for communicating sexual consent, but the most common strategy for both sexes involved not resisting a partner's initiation; in other words, instead of conveying consent by saying yes, people often just don't say no (Hickman & Muehlenhard, 1999). Some strategies were more likely to be used by one sex than another. Women were more likely to use indirect verbal strategies, such as asking her partner if he has a condom, whereas men were more likely to use indirect nonverbal strategies, such as kissing or touching. Sex differences were small, however, and the general pattern of responses for men and women was quite similar.

Communicating about sex sometimes requires that we do more than let a partner know whether we're interested in sex or not. Sometimes we need to discuss particular sexual issues with a partner: "Would you like to try a different position?" "How many sexual partners have you had?" or "Do you like oral sex?" Not surprisingly, research confirms that people often have difficulty discussing specific sexual issues (Fisher, Miller, Byrne, & White, 1980). One study of college students showed that while most had discussed sexual issues with a dating partner, disclosure about nonsexual issues was more common than about sexual ones (Byers & Demmons, 1999). In the same study, both men and women reported that they were more likely to talk with a partner about their sexual likes than about their dislikes. Talking about one's sexual dislikes may be more difficult because it could highlight potential disagreements and might involve hurt feelings. Byers and Demmons (1999) also found that sexual self-disclosure was highest when it was reciprocated by a partner. Thus, we are most comfortable talking with a partner about sex if our partner does the same, presumably because the risks of offending or hurting a partner's feelings are minimized if both partners communicate equally.

Sexual Communication and Satisfaction

Given all the potential landmines of sexual communication, why should we bother? Isn't it easier to just rely on prolonged eye contact or an appropriately timed moan to communicate with a sexual partner? While indirect strategies like these may be easier in the short run, there is good evidence that clear sexual communication leads to partners feeling more satisfied with their sex lives. Communicating with a partner about sexual likes and dislikes is associated with greater sexual satisfaction (Byers & Demmons, 1999; Cupach & Comstock, 1990; Purnine & Carey, 1997).

The importance of good sexual communication was highlighted in a study by Masters and Johnson (1979), which compared the sexual experiences of heterosexuals and homosexuals. In terms of sexual efficiency (defined as reaching orgasm easily and consistently), there was little difference between the homosexual and heterosexual couples who participated in this study, in which couples were observed in sexual activities as well as interviewed about their reactions. Masters and Johnson concluded, however, that the subjective quality of the sexual experience (greater psychological involvement, more total body contact, more enjoyment of each aspect of the sexual experience, and more responsiveness to the needs and desires of the partner) was greater for homosexuals (male and female) than for heterosexuals. Masters and Johnson attributed this high subjective quality to, among other things, good communication. In this study, homosexuals talked more easily and openly about their sexual feelings than did heterosexuals. They would ask each other what was desired, and they would comment on whether what was being done was pleasurable. In contrast, Masters and Johnson noted a "persistent neglect of the vital communicative exchange" by heterosexual couples and their "potentially self-destructive lack of intellectual curiosity about the partner" (p. 219).

Given the differences we discussed earlier in the way women and men think about and evaluate sexual behavior, it may not surprise you to learn that women and men are likely to interpret sexual situations differently, too. In general, men tend to perceive the world as a sexier place to be than women do. Heterosexual men tend to perceive other people, particularly women, to be more interested in sex than women do, and they tend to believe that women's behavior has more sexual meaning than do women (Abbey, 1982; Abbey & Melby, 1986; Shotland & Craig, 1988). When men and women interacted with a woman or just observed or read about her, men rated her as a more sexual person (endorsing such descriptors as "sexy" and "seductive") than did women. What does this difference have to do with sexual communication? Well, imagine that Jim and Sarah are out together for the first time. Jim believes that the way Sarah is glancing up at his face, playing with her hair, and "accidentally" brushing his arm with hers is Sarah's way of communicating sexual desire. Sarah, on the other hand, is preoccupied with the piece of spinach she just noticed on Jim's teeth and by the piece of hair that keeps falling into her face, and she is chastising herself for clumsily bumping into Jim. It isn't hard to imagine that this kind of misreading of another person's signals could lead to awkward or unpleasant consequences. As you will see in the next section, some have argued that these differences in interpretation may contribute to sexual violence, especially date rape. Even if the consequences are not so severe, however, the findings we have reviewed in this section clearly show that people and their relationships benefit from honest, forthright communication about sexual desires and intentions.

SEXUAL AGGRESSION

Our discussion thus far has focused almost exclusively on the positive aspects of sexual interaction. But, of course, we know that not all sexual experiences are satisfying, or even wanted. Sadly, researchers have documented that unwanted sexual experiences are all too common. Exact statistics differ from study to study depending in part on the questions asked and the samples studied. From the earlier studies available to them, Cate and Lloyd (1992, p. 99) concluded that "fully one half to three fourths of college women report experiencing some type of sexual aggression in dating relationships." In a more recent meta-analysis of 120 studies involving over 100,000 participants, Spitzberg (1999) examined five forms of sexual aggression. These were

- Rape: Penile penetration of the vagina via the use or threat of force;
- Attempted rape: unsuccessful rape attempts;
- Sexual assault: use of objects such as the penis or tongue to penetrate any orifices (oral, anal, vaginal) via force or threat of force;
- Sexual contact: unwanted sexual play, kissing, rubbing, disrobing and the like (but not penetration) obtained through force, threat of force, continued arguments or authority; and
- Sexual coercion: intercourse obtained by "symbolic means" such as authority or persistent arguments.

In this meta-analysis, the majority (but not all) of the studies examined dating relationships (Spitzberg, personal communication, September 26, 2000).

Overall (see Table 9.2), in these studies about 13 percent of women and just over 3 percent of men reported having been raped; 18 percent of women and nearly 6 percent of men said they had been the victims of a rape attempt; and 22 percent of women and 14 percent of men reported having been sexually assaulted. Across the five different measures, three general conclusions can be drawn. First, men were more likely than women to report having perpetrated sexually coercive behavior. For instance, 9 percent of men versus 6 percent of women reported having sexually assaulted another person. Second, women reported having been coerced more often than having perpetrated coercion. Again with reference to sexual assault, 22 percent perceived themselves as the victims of assault, but only 6 percent engaged in sexual assaults on their partners. Third, on four of five measures, the percentage of women feeling they had been victims of aggression was higher than the percentage of men who acknowledged having been perpetrators of aggression. It is possible that a small number of men are coercive toward a larger number of women. Alternatively, and perhaps more likely in our opinion, women might be more likely to perceive sexual aggression in a partner's behavior.

People occasionally express resistance when they are actually interested in having sex (Muehlenhard & Hollabaugh, 1988). However, a lack of sensitivity to the use of coercion could contribute to date rape, a serious problem on many college campuses today (Shotland, 1989). Sometimes, of course, there is nothing subtle about rape. When a person is confronted with a gun, a knife, or a fist and told to submit sexually, this is clearly rape, whether it occurs on a date, in a marriage, or in a back alley.

But coercion is not always so clear-cut. A woman can feel physically forced when the man believes he is only being assertive. And a man can believe that a woman has "led him on" to a point where he should not be expected to stop. Or perhaps he really believes that she has communicated her desire for sex, even if

TABLE 9.2 **Statistical Summary of Sexual Aggression Estimates Across Samples and Studies**

	Female Victimization	Female Perpetration	Male Victimization	Male Perpetration
	Mean Percent (Study N)	Mean Percent (Study N)	Mean Percent (Study N)	Mean Percent (Study N)
Rape	12.9 (52)	3 (1)	3.3 (13)	4.7 (11)
Attempted Rape	18.3 (31)	NA (0)	5.6 (7)	10.8 (4)
Sexual Assault	22.0 (32)	6.0 (6)	14.2 (11)	8.9 (8)
Sexual Contact	24.0 (25)	8.8 (4)	7.9 (7)	13.4 (10)
Sexual Coercion	25.0 (28)	29.0 (1)	23.2 (11)	24.1 (11)

Source: Spitzberg, 1999.

she hasn't. As described earlier, some have proposed that men's tendency to perceive women in sexual terms may increase the risk of date rape (Abbey, 1987; Bart & O'Brien, 1985). They argue that if a man perceives a woman as sexy and seductive, he may hear a yes when she is saying no. Others, however, have argued that miscommunication is an unlikely explanation for acquaintance rape, because gender differences in perceptions of sexual intent are small, and it is more plausible "that sexually aggressive men selectively ignore or reinterpret what women say to fit what they want to hear, using miscommunication as an excuse for raping (Christopher & Frandsen, 1990; Warshaw, 1994)" (Hickman & Muehlenhard, 1999, p. 268). Even if miscommunication of sexual intent is a factor in cases of acquaintance rape, it would be overly simplistic and dangerous to characterize rape as a mere problem of communication gone awry.

On the other hand, there is no doubt that better sexual communication and decision making can only help to decrease the risk of sexual aggression. After all, if you put two young people with healthy sexual appetites together with some alcohol, an inadequate understanding of each other's concerns, and a fair amount of insecurity about their own self-worth, you may have a situation ready-made for date rape. But what if we change that scenario? What if both people agree in advance that each of them has veto power over sex? Could date rape be reduced if dating partners fully accepted that no really does mean no and puts an end to the discussion? Perhaps so. However, so long as we regard male sexual activity as a form of conquest, encourage women to "play" hard-to-get, and feel embarrassed by honest talk with a sexual partner, it will be difficult to disentangle problems of power and violence from problems of sexual communication and responsibility.

CHAPTER SUMMARY

Sexual Attitudes

Attitudes about Casual Sex. People's attitudes about sex have generally become more permissive over time. Today, most people endorse a "permissiveness-with-affection" standard that is accepting of sex in the context of a committed relationship. Men are somewhat more likely than women to approve of sex outside of such a relationship, but this difference has decreased over time.

Attitudes about Homosexuality. Americans' attitudes about homosexuality are more negative than their attitudes about casual sex. These attitudes have also become less negative over time, however, and the difference may continue to decrease.

Cultural Differences in Sexual Attitudes. Despite increasing permissiveness among Americans, studies have shown sexual attitudes in the United States to be rather conservative. This is true for attitudes about sex before marriage, sex before the age of 16, extramarital sex, and homosexual sex.

Sexual Behavior

Premarital Sex. Rates of sexual intercourse among adolescents suggest that the trend toward earlier first sexual experiences has dropped off. Young people have many different motives for engaging in or avoiding sexual activity, and many of these reasons are tied to the nature of their relationships (e.g., wanting to please a partner or express their love and affection). Researchers have identified a number of predictors of the age at which adolescents first engage in sex, including an individual's values, a desire to become more "adult," and family structure, among others.

Sex in Committed Relationships. The frequency with which people have sex with a relationship partner depends on several factors. Relationship status, age, sexual orientation, and duration of the relationship all have an influence on how often a couple engages in sex.

Monogamy. Despite most people's general disapproval of extradyadic sex, a sizable minority of people engage in sex with someone other than their current relationship partner. Men are more likely than women, and gay men are more likely than heterosexual men, to be nonmonogamous. Sociosexual orientation is another predictor, as is the degree of equity in a relationship.

Preventing Pregnancy and Sexually Transmitted Diseases. Given the high frequency of casual sex among young adults, researchers have worked to identify the factors that make a person less likely to use birth control and to practice safer sex. These factors include interpersonal obstacles to condom use, the influence of alcohol on sexual decision-making, beliefs of personal invulnerability, and negative attitudes about sex.

Sexual Satisfaction

Sexual Frequency and Satisfaction. Most people report generally high levels of sexual satisfaction, and this is particularly true for people who have sex more often.

Sex and Relationship Satisfaction. Many studies have shown that those partners who are satisfied with their sex lives tend to be more satisfied with their relationships, in general. Other studies suggest a somewhat more complicated association, focusing on the match between ideal and actual sexual frequency, general levels of positivity and negativity in the relationship, and the nature of relationship activities that a couple engages in (sexual and nonsexual).

Exchange Theories and Sexual Satisfaction. The Interpersonal Exchange Model of Sexual Satisfaction focuses on a person's sexual costs and rewards as predictors of sexual satisfaction. Equity theory predicts that a lack of equity (especially if one is the underbenefited partner) is associated with less sexual satisfaction.

Sexual Communication

Communicating Desire. People often try to communicate sexual desire to their sexual partners, but this communication is often nonverbal and indirect. Men are more likely than women to initiate sex, and both sexes use a variety of strategies to indicate a willingness to engage in sexual activity. Talking about specific sexual issues, particularly sexual problems and dislikes, is often difficult for sexual partners.

Sexual Communication and Satisfaction. Direct and honest sexual communication is associated with greater relationship and sexual satisfaction.

Sexual Aggression

Studies show that sexual violence is frighteningly common. Researchers have identified various forms of sexual aggression, and women are more likely than men to be the victims. There is debate about whether sexual miscommunication plays a role in the incidence of sexual aggression, particularly date rape; in any case, power discrepancies between women and men are an important aspect of sexual violence.

PART FOUR

Relationship Issues

CHAPTER 10

Stresses and Strains

SHYNESS ◆ JEALOUSY ◆ Two Types of Jealousy ◆ Who's Prone to Jealousy? ◆
Who Gets Us Jealous? ◆ What Gets Us Jealous? ◆ Responses to
Jealousy ◆ Coping Constructively with Jealousy ◆ DECEPTION
AND LYING ◆ Lying in Close and Casual Relationships ◆
Lies and Liars ◆ So, How Well Can We Detect a
Partner's Deception? ◆ BETRAYAL ◆ Individual
Differences in Betrayal ◆ The Two Sides
to Every Betrayal ◆ Coping with Betrayal ◆
CHAPTER SUMMARY

Let's pause for a moment and take stock. In previous chapters, we have discussed adaptive and maladaptive cognition, good and bad communication, and rewarding and unrewarding social exchange. Until now, we have given equal time to both beneficial and disadvantageous influences on close relationships. But not here. In this chapter, we'll concentrate on various pitfalls, stumbling blocks, and hazards that cause wear and tear in relationships. And importantly, the stresses and strains we cover here—shyness, jealousy, lying, and betrayal—are commonplace events that occur in most relationships somewhere along the way. As we'll see, most people have been shy at some point in their lives, and almost half feel that they are shy now (Carducci, 1999). Sooner or later, almost everyone lies to their intimate partners (DePaulo, Kashy, Kirkendol, Wyer, & Epstein, 1996). Even outright betrayals of one sort or another are surprisingly widespread and hard to avoid (Baxter et al., 1997).

However, the fact that these incidents are commonplace doesn't mean they are inconsequential. Negative events like these can be just as influential as—and sometimes even more powerful than—the rewards people get from their relationships (Rook, 1998). They help explain why most of us report having had a very troublesome relationship within the last five years (Levitt et al., 1996). Perhaps even worse, such problems may even prevent a worthwhile relationship from ever beginning, as we'll see in the next section.

279

SHYNESS

Have you ever felt anxious and inhibited around other people, worrying about their evaluations of you and feeling ill at ease in your interactions with them? Most people have. Over 80 percent of us have experienced **shyness,** the syndrome that combines social reticence and inhibited interactive behavior with nervous discomfort in social settings (Bruch & Cheek, 1995; Leary & Kowalski, 1995). When people are shy, they fret about social disapproval and unhappily anticipate unfavorable judgments from others. They also tend to be preoccupied with their own imagined inadequacies, so they feel self-conscious and inept (van der Molen, 1990). As a result, they interact with others in an impoverished manner. If they don't avoid an interaction altogether, they behave in an inhibited, guarded fashion; they look at others less, smile less, speak less often, and converse less responsively, and they may even stand farther away (Asendorpf, 1990). Compared to people who are not shy, they manage small talk poorly.

Shyness may beset almost anyone now and then. It is especially common when we are in unfamiliar settings, meeting attractive, high-status strangers for the first time. It is unlikely to occur when we are on familiar turf interacting with old friends (Leary & Kowalski, 1995). However, some people are *chronically* shy, experiencing shyness often, and there are three characteristics that distinguish them from people who are less shy. First, people who are routinely shy *fear negative evaluation* from others. The possibility that others might dislike them is rarely far from their minds, and the threat of derision or disdain from others is more frightening to them than it is to most people. Second, they tend to doubt themselves. *Poor self-regard* usually accompanies chronic shyness, and "shy people tend to have fairly extensive problems with low self-esteem" (Cheek & Melchior, 1990, p. 59). Finally, they feel less competent in their interactions with others; overall, they have lower levels of *social skill* than do people who are not shy (Evans, 1993; Jackson, Towson, & Narduzzi, 1997).

This unwelcome combination of perceptions and behavior puts shy people between a rock and a hard place. They worry about what people are thinking of them and dread disapproval from others, but they don't feel capable of making favorable impressions that would avoid such disapproval. As a result, they adopt a cautious, relatively withdrawn style of interaction that deflects interest and enthusiasm from others. For instance, if they find an attractive woman looking at them, shy men won't look back, smile, and say hello; instead, they'll look away and say nothing (Garcia, Stinson, Ickes, Bissonnette, & Briggs, 1991). Pleasant conversations that would have ensued had the men been less shy sometimes do not occur at all. (Do you tend to be chronically shy? See for yourself in Table 10.1).

The irony here is that by behaving in such a timid manner, people who are either temporarily or chronically shy often make the negative impressions on others that they were hoping to avoid. Instead of eliciting sympathy, their aloof, unrewarding behavior often seems dull or disinterested to others. In groups, their quiet reticence leads others to think they're not very smart (Paulhus & Morgan, 1997), and over time, they may be more likely to encounter neglect and rejection than understanding and empathy (Bruch & Cheek, 1995). Indeed,

TABLE 10.1. The Shyness Scale

How shy are you? Rate how well each of the following statements describes you using this scale:

0 = Extremely uncharacteristic of me.
1 = Slightly characteristic of me.
2 = Moderately characteristic of me.
3 = Very characteristic of me.
4 = Extremely characteristic of me.

___1. I am socially somewhat awkward.
___2. I don't find it hard to talk to strangers.
___3. I feel tense when I'm with people I don't know well.
___4. When conversing, I worry about saying something dumb.
___5. I feel nervous when speaking to someone in authority.
___6. I am often uncomfortable at parties and other social functions.
___7. I feel inhibited in social situations.
___8. I have trouble looking someone right in the eye.
___9. I am more shy with members of the opposite sex.

The first thing you have to do to calculate your score is to reverse your answer to number 2. If you gave yourself a 0 on that item, change it to a 4; a 1 becomes a 3, a 3 becomes a 1, and a 4 should be changed to 0. (2 does not change.) Then add up your ratings. The average score for both men and women is about 14.5, with a standard deviation of close to six points. Thus, if your score is 8 or lower, you're less shy than most people, but if your score is 20 or higher, you're more shy.

Source: Cheek & Buss, 1981.

shy people make new friends much more slowly and fall in love much less often than do those who are not shy (Asendorpf & Wilpers, 1998). They also tend to be more lonely, as we'll discuss in chapter 14 (Dill & Anderson, 1999).

Obviously, it's usually better to feel confident than shy in social life. On occasion, shyness can be useful; when people really are confronted with novel situations and don't know how to behave, brief bouts of shy caution may keep them from doing something inappropriate (Leary, 2001a). More often, however, shy people run scared from the threat of social disapproval that hasn't occurred and never will, so their shyness is an unnecessary and counterproductive burden (Miller, in press). Formal programs that help people to overcome chronic shyness often teach them a more positive frame of mind, helping them to manage their anxiety and apprehension about social evaluation, and teach them social skills, focusing on how to initiate conversations and how to be assertive. Both positive thinking and effective behavior are then rehearsed in role-playing assignments and other practice settings until the clients feel comfortable enough to try them on their own (Henderson & Zimbardo, 1998).

TABLE 10.2. Doing Better with an Excuse for Failure

In Leary's (1986) study, when noise that was said to be impossibly "loud" gave shy people an excuse for their interactions to go badly, they behaved no differently than did people who were not shy. In contrast, "soft" noise that was not supposed to interfere with their conversations left them tense and anxious, even though the noise was played at exactly the same volume in both the "loud" and "soft" conditions.

	CHANGE IN HEART RATE (IN BEATS PER MINUTE)	
	Noise	
Participants' Chronic Shyness	"Soft"	"Loud"
Low	5.3	4.7
High	15.8	4.5

However, most shy people probably do not need formal training in interaction skills, because they do just fine when they relax and quit worrying about how they're being judged. If you're troubled by shyness now, you may make better impressions on others if you actually care *less* about what they think. Evidence for this possibility comes from an intriguing study by Mark Leary (1986), who asked people to meet and greet a stranger in a noisy environment that was said to simulate a crowded singles bar. Leary created a multitrack tape of overlapping conversations, three different songs, radio static, and party noise (such as laughing and yelling)—it was definitely "noise"—and played it at a mildly obnoxious level as each couple talked. Importantly, the tape was always played at the same volume, but some people were told that the noise was so loud that it would probably interfere with their conversation and make it hard for them to have a nice chat, whereas others were told that the noise was soft enough that it wouldn't be a problem. Once these expectations were in place, people who were either shy or not shy were left alone with a stranger, a setting that is ordinarily threatening to shy people. Leary monitored the heart rates of his participants to track their anxiety and arousal, and Table 10.2 shows what he found. When the noise was "soft" and there wasn't a good excuse for their interactions to go poorly, shy people exhibited considerably more arousal and apprehension than normal people did; their heart rates increased three times as much. Even worse, they looked obviously shy and uncomfortable to people who later watched videotapes of their conversations. On the other hand, when they had an excuse—the impossibly "loud" noise—that lowered everyone's expectations, they behaved as if they weren't shy at all. They exhibited a normal, moderate increase in heart rate as their interactions began, and they gave observers no clue that they were usually shy.

Interestingly, if they couldn't be blamed for interactions that went badly, the shy people in Leary's (1986) study relaxed and conducted their conversations without difficulty. In a sense, when they were given a nonthreatening way to think about an upcoming interaction, their shyness disappeared. Such people— and that probably includes most people who feel shy—probably don't need ad-

By worrying too much about what others are
thinking of them, shy people may actually convey
to others the negative impressions they fear.

ditional training in basic social skills. What they do need is greater calm and self-
confidence (Glass & Shea, 1986). Although that may not be easy to come by, shy
people should consider the alternative: They're not winning friends and influencing people by acting shy, so what do they have to lose by trusting themselves
and expecting interactions to go well?

JEALOUSY

Once we have an established relationship, a different kind of uncomfortable experience can occur. **Jealousy** is the negative emotional experience that results
from the potential loss of a valued relationship to a real or imagined rival (Salovey, 1991). It often involves a variety of feelings, ranging all the way from sad
dejection to actual pride that one's partner is desirable to others, but the three
feelings that define jealousy best are *hurt, anger,* and *fear* (Guerrero & Andersen,
1998b; Sharpsteen, 1993).[1]

---

[1]Jealousy is sometimes confused with envy, but the two are quite different (Parrott & Smith, 1993).
We envy someone when we wish we had what they have; envy is characterized by a humiliating
longing for another person's possessions. In contrast, jealousy is the confused state of hurt, anger,
and fear that results from the threat of losing what we already have, a relationship that we do not
wish to give up.

Hurt follows from the perception that one's partner has failed to honor his or her commitment to their relationship, and fear and anxiety result from the dreadful prospect of abandonment and loss (Guerrero & Andersen, 1998a). But it's not just the painful loss of a rewarding partnership that creates jealousy; people suffer when they lose a relationship for any reason, ranging from a partner's move overseas to take a wonderful job, to the partner's accidental death. The unique element in jealousy is the romantic rival who threatens to lure a partner away: "To be jealous, one must have a relationship to lose and a rival to whom to lose it" (DeSteno & Salovey, 1994, p. 220). It's being cast aside for someone else that gets people angry (Mathes, Adams, & Davies, 1985), and unless the rival is a friend who is also thought to be guilty of a personal betrayal, most of that anger is directed at the partner who is beginning to stray (Paul, Foss, & Galloway, 1993). Sometimes that anger turns violent; 13 percent of all the murders in the United States result from one spouse killing another, and when that occurs, jealousy is the most common motive (Buss, 2000).

Obviously, jealousy is an unhappy experience. It appears to be a common experience around the world, however (Buss et al., 1999), and it has even been observed in children under two years of age (when their mothers ignored them to play with other children; Masciuch & Kienapple, 1993). Moreover, our cultural reactions to jealousy are not always negative. An analysis of magazine articles from 1945 to 1985 demonstrated that back in the 1950s and 1960s, jealousy was usually considered to prove one's love and to be good for a marriage (Clanton, 1989). In the 1970s and 1980s, the typical view changed to depict jealousy as an improper, unhealthy state born of insecurity and personality defects. In the twenty-first century, our ambivalence continues, with jealousy seeming to be "a two-edged sword—an expression of love on the one hand, of perceived paranoia on the other" (Guerrero & Andersen, 1998a, p. 40). If anything, however, people may be more prone to jealousy than they used to be. In the 1990s, both homosexual and heterosexual men reported more jealousy at the thought of a lover having sex with someone else than did men surveyed 12 years earlier (Bringle, 1995).

Given that, here's an interesting question: How would you feel if you *couldn't* make your lover jealous? Would you be disappointed if nothing you did gave your partner a jealous twinge? Most people probably would be, but whether or not that's a sensible point of view may depend on what type of jealousy we're talking about, why your partner is jealous, and what your partner does in response to his or her jealousy. Let's explore those factors.

Two Types of Jealousy

Reactive jealousy occurs when someone becomes aware of an actual threat to a valued relationship (Bringle & Buunk, 1991; Parrott, 1991). The troubling threat may not be a current event; it may have occurred in the past, or it may be anticipated in the near future (if, for instance, one's partner expresses the intention to date someone else), but reactive jealousy always occurs in response to a realistic danger. A variety of behaviors from one's partner can cause concern; people all over the world become jealous if their partners have sex with someone else (Hupka et al., 1985), but even just fantasizing about or flirting with someone else is considered "unfaithful" by young adults in the United States (Yarab, Allgeier, & Sensibaugh, 1999). Unfortunately, there may be a lot to be jealous about. In one survey of nearly 700 American college students, most young adults reported having dated, kissed, fondled, or slept with someone else at some time while they were in a serious dating relationship with a romantic partner (Wiederman & Hurd, 1999). Two-thirds of the men and half of the women said they had kissed and fondled someone else, and half of the men and a third of the women said they had had intercourse with a rival (most of them more than once).

In contrast, **suspicious jealousy** occurs when one's partner *hasn't* misbehaved and one's suspicions do not fit the facts at hand (Bringle & Buunk, 1991). Suspicious jealousy results in worried and mistrustful vigilance and snooping as the jealous partner seeks to confirm his or her suspicions, and it can range from outright paranoia to a mildly overactive imagination. In all cases, however, suspicious jealousy can be said to be unfounded; it results from situations that would not trouble a more secure and more trusting partner.

The distinction between the two types of jealousy is meaningful, because almost everybody feels reactive jealousy when they realize that their partners have been unfaithful (Bringle & Buunk, 1991; Buss, 2000), but people vary a lot in their tendencies to feel suspicious jealousy in the absence of any provocation. Nevertheless, the distinction between the two isn't quite as sharp as it may seem. A jealous reaction to a partner's affair may linger on as suspicious jealousy years later, as trust, once lost, is never fully regained. Reactive jealousy may create suspicious jealousy that had not been present earlier. And people may differ in their judgments of what constitutes a real threat to their relationship (Buunk & Hupka, 1987). Knowledge that a partner is merely fantasizing about someone else may not trouble a secure partner who is not much prone to jealousy, but it may cause reactive jealousy in a partner who is insecure. What is reactive jealousy in one person may seem like suspicious jealousy to another. So, the boundary between them can be vague, and as we explore individual differences in susceptibility to jealousy in our next section, we'll ask a generic question that refers to both types of jealousy.

Who's Prone to Jealousy?

On the whole, men and women do not differ in their jealous tendencies (Buunk, 1995), but there are individual differences in susceptibility to jealousy that lead some people to feel jealous more readily and more intensely than other people do. One obvious precursor of jealousy is *dependence* on a relationship (Buunk, 1982). When people feel that they need a particular partner because their alternatives are poor—that is, when people have a low CL_{alt}—any threat to their relationship is especially menacing. In contrast, people who have desirable alternatives tend to be less jealous, because they have less to lose if the relationship ends (Hansen, 1985b).

Jealousy also increases with feelings of *inadequacy* in a relationship (White, 1981a, 1981b). People who worry that they can't measure up to their partners' expectations, or who fret that they're not what their lovers are looking for, are more prone to jealousy than are people who feel certain they can keep their partners satisfied. Self-confidence in a relationship is undoubtedly affected by a person's global sense of self-worth, but people with high self-esteem are not always less jealous than those with low self-esteem (Guerrero & Andersen, 1998b). Instead, it's a person's perceptions of his or her adequacy as a partner in the relationship that matters, and that depends more on how much your partner likes and needs you than on how much you like yourself. Even people with generally high self-esteem can be prone to jealousy if they doubt their ability to fulfill a beloved partner.

One of the ingredients in such doubt is a discrepancy in the "mate value" each person brings to the relationship (Buss, 2000). If one partner is more desirable than the other, possessing (for example) more physical attractiveness, wealth, or talent, the less desirable partner is a less valuable mate, and that's a potential problem. The less desirable partner is likely to be aware that others could be a better match for his or her lover, and that may cause a sense of inadequacy that does not exist in other areas of his or her life (or with other partners). Here is another reason, then, why "matching" occurs, with people pairing off with others of similar mate value (see chapter 3): Most of us want the most desirable partners we can get, but it can be threatening to realize that our partners could do better if they really wanted to.

In any case, consider the perilous situation that faces people who feel both dependent on and inadequate in their current relationships: They need their partners but worry that they're not good enough to keep them. It's no wonder that they react strongly to real or imagined signs that a romantic rival has entered the scene.

Attachment styles influence jealousy, too, and to some extent, people with a preoccupied style routinely find themselves in a similar fix: They greedily seek closeness with others, but they remain chronically worried that their partners don't love them enough in return. That's a recipe for jealousy, and sure enough, preoccupied people experience more jealousy than do those with the other three styles (Buunk, 1997; Sharpsteen & Kirkpatrick, 1997). People with a fearful style share the same anxiety over abandonment that preoccupied people do (remember Figure 8.2 back in chapter 8?), so they experience similar worry and suspicion in jealousy-provoking situations, but with their lower comfort with closeness, they tend not to be as sad or scared by competition with a rival (Guerrero, 1998). By comparison, people with secure or dismissing styles don't worry about being abandoned by others, so they tend to be less prone to jealousy than preoccupied or fearful people are. However, secure people do tend to experience more fear than dismissing people do when a valued relationship is imperiled (Guerrero, 1998). Add all this up, and the folks who are least affected across the board when a relationship is threatened are typically those with a dismissing style of attachment. Feeling self-sufficient and trying not to depend on others is apparently one way to stay relatively immune to jealousy.

Other personal characteristics also promote jealousy. People who value *sexual exclusivity*, who want and expect their partners to be monogamous, are

Jealousy is the negative emotional experience—a combination of hurt, anger, and fear—that results from the potential loss of a valued relationship to a real or imagined rival.

likely to experience high levels of reactive jealousy if their partners have affairs (White, 1981a, 1981b). On the other hand, if their partners share their desire for sexual exclusivity and are being faithful, such people tend to experience less suspicious jealousy than others because a sexual betrayal seems unlikely (Pines & Aronson, 1983). By comparison, people who have had (or are planning) affairs of their own tend to be less jealous when their partners stray (Buunk, 1982), but they also tend to worry more that their partners *will* stray in the future (Guerrero & Andersen, 1998b). Overall, then, people who do not value sexual exclusivity tend to experience less reactive jealousy but more suspicious jealousy than do people who emphasize monogamy.

Traditional gender roles also make jealousy more likely (Hansen, 1985a, 1985b). Macho men and feminine women experience more jealousy than androgynous people do, perhaps because the rules of traditional relationships tend to be quite strict. With their rigid expectations, there's little room for idiosyncrasy in traditional partnerships, and that causes greater dismay if the partners break the rules by, for instance, forming a friendship with a coworker of the other sex at work.

Who Gets Us Jealous?

Learning that our partners are interested in someone else can evoke jealousy, but not all rivals are created equal. Romantic rivals who have high mate value and who make us look bad by comparison are worrisome threats to our relationships, and they arouse more jealousy than do rivals who are milder competition. But the particular talents of a rival matter, too. A rival who surpasses us in accomplishments we care about—who has achieved things we wish we had—is especially galling (DeSteno & Salovey, 1996b). A rival who is attractive to our partners is disturbing, too. And what kind of rival is that? It depends on whether a partner is male or female. As we saw in chapter 3, men are particularly interested in women's looks, whereas women are particularly interested in men's resources. The worst rival is one who can beat us at our own game, and men are more jealous of other men who are self-confident, dominant, and assertive (which are traits that suggest one is resourceful) than they are of rivals who are simply very handsome (Dijkstra & Buunk, 1998). In contrast, women are more jealous of other women who are pretty than they are of rivals who are self-confident and dominant. Both men and women experience more jealousy when they encounter rivals who are good at giving the other sex what it wants, but for women the threatening comparison is physical attractiveness, and for men it's dominance.

You might remember that this pattern is consistent with evolutionary psychology's assumption—emerging from the parental investment model—that men seek youth and fertility (thus, beauty) in their partners, whereas women seek resources (thus, dominance) in their men. Evolutionary psychology has also stimulated study of another, more arguable, difference between men and women in the misbehavior from their partners that threatens them most.

What Gets Us Jealous?

An evolutionary perspective suggests that jealousy evolved to motivate behavior designed to protect our close relationships from the interference of others (Buss, 1999, 2000). Presumably, early humans who reacted strongly to interlopers—being vigilant to outside interference, fending off rivals, and working hard to satisfy and fulfill their current partners—maintained their relationships and reproduced more successfully than did those who were blasé about meddlesome rivals. This perspective thus suggests that, because it offered reproductive advantages in the past, jealousy is now a natural, ingrained reaction that is hard to avoid (Buss, 2000). More provocatively, it also suggests that men and women should be especially sensitive to different sorts of infidelity in their romantic partners.

As you may recall (from chapter 1), men face a reproductive problem that women do not have: paternity uncertainty. A woman always knows whether or not a particular child is hers, but, unless he is completely confident that his mate hasn't had sex with other men, a man can't be certain (without using some advanced technology) that he is a child's father. And being cuckolded and raising another man's offspring is an evolutionary dead end; the human race did not descend from ancestors who raised other people's children and had none of their own! Indeed, the potential evolutionary costs of failing to detect a partner's infidelity are so great that natural selection may have favored men who were *too* suspicious of their partners' faithfulness over those who were not suspicious enough (Haselton & Buss, 2000). Unwarranted doubt about a partner's fidelity is divisive and painful, but it may not be as costly and dangerous to men, in an evolutionary sense, as being too trusting and failing to detect infidelity when it occurs. Thus, today, men have more extramarital affairs than women do (Buss, 1994), but husbands tend to be less certain than wives are that their spouses have been totally faithful to them (Paul et al., 1993). Paternity uncertainty may cause men to be more vigilant than women are about the threat of sexual infidelity.

For their part, women presumably enjoyed more success raising their children when they were sensitive to any signs that a man might withdraw the resources that were protecting and sheltering them and their children. Assuming that men were committed to them when the men in fact were not would have been risky for women, so natural selection may have favored those who were usually skeptical of men's declarations of true love. Unfairly doubting a man's commitment may be obnoxious and self-defeating, but believing that a mate was devoted and committed when he was not may have been more costly still. In our ancestral past, women who frequently and naïvely mated with men who then abandoned them probably did not reproduce as successfully as did women who insisted on more proof that a fellow was there to stay. Thus, modern women are probably the "descendants of ancestral mothers who erred in the direction of being cautious," who tended to prudently underestimate the commitment of their men (Haselton & Buss, 2000, p. 83).

As a result of all this, men may experience the most jealousy at the thought of *sexual* infidelity in their mates, whereas women react more to the threat of *emotional* infidelity, the possibility that their partners are falling in love with someone else. Either type of infidelity can provoke jealousy in either sex, but they differ in their evolutionary implications. For a man, it's not a partner's love for someone else that's the bigger threat to his reproductive success, it's the sex; his children may still thrive if his mate loves another man, but he certainly does not want to raise the other man's children. For a woman, it's not a partner's sex with someone else that's more dangerous, it's the love; as long as he continues to provide needed resources, her children may still thrive even if he impregnates other women, but if he falls in love and moves out entirely, her kids' future may be imperiled.

This reasoning led David Buss and his colleagues (Buss, Larsen, Westen, & Semmelroth, 1992, p. 252) to pose this compelling question to research participants:

> Please think of a serious committed romantic relationship that you have had in the past, that you currently have, or that you would like to have. Imagine that you discover that the person with whom you've been seriously involved became interested in someone else. What would distress or upset you more (*please pick only one*):
>
> (A) Imagining your partner forming a deep emotional attachment to that person.
>
> (B) Imagining your partner enjoying passionate sexual intercourse with that other person.

Which one would you pick? Most of the men—60 percent—said the sex would upset them more, but only 17 percent of the women chose that option; instead, a sizable majority of the women—83 percent—reported that they would be more distressed by a partner's emotional attachment to a rival. Moreover, a follow-up study demonstrated that men and women differed in their physiological reactions to these choices (Buss et al., 1992). Men displayed more autonomic changes indicative of emotional arousal when they imagined a partner's sexual, rather than emotional, infidelity, but the reverse was true for women.

On the surface, these results are consistent with an evolutionary perspective. However, they have been challenged by critics who suggested that they are less convincing than they seem. One straightforward complaint is methodological. The use of a "forced-choice" question in which research participants have to pick one option or the other can exaggerate a subtle and relatively minor sex difference (DeSteno & Salovey, 1996a). If men find sexual infidelity only slightly more threatening than women do, a forced-choice question could yield the striking results Buss et al. (1992) obtained even if the actual difference in men's and women's outlooks was rather trivial.

More importantly, men and women may differ in their judgments of the meanings of emotional and sexual infidelity (DeSteno & Salovey, 1996a; Harris & Christenfeld, 1996). If women routinely assume that men can have sex with someone without loving that partner, sexual infidelity may be just that: casual sex. However, if women also assume that when a man is in love with someone else, he's having (or wants to have) sex with her, a man's emotional infidelity would imply that sexual infidelity is occurring as well. Thus, if women think that men's sexual infidelity often occurs by itself, but emotional and sexual infidelity always go together, it would be reasonable for them to consider emotional infidelity the bigger threat. For their part, if men assume that women often love someone without having sex, but usually love those with whom they do have sex, sexual infidelity would seem the more momentous threat to them.

In fact, people do tend to assume that a person conducting an extramarital affair is more likely to be emotionally attached to the illicit lover, and more committed to the extramarital relationship, if the cheating spouse is a woman instead of a man (Sprecher, Regan, & McKinney, 1998). People think that sex and love are more closely connected for women than for men, so the choice between the two types of infidelity probably does mean different things for men than for women.

There are other possible problems with the results obtained by Buss et al. (1992). Other researchers have had trouble getting the same patterns of physiological responses (Grice & Seely, 2000); men do respond with more arousal to imagined scenes of sexual, rather than emotional, infidelity, but they're also affected by *any* scenes with sexual content, whether or not infidelity is involved (Harris, 2000). Even the basic finding that men dread sexual infidelity more than women do is not always obtained (Hupka & Bank, 1996).

Nevertheless, most studies do obtain that finding, and it has now been replicated in Sweden (Wiederman & Kendall, 1999), the Netherlands and Germany (Buunk, Angleitner, Oubaid, & Buss, 1996), and Korea and Japan (Buss et al., 1999). Overall, the extent to which people react jealously to sexual infidelity varies from culture to culture, but men routinely find it more distressing than women do. Moreover, the sex difference still results when people are asked to pick the infidelity that bothers them most after *both* infidelities have occurred (Buss et al., 1999), a finding that answers the criticism that they mean different things to the different sexes. The sex difference is also obtained when people rate their distress in response to the two infidelities instead of just picking the one that bothers them more (Sagarin, Becker, Guadagno, Nicastle, & Millevoi, 2000); the pattern doesn't just depend on how you ask the question.

The most reasonable conclusion from all these studies is that everybody hates both types of infidelity. Here, as in so many other cases, the sexes are more similar to each other than different. Still, to the extent that they differ at all, women are likely to perceive a partner's emotional attachment to a rival as more perilous than men do (e.g., Sagarin et al., 2000). This pattern is consistent with evolutionary assumptions, but it doesn't prove that they are correct; there may be other influences at work, including the simple possibility that—consistent with their predominant gender roles—women are more attuned to their partners' feelings about things than men are (Harris, 2000). In any case, it's clear that the threat of infidelity is a salient, jealousy-provoking event for both men and women (see Box 10.1), and evolutionary psychology offers a fascinating, if arguable, explanation of men's and women's reactions to it.

Responses to Jealousy

People may react to the hurt, anger, and fear of jealousy in ways that have either beneficial or destructive effects on their relationships (Guerrero, Andersen, Jorgensen, Spitzberg, & Eloy, 1995). On occasion, jealous people lash out in ways that are unequivocally harmful, retaliating against their partners with violent behavior or verbal antagonism, or with efforts to make them jealous in return (Guerrero & Andersen, 1998a). On other occasions, people respond in ways that may be intended to protect the relationship but that often undermine it further: spying on their partners, restricting their partners' freedom, or derogating or threatening their rivals. There are times, however, when people respond positively to jealousy by straightforwardly expressing their concerns and trying to work things out with their partners, or by making themselves or their relationships more desirable (by, for instance, improving their appearance, sending the partner gifts, or doing more housework) (Guerrero & Andersen, 1998b).

Attachment styles help determine what people will do. When they become jealous, people who are relatively comfortable with closeness—those with secure or preoccupied attachment styles—are more likely to express their concerns and to try to repair their relationships than are those with more avoidant styles (Guerrero, 1998). By comparison, people who are dismissing or fearful are more likely to avoid the issue or deny their distress by pretending nothing is wrong or by acting like they don't care.

BOX 10.1

Cues to Infidelity

The extent of people's sensitivity to the threat of infidelity from a romantic partner is apparent in the number of different cues they consider to be warning signs of potential unfaithfulness. Todd Shackelford and David Buss (1997) asked a large group of college students to nominate events that would lead them to suspect sexual or emotional infidelity, and the students identified 170 of them! These diverse cues reflected 14 different broad categories of events, and most of them were believed to be more indicative of one type of infidelity than the other. As you can see, the cues ranged from uncharacteristic anger and inconsiderateness to exaggerated displays of affection, so they covered a lot of ground. Have you noticed any of these in your romantic partner?

CUES MORE DIAGNOSTIC OF SEXUAL INFIDELITY

Revelation of an affair: Finding a partner in bed with a rival, or being told by friends;

Physical clues: Encountering an unexpected sexually transmitted disease;

Sexual disinterest or boredom: Finding a partner to be strangely unresponsive;

Changes in the normal routine: New and unusual sexual positions, or changes in sleeping, eating, or clothing habits; and

Exaggerated sexual interest or affection: Sudden, suspicious increases in sexual appetite or affectionate behavior.

CUES MORE DIAGNOSTIC OF EMOTIONAL INFIDELITY

Dissatisfaction with the relationship: Suggestions that you break up or begin seeing others;

Emotional disengagement: Forgetting anniversaries, or neglecting to say "I love you";

Acting guilty or anxious: Being unusually apologetic or avoiding eye contact;

Reluctance to discuss someone: Avoiding talk or acting nervous about some other person;

Avoiding the relationship: Ducking dates, or offering fewer invitations to spend time together;

Increased anger and criticism: Becoming less tolerant and more argumentative; and

Increased inconsiderateness: Becoming rude or less gentle.

CUES EQUALLY DIAGNOSTIC OF EITHER INFIDELITY

Spending time with a rival: Wearing something belonging to a rival, or calling you by a rival's name; and

Acting apathetic: Spending less time on appearance, or becoming less excited to see you.

Interestingly, compared to men, women considered almost all of these signals to be more likely to indicate that their partners were being unfaithful (Shackelford & Buss, 1997). They had a lower threshold than men did for assuming the existence of an affair. On one hand, this is sensible, because men do tend to have more affairs than women do (Buss, 1994). On the other hand, many of these cues—particularly those thought to signal emotional infidelity—are quite ambiguous. We hope that people do not inadvertently poison their relationships by assuming the worst when such conclusions are unwarranted.

Men and women often differ in their responses to jealousy, too, with consequences that can complicate heterosexual relationships. Imagine yourself in
this situation: At a party, you leave your romantic partner sitting on a couch
when you go to refill your drinks. While you're gone, your partner's old
boyfriend or girlfriend happens by and sits for a moment, and they share a light
kiss of greeting just as you return with the drinks. What would you do? In one
of the few experimental studies of jealousy, researchers showed people videotapes of a scenario like this and measured their intentions, and men and
women responded differently (Shettel-Neuber, Bryson, & Young, 1978). Women
said they would react to the rival's interference by seeking to *improve the relationship;* they intended to put on a show of indifference but compete with the
rival by making themselves more attractive to their partners. In contrast, men
said they would strive to *protect their egos;* they planned to get drunk, confront
and threaten the rival, and pursue other women. Whereas women seemed to
focus on preserving the existing relationship, men considered leaving it and
salving their wounded pride with conquests of new partners.

Sex differences like these have also been obtained in other studies (Guerrero & Reiter, 1998), and one thing that makes them worrisome is that women
are much more likely than men to *try* to get their partners jealous (White,
1980a). When they induce jealousy—usually by discussing or exaggerating
their attraction to other men, sometimes by flirting with or dating them—they
typically seek to test the relationship (to see how much he cares) or try to elicit
more attention and commitment from their partners (White, 1980a). They evidently want their men to respond the way they do when they get jealous, with
greater effort to protect and maintain the relationship. The problem, of course,
is that that's not the way men typically react. Women who seek to improve their
relationships by inducing jealousy in their men may succeed only in driving
their partners away.

Coping Constructively with Jealousy

So, near the end of our discussion, would you still be disappointed if you
couldn't make your partner jealous? It's an unhappy mixture of hurt, anger,
and fear that occurs when your partner wants you but isn't sure he or she can
keep you. It sometimes seems to be the glue that keeps people together, but it
can also be "the explosive force that destroys the couple and alienates the persons from each other" (Bringle & Buunk, 1991, p. 149). It may be a natural thing
for humans to feel, but it's often an ugly, awful feeling that results in terribly
destructive behavior (Buss, 2000). Someday, you may find yourself wishing that
you could feel it less intensely, and limit its effects. What can be done?

There are no easy and certain answers to this question, but many of those
who have considered this issue have emphasized two major themes. First, we
have to do away with the notion that jealousy is a sign of "true love." In fact,
jealousy is a sign of dependency and is a reflection of our own desires, our own
self-interest. Jealousy isn't based on generous concern for the well-being of our
partners, it's inherently selfish. The first step in controlling jealousy is to learn
to recognize it for what it is.

A second step is to work on reducing the connection between the exclusivity of a relationship and our sense of self-worth. Finding that someone we love is attracted to a rival can be painful. However, it does not mean that your partner is a horrible, worthless person, or that you are. We react irrationally when we act as though our self-worth totally depended on a particular relationship.

In fact, when they succeed in reducing unwanted jealousy, people tend to use two techniques that help them to maintain a sense of independence and self-worth (Salovey & Rodin, 1988). The first is *self-reliance,* which involves efforts to "stay cool" and avoid feeling angry or embarrassed by refusing to dwell on the unfairness of the situation. The second is *self-bolstering,* giving a boost to one's self-esteem by doing something nice for oneself and thinking about one's good qualities. Maintaining a sense of self-confidence about one's ability to act, and to survive, independently apparently helps keep jealousy at manageable levels.

When people are unable to do that on their own, formal therapy can help. Clinical approaches to the treatment of jealousy usually try to (a) reduce irrational, catastrophic thinking that exaggerates either the threat to the relationship or the harm that its loss would entail; (b) enhance the self-esteem of the jealous partner; (c) improve communication skills, so the partners can clarify their expectations and agree on limits that prevent jealous misunderstandings; and (d) increase satisfaction and fairness in the relationship (White & Mullen, 1989; Pines, 1998). Most of us don't need therapy to cope with jealousy. But it might help some of us if romantic relationships came with a warning label:

> WARNING: It may be dangerous to your and your partner's health if you do not know beyond doubt that you are a valuable and worthwhile human being with *or* without your partner's love.

DECEPTION AND LYING

The last two sources of stress and strain we'll cover in this chapter can certainly cause jealousy when they involve romantic rivals, but they involve rivals only now and then and occur much more often than jealousy does. Indeed, the hazards we'll consider in this section of the chapter, lying and other forms of deception, occur so often in social life that they are commonplace, whether we realize it or not (McCornack, 1997). As we'll see, deception of some sort or another occurs regularly even in intimate relationships that are based on openness and trust (Metts, 1989).

Deception is intentional behavior that creates an impression in the recipient that the deceiver knows is false (Buller & Burgoon, 1994). Outright lying in which people fabricate information and make statements that contradict the truth is the most straightforward example of deceptive behavior, but there are various other ways to convey misleading impressions without coming right out and saying things that are untrue (Buller & Burgoon, 1994). For instance, people may simply *conceal* information and not mention details that would communicate the truth, or they may *divert attention* from vital facts, abruptly changing topics to avoid the discussion of touchy subjects. On other occasions, they may mix truthful and deceptive information into *half-truths* that are misleading. We'll focus on lies in the following discussion because they have been studied much more extensively than other forms of deception, but we'll only be scratching the surface of the various ways intimate partners mislead each other.

Lying in Close and Casual Relationships

Research by Bella DePaulo and her colleagues at the University of Virginia has painted a remarkable portrait of lying in everyday life. College students who keep diaries of their interactions with others report telling two lies a day on average, lying to one out of every three (34 percent) of the people with whom they interact (DePaulo et al., 1996). Adults off campus tell fewer lies, about one per day, lying in one of every five interactions. Very few people, only 5 percent, report having told no lies at all in a given week. Most of these lies are casual, spontaneous events that are not considered to be serious by those who tell them, and most of them are successful; the liars are confident that their lies are accepted 59 percent of the time, but they feel sure that they've been caught lying only 19 percent of the time. (On other occasions, they aren't sure of the result.)

In most interactions, the most common type of lie is one that benefits the liar, warding off embarrassment, guilt, or inconvenience, or seeking approval or material gain. However, one-fourth of all lies are told to benefit others, protecting their feelings or advancing their interests, and when women interact with other women, such lies are as common as self-centered ones are (DePaulo et al., 1996). People are especially likely to misrepresent the truth when brutal honesty would hurt the feelings of someone who is highly invested in the issue at hand. Imagine, for instance, that you really dislike a painting, but are describing your feelings about it to an art student who may have painted it. Would you be totally honest? In just such a situation, no one was (DePaulo & Bell, 1996). People typically admitted that the painting wasn't one of their favorites, but they were much less critical than they had been in prior written evaluations of the piece.

Some lies are obviously undertaken to promote polite, friendly interaction with others. We often claim to agree with others when in fact we do not, and we often say that we are more pleased with events than we really are. Most lies in close relationships, where we expect our partners to be generous and honest, are benevolent, small lies like these (DePaulo & Kashy, 1998). People tell fewer self-serving, greedy lies—and fewer lies overall—to their lovers and friends than to acquaintances and strangers. In particular, spouses are more likely to conceal information, and less likely to make explicitly false statements, than are partners in other relationships (Metts, 1989).

These patterns make lying sound rather innocuous in close relationships. However, people still tell a lot of lies to their intimate partners, and when they do tell serious lies about topics that could destroy their reputations or relationships, they tell them more often to their closest partners than to anyone else (DePaulo, Ansfield, Kirkendol, & Boden, 2000). The biggest deceptions we undertake occur more often in our intimate relationships than anywhere else.

In addition, lies can be consequential even when they go undetected. In general, people consider interactions in which they tell a lie for any reason to be less pleasant and less intimate than interactions in which they are totally honest, and lying to a close partner makes them particularly uncomfortable (DePaulo & Kashy, 1998; DePaulo et al., 1996). Despite its prevalence in social life, most of us judge lying harshly (Gordon & Miller, 2000), and people evidently know they're living dangerously when they lie to others. Moreover, lying in close relationships undermines the liar's trust in the partner who receives the lie (Sagarin, Rhoads, & Cialdini, 1998). This is a phenomenon known as **deceiver's distrust;** when people lie to others, they may begin to perceive the recipients of the lies as less honest and trustworthy as a result. This seems to occur both because liars assume that other people are just like them, so they assume that others share their own deceitful motives, and because they feel better about themselves when they believe their faults are shared by others (Sagarin et al., 1998). In either case, lying can sully a relationship even when the liar is the only one who knows that any lying has taken place.

Liars are also likely to think that their lies are more harmless and inoffensive than the recipients do (Gordon & Miller, 2000). This is a common pattern when someone misbehaves in a partnership, and we'll see it again at the end of this chapter when we discuss betrayals: The recipient (or victim) of a partner's wrongdoing almost always considers it more informative and influential than the perpetrator does (e.g., Mikula, Athenstaedt, Heschgl, & Heimgartner, 1998). When lies are discovered, the recipients usually think them more worrisome and momentous than the liars do (McCornack & Levine, 1990a); what liars consider to be a small fib may be considered to be a harmful and duplicitous deceit by others. But that begs the question, how often do liars get caught? As we'll see, the answer is, "it depends."

Lies and Liars

Some people do lie more than others do (Kashy & DePaulo, 1996). Those who are gregarious and sociable, and those who are more concerned with the impressions they make on others, tell more lies than do those who are less outgoing. However, frequent liars are not necessarily more successful liars. High social skill makes people more convincing (Burgoon, Buller, & Guerrero, 1995), but a liar's performance also depends on the level of motivation (and guilt and fear) with which he or she enacts the lie (Zuckerman, DePaulo, & Rosenthal, 1981). Lies are typically shorter but more confusing statements than truths are, unless the lie is important and the liar is highly motivated to get away with the lie; when liars care enough to send their very best, they create scripts that are more convincing than those authored by liars who are less highly motivated (DePaulo, Lanier, & Davis, 1983). However, when they deliver their lies, motivated liars do a poorer, more suspicious job than do those who have less to lose (DePaulo et al., 1983). People who really want to get away with a lie tend to be more obvious than they would be if they didn't care so much. In particular, people who are lying to make good impressions on attractive people of the other sex tend to be quite transparent, both to the recipients of their lies and to anyone else who's watching (DePaulo, Stone, & Lassiter, 1985)! People who are lying to un-attractive targets, or to members of their own sex, are harder to detect.

What goes wrong when lies are detected? The liar's nonverbal behavior gives him or her away. When people are lying, they often speak hesitantly in a higher pitch and make more grammatical errors and slips of the tongue than they do when they're telling the truth (Porter & Yuille, 1996). In addition, their pupils dilate and they blink more often (DePaulo, 1994). Except for brief flashes ("microexpressions") of honesty when they're gaining control (Ekman & O'Sullivan, 1991), their facial expressions usually don't give them away; people know they're supposed to look sincere and to look others directly in the eye when they're trying to seem honest, and they are usually able to do so. But there tend to be discrepancies and mismatches between their tones of voice and their facial expressions that arouse suspicion (Zuckerman, Driver, & Koestner, 1982). None of these cues is certain evidence of lying all by itself; "there is no one cue that always indicates that a person is lying" (DePaulo, 1994, p. 85). However, the global pattern of a person's paralanguage and body language often indicates that he or she is lying, and this takes place in a manner that is equally obvious in both men and women (Burgoon, Buller, Grandpre, & Kalbfleisch, 1998).

So, How Well Can We Detect a Partner's Deception?

The problem is that the specific reactions that indicate that a person is lying may be quite idiosyncratic. People differ in their mannerisms. Some of us speak hesitantly most of the time, whereas others are more verbally assertive; some people engage in frequent eye contact, whereas others rarely look us in the eye. Lying is usually apparent in changes in a person's ordinary demeanor, but to notice those changes, one may need some prior familiarity with the person's style (DePaulo, 1994). Moreover, deceptive behavior may change in the middle of an interaction as deceivers adjust their actions and adapt to the recipients' re-actions to their lies; the longer a deceptive interaction goes on, the less apparent a person's lying may become (Burgoon, Buller, White, Afifi, & Buslig, 1999). The detection of deception is actually a complex process that requires attention to a complicated array of information. People can learn to detect deception in others: When research participants get repeated opportunities to judge whether or not someone is lying—and are given continuing feedback about the accuracy of their judgments—they do become better judges of that person's truthfulness. However, their improvement is limited to that particular person, and they're no better at detecting lying in anyone else (Zuckerman, Koestner, & Alton, 1984)!

Intimate partners have personal, idiosyncratic knowledge of each other that should allow them to be sensitive judges of each other's behavior. But they also *trust* each other (or their relationship probably isn't very intimate), and that leads them to exhibit a **truth bias** in which they assume that their partners are usually telling the truth (Levine & McCornack, 1992). The net result is that intimate partners make very confident judgments of each other's veracity, but their confidence has nothing whatsoever to do with how accurate they are (De-Paulo, Charlton, Cooper, Lindsay, & Muhlenbruck, 1997). This means that people are sometimes certain that their partners are telling the truth when their partners are actually lying.

There is some evidence that, early in a developing relationship, women (but not men) get better at detecting deception in their partners as they spend more time together (Anderson, DePaulo, Sternglanz, & Walker, 1999). And as we saw in chapter 5, women decode others' nonverbal behavior better than men do, so it wouldn't be surprising if they were more proficient at catching lies (McCornack & Parks, 1990). On the other hand, women are more trusting than men are (Rosenthal & DePaulo, 1979), and people are relatively unlikely to notice deception when they are not alert to the possibility and are not suspiciously looking for it (McCornack & Levine, 1990b). The bottom line, then, is that on the whole women do not seem to be better lie detectors than men (Rosenthal & DePaulo, 1979).

In fact, as relationships become intimate and trust increases, the partners' accuracy in detecting deception in each other doesn't improve, it declines (McCornack & Parks, 1990). Mere practice doesn't seem to be of much use where lie detection is concerned. Indeed, experienced customs inspectors (Kraut & Poe, 1980), agents of the FBI, CIA, or National Security Agency, and psychiatrists (Ekman & O'Sullivan, 1991) all do no better than laypersons do at detecting lies told (or powder smuggled) by strangers. And that means they're not doing well at all. Federal law enforcement officers studied by DePaulo and Pfeifer (1986) correctly identified 52 percent of the lies they encountered in videotaped statements, but because half of the statements they judged were truthful and half were lies, they should have gotten 50 percent right if they were just flipping a coin! Neither their performance nor that of a comparison group of college students (who got 54 percent right) was reliably different than just random guessing.

Now, some people—including some Secret Service agents and some clinical psychologists—*can* catch liars readily (Ekman, O'Sullivan, & Frank, 1999). And if anyone routinely knows when *you're* lying, your intimate partners probably do. However, any belief that our partners are completely transparent to us is probably misplaced. People tend not to be very skilled lie detectors, and despite our considerable experience with our close friends and lovers, we usually do a poorer job of distinguishing their fact from fancy than we realize (DePaulo et al., 1997). In fact, when we're lying, the chances that we'll be caught are usually lower than we think they are (Gilovich, Savitsky, & Medvec, 1998).

Thus, people tell lots of lies, even in close relationships, and they get away with most of them. However, don't pat yourself on the back if you're currently deceiving a partner. Consider the big picture. People tell fewer lies in the relationships they find most rewarding, in part because lying violates shared expectations of honesty and trust. Keeping secrets isn't easy (see Box 10.2). And even if your lies go undetected, they may poison the atmosphere in your relationship, contributing to unwarranted suspicion and doubt. And you run the risk that if they are detected, your lies may seem to your partner to be a despicable example of this chapter's last topic: betrayal of an intimate partner.

BOX 10.2

Keeping Secrets

Sometimes, people interact with others when they are aware of information that they think it best to keep secret. Research by Daniel Wegner and his colleagues has shown that this isn't always easy to do (Wegner & Lane, 1995). Secrecy has consequences that people rarely anticipate. For one thing, it takes effort. In order to keep a secret successfully, we have to monitor our behavior mindfully, carefully checking for any signs that the unwanted information is about to slip out. Ironically, this keeps the forbidden knowledge in the back of our minds so that, if we become tired or distracted and let down our guard, it's actually more likely to intrude on our thoughts than it would have been if we hadn't been trying to keep it secret at all (Lane & Wegner, 1994, 1995). People who are keeping secrets often become preoccupied with the clandestine knowledge they're trying to put behind them,

so they constantly run the risk that it could be revealed at any time (Wegner & Gold, 1995).

Moreover, there's a special allure to secret relationships. In one study in Wegner's lab, a man and a woman who were previously unacquainted followed the researchers' instructions to secretly play "footsie" under a table (keeping their feet in contact) while they were talking with two other strangers who were not covertly carrying on (Wegner, Lane, & Dimitri, 1994). Other couples played footsie publicly, with the knowledge of everyone involved. Afterwards, the partners who had been touching each other secretly were more attracted to each other than were those who had been touching openly. Secret loves not only tend to occupy our thoughts, they sometimes seem sweeter than they would be if they were public and everyone knew about them.

BETRAYAL

People don't always do what we want or expect them to do. Some of the surprises our partners spring on us are pleasant ones (Afifi & Metts, 1998). But sometimes, our partners do harmful things (or fail to do desirable things) that violate the expectations we hold for close confidants. Such acts are **betrayals,** disagreeable, hurtful actions by people we trusted and from whom we reasonably did not expect such treachery (Couch, Jones, & Moore, 1999). Sexual and emotional infidelity and lying are common examples of betrayal, but any behavior that violates the norms of benevolence, loyalty, and trustworthiness that support intimate relationships may be considered treasonous to some degree. People who reveal secrets about their partners, who gossip about them behind their backs, break important promises, fail to support their partners, spend too much time elsewhere, or who simply abandon a relationship are often thought to have betrayed their partners (Metts, 1994).

The common component in such actions, and the active ingredient that hurts our feelings, appears to be **relational devaluation,** the painful realization that our partners do not love, respect, or accept us as much as they used to, or as much as we thought they did (Leary, 2001b). When we are victimized by intimate partners, their betrayals demonstrate that they do not value their relationships with us as much as we had believed, or else, from our point of view, they would not have behaved as they did (Fitness, 2001). The sad irony is that for relational devaluation of this sort to occur, we must have (or think we have) a desired relationship that is injured; thus, casual acquaintances cannot betray us as thoroughly and hurtfully as trusted intimates can (Jones & Burdette, 1994). We're not always hurt by the ones we love, but the ones we love *can* hurt us in ways that no one else can (Miller, 1997b).

In fact, when our feelings get hurt in everyday life, it's usually our close friends or romantic partners who cause us distress (Leary, Springer, Negel, Ansell, & Evans, 1998). Those partners are rarely being intentionally malicious—which is fortunate, because it's very painful to believe that our partners intended to hurt us (Vangelisti & Young, 2000)—but they often disappoint us anyway. Almost all of us have betrayed someone, and have been betrayed by someone else, in a close relationship at some time or another, and a betrayal has occurred in about half of the relationships we have now (Jones & Burdette, 1994). Betrayal is a common event in close relationships.

Because caring and trust are integral aspects of intimacy, this may be surprising, but perhaps it shouldn't be. Most of us are close in some way to more than one person, and when people try to be loyal simultaneously to several different relationships, competing demands are inescapable. When obligations overlap, occasional violations of the norms in a given relationship may be unavoidable (Baxter et al., 1997). If two of your close friends scheduled their weddings in different cities on the same day, for instance, you'd have to disappoint one of them, even without wanting to. Moreover, we occasionally face competing demands within a given relationship, finding ourselves unable to appropriately honor all of the responsibilities of a caring friend or lover. One of your authors (who, in this case, we will not single out!) once learned that the ex-wife of a good friend was now sleeping with the friend's best friend. Honesty and openness required that your author inform the friend of his other friend's—and, arguably, the ex-wife's—betrayal. However, caring and compassion suggested that the friend not be burdened with painful, embarrassing news he could do nothing about. It was a no-win situation. Your author, seeking to protect the friend's feelings, decided not to tell him about his other friend's betrayal, but when he later learned the truth, he was hurt and disappointed that your author had kept such a secret from him. Perceived betrayals sometimes occur when people have the best intentions but simply cannot honor all of the overlapping and competing demands that intimacy and interdependency may make.

Individual Differences in Betrayal

Nevertheless, some of us betray our partners more often than others do. Using a scale designed to assess the frequency with which people engage in various acts of betrayal, Warren Jones and his colleagues at the University of Tennessee have

TABLE 10.3. The Interpersonal Betrayal Scale

How often have you done each of these things? Read each item and respond to it using this scale:

1 = I have never done this.

2 = I have done this once.

3 = I have done this a few times.

4 = I have done this several times.

5 = I have done this many times.

_____ 1.   Snubbing a friend when you are with a group you want to impress.

_____ 2.   Breaking a promise without good reason.

_____ 3.   Agreeing with people you really disagree with so that they will accept you.

_____ 4.   Pretending to like someone you detest.

_____ 5.   Gossiping about a friend behind his or her back.

_____ 6.   Making a promise to a friend with no intention of keeping it.

_____ 7.   Failing to stand up for what you believe in because you want to be accepted by the "in" crowd.

_____ 8.   Complaining to others about your friends or family members.

_____ 9.   Telling others information given to you in confidence.

_____ 10. Lying to a friend.

_____ 11. Making a promise to a family member with no intention of keeping it.

_____ 12. Failing to stand up for a friend when he or she is being criticized or belittled by others.

_____ 13. Taking family members for granted.

_____ 14. Lying to your parents or spouse about your activities.

_____ 15. Wishing that something bad would happen to someone you dislike.

Calculate your score by adding up your answers. The average score for college men and women is 36. The average for adult men and women off campus is 35. However, in a sample of elderly people over age 65, the average score was 27.6. The standard deviation of the scores people get on the scale is eight points, so if your own score is 44 or higher, your betrayal score is higher than average. On the other hand, if your score is 28 or lower, you betray others less often than most other people do.

Source: Jones & Burdette, 1994.

found that betrayal scores are higher among college students majoring in the social sciences, education, and the humanities, and lower among those studying the physical sciences, engineering, and other technical fields (Jones & Burdette, 1994). (You can examine the Interpersonal Betrayal Scale for yourself; it's reprinted in Table 10.3.) Off-campus, white people betray others more often than other folks do, but betrayal is less frequent among those who are older, better educated, and religious. More importantly, those who report repeated betrayals of others tend to be unhappy and maladjusted. Betrayers tend to be resentful, vengeful, and suspicious people. They're prone to jealousy and cynicism, have a higher incidence of psychiatric problems, and are more likely than others to come from broken homes. They also tend to be lonely (Jones, 2000). Overall, betrayers do not trust others much, perhaps because they wrongly attribute to others the same motives they recognize in themselves (Couch & Jones, 1997).

Men and women do not differ in their tendencies to betray others, but they do differ in the targets of their most frequent betrayals (Jones & Burdette, 1994). Men are more likely to betray their romantic partners and business associates than women are, whereas women betray their friends and family members more often than men do. Whether one is at particular risk for betrayal from a man or woman seems to depend on the part one plays in his or her life.

The Two Sides to Every Betrayal

Those who betray their intimate partners usually underestimate the harm they do. As we saw in chapter 4, it's normal for people for perceive their actions in self-serving ways, but when it comes to betrayal, this tendency leads people to excuse and minimize actions that their partners may find quite harmful (Baumeister & Campbell, 1999). Betrayers often consider their behavior to be inconsequential and innocuous, and they are quick to describe mitigating circumstances that vindicate their actions (Stillwell & Baumeister, 1997). However, their victims rarely share those views. Those who are betrayed routinely judge the transgression to be more severe (Kowalski, 2000) and more memorable (Van Lange, Rusbult, Semin-Goossens, Görts, & Stalpers, 1999) than the betrayers do.

These two different perspectives lead to disparate perceptions of the harm that is done. People who are betrayed almost never believe that such events have no effect on their relationships; 93 percent of the time, they feel that a betrayal damages the partnership, leading to lower satisfaction and lingering suspicion and doubt (Jones & Burdette, 1994). In contrast, the perpetrators acknowledge that their behavior was harmful only about half the time. They even think that the relationship has *improved* as a result of their transgression in one of every five cases. Such judgments are clearly ill-advised. We may feel better believing that our occasional betrayals are relatively benign, but it may be smarter to face the facts: Betrayals almost always have a negative, and sometimes lasting, effect on a relationship (Amato & Rogers, 1997). Indeed, they are routinely the central complaint of spouses seeking therapy or a divorce (Geiss & O'Leary, 1981).

Coping with Betrayal

Betrayal can be tough to take. It's more damaging to a relationship to catch a partner in the act or to be informed of a betrayal by others than to have a partner simply confess his or her sins, but no matter how they are detected, betrayals typically have adverse effects on the quality of a relationship (Falato, Meyer, Weiner, Afifi, & Riggs, 1999). Still, when such events occur, some responses are more helpful than others. When they think back to past betrayals, college students report less anxiety and better coping when they say they tried to (a) face up to the betrayal instead of denying that it happened; (b) reinterpret the event in a positive light and use it as an impetus for personal growth; and (c) rely on their friends for support (Ferguson-Isaac, Ralston, & Couch, 1999). People seem to fare less well when they try to pretend it didn't happen, wallow in negative emotions such as bitterness and spite, and resort to drugs and alcohol to blot out the pain. Women often respond more constructively than men do; women are more likely than men to seek support from others and to (try to) think positively about the situation, whereas men are more likely than women to get intoxicated to blunt their distress (Couch, Rogers, & Howard, 2000).

If a relationship is to continue to thrive after a painful incident of betrayal, forgiveness may be necessary (Fincham, 2000). Forgiveness is "a decision to give up your perceived or actual right to get even with, or hold in debt, someone who has wronged you" (Markman, Stanley, & Blumberg, 1994, p. 217). It's not always easy to forgive someone. It takes effort (McCullough, 2000). But forgiveness comes more readily when two important ingredients exist. The first is an *apology*. Victims are more likely to forgive those who betray them when the offenders admit to doing wrong and offer a sincere apology. Forgiveness is less likely to occur when excuses are given, an apology seems insincere, or the betrayer simply begs for understanding and mercy (Couch et al., 1999). If you have misbehaved and a relationship is suffering, you might do well to recognize that your behavior was harmful, and apologize. A second component to forgiveness is *empathy* on the part of the victim (McCullough et al., 1998). People who can imagine why their partners behaved the way they did and who are able to feel some compassion for those partners are much more likely to forgive them than are those in whom empathy is lacking.

Fortunately, forgiveness is more likely to occur in close, committed relationships than in those that are less committed, both because empathy occurs more easily and because the betrayers are more likely to apologize (Couch et al., 1999). Still, the damage done by betrayal is greater in intimate relationships than anywhere else, and that's a pattern that's true of all the stresses and strains we've addressed in this chapter. The stakes are higher in intimate partnerships. It's more painful when our partners misbehave, but there's more reason to work to repair any damage that is done. Intimacy offers the potential for both invaluable, irreplaceable rewards and excruciating costs.

CHAPTER SUMMARY

Some hazards are surprisingly common in close relationships. Shyness, jealousy, lying, and even betrayal occur regularly, and may be very influential.

Shyness

Most people have experienced *shyness*, the syndrome that combines inhibited social behavior with nervous discomfort in social settings. Shy people fret

about social disapproval and manage small talk poorly. Those who are chronically shy display high fear of negative evaluation, low self-esteem, and poor social skills; thus, they worry about what other people are thinking of them but
feel incapable of making favorable impressions that would avoid any disapproval. The irony in this is that by behaving in such a timid manner, shy people
often make the negative impressions that they were hoping to avoid.

Programs designed to reduce shyness usually focus on positive thinking
and social skills. Many shy people do not need skills training, however, because
they stay relaxed and interact comfortably with others when they are given an
excuse for the interaction to go poorly. Greater calm and self-confidence, however obtained, will help most of those who are shy.

Jealousy

When people face the potential loss of a valued relationship to a real or
imagined rival, they often experience *jealousy,* a negative emotional experience that is a combination of hurt, anger, and fear. The unique element that
distinguishes jealousy from other states, such as envy or the sadness that follows a lost relationship, is the rival who threatens to lure a partner away. Our
cultural reactions to jealousy are often mixed; to some people, jealousy may
seem to prove one's love, whereas others may consider it an improper sign of
insecurity.

Two Types of Jealousy. When people get jealous in response to a real
threat to their relationships, *reactive jealousy* is said to occur. In contrast, *suspicious jealousy* occurs when one's partner has not misbehaved and one's suspicions do not fit the facts at hand. The distinction between the two types of
jealousy is important, because almost everybody feels reactive jealousy in response to a partner's unfaithfulness, but people vary considerably in their tendency to feel suspicious jealousy in the absence of any provocation.

Who's Prone to Jealousy? Some people feel jealous more readily and more
intensely than other people do. Those who are dependent on a particular partner tend to be more jealous. So are those who feel inadequate and uncertain
that they can keep their partners satisfied. Needing someone but worrying that
you're not good enough to keep that person is a recipe for jealousy.

Attachment styles influence jealousy, too. People with a preoccupied style
are especially prone to jealousy, whereas people with a dismissing style are not.
In addition, people who value sexual exclusivity experience less suspicious
jealousy—but more reactive jealousy after infidelity occurs—than do those who
value monogamy less. Finally, androgynous people experience less jealousy
than do those who adhere to traditional gender roles.

Who Gets Us Jealous? Not all rivals are created equal. A rival who surpasses us in accomplishments we care about is especially galling. A rival who is
attractive to our partners is disturbing, too. Both men and women experience
more jealousy when they encounter rivals who are good at giving the other sex

what it wants, but for women the threatening comparison is physical attractiveness, and for men it's dominance.

What Gets Us Jealous? An evolutionary perspective suggests that men and women should be sensitive to different kinds of infidelity in their romantic partners. For men, who face the problem of paternity uncertainty, the evolutionary costs of failing to detect a partner's sexual infidelity are so great that natural selection may have favored men who were too suspicious of their partners' faithfulness over those who were not suspicious enough. For a man, it's not a partner's love for someone else that's the bigger threat to his reproductive success, it's the sex. For their part, women presumably became sensitive to any signs that a man might withdraw the resources that were protecting their children. Natural selection may have favored those who were usually skeptical of men's declarations of true love, because a man's emotional infidelity conceivably endangers his female partner's reproductive success more than his sexual infidelity does.

In fact, most men do say that a partner's sexual infidelity would trouble them more than her emotional infidelity would, whereas the reverse is true for women. This finding has engendered criticism, but it has also been replicated in diverse cultures and does not seem to depend on how researchers ask the question. Men and women hate both types of infidelity, but women perceive a partner's emotional attachment to a rival as more worrisome than men do.

Responses to Jealousy. People may react to jealousy in ways that either hurt or help their relationships. People who have secure or preoccupied attachment styles tend to express their concerns and try to repair their relationships, but people who are dismissing or fearful more often pretend that they just don't care. Men and women often differ in their responses to jealousy, too. Women typically seek to improve and repair their relationships, whereas men strive to protect their egos by getting drunk and pursuing other women. Women are more likely than men to try to induce jealousy in their partners, but this is a dangerous strategy: Women who seek to improve their relationships by inducing jealousy in their men may succeed only in driving their partners away.

Coping Constructively with Jealousy. To keep jealousy at manageable levels, we may have to do away with the notion that it is a sign of true love. Jealousy isn't based on generous concern for the well-being of our partners, it's inherently selfish. We may also have to reduce the connection between the exclusivity of a relationship and a personal sense of self-worth. Indeed, people who succeed in reducing unwanted jealousy on their own often practice self-reliance and self-bolstering, maintaining a sense of self-confidence about their ability to act and survive independently. Formal therapies usually try to reduce catastrophic thinking, improve communication skills, enhance the jealous partner's self-esteem, and increase the fairness of the troubled relationship.

Deception and Lying

Deception is intentional behavior that creates an impression in the recipient that the deceiver knows is false. Some deception involves attempts to conceal information or divert attention from the truth, and people sometimes tell half-truths, but outright lying is the most straightforward example of deceptive behavior.

Lying in Close and Casual Relationships. There's a lot of lying in every-day life. College students report lying to one out of every three of the people with whom they interact. Most lies are self-serving, but people also tell many lies that are intended to benefit others. Lies of the latter sort are especially common in close relationships.

However, when people tell lies about serious matters, they tell them more often to their intimate partners than to anyone else. Lies also engender *deceiver's distrust*, which leads liars to perceive the recipients of their lies as untrustworthy. In addition, if lies are discovered, the recipients usually consider them to be more injurious than the liars do.

Lies and Liars. People who are extraverted and who are concerned with the impressions they make on others lie more often than others do. But practice doesn't make perfect. A liar's performance depends on the motivation with which he or she enacts the lie; people who really want to get away with a lie tend to be more transparent than they would be if the lie were less important.

Liars make more speech errors, speak in a higher pitch, and blink often. They often look sincere, however, and no single cue always indicates that a person is lying. Instead, the global pattern of a person's body language and paralanguage—and discrepancies between the person's tone of voice and facial expression—usually indicate whether or not he or she is lying.

So, How Well Can We Detect a Partner's Deception? The reactions that indicate that a person is lying may be quite idiosyncratic. People can learn to detect deception in a certain partner, but such success is usually limited to that person. Intimate partners have detailed knowledge of each other, but they also exhibit a *truth bias* that leads them to assume that their partners are being honest with them. In fact, as relationships become more intimate, the partners' accuracy in detecting deception in each other usually declines.

People tend not to be very skilled lie detectors, and liars get away with most of their lies. Nevertheless, lies have poisonous effects on close relationships even when they go undetected, and they are inherently risky.

Betrayal

Betrayals are hurtful actions by people we trusted and from whom we did not expect such misbehavior. One of the key components of betrayal is *relational devaluation,* the painful realization that our partners do not love and respect us as much as we thought they did. That means that in order for a meaningful betrayal to occur we must have a desired relationship to be injured. Indeed, when our feelings get hurt, it's usually our friends or lovers who cause us distress, and such incidents may be hard to avoid; most people are close to more than one person, and when people try to be loyal simultaneously to several different relationships, competing demands are inescapable.

Individual Differences in Betrayal. Men and women do not differ in their tendencies to betray others, but white people betray others more often than other ethnic groups do, and betrayal is less frequent among those who are older, better educated, and religious. Frequent betrayers tend to be unhappy and maladjusted people who are resentful, vengeful, and suspicious of others.

The Two Sides to Every Betrayal. Betrayers often consider their behavior to be inconsequential and innocuous, but their victims rarely share those views. In almost every case, victims feel that a betrayal damaged their relationship. Perpetrators are much less likely to recognize the harmfulness of their actions.

Coping with Betrayal. Victims who face up to a betrayal, reinterpret it positively, and rely on friends for support cope more constructively than do those who try to pretend it didn't happen and ignore their distress. Women are more likely than men to respond constructively to betrayal.

Forgiveness entails giving up one's right to retaliate for wrongdoing from others. It occurs more readily when the betrayers apologize for their actions and the victims are able to empathize with the offenders. Fortunately, forgiveness is more likely to occur in close, committed relationships than in those that are less committed.

CHAPTER 11

Power in Intimate Relationships

POWER AND SOCIAL EXCHANGE THEORY ◆ Sources of Power ◆ Types of Resources ◆ The Process of Power ◆ The Outcome of Power ◆ POWER AND PERSONALITY ◆ POWER AND UNDERSTANDING ◆ Understanding Stereotypes ◆ CHAPTER SUMMARY ◆

If you were asked to describe what your ideal relationship would be like in terms of the balance of power, what would you say? Do you want to have most of the power? Or do you want to share that power equally with a partner? If you are like most people, you would probably say the latter. Most people say that their ideal relationship would be egalitarian; 95 percent of women and 87 percent of men in one study said they believed that dating partners should have "exactly equal say" about the relationship (Hill et al., 1979). That may not surprise you, but this preference for sharing power is an enormous departure from the traditional model endorsed by previous generations, in which men were the dominant partners in heterosexual relationships, making all the important decisions and calling all the shots. And although today few people say explicitly that they want to emulate this model, figuring out how to achieve equality in a relationship can be much more complicated than it sounds. Consider one aspect of relationships that has been studied extensively by researchers interested in relational power, namely the power to make decisions relevant to the relationship. How does decision making work in an egalitarian relationship—do partners make all decisions together? Or does each partner take responsibility for making exactly half the decisions? Does it matter which decisions are important and which aren't? You can see that while endorsing equality in a relationship is a simple matter, making equality a reality is a much greater challenge.

This chapter will explore the ways in which social power operates in intimate relationships. Social power is the ability to influence the behavior of others and to resist their influence on us (Bannester, 1969; Huston, 1983). It affects all kinds of relationships—between friends as well as lovers, at work as well as in the family, in superficial as well as close encounters. We will identify some of the basic factors that contribute to relational power, the ways in which people exercise power in their relationships, and the consequences of power for individuals and couples.

POWER AND SOCIAL EXCHANGE THEORY

Although there are different ways to analyze social power, one of the most widely adopted perspectives is that of social exchange theory (Burgess & Nielsen, 1977; Emerson, 1962; Thibaut & Kelley, 1959). You should already be familiar with the basic principles of social exchange. In this chapter, the role of power in the social exchange process will be examined in terms of the "three faces of power": the bases on which power is built, the processes by which power is wielded, and the outcomes produced by the use of power (Olson & Cromwell, 1975).

Sources of Power

From a social exchange perspective, power is based on the control of valuable resources. If A possesses something B wants, B will be motivated to comply with A's wishes in order to secure the resource from A. Thus, A will have power over B. There are three major factors involved in this view of social power.

First, the person who has power does not have to possess the desired resources; it is enough if he or she controls access to them. Imagine that you are shopping with a friend and while browsing through the CDs in a music store, you discover the rare recording that you have spent months looking for; better yet, it's on sale! But you don't have any money with you, and you turn to ask your friend to give you the money to buy the elusive CD. Your friend doesn't actually have the object you desire, but his or her power in this situation comes from controlling your ability to get it. Similarly, relationship partners can control our access to things we value about the relationship itself—the ability to spend time together, to express our affection for one another, or to feel understood by someone—and thereby have power over us.

Of course, a person only derives power from having a resource if other people want that resource, and the greater the desire, the greater the power. The example of the rare CD is an illustration of this: If you have only a mild interest in the recording, your friend who might lend you the money to buy it has only a little power over you. But if you want the CD desperately, your friend has a great deal of power over you.

When we're talking about money, the association with power may be obvious. But social exchange theory takes an "economic" view of relationships and argues that relational resources affect power in relationships just the way that financial resources do. In a relationship between two people, the degree to which a person feels dependent on a partner is a form of "power currency." If you are less dependent on the relationship than your partner is, then you have more power over your partner than he or she has over you. Some rather pessimistic-sounding "laws" about intimate relationships put it this way:

> *The Law of Personal Exploitation:* In any relationship, the person who cares less has the power to exploit the person who cares more (Ross, 1921).

> *The Principle of Least Interest:* In any relationship, the person who has less interest in continuing and maintaining the relationship has more power (Waller & Hill, 1951).

These statements may seem harsh, but they have been supported by research (Peplau & Campbell, 1989). Sprecher and Felmlee (1997) conducted a study of dating couples and found that the partner who was less emotionally involved in the relationship had significantly more power in the relationship. The principle of least interest has been demonstrated in lesbian couples (Caldwell & Peplau, 1984) as well as in marriage (Pyke, 1994). Pyke interviewed women who had been married twice, and found that those who reported having been reluctant to get married a second time were more likely than those who wanted to remarry quickly to have egalitarian second marriages. One woman explained that she had not wanted to remarry unless she could find a second husband with whom she could emulate her parents' relationship: "[My father] loves my mother so much that she has him wrapped around her finger. She is quite a dominant person. She can get him to do anything. And he loves her so much that he'll do it. I think Don [her current husband] is a lot like that." (Pyke, 1994, p. 87). This woman's reluctance to rush into a second marriage may have given her the power advantage she was looking for. While few people may explicitly seek out this kind of power imbalance in a relationship, her motivations highlight an enduring reality in human relationships: Whenever we want something badly (be it a rare CD or love) and believe we cannot get it elsewhere, the person who has what we want has the power to exert control over us.

This availability of alternative sources of desired resources is the third critical factor in the social exchange perspective on power. If there is another friend along on the shopping excursion who could also lend you the money you need, the first friend has considerably less power over you. And if there are many people who would loan you the money, then you are not very dependent on any one of them, and no one of them has much power over you at all.

In the same fashion, alternatives also influence the balance of power in an intimate relationship. Social exchange theory argues that a person's relationship alternatives (CL_{alt}) affect commitment to an existing relationship. Those with few alternatives (a low CL_{alt}) outside the existing relationship will tend to be more committed to that relationship than those with many alternatives (a high CL_{alt}). Without the prospect of other options, people are more dependent on what they already have. And as we have just seen, being more dependent means having less power. Within a couple, the balance of power is affected by both partners' alternatives: If one partner has few alternatives, and the other has many, there will be a more severe power imbalance than if the partners' alternatives were more similar.

Whether or not relationship partners know the principles of social exchange theory, there is evidence that they may actively put them to use to exert power in the relationship. Gephart & Agnew (1997) identified several power strategies based on these principles that people might use in a relationship. For example, if having fewer relationship alternatives means having less power, then a person who wants to exert control over the relationship may try to maintain his or her own alternatives and reduce the alternatives available to his or her partner. One study of college students found that those who were less invested in and committed to their dating relationships did just that. For example, students who were not very committed to their relationships were more likely to agree with statements such as, "I work hard to develop meaningful relationships with others besides my partner." In contrast, those who were more invested in their relationships were more likely to work to minimize their partners' alternatives, endorsing statements like, "I do what I can to encourage my partner to spend nearly all his/her free time with me" (Gephart & Agnew, 1997).

Differences in available alternatives have been cited as one possible explanation for the gender differences commonly seen in relational power. In the model of traditional marriage described earlier, the division of labor for women and men provided greater power to men: Employment outside the home allowed men to develop alternative sources of desired resources; women who did not work outside their homes had fewer opportunities (Levinger, 1976). Women with young children are especially likely to be dependent on their husbands both financially and, often, socially (Laws, 1971). While this power imbalance might be partly dictated by societal and social norms, some men may also have used their power to influence the availability of their spouse's alternatives. For instance, an economically more powerful husband can insist that his wife not pursue a career and thereby maintain the existing power structure in their relationship. In fact, there is some evidence that a husband's achievements serve to set a ceiling on his wife's accomplishments, ensuring that she is unlikely to surpass him (Philliber & Vannoy-Hiller, 1990).

Types of Resources

If power is based on the resources we possess, what kinds of resources are involved? Table 11.1 defines and illustrates a classification of types of resource power developed by French and Raven (1959); their scheme has been widely used in research on social power (Frost & Stahelski, 1988; Podsakoff & Schriesheim, 1985) and has been applied to all kinds of interactions, including those between student and teacher (Jamieson & Thomas, 1974), patient and doctor (Raven, 1988), and employee and employer (Hinkin & Schriesheim, 1990). These bases of power apply in intimate relationships, as well. For example, if a husband craves nightly backrubs from his wife, she has *reward power* over him at bedtime: She can rub his back or not, as she chooses, supplying or withholding a reward from him. In a different kind of relationship, parents often see themselves as having *legitimate power* over their children. For example, they may believe they have the authority (by virtue of being parents) to set a curfew for their child.

TABLE 11.1. Types of Resource Power

Type of Power	Resource	Gets People to Do What You Want Them to Do Because:
Reward power	Rewards	You can do something to them they like or take away something they don't like.
Coercive power	Punishments	You can do something to them they don't like or take away something they like.
Legitimate power	Authority: governmental, social status, religious	They recognize your authority to tell them what to do.
Referent power	Respect and/or love	They identify with you, feeling attracted and wanting to remain close.
Expert power	Expertise	You have the broad understanding they desire.
Informational power	Knowledge	You possess some specific knowledge they desire.

Source: Based on French & Raven, 1959.

Others have emphasized more specific types of resources that contribute to social power. One classification scheme, for example, emphasizes particular power resources, including socioeconomic resources, love and affection, expressions of understanding and support, companionship, sex, and services (Safilios-Rothschild, 1976b). Another includes status, money, goods, love, services, and information (Foa, 1971; Foa & Foa, 1980). One study even described the power dynamic involved in arguments over the television remote control (Walker, 1996)! All these resources fit easily within the more general French and Raven typology. For instance, reward power can be gained from many different resources (e.g., money, love, information, sex, even the remote control), depending on how much those resources are valued by others.

But are all resources equal in terms of social power? This question has provoked considerable debate. An early and highly influential version of the social exchange, resource-based view of social power held that socioeconomic resources are particularly important (Blood & Wolfe, 1960). According to this perspective, the person in a family who has more socioeconomic resources will have more influence on family decisions. Research guided by this version of resource theory has typically found that husbands have more power than do wives and that husbands with greater socioeconomic resources have more power than husbands with fewer socioeconomic resources.

But this latter finding has not always been replicated in cross-cultural research. In Greece and Yugoslavia, for example, husbands with greater socioeconomic resources appear to have less power in their families' decisions compared with husbands who have fewer such resources. Trying to account for these cross-cultural differences, Rodman (1972) proposed a normative theory of power. According to Rodman, gaining greater socioeconomic resources creates two opposing effects on social power. First, as husbands acquire these resources, their power in the family increases just as our discussion of resources suggests it should. Second, however, gaining socioeconomic resources and status is also associated with coming to adopt a more egalitarian norm about sharing power in the family.

Rodman combined these two effects to create a four-stage normative theory of power. In the first stage, patriarchy, the husband is the authority in the family and has the greatest power regardless of his socioeconomic status. The second stage, modified patriarchy, involves cultures such as Greece and Yugoslavia, where the upper classes have more egalitarian beliefs than lower socioeconomic classes about power in the family. In the third stage, transitional egalitarianism, the culture does not clearly dictate who should have power, and, therefore, power will be based directly on possession of resources such as money and job prestige. Rodman classified most of the highly industrialized countries in the Western world, including the United States, as being in this third stage. Finally, the fourth stage, egalitarianism, is found in cultures that endorse the equal sharing of power, so that power is not affected by socioeconomic resources. Sweden and Denmark were cited as examples of such fourth-stage cultures.

Rodman's approach emphasizes the importance of cultural norms. According to his view, resource power only works where the culture is unclear about how power should be allocated. Where the culture—or the subgroup in the culture—has a clear norm about power and who should have it, it is the norm that matters, and resources are irrelevant. In fact, if a culture traditionally assigns greater power to men, then simply being male can be a basis of power in that culture (Sprey, 1975). Patriarchal societies value the male gender above all other resources, thus creating what Gillespie (1976) has called the "caste/class" system of male dominance. In modified patriarchal cultures, other resources besides gender are valued, at least in the upper levels of the society. Safilios-Rothschild (1976b) emphasizes, for example, the power of love in upper-class Greek society. Those women who thought their husbands were more in love with them also believed they had more power than did women who felt their husbands were more indifferent. Thus, within the upper classes of these modified patriarchal societies, the interplay of a variety of resources should determine the power that each spouse has.

Similarly, the difference between the last two stages of Rodman's model (i.e., transitional egalitarianism and egalitarianism) may lie in the relative influence of gender and money as resources. Although Rodman located the United States in the third stage, it may be that American values are shifting away from traditional gender norms that give the male breadwinner greater power, placing greater emphasis on egalitarian ideals than on economic resources. One recent study illustrates the complexity of this transition. Tichenor (1999) explored the balance of marital power in American couples in which the wife earned substantially more money than the husband. How did these couples define the balance of power in their marriages? Most couples argued that money did not determine power, and in fact, the relative incomes of the spouses did not pre-dict power differences. On the other hand, many of the wives seemed nervous about being seen as relatively more powerful. They defined "providing for the family" in a way that allowed husband and wife to be viewed as co-providers. More traditional couples in which husbands earned more money than their wives did not experience the same discomfort with the notion of one spouse having greater power. So while money alone did not determine the balance of power, perceptions of power were interpreted through a gendered lens. Thus, American society may be in transition, and the association between norms, so-cioeconomic resources, and power is therefore a complicated one.

Further complicating this discussion of gender and relational power is the fact that men and women may gain power from different sources. For exam-ple, in one study of dating couples, women who reported being more involved in the relationship also reported having less power, as would be predicted by the principle of least interest (Sprecher, 1985). But there was no association be-tween level of involvement and self-reported power among men. On the other hand, men who said they had greater access to alternative relationships re-ported more power, but there was no association between alternatives and power among female subjects. And among those heterosexual couples who took part in the Boston Couples Study, only the women appeared to regard sexual activities with the partner as a social resource. Women who reported they had not had intercourse said they had more power in the relationship than did those who stated they had engaged in intercourse with their partners. The notion that women, but not men, can increase their power in a heterosex-ual relationship by withholding sexual favors is consistent with a traditional view of the resources controlled by each gender. According to this perspective, men have power based on money and status, whereas women have power based on love and sex.

Carli (1999) has made a similar observation about the general bases of power utilized by men and women. Using French and Raven's typology, she ar-gues that men, just by being male, are perceived to have greater expert and le-gitimate power than women. In other words, men are seen as being more competent and having greater expertise, and thus more entitled to exert influ-ence over other people. Those seen as having greater competence and expertise are often rewarded financially, which increases men's access to the socioeco-nomic resources just discussed. Women, on the other hand, are seen as warmer, more nurturing, and more likable than men, and this gives them greater refer-ent power (Carli, 1999).

What does this mean for the balance of power between the sexes? Is it possi-ble for equal power to be based on the control of different resources? In the ab-stract, this seems a reasonable proposition. Women's greater referent power could balance out men's greater legitimate power and access to socioeconomic resources. In practice, however, the issue is more complex. First, we have to con-sider the "tradability" of resources. Foa and Foa (1980) describe some resources (e.g., money) as "universalistic" and others (e.g., love) as "particularistic." Uni-versalistic resources can be exchanged with anyone; whoever owns them automatically has a certain freedom in deciding with whom he or she will exchange them. Particularistic resources are more limited; it is not clear who else will want them. Thus, some resources (such as socioeconomic ones) almost automatically carry with them the possibility of being used in other relationships; other resources (such as love) may be unique to the present relationship. As we have seen, having more alternatives is associated with having more power.

Then there is the matter of ultimate control over the resource. The ownership of money is clear-cut. The person who has it controls it. The vulnerability of money is also clear-cut. Money can be stolen or taken away by superior force. Love, in contrast, is far more complicated. On one hand, it cannot be taken by force. As Blau (1964) has stated, "We cannot force others to give us their approval, regardless of how much power we have over them, because coercing them to express this admiration or praise would make their expression worthless" (p.17). The power of love is that it must be given spontaneously.

On the other hand, love, like any other resource, must be valued to be effective in creating power. Our love, then, is only powerful when the other person loves us. As described by Scott Spencer (1980) in his novel *Endless Love,* when their love dies so does our power:

> There had been a time when Rose had felt she could protect her position in the marriage . . . by simply (and it was simple) withholding her love. But now that her love was no longer sought there was no advantage to be gained in rationing it. It was clear that the power she once had was not real power—it had been bestowed upon her, assigned. It had all depended on Arthur's wanting her, depended on his vulnerability to every nuance of rejection. He had, she realized now, chosen her weapon for her. He had given her a sword that only he could sharpen. (pp. 66–67)

So basing one's sense of power in a relationship on the give and take of love can leave one in a precarious position. But in general, we have seen that many different kinds of resources can contribute to the balance of power in intimate relationships. In the next section, we will consider how these types of power are used in relationships.

The Process of Power

A second major consideration is the process by which power is expressed. The kinds of behaviors that can be used to get our way with others seem almost infinite. Some people use physical violence; others plead. Sometimes power is exercised by talking more than anyone else; at other times, the one who is silent is exerting his or her will most effectively. Although general rules about the process of power are hard to come by (Szinovacz, 1981), it does appear that the way we get our way is affected by the resources we possess as well as by culturally determined norms about how we should behave. In this section, we consider three possible ways in which power could be expressed: language, nonverbal behavior, and general styles of power.

Language

Our use of language may be one of the most subtle and pervasive processes of power. How we talk to another person may be strongly influenced by the balance of power between us. Social scientists have observed that patterns of verbal communication can maintain and enhance the more powerful position of males in heterosexual interactions (Thorne & Henley, 1975). Consider, for example, a study in which conversations between college students were surreptitiously recorded in public places (Zimmerman & West, 1975). Permission to analyze the recordings for research purposes was obtained from subjects after their conversations were completed. In these analyses, the language patterns of same-sex couples (male and female) were compared with those of opposite-sex couples. For same-sex couples, conversational structure was much the same, regardless of whether two males or two females were talking. Cross-sex couples, however, displayed a distinctive gender-based pattern. First, males interrupted their female partners much more often than their female partners interrupted them. Interrupting someone is usually associated with having greater social power (Kollock, Blumstein, & Schwartz, 1985). Second, females were more silent than were males. As described by Zimmerman and West, females were getting "cut off at the pass" during these conversations. The cutoffs could be explicit or implicit. That is, when a woman would make a statement, the man might interrupt her before she was through, or he might let her finish but then just give her a minimum response ("um"). These cutoffs may have contributed to the greater silence among women. What's the point in talking if he isn't interested?

In a subsequent study, West and Zimmerman (1983) examined the cross-sex conversations of unacquainted couples who talked with each other in a laboratory setting. Again, males interrupted females far more often than females interrupted males. Taken together, these two studies suggest that various aspects of conversational style between heterosexual couples (both those who know each other and those who have just met) serve to ensure that males have more active control over the conversation than do females. Although conversational dominance appears to be affected by the topic of discussion, men are more likely to dominate discussions of neutral topics as well as of traditionally masculine topics, while women are more likely to dominate only when traditionally feminine topics are being discussed (Brown, Dovidio, & Ellyson, 1990).

Although it is important to determine whether men and women use language differently to assert power, an even more fundamental issue involves the effects of speaking in a style seen as traditionally masculine or feminine. How are these speakers perceived by their listeners? Does it matter whether the speaker, or the listener, is male or female? Early research on this topic suggested that both sexes may pay a social price for speaking "out of role" (Falbo, Hazen, & Linimon, 1982). In this study, women who used an expert style and men who used a helpless presentation style were liked less by their listeners than were women and men who adopted power styles more in keeping with traditional notions about the behavior of women and men. More recent research, however, raises the possibility that the social cost of speaking out of role may be greater for women than for men (Carli, 1990). After listening to a male or female speaker who spoke in either an assertive or a tentative manner, subjects rated the speaker on a variety of characteristics. In general, the tentative speaker was seen as less confident and less powerful than the assertive speaker, but only the tentative female speaker was perceived as less competent and less knowledgeable. The presentation style of male speakers did not affect their perceived competence and knowledge, nor did it determine their ability to influence the opinions of their audience. For female speakers, however, their influence depended on both their style and the gender of the listener. Compared with assertive female speakers, tentative female speakers were more influential with male listeners and less influential with female listeners. Similarly, male listeners liked the tentative female speaker more, while female listeners responded more positively to the assertive female speaker. Taken together, these studies indicate that women still face a difficult dilemma when trying to influence others. For them, speaking in a way that creates respect (being an expert, behaving assertively) may well decrease liking and influence, especially among the men with whom they interact.

Nonverbal Behavior

Although research findings on power and language have been reasonably consistent, the relationship between power and nonverbal behavior is much less certain. There is no doubt that people often communicate their dominance or power to others nonverbally, through their facial expressions, posture, touch, and the degree of eye contact they maintain with another person (Aguinis, Simonsen, & Pierce, 1998). For example, looking directly at a person while you are speaking, and then looking away while you are listening is one way of communicating "visual dominance" (Brown et al., 1990; Dovidio, Ellyson, Keating, Heltman, & Brown, 1988). But as with other aspects of power, the effectiveness of communicating one's power may depend on the gender of the communicator and on the gender of the intended audience. For example, Carli, LaFleur, and Loeber (1995) conducted a study to examine the relationship between nonverbal behavior, gender, and a person's power to influence someone else. She trained confederates to deliver a persuasive message about changing the student meal plan, using different nonverbal styles. The "task style" involved "a rapid rate of speech, upright posture, moderately high eye contact while speaking, few vocal hesitations or stumbles, and calm restrained hand gestures" (Carli et al., 1995, p. 1032). These are nonverbal behaviors that have generally been associated with greater perceived competence, so we might expect students to be influenced to change their opinions about the meal plan by someone using this style. In general, this was the case: Speakers using a task style were in fact influential. However, when the audience was male, female task-style speakers were less influential than males using the same style. Moreover, men liked women using a task style less than they liked men using the same style (Carli et al., 1995). So nonverbal behavior can communicate power and influence, and it seems that it does so differently, and with different consequences, for women and men.

Another nonverbal behavior that has been considered a source of power is physical touch—who touches whom, in what way, and how often? In her influential book on this issue, entitled *Body Politics,* Henley (1977) maintained that men touch women more than women touch men, and that this difference reflects the use of touch as an expression of higher status and greater power. Recent research confirms a gender difference in touch but indicates that both age and situation influence its occurrence (Major, Schmidlin, & Williams, 1990). Among the adults in this study, but not among the children, males touched females more than females touched males, especially in public, nonintimate settings. In addition, there was more cross-sex touching than same-sex touching among adults and more touching between female pairs in nonintimate settings than between male pairs. Such a complicated set of research findings illustrate that "touch serves multiple functions and has multiple meanings" (Major et al., 1990 p. 641; see also Stier & Hall, 1984; Thayer, 1988). Touch can, of course, be intrusive or demeaning, and it can serve to reinforce dominance over the person being touched. But it can also act as a signal of interest in sexual activities, and it can function as a gesture of solidarity, indicating warmth and concern for the person being touched. In fact, the majority of studies examining these nonverbal behaviors have investigated their association with power in interactions between strangers or mere acquaintances. It is unclear whether these same behaviors influence power in more intimate relationships, such as long-term romantic relationships and close friendships. An adequate understanding of the meaning and consequence of nonverbal behavior undoubtedly requires an appreciation of the context in which it occurs.

Styles of Power

Another way to look at the process of power is to examine the styles people use when they try to influence others. Like verbal interactions, styles of power may reflect gender differences. Johnson (1976, 1978) has proposed that women are especially likely to use personal power (e.g., appeals to affection and/or sexuality) and manipulative power (e.g., appeals based on helplessness). According to Johnson, men are more likely to use more direct forms of power (e.g., coercion, authority) as well as personal power based on competence (e.g., expertise, information).

The findings from a study on marital power appear to support Johnson's contentions. In this research, husbands and wives were asked why they did things their spouses asked them to do (Raven, Centers, & Rodrigues, 1975). The possible answers to this question involved the first five types of power listed in Table 11.1. Most wives indicated two reasons why they complied with their husband's wishes: his superior knowledge (expert power); and the fact that they were both members of the same family and, therefore, should see eye-to-eye on such matters (referent power). Most husbands, in contrast, only cited referent power as the major reason they complied with what their wives wanted them to do. While this study does not tell us directly about the styles of power people use, it does tell us about people's attitudes and beliefs in this area. Wives were viewed by husbands as wielding only personal power (based on their marital relationship); husbands were seen by wives as having both personal power and expert power.

Styles of power among heterosexual and homosexual couples have also been investigated (Falbo & Peplau, 1980). Subjects in this study were male and female, gay and straight; they all responded to instructions to describe "How I get my partner to do what I want." Falbo and Peplau found that two dimensions characterized most of their subjects' replies. The first dimension involved direct power styles (e.g., asking, telling, talking) versus indirect styles (e.g., hinting, being nice, pouting), similar to Johnson's distinction between direct and manipulative power. The second dimension was that of bilateral styles (e.g., attempting persuasion, bargaining, etc.) versus unilateral ones (e.g., withdrawing, just letting each person do what he or she wants).

Comparisons were first made on the basis of sexual orientation and gender. On these analyses, homosexuals did not differ in their styles of power from heterosexuals. Among the homosexual subjects, males did not differ from females. However, among the heterosexuals, males and females differed sharply. Heterosexual males reported much more use of direct and bilateral styles than did heterosexual females. In contrast, heterosexual females reported extensive use of indirect and unilateral styles.

Falbo and Peplau then made two additional comparisons that are very important for interpreting their results. Including all their subjects (male and female, gay and straight) in their analyses, they looked at the association between power styles and subjects' reports of both power and satisfaction in their relationships. It was found that people who reported having greater power in the relationship also reported greater use of a bilateral power style. Greater satisfaction was associated with greater use of a direct power style. Thus, the power styles reported as most characteristic of heterosexual females were also the styles that were used by powerless and dissatisfied people, regardless of gender or sexual orientation. By including homosexual couples, Falbo and Peplau were able to show that different power styles were not simply a matter of gender. Gay males did not differ from lesbians in terms of which styles of power they used more often. In this study, sex differences in power styles were restricted to heterosexual couples.

The research by Falbo and Peplau generated considerable interest and prompted a number of subsequent studies. For example, Clark, Shaver, and Abrahams (1999) studied college students' strategies for initiating a romantic relationship. Consistent with Falbo and Peplau's finding about sex differences in power strategy use (1980), they found that men used more direct strategies to initiate a relationship, such as directly asking a partner for a date, whereas women used indirect strategies, including waiting to be asked for a date or going along with a partner's suggestion. However, other studies have not found a sex difference in the use of power strategies (Aida & Falbo, 1991; Cowan, Drinkard, & MacGavin, 1984; Offermann & Schrier, 1985; Sagrestano, 1992). Still others have shown mixed support (Gruber & White, 1986); for example, although research on several hundred heterosexual and homosexual couples in well-established relationships did find that men reported receiving more indirect power tactics such as manipulation and supplication than did women, men and women did not differ in their reports of being the target of direct tactics such as bargaining (Howard, Blumstein, & Schwartz, 1986).

Research has been more consistently supportive of Falbo and Peplau's other conclusions, however. In general, those in relationships who have more power report using more direct power strategies (Sagrestano, 1992); this finding has even received cross-cultural support (Steil & Hillman, 1993). In fact, just working in a traditionally masculine field, such as accounting or business management, has been associated with greater use of direct strategies among women (Carothers & Allen, 1999). A masculine work environment, in which appearing powerful and influential is important, appears to elicit these direct strategies, regardless of gender.

The association between power and relationship satisfaction has also received general support. Several studies of married couples have found that spouses who use more direct power strategies are generally more satisfied than spouses who used indirect strategies (Aida & Falbo, 1991; Wilkie, Ferree, & Ratcliff, 1998). This finding has been extended to friendship relationships, as well; Veniegas and Peplau (1997) have shown that both men and women are more satisfied with same-sex friendships that are relatively equal in the balance of power.

So what does all this research on power in relationships tell us? It may be that men have traditionally had more power and that this power allows them to use direct strategies, such as asking for something or reasoning with a partner, to get what they want. Women have traditionally had less power in relationships, and they are thus more likely to use indirect strategies such as making a suggestion or withdrawing from their partner to get their way. The mixed results reported by studies in this area may simply reflect shifts over time in traditional gender roles, a change that gives men less automatic authority in a relationship than in the past. Nonetheless, regardless of gender, direct strategies do seem to be the ones preferred by people who generally have more power to begin with. Moreover, those who have little power in their relationship (who may be most likely to use indirect strategies) find it a generally unhappy experience.

The Outcome of Power

The third face of power is its outcome. Most studies on power have defined the outcome of power in terms of which person gets his or her way in decisions made by the couple or family. However, this focus on explicit decision making has been criticized as both too narrow and possibly misleading. Consider, for example, the difference between "implementation" power and "orchestration" power (Safilios-Rothschild, 1976a). The person with orchestration power decides who will decide; the person with implementation power simply carries out delegated power. And whenever power is delegated, it can be recalled. Perhaps, then, studies of decision-making power are only measuring the lower level of implementation power without finding out who controls the decision

TABLE 11.2. Implementation Power versus Orchestration Power

	Daily Decisions (Based on Wives' Questionnaire Responses)		
	Husband-Dominated	Egalitarian	Wife-Dominated
Financial	37%	18%	45%
Social	12	60	28
Child rearing	2	40	58
Major decisions (e.g., changing jobs or residences)	48	50	2
	Authority in the Home (Based on In-Depth Interviews)		
Husband-dominated		54%	
Egalitarian		39	
Wife-dominated		7	

Source: Data from Johnson, 1975.

maker. Research on decision making also has been faulted for not examining more carefully the types and importance of the decisions being studied (Brinkerhoff & Lupri, 1978; Safilios-Rothschild, 1970). Having the power to make trivial decisions is not the same as having the power to make important ones.

These distinctions involving the level of power and the importance of the decisions being made are particularly crucial when we examine the power that wives have in their marriages. Unless these distinctions are taken into account, studies of decision-making power may overestimate the power that wives have. A striking example of this possibility was provided in some research on Japanese-American wives in Hawaii (Johnson, 1975). When these wives filled out the typical questionnaire asking who makes the decisions in a number of areas relevant to married life, they did not indicate a single area where their husbands dominated, although they reported a drastic decline in their own power when "major decisions" were made (see Table 11.2). However, when these same women were interviewed in detail about how decisions were made in their families, their responses (as coded by judges) indicated a great deal of husband dominance (also shown in Table 11.2). It appears that much of the power these women had was delegated by their husbands and restricted to relatively minor, everyday decisions.

On the other hand, research on decision-making power may sometimes underestimate the power of wives. This possibility can be demonstrated by comparing the two most popular ways to measure marital power: (1) self-reports, usually questionnaires but sometimes interviews, and (2) laboratory observations of couples or families carrying out assigned decision-making tasks. Both these methods of research have specific advantages and disadvantages (see chapter 2), but what is of concern here is that they seldom give the same picture

TABLE 11.3. Two Methods of Studying Power

Self-Reports of Who Usually Decides

	Husbands' Reports	Wives' Reports
Husband-dominated	58.4%	62.0%
Egalitarian	31.1	31.6
Wife-dominated	10.5	6.4

Observed Interactions in the Laboratory

Husband-dominated	28.7%
Egalitarian	46.9
Wife-dominated	24.4

Source: Data from Corrales, 1975.

of the marital power structure (Hadley & Jacob, 1976; Olson, 1977; Olson & Cromwell, 1975; Turk & Bell, 1972).

A study on marital power during early marriage (Corrales, 1975) provides a good illustration of the different findings that can result from these two approaches to studying power. In this study, when decision making was observed in the laboratory, wives had a great deal more power than was indicated when husbands and wives answered a questionnaire about who made various decisions in their families (see Table 11.3). This apparent increase in wife power when we go from self-report data to observed interactions is fairly common in those studies that have used both types of measures (Olson & Cromwell, 1975).

In trying to figure out what such a difference might mean, we run into two contradictory possibilities. Probably the most common explanation is that in self-reports people are giving their "authority expectations" (McDonald, 1980). These expectations may be heavily influenced by social norms, such as the greater social acceptability of male dominance. Since interactions in the lab are more like "real behavior," they should be less easily influenced by such norms and should give us a more accurate picture of decision-making power than do self-reports. This reasoning, then, would lead us to conclude that wives are actually a great deal more powerful than they or their husbands realize.

However, the opposite argument can also be made. Huston (1983) has described the power of deciding "when to win" as a higher level of power (somewhat akin to orchestration power). It could be that in the laboratory sessions, where only make-believe decisions are being made, husbands are heavily influenced by the social norm of gallantry. They may decide, since it doesn't really matter, to make their wives happy by letting them win the little game they are playing for the researchers. Husbands acting in this fashion would have good intentions, but their generosity would be firmly based on secure power.

To complicate the matter even further, husbands' and wives' self-reports about how much power each has in the relationship often do not agree (Olson & Cromwell, 1975; Safilios-Rothschild, 1970). Turk and Bell (1972) suggest that many self-reports of power will display what we might call a "powerlessness bias"; each person tends to overestimate the partner's power while underestimating his or her own power. Such a bias may reflect a fundamental distortion in the way we view power in our intimate relationships. We may all be quite sensitive to and aware of the power of our partners, and relatively unaware of our own power. In any event, the disagreements that have been found between methods of studying power (self-report versus observational) and between the self-reports of the partners indicate how difficult it can be to capture the reality of the outcomes of power.

Female Dominance: A Taboo?

Despite these difficulties, however, there is one major conclusion about the outcome of power that is well supported by the research evidence. Even today, female dominance in a heterosexual relationship is less acceptable to both parties than is male dominance. Although both men and women enjoy the benefits of having power and control (Horwitz, 1982; Madden, 1987), they are more comfortable when the balance of power in their relationship is tilted in the male direction than when it is tilted in the female direction. The evidence for this continuing discomfort with female dominance comes from a variety of sources.

You may recall from chapter 9 on sexuality that typical gender scripts call for the man's taking the initiative and the woman's making the response: The man proposes, the woman disposes, as the saying goes. Although depictions of sexual initiation and dominance by females can be found in some pornographic materials, it appears that the appeal of the fantasy does not often translate into a desire for the reality (Kelley & Rolker-Dolinsky, 1987). The socially prescribed roles of a male initiator and a female responder seem widespread in sexual, or at least potentially sexual, heterosexual interactions (Folkes, 1982; Poppen & Segal, 1988). As described in chapter 8, men self-disclose more than women in initial encounters with the opposite sex (Derlega, Winstead, Wong, & Hunter, 1985). In these encounters, self-disclosure is a means of taking the initiative. Since men are expected to be active, dominant, and forceful, they are perceived to be more attractive when they display these characteristics than when they do not (Sadalla, Kenrick, & Vershure, 1987). Both men and women seem more comfortable when the man is masterful and the woman is in distress than when these roles are reversed (Zillmann, Weaver, Mundort, & Aust, 1986). Even physical characteristics may reflect a preference for male dominance. Among heterosexual couples, the man is typically older than the woman; and most men prefer dating shorter women, while most women prefer dating taller men (Shepperd & Strathman, 1989).

The greater acceptability of male rather than female dominance is not restricted to initial heterosexual encounters. Research on marital satisfaction has consistently found that both men and women are less satisfied in female-dominated relationships than in either egalitarian or male-dominated relationships (Centers, Raven, & Rodrigues, 1971; Corrales, 1975; Gray-Little & Burks, 1983). Indeed, in one study, a public display of female dominance was the single best predictor of relationship endurance and satisfaction (Filsinger &

Thoma, 1988). These investigators observed the verbal interactions of 31 dating couples and then were able to keep in touch with 21 of them over a five-year period. To measure female dominance at the time of the initial laboratory session, Filsinger and Thoma classified couples in terms of whether the woman had interrupted the man at that time. As noted earlier in this chapter, interrupting someone is usually associated with having greater power (Kollock et al., 1985). Five years after this conversation in the laboratory had taken place, a full 80 percent of the couples in which the woman interrupted the man had broken up! And among those couples still together, most of them now married, the more often the woman had interrupted the man five years earlier, the less satisfied both partners were with their relationship. Just as female leaders in mixed-sex groups appear to elicit more negative reactions than male leaders (Butler & Geis, 1990), the rather astonishing results of the study by Filsinger and Thoma suggest that intimate relationships in which the woman publicly displays dominance are particularly vulnerable to dissatisfaction and dissolution. Despite the increasing acceptance of an egalitarian norm for heterosexual relationships (Altrocchi & Crosby, 1989; Rogler & Procidano, 1989), the two forms of non-egalitarian relationships are not held in equal regard. It seems reasonable to propose that the way in which men and women respond to female dominance is a highly sensitive measure of the degree of gender equality in a society. So long as female dominance is less acceptable than male dominance, true equality has not been achieved.

POWER AND PERSONALITY

Thus far, we have looked at power as a process of social exchange and examined the way that resources, norms, and gender affect this process. This section describes another way to examine power: in terms of individual personality characteristics. According to personality theorists, people differ on how much they are motivated to obtain power, with some having a strong power motive and others a relatively weak one.

Initial research in this area was conducted by Veroff and his colleagues (Veroff & Feld, 1971; Veroff & Veroff, 1972). Based on the way these investigators measured the need for power, they concluded that this need reflected concerns about weakness; a person who feels weak and insecure desires power in order to gain strength and security. This interpretation allowed Veroff and Veroff (1972) to account for some striking gender differences they obtained in their research. They found, for example, that for men, increasing education was associated with a decreasing need for power, whereas for women, it was associated with an increasing need for power. Single women had the highest need for power in the entire sample. According to the Veroffs, this pattern of results is determined by two factors. First, women who are single violate the cultural norm that places high value on marriage for women. Second, women who have more education are likely to be competing against men in "a man's world" and may feel that being female is a handicap in this situation. Both factors would undermine feelings of security and, from the Veroffs' perspective, result in an increased need for power.

The second major research effort on the need for power has been conducted by Winter and his associates. These investigators tried to create a more "positive" measure of the need for power than that used by Veroff. Specifically, Winter's (1973) measure of the need for power is designed to reflect an interest in strong, vigorous action; a desire to produce strong emotional effects in others; and a concern about reputation and position. (It is possible to suggest, of course, that these are exactly the interests, desires, and concerns that would be felt by someone who also felt weak and insecure.)

Winter's major example of a person strong in the need for power is the literary figure Don Juan, who used the sexual conquest of women to prove his manhood and flaunt his power. Some of the research that has been conducted with Winter's measure of the need for power implies that Don Juan may be alive and well in the United States. The first of these studies (Stewart & Rubin, 1976) involved a subset of the couples participating in the Boston Couples Study (see chapter 5). Although these men and women were equal in their general need for power, the power motive was much more important for the men's relationships than for the women's. For men, a high need for power was associated with low relationship satisfaction (both their own and that of their partners), low love for their partners, and a high number of anticipated problems in the relationship. Among women, the need for power affected only the number of anticipated problems. In addition, men high in the need for power were more likely than other men to indicate being interested in someone else, and they reported having had a larger number of previous relationships. Upon follow-up two years later, men high in the need for power were more likely to have broken up with their partners and less likely to have married them. There was no relationship between the need for power and any of these measures for women. Furthermore, even though the need for power predicted a great deal about men's heterosexual relationships, this need was not related to their plans for future education or their career aspirations.

But what happens to Don Juan when he gets married? Of course, the literary one never did, and, presumably, the modern ones will try not to. But marriage is so highly valued in our society that maybe even Don Juans cannot avoid it. The married life of Don Juan has, in fact, been explored in a longitudinal study (Winter, Stewart, & McClelland, 1977). First measured in 1960 on their need for power when they were college students, male subjects were contacted 14 years later and asked about their current circumstances; among the questions (for those who were married) were some about their wives' careers. Men who were high in the need for power when they were undergraduates were less likely to have wives with full-time careers than were men who were low in the need for power during their undergraduate days. These results suggest that modern, married Don Juans may seek to exercise their power over women economically rather than (or, in addition to) sexually. There is also some indication that among both married and dating couples,

Research suggests that speaking in a way that emphasizes competence has different consequences for women and men.

men high in the need for power may inflict more physical abuse on their female partners than men low in the need for power (Mason & Blankenship, 1987). No association was found for women between the amount of physical abuse they reported inflicting on their male partners and the strength of their need for power.

It is important not to overemphasize the difference between men and women in their need for power. Among both sexes, the need for power varies, with some having a strong need and others a weak one. In addition, the average intensity of the need as defined by Winter is similar for both sexes, and many of the activities associated with the power motive (holding office, seeking a power-related career, displaying visible signs of wealth and prestige) are similar among men and women (Winter, 1988). The difference between the way the power motive operates for men and women seems restricted to two general areas: intimate relationships and what Winter calls "profligate behaviors." As we have seen, men's need for power is closely related to their behavior in intimate relationships, but these associations are not found for women (Stewart & Chester, 1982). Moreover, only among men does a high need for power predict such "profligate behaviors" as drinking, drug use, aggression, and gambling (Winter, 1988).

Winter has suggested that these differences are not a matter of gender per se, but rather a reflection of the different socialization practices applied to males and females (Winter, 1988; Winter & Barenbaum, 1985). According to this perspective, girls receive more training in behaving in a responsible manner than do boys. This training, says Winter, prompts women with a high need for power to channel this need into socially responsible actions, while men express their need for power in both socially responsible and socially irresponsible ways. Winter's emphasis on the importance of responsibility training leads him to focus on other social factors besides gender that might affect how the need for power is expressed. He proposes, for example, that growing up with younger siblings promotes a greater sense of social responsibility and should strengthen the responsible exercise of power. And Winter believes that having children should also tend to increase the socially responsible use of power among both men and women. But if the root of the problem is socialization, then perhaps a full cure requires a change in socialization practices. If Winter's analysis is correct, providing social responsibility training to boys similar to what girls receive should help reduce the destructive effects of the power motive.

POWER AND UNDERSTANDING

Having examined power as part of the social exchange process and as a personality characteristic, let us turn to a third way to look at power in intimate relationships. This approach defines power in a relationship in terms of which of the two individuals has more influence on how the relationship progresses and on whether it is satisfying for both partners. Murstein (1976b), one of the strongest advocates of this way of viewing power, argues that men have more impact on, and thus more power in, heterosexual relationships.

A key aspect of Murstein's proposal about power in heterosexual relationships involves who needs to understand whom. According to Murstein, the weak need to understand the strong if the relationship is to progress successfully. Since the more powerful partner is in a position to demand more rewards, the less powerful person has to understand the other in order to develop ways to please that person. This view of the relationship between power and understanding has also been suggested by a number of feminist scholars (Adams, 1971; Glazer-Malbin, 1975). As Miller (1976) put it, "subordinates . . . know much more about the dominants than vice-versa. They have to" (p. 10). The formulation itself is gender-free: whoever (male or female) has less power will need to understand whoever (male or female) has more power. However, since it is usually assumed that men have more power than women, the typical prediction is that women's understanding of their male partner will have a stronger association with relationship satisfaction than will men's understanding of their female partner.

Much of the research on the relationship between gender and understanding has involved a procedure in which subjects first make ratings from their own point of view and then try to adopt the viewpoint of their partners. Murstein's approach is typical of, but somewhat more elaborate than, that used by other researchers. He has subjects fill out a questionnaire eight separate times! First, they describe themselves in terms of a number of different personality characteristics; then for the same set of characteristics they describe their

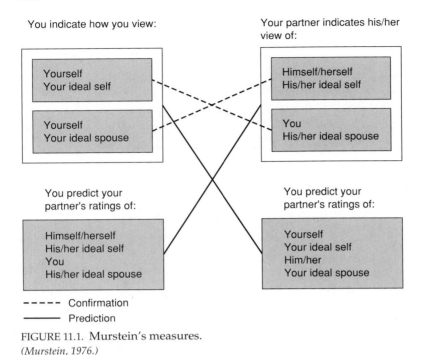

You indicate how you view:

Yourself
Your ideal self

Yourself
Your ideal spouse

Your partner indicates his/her view of:

Himself/herself
His/her ideal self

You
His/her ideal spouse

You predict your partner's ratings of:

Himself/herself
His/her ideal self
You
His/her ideal spouse

You predict your partner's ratings of:

Yourself
Your ideal self
Him/her
Your ideal spouse

- - - - - Confirmation
———— Prediction

FIGURE 11.1. Murstein's measures.
(Murstein, 1976.)

ideal self (the way they would like to be), then their partner (the way they believe he or she really is), and then their ideal spouse. After all this, subjects go back through the same questionnaire predicting how their partner would have described self, ideal self, partner, and ideal spouse.

From the data generated by this procedure, Murstein developed two measures: confirmation and prediction. Confirmation refers to matches between a person's views of self and ideal self in relation to the partner's views of the person and the ideal spouse. Prediction, on the other hand, involves how well the two partners can predict each other's ratings. Figure 11.1 diagrams these various comparisons. On the whole, Murstein's research on confirmation and prediction has tended to support his notions about women needing to understand men more than vice versa (Murstein, 1972a, 1976b; Murstein & Beck, 1972). For both premarital and marital couples, confirmation and prediction by the female of the male's views of himself were associated with enhanced relationship progress and satisfaction. Confirmation and prediction by the male of the female's view of herself showed no such association.

However, there is one major problem with these findings. As Murstein acknowledges, his results could reflect not the power of any individual man, but the importance and power of the masculine stereotype. Perhaps what is being confirmed and predicted by women is simply the way that men are supposed to be.

Understanding Stereotypes

The influence of the masculine stereotype in this kind of research was clearly demonstrated in an early study by Corsini (1956). He used a similar, but less extensive, procedure than that adopted later by Murstein: married couples individually rated themselves and their partners and then predicted their partners' ratings. Corsini's results were similar to Murstein's. Marital adjustment was positively associated with the ability of the wife to predict her husband's view of himself, but not with the ability of the husband to predict his wife's view of herself.

Most investigators would have stopped right there, but Corsini took an interesting further step. He randomly paired questionnaire responses of men and women in his study, creating a set of "partners" who had never met. And these random pairings gave him exactly the same results as those he had obtained for actual married couples! Partners, randomly paired together, were happier in their marriages (to other people, not each other) when the woman could "predict" the man's view of himself. Obviously, this has nothing to do with understanding; you cannot understand a perfect stranger. Trying to figure out what was going on here, Corsini compared the self-description of each person in his study with the self-descriptions of all the other people in the study of the same sex. High scores on this "conformity index" meant that the person viewed himself or herself similarly to the way that others of the same sex viewed themselves. In the final twist to this story, Corsini found that men who scored high on the conformity index tended to have happy marriages; no such relationship was found for women.

Corsini's results strongly suggest that wives' predictions are related to relationship success not because husbands are powerful and wives need to be understanding, but rather because both partners respond favorably to the stereotyped masculine role. To see how this process works, let's take up the pieces one by one. First, happy husbands rate themselves in a stereotyped way, though maybe they really do embody that stereotype in their behavior. Second, happy wives predict that their husbands will rate themselves in accordance with the masculine stereotype. Then, when you put a happy husband from one marriage with a happy wife from another marriage, it will look like she is able, miraculously, to predict how this unknown man views himself! She can't. She is just saying, for example, "My husband says he's strong and silent." And, sure enough, that unknown man from another (happy) marriage says, "As for me, I'm strong and silent."

Unfortunately, not everyone has attended to the potential role of stereotypes in affecting partners' ratings of each other. In addition to Murstein, a host of researchers have claimed that a wife's understanding of her husband makes a greater contribution to marital happiness than a husband's understanding of his wife (Dean, 1966; Kotlar, 1965; Sicoly & Ross, 1978; Stuckert, 1963; Taylor, 1967). None of these studies included random pairings to check for the possible influence of stereotyped concepts. But even if all the research results on the relationship between understanding a spouse and having a happy marriage are a matter of stereotypes, an important question remains.

Why does agreement on the male stereotype—but not on the female stereotype—distinguish happy from unhappy couples? We know from the previous discussion of the taboo against female dominance in a heterosexual relationship that stereotyped expectations about female behavior do play an important role in relationship satisfaction. And yet from the research described in this section, happy and unhappy couples do not appear to differ in their ability to access the female stereotype so as to create the appearance of husbandly "understanding." Perhaps future research will generate some cogent reasons why agreement on the male stereotype is particularly characteristic of happy couples. Or, perhaps, future research will discover that this pattern is no longer so widespread. In more recent studies, predictive accuracy and perspective-taking by both spouses were positively correlated with marital satisfaction (Arias & O'Leary, 1985; Long & Andrews, 1990). These results suggest that either it is becoming important for happy couples to agree on the female stereotype as well as the male one, or that happy couples have learned to understand each other as real, live people and not just as representations of a socially approved stereotype.

CHAPTER SUMMARY

Social power is the ability to influence the behavior of others and to resist their influence on us.

Power and Social Exchange Theory

Sources of Power. From a social exchange perspective, power is based on the control of valuable resources. A powerful person does not need to have direct control over these resources; indirect control can be sufficient. But power based on resources requires that the person over whom power is held values the resource. Resource power also depends on the availability of alternative sources of the resource. The more alternatives you have, the less dependent you are on any one person and the less power any one person has over you. In a dyadic relationship, power and dependency are inversely related: The one who is more dependent has less power.

Types of Resources. Many different types of resources can serve as the basis for many different types of power (see Table 11.1). The social norms within a culture also affect power. These norms may directly allocate power in the society, or they may indirectly distribute power through cultural beliefs about what is valuable. Resource-based power does not necessarily operate the same way for both men and women. Traditionally, it has been expected that men would base their power on money and status, while women would base their power on love and sex. If power is based on different resources, can power be equal? To answer this question, we must consider whether the resources are equally valued, equally easy to exchange across various social interactions, and equally under the control of the person basing his or her power on it.

The Process of Power. The process of power refers to the way that power is expressed. Our use of language may be a subtle means of expressing power. For example, interrupting someone is usually associated with having greater social power, and men tend to interrupt women more than vice versa. The role of touch in expressing power is less clear, as touch can express dominance or solidarity. Men and women may use different power strategies. Some research has found that in heterosexual relationships, men are more likely to use power styles that are direct and bilateral, while women are more likely to use indirect and unilateral styles. Not all research, however, has obtained this gender difference. In one study, the power styles of women were found to be more confined to stereotypically feminine tactics, while men appeared to have more freedom to use a wider variety of power styles, masculine and feminine. When men and women use nontraditional power styles, they may find themselves liked less than those who use the power styles traditionally associated with their sex. Women who speak in an assertive manner are respected more by both male and female listeners. Male listeners, however, are more influenced by a tentative female speaker than by an assertive one.

The Outcome of Power. The outcome of power can have different levels. Orchestration power refers to the authority to decide who will decide; implementation power refers to actions taken once power has been delegated. Research on decision making by husbands and wives has been criticized by some for overestimating the power of wives by mistaking implementation power for orchestration power. On the other hand, it is also possible that research, particularly that involving questionnaires, has underestimated the power of wives, since both husbands and wives may give stereotyped answers emphasizing the power of husbands. In estimating power in an intimate relationship, there may be a general tendency for people to overestimate the partner's power while underestimating their own. It is clear, however, that even today female dominance in a heterosexual relationship is less acceptable to both parties than is male dominance. Men are expected to take the initiative and women to take the role of responder. Both husbands and wives are more comfortable in either egalitarian or male-dominated marriages than in female-dominated marriages. In addition, it appears that heterosexual relationships in which the female publicly displays dominance may be less enduring.

Power and Personality

Individual differences in the need for power have been defined in two different ways. One approach defines the need for power as reflecting concerns about weakness and has found that single women have an especially high need for power. Another approach defines the need for power as an interest in strong, vigorous action that produces strong effects on others. On the basis of this definition, men and women have similar needs but may express them differently. In general, men's need for power has more connections with their intimate relationships than women's need for power. Among men, those high in the need for power are less satisfied and less committed to their relationships than are those low in the need for power. Men high in the need for power when they were young were less likely to have wives with full-time careers when they were thirty-something. In addition, men high in the need for power may inflict more physical abuse on their female partners. Men high in the need for power are also more likely than men low in the need for power to engage in "profligate behaviors" such as drinking and gambling; this association is not found for women. It has been suggested that women are more likely than men to express their need for power in socially constructive ways because women are socialized, more than men, to be socially responsible.

Power and Understanding

It is widely supposed that the weak need to understand the strong: that is, the one who has less power needs to understand the motives and desires of the one who has more power in order to please and placate the more powerful partner. If, then, males are more powerful in heterosexual relationships than females, there should be a positive association between female understanding of the male and progress in the relationship. This finding has been obtained in a number of studies. Most of these studies, however, failed to guard against an alternative explanation: the power of stereotypes.

Understanding Stereotypes. If both a man and a woman describe the man in a stereotyped manner, the woman will appear to understand him. This process accounts for why randomly paired partners were happier in their marriages when the woman could predict the man's view of himself. It is still not understood, however, why agreement on the male stereotype and not on the female stereotype distinguishes happy couples from unhappy ones. More recent research suggests that the gender difference in understanding may be a thing of the past.

Conflict and Violence

It didn't really start out as a fight. Peggy took the family car for the evening to go to her aerobics class. She was supposed to return a set of hedge clippers to her mother-in-law that her husband, Paul, had borrowed. But, she didn't. The next morning Paul realized the clippers were still in the car and that the person who helped his mother with her yard would be working that day. So, on his way to his office, Paul dropped off the clippers at his mother's. However, it took him out of his way on a day when he had a lot to do. He wasn't humored. When he got home that night, he let Peggy know that her forgetfulness had been an inconvenience and extra pressure in an already harried day. Peggy mumbled an apology in an offhand sort of way, saying "Oh, I forgot."

That irked Paul—Peggy didn't really seem to care. Peeved at Peggy's lack of concern, he said, "It would have really helped had you done it." Peggy responded, "Well, you've known all week that your mother would need them today." The unspoken implication: "Paul, why didn't you do it earlier?" Now Paul was getting angry. He could feel his heart rate going up. He conjured up a litany of ways Peggy's behavior was irresponsible and inconsiderate. She failed to pay bills on time; when the gas tank got low, she left it to Paul to fill; her magazines and mail were strewn everywhere; she made social commitments for both of them without consulting Paul. The list went on.

After a few moments, it was really getting to Paul. He blurted out: "Why are you needling me for not having done it? You had said you would drop them off. All you do is complain—about me, about my mother, about our house. When was the last time you filled up the gas tank or picked up your magazines from the kitchen table? Do you care about how things are going here?"

Peggy retorted: "You expect me to do everything. You're like a child who wants to be taken care of. Grow up! You need to do your share, too. You think I'm supposed to work and then come home to do all the chores. This isn't the 1950s. How about you start driving the kids when they need to be taken places and pulling your weight with the Saturday cleanups."

Paul: "No, it isn't the 1950s. In those days people kept their promises."

Peggy: "Well, if you hadn't put the clippers in the back seat, I would have seen them and remembered to do it."

Paul, with his voice rising: "You never remember, and from the looks of things you never will."

Peggy, walking out of the room: "When you are ready to talk civilly, let me know. And if you can't behave that way by this weekend, you can entertain your clients the Olsons by yourself."

Taking back hedge clippers. It doesn't seem to be a life-or-death matter, yet it is just such events that often create conflicts in intimate relations. In this chapter we want to examine conflict and violence in close relationships. Peterson (1983) has provided a developmental model of conflict (see Figure 12.1) in which he sees conflicts as having a beginning (including predisposing and precipitating factors), a middle stage (involving escalation and negotiation) and termination. Influenced in part by Peterson's analysis, we will begin by discussing the nature and sources of conflict. With the sources of conflict in mind, we will look at the attributions (that is, the causal explanations) partners make for negative behaviors and how those attributions are related to marital satisfaction. Then we will look at how conflicts unfold, how they escalate, and how people respond to them. We'll discuss how people can more effectively cope with conflicts and whether conflict can be beneficial to relationships. One strategy people sometimes use for dealing with conflict is to become violent. In the last sections of the chapter, we will look at violence in both marital and dating relationships. The prevalence, types, and correlates of violence will be considered.

THE NATURE AND BEGINNINGS OF CONFLICT

What Is Conflict?

Interpersonal conflict involves incompatibility between people (Canary, Cupach, & Messman, 1995, p. 4). Peterson (1983, p. 365) defines conflict as "an interpersonal process that occurs whenever the actions of one person interfere

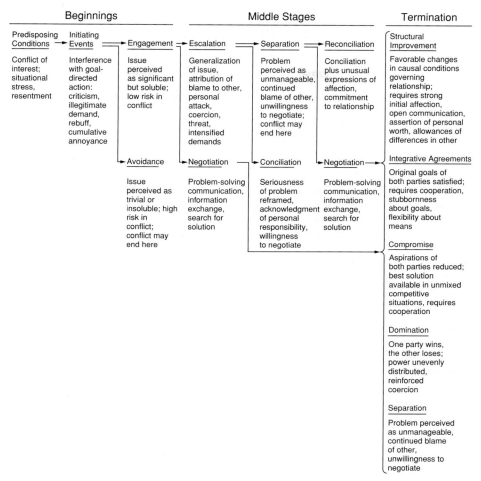

Beginnings	Middle Stages	Termination

Predisposing Conditions →	Initiating Events ⇒	Engagement →	Escalation ⇒	Separation →	Reconciliation	Structural Improvement
Conflict of interest; situational stress, resentment	Interference with goal-directed action: criticism, illegitimate demand, rebuff, cumulative annoyance	Issue perceived as significant but soluble; low risk in conflict	Generalization of issue, attribution of blame to other, personal attack, coercion, threat, intensified demands	Problem perceived as unmanageable, continued blame of other, unwillingness to negotiate; conflict may end here	Conciliation plus unusual expressions of affection, commitment to relationship	Favorable changes in causal conditions governing relationship; requires strong initial affection, open communication, assertion of personal worth, allowances of differences in other

	Avoidance	Negotiation	Conciliation	Negotiation	Integrative Agreements
	Issue perceived as trivial or insoluble; high risk in conflict; conflict may end here	Problem-solving communication, information exchange, search for solution	Seriousness of problem reframed, acknowledgment of personal responsibility, willingness to negotiate	Problem-solving communication, information exchange, search for solution	Original goals of both parties satisfied; requires cooperation, stubbornness about goals, flexibility about means

Compromise

Aspirations of both parties reduced; best solution available in unmixed competitive situations, requires cooperation

Domination

One party wins, the other loses; power unevenly distributed, reinforced coercion

Separation

Problem perceived as unmanageable, continued blame of other, unwillingness to negotiate

FIGURE 12.1. The possible courses of conflict from its beginnings, through its middle stages, to its termination. Arrows indicate the likely sequences, ending with avoidance or any of five possible terminations of the conflict.
Source: Peterson, 1983.

with the actions of another." This definition focuses on actions. For Rubin, Pruitt, and Kim (1994), conflict involves not just actions but also people's goals, plans, and aspirations. Cahn (1990, p. 1) rounds out the domains of interpersonal conflict further by defining it as "interaction between persons expressing opposing interests, views, or opinions." To study conflict, researchers often ask participants to report on irritants in their relationships or to discuss topics related to their relationships on which the partners disagree.

Weiss and Dehle (p. 96) note that "Researchers often use conflict and marital adjustment (or satisfaction) interchangeably (low levels of marital adjustment is said to equal conflict)." Clearly there are conflicted relationships, such as distressed marriages and dealings with enemies (see Box 12.1). Yet we see

---

BOX 12.1

Enemies

Relationships that Result from Conflict

However rich or powerful a man may be, it is the height of folly to make personal enemies; for one unguarded moment may yield you to revenge of the most despicable of mankind.
— LYTTETON

What might be called "enemyships" are relationships between enemies that have resulted from conflict in which negative feelings and actions are central features (Wiseman & Duck, 1995). In many relationships, there are rights and responsibilities. In enemyships, exactly what these are is unclear. Instead of knowing the other person's responsibilities, enemyships generate a sense, often diffuse, of disease. They make us feel on guard.

Very few studies of enemies exist, but Wiseman and Duck have reported on intensive interviews Wiseman did with 140 adults to obtain their views of such relationships. She dealt with several questions, including, "How do enemy relationships evolve?" "How do enemies act and feel toward one another?" "What do people do about their enemies?"

Enemies came from three common sources: people the informant hardly knew, specific contexts such as work, or former friends and lovers. Former friends and lovers were considered uniquely dangerous as enemies, because they could use the confidential information they had gained earlier in the relationship against the informants. Participants in this study thought that women were especially prone to becoming enemies. A substantial portion of participants believed that some people are automatic, "natural" enemies. Some believed that there were people who would never respect them for their abilities, or alternatively, would be jealous of their successes.

For Wiseman's informants, when enemyships emerged, it typically happened suddenly and unexpectedly, based (in the

---

dissatisfaction in relationships as a judgment made by partners, not conflict per se. So we will focus more on conflict in terms of process and interaction, as indicated in Peterson and Cahn's definitions.

Many definitions imply that conflict is "typically marked by significant disagreement indicated by negative emotions or other indexes of intensity" (Canary et al., 1995, p. 7). Fincham and Beach (1999, p. 60), however, note that "not all marital conflicts are overt. Marital conflicts can go undetected by one of the partners." They argue that definitions of conflict should not require overt hostility to exist.

The Frequency of Conflict

How often do partners engage in conflict? Answers vary, probably depending on the number of relationships involved, the way conflict is defined and assessed, the population studied, and the like. Studies of children often show high levels of conflict with both parents and peers (see Canary et al., 1995, pp. 61 and 82). For instance, Eisenberg (1992) found one conflict approximately every 3.6 minutes in the conversations between four-year-olds and their mothers. Vuchinich (1987) informants' minds) on the other person's actions. These might involve actions that let the informant down, betrayed their trust, broke agreements, or were embarrassing or offensive to them. These acts tended to baffle the targets. They typically didn't feel they had done anything to contribute to the situation, so they felt a sense of injustice.

Around their enemies, informants felt uncomfortable and tense. Sometimes they felt sarcastic or disgusted. More often, however, they were inhibited and would leave the scene to avoid confrontations. In interacting with enemies, people tended to be vigilant, focused on interpreting their enemies' interactions. They noticed body language, the enemy's tone of voice and the like, often taking it as an indicator of ill will.

The dominant strategy people said they used for dealing with antagonistic relationships was to avoid their enemies. Working to improve enemyships was rare. Often, informants had no prior faith in the other person, so in many enemyships there was no foundation of relating to reestablish. Neither counterattack nor retaliation were common. Instead, a key

goal was to get enemies out of one's life. People wanted to do this as much as possible in a way that allowed them to maintain their own self-esteem and reduced their worries about the possible actions of their enemies. Often people told their version of the difficulty to friends in the hope that their friends would serve as allies and provide support.

Wiseman and Duck concluded that having an enemy is not simply the opposite of having a friend. Many of the processes in friendship don't operate in enemyships. For example, friendships evolve over time; enemyships tend to erupt suddenly. There are different degrees of friendship. Enemyship tends to be a categorical distinction; people are either our enemies or they are not. We can let friendships lapse, but even if we avoid enemies, the enemy's status in our lives often remains intact. When transgressions occur in friendships, it is often like a bank account in which the other person has credits that can be tapped to help restore the bond. With enemies, that is less likely to happen. In short, enemies are a unique and problematic relationship.

observed family meals, finding 3.3 disputes per dinner. Across various relationships, adolescents report an average of seven disagreements per day (Laursen & Collins, 1994). In a diary study (Lloyd, 1987), premarital dating couples recorded 2.3 conflicts per week. Participants in McGonagle, Kessler, and Schilling's (1992) community sample experienced one to two unpleasant disagreements a month. And, in counting conflicts, one must remember that often conflicts are not addressed. For instance, in a study of Northwestern University students, they did not bring up with their partners 40 percent of the conflicts and irritations they identified in their dating relationships (Roloff & Cloven, 1990; Cahn, 1990). Whatever the exact count, we believe conflict is frequent in close relationships.

Many factors influence the amount of conflict that partners experience. *Personality:* In McGonagle et al.'s study (1992), neuroticism, social extroversion, mastery, and self-esteem were all associated with frequency of disagreements. For both husbands and wives, one of the most powerful predictors of having disagreements was high neuroticism. *Similarity of preferences:* Given that conflict revolves around incompatibility, it is not surprising that in a Texas study the less similarity dating partners had in their preferences for various activities, the more conflict they experienced over engaging in joint activities (Surra & Longstreth, 1990).

Life stage: It is generally believed that adolescence is a time of marked parent-child conflict. Actually, a meta-analysis of studies shows that the rate of parent-child conflict declines with age during adolescence (Laursen, Coy, & Collins, 1998). However, conflict in mid-adolescence is more heated than it is in earlier adolescence. In a comparison of married California couples (N = 156) in their forties versus those in their sixties, those in their forties reported higher levels of disagreement, especially in the areas of children, money, recreation, and religion (Levenson, Carstensen, & Gottman, 1993).

Conflict Topics and Issues

The range of potential issues that trigger conflict seem almost infinite. When Buss (1989) asked midwestern university students to specify things that men do that upset women (and vice versa), he grouped their answers into 147 distinct sources of conflict. Other studies have come up with 65 or 85 categories (see Peterson, 1983, p. 366).

Peterson classified the events that precipitate marital conflicts into four common categories: criticism, illegitimate demands, rebuffs, and cumulative annoyances. **Criticism** involves verbal or nonverbal acts that are perceived as demeaning or unfavorable. For example, in a game of recreational basketball, criticism might involve a player who has just missed a shot being upset by a teammate saying "You're not trying." **Illegitimate demands** involve another person asking you to do things that you believe are unjust (i.e., outside your normal expectations of the relationship). Consider the following from my annals of true stories: My hairdresser asked a customer to take a half day off work to drive her to a routine medical appointment, but the patron's agitated refusal clearly signaled that the patron found it an unreasonable request. **Rebuffs** involve situations in which "one person appeals to another for a desired reaction, and the other person fails to respond as expected." So, not only may our hairdresser's demand for a ride seem unreasonable to the patron, but the patron's refusal to cooperate may be a rebuff to the hairdresser. **Cumulative annoyances** are acts such as blocking someone's view of the television that may initially go unnoticed but with repetition eventually become irritating.

From his evolutionary perspective, Buss (1989) believes that much of the conflict in dating and marital relationships stems from differences in partners' reproductive interests. He contends that women will be angered by aspects of male reproductive strategies that conflict with their own. For instance, women are likely to be upset by men's early initiation of sexual advances, frequent or aggressive sexual advances, and desire for multiple sexual partners. Men are likely to be upset by women's withholding or delaying sexual consummation (such as wanting sex less often, or requiring certain conditions to be met before having sex). Buss has found support for his analysis.

As illustrated in studies of friendships versus romantic relationships, dating couples versus newlyweds, midlife versus older married couples, and het-

TABLE 12.1. Frequently Reported Situations Causing Conflict Between Parents and Young Adolescents

Problem	% of Adolescents Reporting Problem	% of Parents Reporting Problem
Helping out around house	75	87
Cleaning up bedroom	71	85
Putting clothes away	63	84
Fighting with siblings	69	73
Doing homework	58	71
Time for going to bed	50	71
Messing up the house	47	65
Using the television	49	61
Talking back to parents	47	58
Getting low grades	49	51
Telephone calls	45	51
How money is spent	40	59
Making too much noise	38	54
Earning money	38	50
Cleanness	39	48

Note: The four topics that generated the most intense conflicts were fighting with siblings, talking back to parents, lying, and cleaning up bedroom.
Source: Riesch et al., 2000.

erosexual versus same-sex partners, the precipitating factors in conflict vary somewhat by the type of relationship involved.

- Baxter, Wilmot, Simmons, and Swartz (1993) found that the nature of conflict differed between friendships and romantic relationships. Friends were more apt than romantic partners to have mock conflict such as name-calling done for the fun of it. They were also more likely to have nondiscussed and tacit conflicts. Tacit conflicts are those in which the partners discuss the problem in ways that prevent escalation or hurting the other person. Romantic relationships were more commonly characterized by *déjà vu* conflicts, in which the parties enacted the same conflicts over and over like a broken record.
- Buss (1989) found that dating couples were more apt than newlyweds to report being upset about their partners being unfaithful, possessive, and sexually aggressive. Newlyweds were more likely to report being concerned about their partners being abusive, inconsiderate, moody, and disheveled (not taking care of their appearance). Buss believes that when couples get into monogamous relationships, sexual conflict declines. There are other relationships, such as those of parents and their adolescent children, in which sex between the partners is a nonissue. Table 12.1 shows common problems in that form of relationship.

- In Levenson et al.'s study of married couples, children were a relatively more important source of the disagreements experienced by midlife couples, while recreation and communication were relatively more important sources of disagreement for couples in their sixties. Perhaps these shifts reflect the departure of children and the greater leisure time older adults have.
- Kurdek (1994a) looked at the sources of conflict in gay, lesbian, and heterosexual couples who had, on average, been together 11, 7 and 5 years, respectively. He grouped areas of conflict into six clusters: power, social issues, personal flaws, distrust, intimacy, and personal distance. In four of the six domains, no significant differences were found as a function of the partner's sexual orientation. Social issues were a greater source of conflict for heterosexual couples than for lesbians, while trust was a greater source of conflict for gay and lesbian couples than for heterosexuals. To explain these differences, Kurdek suggests that heterosexual partners may vary more than lesbian partners in their social and political attitudes. He also notes that gay men and lesbians are likely to retain previous lovers in their network of friends, thus making issues of trust more salient. He concludes, consistent with points we made in chapter 1, that "Despite these areas of difference among the three types of couples, in balance, the three types of couples were more alike than they were different" (Kurdek, 1994a, p. 932).

ATTRIBUTIONS AND CONFLICT

Basic Propositions about Attributions and Conflict

When we recognize and deal with conflicts, we are often concerned with explaining the causes of our own and our partners' behavior. As noted in chapter 4, these causal explanations are called attributions. Research on intimate relationships has suggested that the interpretations we make of our own and our partner's behavior are a key aspect of conflict, arguably as important as what is actually said and done (Fincham, Bradbury, & Grych, 1990).

In their pioneering work on the cognitive factors involved in intimate conflict, Orvis, Kelley, and Butler (1976) offered the following propositions.

1. Attributional processes will be more active during conflict than at other times. When disagreements arise, people are motivated to search for the causes of their own and others' behavior. When people agree, the reasons for why they agree don't much matter. Subsequent research by Holtzworth-Munroe and Jacobson (1985, 1988) has confirmed this comparison. Married couples make more attributions for negative, unpleasant events in their relationships than for positive, enjoyable ones.
2. During conflict, each person will take a benign view of the causes of his or her own behavior. According to Orvis et al., there is a definite tilt in the way we think about the causes of behavior during conflict. Attributional processes at such times are not objective and impartial; instead, they reflect a self-serving bias. Most of the time, most or us believe that our motives are

good, and we almost always have a good excuse for our less admirable behaviors (Snyder, Higgins, & Stucky, 1983).

3. Attributions made during conflict can create attributional conflict—disagreement about motives—which is usually irresolvable. Most conflict initially concerns the facts about specific behaviors—who did what to whom. But as Orvis et al. point out, disagreements about facts often turn into conflict over motives. Instead of arguing about what people did, attributional arguments focus on why they did it. These sorts of disputes about motives are difficult to resolve.

Attributions: Differences Between Happy and Unhappy Couples

As you will recall from chapter 4, happy and unhappy couples tend to make different attributions for their partners' behaviors. Spouses in happy marriages make benign attributions. In contrast, distressed couples make distress-maintaining attributions. Among these couples, positive behaviors are discounted through the use of external, unstable, and specific attributions. Negative behaviors, however, are viewed as internal, stable, and global. Overall, unhappy couples exaggerate the bad and minimize the good.

Responsibility attributions also differ according to the state of a couple's relationship (Bradbury & Fincham, 1990). Whereas causal attributions involve deciding on the factors that produce an event, attributions of responsibility indicate a person's accountability for an event. Assigning high responsibility for an action involves feeling the actor behaved intentionally, was selfishly motivated, and was blameworthy. Causal and responsibility attributions are empirically associated, but they are not exactly the same (Fincham, Harold, & Gano-Phillips, 2000). It is possible, for instance, to cause something to happen but not be held responsible because of mitigating factors, such as not intending it to happen. In general, unhappy couples are more likely than happy couples to regard the partner as selfishly motivated and behaving with negative intent. Here, too, unhappy couples seem predisposed to emphasize the bad and ignore the good. For them, the glass is always half empty rather than half full.

The findings on the causal and responsibility attributions made by happy and unhappy couples suggest that these attributions act as a screen, magnifying behaviors consistent with the state of the relationship while filtering out discrepant relationships. Over time, such a screen should intensify the initial emotional quality of the relationship. The happy should get happier and the miserable more miserable. This interpretation assumes that attributions can produce differences in satisfaction. But there are some other possibilities (e.g., marital satisfaction leads to more benign attributions).

To check on whether attributions cause marital satisfaction or vice versa, Fincham et al. (2000) studied 130 couples living in small midwestern towns. These participants were contacted 15 to 20 months after their marriages and followed for the next 18 months. The couples were asked about the attributions they made for four negative partner behaviors common to nearly all marriages (e.g., "Your spouse criticizes something you say"). Fincham et al. concluded:

"For both husbands and wives, a cross-lagged effects model showed that the paths from causal attributions to later satisfaction and from satisfaction to later causal attributions were significant" (p. 267). In other words, attributions and marital satisfaction were bidirectionally linked: attributions appear to affect marital satisfaction, and marital satisfaction affects attributions.

Furthermore, Fincham and his associates argued that a key reason why relationship enhancing attributions work is that they increase spouses' confidence in their efficacy in dealing with conflicts. For instance, they lead people to such beliefs as "I am able to do the things needed to settle our conflicts." Fincham et al.'s results were consistent with this path model.

Taken as a whole, research on the attributions made by distressed couples depicts an ever-tightening, increasingly vicious circle. Making what we have called distress-maintaining attributions undermines marital satisfaction and, in turn, low marital satisfaction is likely to foster the kinds of attributions that increase the possibility of further distress. It is hard to break the cycle. Fincham and his associates argue that one way out of this conundrum is to try changing efficacy expectations instead of attributions per se.

THE MIDDLE STAGES OF CONFLICT

Escalation, Threats, and Entrapment

Once partners become engaged in conflicts, Peterson (1983) believes they follow either of two paths (Figure 12.1): escalation or negotiation. Peterson sees the escalation of conflict as involving generalization of issues, attribution of blame to the other person, personal attacks, and intensified demands and threats. Escalation eventually leads to the end of the conflict, but the path along which it travels may meander, cycling though separation (e.g., blaming the partner, being unwilling to negotiate), reconciliation, and/or negotiation.

To illustrate the escalation process, let's go back to Peggy and Paul. Their conflict started over Peggy's failure to return the hedge clippers. Pretty soon, Paul was angry that Peggy failed to pay bills on time, didn't fill their car's gas tank when it was getting empty, and the like. That reflects a generalization or spreading of issues. In terms of blame, Peggy held Paul responsible for the clippers being in the back of the car and therefore not prominent for her. Paul, on the other hand, blamed Peggy, attributing her failure to return the clippers to her irresponsibility and inconsiderateness. In her statement, "You're like a child who wants to be taken care of. Grow up," Peggy engages in a personal attack on Paul. She demands that he should start driving the kids and participating in Saturday cleaning chores. She ends with a threat: "And if you can't behave that way by this weekend, you can entertain your clients the Olsons by yourself." That's the way conflicts go sometimes, spiraling out of control.

Perhaps Peggy uses her threat in the hope that it will get Paul to act in a civil manner. Threatening may give Peggy a sense of power in the heat of the moment. That may make her feel good. Often, however, threats—like guilt induction, bribes, and passive manipulation strategies (see Rubin & Rubin,

1993)—don't really work so well. They can just dig partners into a deeper hole (see Rubin & Rubin, 1993). Threats, for example, have serious problems. Peggy's not socializing with Paul's clients likely prompts a sense of hostility and resentment in Paul. From Peggy's side, if her threat doesn't produce the desired action, she may threaten more dire consequences next time. Even her initial threatening action probably prompts animosity in Paul. Paul may issue counter threats: "Peggy if you don't pick up your magazines, I'm going to throw them out." For either Peggy or Paul, idle threats that aren't carried out also have drawbacks. If Paul doesn't throw out Peggy's magazines, it will convey to Peggy that Paul doesn't really mean what he says. So when the next issue of Peggy's favorite gardening magazine arrives, she is likely to pile it on top of the heap that is already making the dining room table more a storage space than a place for eating. With threats, you seem to be damned if you do and damned if you don't.

MacDonald, Zanna, and Holmes (2000) argue that alcohol fuels conflict. Their view is that alcohol reduces information processing. In conflicts, it increases the salience of negative emotional cues, making intoxicated people feel more negatively than sober ones. Under the influence of alcohol, people should also perceive their partners' being upset with them. This may lead to uncertainty about the partner's affection, which is linked to distancing and blaming the partner for the conflict. The net result is that under the influence of alcohol, conflict should increase. In a study of university males, some of whom were given alcohol while others weren't, MacDonald et al. have provided experimental support for alcohol's role in the processes they believe lead to escalating conflict.

If escalation and threats keep going, partners may get themselves entrapped. They begin making statements and taking actions that commit them to positions from which retreat seems unthinkable and might produce a loss of face. They have too much invested to quit.

The Demand/Withdraw Pattern

While some couples get entrapped, others seem to persist in what has been called a demand/withdraw or pursuer-distancer pattern (see Christensen & Heavey, 1993). Table 12.2 contains a set of questions that have been successfully used with North American and European samples to assess this phenomenon. The **demand/withdraw** cycle involves one partner approaching the other about a problem and the partner responding by avoiding the issue or the person. It is as if one partner is saying, "I nag because you withdraw," while the other is saying, "I withdraw because you nag."

Christensen and Heavey (1993, p. 122) report that "Across several investigations we find that approximately 60 percent of couples would be classified woman demand/man withdraw, about 30 percent would be classified as man demand/ woman withdraw, and about 10 percent are equal on these two variables." This raises the question why women are usually demanders and men usually withdrawers. Various explanations have been suggested, including some arguing for biological or personality differences between men and women. Christensen and Heavey

TABLE 12.2. **Short Self-Report Measure of Demand/Withdraw Interaction**

	Very Unlikely						Very Likely		

When some problem in the relationship arises:

Woman tries to start a discussion while man tries to avoid a discussion.	1	2	3	4	5	6	7	8	9

During a discussion of a relationship problem:

Woman nags and demands while Man withdraws, becomes silent, or refuses to discuss the matter further.	1	2	3	4	5	6	7	8	9
Woman criticizes while Man defends himself.	1	2	3	4	5	6	7	8	9

When some problem in the relationship arises:

Man tries to start a discussion while Woman tries to avoid a discussion.	1	2	3	4	5	6	7	8	9

During a discussion of a relationship problem:

Man nags and demands while Woman withdraws, becomes silent, or refuses to discuss the matter further.	1	2	3	4	5	6	7	8	9
Man criticizes while Woman defends herself.	1	2	3	4	5	6	7	8	9

Source: Christensen & Heavey, 1993.

offer a **conflict-structure hypothesis.** They start by noting that there are conflicts in which one person's goals can only be achieved with the other's cooperation while the other person can achieve his or her goals unilaterally. For instance, suppose one partner wants to have a romantic weekend at the beach but the other wants to spend the weekend alone reading a novel. In conflicts of this sort, Christensen and Heavey claim that the person seeking cooperation is likely to engage in demanding behavior, while the partner who can achieve his or her goal unilaterally is likely to withdraw. If women more often want goals that require the other men's cooperation, then they should often be the ones making demands. Consistent with this interpretation, Christensen and Heavey found evidence that women seek greater closeness and intimacy than men and that seeking closeness was associated with being demanding. In a follow-up study, they had couples discuss conflicts in a laboratory setting in which either the husband or the wife wanted their partner to make changes (Heavey, Christensen, & Malamuth, 1995). They found that only when the wife wanted her husband to change was the wife more demanding. When the husband wanted his wife to change, this effect was not obtained. In essence, these data suggest that the gender difference in demandingness reflects gender-linked differences in the structure of conflict and relationship processes that flow from them rather than necessarily being due to gender per se.

The demand/withdraw pattern is intertwined with other aspects of conflict and its outcomes. In dealing with relationship problems, couples who engage in demand/withdraw interactions tend to use less positive forms of communication (Vogel, Wester, & Heesacker, 1999). Furthermore, in a Dutch study of discussions of the division of household labor, more wife-demand/husband-withdraw interaction led to destructive conflict outcomes (Kluwer, Heesink, & Van De Vliert, 1997). In a longitudinal study of Canadian couples, a woman demand/man withdraw pattern during discussions of problems identified by the women was associated with a decline in women's marital satisfaction over the ensuing 2.5 years. Thus it appears that a woman demand/man withdraw pattern in conflict is a problematic one.

Negotiation and Accommodation

So far we have been discussing the escalation of conflict and the perseverance of nagging. Yet there are other ways of handling conflict besides having them heat up and lock into reciprocal negative cycles. Peterson (1983) identified negotiation as a second major option. It is what might be considered a rational problem-solving approach to conflicts. Partners state their positions, exchange information in a nonbiased manner, and work toward an acceptable solution. Negotiation leads directly to conflict termination.

Complementing negotiation as a more positive response to conflict, Caryl Rusbult and her associates have defined what they call accommodation (Arriaga & Rusbult, 1998; Rusbult, Bissonnette, Arriaga, & Cox, 1998; Rusbult, Verette, Whitney, Slovik, & Lipkus, 1991): When one's partner acts in a destructive way, **accommodation** involves inhibiting the impulse to respond destructively and instead reacting in a constructive manner. Three aspects of Rusbult's work on accommodation are important for us: (a) her model of how people respond to conflicted interactions and dissatisfaction in their relationships, (b) the key dilemma or transformation process at the heart of accommodative situations, and (c) research on the antecedents and consequences of accommodation. Let us look at each of these in turn.

Rusbult has identified four categories of response to conflict:

1. **Exit**—behaving in an actively destructive manner by leaving the partner, threatening to end the relationship, or engaging in abusive acts such as yelling or hitting;
2. **Voice**—behaving in an actively constructive manner by discussing matters with the partner, changing behavior in such a manner as to solve the problem, or obtaining advice from a friend or therapist;
3. **Loyalty**—behaving in a passively constructive manner by optimistically waiting for conditions to improve, defending the partner in the face of criticism, or continuing to display symbols of the involvement; and
4. **Neglect**—behaving in a passively destructive manner by avoiding discussion of critical issues, reducing interdependence with the partner, or nagging the partner about unrelated matters. (Arriaga & Rusbult, 1998, p. 928)

These four categories can be organized around an active (exit, voice) versus passive (neglect, loyalty) dimension and, especially important for accommodation, a destructive (exit, neglect) versus constructive dimension (loyalty, voice). Inasmuch as voice involves discussing matters with the partner and changing behavior to solve problems, it is a process akin to Peterson's negotiation. Rusbult, however, combines this more active style of responding to conflicts with the more passive response of loyalty to form the broader concept of accommodation.

To understand why people make accommodating responses to conflicts, Rusbult and her coauthors have provided an interdependence analysis. They distinguish between "given" and "effective" preferences. Given preferences are what we want to do based on self-centered, immediate reactions to an event. Effective preferences are what we want to do based on broader concerns, including consideration of the long-term consequences of our actions and the implications for our partners. Accommodation is likely to occur when we shift from our given to our effective preferences. Rusbult calls this shift a *transformation of motivation*. From Rusbult's perspective, whether or not a person makes this shift is influenced by three types of variables: personal dispositions, including personality attributes and values; relationship-specific motives (such as commitment) and properties; and finally, social norms (such as the extent to which friends approve of the relationship).

Rusbult and her associates have done several studies of dating and newlywed couples to determine the possible antecedents of accommodation. In terms of individual-level factors, accommodation was likely to occur among people who are more inclined to engage in partner perspective taking and are more psychologically feminine. Augmenting the individual difference findings of Rusbult's group, Scharfe and Bartholomew (1995) found that securely attached people were more likely to engage in accommodating responses, while dismissing people were less likely to use such responses. In terms of dyadic level factors, accommodation was greater among individuals who were more satisfied with their relationships, believed their alternatives were poor, had invested much in their relationships, considered the relationships central to their lives, and felt more committed to their relationships. Finally, people who feel stronger normative support for continuing their relationships are more likely to accommodate. Based on Rusbult et al.'s (1991) early research, Figure 12.2 depicts a possible model of the causal links among these variables. It shows the centrality of commitment as an antecedent of accommodation. The dyadic-level variables of relationship satisfaction, lack of alternatives, investment, and centrality in part influence accommodation because they foster commitment.

Rusbult and her associates see accommodation as setting in motion a reciprocal process. When one partner accommodates, it tends to increase the other's trust and willingness to do so, which increases the first partner's trust and willingness to accommodate, and so on. Over time, in Rusbult et al.'s view (1991, p. 58), "reciprocating accommodation should result in increases in the quality of couple functioning." In a longitudinal study of newlyweds, Rusbult et al. (1998) found support for accommodation being associated with high levels of marital adjustment.

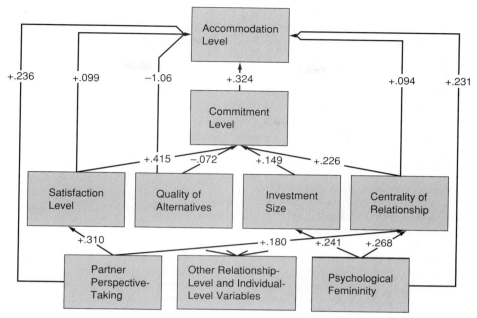

FIGURE 12.2. Links between individual-level variables, relationship-level variables, feelings of commitment, and willingness to accommodate—summary of causal modeling results.
Source: Rusbult et al., 1991.

Dealing with Conflict: Four Types of Couples

To put the various interactions during interpersonal discord together into larger, more organized pictures, John Gottman tried to identify patterns in how different couples deal with conflict. As part of his program of research, he did a seminal study with 79 couples from Bloomington, Indiana (Gottman, 1993, see also Gottman, 1994a, 1999). He videotaped and then rated 15-minute discussions they had about a continuing disagreement in their relationship. In forming his clusters, Gottman looked at how much couples engaged with one another during conflict, the ratio of positive to negative interactions, and finally the partners' efforts to persuade one another during their discussions. Through his analyses, Gottman identified two, five, or eight different types of couples. As some of the types are subtypes of a main category or mixtures of types, we will focus on four main kinds of couples: **volatiles, validators, avoiders,** and **hostiles.**

Box 12.2 provides a simple measure of these types. Before reading further, we encourage you to look at it as a way of assessing your conflict type.

Volatiles, validators, and avoiders all shared a ratio of positive to negative acts of roughly 5:1 during conflict discussion. In other words, their interactions were predominantly positive. For hostile couples, this ratio was much lower, around 1:1 or even less. In terms of persuasion, the volatile couples started off immediately trying to persuade one another. As their conversations continued, their

BOX 12.2

Assessing Your Couple Conflict Type

Following are descriptions of how people in four different types of relationships handle conflict. Which type most closely describes how you and your partner deal with conflict in your relationship? For each description, indicate how often it applies to your conflicts:

A. In our relationship, conflicts may be fought on a grand scale, and that is okay, since our making up is even grander. We have volcanic arguments, but they are just a small part of a warm and loving relationship. Although we argue, we are still able to resolve our differences. In fact, our passion and zest for fighting actually leads to a better relationship with a lot of making up, laughing, and affection.

    1 = Never
    2 = Rarely
    3 = Sometimes
    4 = Often
    5 = Very Often

B. In our relationship, conflict is minimized. We think it is better to "agree to disagree" rather than end up in discussions that will result in a deadlock. We don't think there is much to be gained from getting openly angry with each other. In fact, a lot of talking about disagreements seems to make matters worse. We feel that if you just relax about problems, they will have a way of working themselves out.

    1 = Never
    2 = Rarely
    3 = Sometimes
    4 = Often
    5 = Very Often

C. In our relationship, when we are having conflict, we let each other know the other's opinions are valued and their emotions valid, even if we disagree with each other. Even when discussing a hot topic, we display a lot of self-control and are calm. When fighting we spend a lot of time validating each other as well as trying to persuade our partner or try to find a compromise.

    1 = Never
    2 = Rarely
    3 = Sometimes
    4 = Often
    5 = Very Often

D. We argue often and hotly. There are a lot of insults back and forth, name-calling, put-downs, and sarcasm. We don't really listen to what the other is saying, nor do we look at each other very much. One or the other of us can be quite detached and emotionally uninvolved, even though there may be brief episodes of attack and defensiveness. There are clearly more negatives than positives in our relationship.

    1 = Never
    2 = Rarely
    3 = Sometimes
    4 = Often
    5 = Very Often

Source: Holman & Jarvis (2000). Reprinted with permission. In terms of Gottman's couple types, scenario A reflects a volatile approach, B an avoiding approach, C a validating approach, and D a hostile approach.

efforts at persuasion decreased somewhat compared to their initial high levels, but they remained high compared to other conflict types. Validators initially refrained from trying to influence one another but engaged in persuasion in the middle of their discussions. The four groups differed in engagement both in their positive and negative interactions and in their persuasion. The volatile couples were most engaged with one another, the validators moderately engaged, and the hostiles and avoiders less engaged. The avoiders were low in emotion.

Of the four groups, the hostiles are arguably the most unique. As suggested by their positive-to-negative ratio, their interactions were marked by negativity. Gottman notes that some hostile couples were actively engaged in a great deal of direct conflict, with at least one person attentively listening and often both partners behaving defensively. Gottman depicts another more detached subset of hostile couples as emotionally uninvolved with one another, but prone to brief episodes of reciprocated attack and defensiveness, often over trivial matters. In comparisons of hostile versus nonhostile (or what Gottman sometimes called regulated versus nonregulated) couples, the hostile group was more likely to engage in criticism, contempt, defensiveness, and withdrawal (Gottman, 1994a, p. 123). These forms of interaction undermine the stability of relationships. Hostile couples are also prone to what Gottman calls "flooding," the unexpected eruption of negative emotions that is overwhelming and disorganizing for partners (Holman & Jarvis, 2000). Hostile couples report low marital satisfaction.

The three other types of couples have higher marital satisfaction. Gottman lumps the volatiles and validators into a broader category he calls the engagers. Both volatiles and validators confront conflict openly, being willing to disagree and trying to persuade one another. But there are subtle differences between them. Gottman describes the conflicts of volatiles by saying:

> For volatile couples, there was a high level of both positive and negative affect in these marriages. The husbands were extremely expressive and involved. There was a great deal of negativity in these interactions, and also a lot of humor and affection. There seems to be a premium placed on arguing in these couples, apparently in the service of preserving their individuality and separateness. (Gottman, 1993, p. 10)

In contrast to volatiles,

> Validating couples . . . had conversations that involved conflict, but there was a lot of ease and calm in the discussion. The conversation was initially characterized by one spouse validating the other's description of a problem. Validation can be as minimal as vocal listener backchannels such as "mmhmm" and "yeah." . . . At a more extreme level, the validating spouse provides support, perhaps empathy for the partner's feelings, communicating that he or she understands expressed feelings, that it makes sense for the partner to feel that way, given his or her position and vantage point. The validator still may not feel the way the partner does, but he or she communicates, verbally or nonverbally, that he or she understands and accepts the expressed feelings as valid. . . . In the conversation of validating couples, there is often the sense that, although there is disagreement between them, they are both working together on a problem.

However, in the disagreement part of the interaction there is a great deal of belligerent argument by each person for his or her position. (Gottman, 1993, p. 10)

In describing the avoiders, Gottman observed:

The interviewer had a great deal of difficulty setting up the conflict discussion. Although conflict/avoiders did not describe themselves as avoidant of conflict, these couples did not have specific strategies for resolving conflict. For example, they often referred to the passage of time alone as solving problems, and to working things out alone. . . . The interactions are not psychologically minded or introspective. Once each person has stated his or her case, they tend to see the discussion as close to an end. They consider accepting these differences as a complete discussion. Once they understand their differences, they feel that the common ground and values they share overwhelm these differences and make them unimportant and easy to accept. Hence, there is very little give and take and little attempt to persuade one another. The discussion has very little emotion, either positive or negative. Often the proposed solutions to issues are quite nonspecific. (Gottman, 1993, p. 10)

THE TERMINATION AND OUTCOMES OF CONFLICT

Ways of Terminating Conflict

Whether couples are volatiles, validators, avoiders, or hostiles, most conflicts eventually end. Peterson (1983) describes five ways they can terminate: separation, domination, compromise, integrative agreement, and structural improvement. He sees the order in which these endings are listed as forming, at least roughly, a continuum from most destructive to most constructive.

Separation is the withdrawal of one or both partners without the conflict having been resolved. It is how Peggy and Paul ended their conflict about the clippers that we presented at the beginning of the chapter. As is common in this sort of ending, Peggy got in an aggressive twist, a parting shot at the end: "And if you can't behave that way by this weekend, you can entertain your clients the Olsons by yourself." If their tempers flare, separation gives combatants time to cool off and to think about the situation more constructively. However, even if partners return to their problem more calmly, unless there are changes in the underlying conditions that lead to the conflict, Peterson believes further quarreling is likely.

In **domination,** one person continues to pursue his or her goals, while the other capitulates. This is apt to happen in relationships in which one person is more powerful than the other. Unfortunately, the consequences for the person giving in are usually negative.

Compromise occurs when both parties reduce their aspirations so that a mutually acceptable alternative can be found. If Paul wanted to go to a favorite Greek restaurant and Peggy wanted to go to a favorite Italian restaurant, they could compromise by going to a less good restaurant that served both Greek and Italian food. Both would get some of their aspirations fulfilled, but neither would be totally satisfied. Often better solutions can be found.

Integrative agreements satisfy both partners' original aspi[...] goals. Integrative agreements are most commonly sought for conflic[...] mediate intensity, but they are difficult to achieve. They require the p[...] one's central goals but flexibility in the means of achieving the[...] "logrolling" (making concessions on one issue if your partner will make [...] cessions on another).

When intense issues are discussed and reconciled, the partners may be left as weary warriors. But fundamental change may occur in their relationships. With reference to **structural improvement,** Peterson (1983, p. 382) writes:

> Some change will take place in one or more of the causal conditions governing the relationship. Each person will know more about the other than before. Each person may attribute more highly valued qualities to the other than before. Having weathered the storm of previous conflict, each person may trust the other and their relationship more than before, and thus be willing to approach other previously avoided issues in a more hopeful and productive way. With these changes, the quality of the relationship will be improved over many situations and beyond the time of the immediate conflict with which the process began.

Can Fighting Be Good for a Relationship?

> "The most important advice I can give to men who want their marriages to work is to try not to avoid conflict." John Gottman, *Why Marriages Succeed or Fail.* New York: Simon & Schuster, 1994, p. 159.

Even if we admit that conflict is inevitable in an intimate relationship, most of us probably still feel that it would be better not to have the unpleasantness of quarrels, disagreements, and arguments. But perhaps this negative view of conflict is mistaken. Social scientists such as John Gottman, whom we have quoted here, believe that conflict is an essential aspect of promoting intimacy. Consistent with this view, questionnaire research shows that the more unexpressed irritants participants have in their relationships, and the more they report minimizing or avoiding the discussion of conflicts, the less satisfied they are (Canary & Cupach, 1988; Roloff & Cloven, 1990, p. 62). Noller, Feeney, Bonnell, and Callan (1994) obtained complementary results in an interaction study that involved coding how couples discussed a problem just prior to their marriage as well as one and two years later. Disengagement (mutual withdrawal and avoidance of conflict) before marriage was related to wives being less happy after marriage and was associated with concurrent dissatisfaction for both husbands and wives at two of the three times when data were collected. Of course, simply confronting conflict isn't a guarantee that satisfaction with the relationship will grow (see Fincham & Beach, 1999, pp. 52–54). Given findings such as these, an increasingly common view is that it is the handling of conflict—not its absence—that allows relationships to grow and prosper (Holmes & Boon, 1990; Peterson, 1983).

In their book *The Intimate Enemy,* Bach and Wyden (1968) consider this proposition in great detail, contending that, when fairly and skillfully done, fighting increases intimacy. Many of their suggestions for how to "fight fair" have already been described (e.g., listening, validating, owning our feelings),

'ond providing rules for how to fight. They also pro-
lts that should occur: a "fight effects profile." The
;hown in Table 12.3. A "good fight" (i.e., one that is
the positive effects listed in this table and thereby
;ood relationship.
hat there is no acceptable substitute for making
t when disagreements arise. The available alter-
...ch worse. Bad fighting is one of these unaccept-
.. i iere, the partners go at each other, with no holds barred. The
... or bad fights can range from psychological distress to severe physical injury or even death. It is possible that the lack of communication skills needed to
handle conflict and keep it within bounds makes a significant contribution to
the escalation of conflict that can end in physical violence (Dutton, 1987).

Another alternative to having a good fight is to avoid fighting altogether. If
there are no disagreements, fight avoidance seems reasonable. However, it is
unlikely that intimate partners, particularly those who live together, could have
a lasting partnership without any disagreements. More often, fight avoidance
"papers over" problems, preventing serious issues in the relationship from
being confronted (Baxter & Wilmot, 1985; Gottman & Krokoff, 1989). At best,
such avoidance tactics can create a relatively comfortable, though perhaps increasingly superficial, relationship. At worst, the partners collect "gunnysacks"
of unresolved complaints that at some point burst open with explosive rage.

Bach and Wyden do not underestimate how hard it is to fight fair and have
a "good" fight. It requires strong self-discipline and genuine caring about the
other person. But the outcome is worth the effort. Instead of being seen as a
dreadful problem, conflict can be seen as a challenging opportunity—the chance
to learn about both partner and self, the possibility for the relationship to grow
in strength and intimacy. Try to remember what you have learned about fighting
fair the next time conflict puts your communication skills to the test.

VIOLENCE AND ABUSE IN RELATIONSHIPS

Bach and Wyden use the word *fighting* in the sense of verbally dealing with disagreements, but the word also describes physical fighting. Such fighting is a form
of **violence,** "an act carried out with the intention of, or an act perceived as having the intention of, physically hurting another person" (Steinmetz, 1987, p. 729).
There is a close link between conflict and violence. In the **Conflict Tactics Scale,** a
classic tool for assessing violence among couples, participants are asked to think
about how they settle differences. That the developers of the scale used this framing of their questions implies that they saw a link between conflict and violence.
Empirical studies show a strong association between the two (see Lloyd & Emery,
1994, p. 29). Lloyd and Emery (1994, p. 29) note that "Physical aggression can be
conceptualized as a conflict negotiation strategy." Of course, violence is only one
way of handling conflict, perhaps preferred by some but used by others when
they cannot think of a better strategy (Klein, 1998, p. 7).

TABLE 12.3. The Fight Effects Profile

Each fight is scored by each person from his or her point of view. In a good fight, both partners win. That is, both partners have considerably more positive outcomes than negative ones.

Category	Positive Outcome	Negative Outcome
Hurt	Person feels less hurt, weak, or offended.	Person feels more hurt, weak, or offended.
Information	Person gains more information about relationship or partner's feelings.	Person learns nothing new.
Resolution	Open conflict has made it more likely the issue will be resolved.	Possibility of a solution is now less likely.
Control	Person has gained more mutually acceptable influence over the partner's behavior.	Person now has less mutually acceptable influence over the partner.
Fear	Fear of fighting and/or the partner is reduced.	Fear has increased.
Trust	Person has more confidence that the partner will deal with him or her "in good faith, with good will, and with positive regard."	Person has less confidence in partner's goodwill.
Revenge	Intentions to take revenge are not stimulated by the fight.	Intentions to take revenge are stimulated by the fight.
Reconciliation	Person makes active efforts to undo any harm he or she has caused and welcomes similar efforts by the partner.	Person does not attempt or encourage reconciliation.
Centricity	Person feels he or she is more central to the other's concern and interest.	Person feels he or she "counts less" with partner.
Self-Count	Person feels better about himself or herself: more confidence, more self-esteem.	Person feels worse about himself or herself.
Catharsis	Person feels cleared of tension and aggression.	Person feels at least as much tension and aggression as before the fight.
Cohesion-Affection	Closeness with and attraction to the partner have increased.	Closeness with and attraction to the partner have decreased.

Source: Adapted from Bach & Wyden, 1968.

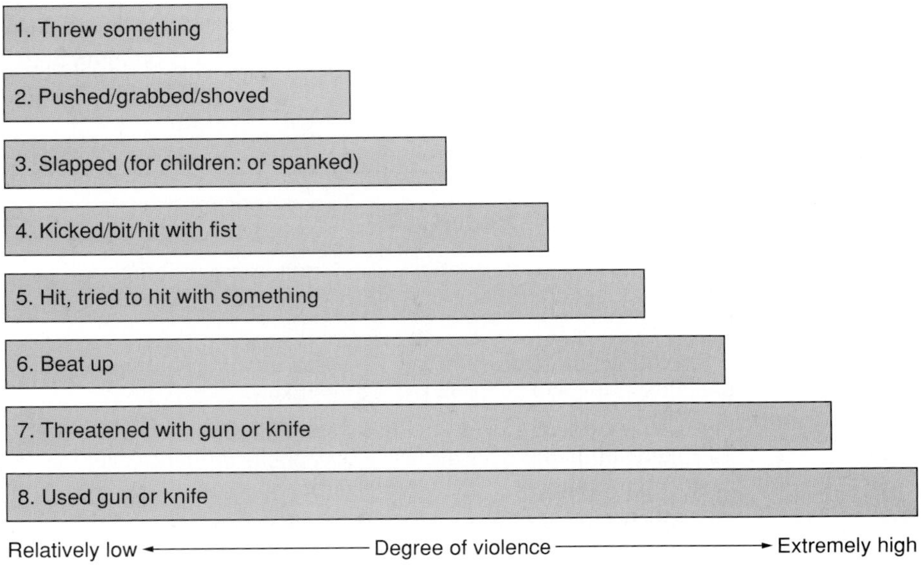

1. Threw something

2. Pushed/grabbed/shoved

3. Slapped (for children: or spanked)

4. Kicked/bit/hit with fist

5. Hit, tried to hit with something

6. Beat up

7. Threatened with gun or knife

8. Used gun or knife

Relatively low ◄─────────────── Degree of violence ───────────────► Extremely high

FIGURE 12.3. The Conflict Tactics Scale: Physical violence.
(Straus, 1979.)

Until the 1970s, little attention was paid to the role of physical abuse and violence in families; it was an almost unthinkable topic. However, when investigators did begin to examine family violence, they rapidly discovered that it was more common than anyone thought (Steinmetz & Lucca, 1988). The use of physical force in families occurs both across generations (between parents and children) and within generations (between spouses as well as among siblings). In chapter 9, we examined sexual aggression. Here we focus primarily on violence between husbands and wives.

The Prevalence of Violence

Because so much of family life occurs in private, it is difficult to obtain accurate statistics on the extent of spouse abuse. Early estimates came from three national surveys conducted by Murray Straus and his colleagues in 1975, 1985 and 1992 (Hampton, Gelles, & Harrop, 1989; Straus, Gelles, & Steinmetz, 1980; Straus, 1995). Those who participated in these surveys were asked to indicate how frequently they engaged in each of the eight types of physical aggression included in the Conflict Tactics Scale (see Figure 12.3). More recently (1995–96), the U.S. government-sponsored National Violence Against Women Survey (Tjaden & Thoennes, 1999) posed a 12-item version of the Conflict Tactics Scale to a representatively selected sample of 16,000 U.S. women and men.

Violence is as American as apple pie. In the National Violence Against Women Survey, 51.9 percent of women and 66.4 percent of men reported that at

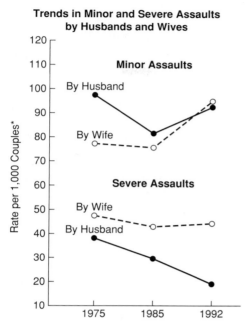

*Weighted to adjust for oversamples

FIGURE 12.4. Spouse abuse in the United States, 1975, 1985, and 1992.
Source: Straus, 1995.

some time in their lives they had been physically assaulted; 22.1 percent of women and 7.4 percent of men indicated an intimate partner had assaulted them during their lives. The most common forms of violence are slapping or hitting followed by pushing, grabbing, or shoving. Using knives and guns is less common, although 9.6 percent of men say they have been the victims of knife attacks.

Interpersonal violence is nothing new. In Straus's 1976 study nearly twice as many couples (38 per thousand) reported severe recent male violence against women as did in his 1992 survey (19 per thousand). These results, including a trend for women to engage in more assaults of a minor nature, are shown in Figure 12.4. The most current estimates based on the National Violence Against Women Survey are that someone physically assaults 1.9 million U.S. women annually. That means one American woman is assailed physically every 17 seconds.

Ethnic comparisons have traditionally shown higher levels of partner violence among blacks than among whites (Johnson & Ferraro, 2000). In the National Violence Against Women Survey (Tjaden & Thoennes, 1999, pp. 22–26) rates for being physically assaulted by an intimate partner were: American Indian/Alaska Natives, 31 percent; Mixed Race, 27 percent; African Americans, 26 percent; whites, 21 percent; and Asian/Pacific Islanders 13 percent.

Types of Couple Violence

In a provocative set of papers, Johnson and his coauthors (Johnson, 1995; 2000; in press; Johnson & Leone, 2000; Johnson & Ferrero, 2000) have argued that there are multiple forms of couple violence. Johnson (1995) began his analysis by noting a family violence and a feminist perspective for studying domestic violence. The family violence perspective has been developed by researchers like sociologist Straus who do surveys with samples from the general public. The feminist perspective has been developed by researchers who typically find their participants from places such as shelters for abused women, hospital emergency rooms, and criminal divorce courts. Johnson noted that these two groups of scholars have different views of key aspects of couple violence. Johnson initially distinguished between two types of violence: common couple violence, linked with the sociological tradition, and patriarchal terrorism, linked with the feminist tradition.

In later publications Johnson and his coauthors have distinguished up to four types, based on each partner's use or nonuse of violence as a means of controlling the other partner. A third type, **mutual violent control,** includes couples in which both partners are controlling and violent. The fourth type, **violent resistants,** includes couples in which both partners are violent but the resistant partners, almost always the women, are not trying to control their spouses but instead seem to be acting in self-defense. As the third type is very rare and the fourth group could be the partners of patriarchal terrorists, we will focus mostly on Johnson's original types.

Johnson believes that **common couple violence** typically erupts from conflicts that occasionally get out of hand. He sees it as usually leading to minor forms of violence that rarely escalate into serious, life-threatening forms of aggression. Neither partner is using violence primarily as means of asserting control or power over the other. Johnson believes that **patriarchal terrorism** is a product of patriarchal traditions in society that result in men who desire to control "their" women. Patriarchal terrorism involves not only violence, but also other control tactics such as threats, isolation, and economic subordination (see Figure 12.5). In patriarchal terrorism, abuse escalates in frequency and intensity over time. Compared with victims of common couple violence, victims of patriarchal terrorism are less likely to fight back physically, are twice as likely to get injured, are more likely to experience post-traumatic stress syndrome and depression, are more likely to have missed work or school, and are four times as likely to have left their husbands multiple times (Johnson & Leone, 2000). Common couple violence is much more prevalent but seemingly less severe than patriarchal terrorism. In part because common couple violence is more common, it is often what is studied. Johnson and his colleagues underscore, however, that the correlates of violence may vary, depending on the type of conflict being investigated.

Gender Differences in Partner Violence

For many people, one of the most surprising aspects of the data collected by Straus and his colleagues was a high level of wife-to-husband abuse. For in-

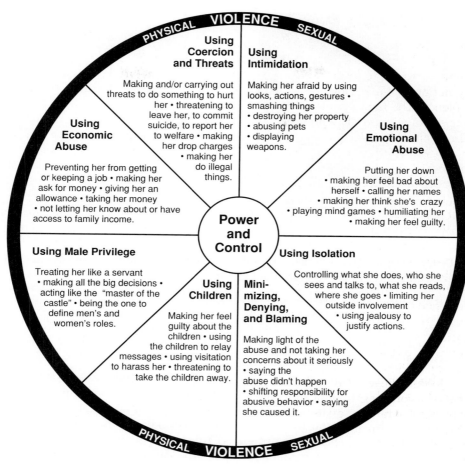

FIGURE 12.5. Power and control wheel.
Source: Johnson, 1995.

stance, in the 1985 Family Violence survey, 12.1 percent of women versus 11.3 percent of men reported having committed a violent act against their spouse in the preceding year (see Barnett, Miller-Perrin, & Perrin, 1997, p. 189). For severe acts (items 4 through 8 in Figure 12.3), 4.4 percent of women versus 3.0 percent of men indicated they had acted violently. In a more recent meta-analysis of 82 studies, John Archer (2000, p. 664) reached a similar conclusion: "women were more likely than men to have used physical aggression toward their partners and to have used it more frequently, although the effect size was very small."

This greater prevalence of wife-to-husband abuse has been the subject of considerable controversy and discussion (e.g., Dobash, Dobash, Wilson, & Daly, 1992; O'Leary, 2000). For instance, in a commentary on Archer's meta-analysis,

Abused women often turn to shelters
and crisis centers for assistance and
emotional support.

O'Leary accepted his conclusions as they apply to community samples and to specific measures of aggression. But O'Leary contended that:

> If conclusions are based on clinical samples, men appear to engage in aggression against their partners more frequently than women . . . If conclusions are based on a broader definition of physical aggression that includes sexual aggression and murder, men would be deemed more aggressive. (O'Leary, 2000, p. 685)

Others in this debate have noted that the Conflict Tactics Scale does not assess whether the violence involved was offensive or defensive in nature. According to some researchers, wife-to-husband abuse is often a defense against, or provoked by, husband-to-wife abuse (e.g., Walker & Browne, 1985). The Conflict Tactics Scale also does not include questions about the severity of injury resulting from abuse incidents. Research indicates that women suffer serious injury more often than do men (Archer, 2000), and women are twice as likely as men to be killed by their spouses (O'Leary & Vivian, 1990). In general, women are far more vulnerable to violent attack from someone they know intimately (family member, former spouse, current or former romantic partner) than are men. Among the female victims included in national crime surveys conducted in 1994, 20.4 percent knew their attacker intimately, compared with only 2.6 percent of male victims (Craven, 1997).

In essence, then, although extensive evidence from broad cross-sectional samples can be found showing that women engage in as much or possibly even more violence than men, it appears that it is women who are generally hurt by such violence. Researchers are increasingly entertaining the possibility that the gender difference in aggression may be sample specific, with a different pattern of results for extreme groups. Consistent with this view, when Johnson (in press) examined gender differences in violence as a function of his types, he found that patriarchal terrorism was almost exclusively perpetrated by men, that common couple violence was roughly gender symmetric, and that violent resistance was almost exclusively a response of women.

Social scientists and others have offered many explanations for couple violence (for explanations of spousal violence see Barnett et al., 1997, chapter 2). One of these is related to Johnson's patriarchal terrorism, namely that couple violence reflects a patriarchal belief system that gives men more privilege and power than women. According to this explanation, cultural standards still permit husband-to-wife violence but should foster women's being more docile and submissive. From this perspective, high levels of wife-to-husband conflict are perplexing. It could, of course, be that patriarchal explanations account for patriarchal terrorism but not for common couple violence, reinforcing Johnson's idea that there may be different antecedents for different kinds of violence.

Another issue for which the patriarchal explanation of violence has implications is sexual orientation. If violence is a result of a patriarchal power structure and sex roles, then to the extent that gay and lesbian couples are more egalitarian, they should be able to avoid interpersonal violence. Peplau and Spalding (2000), however, cite evidence that nearly 50 percent of lesbian and 30 to 40 percent of gay respondents report having been victims of relationship violence. In a representatively selected sample of gay men living in the west end district of Vancouver, British Columbia, an area with a high proportion of gay residents, 41 percent reported having been the recipient of at least one act of violence from a male partner during their lifetimes (Bartholomew, Landolt, & Oram, 1999). In this study, 12 percent of gay men, a number very similar to that in Straus's studies, reported having acted violently during the past year. Thus, the relatively high level of violence among gay and lesbian couples suggests to us that other theoretical models besides patriarchal terrorism may be more useful for explaining violence in gay couples.

Correlates of Violence

Just as it crosses gender and sexual orientation lines, partner abuse is not restricted to any one social class, race, or ethnic background; it occurs throughout society (Lockhart, 1987). But there are a number of specific factors associated with increased rates of spouse abuse (Barling, 1990; Fergusson, Horwood, Kershaw, & Shannon, 1986; Gelles & Straus, 1988; Straus et al., 1980):

Stressful events, such as unemployment and unplanned pregnancy

Low socioeconomic status involving such factors as low income and little education

Family background, including growing up in a violent family

That last factor, family background, has received particular attention from researchers and the mass media. In their review of research, Kantor and Jasinski (1998, p. 16) proclaimed, "violence in the family of origin is probably the most widely accepted risk marker for the occurrence of partner violence." There is reasonably consistent evidence of a cycle of family violence (e.g., Steinmetz, 1978; Stets, 1990). Adults who witnessed parental violence during their childhood are more likely to be involved in spouse abuse, as an abuser and perhaps as a victim. They are also more likely to abuse their own children. The

Family conflict can be emotionally stressful for
parents and children, too.

long-term effects on spouse abuse of having been abused as a child are less well
understood and may not be a major factor in the cycle of family violence (De-
Maris, 1990). Regardless of the exact determinants of this intergenerational
transmission of aggression, it is important to realize that it is not inevitable.
Using data from the 1975 National Family Violence Survey, Johnson and Ferraro (2000) acknowledge that the sons of the most violent parents have a whop-
ping 1,000 percent greater chance than the sons of nonviolent parents to engage
in "wife beating" (i.e., severe violence). Yet even in this extreme group of offspring, only 20 percent had committed severe acts of violence against their
spouses in the past 12 months. The other 80 percent of the children of very violent parents had not been severely violent recently in their adult relationships.
Thus, the cycle of violence refers to an average tendency, not an absolute certainty. But even an average tendency in this matter is most disturbing, because
it translates into enormous suffering for many people. In the cycle of family violence, the evil that people do does, in fact, live after them.

Why Don't They All Leave?

When spouse abuse occurs, what is the prognosis for the relationship? Studies of women who seek aid at women's shelters suggest that over 40 percent of them return to their partners (Rusbult & Martz, 1995, p. 559). Campbell, Miller, Cardwell, and Belknap (1994) followed 51 battered women over a 2.5-year period. At the end of this study,

> 43 percent of the participants had left their partners remaining unattached (20 percent) or in a nonabusive relationships (23 percent),
>
> 23 percent remained with their partners but had successfully attained an end to the violence for at least one year's period of time, and
>
> 33 percent were still in an ongoing abusive relationship, either as victims (25 percent) or as both victims and perpetrators of violence (8 percent).

Perhaps one of the most puzzling aspects of marital violence is why many of its victims remain in the relationship. Research on this issue has pointed to three important factors (Gelles, 1976; Strube, 1988). First, the victim's economic status is crucial. Women who leave abusing relationships are more likely to be employed than women who stay. Second, commitment to the relationship can turn into entrapment. In one study of abused women, those in longer-lasting relationships were less likely to leave than those in more short-term relationships (Strube & Barbour, 1983). Finally, women who spontaneously cited "love" as a reason for staying were less likely to leave. The more these women had invested in terms of both time and affection, the greater was their commitment to the relationship and the harder it was for them to leave it. Rusbult and Martz (1995) have conceptualized these factors in terms of Rusbult's investment model. From that perspective, greater investment, lack of alternatives, and high satisfaction should lead to commitment, which in turn should lead to staying in the relationship. Rusbult and Martz's 12-month follow-up study of 100 women who had gone to a shelter found general support for this model, especially for the role of investment, alternatives, and commitment.

In addition to economic dependence and psychological commitment, fear of even greater violence may also prevent the victims of spouse abuse from leaving the relationship. Dutton (1987) describes what he calls "abandonment panic" among some assaultive husbands who may react with extreme anger against the wife if she tries to leave. The possibility of such violent reactions, says Dutton, "argues strongly for maximum protection of women who are attempting to leave abusive relationships" (p. 247).

Violence in Premarital Relationships

Research on family violence has made it clear that the use of physical power to control others is not restricted to the battlefield. Nor is the use of physical force restricted to married couples. There has also been increasing concern with physical violence among dating couples (Lloyd & Emery, 2000). It appears that dating violence is widespread. In an early study, for example, 22.3 percent of 355 undergraduates surveyed reported that violence had occurred in their relationships (Cate, Henton, Koval, Christopher, & Lloyd, 1982). The vast majority of these students indicated that only mild or moderate levels of violence had occurred (types 1 to 5 on the Conflict Tactics Scale shown in Figure 12.3). In this sample, none reported the use of a knife or gun, but a few did state that beatings or threats with a weapon had taken place. The majority of those who indicated that violence had occurred in their relationships said this violence was reciprocal, with both partners engaging in physical force. Among subjects who said that only one person had used force, more females (22 percent) were said to have used force than males (10 percent). In a much larger study of over 4,700 U.S. college students at 32 different institutions, 37 percent of the men and 35 percent of the women reported having used some form of physical aggression in the previous year (White & Koss, 1991). More men (39 percent) than women (32 percent) indicated that their partners had used force against them.

In comparisons among different types of relationships, it appears that cohabiting couples are more violent than either noncohabiting dating couples or married couples (Johnson & Ferraro, 2000). Although the exact reasons for the association between cohabitation and physical violence are still being clarified, the in-between status of cohabitation could be an important factor. On one hand, cohabiting couples have more extensive contact and, therefore, more opportunity for conflict than do noncohabiting dating couples. On the other hand, cohabitation is legally, and often socially, a less committed state than marriage. At least among 8th and 9th grade dating couples, evidence is available showing that the less committed partners are to one another, the more likely they are to engage in violence (Gaertner & Foshee, 1999). It seems possible that this combination of more contact and less commitment could create a greater risk for violent altercations.

O'Keefe (1997) drew on a social learning perspective plus findings from the past literature in trying to predict dating violence among 939 ethnically diverse (53 percent Latino, 20 percent white) Los Angeles high school students. According to the version of the social learning perspective that O'Keefe used, adolescents learn violent behavior from their larger context (e.g., their families) and react to more immediate situational factors, such as whether they have been drinking alcohol or their partner's actions. When students were simply asked why they acted violently, the most frequent reason given by both males and females was anger. The second most common reason for boys was to get control over their partners, while for girls it was self-defense. When O'Keefe used statistical procedures to predict who was most violent, she found that four factors predicted the actions of both males and females: a belief that male-to-female dating violence is justifiable, being the recipient of dating violence, alcohol/drug use, and greater conflict in the dating relationship. For males, witnessing interparental violence also was a useful predictor, and for females the belief that female-to-male violence is justifiable as well as being in a more serious relationship added to the success of the prediction. Thus, these results suggest that both contextual factors and situational factors contribute to violence. The findings (e.g., intergenerational transmission) also complement some of those for marital couples.

CHAPTER SUMMARY

The Nature and Beginnings of Conflict

What Is Conflict? *Interpersonal conflict* involves incompatibility between people—their actions, goals, desires, opinions, and the like. Often, but not necessarily, it involves negative emotions.

The Frequency of Conflict. Conflict occurs often. The frequency of conflicts in relationships has been shown to be associated with personality characteristics (e.g., neuroticism), having incompatible preferences, and life stage factors.

Conflict Topics and Issues. Intimate partners experience conflict over a wide range of issues. These vary somewhat by type of relationship with, for instance, differences in reproductive strategies being a key source of conflict in dating relationships, while "helping out around house" has been identified as a key conflict in young adolescents' relationships with their parents. According to Peterson, four common categories of events that precipitate marital conflicts are *criticism, illegitimate demands, rebuffs,* and *cumulative annoyances.* The type of couple (gay, lesbian, or heterosexual) has some but not a major influence on the sources of conflict between partners.

Attributions and Conflict

Basic Propositions about Attributions and Conflict. People are more active in their search for explanations during conflict than during more pleasant, peaceful interactions. During conflict, people will tend to take a benign view of the causes of their own behavior, easily finding excuses for what they do. Although conflict may start as a dispute about facts, it can readily turn into an attributional conflict over motives.

Attributions: Differences Between Happy and Unhappy Couples. Despite these general trends in attributional behavior during conflict, there are major differences in the patterns of attributions of happy versus unhappy couples. Unhappy couples make distress-maintaining causal attributions: emphasizing the bad by making internal, stable, and global attributions for a partner's negative behavior and discounting the good by making external, unstable, and specific attributions for the partner's positive behavior. Happy couples make relationship-enhancing causal attributions, which are the mirror image of those made by unhappy couples. Attributions of responsibility (indicating a person's accountability for an event) also differ depending on the state of the relationship. Unhappy couples are more likely than happy ones to see selfish motives and negative intentions in their partners' behavior. There is evidence of bidirectional influence between attributions and marital distress, thus setting in motion a continuous cycle.

The Middle Stages of Conflict

Escalation, Threats, and Entrapment. Once conflict surfaces, two responses are escalation or negotiation. Escalation involves such processes as the generalization of issues, the attribution of blame to the other person, personal attacks, intensified demands, and threats. Alcohol triggers processes that exacerbate conflict. The escalation of conflict can lead to entrapment, taking positions from which retreat seems unthinkable.

The Demand/Withdraw Pattern. In dealing with conflicts, many couples become bogged down in a *demand/withdraw* cycle in which one partner approaches the other about a problem and the partner responds by avoiding the issue or the person. Women are twice as likely as men to be the person making demands. Christensen and Heavey offer a *conflict-structure hypothesis* to explain this gender difference. Women are more likely than men to be wanting change in their partners, and the person wanting change occupies the demand role. Available evidence suggests the detrimental impact on relationships of a woman demand/man withdraw conflict pattern.

Negotiation and Accommodation. Negotiation and *accommodation* are positive responses to conflict. In the view of Rusbult and her associates, commitment is a key factor in accommodation. Partner's perspective taking, femininity, relationship satisfaction, investment, a lack of alternatives, and support of the relationship by others are all also associated with accommodation. In the case of relationship factors, their impact on accommodation may be in part because they foster commitment. Evidence suggests that accommodation, in turn, is linked to marital adjustment.

Dealing with Conflict: Four Types of Couples. In considering patterns of how couples interact over disagreements, Gottman identifies four main types: *volatiles, validators, avoiders,* and *hostiles.* The first three groups generally have a high ratio of positive-to-negative interactions, but they differ in their engagement with one another and their use of persuasion. In volatile relationships, there is extreme expressiveness and involvement. Validators have calmer, more relaxed discussions in which they appear to be working together on the problem. Volatiles begin conflict discussions by trying to persuade one another; validators take stock at the beginning of their discussions before trying to persuade one another. Avoiders tend not to have specific strategies for resolving conflicts; they hope that with the passage of time, things will work out. In their discussions, they engage in very few influence attempts. The conflict discussions of hostiles are marked by negativity. These couples tend to engage in such behaviors as criticism, contempt, defensiveness, withdrawal, and flooding.

The Termination and Outcomes of Conflict

Ways of Terminating Conflict. Peterson (1983) describes five ways conflicts can end: *separation, domination, compromise, integrative agreement,* and *structural improvement.* In separation, one or both parties withdraw without immediate resolution of the conflict. In domination, one person gets his or her way and the other gives in. In compromise the two parties find an alternative that is acceptable to both but optimal to neither. In integrative agreement, both partners' original goals and aspirations are met. In structural agreements, the partners' relationship is likely to be "improved over many situations and beyond the time of the immediate conflict" (Peterson, 1983, p. 382).

Can Fighting Be Good for a Relationship? It has been suggested that a good fight, fought fairly and with respect for the other participant, can promote intimacy (see Table 12.3). The alternatives to having a good fight are to have bad ones or to avoid having any fights at all. Bad fights can produce psychological and sometimes physical damage to the participants. Fight avoidance can create superficial relationships, in which people fear to tread into sensitive areas, or relationships in which resentments build up and then explode. It is possible to view conflict as an opportunity to learn more about oneself and one's partner and as a way to strengthen the relationship.

Violence and Abuse in Relationships

The Prevalence of Violence. According to national surveys conducted in 1975, 1985, and 1995–96, marital abuse was high in the United States at the end of the twentieth century.

Types of Couple Violence. Johnson has distinguished between *common couple violence* and *patriarchal terrorism.* Common couple violence is the more prevalent and less intense type. Patriarchal terrorism typically involves not only frequent, intense violence, but also a desire to control one's partner. Patriarchal terrorism, typically perpetrated by men, has negative effects such as depression and missing work.

Gender Differences in Partner Violence. Surprisingly, a number of studies involving broad cross-sections of the population have indicated that wife-to-husband abuse is often as common as husband-to-wife abuse. It appears, however, that women are more likely to suffer serious injury than are men. Same-sex couples also have relatively high levels of violence, which challenges patriarchal explanations of common couple violence.

Correlates of Violence. Spouse abuse is associated with experiencing stressful events, having a low socioeconomic status, and growing up in a violent home. In the cycle of family violence, children who witness parental abuse are more likely as adults to be involved in spouse abuse (as abuser or victim) and to abuse their own children.

Why Don't They All Leave? Some victims of abuse leave their relationships, others achieve a reduction in violence, and others remain in an abusive situation. Research on spouse abuse indicates that victims are less likely to leave the relationship when they do not have adequate economic resources and when they have invested more (in terms of time and affection) in the relationship. In terms of Rusbult's investment model, high investment, few alternatives, and high commitment are associated with staying. Victims may fear that if they try to leave, they will suffer even greater physical harm.

Violence in Premarital Relationships. Although different studies have obtained different estimates, it is clear that physical violence occurs in a large number of premarital relationships, especially between cohabiting couples. The predictors of acting violently in a Los Angeles study of dating relationships varied slightly by gender, but four factors help us to identify both males and females who are likely to act violently: a belief that male-to-female dating violence is justifiable, being the recipient of dating violence, alcohol/drug use, and greater conflict in the dating relationship.

PART FIVE

Losing and Enhancing Relationships

CHAPTER 13

The Dissolution and Loss
of Relationships

*For a long time after I left my wife I continued to wear my wedding ring. . . .
It reminded me of how much there was I loved about my marriage, even when
so little worked, and of how much I missed it, and would always miss it, my
marriage and the vanished, unrecoverable family that my wife and my daughter and I had once formed.*

JOHN TAYLOR, *Falling: The Story of One Marriage*

No two divorces are exactly the same, but a brief synopsis of journalist John
Taylor's account of the unraveling of his marriage is a useful starting point for
this chapter on the dissolution and loss of relationships. At 26, John met Maureen while he was working for a magazine. Maureen was a journalist from
Great Britain who was in New York writing pieces for a Paris paper. She was six
years John's senior. John "was immediately taken with her." They began dating, started living together four months later, and were married in an interfaith,
Jewish service a year after that.

For reasons John never fully understood, their wedding night was a disappointment to Maureen. Within two years, they had a baby, Jessica, and Maureen
was diagnosed with Parkinson's disease. And their marriage began to go wrong.
It was nothing dramatic but rather a slow, gradual decay. Maureen felt confined

by her role and by being in Brooklyn; she became dependent and resentful. John's career prospered but he withdrew from their relationship. A core dispute emerged: Each partner felt that the other had too little respect for the contributions he or she gave to their partnership. When the decay first started, they tried talking, but that often led to complaining; after a while, they began withholding their feelings and talked less. John was repeatedly losing his temper.

John began an affair. He felt dishonest and guilty, but the affair continued for some time. Eventually, John ended the affair when his lover wanted him to leave his wife.

Outwardly, John's life with Maureen seemed normal, but they talked little, saw few people, and did little together. He decided to try a "trial separation." Maureen resisted, but John packed some belongings and left while she was out. They tried marriage counseling but stopped going after a few sessions. John had another short affair. Still, he missed his wife and daughter and felt he belonged with them. He returned "home."

He and Maureen started seeing a new therapist. In their sessions, they engaged in reciprocal accusations, each complaining about the other. Maureen attributed their arguments to John's drinking; John acknowledged having two to three drinks after work but didn't think his drinking was problematic. Their therapist encouraged better communication patterns, but they had lost their desire for such changes.

Over the next few years, John "tried not to complain" about bothersome aspects of their marriage. He and Maureen slipped into a pattern of separate activities, each doing different things with their daughter. John often slept in the living room. He still wanted to stay with his wife, but began yet another affair.

Finally, eleven-and-a-half years after their marriage, Maureen told John they had to separate—that it would be better for Jessica than persisting marital tensions. It was a moment John "had both dreaded and longed for." He realized that despite Maureen's medical condition, she didn't need him as much as he had thought. Instead, he felt his "obligation was to set her free."

Nothing happened immediately. John was drinking heavily, and after he had a panic attack that required a trip to the hospital, Maureen insisted that he find his own place. They began working on a divorce agreement.

Wanting to remain amicable, John and Maureen went to a mediator and reached agreement on a tentative settlement in which John would pay maintenance to Maureen until Jessica reached age 18. However, before the deal was signed, the mediator advised them to get a lawyer's opinion, and Maureen's lawyer advised her to seek lifetime maintenance. John felt that Maureen had chosen to leave the workforce, and a shouting match ensued. John agreed to her demands when the mediator injected that Maureen could probably get a lifetime maintenance settlement from the courts because of her medical condition. Outside the mediator's office, they kissed, John taking "some satisfaction in shouldering my responsibilities."

Soon thereafter John found an apartment. After multiple rehearsals, John and Maureen told Jessica. Jessica cried but listened to what was being said. She seemed most concerned by the finality of a divorce. When John said it would be for the best, she nodded.

After moving out, John was intensely lonely. He felt "bewilderment and despair . . . even more brittle and snappish than before." He worried about Maureen and became preoccupied with how unhappy he had made her. They did, however, become more open in their conversations and accepted each other's limitations. Their postmarital relationship brought out "the best" in both of them. A year later, John still had nights when he was overwhelmed with grief. But, on other nights he felt "our lives seemed in order; we had done the right thing after all."

Various issues underlie Taylor's memoirs: the historical change in divorce rates, the sources of marital dissatisfaction, the steps he and Maureen passed through in dissolving their marriage, the experiences he had afterwards, and the consequences for himself, his wife, and his daughter. These are all the sorts of questions that social scientists have addressed in analyzing the termination of relationships. They will be the central concerns of this chapter.

The chapter will focus on the ending of marital relationships, but other forms of intimate relationships—such as cohabiting partnerships, dating relationships, and friendships—also end. (Of course, in many cases, calling the experience an "ending" is an overstatement. What the partners are actually doing is transforming their relationship to a less intimate, less interdependent stage.) Also, in addition to separation and divorce, relationships may end through death. In 1995, 46 percent of American women and 16 percent of men age 65 and older were widowed (U.S. Bureau of the Census, 1998b).

THE CHANGING RATE OF DIVORCE

The Prevalence of Divorce

In his memoir, Taylor expressed the view that we live in "faithless" times that provide little encouragement for couples to stay together. He may be right. The U.S. Census Bureau has been keeping track of divorce for some time. A frequently reported statistic is the **refined divorce rate,** the number of divorces per 1,000 married women over age 15 that occur in any given year. It is a better measure than the total number of divorces per year—or even the number of divorces per 1,000 population—because it avoids problems of changes in the size and composition of the population.

Changes in the refined divorce rate seem to support John's contention that marital fidelity and commitment have eroded. During the twentieth century, the divorce rate in the United States generally increased (albeit with a few twists and turns; see Figure 1.2). Current divorce rates are much higher than they were when your grandparents were married (U.S. Bureau of the Census, 1976; U.S. Bureau of the Census, 1998b; U.S. National Center for Health Statistics, 1995).

Many divorced people remarry, but paralleling the divorce rate, there has been a marked increase in the percentage of all adults who are currently divorced and who have not remarried. In 1960, this was true of only 1.8 percent of men and 2.6 percent of women, but by 1998 these percentages had quadrupled to 8.2 percent and 10.6 percent, respectively (Popenoe & Whitehead, 1999). In other words, in the United States, 8.3 million men and 11 million women were divorced.

As a result, by the late 1990s, 20 million children—more than one out of every four people under age 18—lived in one-parent families, most of them headed by their mothers (U.S. Bureau of the Census, 1998a). Overall, 35 percent of U.S. children were living apart from their biological fathers, up from 17 percent in 1960 (Popenoe & Whitehead, 1999). Remarkably, about half of all children will probably spend some of their childhood in a single-parent household.

Looking ahead, researchers estimate that 45 to 50 percent of marriages started in the United States today will end in divorce (Popenoe & Whitehead, 1999). These projections typically assume that the current divorce and death rates will continue. If prevailing social trends change, these rates may change. Nevertheless, as you read this, the best guess is that the chances that the average marriage will end in divorce are about the same as getting "heads" when you flip a coin.

The typical American couple that divorced in 1990 had been married just over seven years. When they married, the husband was 28 and the wife 26. On average, divorced couples had .90 children (U.S. Bureau of the Census, 1998b). Overall, younger people are more likely to divorce than older ones, and divorce is more common early in a marriage (particularly in the first two or three years) than later on (Bumpass, Sweet, & Castro Martin, 1990; London & Wilson, 1988).

U.S. Divorce Rates in Comparative Perspectives

Although divorce rates increased in virtually all Western countries during the second half of the twentieth century, the United States had the dubious distinction of leading the pack. In 1995, the United States had a crude divorce rate (that's the number of divorces per 1,000 population) of 4.5 (United Nations, 1999). Most other countries had substantially lower rates (e.g., Mexico, 0.4; Chile, 0.4; South Africa, 0.8; Japan, 1.8; Netherlands, 2.2, Sweden, 2.4; Canada, 2.6; the United Kingdom, 2.9). Only a few countries (e.g., Russia, 4.5) have divorce rates close to that of the United States.

While the current divorce rate represents a significant change in our society, the ending of large numbers of marriages after a relatively short period is not a new phenomenon. In former times, many marriages were terminated by the early death of one of the partners. The hazards of childbirth made it especially likely that a married woman would die young and that her husband would remarry. As historian Lawrence Stone put it, divorce can be considered "a functional substitute for death: both are means of terminating marriage at a premature stage" (1988, p. 21). In addition, many marriages in the past were ended by desertion, without a legal divorce ever being obtained. Those young men encouraged to go west in America during the 1800s often left wives and children behind. Actually, the average duration of marriage seems to have increased "from about fifteen to twenty years in preindustrial Europe to about thirty-five years in 1900, and then to almost fifty years" in the late 1980s (Phillips, 1988, p. S93). And when anything has the possibility of lasting a longer time, it also has an increased possibility of breaking down. Taken in their broader historical context or in comparison with the breakup of other forms of close relationships (see Box 13.1), the current high rates of divorce in the United States seem less deviant, less shocking. Nevertheless, what has clearly changed is the way that marriages end.

BOX 13.1

Dissolution in Four Types of Relationships

Separation Rates in Four Types of Relationships

Study	Marital	Cohabiting	Gay	Lesbian
Blumstein & Schwartz, 1983	4%	17%	16%	22%
Kurdek, 1998	7%		14%	16%
Bumpass & Sweet, 1989	20%	45%		
Wu & Balakrishnan, 1995	< 5%	24%		
Leridon, 1990	8%	16%		

Note: Blumstein and Schwartz (1983) solicited volunteer participants via the media; their index of relationship termination is the percentage of participants (N = 2,082) who broke up within 18 months of originally completing a questionnaire. Kurdek (1998) conducted a five-year longitudinal study of 353 married, gay, and lesbian couples, who had respectively been living together, on average, for 4.7, 10.9, and 7.1 years at the beginning of the study; he assessed the percentage in each group that separated over the study period. Using the 1987–1988 National Survey of Families and Households, Bumpass and Sweet (1989) examined dissolution rates over the first five years of their relationship among 4,184 people involved in "first unions." Wu and Balakrishnan (1995) used data from Statistics Canada's 1990 General Social Survey (Family and Friends section). They report the percentage of marriages and first cohabitations (N = 2,876) that end in separation within three years. Leridon (1990) analyzed data from a French Family History Survey involving participants who became involved in first unions during the period 1968–1985. Breakdown results are the outcomes over the first five years for unions formed in the period 1977–1979.

The table presents the dissolution rates among married, cohabiting, gay, and lesbian couples in five different studies. What these studies show is that married couples have less likelihood of separating over a given period of time than do cohabiting or same-sex couples. In the only study (Blumstein & Schwartz, 1983) comparing all four kinds of couples, the difference between marriages and all other relationships was considerably greater than that between heterosexual cohabiting and same-sex couples, so marriage appeared to be more crucial to stability than sexual orientation per se.

Investigators have also examined the factors associated with breakups in different types of relationships. Peplau and Spalding (2000) found that partners in gay, lesbian, cohabiting, and marital relationships report similar levels of attraction to one another. However, married couples have more barriers around their relationships than do members of other types of couples. As Peplau and Spalding noted, gay and lesbian couples "cannot marry legally, are less likely to own property jointly, are less likely to have children in common, may lack support from their families of origins, and so on (pp. 120–121)." Cohabiting heterosexual partners are also more likely to break up if they have no children (Wu & Balakrishnan, 1995). All in all, it appears that an important factor in the lower dissolution rates of married couples are the barriers linked with marriage that make it harder to leave the relationship.

Why Has the Divorce Rate Increased?

When important social changes occur, we like to understand their causes. In many cases, however, it is difficult to know for certain why something took place. And so it is with the increase in divorce in the second half of the twentieth century. We don't know exactly why it happened. But a number of possible reasons for the "divorce epidemic" have been suggested. Some answers have focused on the partners' expectations and satisfaction with their marriages; others have turned to societal factors and the connections among areas of social change.

At the individual level, one possibility involves the expectations that people have about the benefits of marriage. In 1968, Slater noted that:

> Spouses are now asked to be lovers, friends, and mutual therapists in a society which is forcing the marriage bond to become the closest, deepest, most important and most enduring relationship of one's life. Paradoxically, then, it is increasingly likely to fall short of the emotional demands placed upon it and be dissolved. (p. 99)

Twenty years later, Phillips (1988) expressed a similar point of view:

> The same stress on romantic love, emotional intensity, and sexual satisfaction that has long been associated with premarital and extramarital relationships has spilled over into marriage . . . The higher these emotional expectations rise, the less likely they are to be fulfilled. (pp. 623–624)

People may simply be expecting too much of marriage. Married spouses are certainly less content than they used to be. Since the early 1970s, the National Opinion Research Center at the University of Chicago has asked large, representative samples of Americans to rate their marriages as "very happy," "pretty happy," or "not too happy." A smaller percentage of people reported "very happy" marriages in 1996 than did so in the period 1973–1976 (Popenoe & Whitehead, 1999). In a complementary study, Rogers and Amato (1997) interviewed two samples of married people age 20 to 35, the first in 1980 and the second in 1992. The cohort interviewed in 1992 reported more marital conflict, more marital problems, and less marital interaction than did the cohort interviewed in 1980. So, converging evidence suggests a decline in marital quality since the early 1970s. From marital conflict and dissatisfaction to divorce is a short step.

If dissatisfaction influences divorce rates, what are the more remote changes that may contribute both to marital dissatisfaction and divorce? In Rogers and Amato's study, the 1992 cohort differed from the 1980 cohort in some important ways. The 1992 group experienced more work-family conflicts and had less traditional attitudes about gender roles (e.g., they were less likely to endorse such statements as "A woman's most important task in life should be taking care of her children"). Both these factors were linked to lower marital quality, suggesting that they may be implicated in rising divorce rates.

Associated with work-family conflict and the changing views of women's roles is the changing economic status of women (Phillips, 1988). Cross-cultural comparisons indicate that the level of socioeconomic development and women's participation in the labor force have U-shaped relationships with divorce rates (Trent & South, 1989). Divorce is frequent at the two ends of the continuum: (1) where the level of development is low and women rarely work, and (2) where the level of development is high and most women work. It seems likely that these two cultural conditions involve very different kinds of divorce. In the first, women's status is very low, and men have easier access to divorce. In the second, women are less economically dependent on men, perhaps making divorce a more financially acceptable alternative for both spouses.

Indeed, money may affect marriage in at least two different ways. An **independence hypothesis** postulates that paid employment increases a person's freedom to choose divorce, so there should be a higher divorce rate among women who work outside the home. Alternatively, a **stabilization hypothesis** proposes that people with money are more likely to invest in marriage-related assets (such as possessions and children) that increase their commitment to the marriage; this perspective predicts a decreased divorce rate among working women. Which is the more accurate hypothesis? Remarkably, a careful study by Greenstein (1990) provided some support for both views. On one hand, women who worked 35 or more hours per week had a higher divorce rate than did those who worked fewer hours. On the other hand, women who earned more money had a lower divorce rate than did those who earned less. Combining these two effects, the greatest risk of divorce was found for low-income wives who worked 35 to 40 hours a week. For such women, paid employment may be neither liberating nor stabilizing. Instead, it may be just another stressor that makes life more difficult and marital conflict more likely. Whatever the case, women's participation in the labor force is clearly correlated with divorce in the United States; during the twentieth century, as the proportion of women employed outside the home increased so, too, did the divorce rate (Ruggles, 1997).

Other broad sociological changes may also have influenced recent divorce rates. Consider no-fault divorce laws: To accommodate people's increasing desire to divorce, divorce laws were changed to make divorce easier to obtain. Then, as the prevalence of divorce increased, people's attitudes toward divorce became more tolerant, which reduced the social barriers against divorce even further (Thornton, 1989). Legal changes may have made divorce more socially acceptable (Rodgers, Nakonezny, & Shull, 1999). Moreover, divorce, like many other social customs, is passed down from one generation to the next. Children who experience the divorce of their parents are more likely to be divorced themselves when they become adults (Glenn & Kramer, 1987). Thus, there may be historical periods in which the causes and consequences of divorce reciprocally influence one another to increase the divorce rate. Conceivably, this cycle may be broken at some point and new social norms may reduce the divorce rate.

THE PREDICTORS OF DIVORCE

John and Maureen's divorce may have been influenced in part by the historical period in which we are living, but even so, some of their contemporaries got divorced while others did not. Why? What predicts who will and will not separate?

Levinger's Model

George Levinger (1976) has offered a simple yet useful model for conceptualizing the factors leading to the breakup of relationships. He identifies three types of influences that are reminiscent of the building blocks of interdependency that we discussed in chapter 6. The first of these is *attraction*. For Levinger, attraction is enhanced by the rewards a relationship offers (e.g., enjoyable companionship, sexual fulfillment, security, social status, a sense of validation) and is diminished by its costs (e.g., irritants, the investment of time and energy). The second key influence on breakups is the *alternatives* available. The most obvious of these is other partners, but Levinger uses "alternatives" in a broader sense. Besides another relationship, alternatives might include the attractiveness of being single or of achieving occupational success. Finally, there are the *barriers* around the relationship that make it hard to leave; these include the legal and social pressures to remain married, religious and moral constraints, and the financial costs of obtaining a divorce and maintaining two households. In general, (a) the more the partners are attracted to one another, (b) the stronger the barriers, and (c) the less appealing the alternatives, the more likely the couple is to stay together. Conversely, the less attraction between the partners, the weaker the barriers, and the stronger the alternatives, the more likely the couple is to separate.

Clearly, Levinger thinks that attraction to one's partner is a key influence on divorce. However, liking for one's partner is obviously not the only consideration. Seemingly dissatisfied couples are likely to stay together if the barriers to separation are high and/or their alternatives are poor. Happily married couples may end their relationships if there are strong alternatives and few costs to breaking up.

In John and Maureen's relationship, their level of attraction seemed to be fairly low. One might feel John had good alternatives. Certainly, he had extramarital relationships. But, he was not passionately attracted to these partners, and when they became demanding, he withdrew from them. Barriers did appear to prevent John from leaving Maureen. He realized it is cheaper to remain married, and his daughter was a consideration. Most of all, he had a strong sense of duty and responsibility that tied him to Maureen. When that barrier of feeling that his wife depended upon him finally eroded, he moved out for good.

Specific Factors Associated with Divorce

Moving beyond Levinger's general framework, a large number of studies have examined how specific factors are associated with the rate of divorce. (See Cate & Lloyd, 1992, for a short review of how premarital factors predict marital stability; Kitson, Barbi, & Roach, 1985, for a review of findings from family science research up to the mid-1980s; White, 1990, for a review of findings from family science research in the 1980s; and Karney & Bradbury, 1995, for a meta-analysis of longitudinal studies examining how the development of marital relationships over time influences marital outcomes). Some of the diverse types of influences used to predict marital outcomes include broad societal forces, demographic factors, life course factors, personality attributes, interactional variables, and evaluation of the relationship itself.

When we try to draw conclusions about the factors that put people at risk for divorce, we face at least three challenges. First, many researchers treat separation and divorce as equivalent outcomes, although not all couples that separate get legally divorced. A marriage may be a failure in either case, but those who divorce may differ in important ways from those who merely separate. Second, the samples of participants in studies of divorce often have unique characteristics. In Karney and Bradbury's (1995) meta-analysis of 115 longitudinal research projects, only 17 percent of the studies sought nationally representative samples. Only 8 percent specifically used both blacks and whites, while 75 percent had samples consisting primarily of middle-class whites. Finally, statements of general trends often gloss over important qualifications: Some generalizations hold in many but not all samples, predictors of divorce may change over time, predictors may hold for some groups or stages of marriage but not others, and the meaning of the findings may reflect the other factors investigated and/or the statistical procedures used. Two examples of such qualifications will suffice. While having a child before marriage is generally associated with high divorce rates, one key study found that this effect was noticeable among blacks in the first years after marriage but *not* in a ten-year follow-up (Billy, Landale, & McLaughlin, 1986). Those couples that stayed together may have been able to gradually overcome the stresses of premarital childbirth, or—perhaps in wanting a child more—they may have been less susceptible to those stresses in the first place. Whatever the case, an important predictor of the risk of divorce lost its power as time went by. Similarly, a study of several classic correlates of divorce (age at marriage, poor health, low social integration, and low income) concluded that, "In general, these factors seem to operate almost exclusively among young people and young marriages" (Booth, Johnson, White, & Edwards, 1986, p. 421). You should keep these caveats in mind while inspecting Table 13.1, which presents a summary of key predictors of marital stability identified by modern research.

Social scientists don't expect statistical generalizations to apply to every case. Nonetheless, it is interesting to look at the risk factors in John and Maureen's marriage. In terms of demographic factors, there seems to be little reason to have expected their divorce. Neither of their parents had gotten divorced, they were middle-class whites, it was the first marriage for each of them, and Maureen was a bit old when they married, but they certainly weren't in the highest risk category on that score. Their interfaith relationship created some risk, but it did not appear to be a salient source of contention in their marriage.

In terms of personality attributes, John's neuroticism may have played some role. He had a panic attack when his marriage was breaking down. He also "seethed with ambition"(p. 37) and sometimes lost (e.g., p. 131) his temper to the point where he engaged in occasional erratic, aggressive actions (such as smashing through a car window with a baseball bat to silence its alarm system).

TABLE 13.1. Predictors of Divorce: A Synthesis of the Literature

Predictor	Findings
Sex ratios	Cross-cultural research shows that the higher the ratio of women to men in a society, the higher the rate of divorce (Trent & South, 1989). In this research, the level of economic development in the 66 societies studied was statistically held constant.
Race	Consistent, strong evidence shows black Americans are more likely than white Americans to divorce (see White, 1990).
Intergenerational transmission	Parents who divorce increase the chances that their children will divorce (see Karney & Bradbury, 1995; White, 1990). However, this effect is declining. Before 1975, adults whose parents had divorced were about 2.5 times as likely to divorce as those whose parents hadn't divorced. By 1996, this ratio had declined to 2.0 (Wolfinger, 1999).
Age at marriage	Teenage marriages are the most likely to end in divorce, although there is evidence that age has a curvilinear relation to divorce rates: That is, the rate drops for people who marry in their twenties but then goes back up again a bit for people who marry at older ages (see Karney & Bradbury, 1995; Kitson et al., 1985; White, 1990; Booth, Johnson, White, & Edwards, 1986).
Prior marriage	Second marriages have higher rates of divorce than first marriages (see White, 1990).
Socioeconomic status	"For the most part, research has found that individuals with low-status occupations, less education, and lower income have a higher probability of divorce" (Kitson et al., 1985, p. 268; see also Karney & Bradbury, 1995; White, 1990).
Religion	Earlier studies consistently showed Catholics and Jews to have lower divorce rates than Protestants (Kitson et al., 1985). A more recent investigation of the first five years of marriage failed to find denominational differences except for a low divorce rate among Mormons (Lehrer & Chiswick, 1993). Frequent church attendance has been associated with lower divorce rates (Mahoney, Pargament, Tarakeshwar, & Swank, in press). Nonbelievers and religiously mixed couples are more prone to divorce (Kitson et al., 1985; Lehrer & Chiswick, 1993).
Premarital cohabitation	Most studies show that premarital cohabitation is associated with higher divorce rates (Karney & Bradbury, 1995; Krishnan, 1998; White, 1990).

John appears to have some of the qualities of a **Type A** person, someone who is competitive, constantly concerned with getting ahead, easily irritated, and aggressive. Burke, Weir, and DuWors (1979) found low levels of marital satisfaction in the wives of Type A husbands.

More risk factors lay in the dyadic and interactional aspects of their relationship. They had cohabited. For a reasonably young, newlywed couple, Mau-

TABLE 13.1. Predictors of Divorce: A Synthesis of the Literature

Predictor	Findings
Premarital conception	Premarital pregnancy is positively associated with divorce (Kitson et al., 1985), but if researchers distinguish premarital *births* from children who were *conceived* premaritally but born after marriage, it turns out there is "unassailable documentation of the fact that premarital child-bearing increases the risk of divorce but that, by itself, a premarital conception does not" (White, 1990, p. 906).
Fertility within marriage	Several—though not all—investigators concerned with this phenomenon have reported that childlessness is associated with higher divorce rates. Converging evidence suggests that the risk-reducing effect of children is most noticeable in the first few years of marriage.
Children	The presence of teenage children modestly elevates divorce rates. Parents who have sons are less likely to divorce than are those who have daughters (see Katvez, Warner, & Acock, 1994; Waite & Lillard, 1991; White, 1990).
Attitude similarity	Longitudinal studies show that spouses with similar attitudes are less likely to divorce (Karney & Bradbury, 1995).
Personality attributes	Neuroticism has been associated with higher divorce rates in several longitudinal studies (Karney & Bradbury, 1995).
Stressful life events	The occurrence of stressful life events (other than parenthood) increases the likelihood of divorce (Karney & Bradbury, 1995).
Time together	Couples who share more time together are less likely to divorce (White, 1990).
Interaction patterns	After combining specific aspects of marital interaction into broad categories, Karney and Bradbury (1995) found that positive interactions predicted stability and negative interactions predicted divorce.
Sexual satisfaction	Greater satisfaction with the sexual aspects of marriage is associated with a lower likelihood of divorce (Karney & Bradbury, 1995).
Marital satisfaction	"Marital satisfaction has larger effects on marital stability than do most other variables" (Karney & Bradbury, 1995, p. 20; see also White, 1990). People who are more satisfied with their marriages are less likely to divorce. Even so, satisfaction is far from being a perfect predictor of divorce.

reen's health problems were certainly a stressor. They spent little time together. There is little evidence that they had much positive interaction. Instead, John describes an initial pattern of complaining followed by withdrawal. John's description is reminiscent of the destructive communication patterns identified in chapter 5:

> One can describe a couple as on a cascade toward marital dissolution. . . . The process cascade I propose, which predicts marital dissolution, is the following: Complaining and criticizing leads to contempt, which leads to defensiveness, which leads to listener withdrawal from interaction (stonewalling). I refer to these four corrosive marital behaviors as the "Four Horsemen of the Apocalypse." (Gottman, 1994, p. 110)

Another prominent feature of John's marriage was his sexual infidelity. Several studies have demonstrated that extramarital sex is linked to a greater probability of divorce (see Wiederman, 1997); however, the role this stressor plays in divorce is open to interpretation. People who engage in extramarital sex are likely to believe that they did so because of preexisting problems in their marriages. On the other hand, their partners are more apt to see their infidelity as a cause of marital breakdown (Spanier & Margolis, 1983). To some degree, extramarital affairs may be both a symptom and a cause of marital distress.

In therapy, Maureen blamed their marital problems on John's drinking. This is one of a variety of answers people often give when they are asked why their marriages broke down. Other common reasons include communication difficulties, general incompatibility, sexual infidelity, not spending enough time at home, and financial disagreements (see Kitson et al., 1985). Evidence from longitudinal studies suggests that a wife's concern about her husband's drinking is one of a half dozen complaints associated with later marital disruption (Amato & Rogers, 1997).

THE ROAD TO DIVORCE

The literature on the prediction of divorce tells us a good deal about who is likely to get divorced, but it sheds less light on the processes people go through in separating. In intensive interviews with 30 divorcing people, Joseph Hopper (1993) determined that most divorce experiences were characterized by a long period of discontent, multiple complaints about their partners that were coupled with things they liked, and ambivalence about getting separated. Hopper writes:

> Prior to nearly every divorce, there was a long period of assessment, with both initiators and noninitiating partners describing similar experiences and feelings of indecision and ambivalence. They described pain, dissatisfaction, and feelings of being trapped; at the same time, they described good things that they did not want to forego. That is what made divorce such an agonizing decision and process, no matter what side of the divorce they were on. (Hopper, 1993, p. 806)

Various formal models of the steps leading to separation have been offered. We will first consider Karney and Bradbury's (1995) **vulnerability-stress-adaptation** model of marital dissolution. Then we will consider models of the steps people go through en route to the breakdown of romantic relationships.

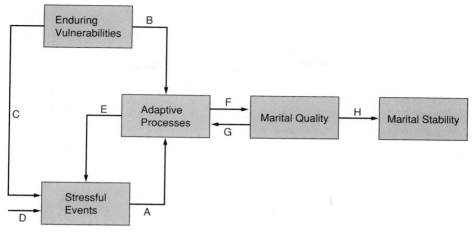

FIGURE 13.1. A vulnerability-stress-adaptation model of marriage.
Source: Karney & Bradbury, 1995.

Karney and Bradbury's Vulnerability-Stress-Adaptation Model

Karney and Bradbury's model of marital instability is shown in Figure 13.1. According to their view, some people enter marriage with enduring vulnerabilities. These might include adverse experiences in one's family of origin, poor education, maladaptive personality traits, bad social skills, or dysfunctional attitudes about marriage. These enduring vulnerabilities are presumed to interact with the circumstances people encounter to help determine the number of stressful events couples face in their marriages (such as unemployment). How well partners adapt to their stresses is a function of the stresses themselves and of the partners' enduring attributes. Some people cope better than others. Failure to cope successfully can exacerbate the stresses one is experiencing. Poor coping is postulated to lead to marital dissatisfaction, which in turn leads to instability or divorce.

Overall, this is a general model that suggests that the roots of divorce can begin in childhood. Subsequent events such as one's choice of a partner are influential, too, however (see Duck, 1982), and intolerable stresses ultimately affect some marriages but not others. When they occur, satisfaction erodes, and divorce eventually follows.

Steps to Separation

In the 1980s, Baxter (1984), Duck (1982), and Lee (1984) each proposed a model of the steps that partners go through in ending their relationships. Duck based his model on a conceptual analysis; Baxter and Lee had participants give narrative accounts of their experiences, and Lee also collected questionnaire information. Although these models differ in some of their specifics (e.g., Duck has four stages, Lee five, and Baxter seven), a general pattern emerges from them: They all agree that separation involves discovery of the problem, exposure, negotiations, transformation, and grave dressing.

Discovery of the Problem

All three models start with the discovery of the problem. This may be a gradual recognition of various concerns or a sudden, striking event. In this phase, the dissatisfied person assesses his or her partner's behavior, notes the problems, evaluates the costs of leaving, considers the benefits of alternatives, and the like. Common emotions during this phase are frustration and disgruntlement. The discovery phase culminates when a partner concludes that he or she wants to end the relationship.

Exposure

The disgruntled person then reveals his or her discontent. Here, the dissatisfied party can be either indirect or direct in expressing his or her desire to leave. If people use the indirect approach, they begin to extricate themselves without ever straightforwardly announcing their wish to end the relationship. For instance, a student in Baxter's (1984) study told his partner he couldn't see her because he had too much homework to do; he also ignored her messages and kept phone conversations short. Besides this form of withdrawal, other indirect strategies involve telling a partner you just want to be friends (when you really want to end the relationship entirely) or making it costly in various ways for the partner to continue the relationship. In more direct approaches, the dissatisfied partner may reveal his or her feelings about the state of the relationship and thereby start a mutual discussion of separating, or simply announce that the relationship is over ("I'm not going to see you again!"). Common feelings in this phase include shock, anger, hurt, and, sometimes, relief.

Negotiation

Once the problem is known, there may be negotiations. Baxter (1984) found that if the initiator has been direct in expressing discontent, the partner may accept the termination of the relationship. However, the spurned party often resists termination, perhaps offering to make the relationship better and more rewarding. In discussing their grievances, partners may try to create shared norms for negotiation, articulate their own needs, or evaluate their partner's point of view. They may try to placate their partner or bargain, or they may say or do things that cause the discord to grow. During this phase, partners may try to manage their stress and ambivalence as they try to work toward a solution. The person seeking to separate may have a change of mind. In that case, the couple is likely to try to repair their relationship. Ultimately, negotiation reaches what Lee (1984) calls resolution: the couple reaches a decision about their relationship.

Transformation

Once the decision is reached, the relationship still has to be transformed. There may be "farewell addresses." For cohabiting couples, one party will typically get a new residence. There will be changes in the frequency, nature, and duration of interactions as well as the way the relationship is defined. Doubts no longer center on the future of the relationship but rather on one's personal future. Physical and psychological stresses stem from a sense of loss and a change in status. A process of mourning is likely to begin. Partners will begin publicizing the changed status of their relationship. For themselves and for members of their networks, they will give explanations for the breakup of their relationship. (See Box 13.2.) According to Duck (1982), ex-partners may "market" their version of the situation and try to avoid loss of face.

Grave-Dressing

Finally, in Duck's (1982) model there is what he calls the *grave-dressing* phase. Here, the goal is to put the relationship behind oneself and get over it. The work in this phase is largely cognitive, tidying up the memories associated with the relationship and creating an acceptable story for the course of the relationship from its beginning to its end. Simplification and rationalization are likely to occur.

Trajectories as a Whole

Most intimate relationships don't end overnight. Lee's (1984) participants said that on average it took them about 30 weeks to go from the discovery of discontent to the transformation point of their breakups. For marriages that end in divorce, the average period of contemplating separation is probably much longer. For instance, in one study of couples who stayed married for about a dozen years, the women—who seem to lose confidence in their relationships faster than men do (Rands, 1988, p. 136)—typically spent the last five years of their relationships thinking about separating (Stewart, Copeland, Chester, Malley, & Barenbaum, 1997, p. 50).

Not all these steps always occur, and relationships may end in idiosyncratic ways. Nevertheless, certain trends do exist. In Baxter's study (1984), the most common pathway to separation was one she labeled "Persevering Indirectness." It was followed by 30 percent of her informants. These modal trajectories started with one partner (rather than both) wanting to separate, with that partner using an indirect strategy, trying to end the relationship without saying so. Several tries were needed, but if the disgruntled partner persisted, the couple finally separated without any formal efforts to repair the relationship.

Lee (1984) examined how the manner in which partners dissolved their relationships affected their feelings about each other afterwards. In general, couples who avoided identifying and discussing their sources of dissatisfaction had less positive feelings toward each other and were less likely to stay in touch. Lee also compared couples who decided on separating and followed through on their decision versus those who oscillated between withdrawal and reconciliation. Those who swung back and forth before taking final action felt more hurt, angry, lonely, and confused after they finally separated.

BOX 13.2

Accounts: What Are They? What Are Their Functions?

Before you read the rest of this box, we encourage you to try a short exercise proposed by Weber and Harvey (1994, p. 294):

1. Think of a difficult or troublesome experience you have had in a close relationship.
2. If you are recalling a past experience, what do you remember? What happened? What did you do? How did you feel?
3. Why did these events occur in your relationship?
4. Have you ever told anyone about this experience, and your interpretation of what happened?

In doing this exercise, you are giving an account. We have prompted it, but in our daily lives, as the following description of bereavement implies, people often form accounts without any external encouragement:

The death of my first husband, [when I was] 44, was the most devastating experience of my life. He was 49, and died suddenly . . . My first husband and I were extremely close. He was 30 when we married and I was 25. It was the first marriage for both of us . . . I went to the cemetery where my husband was buried quite often at first, then it tapered off. I wrote down my feelings. I wrote and wrote things . . . I talked about my feelings a lot, too. (60-year-old woman attending an Elderhostel program, Weber, 1992, pp. 184–185)

According to Weber (1992, p. 178) "An **account** is a story-like narrative or explanation of one's experience, such as in a personal relationship, emphasizing the characters and events that have marked its course." Accounts are awash with descriptions, expectations, feelings, interpretations of people's actions, and explanations of how events occurred. Yet even with their richness, they tend to bring order and a plot sequence to life's complex, messy events. Accounts of the ending of relationships may provide a history of the relationship's beginning, an identification of factors that led to eventual breakup, identification of the relationship problems and partners' flaws that in retrospect had existed all along, reactions to separation, and ways of coping. In accounting for a relationship, there may be a master account covering the whole story and several subaccounts, covering specific parts of the relationship. Accounts are the narrator's perceptions; they aren't necessarily "true." Indeed, it is likely that many aspects of the ex-partners' accounts will differ.

Accounts may serve several functions. In them we often paint ourselves in a favorable light to justify our behaviors and help maintain self-esteem. We can use accounts to influence the way others think of us. We might even offer our accounts as lessons so others can learn from our experiences. In sharing our accounts with others, we get a chance to express and work through our emotions. Formulating narratives helps us to find meaning in what has happened in our lives. Even if memories of past relationships persist indefinitely, account making may help to bring some measure of closure to events. With this completion may come a new sense of identity, as when a widow no longer thinks of herself as dependent on her husband but sees herself as more self-reliant. Finally, research shows that confiding in others can help us overcome traumatic events. Weber and Harvey contend that accounts "are essential to recovery from loss" (p. 304).

Application to John and Maureen

The multiyear trajectory that John and Maureen followed toward separation was one that involved oscillation between withdrawal and reconciliation. John initiated their first separation, Maureen their second. Clearly, the recognition of their problems was a slow process rather than a sudden event. John was direct when he initiated their first separation, but he called it a trial separation, presumably still open to further review. Maureen also used a direct approach in telling John their marriage was ending, but she did not leave it open to discussion. Their getting back together and their attempts at counseling testify to their efforts to discuss their problems and attempt reconciliation. Characteristic of the transformation stage, they told their daughter of the impending separation, marketing it to her as something that would be mutually positive. Once they had communicated this information to their daughter, all three of them had the experience, akin to the emotions identified by Duck, of being "mourners grieving at the death of the family we had been." Once their final decision to separate was reached, John got a new residence, their interaction patterns changed, and they used a mediator to help them reach a divorce agreement. This is an approach that frequently works better than adversarial legal procedures (see Box 13.3).Presumably writing a book about his experiences gave John ample opportunity to do the "tidying up" activities that Duck associates with the grave-dressing phase.

THE AFTERMATH OF SEPARATION AND DIVORCE

Over the past three decades, when people have been asked how much stress and change various events would cause in their lives, the death of a spouse and a divorce have been consistently rated at the top of the list (Miller & Rahe, 1997). What are the consequences of divorce? The spouses' lives change, of course, but so do their children's.

The Aftermath of Separation from the Individual's Perspective

In one ambitious study, Stewart and her colleagues (1997) followed 160 Boston-area families with elementary school-aged children for 18 months after they legally indicated their intent to divorce. Among other things, Stewart et al. examined the participants' adjustment, their interpersonal relationships, their household labor, and, incidentally, their economic situations. In addition to examining effects on the adults, Stewart et al. also looked at what happened to the children who were involved.

Adjustment

To assess well-being and adjustment, Stewart et al. asked participants in both initial and follow-up interviews about the emotions and stress they were experiencing. Not surprisingly, shortly after filing for divorce participants generally had lower well-being than they did later. For instance, they were at first likely to feel anxious, depressed, confused, and hostile. Both men and women expressed concern about "being alone."

Complementing this finding, a study of the driving records of people involved in divorce proceedings showed that they had more accidents and got

BOX 13.3

Divorce Mediation

Since the late 1970s, divorce mediation has become a commonly used approach to assist divorcing couples (Coogler, 1978; Haynes, 1981; Twaite, Keiser, & Luchow, 1998). It was created as an alternative to the adversarial model of the legal system—"You get your lawyer; I'll get mine; and we'll settle this in court." Over the years, mediation has become a more common practice, and even can be mandated in some jurisdictions. Although today there are various models of mediation, they generally emphasize open communication, negotiation, and mutual resolution of the emotional, financial, and child-related issues in divorce. Mediators are typically from legal or behavioral science backgrounds and need to be knowledgeable in both these fields. Agreements formulated during the course of mediation are put in written form, in order to serve as the basis for the divorce petition to the court. Mediators do not, however, serve as the lawyers in the divorce action itself, and most mediators require their clients to have separate legal counsel to inspect all agreements resulting from mediation.

A growing body of research testifies to the effectiveness of divorce mediation (see Benjamin & Irving, 1995; Kelly, 1996; Twaite et al., 1998). At least 40 per cent of couples that go through mediation can reach complete agreement and up to 80 per cent reach at least partial agreement (see Benjamin & Irving, 1995, p. 53). Emery (1999a) notes that: Compliance with agreements reached in mediation is somewhat better than with adversary settlements; parents, particularly fathers, are more satisfied with their experiences with mediation than with adversary procedures; and even many years later, mediation leads to less conflict and more cooperation in coparenting (p. 125).

Concerns have been expressed that mediation does not afford the weaker spouse the benefits that litigation provides. But this does not seem to be the case: in both U. S. and Canadian studies women received higher child support and maintenance awards via mediation than litigation (see Twaite et al., 1999, p. 369). Indeed, wives often find that in the mediation process they develop confidence in their ability to stand up for themselves (Twaite et al., 1998, p. 370).

Participants believe that mediation helps them focus on the needs of their children, gives them an opportunity to express their feelings and grievances, and deal with fundamental issues in greater depth than would occur in court procedures (Twaite et al., 1998, p. 366). Although it does not always work, mediation does appear to usually offer a less acrimonious, more constructive approach to the divorce process. As such, it may help protect both adults and children from the sometimes-disastrous consequences of an embittered, embattled divorce.

more tickets than usual in the six months before and after filing for divorce (McMurray, 1970). Both accidents and driving violations reached their peak in the three months that followed the formal beginnings of their divorces.

Interpersonal Relations

In the early separation period, most of Stewart et al.'s participants maintained frequent contacts with friends. These findings complement the National Survey of Families and Households data, which show that social time with friends increases after divorce, especially in the first year (Hanson, McLanahan,

& Thomson, 1998). Friends and, to a lesser degree, various kin (such as parents, siblings, and children) were the most important sources of people's support during a separation (Duran-Aydintug, 1998). In general, women rely on their social supports more than men do, except that men are slightly more likely than women to get support from new romantic partners.

Of course, not all post-separation relationships are supportive. For about half of the participants in Stewart et al.'s study, their interactions with their estranged spouses were hostile or tense. Half of them also reported that they had relatives who disapproved of their separation.

Furthermore, people usually lose about half of their friends and other members of their social networks (such as in-laws) after a divorce (Rands, 1988). Over time, some new network members are usually added, but two years later an ex-spouse's social network is typically 14 percent smaller on average than it was before the separation. The composition of the networks also changes, usually including fewer married people but more same-sex friends.

Household Chores

In looking back at their division of labor before they separated, most women reported that they had typically handled traditionally feminine household tasks (e.g., shopping, cooking, cleaning, laundry), whereas most men reported they had typically handled masculine tasks (e.g., yard work, repairs, the car). (About half of men felt they had also participated in traditionally feminine tasks.) After their separation, both the men and the women were doing more tasks. For instance, most women were doing household repairs, seeing to their cars, and paying bills. Many (44 percent) were doing yard work. Children's responsibilities had also increased.

Economic Resources

Two-thirds of the mothers in Stewart et al.'s (1997) study indicated that their financial situation deteriorated after separation. This is a routine finding. For instance, in the National Survey of Families and Households, over 13,000 people were interviewed in 1987, and most were interviewed again in 1993; inspecting these data, Hanson et al. (1998) found that the household incomes of women who divorced between interviews dropped an average of 20 percent. More detailed analyses showed household incomes dropped sharply immediately after divorce, but recovered over the ensuing four to five years, especially for women who remarried or established a cohabiting relationship.

Part of the reason why mothers suffer economically is that only about 50 percent of fathers pay all the child support they are supposed to pay; 25 percent ignore custody payments altogether (U.S. Bureau of the Census, 1995). Fathers are more likely to provide custody support if their own incomes are higher and if there are enforcement systems, such as mandated deduction of payments from their paychecks (Meyer, 1999).

Men's economic conditions are less likely than women's to decline after divorce. Using a large national sample, Stroup and Pollock (1994) found that the incomes of divorced men were about 10 percent lower than those of married men. But after divorce, men are more likely to live by themselves, while women are more likely to have children in their households. With that in mind, economists have calculated how spouses' incomes change in relation to their needs; need is typically taken as the poverty level for households of a given size. Using a needs-adjusted measure, Bianchi, Subaiya, and Kahn (1999) found that noncustodial fathers' incomes increased 28 percent in the year after they got divorced, while custodial mothers' incomes dropped 36 percent. Thus, from a needs-adjusted perspective, men's incomes fared well and women's poorly immediately after a divorce.

Relationships Between Former Partners

Let's not forget that one of the key things that changes with separation is the partners' relationship to one another. In some cases, partners will no longer have any contact with each other. For most people, however, the bonds are not broken immediately. Based on clinical work, Robert Weiss (1979, p. 204) contended that "there persists after the end of most marriages . . . a sense of bonding to the spouse." These bonds may fade slowly. They are like the attachment bonds children have with their parents. In both childhood and adulthood, Weiss asserted, the loss of attachment can lead to separation distress, provoking such emotions and reactions as rage, protest over desertion, anxiety, restlessness, feelings of fear or panic, and hyperalertness to indications of the lost partner's return. Moments of euphoria and enhanced self-confidence can also occur. "Because they remain attached to each other and are simultaneously angry with each other," Weiss wrote, "the relationship of separated spouses is intensely ambivalent" (p. 209). There may be a paradoxical desire to rejoin the partner followed by outbursts of anger.

Still, certain patterns may underlie these conflicting feelings. Ahrons (1994) has identified four types of postmarital relationships: **Fiery Foes, Angry Associates, Cooperative Colleagues,** and **Perfect Pals.** For both Fiery Foes and Angry Associates, the spouses' anger with each other is still part of their relationship. Angry Associates have some capacity to work together in coparenting their children; Fiery Foes have very little. Cooperative Colleagues aren't good friends yet they are able to cooperate successfully in parenting tasks. Finally, Perfect Pals maintain "a strong friendship with mutual respect that did not get eroded by their decision to live separate lives" (p. 116). In a midwestern sample of divorced parents, Ahrons found that a year after their divorces, half the ex-spouses had amicable relationships (38 percent Cooperative Colleagues, 12 percent Perfect Pals) and half had distressed relationships (25 percent Angry Associates and 25 percent Fiery Foes).

Children Whose Parents Divorce

Like many others thinking about divorce, John Taylor fretted about the effect it would have on his daughter. In fact, an extensive body of research addresses this question (see Amato & Keith, 1991a, 1991b; Emery, 1999a, 1999b; Hetherington, Bridges, & Insabella, 1998). One meta-analysis combined 129 studies involving roughly 95,000 participants to compare youngsters whose parents divorced to those whose parents remained continuously married (Amato & Keith, 1991a, 1991b). Various outcomes were examined among both children and adults.

Across the board, "adults who experienced parental divorce exhibited lower levels of well-being than did adults whose parents were continuously married" (Amato & Keith, 1991a, p. 43). Children of divorced parents were more likely to

Although many children's parents will divorce, low levels of postmarital conflict can contribute to children's well-being.

head one-parent families, have lower psychological adjustment (e.g., more depression and anxiety, and lower satisfaction with life), have more behavioral conduct problems (e.g., alcoholism, drug use, criminal behavior, suicide, teen pregnancy, or marriage), and lower educational attainment. However, these effects were usually not large. In other words, the global impact of having parents who divorced was consistently negative but relatively modest.

Some other findings from these meta-analyses are also worth noting. Among both children and adults, the detrimental implications of parental divorce were greater in studies done earlier (e.g., in the 1960s) than in those done more recently (e.g., the 1980s). Further, studies that have been done outside the United States typically find more problems for the children of divorce than those done within the United States.

There may be several reasons why divorce might detrimentally affect children: Divorce often involves economic deprivation, parental loss, parental stress, and family conflict (Amato, 1993; Amato & Keith, 1991b; Hetherington et al., 1998). For instance, according to the **parental loss** view, children are presumed to benefit from having two parents. If this is the case, children who experience the death of a parent should manifest levels of well-being comparable to those whose parents are divorced, and both groups should have lower well-being than those children whose parents remain married. Furthermore, children whose custodial parents remarry should show higher levels of well-being than those whose parents remain single. However, neither of these expectations are consistently confirmed. Most studies show that children who experience the death of a parent enjoy well-being that falls between that of children whose parents divorce and those whose parents remain married.

According to the **parental stress** model, stress impairs the quality of parenting and therefore has detrimental effects on children. According to this view, a child's well-being should be associated with the post-divorce psychological adjustment of the custodial parent and the quality of the child's relationship with the custodial parent. Both these expectations have been supported (Amato, 1993). Apropos of **economic hardship,** most studies demonstrate that if economic differences between divorced and nondivorced families are taken into consideration, the difference in the well-being of children in these households is reduced.

Amato (1993) concludes that more than one explanation may have some merit but that the **conflict explanation** has the strongest and most consistent support. The basic premise of this explanation is that parental conflict has detrimental consequences for children. Consistent with this model, there is reasonable support for the following propositions:

- Since conflict typically occurs in the period leading to divorce, the lower levels of well-being that children of divorce experience should be apparent before the marriage ends;
- The greater the postmarital conflict between parents, the lower the children's well-being; and
- Children in highly conflicted but intact marriages should have low levels of well-being.

On the latter point, evidence suggests that children in chronically conflicted but intact families often fare less well than children whose parents divorce (Amato & Keith, 1991b). Thus, for some couples, staying together for the sake of the children may not actually benefit the children at all.

Among college students, nearly half (48 percent) of those whose parents had divorced felt their childhoods had been harder than average, whereas only 14 percent of those from intact families felt that way (Emery, 1999b). On the other hand, longitudinal investigations indicate that children's functioning improves with the passage of time after a divorce (Amato & Keith, 1991b). People are resilient. As Robert Emery has written:

> Divorce is a risk factor for a number of significant problems, but some problems were present prior to the marital separation, and in any case, the majority of children from divorced families successfully adjust to their new family and their new life circumstances. However, the successful adjustment does not mean that children have not struggled both directly with the stressors of divorce and less obviously with inner fears, worries, and regrets. To use a familiar metaphor, some children are irreparably wounded by divorce; the wounds of most children heal; but even healed wounds leave a scar. (Emery, 1999b, p. 18)

To Emery's reflections, we would add that it is one thing to analyze the effects of divorce on children and another to make sure that children receive what they need. Divorcing or remarrying parents may find it helpful to remember that with children the basics are what count: loving, effective parenting; peace between parents; and freedom from poverty.

Application to John and Maureen

The first time John left Maureen he experienced reactions much like separation anxiety. His panic attack, his feelings of loneliness, and his despair and bewilderment all illustrate the types of stress and emotional upheaval that are common in the period around and after separation. His support payments also severely stretched his financial resources. Happily, there was little long-term hostility between John and Maureen; they seemed to be Cooperative Colleagues. As with many people going through a divorce, after a year, the clouds began to lift. His life went on.

CHAPTER SUMMARY

In this chapter we have examined separation and divorce. In particular we have covered the changing rate of divorce, what predicts who will divorce, the steps people take in separating, and the aftermath of separation.

The Changing Rate of Divorce

The rate of divorce generally increased in the U.S. during the twentieth century, peaking around 1980 and then staying on a plateau. The U.S. divorce rate is high in cross-national comparisons but lower than the separation rate for cohabiting couples, for whom the barriers to leaving a relationship are lower. Several possible explanations exist for why the divorce rate is high. These include the high expectations people have for marriage, declining levels of the quality of marriages, and the changing economic status of women. Cyclical processes may have been set in motion with divorce rates and attitudes, divorce laws, and the intergenerational transmission of divorce reciprocally influencing one another.

The Predictors of Divorce

Levinger has offered a model of divorce that emphasizes attraction between partners, barriers around their relationship, and alternative attractions. When attraction and barriers are low but alternative attractions are high, divorce is likely. Recent reviews have found many predictors of divorce, including demographics and life-span factors (e.g., sex ratios, race, intergenerational transmission, age at marriage, prior marriage, premarital child bearing, socioeconomic status, religion), personality attributes (e.g., neuroticism), properties of the couple and the way the partners interact (e.g., premarital cohabitation, having children together, attitude similarity, time together, engaging in negative interactions), stressful life events, and satisfaction with both sex and the relationship.

The Road to Divorce

Karney and Bradbury believe we bring enduring vulnerabilities to our relationships. These are exacerbated by stress and, if we do not cope effectively, divorce is likely to follow. There appears to be a coherent pathway to divorce, which starts with the recognition of relational problems. This is followed by exposure of the problems to one's partner, negotiation, transformation of the relationship to a new form, and finally grave-dressing, or putting the relationship behind oneself. The process of dissolving a relationship may affect the feelings and interactions ex-partners experience after they separate.

The Aftermath of Separation and Divorce

Separation is a major life event. After separation, attachment bonds may linger. The well-being and life satisfaction of the separating people are likely to drop. Their social networks are likely to shrink, although friends and kin remain important sources of support. After going through a separation, both men and women are likely to engage in more household chores and women are likely to have a reduced standard of living. Many ex-spouses have tense, con-flicted relationships, others can work together effectively in child rearing, and still others, a small subgroup, have positive friendships. The children of di-vorced parents typically exhibit lower well-being than the children of parents who remained married. The stress on parents, accompanied by less effective parenting, economic factors, and especially parental conflict, have been found to play a role in the adjustment of children of divorce.

Concluding Reflections

Two conceptual viewpoints have guided much of the work on the an-tecedents and particularly the aftermath of divorce (Kitson & Morgan, 1990): a selection perspective and a crisis perspective. According to the selection per-spective, those who divorce are considered deficient or pathological. They are seen as inept at picking partners, maintaining relationships, and coping with stress. Karney and Bradbury's model embodies many aspects of this position. A crisis model, on the other hand, "implies a relatively self-contained and limited period of distress" (Kitson & Morgan, 1990, p. 915) resulting from events that could befall most couples, no matter who they are. There is also a third view that divorce is a developmental transition, an ordinary phase for many contem-porary couples that must be addressed and worked through. Some advocates of this view (e.g., Ahrons, Stewart et al.) believe that much of the existing liter-ature is negatively biased, painting too bleak a picture of divorce. They ac-knowledge that divorce is a significant event, typically accompanied, at least in part, by pain. Yet they also see it as a chance for individual change and growth. Certainly, in deciding to divorce, many people must believe that being sepa-rated will be a better state than their marriage. And in talking to divorced peo-ple, one often hears comments about the positive side of separation (e.g., being in control of their own lives, no longer being belittled by their spouse, etc.).

Given the complexity of divorce as a life event and the variability in peo-ple's experiences, we believe all three of these viewpoints offer a useful kernel of truth. As we step back from the details of this discussion, the available evidence suggests to us that divorce is a significant life event, usually—but not totally—a painful one. We believe some people are more vulnerable to becoming divorced than others, but situational and historical-cultural factors also influence whether couples actually dissolve their intimate ties. Akin to Emery's earlier observa-tions, we believe many people experience wounds due to divorce, but injuries do heal. Members of divorced families often show remarkable resiliency in ad-justing to their new family and their new life circumstances.

CHAPTER 14

Loneliness

Before beginning this chapter, we encourage you to go to Box 14.1 to do a loneliness assessment exercise. Then read on!

> Jim, aged 18, is a first year student in University. He is very quiet and reserved,
> and he spends a lot of his time thinking about himself and his situation. Jim
> feels that he is alienated from other students on campus and that he is excluded
> from events that are happening around him. There is no one he feels he can
> turn to or depend upon. He has no close friends, although he often wishes he
> did. However, he feels that he doesn't know how to make friends, so he tends
> to avoid any social contacts. He never initiates any social activities, and when-
> ever he is with a group of people, he feels an outsider and doesn't have a good
> time. Therefore Jim isolates himself from others, spending long hours concen-
> trating on his course work. Often Jim feels that he is inferior and rejected and
> wonders if something is wrong with him. He feels other people don't like him
> and this makes him unhappy. Sometimes he becomes angry and can see only
> the worst in everything.
>
> Borys & Perlman, 1985, pp. 69–70

Jim is a prototypical lonely person. Not everyone is as lonely as Jim, but loneliness
is a nearly universal human experience. It is hard even to imagine someone who
has not at some time felt lonely. After the end of an intimate relationship, feelings

---

BOX 14.1

Loneliness Self-Exploration Exercise

Ask yourself the following questions. What does loneliness mean to you? When have you felt lonely? What led up to your feeling lonely? Describe how it felt. What thoughts have you had when you're lonely? What did you do when you have felt lonely?

To what degree did doing this ease your loneliness? What have you done to improve your situation? How well did your efforts work?

Adapted from Dayoff, 2000.

---

of loneliness can be intense and extremely painful. But loneliness occurs in many other situations as well: trying to get to know people in a new school or on a new job; traveling alone in a foreign country; finding yourself at loose ends on a Saturday night. In this chapter, we examine the experience of being lonely, factors that may cause or intensify loneliness, and some ways to cope with lonely feelings.

WHAT IS LONELINESS?

Loneliness is not the same as physical isolation; people can feel happy as a clam in complete solitude but lonely in a crowd. Instead, **loneliness** has been defined as a feeling of deprivation and dissatisfaction produced by a discrepancy between the kind of social relations we want and the kind of social relations we have (Perlman & Peplau, 1981). We feel lonely when we are alone if we would rather be with someone. We feel lonely when we are with other people if we would rather be with someone else.

Weiss (1973) has suggested that there are two different types of loneliness. In **social isolation,** people are dissatisfied and lonely because they lack a social network of friends and acquaintances. In **emotional isolation,** people are dissatisfied and lonely because they lack a single intense relationship. According to Weiss, it is not possible to ease one type of loneliness by substituting the other type of relationship. So, for example, if a couple has just moved to a new town where they do not know anyone, they will experience the loneliness of social isolation even though they have a close relationship with each other. On the other hand, a person can have an extensive social network and a very active social life but still feel lonely if he or she does not have a romantic partner. Although these two types of loneliness may co-occur, and Russell, Peplau, and Cutrona (1980) have described them as two routes to a single generalized experience, researchers have resonated to this distinction. At least modest evidence supports its validity (DiTommaso & Spinner, 1995; Russell, Cutrona, Rose, & Yurko, 1984; Vaux, 1988a). If we lack the kind of relationship we desire, we can be lonely despite having other, quite rewarding social interactions.

A Discrepancy Model for Conceptualizing Loneliness

Complementing their aforementioned definition of loneliness, Perlman and Peplau (for example, see Perlman & Peplau, 1998) have offered a **discrepancy framework** for conceptualizing the experience of loneliness. A schematic representation of their analysis is shown in Figure 14.1. Central to their thinking is the idea that loneliness stems from a discrepancy between the social relationships people need (or desire) and the relationships they actually have. Like Peterson's model of conflict discussed in chapter 12, Perlman and Peplau believe there are both predisposing and precipitating factors that contribute to this mismatch. Yet not everyone perceives and interprets the mismatch in exactly the same way. Instead, people engage in cognitive processes such as causal attributions, social comparisons, and perceived control. These cognitive processes can moderate how intensely people react to their social deficiencies. Having experienced loneliness, they then try to cope with it.

Perlman and Peplau have presented their diagram as a general framework that helps organize thinking about important elements of the loneliness experience. They have not intended it as a fully developed theory of loneliness. Much of the material we will present in this chapter can be fit into this schematic diagram. We will start at the heart of this model, with the measurement of loneliness itself and the feelings associated with being lonely. Then we will go back to the top of the figure and loosely work our way from predisposing factors downward to coping. We will take a small detour to reflect on loneliness across the life-span perspective.

Measuring Loneliness

A basic approach to measuring loneliness has been to simply ask people a direct question about whether or not they are lonely. Usually the answers to single questions such as this are less reliable than answers to a set of questions, and people's answers to such direct questions may be influenced by the respondents' trying to present themselves in a socially desirable light. So loneliness researchers have developed several longer scales for assessing loneliness in children and adults (Russell, 1996; Russell et al., 1980; Shaver & Brennan, 1990; Terrell-Deutsch, 1999). Over the years the UCLA Loneliness Scale has been the most widely used measure of adult loneliness. The items in the third version of this scale are shown in Table 14.1.

The first version of the UCLA Loneliness scale was developed in the mid-1970s. Russell and his colleagues began with an initial pool of 75 items written by psychologists to describe the experience of loneliness. Initially the items were all phrased in a pro-trait manner (i.e., agreeing with each item was indicative of loneliness). The number of items was reduced via statistical procedures, and then the resulting scale's reliability and validity were established. Other noteworthy advances have subsequently occurred. In particular, since its original publication:

- Russell's revisions of the scale have simplified the wording of the items and balanced the response pattern so that agreeing with some items and disagreeing with others reflects loneliness,

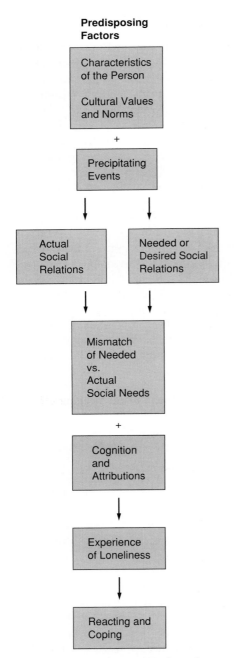

FIGURE 14.1. Peplau and Perlman's
discrepancy view of loneliness.

TABLE 14.1. The UCLA Loneliness Scale (Version 3)

Instructions: The following statements describe how people sometimes feel. For each statement, please indicate how often you feel the way described by writing a number in the space provided. Here is an example:

How often do you feel happy?

If you never felt happy, you would respond "never"; if you always feel happy, you would respond "always."

NEVER	RARELY	SOMETIMES	ALWAYS
1	2	3	4

*1. How often do you feel that you are "in tune" with the people around you? ____

2. How often do you feel that you lack companionship? ____

3. How often do you feel that there is no one you can turn to? ____

4. How often do you feel alone? ____

*5. How often do you feel part of a group of friends? ____

*6. How often do you feel that you have a lot in common with the people around you? ____

7. How often do you feel that you are no longer close to anyone? ____

8. How often do you feel that your interests and ideas are not shared by those around you? ____

*9. How often do you feel outgoing and friendly? ____

*10. How often do you feel close to people? ____

11. How often do you feel left out? ____

12. How often do you feel that your relationships with others are not meaningful? ____

13. How often do you feel that no one really knows you well? ____

14. How often do you feel isolated from others? ____

*15. How often do you feel you can find companionship when you want it? ____

*16. How often do you feel that there are people who really understand you? ____

17. How often do you feel shy? ____

18. How often do you feel that people are around you but not with you? ____

*19. How often do you feel that there are people you can talk to? ____

*20. How often do you feel that there are people you can turn to? ____

Note: Copyright by Daniel W. Russell. Reprinted with permission.
*Reverse score item (i.e., 1 = 4, 2 = 3, 3 = 2, 4 =1).
Mean score among 489 college students in Russell's (1996) validation sample = 40.08.

- Russell and his colleagues have demonstrated the scale's discriminant validity for constructs such as social desirability, self-esteem, and anxiety, and
- the UCLA scale has been translated into several different languages (e.g., French, German, Greek, Japanese, Persian, Portuguese, Russian, Spanish).

The questions in the UCLA Scale ask respondents about the frequency of their feelings. Some observers have noted that the scale does not provide a clear time perspective; many respondents probably respond with regard to their current feelings, but others may interpret the questions with regard to their overall life histories. Some loneliness researchers have argued that a clearer distinction should be made between a passing form of "state" loneliness and a persisting form of "trait" loneliness. Among others, Shaver, Furman, and Buhrmester (1985) have constructed scales to do this. As we will see later in this chapter, this difference between a chronic, enduring loneliness characteristic of some people and a more temporary state of affairs created by specific situations is an important issue in research on the beliefs and behavior of lonely people.

How Does It Feel to Be Lonely?

When we are lonely, we feel dissatisfied, deprived, and distressed. This does not mean, however, that feelings associated with loneliness are all the same. In fact, different people in different situations may have different kinds of feelings when they are lonely. A study on the loneliness of widows illustrated how many kinds of emotions and desires can become bound up with the experience of being lonely (Lopata, 1969). For these women, loneliness was associated with one or more of the following:

Desiring to be with the husband

Wanting to be loved by someone

Wanting to love and take care of someone

Wanting to share daily experiences with someone

Wanting to have someone around the house

Needing someone to share the work

Longing for the previous form of life

Experiencing loss of status

Experiencing loss of other people as a consequence of having lost the husband

Fearing the inability to make new friends

Thus, loneliness included longing for the past, frustration with the present, and fears about the future.

Even for those who have not experienced the often devastating blow of losing a spouse, loneliness can involve many different kinds of feelings. Based on a survey of loneliness in the general population, Rubenstein, Shaver, and Peplau (1979) described four different sets of feelings that people say they have when they are lonely: desperation, impatient boredom, self-deprecation, and depression. The specific feelings reported in each of these clusters are given in Table 14.2. Though there are huge differences between some of these feelings (e.g., desperation versus boredom), loneliness is complex enough to encompass all of them.

TABLE 14.2. Feelings When Lonely

Desperation	Impatient Boredom	Self-Deprecation	Depression
Desperate	Impatient	Feeling unattractive	Sad
Helpless	Bored	Down on self	Depressed
Afraid	Desire to be elsewhere	Stupid	Empty
Without hope	Uneasy	Ashamed	Isolated
Abandoned	Angry	Insecure	Sorry for self
Vulnerable	Unable to concentrate		Melancholy
			Alienated
			Longing to be with one special person

Source: Rubenstein, Shaver, & Peplau, 1979.

Does Loneliness Matter?

Inasmuch as loneliness is often temporary, you might think that it is typically a fleeting experience of little consequence. Undoubtedly that is sometimes true. Yet substantial evidence suggests that loneliness is linked with a variety of serious conditions. Consider some examples:

Via doing secondary analysis of several large surveys of American youths, Brennan and Auslander (1979) found that loneliness was associated with running away from home and delinquent acts such as gambling, theft, and vandalism.

Among college students, the evidence is perhaps not as consistent as it might be, but some studies show lonely students to be more likely to obtain low grades (see Burleson & Samter, 1992, especially p. 171) and to drop out (Rotenberg & Morrison, 1993). While lonely students may have more time to study, they may be more easily distracted (see Cacioppo et al., 2000) and less effective in their study habits.

Among older adults, loneliness is associated with memory problems (Bazargan & Barbre, 1992).

Jones and Carver (1991, p. 406) note that there is an "extensive pattern of correlations between loneliness and various negative psychological conditions." They review evidence showing three points: (a) groups undergoing treatment, counseling or imprisonment tend to have high loneliness scores; (b) significant correlations exist between loneliness and self-reported measures of clinical syndromes, including lack of personality integration, neurosis, general maladjustment, personality disorder, rape potential, and suicide risk; and (c) loneliness has been associated with practitioners' ratings of older adults' mental status and adjustment. Ernst and Cacioppo (1999) reach very similar conclusions to Jones and Carver's. Ernst and Cacioppo cite additional evidence showing loneliness to be associated with schizophrenia, bulima nervosa, and alcohol abuse (see Akerlind & Hornquist, 1992). Both Jones and Carver and Ernst and Cacioppo point out that it is difficult to determine a causal direction in these studies—loneliness may contribute to psychological difficulties, or psychological difficulties may lead to loneliness.

Based on questionnaire responses and physiological measures taken while students slept in a laboratory, Cacioppo et al. (2000) concluded that lonely people have more difficulty sleeping and benefit from it less. More specifically, their participants reported taking longer to get to sleep and had greater daytime dysfunction due to sleepiness. Laboratory recordings showed parallel findings that lonely people took longer to get to sleep and that they awoke more often during the night.

Trait-lonely people have high mean levels of cortisol, a physiological indicator of anxiety (Cacioppo et al., 2000).

Loneliness has also been linked with poor health outcomes. In a 14-year longitudinal study of 1,752 older Danes, loneliness was associated with increased mortality due to cardiovascular disease among men (Olsen, Olsen, Gunner-Svensson, & Waldstrom, 1991). Complementing this finding, Cutrona, Russell, de la Mora, and Wallace (1997) followed 3,000 older Iowa residents over a four-year period. At the beginning of the study, none of the participants were living in nursing homes. At the end of the four-year period, over 40 percent of the seniors high in loneliness were in nursing facilities but less than 10 percent of those who were low in loneliness had left their homes (see Figure 14.2). Even after control variables such as age, health at the beginning of the study, initial morale, and social ties were taken into consideration, those who had reported the highest levels of loneliness at the beginning of the study were more likely to have subsequently been admitted to a nursing home.

Several models of the association between loneliness and health are possible. Perhaps both are caused by some third factor, such as income, or perhaps poor health leads to loneliness. Nonetheless, it seems plausible that loneliness contributes to poor health. How might this work? One way might be that loneliness leads to demoralization, leading lonely people to neglect their self-care. Another way might be that lonely people may lack relationships with others that could promote improved health. Intimate friends and family members can promote health by encouraging health-promoting behaviors (e.g., eating a healthy diet or exercising), discouraging risky behaviors (e.g., smoking), encouraging the seeking of medical treatment as needed, helping with recovery from illnesses, and helping with activities such as taking medications. Regardless of whether the key is apathy or help from intimate others, intervening physiological processes are probably involved in the link between loneliness and health. For example, lonely medical students were shown to have less effective immune systems than nonlonely medical students (Kiecolt-Glaser et al., 1984). Thus, the weakened immune systems of lonely people appear to leave them more vulnerable to infection and illness. In essence, there may be both psychological and physiological truth to the view that loneliness means having a broken heart.

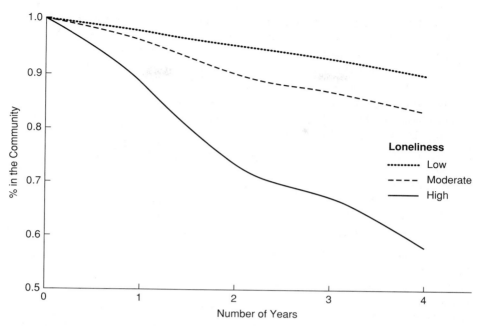

FIGURE 14.2. Loneliness and survival in the community.
Source: Cutrona et al., 1997.

Who Are the Lonely?

In an early national survey of United States citizens, 26 percent said they had felt "very lonely or remote from other people" in the past few weeks (Weiss, 1973, p. 23). Naturally, the proportion of people who acknowledge loneliness varies as a function of the exact wording of the question posed (the nature of the loneliness described, the time span involved, etc.). Yet, regardless of exactly how the question is posed, are there some people who are more vulnerable (or predisposed) to loneliness than others? The answer, consistent with the discrepancy model shown in Figure 14.1, is yes, with the major differences involving nationality, socioeconomic status, marital status, and gender.

Nationality

From a sociocultural perspective, one might expect nationality differences in loneliness. Data from the World Values Survey conducted in the early 1980s on how often people feel lonely support this expectation (Stack, 1995; see also Stack, 1998). Among adults in 18 countries, Italians and Japanese respondents reported the most frequent feelings of loneliness; Danes reported the least frequent feelings of loneliness (see Table 14.3). Respondents from the U.S. ranked high (fourth) in the extent of their loneliness. Perhaps this in part reflects the individualistic, competitive nature of life in the United States. In a comparative European study of Tuscany (Italy) versus the Netherlands, van Tilburg, de Jong Gierveld, Lecchini, and Marsiglia (1998) found that most of the national

TABLE 14.3. **Mean Level of Loneliness, 18 Nations, World Values Surveys, 1981–1983**

Country	Males	Females	Country	Males	Females
Italy	1.30	1.67	Britain	.70	1.16
Japan	1.32	1.41	N. Ireland	.72	1.12
Spain	1.12	1.33	Australia	.76	1.05
U.S.	1.04	1.33	Iceland	.70	1.11
Canada	.92	1.22	Belgium	.70	1.09
France	.85	1.20	Norway	.71	1.03
USSR	.81	1.11	Sweden	.68	1.02
Ireland	.81	1.08	Netherlands	.70	.87
W. Germany	.74	1.14	Denmark	.57	.65

Note: Higher scores reflect greater loneliness.
Source: S. Stack, 1995.

differences in loneliness could be accounted for by nationality differences in social integration. In the Netherlands, where loneliness was low, even though many people lived alone, they were socially integrated in terms of having more people in their social networks, being involved in civic organizations and volunteer work, receiving more emotional support, and the like.

Socioeconomic Factors

In his early classic volume, Weiss (1973, p. 26) reported evidence that lower income groups tend to be lonely. Subsequent studies have produced similar findings. For instance, in Page and Cole's (1991) survey of households (N = 8,634) in a large, predominantly urban southwestern U.S. county, members of families with incomes of under $10,000 were 4.6 times more likely to report loneliness than members of families with incomes of $75,000 or more. In that study, education also showed an inverse relationship to loneliness.

Marital Status

In general, married people are less lonely than unmarried people (Page & Cole, 1991; Perlman & Peplau, 1981; Stack, 1998). When the unmarried are categorized into subgroups (never married, separated or divorced, widowed), the results vary somewhat by study. The general trend appears to be for the never-married to be less lonely. Thus, loneliness seems to be a reaction to the loss of a marital relationship rather than a response to its absence.

In Stack's 17-nation survey, the strength of the marital status-loneliness association was roughly the same in all 17 cultures, suggesting the near universality of this effect. The relationship was obtained for both men and women. Cohabitation also buffered people from loneliness but not as much as marriage per se.

Although marital status is a reliable, important predictor of loneliness, it is not a guarantee against loneliness. Consider briefly the situation of married people and then of nonmarried people. As a recent Turkish study demonstrates (Demir & Fisiloglu, 1999), loneliness is associated with marital satisfaction, so that those with unhappy marriages are at risk for loneliness. Even among newlyweds, those with communication difficulties are vulnerable to loneliness (Sadava & Matejcic, 1987). From the vantage point of the single, Dykstra's (1995) study of older Dutch adults without partners showed that they can be relatively free of feelings of loneliness when:

They are more accepting of their single status,

They are well supported by friends, and

They see opportunities for changing their status if they wish.

Gender

Although many studies of loneliness do not indicate any overall difference between men and women, some research using the UCLA scale has found that men have higher loneliness scores than do women (Schultz & Moore, 1986, 1988; Stokes & Levin, 1986). According to Borys and Perlman (1985), however, the gender difference you get will depend upon the kind of question you ask. When these investigators combined loneliness scores on the UCLA scale from 28 different subject samples, they also found that men reported greater loneliness than did women. But when they combined 11 different samples in which subjects provided self-ratings of loneliness, they obtained exactly the opposite result: Here, women reported greater loneliness than men. These later findings are echoed in Stack's study—in every culture, women were more likely to report loneliness than were men (see Table 14.3).

For Borys and Perlman, the critical difference between the UCLA scale and self-ratings boils down to one word: loneliness. The UCLA scale never uses the word; subjects never have to state directly whether they are lonely. Self-ratings (as well as the NYU scale) do require this direct statement. Borys and Perlman believe that it is more difficult for men to explicitly acknowledge that they are lonely, and with good reason. When they had undergraduates read the brief description of a lonely person presented at the beginning of the chapter, identified either as a man (Jim) or as a woman, the man was evaluated more negatively than the woman. The social price of admitting loneliness appears, then, to be higher for men than for women, and men may learn to avoid this "L-word." But when asked about their experiences without the word "lonely" being used, men's responses often indicate that they suffer more loneliness than women do.

In addition to overall differences between men and women, gender also interacts with marital status. Returning to Stack's (1998) cross-national study, marriage reduced the likelihood of male loneliness more than it did female loneliness. In other investigations, wives have reported greater loneliness than have husbands (Peplau, Bikson, Rook, & Goodchilds, 1982; Rubenstein & Shaver, 1982). In these investigations, men reported greater loneliness than women when they were never married, were separated or divorced, or were widowed (Peplau et al., 1982; Rubenstein & Shaver, 1982). These findings suggest that men and women may differ in their vulnerability to the two types of loneliness described earlier. Men, it appears, are most likely to be lonely when they experience the emotional isolation of not having an intimate partner. Women, however, may be most susceptible to loneliness if the intimate tie of marriage reduces their access to a larger social network (Fischer & Phillips, 1982). This kind of social isolation would seem particularly likely for wives who are unemployed, who have left their friends and family because of a change in the location of their husband's job, or who have young children.

LONELINESS ACROSS THE LIFE SPAN

Just as friendship varies as we grow older and go through life (chapter 7), so too does loneliness have a life-span developmental course (see Perlman, 1988). We will consider three aspects of this: (a) how early family environments predispose people for loneliness, (b) how the prevalence of loneliness varies across the life span, and (c) age-related predictors of loneliness.

Family Antecedents of Loneliness

Both parent-child relationships and family structure are related to loneliness. One can generally conclude that lonely people had (or at least report that they had) cold, less nurturant parents (see Perlman, 1988, p. 196). For instance, in Rubenstein and Shaver's (1982) large-scale study, their lonely respondents recalled their parents as being remote, disagreeable, and less trustworthy. They felt their parents didn't spend enough time with them. In other studies, lonely adolescents and university students, compared to nonlonely participants, have reported having parents who were less likely to be positively involved with them and who administered higher levels of punishment. In the relationship domain, lonely offspring remember greater parental dissatisfaction with their choice of friends and felt their parents gave them little encouragement to strive for popularity. Collectively, these studies demonstrate that parent-child relations are important in identifying who is lonely.

In terms of family structure, Rubenstein and Shaver (1982) found that people whose parents had been divorced reported feeling more lonely than people whose parents had not divorced (see also Shaver & Rubenstein, 1980). Moreover, the younger the person was when his or her parents divorced, the more loneliness the person experienced as an adult (see Figure 14.3). This difference did not apply to people who had lost a parent by death: People who had been bereaved during childhood reported no more loneliness as adults than did people whose families remained intact throughout their childhood and adolescence. Thus, there seems to be something specific to divorce that increases the potential for feelings of loneliness as an adult. (See chapter 13 for an extended discussion of the effects of divorce on children.)

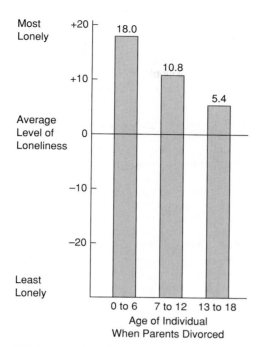

FIGURE 14.3. Loneliness scores by age at parents' divorce.
(Rubenstein, Shaver, & Peplau, 1979.)

Age Changes in Loneliness

Prominent earlier writers believed that young children could not experience loneliness. For example, Robert Weiss (1973, p. 90) maintained, "Loneliness proper becomes a possible experience only . . . in adolescence." He felt it wasn't until we gained independence from our families that we could fully experience loneliness. At that point, it becomes "possible for individuals to scan their social worlds for attachment and see only unsatisfactory friendly acquaintances" (Weiss, 1973, p. 90). He also depicted adolescents as being able to experience the grief of lost love affairs.

In light of more recent research (see Rotenberg & Hymel, 1999), however, we are convinced that loneliness can occur at a much earlier age than adolescence. Our conclusion is based on at least three points (see Perlman & Landolt, 1999). First, Cassidy and Asher (1992) found that a majority of children at an early age (i.e., as young as age five) seem to understand the nature of loneliness; in some cases this was probably based on their own experience with it. Along these same lines, Hymel, Tarulli Hayden, Thompson, and Terrell-Deutsch (1999) were able to get eight-year-olds to define and describe loneliness. Second, children as young as those in kindergarten give internally

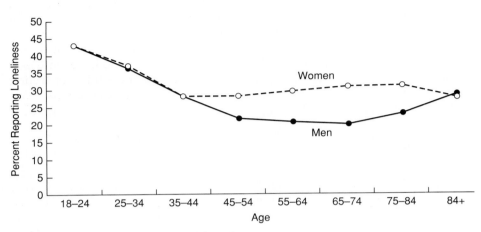

FIGURE 14.4. Loneliness across the life cycle.
Source: Perlman, 1991.

consistent answers to measures designed to assess children's loneliness. This implies that something, presumably loneliness, is being reliably assessed. Finally, even at that age, scores on childhood loneliness measures are relating to other factors as one might expect. This gives confidence that these scales are measuring what they were designed to measure even in five- and six-year-olds.

Looking at the fluctuations in loneliness over the life cycle, there is a stereotype in our society of the lonely old person. Both young and old agree that the older one gets, the lonelier one becomes (Rubenstein & Shaver, 1982). When we ask people about their own experiences of loneliness, however, we discover that this stereotype is questionable. To examine life-cycle changes in loneliness, Perlman (1991) combined results from six U.S. and Canadian surveys (N = 18,682) containing similar self-labeling questions about loneliness. In each of these surveys, there were both younger and older adult respondents. As seen in Figure 14.4, loneliness appears to have a "backward" check-shaped curve, with slightly different results for men and women. Complementing several U.S. studies, Perlman's analysis shows that the loneliest people are adolescents and young adults (Peplau et al., 1982; Rubenstein & Shaver, 1982). Loneliness actually declines with age, at least until people are into the later stages of old age, when it may begin to increase (e.g., Peplau et al., 1982). These findings are not restricted to North America. A representative study of 2,795 Swedes shows basically similar results, with loneliness declining with age, especially among those who were married (Tornstam, 1992). In this study, the results for men and women were more parallel than in Perlman's.

Although the association between youth and loneliness goes against our stereotype of the elderly lonely, it is not really so surprising when we think about it. Young people face the enormously difficult task of defining their own identities as individuals. Without a solid sense of self, it is all too easy to feel unappreciated and unloved by others. Moreover, young people are constantly having to develop new relationships as they go through school and into employment settings; each new social situation creates the possibility of feeling lonely. Finally, it may be that younger people have greater expectations about their relationships than do older people, who have learned to live with less-than-perfect understanding and compatibility.

There is some controversy over exactly what happens in later life. In studies involving older adults (ages 55 and over), findings on loneliness vary, some studies showing marked later-life increases in loneliness, others showing none at all. In Tornstam's study, both effects were observed: Respondents in their seventies had low levels of loneliness if they were married but showed a modest upturn in loneliness if they were not married. Scrutiny of these and other findings (e.g., Townsend, 1968) suggests that the magnitude of any possible increase in loneliness among older adults may depend on the proportions of incapacitated persons and widows in older subgroups. Especially when they include many incapacitated and widowed people, older samples may show elevated loneliness.

Age-Related Predictors of Loneliness

Not only does the magnitude of loneliness change, but also the factors precipitating loneliness may change. For example, in late adolescence, going away to college is apt to increase loneliness, especially among youths who are less socially skilled at initiating relationships (Shaver et al., 1985). Among older adults, the loss of a spouse is a common factor prompting loneliness (Lopata, 1969).

Looking at the patterns between other factors and loneliness at different points in the life cycle, Schmitt and Kurdek (1985) speculate that the loneliness of college women may "be related to transient changes in identity and relationship status," while elderly women's loneliness "apparently results from more permanent losses" (p. 494). Complementing this conclusion, Schultz and Moore (1988) found that personality and adjustment factors were less predictive of loneliness among retirees than among younger adults.

SOME POSSIBLE CAUSES AND MODERATORS OF LONELINESS

Although life-span developmental factors are important, there are many different causes of loneliness (de Jong-Gierveld, 1987). This section will review other possible causes of loneliness that have received extensive attention from social scientists. Before doing that, however, we will return to the discrepancy framework of Figure 14.1 to consider how it acts as a key generic antecedent of loneliness.

Loneliness theorists generally agree that loneliness stems from social deficits, but they differ in exactly how they conceptualize these deficits. Perlman and Peplau look for a difference between desired and achieved levels. They envision that two people with the same level of interpersonal attachment could differ in their social desires or needs. Perlman and Peplau would expect the person with higher social desires to be at greater risk for loneliness. Other theorists, drawing on the writings of Robert Weiss, 1973 (see Archibald, Bartholomew, & Marx, 1995), believe that there are enduring social needs; they see loneliness as occurring whenever social needs are not meet. These theorists emphasize the social provisions people receive. For them, receiving few social provisions is presumably inadequate for one's needs, but they contend that loneliness can be successfully predicted simply from the levels of social provisions that people derive from their social ties. In a test comparing the cognitive discrepancy versus the social provision views, Archibald et al. found that the actual provisions received were the primary predictor of loneliness but that discrepancies did add a small improvement in prediction. They conclude that "The results provide limited support for a cognitive discrepancy model of loneliness" (p. 296).

Inadequacies in Our Relationships

There are any number of reasons why we might feel dissatisfied with the relationships that we have. Rubenstein and Shaver (1982) found that most of the reasons that the people in their survey gave for being lonely could be classified into five major categories:

1. Being unattached: Having no spouse; having no sexual partner; breaking up with spouse or lover
2. Alienation: Feeling different; being misunderstood; not being needed; having no close friends
3. Being alone: Coming home to an empty house; being alone
4. Forced isolation: Being housebound; being hospitalized; having no transportation
5. Dislocation: Being far from home; starting in a new job or school; moving too often; traveling often

The first two categories parallel Weiss's distinction between loneliness based on emotional isolation (being unattached) and loneliness due to social isolation (alienation). There also appears to be an important difference between relationship deficits that are produced purely by the situation (forced isolation; dislocation) versus those (being unattached; alienation; being alone) that could come about in a variety of ways, such as being caused by characteristics of the other people in the lonely person's environment or by characteristics of the lonely person.

Changes in What We Want from a Relationship

In terms of Perlman and Peplau's model (Figure 14.1), loneliness can also develop because of changes in our ideas about what we want out of our relationships. At one time in our life, our social relations may be quite satisfying, and so we do not feel lonely. These relationships may then continue but at some point fail to be satisfying because we have changed in what we want. Peplau and her associates have noted that these changes can come from many different sources (Peplau, Russell, & Heim, 1979; Perlman & Peplau, 1981). Our moods change, and the kinds of relationships we want when we are happy may differ from those we want when we are sad. As we age, we go through developmental changes that may affect our relational desires. The kind of friendship that was very satisfying when we were 15 may fail to satisfy us when we are 25. Situational changes also can be involved. Many people do not want a close, emotional involvement when they are preparing for their careers. Later on, however, when their careers are established, they may feel a great need for an emotionally committed relationship. Whatever the reason, we do change our minds about what we want from relationships, and if our relationships do not also change accordingly, we may experience loneliness.

Self-Esteem

Although it seems reasonable to believe that certain circumstances (e.g., the loss of an intimate partner; a move to a new place) as well as changes in what we want out of a relationship could cause us to feel lonely, the causal connection gets considerably more problematic when we consider people's personal and social characteristics. For example, the feeling of alienation cited by respondents in the survey by Rubenstein and Shaver (1982) could be a direct cause of loneliness (feeling alienated from others makes you feel lonely too), an indirect cause (people who feel alienated act in ways that drive others away and, thus, become lonely), or an effect of loneliness (feeling lonely makes you feel alienated, too). There probably are some personal characteristics that make it more likely that a person who has them will experience loneliness. But loneliness does not occur in a psychological vacuum, and feeling lonely will have personal and social consequences. In the following pages, we examine some factors whose connection with loneliness could go either way: as a cause or as an effect.

Whatever the causal relationship involved, loneliness is associated with having low self-esteem (McWhirter, 1997; Rubenstein & Shaver, 1980). People who report themselves as lonely also tend to regard themselves as unworthy and unlovable. Perhaps because of this lack of self-esteem, lonely people expect to be uncomfortable in risky social situations (Vaux, 1988b). This anticipated discomfort may motivate lonely people to reduce their social contacts, which could make it more difficult for these people to establish the kinds of relationships they need in order not to be lonely anymore.

Interpersonal Behaviors

This difficulty of distinguishing cause from effect also occurs in research on the interpersonal behavior of lonely people. As you will see, lonely people behave differently from nonlonely people in a variety of ways. But why? Does being lonely cause us to act differently? Or does acting differently create the social circumstances that produce loneliness? We don't know, although it seems likely that causation here goes in both directions. What we do know is that the interpersonal behavior of lonely people makes it harder for them to establish rewarding relationships with others.

Compared with people who are not lonely, lonely people evaluate others more negatively (Jones, Freemon, & Goswick, 1981; Jones, Sansome, & Helm, 1983; Wittenberg & Reis, 1986). They don't like others very much (Rubenstein & Shaver, 1980); mistrust others (Vaux, 1988b); interpret others' actions and intentions negatively (Hanley-Dunn, Maxwell, & Santos, 1985); and are more likely to hold hostile attitudes (Check, Perlman, & Malamuth, 1985; Sermat, 1980).

Lonely people also lack social skills in their behavior with others (Solano & Koester, 1989). They are more passive than nonlonely people in social interactions, hesitating to express their opinions in public (Hansson & Jones, 1981). In addition, lonely people tend to be socially unresponsive and insensitive. During conversations between lonely and nonlonely people, lonely people made fewer statements focusing on their conversational partners, asked fewer questions of their partners, were slower to respond to statements made by their partners, and were less likely to continue discussing the topic initiated by their partners (Jones, Hobbs, & Hackenbury, 1982). Lonely people also appear challenged in developing intimacy in their relations with others, and their level of self-disclosure is low (Davis & Franzoi, 1986; Schwab, Scalise, Ginter, & Whipple, 1998; Solano, Batten, & Parish, 1982; Williams & Solano, 1983). Finally, there is some evidence that lonely men are more likely than nonlonely men to behave in physically aggressive ways (Check et al., 1985).

Given these negative attitudes and socially inept or undesirable behaviors, you might expect that lonely people would elicit negative reactions from others. And in some circumstances, though not all, this is the case (Jones, 1990; Jones, Cavert, Snider, & Bruce, 1985; Rook, 1988). The conversational partners of lonely people feel they do not know the person very well (Solano et al., 1982) and regard the lonely person as socially incompetent (Spitzberg & Canery, 1985). Overall, then, lonely people seem caught in a downward social spiral. They reject others, lack social skills in their behavior with others, and, at least in some instances, are rejected by others (see Figure 14.5). Regardless of where this pattern begins, all of its components reinforce each other and make social life more difficult and less rewarding.

Social Anxiety and Shyness

Loneliness is only one of a number of common problems that involve personal distress and social dissatisfaction. Another such problem, *social anxiety,* refers to feelings of discomfort in the presence of others (Leary, 1983). There are many different types of social anxiety, including fear of public

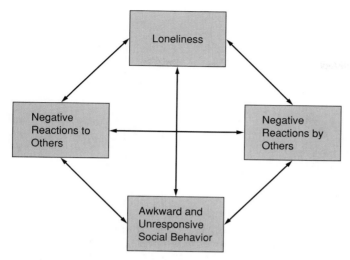

FIGURE 14.5. Loneliness: A vicious circle.

speaking (called "speech anxiety") and shyness, which combines social inhibition and avoidance with feelings of discomfort in interpersonal interactions (Jones, Cheek, & Briggs, 1986; Zimbardo, 1977). A self-report scale measuring shyness is reprinted in Table 10.1. Loneliness, shyness, and social anxiety are all interrelated; those suffering from one often suffer from the others as well (Bruch, Gorsky, Collins, & Berger, 1989; Cheek & Busch, 1981; Jones & Carpenter, 1986; Solano & Koester, 1989). In particular, the interpersonal behaviors of shy and socially anxious people closely resemble those of lonely people: negative attitudes toward others, passive and unresponsive behavior with others, and negative reactions from others in some circumstances (Gurtman, Martin, & Hintzman, 1990; Jones & Carpenter, 1986; Langston & Cantor, 1989).

Socially anxious feelings can have many causes (Leary, 1987). They can be a learned response to an unpleasant social encounter; social difficulties in the past can contribute to social anxiety in the future. Social anxiety also appears to have an important cognitive component. People who are anxious about social encounters often believe that they lack the skills necessary for social success (Maddux, Norton, & Leary, 1988). Even if, in fact, they have such skills, their belief that they lack them is likely to cause concern. When a person wants to make a favorable impression on others but is convinced that he or she is unable to do so, awareness of this discrepancy can create considerable anxiety (Schlenker & Leary, 1982).

Depression

In an attempt to discriminate among a variety of problems in living, Anderson and Harvey (1988) examined the relationship among a number of self-report scales measuring loneliness, social anxiety, shyness, and depression.

These four scales yielded three basic factors: loneliness, social anxiety/shyness, and depression. And all three were positively correlated with each other. Thus, just as loneliness is associated with social anxiety and shyness, so it is associated with depression. Depression is characterized by negative mood (such as feelings of sadness and despair), low self-esteem, pessimism, lack of initiative, and slowed thought processes (Holmes, 1991). It may involve disturbances in sleeping and eating patterns along with reduced sexual desire. Approximately 5 percent of the population will experience a major depression sometime during their lives (Robins et al., 1984), but many more will suffer from brief, relatively mild bouts with the "blues."

Like those suffering from loneliness or social anxiety, depressed people seem caught in an ever-worsening, downward spiral of interpersonal behaviors. Complementing points made in chapter 7, depressed people reject others, exhibit awkward or inadequate social skills, and are rejected by others (Burchill & Stile, 1988; Gurtman et al., 1990; Hokanson, Loewenstein, Hedeen, & Howes, 1986; Strack & Coyne, 1983). In addition, depressed people are similar to lonely people in their discomfort with, and avoidance of, risky social interactions (Pietromonaco & Rook, 1987).

Although depression and loneliness often occur together, they are not identical conditions. Consider, for example, these findings from another study of college freshmen (Bragg, 1979; Weeks, Michela, Peplau, & Bragg, 1980). First, while dating (even in a very casual way) was associated with less loneliness and with less depression, knowing people was associated only with less loneliness. Second, in terms of satisfaction with their lives, lonely students indicated low satisfaction only with their social lives, but depressed students reported low satisfaction with both the social and nonsocial aspects of the way they were living. Taken together, these results suggest that depression is a more global state of dissatisfaction and discontent that can be particularly sensitive to success or failure in romantic relationships. On the other hand, loneliness appears more specifically interpersonal, but affected by a broader range of social interactions. Despite these differences, however, the close connection between depression and loneliness is evident. When the first-semester college students in this study were recontacted five weeks after their initial participation, those who were still lonely had become even more depressed than they were initially. It's depressing to stay lonely, and being depressed makes it harder to engage in an active effort to improve our social life.

Causal Attributions

In terms of Perlman and Peplau's model of loneliness (see Figure 14.1), personal attributes such as self-esteem and social skills can be classified as predisposing causes of loneliness. In their model, once people experience a discrepancy between their desired and achieved levels of social contact, they engage in interpretive activity. According to this perspective, loneliness is apt to be especially intense and long-lasting when people believe that their

TABLE 14.4. Explanations of Loneliness

	LOCUS OF CAUSALITY	
STABILITY	Internal	External
Stable	I'm lonely because I'm unlovable, I'll never be worth loving.	The people here are cold and impersonal; none of them share my interests. I think I'll move.
Unstable	I'm lonely now, but I won't be for long. I'll stop working so much and go out and meet some new people.	The first semester in college is always the worst, I'm sure things will get better.

Source: Based on Shaver & Rubenstein, 1980. From Brehm & Kassin, 1990.

own enduring characteristics cause their loneliness (Michela et al., 1982; Peplau et al., 1979). Explanations for the cause of loneliness seem to lock loneliness in place.

This kind of internal, stable attribution paints a depressing picture—we are the cause of our own misery, and things are unlikely to change. Such attributions may discourage people from trying to meet people and make friends. In contrast, explanations for loneliness that rely on attributions that are external, unstable, or both offer some hope that things can change for the better (see Table 14.4). This more hopeful attitude may, in turn, reduce emotional distress and promote more active, constructive efforts to cope with feelings of loneliness. The results of research by Cutrona (1982) on the loneliness experienced by new college students were consistent with this line of reasoning. Those who made internal, stable attributions for their loneliness in the fall semester (saying they were lonely because of shyness, their personality, their fear of being rejected, and their not knowing what to do to start a relationship) were more likely to still be lonely in the spring than were those students who made other kinds of attributions in the fall.

Subsequent to Cutrona's study, Anderson, Miller, Riger, Dill, and Sedikides (1994) distinguished between characterological and behavioral attributional styles. **Characterological self-blame** involves attributions to one's nonmodifiable, enduring character. The blame for failure is placed on the internal, stable, and uncontrollable aspects of one's behavior. **Behavioral self-blame** involves attributions to one's modifiable actions. Here the blame for failure is placed on the internal, unstable, and controllable aspects of one's behavior. In Anderson et al.'s study, students who tended to make characterological attributions for their failures were more lonely. Those who tended to make behavioral attributions for their failures were less lonely. So, it is not simply considering oneself responsible for life's difficulties that fosters loneliness, it is the precise way one accepts responsibility.

TABLE 14.5. What People Do When They Feel Lonely

Sad Passivity	Active Solitude	Social Contact	Distractions
Cry	Study or work	Call a friend	Spend money
Sleep	Write	Visit someone	Go shopping
Sit and think	Listen to music		
Do nothing	Exercise, walk		
Overeat	Work on a hobby		
Take tranquilizers	Go to a movie		
Watch TV	Read		
Get drunk or stoned	Play music		

Source: Rubenstein & Shaver, 1982.

COPING WITH LONELINESS

In this section, we examine the process of coping with loneliness, the last step in Perlman and Peplau's discrepancy model (see Figure 14.1). First, we consider the actions, constructive and destructive, that people engage in when they are lonely. Then, we turn to some specific coping responses that might be useful in reducing feelings of loneliness. Some closing comments offer a somewhat different perspective: that loneliness can make a positive contribution to personal growth and intimacy with others.

What Do People Do When They Are Lonely?

As we know from our own experience and the observations of others, there are many different reactions to loneliness. Table 14.5 summarizes the four major types of responses to loneliness mentioned by participants in the survey conducted by Rubenstein and Shaver (1982). As you can see, two of these categories involve positive, constructive coping behaviors: social contact and active solitude. In contrast, some of the behaviors categorized as sad passivity are potentially self-destructive. The distractions of going shopping and spending money are harder to classify. A moderate spree based on a flush bank account seems a reasonable way to get your mind off things, but self-induced impoverishment created by reckless spending is unlikely to be an effective cure for social dissatisfaction.

In their discussion of the self-help strategies of lonely people, Rook and Peplau (1982) distinguish between cognitive and behavioral coping strategies. Various examples of these two types are listed in Tables 14.6 and 14.7, which also indicate the extent to which they were used by the college students surveyed. The majority of these strategies are positive and constructive: for example, reminding yourself that you have good relationships with other people, or

TABLE 14.6. Cognitive Strategies College Students Used to Cope with Loneliness

Strategy	Never	Sometimes	Often
Thought about things you could do to overcome your loneliness	4%	52%	44%
Reminded yourself that you actually do have good relationships with other people	7	33	60
Tried to figure out why you were lonely	7	54	39
Thought about good qualities that you possess (such as being warm, intelligent, sensitive, self-sufficient, etc.)	7	68	25
Told yourself that your loneliness would not last forever, that things would get better	10	38	52
Thought about things you can do extremely well (excelling at schoolwork, athletics, artwork, gourmet cooking, etc.)	10	47	23
Told yourself that most other people are lonely at one time or another	11	56	33
Took your mind off feeling lonely by deliberately thinking about other things (anything other than your loneliness)	13	61	26
Told yourself that you were overreacting, that you shouldn't be so upset	14	62	24
Thought about possible benefits of your experience of loneliness (such as telling yourself that you were learning to be self-reliant, that you would grow from the experience, etc.)	21	42	37
Changed your goals for social relationships (such as telling yourself that it is not that important to be popular, that at this point in you life it's all right not to have a boyfriend or girlfriend, etc.)	22	55	23

Source: Rook & Peplau, 1982.

trying to find new ways to meet people. But some negative, self-destructive reactions (e.g., taking your mind off feeling lonely by using drugs or alcohol) were also reported fairly often.

What Helps People to Feel Less Lonely?

It is obvious that mindlessly watching TV, drinking to excess, or eating when you are not even hungry are all poor ways to cope with loneliness. These activities do not produce a more satisfying social life and, indeed, could well make it more difficult to establish good relationships. It is clearly better to cope actively

TABLE 14.7. Behavioral Strategies College Students Used to Cope with Loneliness

Strategy	Never	Sometimes	Often
Tried harder to be friendly to other people (such as making an effort to talk to people in your classes, etc.)	2%	62%	36%
Took you mind off feeling lonely through some mental activity (such as reading a novel, watching TV, going to a movie, etc.)	6	60	34
Worked particularly hard to succeed at some activity (such as studying extra hard for an exam, putting extra effort into practicing an instrument, pushing yourself on an athletic skill, etc.)	7	53	40
Did something helpful for someone else (such as helping a classmate with homework, doing volunteer work, etc.)	7	64	29
Did something you are very good at (schoolwork, athletics, artwork, etc.)	7	66	27
Took your mind off feeling lonely through some physical activity (such as jogging, playing basketball, shopping, washing the car, etc.)	12	51	37
Tried to find new ways to meet people (such as joining a club, moving into a dorm, going to dances, etc.)	18	64	18
Did something to make yourself more physically attractive to others (going on a diet, buying new clothes, changing your hairstyle, etc.)	20	61	19
Did something to improve your social skills (such as learning to dance, learning to be more assertive, improving conversational skills, etc.)	25	66	9
Talked to a friend or relative about ways to overcome your loneliness	40	45	15
Took you mind off feeling lonely by using drugs or alcohol	74	25	1
Talked to a counselor or therapist about ways to overcome your loneliness	91	6	3

Source: Rook & Peplau, 1982.

and positively with loneliness (Rook, 1984a). But how can we do this? The actions reported by participants in the surveys just summarized offer some suggestions, some of them quite helpful. On the basis of their research, social scientists have also come up with some ideas.

Earlier in this chapter, four self-defeating characteristics of lonely people (and of those who are socially anxious or depressed) were described:

1. Expecting discomfort in socially risky situations
2. Making internal, stable attributions for unpleasant experiences and feelings

3. Having negative attitudes toward others
4. Behaving in passive and unresponsive ways with others

Regardless of whether these characteristics cause or are produced by loneliness, they make it difficult to establish the kinds of rewarding social relationships needed to get over being lonely. It would therefore seem to be important for people experiencing loneliness to try to counteract these thoughts and behaviors. Here are some suggestions for how to do so.

1. If the fear of possible social failure is keeping you from getting involved in some potentially interesting social interactions, try some rational cost analysis. If you go to that party, for example, and don't meet anyone, are you any worse off than you were? But if you go and have some enjoyable interactions, aren't you much better off than you were? Isn't the potential benefit worth the risk?

2. If you find yourself blaming your own inadequacies for feeling lonely, look around. Are you the only lonely person in your current situation? Usually, if you look carefully, you will discover that the answer is no; others are lonely too, which suggests that situational factors are involved. The sometimes extremely strong impact of the situation on loneliness was illustrated in the study of first-semester college freshmen mentioned earlier (Bragg, 1979; Weeks et al., 1980). At the first testing session two weeks after classes started, 75 percent of the more than 300 subjects who participated reported experiencing at least occasional loneliness, and 43 percent said they were moderately or severely lonely. Five weeks later, loneliness had decreased, but the prevalence of loneliness was still very high: 66 percent reported occasional loneliness, and 30 percent indicated that they were experiencing moderate or severe loneliness. Significant numbers of these students blamed their own inadequacies for being lonely, and yet, obviously, the situation of being new at school was by far the most important factor. The next time you are tempted to blame yourself for being lonely, think about this research and look for some situational influences that might be involved.

3. Identifying situational influences does not, however, mean that you should just sit back and wait for things to get better. The situation may be the root cause for loneliness, but often it takes individual effort to turn things around (Peplau et al., 1979; Revenson, 1981). Sometimes that effort involves taking some social risks. But attitudes are also important. Do you find yourself getting more and more critical of others? Home alone, do you think of them as selfish, shallow, and uncaring? Such negative attitudes can have the force of a self-fulfilling prophecy: What you expect is what you get. Armed with negative, even hostile, attitudes about others, your behavior is unlikely to be all sweetness and light—and their reaction is unlikely to be the warm acceptance you desire. Taking a more positive approach—actively looking for others' good qualities—has a much better chance of success.

4. But what if you dutifully do "all of the above" and you are still lonely? Does this mean that, despite your good intentions, you are being tripped up by inadequate social skills? Possibly. Some people can benefit from social skills

Solitary activities can help widows and others avoid loneliness.

training provided by therapists, counseling centers, or various community groups. But there is another possible factor involved. What sort of relationship are you looking for? In Cutrona's (1982) study of freshmen who did or did not stay lonely for their entire first year in college, those who stayed lonely seemed to believe that only a successful romance could reduce their loneliness. However, the students who became less lonely as the school year progressed placed greater emphasis on the satisfaction that could be derived from friendship. Other investigators have also highlighted the role of friendship in reducing or preventing loneliness (Rook & Peplau, 1982; Schmidt & Sermat, 1983). Putting some effort into deepening and enriching our relationships with our friends may be a better way of coping with loneliness than desperately seeking Mr. or Ms. Right.

Loneliness as a Growth Experience

Thus far we have concentrated on how to reduce or avoid loneliness by improving our social relations. You might assume that loneliness should always be avoided or reduced. Actually, that isn't true. There may be times when loneliness can be transformed into a constructive experience.

One transformation process involves turning the negative, unpleasant state of loneliness into the positive, enjoyable state of solitude. Too often our reaction to even mild feelings of loneliness is to immediately seek companionship or try to kill time by mindless activities. As an alternative, we might consider those examples of active solitude listed in Table 14.5, especially those that are pleasure-oriented rather than work-related. We all have things we really like to do but never seem to have the time for. When we start feeling bored, restless, and lonely, this can be a signal that now we do have the time. Perhaps we like long, leisurely bubble baths, or walking in the woods, or perhaps just sitting around and daydreaming about the future. To turn loneliness into solitude, it is not the activity we engage in that matters; what counts is our attitude about the activity. If we seek distraction or oblivion, we have not found solitude. But if we immerse ourselves in the activity, enjoying it for its own sake, then we can appreciate our moment of solitude without fretting over being lonely.

One of the great benefits of being able to enjoy solitude is that we learn that we can take good care of ourselves and need not always depend on other people to make us happy. Such an awareness is not a barrier to having intimate ties with others. Indeed, the ability to be comfortably alone with oneself may enhance our capacity to love others (Branden, 1980; Moustakas, 1972; Safilios-Rothschild, 1981). If we always need rewarding interactions with other people in order to be happy, this places a terrible burden on them—one they may not be willing or able to bear. Furthermore, being alone (physically or psychologically) can be used to develop an understanding of our own needs, feelings, and perspective on life. And, it is hoped, the more self-knowledge we have, the better equipped we are to have realistic, accepting, and loving relationships with others. It is by no means easy to face ourselves and our aloneness in the world; it can, however, be an enormously enriching experience. As the British historian Edward Gibbon once remarked, "I was never less alone than when by myself."

These two strategies of transformation—turning loneliness into solitude and using aloneness to gain self-knowledge—provide a balance to reducing loneliness through improving or extending our social relations. Much of healthy personal growth consists of promoting such a balance—of trying to develop satisfying relationships with other people and of trying to create a secure, internal base of satisfaction within ourselves.

CHAPTER SUMMARY

What Is Loneliness?

Loneliness is not the same as physical isolation. Instead, it is a feeling of deprivation and dissatisfaction produced by a discrepancy between the kinds of social relations one has and the kinds one desires. Two different types of loneliness have been identified: *social isolation* created by the lack of a social network, and *emotional isolation* based on the lack of a single intense relationship.

A Discrepancy Model for Conceptualizing Loneliness. Perlman and Peplau have offered a *discrepancy framework* for conceptualizing the experience of loneliness. Central to their thinking is the idea that loneliness stems from a discrepancy between the social relationships a person needs (or desires) and the relationships they actually have. They believe there are predisposing and precipitating factors that lead to discrepancies, and that people make cognitive interpretations of why their actual and achieved levels of contact differ. These explanations may moderate the experience of loneliness. Once people are lonely, they react and try to cope.

Measuring Loneliness. The UCLA Loneliness Scale, which has been translated into several languages, is the most widely used measure of adult loneliness. It has been shown to have good reliability and validity. Other measures for assessing state versus trait loneliness are also available. Trait measures of loneliness reflect a long history of frequent and intense feelings of loneliness. In contrast, measures of the state of loneliness reflect variations in loneliness across time and different situations.

How Does It Feel to Be Lonely? A variety of emotions and desires can be bound up with the experience of being lonely. In one survey, respondents reported four major categories of feelings they have when lonely: desperation, impatient boredom, self-deprecation, and depression.

Does Loneliness Matter? Although some forms of loneliness are fleeting, minor experiences, loneliness is associated with several serious problems. These include adolescents running away from home, crime and delinquency, academic problems, sleep disturbances, elevated cortisol levels (indicative of anxiety), poor mental health, poor physical health, and mortality rates.

Who Are the Lonely? Wealthier people are less prone to loneliness. In multinational comparisons, U.S. samples have been moderately high in loneliness, perhaps because of the more individualistic, competitive nature of U.S. society. In a European study, nationality differences in social integration helped to account for national differences in loneliness. Married people are less lonely than are those who have experienced the loss of a relationship through separation, divorce, or the death of a partner. When responding to the UCLA Loneliness Scale (which does not use the word *lonely*), men tend to report greater loneliness than do women. When providing self-ratings of loneliness, however, women tend to report greater loneliness than do men. Since lonely men are evaluated more negatively than lonely women, men may be reluctant to explicitly acknowledge their lonely feelings. Among married couples, wives report greater loneliness than husbands. Among those who are not married, men report greater loneliness than women.

Loneliness Across the Life Span

Family Antecedents of Loneliness. Lonely people recall having had cold, remote parents. With regard to family structure, parental divorce—especially when it occurs early in the child's life—but not parental death, has been associated with adult loneliness.

Age Changes in Loneliness. In general, loneliness decreases with age from adolescence to the preretirement years; adolescents and young adults report the greatest amount of loneliness. Loneliness may increase modestly in old age, especially among those who are incapacitated and widowed.

Age-Related Predictors of Loneliness. Life events such as going away to college or the death of a spouse may precipitate loneliness. Personality factors as well as transient changes in identity and relationship status may be more important to the loneliness of young adults, while more permanent losses may be more important to the loneliness of older people.

Some Possible Causes and Moderators of Loneliness

Theorists generally believe that loneliness stems from social deficits, but there is disagreement about whether deficits per se are crucial or whether one needs to consider both actual and desired levels of social contact. In a study comparing these viewpoints, Archibald et al. (1995, p. 296) concluded that levels of social provisions were most important, yet their results also "provide limited support for a cognitive discrepancy model."

Inadequacies in Our Relationships. The reasons participants in one survey gave for being lonely involved five major categories: being unattached, alienation, being alone, forced isolation, and dislocation. These reasons cover a broad range, with some being situational in nature and others possibly reflecting personal characteristics of the lonely person.

Changes in What We Want from a Relationship. As people change (in their mood, their age, or their external situation), what they want from their relationships may also change. If their relationships do not change accordingly, they may experience loneliness.

Self-Esteem. Loneliness is associated with having low self-esteem. Lonely people also expect to be uncomfortable in risky social situations; these expectations may serve to maintain loneliness by motivating lonely people to avoid certain social contacts.

Interpersonal Behaviors. Lonely people appear to be caught in a downward social spiral. Relative to nonlonely people, they hold more negative attitudes toward others, are more passive and unresponsive in their social interactions, and sometimes elicit more negative reactions from others. Each of these components reinforces the others and makes it more difficult for the lonely person to establish the rewarding social relationships necessary to eliminate loneliness. Another problem in living, social anxiety, involves feelings of discomfort in the presence of others. Shyness includes feelings of discomfort in social situations, along with social inhibition and avoidance. Social anxiety and shyness are often associated with each other, and each is often associated with loneliness. The interpersonal behavior of socially anxious and shy people closely resembles that of lonely people. Socially anxious concerns can be a learned response to an unpleasant social encounter; they may also reflect the belief, accurate or not, that the person is not able to have the social success that he or she wants. Depression is also associated with loneliness, and with shyness and social anxiety as well. Like those who are lonely, depressed people experience difficulties in their social interactions and are uncomfortable with risky social situations. Depression and loneliness are not, however, identical psychological conditions. Depression is a more global state of dissatisfaction, while loneliness is more specifically interpersonal in nature. Depressed people, at least those of college age, may be especially sensitive to success or failure in romantic relationships, while loneliness is affected by a broad range of social interactions.

Causal Attributions. Explanations for loneliness may also increase its duration. In one study, college freshmen who made internal, stable attributions for their loneliness in the fall semester were more likely to still be lonely in the spring than were those who made different kinds of attributions. It is, however, *characterological* (internal, stable, uncontrollable) acceptance of blame for failures, rather than *behavioral self-blame* involving internal, unstable, controllable attributions that is associated with greater loneliness.

Coping with Loneliness

What Do People Do When They Are Lonely? According to their responses to survey questions, people appear to engage in a wide variety of behaviors when they are lonely. Some of these behaviors involve active, constructive coping; others are potentially self-destructive.

What Helps People to Feel Less Lonely? In addition to the active, constructive coping behaviors reported in surveys, some suggestions for coping with loneliness can be derived from the research described in this chapter. Possible ways to reduce loneliness would include (1) doing a rational cost analysis of risky social situations to decide whether the potential gain warrants taking the risk, (2) looking for situational causes of loneliness, rather than blaming your own personal characteristics, (3) maintaining a positive attitude toward others, and (4) concentrating on enriching friendships rather than searching for a romantic partner.

Loneliness as a Growth Experience. Loneliness does not always have to be reduced or avoided; sometimes it can be transformed into a constructive experience. One such transformation involves turning loneliness into solitude by using alone time to engage in pleasurable behaviors. It is also possible that learning to be alone with oneself can contribute to self-knowledge, which may strengthen our capacity for establishing intimate relationships with others. Healthy personal growth consists of establishing a balance between satisfying relationships with others and a secure base of satisfaction within ourselves.

CHAPTER 15

Fostering Relationships: Getting, Maintaining, and Repairing Them

If you want, as most people do, successful intimate relationships, there are many pathways to achieving your goal. In this chapter we will examine some of the ways of fostering relationships. We will divide our analysis along two dimensions: first, we will look at what people can do on their own and how professionals can help them. Second, we will look at three different relational objectives: fostering social bonding, maintaining existing relationships, and repairing relationships that are encountering difficulties.

Before discussing how professionals can help foster relationships, it is worth considering people's tendency to turn to them for assistance with interpersonal issues. From the perspective of people who go for therapy, interpersonal problems are the most commonly mentioned reason for seeing a therapist (Horowitz, 1979). However, a 1994 survey of 7,000 readers of *Consumer Reports* magazine (Seligman, 1995) found that only 41 percent had seen a mental health professional for any reason in the last three years. So, it is undoubtedly fair to say that people typically try to enhance or repair their relationships without professional help, perhaps turning to their informal networks for advice and support.

Even if they don't seek the direct services of mental health professionals, another way members of the general public get professional advice is through the mass media, including television shows, magazine articles, and popular books, especially self-help books. There are many books on how to find or improve relationships. Both those who read these books and the mental health practitioners who recommend them to their clients overwhelmingly believe that they have a positive effect (Ellis, 1993; Halliday, 1991). Yet there has been debate over the pros and cons of self-help books. On the skeptical side, the backgrounds of people who write self-help books are quite varied, as is what they say. Some self-help authors express dogmatic, ill-informed positions. They sometimes imply that change is easy to achieve, thus encouraging readers to be overly optimistic about their abilities to resolve their difficulties. Self-help books leave readers, who lack the skills, experience, and objectivity of professionals, to diagnose their own problems. Because they are written for a general readership, their discussion of problems and solutions are not tailored to an individual reader's situation. Self-help manuals often lack explicit directions on what to do, and even if their guidelines are fairly clear, there is no one to monitor compliance or to provide corrective feedback on how well readers are following the prescription.

On the more positive side, self-help books are inexpensive. They may seem acceptable to people who are ashamed or for other reasons don't want to go for therapy. Readers can refer to them many times, going back to absorb material at their own pace. In remote communities without mental health professionals they offer some form of assistance, and in communities with only a few mental health practitioners, they expand the variety of methods people can consider. Such books often give many readers a positive attitude and general encouragement that may help them to overcome problems.

Besides self-help books, in reading academic texts like this one, you can consider the practical relevance of the scientific information they convey. The eminent social psychologist Kurt Lewin is famous for his remark that "There is nothing so practical as a good theory." This volume has not been designed as a guide to promoting the well-being of your relationships. Yet, as you go back over the available knowledge we have presented, much of it has relevance for how you might have more satisfying relationships. Remember, as one example, the discussion of dysfunctional communication in chapter 5. There we spelled out for you ways of being more effective. Even where we have not explicitly identified the practical implications of our knowledge about relationships, relationship knowledge often has implications for how we might foster our own well-being. As you near the end of this volume, we encourage you to review the relevance of material throughout the book to your own situation. Hopefully we have given you concepts and information for analyzing your own relationships more richly, sophisticatedly, and constructively.

FOSTERING SOCIAL BONDING

Judy is a 25-year-old clerk working for the data entry department of an insurance company headquartered in the Washington, DC area. The worst thing about her life? Eating alone. She jokes that if she could just stop eating alone, she would move in with a man immediately. But since coming to the Washington area a few months ago, she hasn't had much luck meeting anyone, let alone Mr. Right. At work she stares at a computer screen all day. She has a lot of coworkers, but the company demands productivity, and everyone knows management could move data entry to another community or even country where labor costs are lower. Judy would like to socialize with the computer technicians and other professional staff who work for the company, but even though she went to college for a couple of years, there is prejudice among them against fraternizing with clerical staff. After work, she's gone to singles bars a few times. That hasn't been very fulfilling. Being in a noisy environment, having to strike up a conversation with a complete stranger, and having the sense they were evaluating you isn't exactly Judy's idea of fun. Watching TV at home is a bit boring, but at least she feels comfortable doing it. She does, however, want to make more friends.

Strategies People Use to Initiate New Relationships

For many people, the development of new friendships is largely an outgrowth of their daily work and social activities. For example, through our existing social networks, we often meet the friends of our friends. As you will remember from chapter 3, friendships emerge out of physical proximity and repeated interaction. When we work together with people on cooperative tasks, we are likely to become friendly with them. Whether we consciously plan them or not, we become involved in situations and activities that foster friendly interactions. With enough time, these interactions often result in new relationships.

Loneliness Businesses

However, as Judy's situation illustrates, sometimes these steps aren't enough. People turn to more conscious strategies for making new friends. Journalist Suzanne Gordon (1976) contends that there are a variety of "loneliness businesses" to help people form new friendships and dating relationships. These include dating services, the singles bars of the sort Judy tried, personal development groups, cruises, and the like. Such businesses flourish largely, or at least partially, to help their customers find new relationships. In the nonprofit sector, religious organizations, clubs, adult education classes, self-help groups and the like fill a similar niche.

Rook (1984b) argues that an important distinction between many of the profit-centered businesses and the not-for-profit activities is that the for-profit businesses typically have the sole purpose of helping people to find a partner. She contends that the self-consciousness created by explicitly seeking new relationships may undermine encounters, especially for those who are shy and socially anxious. She speculates that people seeking new relationships may "benefit from social interactions structured in ways that distract them from their self-consciousness" (p. 1396). Thus, the more task-oriented meetings and activities of groups like sailing clubs may actually make it easier for members to get acquainted.

Personal Ads and Dating Services

Since the 1970s, close relationships scholars have been researching another mechanism people use for seeking new relationships, personal ads placed in newspapers and on the Web (see Lynn & Bolig, 1985). Many of these studies have been largely descriptive, examining how people describe themselves and what they want in a partner. Several studies of these ads reveal sex role traditionalism. Men often want someone physically attractive and younger than themselves. Women offer physical attractiveness and specify they would like a partner with high economic status. Sociologist Erich Goode (1996) made up four ads to determine how the advertisers' gender, attractiveness, and occupational status influences the number of responses advertisers receive. The fictitious advertisers were a beautiful waitress, an average-looking female lawyer, an average-looking male lawyer, and a handsome cabdriver. The women advertisers generally got more responses than did the men. For the two female ads, the beautiful waitress got more replies, whereas for the two male ads, the average-looking male lawyer got more. These results are consistent with the view that women who offer good looks and men who offer high occupational status are valued as dates.

Besides personal ads, some people use video dating services. These agencies typically have clients do a short video (approximately 10 minutes) of themselves so others can view it. (Often these services also have clients provide a picture and some written information so others can more quickly determine whose video they would like to watch.) Usually these services serve as an intermediary, not a matchmaker, giving out only first names and having clients themselves determine if they would like to get together.

Woll and Crosby (1987) conducted a multifaceted study of the users of a southern California video dating service. They found that in making their videos, people generally tried to give fairly realistic self-portraits, hoping to appeal to one special person rather than a broad range of people. In deciding which videos to view, participants appeared to use the age and attractiveness information from the cover sheets. When viewers were asked what they looked for in videos, they said attractiveness plus more dynamic and personal attributes uniquely available via video (personality, expressive behavior, sense of humor, and compatibility). Expressive behavior (including good eye contact) manifested in one's video did predict the number of times men were chosen as dates, although the results for women were more complex. Nonexpressive women were approached for dates, but expressive women's requests for dates were accepted.

In terms of outcomes, Woll and Crosby state "Clients report they are relatively disappointed with the individuals who have been selecting them" (p. 93).

From their examination of the list of "success stories" maintained by one branch of the video dating agency they studied, Woll and Crosby inferred that only 10 to 15 percent of the past and present members achieved "success" through video dating. Nonetheless, users of the video dating services liked the capacity to prescreen and the number of potential dates available. Going through profiles and viewing videos shortens the time needed to get an impression of another person.

Use of the Internet is another option for starting relationships (see Merkle & Richardson, 2000). While physical appearance is prominent in personal ads and video dating, it is minimized in computer interactions. Nonverbal behaviors (e.g., voice, eye gaze, posture) are also absent. In contrast to the typical development of face-to-face friendships, geographical proximity is insignificant in computer-mediated interactions. Nonetheless, Internet users can get to know one another rather quickly and intimately, achieving both breadth and depth in their online relationships (Parks & Floyd, 1996a). Merkle and Richardson contend that mutual self-disclosure and intimate sharing of private worldviews are keys to these relationships blossoming. Many friendships formed by electronic communication migrate to other means of interacting, including conventional mail, phoning, and face-to-face interaction (Parks & Floyd, 1996a).

While computer use can foster new relationships, we should also note that a two-year study of the introduction of computers into 73 Pittsburgh families (169 individuals) shows that greater use of the Internet was associated with declines in participants' communication with family members in the household, declines in the size of their social circles, and increases in their loneliness (Kraut et al., 1998). One of the main personal uses of the Internet, however, is for interpersonal communication. Perhaps the Internet fosters contact with distant family and close friends, but many of the new friendships formed by electronic communication may be weaker than those established by face-to-face interaction.

Interaction Strategies

Regardless of how we meet others, there are processes of interaction that are used to foster friendships. These are illustrated in Wentzel and Erdley's (1993) study of 423 midwestern grade 6 and 7 students. They were asked what advice they would have for an incoming student on the things one should and shouldn't do to make friends in their new school. From the answers the students gave, Wentzel and Erdley identified five strategies students believed they should use to foster friendships: initiate interaction, be nice, engage in prosocial behavior, have respect for others, and provide social support. They identified three strategies students believed should be avoided: being psychologically aggressive, engaging in negative self-presentation, and acting antisocially (see Table 15.1). Some of the same types of positive strategies emerged in Baxter and Philpott's (1982) study of adults, but a few additional tactics were also apparent: similarity (demonstration of similarity with the other person), self-presentation (presentation of a unique and favorable image of oneself), and information acquisition (soliciting information about the other).

TABLE 15.1. Categories of Appropriate and Inappropriate Strategies for Making Friends at School

Category	Examples	% Students
	Strategies appropriate for making friends	
Initiate interaction	Learn about friend: ask for their name, age, favorite activities. Prosocial overtures: introduce self, start a conversation, invite them to do things.	49
Be nice	Be nice, kind, considerate.	57
Prosocial behavior	Honesty and trustworthiness: tell the truth, keep promises. Be generous, sharing, cooperative.	28
Respect for self and others	Respect others, have good manners: be polite, courteous, listen to what others say. Have a positive attitude and personality: be open to others, be friendly, be funny. Be yourself. Enhance your own reputation: be clean, dress neatly, be on best behavior.	81
Provide social support	Be supportive: help, give advice, show you care. Engage in activities together: study or play, sit next to one another, be in same group. Enhance others: compliment them.	23
	Strategies inappropriate for making friends	
Psychological aggression	Show disrespect, bad manners: be prejudiced, inconsiderate, use others, curse, be rude. Be exclusive, uncooperative: don't invite them to do things, ignore them, isolate them, don't share or help them. Hurt their reputation or feelings: gossip, spread rumors, embarrass them, criticize them.	36
Negative self-presentation	Be self-centered: be snobby, conceited, jealous, show-off, care only about yourself. Be mean, have bad attitude or affect: be mean, cruel, hostile, a grouch, angry all the time. Hurt own reputation: be a slob, act stupid, throw temper tantrums, start trouble, be a sissy.	49
Antisocial behavior	Physical aggression: fight, trip, spit, cause physical harm. Verbal aggression or control: yell at others, pick on them, make fun of them, call them names, be bossy. Dishonesty, disloyalty: tell lies, steal, cheat, tell secrets, break promises. Break school rules: skip school, drink alcohol, use drugs.	75

Note: From "Strategies for Making Friends: Relations to Social Behavior and Peer Acceptance in Early Adolescence," by K. R. Wentzel and C. A. Erdley, 1993, *Developmental Psychology, 29*, p. 8. Copyright 1993 by the American Psychological Association. Reprinted with permission.

Interventions Professionals Offer to Help Clients Initiate New Relationships

Clinical psychologists are prone to giving person-centered explanations for social isolation. In working with a client such as Judy, they might be concerned with how low self-esteem, social skill deficits, or dysfunctional interpersonal beliefs and strategies contribute to her having fewer friends than she wants.

Rook (1984b) has reviewed ways professionals have for fostering new social bonds. Two major approaches include social skill training programs and cognitively oriented therapies. Social skill training programs are often done in group sessions lasting 10 to 12 weeks. They typically are rooted in the behavioral tradition. These programs offer training in skills such as initiating conversations, fostering the flow of conversations (e.g., handling silence, topic continuity), giving and receiving compliments, enhancing physical attractiveness, and the like. Training often consists of a socially skilled person showing the participants the desired behavior, the participants trying it themselves, feedback on their performance, and reinforcement of positive actions. Social skill training is sometimes done preventively with people who are at high risk of becoming isolated (e.g., children of divorced parents) as well as with those who already feel socially isolated.

Cognitively oriented therapies assume that people have self-defeating thought patterns. For instance, when meeting a stranger, an isolated client may feel "I'm dull and boring." Cognitively oriented therapists try to help clients to identify their recurring thought patterns. The therapist would likely encourage the client to test whether these thoughts are correct. The therapist might also help clients to discover inconsistencies in their recurring thoughts and offer alternative interpretations that cast the situation in a more positive light.

MAINTAINING AND ENHANCING EXISTING RELATIONSHIPS

Jim and Linda met at a summer concert in the park. Before the concert began, they started talking and realized immediately that they liked the same types of music. They exchanged phone numbers, began getting together for weekend walks, and before long their relationship just took off. Within three to four months they were expressing love for one another. Linda really appreciated Jim's accepting, supportive nature. Jim, being a touch reserved, liked Linda's more outgoing, emotionally expressive nature. They decided to get married. Everything for their wedding and their honeymoon was perfect. For their honeymoon, they went to Hawaii, where they stayed in a thatched-roof hale (or cottage). They swam, learned about Hawaiian handicrafts, and went to a luau. During the first year of their marriage, there was some adjusting to do (e.g., she liked the bedroom window open, he preferred it shut). They worked out compromises and settled into routines. They still took weekend walks, but they were shorter now so that they could do chores like the laundry and grocery shopping. Instead of being so absorbed with one another, they were getting together more as a couple and sometimes individually with friends and family. The prolonged rapture they had initially experienced in their physical intimacy was a little less intense now. They knew that many of their friends' marriages seemed to drift apart, with the partners becoming bored or even embittered with one another. But Jim and Linda were strongly attached to each other and cherished their marriage. What they wanted was to keep the love and vitality in their relationship.

During most of the twentieth century, social scientists seemed more interested in how relationships like Jim and Linda's got started or ended than in how to keep them going. As noted in chapter 13, marriages that are uninterrupted by divorce now last nearly 50 years on average. In a study of men's friendships, the median duration of the closest friendships of married fathers ages 35 to 50 was about 13 years (Stueve & Gerson, 1977). Perhaps it is less exciting than newfound love and less dramatic than separation, but effectively keeping alive the successful relationships you have already formed can contribute substantially to achieving a rich, rewarding set of close relationships.

Canary and Stafford (in press) write:

> We define **relational maintenance** behaviors *as actions and activities used to sustain desired relational qualities.* This definition implies that people strategically engage in behaviors for the purpose of sustaining important characteristics that are fundamental to intimate relationships. . . . Such characteristics include features such as liking the partner, control mutuality (i.e., the extent to which partners agree on who has rightful influence power in various domains of decision-making), trust, commitment and satisfaction.

According to this definition, maintenance is behavior or a process rather than, as some have argued, a stage between escalation and deterioration. Furthermore, according to this definition, maintenance only occurs once the relationship has developed to a certain level. There is disagreement over whether relational maintenance focuses on simply maintaining the current level of intimacy or on either maintaining or enhancing that level. We will be concerned with both. Canary and Stafford see maintenance activities as being directed at sustaining important relationship characteristics, including stability, persisting levels of trust, commitment, and satisfaction. The other aspects, such as enhancing intimacy, are not part of relationship maintenance per se. As outcomes of relational maintenance, they are separate constructs.

Partners Maintaining Their Own Relationships

What do people do to maintain their relationships? Canary and his associates (Canary & Stafford, in press; Messman, Canary, & Hause, 2000; Stafford & Canary, 1991) have developed what has been called the dominant typology of relational maintenance strategies (Dindia, 2000, p. 291). Canary's group used a combination of procedures: They reviewed the past literature on maintenance, asked people to describe what strategies they used, and then developed these descriptions into lists of strategies that they presented to participants on questionnaires. Early in this program of work, Stafford and Canary derived five relational maintenance strategies: positivity (being positive and cheerful),

TABLE 15.2. Relational Maintenance Strategies

Strategy	Examples
Positivity	Try to act nice and cheerful Attempt to make our interactions enjoyable Ask how his/her day has gone
Openness	Encourage him/her to disclose thoughts and feelings to me Seek to discuss the quality of our relationship Remind him/her about relationship decisions we made in the past
Assurances	Stress my commitment to him/her Imply that our relationship has a future Show myself to be faithful to him/her
Social Networking	Like to spend time with our friends Focus on common friends and affiliations Show that I am willing to do things with his/her friends and family
Sharing Tasks	Help equally with tasks that need to be done Do my fair share of the work we have to do Perform my household responsibilities
Joint Activities	Spend time hanging out Attend Saturday football games Visit my brother when he is away at school
Mediated Communication	Write letters Use e-mail to keep in touch Communicate on the phone
Avoidance	Avoid discussing certain topics Avoid the person Respect each other's privacy and need to be alone
Antisocial Behaviors	Act rude to him/her Act moody Lie to him/her about where I have been
Humor	Call him/her by a funny nickname Tease him/her Be sarcastic in a funny way
No Flirting	Avoid flirting with him/her Do not allow myself to be in a romantic place with him/her Do not encourage overly familiar behavior

Note: From "Equity in the Preservation of Personal Relationships," by Daniel J. Canary and Laura Stafford. In J. M. Harvey and A. E. Wenzel (Eds.), (in press), *Close romantic relationships: Maintenance and enhancement*. Mahwah, NJ: Lawrence Erlbaum Associates. Copyright 200X by Lawrence Erlbaum Associates. Reprinted with permission.

openness (self-disclosure and open discussion about the relationship), assurances (showing love and faithfulness, stressing commitment), networking (spending time with common friends), and sharing tasks (especially household chores). Through continued research, Canary and Stafford (in press) have added six more strategies (see Table 15.2). Five of these include: joint activities, mediated communication (keeping in touch without face-to-face contact), avoidance, humor, and antisocial behavior, which appears to be a paradoxical effort to enhance the relationship by acting negatively. Most of these strategies apply to a variety of relationships, but the most recently found strategy, no flirting, emerged only in a study of cross-sex relationships.

Besides Canary's strategies, several other authors have identified ways that people go about sustaining relationships.

- Aron, Norman, and Aron (in press) identify engaging in activities as a maintenance strategy but show the importance of these activities being novel and arousing.
- Acitelli (in press) focused on attending to one's partner as a key maintenance activity. For Acitelli, attending includes how often people think about their partners, talk about their relationships, and do leisure-type activities with their partners.
- Rusbult, Olsen, Davis, and Hannon (in press) identify both cognitive and behavioral maintenance mechanisms: accommodative behavior (responding positively to a partner's potentially destructive acts), willingness to sacrifice, forgiving betrayals, cognitive interdependence (seeing oneself as interdependent with one's partner), positive illusions, and derogation of tempting alternatives.
- The first three components of what Omarzu, Whalen, and Harvey (in press) call "minding" are essentially ways that people use to maintain relationships: (a) gaining knowledge about the other person by self-disclosure, (b) accepting the other person, and (c) making relationship-enhancing attributions that give the other person the benefit of the doubt.
- In threatening situations where a partner's feelings and thoughts are ambiguous, Simpson, Ickes, and Orina (in press) highlight motivated inaccuracy (failure to correctly infer the contents of their partner's hurtful thoughts and feelings) as a maintenance tactic.
- Karney, McNulty, and Fry (in press) believe that we generally have more positive global evaluations of our partners than we have of their specific behaviors. Starting with this observation, they believe that cognitive processes (e.g., attributions) that separate global beliefs about one's partner from cognitions of the partner's more specific behaviors are mechanisms for maintaining relationship satisfaction.

Clearly there are many strategies that help to maintain relationships, some done consciously, others unconsciously. For the most part, people use similar maintenance activities in a variety of relationships. Yet different strategies may be used at different points in a relationship's development or in different types of relationships. For example, Stafford and Canary (1991) found that married partners engaged more in social networking and assurance mechanisms than did dating partners; however, married partners engaged in less openness than did dating partners. Cross-sex friendships have "no flirtation" as a unique maintenance strategy. Similarly, Haas and Stafford (1998) found that gay and lesbian partners used seeking out gay/lesbian environments as a distinctive

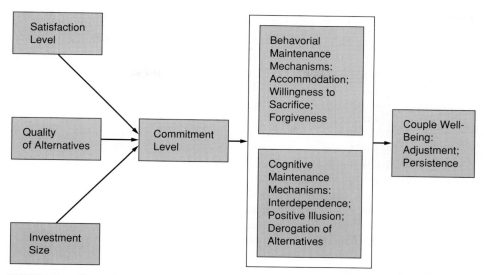

FIGURE 15.1. Commitment and relationship maintenance mechanisms. From "Commitment and relationship maintenance mechanisms," by Caryl Rusbult, Nils Olsen, Judy L. Davis, and Margaret A. Hannon in J. M. Harvey & A. E. Wenzel (Eds.), (in press), *Close romantic relationships: Maintenance and enhancement.* Mahwah, NJ: Lawrence Erlbaum Associates. Copyright 2001 by Lawrence Erlbaum Associates. Reprinted with permission.

way of strengthening their relationships. Like other couples, gays and lesbians relied on their social networks to help them maintain their relationships, but this often involved having one another's friends and family accept their "coming out." Gaines and Brennan (in press) argue that appreciating ethnic and cultural differences, building a relationship culture, and being open to divergent viewpoints foster multicultural relationships. Coleman and Ganong (in press) spell out how mothers in blended families maintain spousal relationships by using four strategies to control the development of relationships between their new husbands and their children: defending children's behavior, gatekeeping access to them, mediating disagreements, and interpreting family members to each other.

In chapter 6, the interdependence model was presented. Rusbult et al. (in press) have applied this model to relationship maintenance (see Figure 15.1). According to their analysis, being satisfied in one's relationship, lacking attractive alternatives, and having made substantial investments all lead to commitment. This in turn leads to maintenance mechanisms that foster relational well-being. Perhaps what might be considered the bottom line of all this is that evidence shows that engaging in maintenance activities is associated with relationship satisfaction and well-being (see for example Canary & Stafford, in press).

Professionals Helping Partners to Maintain Their Relationships

Many couples think they should get professional help only when the relationship is in serious trouble. Actually, mental health professionals are becoming increasingly interested in working with couples like Linda and Jim before there are any serious problems in the relationship. Besides helping couples in distress, professional counselors can help couples to maintain and enrich relationships that are already rewarding.

Premarital Programs

The high divorce rate in the United States has revealed the need to prepare people better for the long-term commitment of marriage. Religious groups have strengthened and expanded their traditional roles in premarital counseling. Since, however, there is serious question about the effectiveness of the standard premarital lectures offered by many churches (Olson, Russell, & Sprenkle, 1980), many mental health professionals from both the religious and secular communities have become interested in premarital programs that require more active learning by the participants. A number of structured, systematic programs for premarital counseling have been developed. The following are some examples of these sorts of programs.

Based on the assumption that the best way to prevent later marital problems is to teach premarital couples better communication skills, the **Couples Communication Program** (CCP) concentrates on four major areas of the communication process (Miller, Miller, Nunnally, & Wachman, 1991; Miller, Nunnally, & Wackman, 1976).

1. Training in awareness and expression of thoughts, feelings, and intentions.
2. Training in better communication through the sender-receiver-clarification sequence: The sender states his or her feelings or beliefs. The receiver listens carefully and summarizes what the sender has said. The sender clarifies for the receiver if the summary is inaccurate or incomplete.
3. Training in various types of communications that can occur in a relationship so that partners can understand the options available to them in communicating with each other and the impact of each type of communication on each of them.
4. Training in ways to build one's own self-esteem and that of the partner.

The **Premarital Relationship Improvement by Maximizing Empathy and Self-Disclosure** (PRIMES) program is similar to CCP in its emphasis on developing better communication skills as a way to prevent problems in the relationship (Ginsberg & Vogelsong, 1977). PRIMES also has four major areas of concentration, with the first two bearing a close resemblance to the first two areas of CCP:

1. Training in the expressive mode of communication. The skills taught here are very similar to those guidelines for good communication discussed in chapter 5: Express feelings; be clear that they are your feelings ("I feel . . . " rather than "You make me feel . . . "); make positive statements as much as

possible; be specific about your feelings and about any changes you ask your partner to make.

2. Training in empathic responding: Put yourself in your partner's shoes; try to feel the way he or she does; reflect back to your partner what you think he or she said and how you think he or she feels; do not interrupt, make judgments, or ask for new information.

3. Training in how and when to switch from the expressive mode to the responding mode.

4. Training in how to facilitate good communication on the part of other people.

The **Premarital Relationship Enhancement Program** (PREP) seeks to apply the principles of behavioral marital therapy (described later in this chapter) to premarital relationships (see Stanley, Blumberg, & Markman, 1999). In this program, couples are taught communication and conflict-resolution skills and are introduced to some of the basic features of the behavioral approach, such as:

Monitoring their own and their partners' behaviors

Learning what behaviors please or displease the partner, and

Making contractual agreements about changes in behavior.

All these programs take an educational approach to premarital counseling. Typically, the programs are carried out by a trainer (or cotrainers) working with a group of couples. The trainer explains the rationale of the program, models the skills to be learned, and encourages and coaches the participants in their efforts. Participants actively engage in communication with others in the group, role-play specific problem areas, read a text discussing how to improve relationship skills, and practice their skills at home with each other. All three programs are intensive, highly structured, and time-limited (e.g., five to eight weeks). The effectiveness of these programs in teaching skills and promoting more satisfying relationships will be discussed later in this chapter.

Marital Enrichment Programs

Marital enrichment programs share the preventive philosophy of premarital programs: Relationship improvement now will reduce problems later. In addition, enrichment programs take a purely positive, growth-oriented approach to long-term relationships, maintaining that every relationship can become more satisfying and more meaningful. Here, too, religious groups have played a leading role (Garland, 1983). One church-sponsored program, the multidenominational Marriage Encounter program, involves a 44-hour experience held over a single weekend (Lester & Doherty, 1983). Among secular groups, the largest organization involved in marital enrichment is the Association of Couples for Marriage Enrichment (ACME). ACME provides organizational support for retreats and growth groups for interested couples (Mace & Mace, 1976). Although these groups do not have any structured program specified in advance, the usual goals are for partners to experience and express more positive feelings and to formulate growth plans for their relationships.

There are also a number of structured programs that have been designed for enrichment purposes. CCP, for example, is used as an enrichment program, as is the Conjugal Relationship Enhancement (CRE) program (Guerney, 1977; Guerney, Brock, & Coufal, 1986)—the latter being the parent program from which its premarital offspring, PRIMES, evolved.

A more behavioral approach to enrichment has been developed by Harrell and Guerney (1976). Their behavioral-exchange program puts particular emphasis on learning conflict-management skills. The program consists of nine major steps:

1. Listen carefully—summarize what your partner said.
2. Locate a relationship issue, something that both partners want to change.
3. Identify your own contribution to this issue.
4. Identify alternative solutions, more than one.
5. Evaluate these alternative solutions.
6. Make an exchange; select one behavior change for each partner.
7. Place conditions on this exchange—bonuses for making the behavior change, penalties for not making it.
8. Implement the exchange: keep trying; keep records.
9. Renegotiate to see if additional or alternative behavior changes are necessary.

The Effectiveness of Premarital and Marital Enrichment Programs

General reviews of the effectiveness of various premarital and marital enrichment programs suggest that, on the average, these programs are modestly successful (Butler & Wampler, 1999; Giblin, Sprenkle, & Sheehan, 1985; Guerney & Maxson, 1990; cf. Christensen & Heavey, 1999). The longer the programs, the more successful they tend to be (Giblin et al., 1985), but over time, after they end, the benefits of programs such as the couples communications approach are prone to deteriorate (Butler & Wampler, 1999). Available research on the PREP program, however, shows that participants in it, as compared to controls, fare better in terms of staying married, constructiveness of communication, avoiding physical violence, and marital satisfaction up to five years postintervention (see Christensen & Heavey, 1999, p. 181).

Although some distressed couples may benefit from enrichment programs (Giblin et al., 1985), there may be a small proportion of couples for whom these programs may have damaging effects on their relationships and their personal well-being (Lester & Doherty, 1983). Because of this possibility for harm, highly distressed couples should be identified before their participation in an enrichment program and given a referral to appropriate therapeutic services (Doherty & Walker, 1982). Even couples with a more stable and satisfying relationship should be cautioned against exaggerated expectations about the benefits of participating in a premarital or marital enrichment program. These programs can help many couples to develop a better relationship, but they cannot create happiness or guarantee endurance.

Sexual Enrichment Programs

The pioneering work by Masters and Johnson (1970) in the treatment of sexual dysfunction resulted in two important principles that have been generally adopted by clinicians. First, Masters and Johnson developed systematic, behavioral treatment programs for specific sexual problems. In addition to this improved treatment technology, however, Masters and Johnson emphasized that sexuality occurs in the context of a relationship. With committed partners, both people need to be involved in the treatment, even if only one of them has a sexual problem. Some researchers in the area of human sexual functioning have questioned the extremely high improvement rates reported by Masters and Johnson (Heiman & Verhulst, 1990) and have urged the need for more carefully controlled research to evaluate treatment effectiveness (Heiman, LoPiccolo, & LoPiccolo, 1981). On the whole, however, the behavioral techniques and relationship approach advocated by Masters and Johnson "have received significant empirical support and should be considered the treatment of choice" (Gurman & Kniskern, 1981, p. 749).

Sexuality may be an especially appropriate focus for enrichment efforts. Consistent with Masters and Johnson's two key points, Hurlbert and Apt (1995) conducted an enrichment program for women who were experiencing difficulty achieving orgasm during coitus. The women and their spouses attended eight weekly, 90-minute sessions. The first four sessions covered general topics. The last four sessions were devoted to teaching either of two sexual techniques: coital alignment or directed masturbation (i.e., women engaging in self-stimulation during heterosexual intercourse). Coital alignment involves a "high riding" variation of the missionary sexual position plus appropriate coordination of movements during intercourse. Prior to the workshop, these women achieved orgasm less than 20 percent of the time when they had intercourse. After the program this number rose to 42 percent of the time for those in the directed masturbation group and 55 percent of the time in the coital alignment group.

REPAIRING RELATIONSHIPS

Henry and Nancy have been married for four years. When they were dating, Nancy thought Henry was a real sweetheart—charming, romantic, and attentive. Whatever they did together made them happy. Now the spark has left their relationship; the only sparks around are the ones that fly. Nancy sees Henry as glum and irritable. If they talk at all, it seems to be to argue. Whenever she tries to bring up the problems they are having, she feels Henry gets bothered and becomes noncommunicative. For Nancy, the little gestures that Henry used to do to show his affection, like holding her hand or making her morning coffee, are gone. She wishes they were back. When Nancy suggests things they might do together, Henry often shrugs them off, claiming he is too tired or too busy. Nancy thinks Henry has become a workaholic. Nancy is feeling stuck and frustrated.

For his part, Henry feels Nancy no longer understands him. All she does is nag and complain that he doesn't do things with her. He thinks back to those golden days at the beginning of their relationship when she had her friends and she wasn't upset by Henry hanging out with his buddies. Now, he sometimes does things just to try to make Nancy happy. But, he seems to be damned if he does and damned if he doesn't. When he suggested they go to an opera he knew she would like, Nancy questioned whether he really wanted to go and asked if he would fidget once they got there. He feels she never seems to appreciate his efforts. Instead, she criticizes him. Henry realizes he isn't perfect, but he works hard and thinks they will both benefit from the advances he is making in his career.

The day of their wedding anniversary, Henry was working on a big assignment due at the end of that week. He and his boss got caught up in doing calculations; before he knew it, it was 6:30. Henry was supposed to be at the restaurant at 7:00. It was summer and road repairs had traffic backed up. He knew he should get Nancy flowers or something but he decided it was best to just get to the restaurant as soon as possible. He arrived 20 minutes late. Nancy was fuming. She felt: Of all days, he doesn't even respect our anniversary. He comes up with yet another excuse. He used to know me so well, now he doesn't understand or care. During dinner Henry and Nancy hardly talked. She went home near tears. In the morning she woke up realizing that they had to fix their relationship or she didn't want it to go on any more. She wanted to at least try fixing it.

Partners Repairing Their Own Relationships

Conceptually, the repair and maintenance of relationships can be separated: the repair of a relationship implies correcting something that has gone wrong; maintenance involves continuing a situation that may be satisfactory. In our daily lives, however, these activities may not be so separate. When Dindia and Baxter (1987) asked a community sample of married partners how they maintained and repaired their marriages, there was a considerable overlap in the strategies they used for these two purposes. The participants in this research generally reported doing less to repair relationships than they did to maintain them. The strategy mentioned most often for repairing relationships was talking, especially about the problem, and spending time together. Other commonly mentioned tactics included giving in, being warm, expressing affection, and giving gifts. Introducing variety, spontaneity, and novelty were less important for repair than they were for maintenance.

Professionals Helping Partners to Repair Relationships: History and Formats

History

The history of marital and couple therapy in the United States dates back to the late 1920s, when professional marriage counselors first became available for couples having difficulties in their relationships (Broderick & Schrader, 1981; Humphrey, 1983; Prochaska & Prochaska, 1978). Marital therapy has always involved a number of different disciplines, such as marriage and family counseling, pastoral counseling, psychiatry, psychology, social work, and sociology. Moreover, marital therapy is essentially a grassroots movement. Professionals began to offer marital therapy in response to clients who came and asked for

Couple therapy is available for distressed relationships; roughly 65 percent of couples going for marital therapy show improvement.

help. Family therapy, on the other hand, developed mainly in response to professional concern. During the 1950s, while working with severely disturbed young people, a number of therapists became convinced that adequate treatment was only possible when the entire family unit was involved in therapy. This decision to focus on the family system rather than the psychopathology of the individual who was identified as "sick" marked the beginning of family therapy as a distinct form of treatment.

Because of these different developmental histories, there were initially some important differences between marital therapy and family therapy. Marital therapists usually worked with the two marital partners, neither of whom was severely disturbed. Family therapists typically worked with at least three family members (parents and child), at least one of whom was severely disturbed. Over time, however, these differences have tended to fade as the originally parallel fields of marital therapy and family therapy began to merge. Many marital therapists have adopted the systems approach (discussed later in the chapter) that was the hallmark of family therapy, and many family therapists work primarily with the marital dyad, even when the identified patient is the child. Both marital and family therapies can be distinguished from individual therapies by their focus on relationships. In these therapies, the relationship between the individuals receives at least as much attention as the individuals themselves (Whitaker, 1975).

Since this book focuses primarily on intimate relationships between two adults, this chapter will only describe therapeutic interventions appropriate for couples and will not review interventions specifically designed for parents and children. Consistent with the increasing overlap between the domains of marital and family therapy, however, many of the therapeutic perspectives and techniques discussed here are also highly relevant to the treatment of families. Also, marital therapy is often used to address such problems as alcoholism, anxiety disorders and the like that may reside with one partner. Some of the assessments of marital therapy are concerned with its use for various problems. We will focus as much as possible on the use of intervention for repairing the relationships.

Most of the work described here has focused on marriage. This doesn't mean that the value of these programs and therapies is restricted to married couples or to heterosexuals. Many of the interventions can be useful for any significant intimate relationship, regardless of the legal status of that relationship or the sexual orientation of the partners.

Formats

Even when we restrict our discussion to couples therapy, there are many ways that therapy can take place:

Individual. One therapist and one client discuss together the client's relationship.

Collaborative. Each of two clients has a therapist, and the two therapists consult each other about their clients.

Concurrent. One therapist sees each of the two clients in separate, individual sessions.

Conjoint. One therapist sees both clients together in the same session. Sometimes, there are cotherapists (often one man and one woman) involved in the conjoint sessions.

Conjoint group. One therapist (or a pair of therapists) works with a group of couples in group sessions.

As you read this list of the different types of therapeutic modalities used in marital therapy, you may have noticed that they line up on a dimension running from more individually oriented to more relationally oriented. In many ways, this dimension reflects the development of the field, as more individually oriented approaches have given way to the more relationally oriented formats. Currently, conjoint therapy is chosen most often, and the use of conjoint groups is increasing.

Professionals Helping Partners to Repair Relationships: Five Theoretical Orientations

Theoretical discussions about therapy often resemble theological disputes from the Middle Ages: passionate, seemingly endless, and sometimes extraordinarily obscure. They are also necessary, as therapists try to find some guidelines to help them in the incredibly complicated task of trying to help other people. Let's consider briefly some of the classic, major theoretical frameworks adopted by marital therapists.

Psychodynamic Approaches

Orthodox psychoanalysis as developed by Sigmund Freud in the early twentieth century was a resolutely one-at-a-time process. There was one therapist (the "analyst") and one client, and this arrangement was seen as critical to the effectiveness of the treatment. The client was expected to transfer his or her central unconscious conflicts onto the relationship with the analyst (the "transference neurosis"); only by working through this transference relationship could the client gain insight and be in a position to change his or her feelings and behavior. It was believed that if other people were present during therapy, the transference relationship would be damaged, and therapeutic improvement would not occur.

Many of the founders of family therapy came from psychoanalytic backgrounds, and their insistence on seeing more than one client at a time represented a dramatic break with the analytic tradition. In recent years, however, it has become more accepted that basic Freudian and more general psychodynamic principles can coexist with a relational focus and a conjoint form (Dare, 1986; Scharff, 1995).

Most marital therapists working from a psychodynamic orientation stress three fundamental propositions:

1. In the way they choose a mate and the manner in which they interact in marriage, people are often acting out their unconscious conflicts.
2. Many unconscious conflicts stem from events that took place in a person's family of origin.
3. The major therapeutic goal is for the clients to gain insight into their unconscious conflicts—to understand why they feel and act the way they do, so that they may have the freedom to choose to feel and act differently.

Box 15.1 provides an example of marital therapy from a psychodynamic perspective.

Rogerian Approaches

Based on work by Carl Rogers, Rogerian (or "client-centered") therapy views psychological difficulties as being caused by faulty socialization. As people grow up, they can become engulfed by the need to gain love and approval; thus, they may grow away from their true needs and desires, substituting instead a "false self" designed to win social acceptance. Rogerian therapists try to help their clients to discover their "true selves"—their true feelings and needs—by providing clients with acceptance ("unconditional positive regard") and empathic understanding. This acceptance is directed toward the person and does not mean that the Rogerian therapist approves or encourages destructive behavior. Indeed, helping clients to make the distinction between respect for a person and reaction to his or her behavior is one of the major goals of client-centered therapy. Although Guerney's (1977) Conjugal Relationship Enhancement program is more structured and directive than most Rogerian approaches, the aim of the CRE program to increase warmth, acceptance, and empathy between partners fits well within the Rogerian perspective.

BOX 15.1

A Psychodynamic Approach to Marital Therapy

A common problem within couples is the dispute over who is to assume how many and which household tasks. Although the wife may be operating from a vantage point of equality and symmetry, neither she nor her husband may recognize that a shaky sense of masculine identity underlies his stubborn resistance to sharing the household duties. The therapist must keep in mind that any adequate solution must consider both spouses' positions.

Negotiating cannot be a simple matter of working out percentages of time or the availability of each. Since unconscious feelings play a part in creating the problem, a purely cognitive negotiating approach is doomed to failure. Absolutely essential is that the therapist have at least some awareness of the contributing problems. Without necessarily working toward greater awareness of the threat posed to the husband by his wife's requests, the therapist may guide them toward some resolution wherein more feminine-related duties are undertaken by the wife and those less feminine by the husband. In this way the therapist, through added awareness, can prevent the negotiating approach from completely failing.

The following example is one that on the surface would appear open to negotiating but where initially it failed completely. In one session the spouses were disputing the wife's opening of her husband's mail. Because of the intensity of their convictions, these seemed like irreconcilable differences not open for compromise, since each spouse remained fixed in the rightness of his or her position.

Any simple and immediately obvious compromise solution, such as the husband agreeing to let his wife see his mail after he had opened it, was no solution for either. The wife felt she had a right to share her husband's mail; he felt she was intruding on his rights. Obviously, reality negotiations about how to deal with the letter-opening disagreements were not going to work. Much more was necessary for the spouses to understand what their disagreement was all about. It is axiomatic, when obvious solutions are not grasped, that the therapist must point the couple toward the task of understanding why not.

The therapist began by encouraging both to discuss their feelings and thoughts with respect to the problem. After some time and effort, both spouses began to better understand the reasons for the intensity of each other's feelings, and each became less entrenched in maintaining his or her own view. The husband's reluctance was expressed as feeling like a child again with "mother" snooping into his affairs. Once his wife viewed his protest in this context, her own attitude changed; she had previously interpreted the behavior as her husband's wish not to share things with her. Being able to understand his behavior as not aimed at her allowed her to feel less need to press for inclusion in this way. At the same time it opened up an opportunity for them to discuss her feelings of being left out more than she wished, and it allowed them to explore more acceptable ways of alleviating both of these feelings. Examples like these stress how superficial the therapeutic work may be if it stays with and focuses only on a solution to the surface problem without promoting an understanding of what needs are served by the resistance to negotiating.

Source: Ables & Brandsma, 1977.

Systems Approaches

When family therapists decided they needed to see the whole family in therapy, they also realized they needed a different conceptualization of psychological problems. Instead of locating the problem in a person, they tried to see the problem as part of the entire family system. Thus, symptomatic behavior on the part of one member of the family (e.g., a drug-abusing teenager) was viewed:

Not as an individual problem—e.g., the emotional disturbance of the teenager

Not as an individual problem caused by the social environment—e.g., by the poor parenting of a resentful mother and withdrawn father

But as behavior that is functional for the entire family system—e.g., the mother and father are able to feel closer to each other as they try to manage the child, and the child receives the attention of both parents.

This concept of the family—or any other relational unit—as a system that is maintained by the behaviors (both healthy and unhealthy) of its members is shared by all existing family system theories (Aylmer, 1986; Todd, 1986). Beyond this basic concept, however, these theories differ widely. Steinglass (1978, 1987), for example, has examined some of the considerable variation in both practice and belief among system theorists. The range of this variation is strikingly evident in Hoffman's (1981) survey of the field, where she describes five major "schools" of family system theories and five "great originals"—charismatic leaders in the family therapy movement who each established separate approaches of their own. Looking for shared assumptions is a dangerous enterprise in the face of such diversity, but a few constants do seem to emerge:

A focus on the individual's differentiation from the family system—that is, on the need to learn how to be both separate and close in relationships.

An emphasis on the process of communication, as communication both reflects how the system operates and serves to stabilize its operation.

An emphasis on the structure of the relationship system: the roles people play, the coalitions they form, their places in the family intergenerational hierarchy.

The assumption that unhealthy people reflect unhealthy but stable relationship systems. Thus, a major goal of systems therapy is to destabilize the system so that healthier, more flexible relationships can develop.

An example of marital therapy from a systems approach is presented in Box 15.2.

Behavioral Approaches

As with psychodynamic and Rogerian approaches, behavioral marital therapy (BMT) evolved from an individual approach into a set of techniques to be used with couples. The behavioral approach to marital therapy was first described in a 1969 article by Stuart, in which he established its fundamental principles. For

---

BOX 15.2

A Systems Approach to Marital Therapy

A couple was seen in conjoint therapy after one interview with the woman triggered a stormy depression, which was accompanied by bursts of unbearable anxiety and somatic symptoms such as daily vomiting, headaches, and abdominal pain. The proposition of the therapist that there was some behavior in the non-symptomatic partner that preceded and contributed to explain the [wife's] symptoms was met with total incredulity by both partners. In a subsequent crisis of the symptomatology that followed a period of quiescence, the therapist was able to detect and show to both members that when the husband started to experience anxiety due to mounting responsibilities in his complex job, the wife would respond to that cue with a flare of symptoms. Immediately, the husband would become involved in taking care of her, and simultaneously his anxiety would vanish, freeing him for

an effective performance at work (which became quite shaky due to his anxiety once when she was on vacation and a new requirement of his job took place). As a result of this observation, the therapist expressed his worries about what would happen to the husband if her symptoms subsided . . ., suggested to her that she produce symptoms out of phase . . . and centered his attention on the husband's anxiety, acknowledging the wife's valuable contribution whenever she reported experiencing symptoms. . . . The whole symptomatic pattern broke within three months, after five years of plaguing the couple's life, as they replaced their hidden homeostatic agreement with one that was more mutual and did not require the presence of symptoms.

Source: Sluzki, 1978.

Stuart and the behavioral marital therapists who came after him, a distressed marriage is defined in terms of a low level of reinforcing exchanges between the partners. Because they do not reinforce positive behavior toward each other, the partners either withdraw from the marital interaction or try to control each other's behavior in coercive, punishing ways. BMT tries to increase the level of positive, reinforcing exchanges between the two people, as well as to decrease their negative, punishing exchanges.

Although BMT has many variations (Weiss, 1978), there seems to be a set of three common procedures that are used by most behavioral marital therapists to increase reinforcing exchanges (Jacobson & Margolin, 1979; Liberman, Wheeler, de Visser, Kuehnel, & Kuehnel, 1980; Stuart, 1980):

1. Direct instructions by the therapist to increase positive behaviors that the partners want. These can be actions that a partner requests ("I really enjoy it when you rub my back") or actions generated by general efforts to please the partner. For example, on "love days" (Weiss, Hops, & Patterson, 1973), one partner deliberately sets out to please the other partner in as many different ways as he or she can think of.

2. Teaching the partners communication and problem-solving skills. Communication skills training in BMT is similar to that used in the PRIMES pro-

TABLE 15.3. Two Different Types of Contingency Contracts

QUID PRO QUO
Husband agrees to clean the bathroom every Saturday. Wife agrees to do laundry every Sunday. Wife does laundry on Sunday only when husband has cleaned bathroom on Saturday. Husband cleans bathroom only if wife did laundry on previous Sunday.

GOOD FAITH
Contract A
Husband agrees to clean bathroom every Saturday. On those Saturdays when he does, he chooses the activity for the evening, and the wife assumes responsibility for reservations and a babysitter.
Contract B
Wife agrees to do laundry every Sunday. When and only when she does, husband will assume all responsibility for children on Sunday nights, including baths, undressing, and putting to bed.

Source: Jacobson & Margolin, 1979.

gram. In contrast to the PRIMES program, however, the emphasis in BMT is on the instrumental value of communication as a necessary ingredient for good problem solving. BMT also directly teaches problem-solving skills, such as those included in Harrell and Guerney's (1976) behavioral-exchange enrichment program.

3. Working out contracts. The last step in problem solving during behavioral marital therapy is making a written agreement about behavior change. Often such contracts are unilateral, noncontingent ones where one partner agrees to perform a certain behavior on specified occasions without any reward for performance or penalty for noncompliance. BMT may also include contingency contracts. Some behavioral therapists advocate a **quid pro quo contingency contract,** in which behavior change by one partner is directly linked to behavior change by the other (Jacobson & Margolin, 1979). Other BMT therapists, concerned about the "who's going to change first" dilemma, suggest **"good-faith" contracts**—parallel agreements in which the behavior change of each partner is reinforced by privileges earned (Weiss, Birchler, & Vincent, 1974). An example of the difference between quid pro quo and good-faith contracts is provided in Table 15.3. Box 15.3 describes a marital therapy case from the behavioral perspective.

Cognitive Approaches

The importance of beliefs and expectations in affecting behavior is central to rational-emotive therapy as developed by Albert Ellis. In their 1961 book, Ellis and Harper applied this perspective to marital problems. At first, the response to this kind of cognitive approach to marital difficulties was less than overwhelming. During the 1980s, however, the "cognitive revolution" in all of psychology began to have a major effect on therapeutic interventions with couples

---

BOX 15.3

A Behavioral Approach to Marital Therapy

Mr. and Mrs. O'Sullivan were referred to the Stony Brook marital therapy program by a local mental health clinic that had a lengthy waiting list. They presented themselves as follows in the initial interview.

Sharon: An attractive 32-year-old woman who said that the major marital problems were lack of communication, lack of mutual interests, sexual naiveté, and decreasing affection. She felt that she had a low tolerance for frustration and that she was depressed. She was a housewife with three children, ages eight, five, and three. Sharon was very dissatisfied with the marriage, she reported feeling like a prisoner, and she resented her husband's "overinvolvement" in Alcoholics Anonymous.

Paul: A neat, reserved 35-year-old salesman who noted only one major marital problem, lack of communication. However, he reported that his wife displayed misdirected anger and had a minimal tolerance for the shortcomings of others. Paul had been a heavy drinker since his college graduation and throughout their 12 years of marriage. Fortunately, he had been abstinent for the past three years, during which he was an active member of A.A.

This couple was seen for a total of 10 conjoint sessions and one initial one-hour interview with each spouse. Therapy was deemed successful by the therapist and both clients. The major treatment procedures included:

1. Teaching communication skills—particular emphasis was placed on listening without interrupting and minimizing punitive statements and questions that sounded like declarations.

2. Encouraging Sharon to engage in more activities outside the home (for example, a prayer group, a women's

---

(Epstein, 1982; Fincham, Bradbury, & Beach, 1990). Many therapists from differing theoretical orientations are now sensitive to cognitive factors. Two cognitive factors that are commonly addressed in marital therapy are unrealistic expectations and causal attributions (Baucom & Epstein, 1990; Beck, 1988; Margolin, 1987).

According to Ellis and Harper (1961), marital problems come about when a person's unrealistic expectations for a spouse's perfection are disconfirmed by the spouse's behavior. This disconfirmation leads to irrational and catastrophic thoughts about the self ("I must be worthless for him or her to act like this") or the partner ("He or she is a terrible, vicious person to act like this"). Such thoughts trigger an intense emotional reaction of rage and despair, as well as an escalating level of irrational behavior toward the partner.

In developing their Relationship Belief Inventory, Eidelson and Epstein (1982) identified five dysfunctional expectations about intimate relationships:

1. Disagreement is destructive. The belief that any kind of disagreement between intimate partners is necessarily harmful and destructive to their relationship.

group, and Al Anon) to increase the positive feedback she might obtain from people other than her husband.

3. Encouraging both Sharon and Paul to volunteer to do things that satisfied each other's needs. They were asked to sign a weekly therapy plan sheet to indicate that they understood the nature of their behavior change agreements and that they were committed to making these changes. The necessity of mutual compromise as a vehicle for alleviating distress was emphasized.

4. Prompting Paul to display some form of affectionate behavior once per day as improvements were made in the relationship.

5. Helping Sharon learn to ask Paul directly to meet more of her needs—especially her needs for his affection. In brief, she was encouraged to be more expressive of her needs.

6. Asking Sharon and Paul to entertain the notion that her criticism of A.A. and Paul's involvement in it (for example, "Most of the members are sick," and "You spend too much time there") resulted from his failure to be affectionate and to tell her at least several hours before going to an A.A. meeting that he needed to go that evening.

7. Having Sharon contemplate the possibility that when Paul went to bed before she did and politely said "Good night," he was not putting her down and she need not feel jealous.

In summary, the treatment procedures included:

1. Communication training
2. Negotiation and compromise
3. Therapist's suggestions that Sharon find social reinforcers outside the marriage
4. Therapist's suggestion that Paul be more affectionate
5. Insight, that is, reinterpretation or relabeling of certain behaviors

Source: O'Leary & Turkewitz, 1978.

2. Mindreading is expected. The belief that partners who truly love each other should be able to sense each other's needs without direct communication.
3. Partners cannot change. The belief that people cannot change, and, therefore, the relationship is also fixed and unchangeable.
4. Sexual performance must be perfect. The belief that one's sexual performance must always be perfect and without flaw.
5. The sexes are different. The belief that men and women differ so radically in their personalities and in what they want in relationships that they cannot find common ground.

Many of these beliefs, and the problems they can create, have been discussed in previous chapters in this book. In their research, Eidelson and Epstein found that reduced marital satisfaction was associated with each of them. The belief that disagreement is destructive had a particularly high association with marital dissatisfaction among both distressed and nondistressed couples. Satir (1967), a leading family systems therapist, has vividly described the way that some families expect total love to equal total agreement. When, inevitably, disagreement arises, it cannot be acknowledged openly because it threatens the security of all the members of the family; thus, disagreements must go "underground." Such hidden disagreements are then revealed only indirectly through destructive patterns of behavior and communication within the family.

For therapists who emphasize the role of irrational expectations in contributing to marital distress, one of the major goals of therapy is to replace irrational beliefs with more rational ones. Typically, this involves helping the couple to realize that both have unrealistic expectations and standards, to understand the damage that such beliefs can cause, and to develop more explicit and flexible perspectives.

Causal attributions are a second cognitive factor associated with marital dissatisfaction. As described in chapter 12, distressed couples are more likely to rely on distress-maintaining attributions, blaming their partners' unchangeable characteristics for their negative behaviors and dismissing their positive behaviors as temporary. Distress-maintaining attributions involve both the locus of attribution (internal to the partner versus external) and the stability of the perceived cause (enduring versus temporary). In his discussion of the role of cognitive factors in marital therapy, Hurvitz (1970) placed particular emphasis on the stability dimension. According to Hurvitz, one of the major problems in distressed marriages is that partners generate "terminal hypotheses" for each other's behavior, blaming the behavior on unchangeable factors. Such hypotheses are terminal because they are a dead end for the relationship, indicating that change and improvement are not possible. In contrast, "instrumental hypotheses" link the current behavior to causes that are subject to change. Hurvitz proposed that a major goal in marital therapy is to help guide the couple away from their terminal hypotheses into considering and exploring instrumental hypotheses.

Some support for Hurvitz's formulation was obtained in the research by Eidelson and Epstein (1982) on irrational beliefs. Among nondistressed couples in their sample, the belief that partners cannot change was not associated with marital satisfaction. However, among the distressed couples, who were all beginning marital therapy, the belief that partners cannot change was strongly associated with lower levels of marital satisfaction. For these couples, a terminal hypothesis of the impossibility of change may have been doubly stressful. Not only did they regard the negative events in their marriages as unchangeable, but they may well have been applying the same hypothesis to therapy itself. Thus, they found themselves committed to a process of change without having much, if any, hope that change could occur. It seems reasonable to suppose that before therapy can be effective, those participating in it must believe that it has some chance of working.

Recent Directions in Therapy

During the 1980s and 1990s, approaches to therapy became more integrative (Jacobson & Gurman, 1986). Behavior therapists made a serious effort to expand their therapeutic vision and procedures, asking such questions as, "Is there a place for passion, play, and other nonnegotiable dimensions?" in marital therapy (Margolin, 1983). Similarly, psychodynamic and family therapists became more comfortable with using behaviorally based training programs to improve communication and problem-solving skills (Robin & Foster, 1989). And, today, marital therapists of all persuasions are relying more on systems theory and focusing more on cognitive factors. New therapies combining cognitive and behavioral approaches have emerged (Jacobson & Christensen, 1996).

Emotionally focused couple therapy (EFT) has also gained prominence (Johnson & Greenberg, 1995; Johnson, Hunsley, Greenberg, & Schindler, 1999). This approach draws heavily on an attachment perspective. From the perspective of EFT, the key factors in marital distress are "absorbing states of distressed affect and the constrained, destructive interactional patterns" linked to this affect (Johnson et al., 1999, p. 68). In attachment terms, marital distress is understood as separation distress and an insecure bond—the partners have lost connection such that the relationship no longer provides a secure base. EFT therapists see threats to attachment triggering a predictable sequence of affects: Typically protest and anger will occur first, followed by clinging and seeking, then depression and despair, and finally, if the attachment figure does not respond, detachment and separation.

Emotionally focused therapists are concerned with both emotional responses and the patterns of interaction between the partners. They try to access and reprocess the partners' emotional experiences and restructure their interaction patterns. EFT therapy builds on nine steps clustered into three basic components. First, by creating an alliance with the clients and identifying interaction patterns that maintain attachment insecurity, EFT therapists try to de-escalate problematic interaction cycles. Second, they try to shift the interaction patterns. This involves getting partners to (a) accept their own disowned needs, (b) accept their partner's evolving construction of the situation, and (c) create emotional engagement between themselves. Third, EFT therapists try to bring about new cycles of attachment behavior. By establishing more effective ways of interacting, the marital partners can better satisfy their attachment needs. Johnson et al. (1999, p. 67) claim that EFT is "now recognized as one of the most researched and most effective approaches to changing distressed marital relationships."

The Success of Professional Help in Repairing Relationships

Both therapists and clients invest much energy, expense, and time in marital therapy, so presumably they feel it has a chance of working. That seems reasonable, but how do we know if it's true? Efforts to assess the success of therapy have been classified into two categories: efficacy (including clinical trials) and effectiveness research (Seligman, 1995). **Treatment efficacy** refers to validly determining the effects of a given treatment in comparison to an alternative or no treatment, as tested under controlled conditions. The fundamental question in efficacy research is whether a beneficial effect of treatment can be demonstrated.

A common feature of this approach is the random assignment of clients to conditions, with some receiving treatment and others assigned to either a waiting list control or placebo treatment condition. The type of treatment (e.g., behavioral, cognitive) offered to clients is tightly prescribed and monitored to insure that it is being faithfully administered. Unlike so-called double-blind drug studies, in which neither patients nor doctors know which patients are getting the experimental treatment, in psychotherapy outcome research therapists, and often patients, know which patients are assigned to which treatment conditions. Patients are usually seen for a fixed number of sessions, and their progress is usually assessed on specific, carefully measured outcomes. Outcome measures are usually taken at the end of treatment and are often taken at one or more intervals after the conclusion of the therapy. These follow-up assessments are usually for periods of weeks or months rather than years.

Critics of efficacy research have argued that the conditions under which therapy is normally provided are typically not like those in neatly controlled studies. Patients usually keep seeing therapists until they have improved or quit. If one treatment approach doesn't work, practicing therapists are likely to try another. Practicing therapists usually help clients to improve in many domains of life, not just along certain parameters.

To augment efficacy research, Seligman (1995) has proposed **effectiveness** studies to focus on what patients get from therapy that is conducted under ordinary, nonexperimental conditions. To assess effectiveness, Seligman used data from a *Consumer Reports* satisfaction survey of people who had participated in therapy. They were asked various questions pertaining to their problems, the therapists they saw, length of treatment, costs, their satisfaction with treatment, their judgment of how much they improved, and the like. Effectiveness research has its limitations, too, such as sampling biases, lack of control conditions, having to ask patients to retrospectively recall their experiences, and lack of specificity about the problems being treated or the techniques being used (see Jacobsen & Christensen, 1996).

Efficacy or clinical trials research is by far the most common form of therapy outcome assessment. When done well, it allows researchers to confidently infer that the treatment administered in the study caused the patient to improve. Effectiveness research, although much less common, solicits information about treatment outcomes under conditions that reflect the experiences of most clients. Despite the debate about the merits and demerits of these approaches, we believe that having both ultimately provides a stronger basis on which to evaluate therapy. Interestingly, several of the key conclusions reached by each tradition are the same (Jacobsen & Christensen, 1996).

To get to the bottom line: *therapy works!* There have been thousands of studies of the efficacy and effectiveness of psychological treatments. Consistently, and with what some authors have called "monotonous regularity," they have demonstrated that therapy clients improve. This conclusion holds for efficacy studies, for effectiveness studies, and for studies of interventions for couples experiencing marital distress. For our purposes, let us look at interventions for couples. Christensen and Heavey (1999) note that couples in marital therapy are almost twice as likely to improve as those in control conditions. According to calculations they report, roughly 65 percent of couples in marital therapy show improvement, with perhaps about half of that group starting out as distressed yet becoming nondistressed after therapy (Christensen & Heavey, 1999, pp. 167 and 168). This certainly is not a perfect record, and there may be times when therapists believe the best outcome of treatment is separation rather than repair. But, in our opinion, for couples wanting to stay together (or separate more constructively), therapy is worth a try.

The practice and study of the effectiveness of psychotherapy has been marked by disputes over which theoretical tradition is most effective. In the latter part of the twentieth century, there were usually two opposing sides on this issue: the behaviorists and the "nonbehaviorists" (including psychodynamic, client-centered, and systems approaches). Simple comparisons between behavioral and eclectic, humanistic, and unclassified orientations have shown behavioral approaches to be superior (Shadish, Ragsdale, Glaser, & Montgomery, 1995), but this may reflect that behavioral studies often have other characteristics associated with treatment success (e.g., the use of specific outcome criteria). Overall the authors of this meta-analysis as well as Christensen and Heavey (1999) agree that "No orientation is yet demonstrably superior to any other" Shadish et al., 1995, p. 345). Often when studies do find one therapy superior to another, there is an alliance effect: the outcome favors the treatment with which the senior investigator is associated.

Another aspect of the dialogue occurring among therapists and researchers from different theoretical backgrounds involves their recognition of nonspecific factors that influence the course of all therapies. Most would agree that two such factors are particularly important in marital therapy. First, couples need to learn and use methods of good communication. As emphasized in chapter 5, clear and constructive communication is essential for a good relationship. The second factor is the therapist's skill in establishing a positive working relationship with both partners (Martin, Garske, & Davis, 2000). Regardless of the therapist's theoretical inclination, if such a relationship is not established, therapy is unlikely to work. These two factors are essential in marital therapies where the couple want to bring their relationship back from the brink of dissolution. Even when dissolution occurs, these factors are likely to help partners through their transition into a positive postromantic relationship.

CHAPTER SUMMARY

This chapter was organized around what people themselves versus professionals do for three relational challenges: forming new social bonds, maintaining and enhancing existing relations, and repairing distressed relationships. Available evidence suggests that people more commonly deal with relationship issues without professional help than with it.

Fostering Social Bonding

Strategies People Use to Initiate New Relationships. Among the strategies people use to develop new relationships are personal ads, dating services, and so-called loneliness businesses, such as singles bars that offer their patrons opportunities for meeting others. Traditional sex roles are often manifested in the personal ads that people place and to which they most often respond. In using video dating services, clients focus on fairly simple information, such as the physical appearance and age of potential dates. The success rate of such services appears to be fairly low, but users like the number of people they can consider as partners and the speed with which they can review potential dates.

Once people meet, both children and adults report various interaction strategies, such as being nice and showing respect, that they use to promote the development of a relationship.

Interventions Professionals Offer to Help Clients Initiate New Relationships. Clinical psychologists often give person-centered explanations for why clients have difficulty forming new relationships (e.g., the client's deficient interpersonal skills or dysfunctional beliefs). They offer social skill training and cognitive therapies as remedies.

Maintaining and Enhancing Existing Relationships

Partners Maintaining Their Own Relationships. People have a large variety of conscious and unconscious strategies that they use to maintain and enhance existing relationships. For instance, people use positivity (being positive and cheerful), openness (self-disclosure and open discussion about the relationship), assurances (showing love and faithfulness, stressing commitment), networking (spending time with common friends), and sharing tasks (especially household chores). These strategies tend to be used in a variety of different relationships, but there are other strategies that are unique or adapted in special ways for specific forms of relationships such as gay relationships, blended families, multicultural relationships, and cross-sex friendships.

Professionals Helping Partners to Maintain Their Relationships. Both religious and secular groups provide professionally developed premarital programs, which range from lectures to more active learning experiences for the participants. The more structured programs emphasize improvement in communication skills; behavioral programs also teach basic features of the behavioral approach, such as how to make contracts about behavior changes. Typically, the more structured educational programs are carried out by a trainer (or cotrainers) working with a group of couples. Procedures include role plays, assigned reading, and practicing at home.

As relationships mature, both religious and secular groups provide professionally developed marital enrichment programs, which aim to enhance the relationship and prevent problems before they develop. There are a number of more structured marital enrichment programs; some emphasize communication skills, while others are more behavioral in their approach. On average, premarital and marital enrichment programs appear to be modestly effective, with communication skills showing the most lasting improvement. These programs are probably not suitable for highly distressed couples, who should be referred to more appropriate therapeutic services.

Professionals have also developed enrichment programs for partners wishing to have a more dynamic sexual relationship. Hurlbert and Apt's (1995) program resembles Masters and Johnson's approach to the treatment of sexual dysfunction: It includes both systematic behavioral techniques (i.e., coital alignment and self-stimulation) and an emphasis on the relational context of sexuality. This program has succeeded in helping women to achieve orgasm during intercourse.

Repairing Relationships

Partners Repairing Their Own Relationships. There is an overlap in what people report they do to maintain and repair their relationships. In one study, commonly mentioned repair strategies included talking, especially about the problem, and spending time together.

Professionals Helping Partners to Repair Relationships: History and Formats. Marital therapy developed in response to clients who came and asked for help. Family therapy, on the other hand, developed in response to professional concerns that adequate treatment of one family member required the participation of all family members. Both marital and family therapies can be distinguished from individual therapies by their focus on relationships.

There are many different formats for marital therapy. Currently, conjoint therapy (where one therapist or two cotherapists see both clients in the same session) is widely used. The use of conjoint groups (where a group of couples participate in group sessions) is also quite common.

Professionals Helping Partners to Repair Relationships: Five Theoretical Orientations. Some of the major theoretical orientations adopted by marital therapists include the following: The psychodynamic approach emphasizes the role of unconscious conflicts in influencing behavior and the need for insight into these conflicts as a prerequisite for change. The Rogerian (or client-centered) approach views therapy as a process during which the therapist provides acceptance and empathic understanding in order to help clients regain a sense of their true feelings and needs. In a systems approach to therapy, it is assumed that a person's unhealthy behavior reflects an unhealthy but stable relational system; for change to occur, the system must be destabilized. Behavioral approaches define a distressed relationship in terms of a low level of reinforcing exchanges between the partners. Contracting is a behavioral technique used to increase positive exchanges. Contracts may be noncontingent—where one partner agrees to perform a certain behavior desired by the other partner without any reward or penalty—or contingent. Contingency contracts may be *quid pro quo*, in which behavior change by one partner is directly linked to behavior change by the other, or they may be *good-faith* parallel agreements, in which the behavior change of each partner is reinforced by earned privileges. Cognitive approaches to marital therapy emphasize the role of unrealistic expectations and causal attributions in contributing to marital distress. Some of the irrational beliefs associated with low levels of marital satisfaction include assuming that disagreement is always destructive and that change is impossible. The irrational belief that change is impossible is similar to a certain kind of causal attribution, "terminal hypotheses," in which negative behaviors are attributed to unchangeable factors within the partners or outside the marriage. A more hopeful kind of causal attribution, "instrumental hypotheses," views current behavior as produced by causes that are subject to change.

In recent years, more integrated approaches, such as those combining cognitive and behavioral approaches, have been developed. Another promising approach is *emotionally focused couple therapy* (EFT), which builds in part on an attachment theoretical framework.

The Success of Professional Help in Repairing Relationships. Two ways of studying the success of psychotherapy are *efficacy* and *effectiveness* research. Efficacy studies involve rigorous experimental procedures and designs, while effectiveness studies focus on the experiences of clients who obtain therapy under more typical, nonexperimental conditions. A great deal of evidence demonstrates that therapy in general, and couples therapy in particular, have beneficial outcomes. Estimates suggest that roughly 65 percent of couples in marital therapy show improvement, with perhaps about half of that group starting out as distressed and becoming nondistressed after therapy. Although there has been considerable debate over which form of treatment is most effective, once appropriate controls are imposed, no single approach appears to be clearly superior to the rest. Therapy outcome research does, however, show the importance of nonspecific factors such as clear, constructive communication between partners and the development of a trusting relationship between the therapist and both partners.

Concluding Reflections. In this chapter we have examined ways of fostering relationships. As our analysis implies, there are challenges to getting and keeping relationships. Throughout this book we have tried to identify both the benefits and the difficulties of ongoing relationships. But when all is said and done, in our opinion the benefits of relationships outweigh the costs. People consider relationships among the ingredients that make their lives most meaningful. As Aristotle stated centuries ago, humans are social animals. The survival and success of our species is built on our capacity for interdependency.

Relationships have varied across time and cultures. Social trends come and go. We see such changes as longer life expectancy, a high divorce rate, urbanization, and greater tolerance of diverse groups. Each of these trends undoubtedly intertwines with our relationships. Besides societal changes that affect relationships, we as individuals have different relational needs and orientations. Dyads have their own properties. Relationships are diverse and will undoubtedly remain so.

Yet we agree with Baumeister and Leary's (1995) assertion that humans have a pervasive need to belong. As they state:

> More precisely, the belongingness hypothesis is that human beings have a pervasive drive to form and maintain at least a minimum quantity of lasting, positive, and significant interpersonal relationships. Satisfying this drive involves two criteria: First, there is a need for frequent, affectively pleasant interactions with a few other people, and, second, these interactions must take place in the context of a temporally stable and enduring framework of affective concern for each other's welfare. (Baumeister & Leary, 1995, p. 497)

There are and will be many ways of getting to this goal, yet in one way or another we believe people will continue striving for it. As you pursue your relationships, we wish you the very best in the process.

References

Abbey, A. (1982). Sex differences in attributions for friendly behavior: Do males misperceive females' friendliness? *Journal of Personality and Social Psychology, 42,* 830–838.

Abbey, A. (1987). Misperceptions of friendly behavior as sexual interest: A survey of naturally occurring incidents. *Psychology of Women Quarterly, 11,* 173–194.

Abbey, A., & Melby, C. (1986). The effects of nonverbal cues on gender differences in perceptions of sexual intent. *Sex Roles, 15,* 283–298.

Ables, B. S., & Brandsma, J. M. (1977). *Therapy for couples.* San Francisco: Jossey-Bass.

Acitelli, L. K. (1997). Sampling couples to understand them: Mixing the theoretical with the practical. *Journal of Social and Personal Relationships, 14,* 243–261.

Acitelli, L. K. (2001). Maintaining and enhancing a relationship by attending to it. In J. H. Harvey & A. E. Wenzel (Eds.), *Close romantic relationships: Maintenance and enhancement,* (pp. 153–167). Mahwah, NJ: Erlbaum.

Acitelli, L. K., Douvan, E., & Veroff, J. (1993). Perceptions of conflict in the first year of marriage: How important are similarity and understanding? *Journal of Social and Personal Relationships, 10,* 5–19.

Acitelli, L. K., & Young, A. M. (1996). Gender and thought in relationships. In G. J. O. Fletcher & J. Fitness (Eds.), *Knowledge structures in close relationships: A social psychological approach* (pp. 147–168). Mahwah, NJ: Erlbaum.

Acker, M., & Davis, M. H. (1992). Intimacy, passion and commitment in adult romantic relationships: A test of the Triangular Theory of Love. *Journal of Social and Personal Relationships, 9,* 21–50.

Adams, J. M., & Jones, W. H. (1997). The conceptualization of marital commitment: An integrative analysis. *Journal of Personality and Social Psychology, 72,* 1177–1196.

Adams, J. M., & Jones, W. H. (1999). Interpersonal commitment in historical perspective. In J. M. Adams & W. H. Jones (Eds.), *Handbook on interpersonal commitment and relationship stability* (pp. 3–33). New York: Kluwer Academic/Plenum.

Adams, M. (1971). The compassion trap. In V. Gornick & B. K. Moran (Eds.), *Woman in sexist society* (pp. 401–416). New York: Basic Books.

Adams, R. G., & Blieszner, R. (1995). Aging well with friends and family. *American Behavioral Scientist, 39,* 209–224.

Adams, R. G., & Blieszner, R. (1996). Midlife friendship patterns. In N. Vanzetti & S. Duck (Eds.), *A lifetime of relationships* (pp. 336–363). Pacific Grove, CA: Brooks/Cole.

Afifi, W. A., & Metts, S. (1998). Characteristics and consequences of expectation violations in close relationships. *Journal of Social and Personal Relationships, 15,* 365–392.

Agnew, C. R., Van Lange, P. A. M., Rusbult, C. E., & Langston, C. A. (1998). Cognitive interdependence: Commitment and the mental representation of close relationships. *Journal of Personality and Social Psychology, 74,* 939–954.

Aguinis, H., Simonsen, M. M., & Pierce, C. A. (1998). Effects of nonverbal behavior on perceptions of power bases. *Journal of Social Psychology, 138,* 455–470.

Ahrons, C. (1994). *The good divorce.* New York: HarperCollins.

Aida, Y., & Falbo, T. (1991). Relationships between marital satisfaction, resources, and power strategies. *Sex Roles, 24,* 43–56.

Ainsworth, M. D. S., Blehar, M. C., Waters, E., & Wall, S. (1978). *Patterns of attachment: A psychological study of the strange situation.* Hillsdale, NJ: Erlbaum.

Akerlind, I., & Hornquist, J. O. (1992). Loneliness and alcohol abuse: A review of evidences of an interplay. *Social Science and Medicine, 34,* 405–414.

Albrecht, S. L., & Kunz, P. R. (1980). The decision to divorce: A social exchange perspective. *Journal of Divorce, 3,* 319–337.

Allen, J. B., Kenrick, D. T., Linder, D. E., & McCall, M. A. (1989). Arousal and attribution: A response facilitation alternative to misattribution and negative-reinforcement models. *Journal of Personality and Social Psychology, 57,* 261–270.

Allen, K., & Ferrari, A. (1997). *101 of the world's most effective pickup lines.* New York: Ace Company Publishing.

Altman, I. (1973). Reciprocity of interpersonal exchange. *Journal of Theory of Social Behavior, 3,* 249–261.

Altman, I., & Taylor, D. A. (1973) *Social penetration: The development of interpersonal relationships.* New York: Holt, Rinehart & Winston.

Altman, I., Vinsel, A., & Brown, B. A. (1981). Dialectic conceptions in social psychology: An application to social penetration and privacy regulation. In L. Berkowitz (Ed.), *Advances in experimental social psychology* (Vol. 14, pp. 107–160), New York: Academic Press.

Altrocchi, I., & Crosby, R. D. (1989). Clarifying and measuring the concept of traditional vs. nontraditional roles in marriage. *Sex Roles, 20,* 639–648.

Amato, P. R. (1993). Children's adjustment to divorce: Theories, hypotheses, empirical support. *Journal of Marriage and the Family, 55,* 23–38.

Amato, P. R., & Gilbreth, J. G. (1999). Nonresident fathers and children's well-being: A meta-analysis. *Journal of Marriage and the Family, 61,* 557–573.

Amato, P. R., & Keith, B. (1991a). Parental divorce and adult well-being: A meta-analysis. *Journal of Marriage and the Family, 53,* 43–58.

Amato, P. R., & Keith, B. (1991b). Parental divorce and the well-being of children: A meta-analysis. *Psychological Bulletin, 110,* 26–46.

Amato, P. R., & Rogers, S. J. (1997). A longitudinal study of marital problems and subsequent divorce. *Journal of Marriage and the Family , 59,* 612–624.

Ambady, N., Hallahan, M., & Conner, B. (1999). Accuracy of judgments of sexual orientation from thin slices of behavior. *Journal of Personality and Social Psychology, 77,* 538–547.

Ambady, N., Hallahan, M., & Rosenthal, R. (1995). On judging and being judged accurately in zero-acquaintance situations. *Journal of Personality and Social Psychology, 69,* 518–529.

Ambady, N., & Rosenthal, R. (1993). Half a minute: Predicting teacher evaluations from thin slices of nonverbal behavior and physical attractiveness. *Journal of Personality and Social Psychology, 64,* 431–441.

Andersen, P. A., & Guerrero, L. K. (1998). Principles of communication and emotion in social interaction. In P. A. Andersen & L. K. Guerrero (Eds.), *Handbook of communication and emotion* (pp. 49–96). San Diego: Academic Press.

Anderson, C. A., & Harvey, R. J. (1988). Discriminating between problems in living: An examination of depression, loneliness, shyness, and social anxiety. *Journal of Social and Clinical Psychology, 6,* 482–491.

Anderson, C. A., Miller, R. S., Riger, A. L., Dill, J. C., & Sedikides, C. (1994) Behavioral and characterological attributional styles as predictors of depression and loneliness: Review, refinement, and test. *Journal of Personality and Social Psychology, 66,* 549–558.

Anderson, D. E., DePaulo, B. M., Sternglanz, W., & Walker, M. (1999, June). *Eagle-eyed or starry-eyed? Deception detection in close relationships.* Paper presented at the meeting of the International Network on Personal Relationships, Louisville, KY.

Anderson, J. L., Crawford, C. B., Nadeau, J., & Lindberg, T. (1992). Was the Duchess of Windsor right? A cross-cultural review of the socioecology of ideals of female body shape. *Ethology and Sociobiology, 13,* 197–227.

Andres, D., Gold, D., Berger, C., Kinch, R., & Gillett, P. (1983). Selected psychosocial characteristics of males: Their relationship to contraceptive use and abortion. *Personality and Social Psychology Bulletin, 9,* 387–396.

Antill, J. K. (1983). Sex role complementarity versus similarity in married couples. *Journal of Personality and Social Psychology, 45,* 145–155.

Archer, J. (2000). Sex differences in aggression between heterosexual partners: A meta-analytic review. *Psychological Bulletin, 126,* 651–680.

Archibald, F. S., Bartholomew, K. & Marx, R. (1995). Loneliness in early adolescence: A test of the cognitive discrepancy model of loneliness. *Personality and Social Psychology Bulletin, 21,* 296–301.

Argyle, M., & Henderson, M. (1984). The rules of friendship. *Journal of Social and Personal Relationships, 1,* 211–237.

Argyle, M., & Henderson, M. (1985). *The anatomy of friendships.* London: Penguin Books.

Arias, H., & O'Leary, K. D. (1985). Semantic and perceptual discrepancies in discordant and nondiscordant marriages. *Cognitive Therapy and Research, 9,* 1183–1197.

Aron, A., & Aron, E. N. (2000). Self-expansion motivation and including other in the self. In W. Ickes & S. Duck (Eds.), *The social psychology of personal relationships* (pp. 109–128). Chichester, England: Wiley.

Aron, A., Aron, E. N., & Allen, J. (1998). Motivations for unreciprocated love. *Personality and Social Psychology Bulletin, 24,* 787–796.

Aron, A., Dutton, D. G., Aron, E. N., & Iverson, A. (1989). Experiences of falling in love. *Journal of Social and Personal Relationships, 6,* 243–257.

Aron, A., Melinat, E., Aron, E. N., Vallone, R. D., & Bator, R. J. (1997). The experimental generation of interpersonal closeness: A procedure and some preliminary findings. *Personality and Social Psychology Bulletin, 23,* 363–377.

Aron, A., Norman, C. C., & Aron, E. N. (2001). Shared self-expanding activities as a means of maintaining and enhancing close romantic relationships. In J. H. Harvey & A. E. Wenzel (Eds.), *Close romantic relationships: Maintenance and enhancement,* (pp. 47–66). Mahwah, NJ: Erlbaum.

Aron, A., Norman, C. C., Aron, E. N., McKenna, C., & Heyman, R. E. (2000). Couples' shared participation in novel and arousing activities and experienced relationship quality. *Journal of Personality and Social Psychology, 78,* 273–284.

Aron, A., Paris, M., & Aron, E. N. (1995). Falling in love: Prospective studies of self-concept change. *Journal of Personality and Social Psychology, 69,* 1102–1112.

Aron, A., & Westbay, L. (1996). Dimensions of the prototype of love. *Journal of Personality and Social Psychology, 70,* 535–551.

Aronson, E., & Cope, V. (1968). My enemy's enemy is my friend. *Journal of Personality and Social Psychology, 8,* 8–12.

Arriaga, X. B., & Rusbult, C. E. (1998). Standing in my partner's shoes: Partner perspective taking and reactions to accommodative dilemmas. *Personality and Social Psychology Bulletin, 24,* 927–948.

Asch, S. E. (1946). Forming impressions of personality. *Journal of Abnormal and Social Psychology, 41,* 258–290.

Asendorpf, J. (1990). The expression of shyness and embarrassment. In W. R. Crozier (Ed.), *Shyness and embarrassment: Perspectives from social psychology* (pp. 87–118). Cambridge: Cambridge University Press.

Asendorpf, J. B., & Wilpers, S. (1998). Personality effects on social relationships. *Journal of Personality and Social Psychology, 74,* 1531–1544.

Asher, S. R., & Coie, J. D. (Eds.). (1990). *Peer rejection in childhood.* New York: Cambridge University Press.

Assh, S. D., & Byers, E. S. (1996). Understanding the co-occurrence of marital distress and depression in women. *Journal of Social and Personal Relationships, 13,* 537–552.

Attridge, M., & Berscheid, E. (1994). Entitlement in romantic relationships in the United States: A social-exchange perspective. In M. J. Lerner & G. Mikula (Eds.), *Entitlement and the affectional bond: Justice in close relationships* (pp. 117–147). New York: Plenum.

Aubé, J., Norcliffe, H., Craig, J., & Koestner, R. (1995). Gender characteristics and adjustment-related outcomes: Questioning the masculinity model. *Personality and Social Psychology Bulletin, 21,* 284–295.

Ault, L. K., Cunningham, M. R., & Bettler, R. F., Jr. (1999, June). *The role of others in individuals' embarrassing predicaments: Preventative face-saving as a social support behavior.* Paper presented at the meeting of the International Network for Personal Relationships, Louisville, KY.

Averill, J. R. (1982). *Anger and aggression: An essay on emotion.* New York: Springer.

Axtell, R. E. (1991). *Gestures: The do's and taboos of body language around the world.* New York: Wiley.

Aylmer, R. C. (1986). Bowen family systems marital therapy. In N. S. Jacobson & A. E. Gurman (Eds.), *Clinical handbook of marital therapy* (pp. 107–148). New York: Guilford.

Babad, E., Bernieri, F., & Rosenthal, R. (1989). Nonverbal communication and leakage in the behavior of biased and unbiased teachers. *Journal of Personality and Social Psychology, 56,* 89–94.

Bach, G. R., & Wyden, P. (1968). *The intimate enemy.* New York: Morrow.

Baeccman, C., Folkesson, P., & Norlander, T. (1999). Expectations of romantic relationships: A comparison between homosexual and heterosexual men with regard to Baxter's criteria. *Social Behavior and Personality, 27,* 363–374.

Bakeman, R., & Gottman, J. M. (1997). *Observing interaction: An introduction to sequential analysis* (2nd ed.). New York: Cambridge University Press.

Baldwin, M. W. (1995). Relational schemas and cognition in close relationships. *Journal of Social and Personal Relationships, 12,* 547–552.

Baldwin, M. W., & Fehr, B. (1995). On the instability of attachment style ratings. *Personal Relationships, 2,* 247–261.

Baldwin, M. W., & Keelan, J. P. R. (1999). Interpersonal expectations as a function of self-esteem and sex. *Journal of Social and Personal Relationships, 16,* 822–833.

Bank, B. J., & Hansford, S. L. (2000). Gender and friendship: Why are men's best same-sex friendships less intimate and supportive? *Personal Relationships, 7,* 63–78.

Bannester, E. M. (1969). Sociodynamics: An integrative theorem of power, authority, interfluence and love. *American Sociological Review, 34,* 374–393.

Barber, N. (1998). Secular changes in standards in bodily attractiveness in women: Tests of a reproductive model. *International Journal of Eating Disorders, 23,* 449–453.

Barber, N. (1999). Women's dress fashions as a function of reproductive strategy. *Sex Roles, 40*, 459–471.

Barenboim, C. (1981). The development of person perception in childhood and adolescence: From behavioral comparisons to psychological constructs to psychological comparisons. *Child Development, 52*, 129–144.

Barling, J. (1990). Employment and marital functioning. In F. D. Fincham & T. N. Bradbury (Eds.), *The psychology of marriage: Basic issues and applications* (pp. 201–225). New York: Guilford Press.

Barnes, K. E. (1971). Preschool play norms: A replication. *Developmental Psychology, 5*, 99–103.

Barnett, O. W., Miller-Perrin, C. L., & Perrin, R. D. (1997). *Family violence across the lifespan: An introduction.* Thousand Oaks, CA: Sage.

Bart, P. B., & O'Brien, P. H. (1985). *Stopping rape: Successful survival strategies.* New York: Pergamon.

Bartholomew, K. (1990). Avoidance of intimacy: An attachment perspective. *Journal of Personal and Social Relationships, 7*, 147–178.

Bartholomew, K., & Horowitz, L. M. (1991). Attachment styles among young adults: A test of a four-category model. *Journal of Personality and Social Psychology, 61*, 226–244.

Bartholomew, K., Landolt, M., & Oram, D. (1999). *Violence in male same-sex relationships: Prevalence, incidence, and injury.* Paper presented at the meeting of the American Psychological Association, Boston, MA.

Bartholomew, K., & Shaver, P. R. (1998). Methods of assessing adult attachment: Do they converge? In J. A. Simpson & W. S. Rholes (Eds.), *Attachment theory and close relationships* (pp. 25–45). New York: Guilford Press.

Baucom, D. H., & Epstein, N. (1990). *Cognitive-behavioral marital therapy.* New York: Brunner/Mazel.

Bauman, L. J., & Siegel, K. (1987). Misperception among gay men of the risk for AIDS associated with their sexual behavior. *Journal of Applied Social Psychology, 17*, 329–350.

Baumeister, R. F., & Bratslavsky, E. (1999). Passion, intimacy, and time: Passionate love as a function of change in intimacy. *Personality and Social Psychology Review, 3*, 49–67.

Baumeister, R. F., & Campbell, W. K. (1999). The intrinsic appeal of evil: Sadism, sensational thrills, and threatened egotism. *Personality and Social Psychology Review, 3*, 210–221.

Baumeister, R. F., Frankenauer, C., & Bratslavsky, E. (1999, October). *Bad is stronger than good.* Paper presented at the meeting of the Society for Experimental Social Psychology, St. Louis.

Baumeister, R. F., & Leary, M. R. (1995). The need to belong: Desire for interpersonal attachments as a fundamental human motivation. *Psychological Bulletin, 117*, 497–529.

Baumeister, R. F., & Wotman, S. R. (1992). *Breaking hearts: The two sides of unrequited love.* New York: Guilford Press.

Baumeister, R. F., Wotman, S. R., & Stillwell, A. M. (1993). Unrequited love: On heartbreak, anger, guilt, scriptlessness, and humiliation. *Journal of Personality and Social Psychology, 64*, 377–394.

Baxter, L. A. (1984). Trajectories of relationship disengagement. *Journal of Social and Personal Relationships, 1*, 29–48.

Baxter, L. A. (1987). Self-disclosure and relationship disengagement. In V. Derlega & J. H. Berg (Eds.), *Self-disclosure: Theory, research, and therapy* (pp. 155–174). New York: Plenum.

Baxter, L. A., Mazanec, M., Nicholson, J., Pittman, G., Smith, K., & West, L. (1997). Every-day loyalties and betrayals in personal relationships. *Journal of Social and Personal Relationships, 14,* 655–678.

Baxter, L. A., & Montgomery, B. M. (1997). Rethinking communication in personal relationships from a dialectical perspective. In S. Duck (Ed.), *Handbook of personal relationships: Theory, research, and interventions* (2nd ed., pp. 325–349). Chichester, England: Wiley.

Baxter, L. A., & Philpott, J. (1982). Attribution-based strategies for initiating and terminating relationships. *Communication Quarterly, 30,* 217–224.

Baxter, L. A., & Widenmann, S. (1993). Revealing and not revealing the status of romantic relationships to social networks. *Journal of Social and Personal Relationships, 10,* 321–337.

Baxter, L. A., & Wilmot, W. M. (1984). "Secret tests": Social strategies for acquiring information about the state of the relationship. *Human Communication Research. 11,* 171–201.

Baxter, L. A., & Wilmot, W. W. (1985). Taboo topics in close relationships. *Journal of Social and Personal Relationships, 2,* 253–269.

Baxter, L. A., Wilmot, W. W., Simmons, C. A., & Swartz, A. (1993). Ways of doing conflict: A folk taxonomy of conflict events in personal relationships. In P. J. Kalbfleisch (Ed.), *Interpersonal communication: Evolving interpersonal relationships* (pp. 89–107). Hillsdale, NJ: Erlbaum.

Bazargan, M., & Barbre, A. R. (1992). Self-reported memory problems among the Black elderly. *Educational Gerontology, 18,* 71–82.

Beck, A. T. (1988). *Love is never enough.* New York: Harper & Row.

Bell, R. A., Buerkel-Rothfuss, N. L., & Gore, K. E. (1987). "Did you bring the yarmulke for the cabbage patch kid?" The idiomatic communication of young lovers. *Human Communication Research, 14,* 47–67.

Belsky, J. (1990). Children and marriage. In F. D. Fincham & T. N. Bradbury (Eds.), *The psychology of marriage: Basic issues and applications* (pp. 172–200). New York: Guilford.

Bem, S. L. (1993). *The lenses of gender: Transforming the debate on sexual inequality.* New Haven: Yale University Press.

Benin, M. H., & Agostinelli, J. (1988). Husbands' and wives' satisfaction with the division of labor. *Journal of Marriage and the Family, 50,* 349–361.

Benjamin, M., & Irving, H. H. (1995). Research in family mediation: Review and implications. *Mediation Quarterly, 13,* 53–82.

Benschop, Y., & Doorewaard, H. (1998). Covered by equality: The gender subtext of organizations. *Organization Studies, 19,* 787–805.

Berg, J. H. (1984). Development of friendship between roommates. *Journal of Personality and Social Psychology, 46,* 346–356.

Berg, J. H., & Clark, M. S. (1986). Differences in social exchange between intimate and other relationships: Gradually evolving or quickly apparent? In V. J. Derlega & B. A. Winstead (Eds.), *Friendship and social interaction* (pp. 101–128). New York: Springer-Verlag.

Berg, J. H., & McQuinn, R. D. (1986). Attraction and exchange in continuing and noncontinuing dating relationships. *Journal of Personality and Social Psychology, 50,* 942–952.

Berger, C. R. (1994). Power, dominance, and social interaction. In M. L. Knapp & G. R. Miller (Eds.), *Handbook of interpersonal communication* (2nd ed., pp. 450–507). Thousand Oaks, CA: Sage.

Berger, D. G., & Wenger, M. G. (1973). The ideology of virginity. *Journal of Marriage and the Family, 35,* 666–676.

Berkman, L. F., & Glass, T. A. (2000). Social integration, social networks, social support and health. In L. F. Berkman & I. Kawachi (Eds.), *Social epidemiology* (pp. 137–174). New York: Oxford University Press.

Berkman, L., & Syme, S. (1979). Social networks, host resistance, and mortality: A nine year follow-up study of Alameda County residents. *American Journal of Epidemiology, 109,* 186–204.

Berman, J. S., & Bennett, J. B. (1982, August). *Love and power: Testing Waller's principle of least interest.* Paper presented at the meeting of the American Psychological Association, Washington, DC.

Berndt, T. J. (1996). Friendships in adolescence. In N. Vanzetti & S. Duck (Eds.), *A lifetime of relationships* (pp. 181–212). Pacific Grove, CA: Brooks/Cole.

Bernieri, F. J., Zuckerman, M., Koestner, R., & Rosenthal, R. (1994). Measuring person perception accuracy: Another look at self-other agreement. *Personality and Social Psychology Bulletin, 20,* 367–378.

Bernstein, W. M., Stephenson, B. O., Snyder, M. L., & Wicklund, R. A. (1983). Causal ambiguity and heterosexual affiliation. *Journal of Experimental Social Psychology, 19,* 78–92.

Berscheid, E. (1983). Emotion. In H. H. Kelley, E. Berscheid, A. Christensen, J. H. Harvey, T. L. Huston, G. Levinger, E. McClintock, L. A. Peplau, & D. R. Peterson (Eds.), *Close relationships* (pp. 110–168). New York: Freeman.

Berscheid, E. (1999). The greening of relationship science. *American Psychologist, 54,* 260–266.

Berscheid, E., & Lopes, J. (1997). A temporal model of relationship satisfaction and stability. In R. J. Sternberg & M. Hojjat (Eds.), *Satisfaction in close relationships* (pp. 129–159). New York: Guilford Press.

Berscheid, E., & Reis, H. T. (1998). Attraction and close relationships. In D. T. Gilbert, S. T. Fiske, & G. Lindzey (Eds.), *The handbook of social psychology* (Vol. 2, 4th ed., pp. 193–281). New York: McGraw-Hill.

Berscheid, E., & Walster, E. (1974). A little bit about love. In T. Huston (Ed.), *Foundations of interpersonal attraction* (pp. 355–381). New York: Academic Press.

Bettor, L., Hendrick, S. S., & Hendrick, C. (1995). Gender and sexual standards in dating relationships. *Personal Relationships, 2,* 359–369.

Bianchi, S. M., Subaiya, L., & Kahn, J. R. (1999). The gender gap in the economic well-being of nonresident fathers and custodial mothers. *Demography, 36,* 195–203.

Bigelow, B. J., Tesson, G., & Lewko, J. H. (1996). *Learning the rules: The anatomy of children's relationships.* New York: Guilford Press.

Billy, J. O. G., Landale, N. S., & McLaughlin, S. D. (1986). The effect of marital status at first birth on marital dissolution among adolescent mothers. *Demography, 23,* 329–349.

Billy, J. O., & Udry, J. R. (1985). The influence of male and female best friends on adolescent sexual behavior. *Adolescence, 20,* 21–32.

Birchler, G. R., & Webb, L. J. (1977). Discriminating interaction behavior in happy and unhappy marriages. *Journal of Consulting and Clinical Psychology, 45,* 494–495.

Blasband, D., & Peplau, L. A. (1985). Sexual exclusivity versus openness in gay male couples. *Archives of Sexual Behavior, 14,* 395–412.

Blau, P. M. (1964). *Exchange and power in social life.* New York: Wiley.

Blieszner, R., & Adams, R. G. (1992). *Adult friendship.* Thousand Oaks, CA: Sage.

Blieszner, R., & Adams, R. G. (1998). Problems with friends in old age. *Journal of Aging Studies, 12,* 223–238.

Blood, R. O., & Wolfe, D. M. (1960). *Husbands and wives: The dynamics of married living.* New York: Free Press.

Blumstein, P., & Schwartz, P. (1983). *American couples: Money, work, sex.* New York: William Morrow.

Bombar, M. L., & Littig, L. W., Jr. (1996). Babytalk as a communication of intimate attachment: An initial study in adult romances and friendships. *Personal Relationships, 3,* 137–158.

Booth, A., Johnson, D. R., White, L. K., & Edwards, J. N. (1986). Divorce and marital instability over the life course. *Journal of Family Issues, 7,* 421–442.

Bornstein, R. F. (1989). Exposure and affect: Overview and meta-analysis of research, 1968–1987. *Psychological Bulletin, 106,* 265–289.

Borys, S., & Perlman, D. (1985). Gender differences in loneliness. *Personality and Social Psychology Bulletin, 11,* 63–76.

Botwin, M. D., Buss, D. M., & Schackelford, T. K. (1997). Personality and mate preferences: Five factors in mate selection and marital satisfaction. *Journal of Personality, 65,* 107–136.

Bouchard, G., Lussier, Y., & Sabourin, S. (1999). Personality and marital adjustment: Utility of the five-factor model of personality. *Journal of Marriage and the Family, 61,* 651–660.

Bowlby, J. (1969). *Attachment and loss: Vol. 1. Attachment.* New York: Basic Books.

Bradbury, T. N. (1994). Unintended effects of marital research on marital relationships. *Journal of Family Psychology, 8,* 187–201.

Bradbury, T. N. (Ed.). (1998). *The developmental course of marital dysfunction.* Cambridge, England: Cambridge University Press.

Bradbury, T. N., Campbell, S. M., & Fincham, F. D. (1995). Longitudinal and behavioral analysis of masculinity and femininity in marriage. *Journal of Personality and Social Psychology, 68,* 328–341.

Bradbury, T. N., & Fincham, F. D. (1990). Attributions in marriage: Review and critique. *Psychological Bulletin, 107,* 3–33.

Bradbury, T. N., & Fincham, F. D. (1992). Attributions and behavior in marital interaction. *Journal of Personality and Social Psychology, 63,* 613–628.

Bragg, M. (1979). *A comparative study of loneliness and depression.* Unpublished doctoral dissertation, University of California, Los Angeles.

Branden, N. (1980). *The psychology of romantic love.* Los Angeles: Tarcher.

Brehm, S. S., & Brehm, J. W. (1981). *Psychological reactance: A theory of freedom and control.* New York: Academic Press.

Brehm, S. S., & Kassin, S. M. (1990). *Social psychology.* Boston: Houghton Mifflin.

Brennan, K. A., Clark, C. L., & Shaver, P. R. (1998). Self-report measurement of adult attachment: An integrative overview. In J. A. Simpson & W. S. Rholes (Eds.), *Attachment theory and close relationships* (pp. 46–76). New York: Guilford Press.

Brennan, K. A., & Morris, K. A. (1997). Attachment styles, self-esteem, and patterns of seeking feedback from romantic partners. *Personality and Social Psychology Bulletin, 23,* 23–31.

Brennan, T., & Auslander, N. (1979). *Adolescent loneliness: An exploratory study of social and psychological pre-dispositions and theory.* Boulder, CO: Behavioral Research Institute. (ERIC Document Reproduction Service No. ED 194822).

Bringle, R. G. (1995). Sexual jealousy in the relationships of homosexual and heterosexual men: 1980 and 1992. *Personal Relationships, 2,* 313–325.

Bringle, R. G., & Buunk, B. P. (1991). Extradyadic relationships and sexual jealousy. In K. McKinney & S. Sprecher (Eds.), *Sexuality in close relationships* (pp. 135–153). Hillsdale, NJ: Erlbaum.

Brinkerhoff, M., & Lupri, E. (1978). Theoretical and methodological issues in the use of decision-making as an indicator of conjugal power: Some Canadian observations. *Canadian Journal of Sociology, 3,* 1–20.

Broderick, B. B. (1988). To arrive where we started: The field of family studies in the 1930s. *Journal of Marriage and the Family , 50 , 569–584.*

Broderick, C. B., & Schrader, S. S. (1981). The history of professional marriage and family therapy. In A. S. Gurman & D. P. Kniskern (Eds.), *Handbook of family therapy* (pp. 5–35). New York: Brunner/Mazel.

Brody, L. R., & Hall, J. A. (1993). Gender and emotion. In M. Lewis & J. M. Haviland (Eds.), *Handbook of emotion* (pp. 447–460). New York: Guilford Press.

Brown, B. B. (1989). The role of peer groups in adolescents' adjustment to secondary school. In T. J. Berndt & G. W. Ladd (Eds.), *Peer relationships in child development* (pp. 188–215). New York: Wiley-Interscience.

Brown, C., Dovidio, J. F., & Ellyson, S. L. (1990). Reducing sex differences in visual displays of dominance. *Personality and Social Psychology Bulletin, 16, 358–368.*

Brown, E. M. (1991). *Patterns of infidelity and their treatment.* New York: Brunner-Mazel.

Brown, G. W., & Harris, T. (1978). *Social origins of depression: A study of the psychiatric disorder in women.* London: Tavistock.

Brown, M., & Auerback, A. (1981). Communication patterns in initiation of marital sex. *Medical Aspects of Human Sexuality, 15, 105–117.*

Browning, J. R., Hatfield, E., Kessler, D., & Levine, T. (2000). Sexual motives, gender, and sexual behavior. *Archives of Sexual Behavior, 29, 135–153.*

Bruch, M. A., & Cheek, J. M. (1995). Developmental factors in childhood and adolescent shyness. In R. G. Heimberg, M. R. Liebowitz, D. A. Hope, & F. R. Schneier (Eds.), *Social phobia: Diagnosis, assessment, and treatment* (pp. 163–182). New York: Guilford Press.

Bruch, M. A., Gorsky, J. M., Collins, T. M., & Berger, P. A. (1989). Shyness and sociability examined: A multicomponent analysis. *Journal of Personality and Social Psychology, 57, 904–915.*

Bruess, C. J. S., & Pearson, J. C. (1993). "Sweet pea" and "pussy cat": An examination of idiom use and marital satisfaction over the life cycle. *Journal of Social and Personal Relationships, 10, 609–615.*

Buehlman, K. T., Gottman, J. M., & Katz, L. F. (1992). How a couple views their past predicts their future: Predicting divorce from an oral history interview. *Journal of Family Psychology, 5, 295–318.*

Buhrmester, D., & Furman, W. (1986). The changing functions of friends in childhood: A neo-Sullivanian perspective. In V. J. Derlega & B. A Winstead (Eds.), *Friendship and social interaction* (pp. 41–62). New York: Springer-Verlag.

Bui, K. T., Peplau, L. A., & Hill, C. T. (1996). Testing the Rusbult model of relationship commitment and stability in a 15-year study of heterosexual couples. *Personality and Social Psychology Bulletin, 22, 1244–1257.*

Bukowski, W. M., & Cillessen, A. H. (Eds.). (1998). *Sociometry then and now: Building on six decades of measuring children's experiences with the peer group.* San Francisco: Jossey-Bass.

Bukowski, W. M., Newcomb, A. F., & Hartup, W. W. (Eds.). (1996). *The company they keep: Friendship in childhood and adolescence.* New York: Cambridge University Press.

Bulcroft, R. A., & White, J. M. (1997). Family research methods and levels of analysis. *Family Science Review, 10, 136–153.*

Buller, D. B., & Burgoon, J. K. (1994). Deception: Strategic and nonstrategic communication. In J. A. Daly & J. M. Wiemann (Eds.), *Strategic interpersonal communication* (pp. 191–223). Hillsdale, NJ: Erlbaum.

Bumpass, L. L., & Sweet, J. A. (1989). National estimates of cohabitation. *Demography, 26, 615–625.*

Bumpass, L. L., Sweet, J., & Castro Martin, T. (1990). Changing patterns of remarriage. *Journal of Marriage and the Family, 52,* 747–756.

Burchill, S. A. L., & Stiles, W. B. (1988). Interactions of depressed college students with their roommates: Not necessarily negative. *Journal of Personality and Social Psychology, 55,* 410–419.

Burger, J. M., & Burns, L. (1988). The illusion of unique invulnerability and use of effective contraception. *Personality and Social Psychology Bulletin, 14,* 264–270.

Burgess, R. L., & Nielsen, J. M. (1977). Distributive justice and the balance of power. In J. H. Kunkel (Ed.), *Behavioral theory in sociology* (pp. 139–169). New Brunswick, NJ: Transaction Books.

Burgoon, J. K. (1994). Nonverbal signals. In M. L. Knapp & G. R. Miller (Eds.), *Handbook of interpersonal communication* (2nd ed., pp. 229–285). Thousand Oaks, CA: Sage.

Burgoon, J. K., Buller, D. B., Grandpre, J. R., & Kalbfleisch, P. (1998). Sex differences in presenting and detecting deceptive messages. In D. J. Canary & K. Dindia (Eds.), *Sex differences and similarities in communication: Critical essays and empirical investigations of sex and gender in interaction* (pp. 321–350). Mahwah, NJ: Erlbaum.

Burgoon, J. K., Buller, D. B., & Guerrero, L. K. (1995). Interpersonal deception: IX. Effects of social skill and nonverbal communication on deception success and detection accuracy. *Journal of Language and Social Psychology, 14,* 289–311.

Burgoon, J. K., Buller, D. B., White, C. H., Afifi, W., & Buslig, A. L. S. (1999). The role of conversational involvement in deceptive interpersonal interactions. *Personality and Social Psychology Bulletin, 25,* 669–685.

Burgoon, J. K., Buller, D. B., & Woodall, W. G. (1989). *Nonverbal communication: The unspoken dialogue.* New York: Harper & Row.

Burke, R. J., Weir, T., & DuWors, R. E. (1979). Type A behavior of administrators and wives' reports of marital satisfaction and well-being. *Journal of Applied Psychology, 64,* 57–65.

Burleson, B. R., Kunkel, A. W., Samter, W., & Werking, K. J. (1996). Men's and women's evaluations of communication skills in personal relationships: When sex differences make a difference—and when they don't. *Journal of Social and Personal Relationships, 13,* 201–224.

Burleson, B. R., & Samter, W. (1992). Are there gender differences in the relationship between academic performance and social behavior? *Human Communication Research, 19,* 155–175.

Burman, B., Margolin, G., & John, R. S. (1993). America's angriest home videos: Behavioral contingencies observed in home reenactments of marital conflict. *Journal of Consulting and Clinical Psychology, 61,* 28–39.

Burn, S. M. (1996). *The social psychology of gender.* New York: McGraw-Hill.

Burns, G. L., & Farina, A. (1992). The role of physical attractiveness in adjustment. *Genetic, Social, and General Psychology Monographs, 118,* 157–194.

Buss, D. M. (1989a). Conflict between the sexes: Strategic interference and the evocation of anger and upset. *Journal of Personality and Social Psychology, 56,* 735–747.

Buss, D. M. (1989b). Sex differences in human mate preferences: Evolutionary hypotheses tested in 37 cultures. *Behavioral and Brain Sciences, 12,* 1–14.

Buss, D. M. (1994). *The evolution of desire: Strategies of human mating.* New York: Basic Books.

Buss, D. M. (1995). Psychological sex differences: Origins through sexual selection. *American Psychologist, 50,* 164–168.

Buss, D. M. (1999). *Evolutionary psychology: The new science of the mind.* Boston: Allyn & Bacon.

Buss, D. M. (2000). *The dangerous passion: Why jealousy is as necessary as love and sex.* New York: The Free Press.

Buss, D. M., & Barnes, M. (1986). Preferences in human mate selection. *Journal of Personality and Social Psychology, 50,* 559–570.

Buss, D. M., & Kenrick, D. T. (1998). Evolutionary social psychology. In D. T. Gilbert, S. T. Fiske, & G. Lindzey (Eds.), *The handbook of social psychology* (Vol. 2, 4th ed., pp. 982–1026). New York: McGraw-Hill.

Buss, D. M., Larsen, R. J., Westen, D., & Semmelroth, J. (1992). Sex differences in jealousy: Evolution, physiology, and psychology. *Psychological Science, 3,* 251–255.

Buss, D. M., & Schmitt, D. P. (1993). Sexual strategies theory: An evolutionary perspective on human mating. *Psychological Review, 100,* 204–232.

Buss, D. M., Shackelford, T. K., Kirkpatrick, L. A., Choe, J. C., Lim, H. K., Hasegawa, M., Hasegawa, T., & Bennett, K. (1999). Jealousy and the nature of beliefs about infidelity: Tests of competing hypotheses about sex differences in the United States, Korea, and Japan. *Personal Relationships, 6,* 125–150.

Butler, D., & Geis, F. L. (1990). Nonverbal affect responses to male and female leaders: Implications for leadership evaluations. *Journal of Personality and Social Psychology, 58,* 48–59.

Butler, M. H., & Wampler, K. S. (1999). A meta-analytical update of research on the couple communication program. *American Journal of Family Therapy, 27,* 223–237.

Buunk, B. (1982). Anticipated sexual jealousy: Its relationship to self-esteem, dependency, and reciprocity. *Personality and Social Psychology Bulletin, 8,* 310–316.

Buunk, B. (1987). Conditions that promote breakups as a consequence of extra-dyadic involvements. *Journal of Social and Clinical Psychology, 5,* 271–284.

Buunk, B., & Hupka, R. B. (1987). Cross-cultural differences in the elicitation of sexual jealousy. *Journal of Sex Research, 23,* 12–22.

Buunk, B. P. (1995). Sex, self-esteem, dependency and extradyadic sexual experience as related to jealousy responses. *Journal of Social and Personal Relationships, 12,* 147–153.

Buunk, B. P. (1997). Personality, birth order and attachment styles as related to various types of jealousy. *Personality and Individual Differences, 23,* 997–1006.

Buunk, B. P., Angleitner, A., Oubaid, V., & Buss, D. M. (1996). Sex differences in jealousy in evolutionary and cultural perspective: Tests from the Netherlands, Germany, and the United States. *Psychological Science, 7,* 359–363.

Buunk, B. P., & Mutsaers, W. (1999). Equity perceptions and marital satisfaction in former and current marriage: A study among the remarried. *Journal of Social and Personal Relationships, 16,* 123–132.

Buunk, B. P., & van der Eijnden, R. J. J. M. (1997). Perceived prevalence, perceived superiority, and relationship satisfaction: Most relationships are good, but ours is the best. *Personality and Social Psychology Bulletin, 23,* 219–228.

Buunk, B. P., & VanYperen, N. W. (1991). Referential comparisons, relational comparisons, and exchange orientation: Their relation to marital satisfaction. *Personality and Social Psychology Bulletin, 17,* 709–717.

Byers, E. S., & Demmons, S. (1999). Sexual satisfaction and sexual self-disclosure within dating relationships. *Journal of Sex Research, 36,* 180–189.

Byers, E. S., Demmons, S., & Lawrance, K. (1998). Sexual satisfaction within dating relationships: A test of the interpersonal exchange model of sexual satisfaction. *Journal of Social and Personal Relationships, 15,* 257–267.

Byers, E. S., & Heinlein, L. (1989). Predicting initiations and refusals of sexual activities in married and cohabiting heterosexual couples. *Journal of Sex Research, 26,* 210–231.

Byrne, D., & Blaylock, B. (1963). Similarity and assumed similarity of attitudes between husbands and wives. *Journal of Abnormal and Social Psychology, 67,* 636–640.

Byrne, D., & Clore, G. L. (1970). A reinforcement model of evaluative processes. *Personality: An International Journal, 1,* 103–128.

Byrne, D., Clore, G. L., & Smeaton, G. (1986). The attraction hypothesis: Do similar atti- tudes affect anything? *Journal of Personality and Social Psychology, 51,* 1167–1170.

Byrne, D., Ervin, C. E., & Lamberth, J. (1970). Continuity between the experimental study of attraction and real-life computer dating. *Journal of Personality and Social Psychology, 16,* 157–165.

Byrne, D., & Fisher, W. A. (1983). *Adolescents, sex, and contraception.* Hillsdale, NJ: Erlbaum.

Byrne, D., & Murnen, S. K. (1988). Maintaining loving relationships. In R. J. Sternberg & M. L. Barnes (Eds.), *The psychology of love* (pp. 293–310). New Haven, CT: Yale Uni- versity Press.

Byrne, D., & Nelson, D. (1965a). Attraction as a linear function of proportion of positive reinforcements. *Journal of Personality and Social Psychology, 1,* 659–663.

Byrne, D., & Nelson, D. (1965b). The effect of topic importance and attitude similarity- dissimilarity on attraction in a multistranger design. *Psychonomic Science, 3,* 449–450.

Cacioppo, J. T., Ernst, J. M., Burleson, M. H., McClintock, M. K., Malarkey, W. B., Hawkley, L. C., Kowalewski, R. B., Paulsen, A., Hobson, J. A., Hugdahl, K., Spiegel, D., & Berntson, G. G. (2000). Lonely traits and concomitant physiological processes: The MacArthur social neuroscience studies. *International Journal of Psychophysiology, 35,* 143–154.

Cahn, D. D. (1990). Intimates in conflict: A research review. In D. D. Cahn (Ed.), *Intimates in conflict: A communication perspective* (pp. 1–22). Hillsdale, NJ: Erlbaum.

Caldwell, M. A., & Peplau, L. A. (1984). The balance of power in lesbian relationships. *Sex Roles, 10,* 587–599.

Call, V., Sprecher, S., & Schwartz, P. (1995). The incidence and frequency of marital sex in a national sample. *Journal of Marriage and the Family, 57,* 639–652.

Cameron, P., & Cameron, K. (1998). "Definitive" University of Chicago sex survey over- estimated prevalence of homosexual identity. *Psychological Reports, 82,* 861–862.

Campbell, J., Miller, P., Cardwell, M., & Belknap, R. A. (1994). Relationship status of bat- tered women over time. *Journal of Family Violence, 9,* 99–111.

Campbell, S. M., Peplau, L. A., & DeBro, S. C. (1992). Women, men and condoms: Atti- tudes and experiences of heterosexual college students. *Psychology of Women Quar- terly, 16,* 273–288.

Canary, D. J., & Cupach, W. R. (1988). Relational and episodic characteristics associated with conflict tactics. *Journal of Social and Personal Relationships, 5,* 305–325.

Canary, D. J., Cupach, W. R., & Messman, S. J. (1995). *Relationship conflict: Conflict in par- ent-child, friendship, and romantic relationships.* Thousand Oaks, CA: Sage.

Canary, D. J., & Dindia, K. (Eds.). (1998). Prologue: Recurring issues in sex differences and similarities in communication. In D. J. Canary & K. Dindia (Eds.), *Sex differences and similarities in communication: Critical essays and empirical investigations of sex and gender in interaction* (pp. 1–17). Mahwah, NJ: Erlbaum.

Canary, D. J., & Emmers-Sommer, T. M. (1997). *Sex and gender differences in personal rela- tionships.* New York: Guilford Press.

Canary, D. J., & Stafford, L. (2001). Equity in the preservation of personal relationships. In J. H. Harvey & A. E. Wenzel (Eds.), *Close romantic relationships: Maintenance and enhancement,* (pp. 133–151). Mahwah, NJ: Erlbaum.

Cantor, J. R., Zillmann, D., & Bryant, J. (1975). Enhancement of experienced sexual arousal in response to erotic stimuli through misattribution of unrelated residual arousal. *Journal of Personality and Social Psychology, 32,* 69–75.

Caporael, L. R., Lukaszewski, M. P., & Culbertson, G. H. (1983). Secondary baby talk: Judgments by institutionalized elderly and their caregivers. *Journal of Personality and Social Psychology, 44,* 746–754.

Carducci, B. J. (1999). *Shyness: A bold new approach.* New York: HarperCollins.

Carli, L. L. (1990). Gender, language, and influence. *Journal of Personality and Social Psychology, 59,* 941–951.

Carli, L. L. (1999). Gender, interpersonal power, and social influence. *Journal of Social Issues, 55,* 81–98.

Carli, L. L., Ganley, R., & Pierce-Otay, A. (1991). Similarity and satisfaction in roommate relationships. *Personality and Social Psychology Bulletin, 17,* 419–426.

Carli, L. L., LaFleur, S. J., & Loeber, C. C. (1995). Nonverbal behavior, gender, and influence. *Journal of Personality and Social Psychology, 68,* 1030–1041.

Carnelley, K. B., & Janoff–Bulman, R. (1992). Optimism about love relationships: General vs specific lessons from one's personal experiences. *Journal of Social and Personal Relationships, 9,* 5–20.

Carothers, B. J., & Allen, J. B. (1999). Relationships of employment status, gender roles, insult, and gender with use of influence tactics. *Sex Roles, 41,* 375–386.

Carrère, S., & Gottman, J. M. (1999). Predicting divorce among newlyweds from the first three minutes of a marital conflict discussion. *Family Process, 38,* 293–301.

Carroll, L. (1988). Concern with AIDS and the sexual behavior of college students. *Journal of Marriage and the Family, 50,* 405–411.

Carstensen, L. L., Isaacowitz, D. M., & Charles, S. T. (1999). Taking time seriously: A theory of socioemotional selectivity. *American Psychologist, 54,* 165–181.

Carton, J. S., Kessler, E. A., & Pape, C. L. (1999). Nonverbal decoding skills and relationship well-being in adults. *Journal of Nonverbal Behavior, 23,* 91–100.

Carver, C. S. (1997). Adult attachment and personality: Converging evidence and a new measure. *Personality and Social Psychology Bulletin, 23,* 865–883.

Cary, M. S. (1978). The role of gaze in the initiation of conversation. *Social Psychology, 41,* 269–271.

Cashdan, E. (1998). Smiles, speech, and body posture: How women and men display sociometric status and power. *Journal of Nonverbal Behavior, 22,* 209–228.

Caspi, A., & Herbener, E. S. (1990). Continuity and change: Assortative marriage and the consistency of personality in adulthood. *Journal of Personality and Social Psychology, 58,* 250–258.

Cassidy, J., & Asher, S. R. (1992). Loneliness and peer relations in young children. *Child Development, 63,* 350–365.

Cassidy, J., & Shaver, P. R. (Eds.). (1999). *Handbook of attachment: Theory, research and clinical applications.* New York: Guilford Press.

Catania, J. A., Coates, T., Peterson, J., Dolcini, M., Kegeles, S., Siegel, D., Golden, E., & Fullilove, M. T. (1993). Changes in condom use among black, Hispanic, and white heterosexuals in San Francisco: The AMEN cohort survey. *Journal of Sex Research, 30,* 121–128.

Catania, J. A., Dolcini, M. M., Coates, T. J., Kegeles, S. M., Greenblatt, R. M., & Puckett, S. (1989). Predictors of condom use and multiple partnered sex among sexually-active adolescent women: Implications for AIDS-related health interventions. *Journal of Sex Research, 26,* 514–524.

Catania, J. A., Gibson, D. R., Chitwood, D. D., & Coates, T. J. (1990). Methodological problems in AIDS behavioral research: Influences on measurement error and participation bias in studies of sexual behavior. *Psychological Bulletin, 108,* 339–362.

Cate, R. M., Henton, J. M., Koval, J., Christopher, F. S., & Lloyd, S. (1982). Premarital abuse: A social psychological perspective. *Journal of Family Issues, 3,* 79–90.

Cate, R. M., & Lloyd, S. A. (1992). *Courtship.* Thousand Oaks, CA: Sage.

Cate, R. M., Lloyd, S. A., & Henton, J. M. (1985). The effect of equity, equality, and reward level on the stability of students' premarital relationships. *Journal of Social Psychology, 125,* 715–721.

Cate, R. M., Lloyd, S. A., Henton, J. M., & Larson, J. (1982). Fairness and reward level as predictors of relationship satisfaction. *Social Psychology Quarterly, 45,* 177–181.

Cate, R. M., Lloyd, S. A., & Long, E. (1988). The role of rewards and fairness in developing premarital relationships. *Journal of Marriage and the Family, 50,* 443–452.

Caughlin, J. P., Huston, T. L., & Houts, R. M. (2000). How does personality matter in marriage? An examination of trait anxiety, interpersonal negativity, and marital satisfaction. *Journal of Personality and Social Psychology, 78,* 326–336.

Centers, R., Raven, B. H., & Rodrigues, A. (1971). Conjugal power structure: A reexamination. *American Sociological Review, 36,* 264–278.

Chan, C., & Margolin, G. (1994). The relationship between dual-earner couples' daily work mood and home affect. *Journal of Social and Personal Relationships, 11,* 573–586.

Check, J. V. P., Perlman, D., & Malamuth, N. M. (1985). Loneliness and aggressive behavior. *Journal of Social and Personal Relationships, 2,* 243–252.

Cheek, J. M., & Busch, C. M. (1981). The influence of shyness on loneliness in a new situation. *Personality and Social Psychology Bulletin, 7,* 572–577.

Cheek, J. M., & Buss, A. H. (1981). Shyness and sociability. *Journal of Personality and Social Psychology, 41,* 330–339.

Cheek, J. M., & Melchior, L. A. (1990). Shyness, self–esteem, and self-consciousness. In H. Leitenberg (Ed.), *Handbook of social and evaluation anxiety* (pp. 47–82). New York: Plenum.

Chelune, G. J., Robison, J. T., & Kommor, M. J. (1984). A cognitive interactional model of intimate relationships. In V. J. Derlega (Ed.), *Communication, intimacy, and close relationships* (pp. 11–40). Orlando: Academic Press.

Choice, P., & Lamke, L. K. (1999). Stay/leave decision-making processes in abusive dating relationships. *Personal Relationships, 6,* 351–367.

Christensen, A. (1979). Naturalistic observation of families: A system for random audio recordings. *Behavior Therapy, 10,* 418–427.

Christensen, A., & Heavey, C. L. (1993). Gender differences in marital conflict: The demand/withdraw interaction pattern. In S. Oskamp & M. Costanzo (Eds.), *Gender issues in contemporary society* (pp. 113–141). Newbury Park, CA: Sage.

Christensen, A., & Heavey, C. L. (1999). Intervention for couples. *Annual Review of Psychology, 50,* 165–190.

Christensen, A., Sullaway, M., & King, C. (1983). Systematic error in behavioral reports of dyadic interaction: Egocentric bias and content analysis. *Behavioral Therapy, 5,* 129–140.

Christopher, F. S., & Frandsen, M. M. (1990). Strategies of influence in sex and dating. *Journal of Social and Personal Relationships, 7,* 89–105.

Christopher, F. S., & Sprecher, S. (2000). Sexuality in marriage, dating, and other relationships: A decade review. *Journal of Marriage and the Family.*

Cialdini, R. B., Borden, R. J., Thorne, A., Walker, M. R., Freeman, S., & Sloan, L. R. (1976). Basking in reflected glory: Three (football) field studies. *Journal of Personality and Social Psychology, 34,* 366–375.

Clanton, G. (1989). Jealousy in American culture 1945–1985: Reflections from popular literature. In D. D. Franks & E. D. McCarthy (Eds.), *The sociology of emotions: Original essays and research papers* (pp. 179–193). Greenwich, CT: JAI Press.

Clark, C. L., Shaver, P. R., & Abrahams, M.F. (1999). Strategic behaviors in romantic relationship initiation. *Personality and Social Psychology Bulletin, 25,* 707–720.

Clark, M. S. (1981). Noncomparability of benefits given and received: A cue to the existence of friendship. *Social Psychology Quarterly, 44,* 375–381.

Clark, M. S. (1984). Record keeping in two types of relationships. *Journal of Personality and Social Psychology, 47,* 549–577.

Clark, M. S. (1986). Evidence of the effectiveness of manipulations of communal and exchange relationships. *Personality and Social Psychology Bulletin, 12,* 414–425.

Clark, M. S., & Chrisman, K. (1994). Resource allocation in intimate relationships. In A. L. Weber & J. H. Harvey (Eds.), *Perspective on close relationships* (pp. 176–192). Boston: Allyn & Bacon.

Clark, M. S., & Grote, N. K. (1998). Why aren't indices of relationship costs always negatively related to indices of relationship quality? *Personality and Social Psychology Review, 2,* 2–17.

Clark, M. S., & Mills, J. (1979). Interpersonal attraction in exchange and communal relationships. *Journal of Personality and Social Psychology, 37,* 12–24.

Clark, M. S., & Mills, J. (1993). The difference between communal and exchange relationships: What it is and is not. *Personality and Social Psychology Bulletin, 15,* 684–691.

Clark, M. S., Mills, J. R., & Corcoran, D. M. (1989). Keeping track of needs and inputs of friends and strangers. *Personality and Social Psychology Bulletin, 15,* 533–542.

Clark, M. S., Mills, J., & Powell, M. C. (1986). Keeping track of needs in communal and exchange relationships. *Journal of Personality and Social Psychology, 51,* 333–338.

Clark, M. S., Pataki, S. P., & Carver, V. H. (1996). Some thoughts and findings on self-presentation of emotions in relationships. In G. J. O. Fletcher & J. Fitness (Eds.), *Knowledge structures in close relationships: A social psychological approach* (pp. 247–274). Mahwah, NJ: Erlbaum.

Clark, M. S., & Waddell, B. (1985). Perceptions of exploitations in communal and exchange relationships. *Journal of Social and Personal Relationships, 2,* 403–418.

Clark, R. A. (1998). A comparison of topics and objectives in a cross section of young men's and women's everyday conversations. In D. J. Canary & K. Dindia (Eds.), *Sex differences and similarities in communication: Critical essays and empirical investigations of sex and gender in interaction* (pp. 303–319). Mahwah, NJ: Erlbaum.

Clarke, S. C. (1995). Advance report of final divorce statistics, 1989 and 1990. *Monthly Vital Statistics Reports, 43 (9),* 1–32.

Clore, G. L., & Byrne, D. (1974). A reinforcement-affect model of attraction. In T. L. Huston (Ed.), *Foundations of interpersonal attraction* (pp. 143–170). New York: Academic Press.

Coie, J. D., & Koeppl, G. K. (1990). Adapting interventions to the problems of aggressive and disruptive rejected children. In S. R. Asher & J. D. Coie (Eds.), *Peer rejection in childhood* (pp. 309–337). New York: Cambridge University Press.

Coleman, M., Ganong, L., & Weaver, S. (2001). Relationship maintenance and enhancement in remarried families. In J. H. Harvey & A. E. Wenzel (Eds.), *Close romantic relationships: Maintenance and enhancement,* (pp. 256–276). Mahwah, NJ: Erlbaum.

Collins, N. L. (1996). Working models of attachment: Implications for explanation, emotion, and behavior. *Journal of Personality and Social Psychology, 71,* 810–832.

Collins, N. L., & Miller, L. C. (1994). Self-disclosure and liking: A meta-analytic review. *Psychological Bulletin, 116,* 457–475.

Colvin, C. R., Vogt, D., & Ickes, W. (1997). Why do friends understand each other better than strangers do? In W. Ickes (Ed.), *Empathic accuracy* (pp. 169–193). New York: Guilford Press.

Condon, J. W., & Crano, W. D. (1988). Inferred evaluation and the relation between attitude similarity and interpersonal attraction. *Journal of Personality and Social Psychology, 54,* 789–797.

Conger, R. D., Cui, M., Bryant, C. M., & Elder, G. H., Jr. (2000). Competence in early adult romantic relationships: A developmental perspective on family influences. *Journal of Personality and Social Psychology, 79,* 224–237.

Connidis, I. A., & Davies, L. (1992). Confidants and companions: Choices in later life. *Journals of Gerontology, 47,* S115–S122.

Connolly, J., Craig, W., Goldberg, A., & Pepler, D. (1999). Conceptions of cross-sex friendships and romantic relationships in early adolescence. *Journal of Youth and Adolescence, 28,* 481–494.

Coogler, O. J. (1978). *Structured mediation in divorce settlement.* Lexington, MA: Lexington Books.

Cook, W. L. (2000). Understanding attachment security in family context. *Journal of Personality and Social Psychology, 78,* 285–294.

Corrales, C. G. (1975). Power and satisfaction in early marriage. In R. E. Cromwell & D. H. Olson (Eds.), *Power in families* (pp. 197–216). New York: Wiley.

Corsini, R. J. (1956). Understanding and similarity in marriage. *Journal of Abnormal and Social Psychology, 52,* 327–342.

Couch, L. L., & Jones, W. H. (1997). Conceptualizing levels of trust. *Journal of Research in Personality, 31,* 319–336.

Couch, L. L., Jones, W. H., & Moore, D. S. (1999). Buffering the effects of betrayal: The role of apology, forgiveness, and commitment. In J. M. Adams & W. H. Jones (Eds.), *Handbook of interpersonal commitment and relationship stability* (pp. 451–469). New York: Kluwer Academic/Plenum.

Couch, L. L., Rogers, J., & Howard, A. (2000, February). *The impact of event characteristics on coping with interpersonal betrayal.* Paper presented at the meeting of the Society for Personality and Social Psychology, Nashville.

Cowan, G., Drinkard, J., & MacGavin, L. (1984). The effects of target, age, and gender on use of power strategies. *Journal of Personality and Social Psychology, 47,* 1391–1398.

Coyne, J. C. (1976). Depression and the response of others. *Journal of Abnormal Psychology, 85,* 186–193.

Crane, R. D., Dollahite, D. C., Griffin, W., & Taylor, V. L. (1987). Diagnosing relationships with spatial distance: An empirical test of a clinical principle. *Journal of Marital and Family Therapy, 13,* 307–310.

Craven, D. (1997). Sex differences in violent victimization, 1994. (1997). Washington, DC: U.S. Department of Justice, Bureau of Justice Statistics. Retrieved September 26, 2000 from the World Wide Web: http://www.ojp.usdoj.gov/bjs/pub/pdf/sdvv.pdf.

Crawford, C. (1998). Environments and adaptations: Then and now. In C. Crawford & D. L. Krebs (Eds.), *Handbook of evolutionary psychology: Ideas, issues, and applications* (pp. 275–302). Mahwah, NJ: Erlbaum.

Critelli, J. W., Myers, E. J., & Loos, V. E. (1986). The components of love: Romantic attraction and sex role orientation. *Journal of Personality, 54,* 354–370.

Crohan, S. E. (1992). Marital happiness and spousal consensus on beliefs about marital conflict: A longitudinal investigation. *Journal of Social and Personal Relationships, 9,* 89–102.

Cromwell, R. E., & Olson, D. G. (1975). Multidisciplinary perspectives of power. In R. E. Cromwell & D. H. Olson (Eds.), *Power in families* (pp. 15–37). New York: Wiley.

Cumming, E., & Henry, W. E. (1961). *Growing old: The process of disengagement.* New York: Basic Books.

Cunningham, M. R. (1986). Measuring the physical in physical attractiveness: Quasi-experiments on the sociobiology of female facial beauty. *Journal of Personality and Social Psychology, 50,* 925–935.

Cunningham, M. R. (1989). Reactions to heterosexual opening gambits: Female selectivity and male responsiveness. *Personality and Social Psychology Bulletin, 15*, 27–41.

Cunningham, M. R., Barbee, A. P., & Druen, P. B. (1997). Social allergens and the reactions they produce: Escalation of annoyance and disgust in love and work. In R. Kowalski (Ed.), *Aversive interpersonal interactions* (pp. 189–214). New York: Plenum.

Cunningham, M. R., Barbee, A. P., & Pike, C. L. (1990). What do women want? Facial-metric assessment of multiple motives in the perception of male facial physical attractiveness. *Journal of Personality and Social Psychology, 59*, 61–72.

Cunningham, M. R., Druen, P. B., & Barbee, A. P. (1997). Angels, mentors, and friends: Trade-offs among evolutionary, social, and individual variables in physical appearance. In J. A. Simpson & D. T. Kenrick (Eds.), *Evolutionary social psychology* (pp. 109–140). Mahwah, NJ: Erlbaum.

Cunningham, M. R., Roberts, A. R., Barbee, A. P., Druen, P. B., & Wu, C. (1995). "Their ideas of beauty are, on the whole, the same as ours": Consistency and variability in the cross-cultural perception of female physical attractiveness. *Journal of Personality and Social Psychology, 68*, 261–279.

Cupach, W. R., & Comstock, J. (1990). Satisfaction with sexual communication in marriage: Links to sexual satisfaction and dyadic adjustment. *Journal of Social and Personal Relationships, 7*, 179–186.

Curtin, S. C., & Martin, J. A. (2000). Births: Preliminary data for 1999. *National Vital Statistics Reports, 48 (14)*, 1–21.

Curtis, R. C., & Miller, K. (1986). Believing another likes or dislikes you: Behaviors making the beliefs come true. *Journal of Personality and Social Psychology, 51*, 284–290.

Cutrona, C. E. (1982). Transition to college: Loneliness and the process of social adjustment. In L. A. Peplau & D. Perlman (Eds.), *Loneliness: A sourcebook of current theory, research, and therapy* (pp. 291–309). New York: Wiley Interscience.

Cutrona, C. E., Russell, D. W., de la Mora, A., & Wallace, R. B. (1997). Loneliness and nursing home admissions among rural older adults. *Psychology and Aging, 12*, 574–589.

Daigen, V., & Holmes, J. G. (2000). Don't interrupt! A good rule for marriage? *Personal Relationships, 7*, 185–201.

Daly, J. A., Hogg, E., Sacks, D., Smith, M., & Zimring, L. (1983). Sex and relationship affect social self-grooming. *Journal of Nonverbal Behavior, 7*, 183–189.

Dare, C. (1986). Psychoanalytic marital therapy. In N. S. Jacobson & A. S. Gurman (Eds.), *Clinical handbook of marital therapy.* (pp. 13–28). New York: Guilford Press.

Darley, J. M., & Gross, P. H. (1983). A hypothesis-confirming bias in labeling effects. *Journal of Personality and Social Psychology, 44*, 20–33.

Data reveal another change in U.S. families. (1999, November 24). *Houston Chronicle*, p. 3A.

Davidson, B. (1984). A test of equity theory for marital adjustment. *Social Psychology Quarterly, 47*, 36–42.

Davidson, L. R., & Duberman, L. (1982). Friendship: Communication and interactional patterns in same-sex dyads. *Sex Roles, 8*, 809–822.

Davila, J., Burge, D., & Hammen, C. (1997). Why does attachment style change? *Journal of Personality and Social Psychology, 73*, 826–838.

Davis, D. (1981). Implications for interaction versus effectance as mediators of the similarity-attraction relationship. *Journal of Experimental Social Psychology, 17*, 96–117.

Davis, K. E., & Latty-Mann, H. (1987). Love styles and relationship quality: A contribution to validation. *Journal of Social and Personal Relationships, 4*, 409–428.

Davis, K. E., & Todd, M. L. (1985). Assessing friendship: Prototypes, paradigm cases, and relationship description. In S. Duck & D. Perlman (Eds.), *Understanding personal relationships: An interdisciplinary approach* (pp.17–38). London: Sage.

Davis, M. H., & Franzoi, S. L. (1986). Adolescent loneliness, self-disclosure, and private self-consciousness: A longitudinal investigation. *Journal of Personality and Social Psychology, 51,* 595–608.

Davis, M. H., & Kraus, L. A. (1997). Personality and empathic accuracy. In W. Ickes (Ed.), *Empathic accuracy* (pp. 144–168). New York: Guilford Press.

Davis, P. J. (1999). Gender differences in autobiographical memory for childhood emotional experiences. *Journal of Personality and Social Psychology, 76,* 498–510.

Day, R. (1992). The transition to first intercourse among racially and culturally diverse youth. *Journal of Marriage and the Family, 54,* 749–762.

Dayhoff, S. A. (2000). *Diagonally-parked in a parallel universe: Working through social anxiety.* Placitas, NM: Effectiveness-Plus Publications.

Dean, D. G. (1966). Emotional maturity and marital adjustment. *Journal of Marriage and the Family, 28,* 454–457.

DeBuono, B. A., Zinner, S. H., Daamen, M., & McCormack, W. M. (1990). Sexual behavior of college women in 1975, 1986, and 1989. *The New England Journal of Medicine, 322,* 821–825.

de Jong Gierveld, J. (1995). Research into relationship research designs: Personal relationships under the microscope. *Journal of Social and Personal Relationships, 12,* 583–588.

de Jong Gierveld, J. (1987). Developing and testing a model of loneliness. *Journal of Personality and Social Psychology, 53,* 119–128.

DeLamater, J. (1987). Gender differences in sexual scenarios. In K. Kelley (Ed.), *Females, males, and sexuality: Theories and research* (pp. 127–139). Albany: State University of New York Press.

De La Ronde, C., & Swann, W. B., Jr. (1998). Partner verification: Restoring shattered images of our intimates. *Journal of Personality and Social Psychology, 75,* 374–382.

DeMaris, A. (1990). The dynamics of generational transfer in courtship violence: A biracial exploration. *Journal of Marriage and the Family, 52,* 219–231.

Demir, A., & Fisiloglu, H. (1999). Loneliness and marital adjustment of Turkish couples. *Journal of Psychology, 133,* 230–240.

DeNeve, K. M., & Cooper, H. (1998). The happy personality: A meta–analysis of 137 personality traits and subjective well-being. *Psychological Bulletin, 124,* 197–229.

DePaulo, B. M. (1992). Nonverbal behavior and self-presentation. *Psychological Bulletin, 111,* 203–243.

DePaulo, B. M. (1994). Spotting lies: Can humans learn to do better? *Current Directions in Psychological Science, 3,* 83–86.

DePaulo, B. M., Ansfield, M. E., Kirkendol, S. E., & Boden, J. M. (2000). *Serious lies.* Manuscript submitted for publication.

DePaulo, B. M., & Bell, K. L. (1996). Truth and investment: Lies are told to those who care. *Journal of Personality and Social Psychology, 71,* 703–716.

DePaulo, B. M., Charlton, K., Cooper, H., Lindsay, J. J., & Muhlenbruck, L. (1997). The accuracy-confidence correlation in the detection of deception. *Personality and Social Psychology Review, 1,* 346–357.

DePaulo, B. M., & Friedman, H. S. (1998). Nonverbal communication. In D. T. Gilbert, S. T. Fiske, & G. Lindzey (Eds.), *The handbook of social psychology: Vol. 2* (4th ed., pp. 3–40). New York: McGraw-Hill.

DePaulo, B. M., & Kashy, D. A. (1998). Everyday lies in close and casual relationships. *Journal of Personality and Social Psychology, 74,* 63–79.

DePaulo, B. M., Kashy, D. A., Kirkendol, S. E., Wyer, M. M., & Epstein, J. A. (1996). Lying in everyday life. *Journal of Personality and Social Psychology, 70,* 979–995.

DePaulo, B. M., Lanier, K., & Davis, T. (1983). Detecting the deceit of the motivated liar. *Journal of Personality and Social Psychology, 45,* 1096–1103.

DePaulo, B. M., & Pfeifer, R. L. (1986). On-the-job experience and skill at detecting deception. *Journal of Applied Social Psychology, 16,* 249–267.

DePaulo, B. M., Stone, J. I., & Lassiter, G. D. (1985). Telling ingratiating lies: Effects of target sex and target attractiveness on verbal and nonverbal deceptive success. *Journal of Personality and Social Psychology, 48,* 1191–1203.

Derlega, V. J., & Chaiken, A. L. (1977). Privacy and self-disclosure in social relationships. *Journal of Social Issues, 33*(3), 102–115.

Derlega, V. J., Wilson, M., & Chaikin, A. L. (1976). Friendship and disclosure reciprocity. *Journal of Personality and Social Psychology, 34,* 578–587.

Derlega, V. J., Winstead, B. A., Wong, P. T. P., & Hunter, S. (1985). Gender effects in an initial encounter: A case where men exceed women in disclosure. *Journal of Social and Personal Relationships, 2,* 25–44.

Dermer, M., & Pyszczynski, T. A. (1978). Effects of erotica upon men's loving and liking responses for women they love. *Journal of Personality and Social Psychology, 36,* 1302–1309.

Dermer, M., & Thiel, D. L. (1975). When beauty may fail. *Journal of Personality and Social Psychology, 31,* 1168–1176.

de Rougemont, D. (1956). *Love in the Western world.* New York: Harper & Row.

DeSteno, D. A., & Salovey, P. (1994). Jealousy in close relationships: Multiple perspectives on the green-ey'd monster. In A. L. Weber & J. H. Harvey (Eds.), *Perspectives on close relationships* (pp. 217–242). Boston: Allyn & Bacon.

DeSteno, D. A., & Salovey, P. (1996a). Evolutionary origins of sex differences in jealousy? Questioning the "fitness" of the model. *Psychological Science, 7,* 367–372.

DeSteno, D. A., & Salovey, P. (1996b). Jealousy and the characteristics of one's rival: A self-evaluation maintenance perspective. *Personality and Social Psychology Bulletin, 22,* 920–932.

de Vries, B. (1991). Friendship and kinship patterns over the life course: A family stage perspective. In L. Stones (Ed.), *Caring communities: Proceedings of the symposium on social support* (pp. 99–107). Ottawa: Industry, Science and Technology.

de Vries, B. (1996). The understanding of friendship: An adult life course perspective. In C. Magai & S. McFadden (Eds.), *Handbook of emotion, aging, and the life course* (pp. 249–268). New York: Academic Press.

Dewsbury, D. A. (1981). Effects of novelty on copulatory behavior: The Coolidge effect and related phenomena. *Psychological Bulletin, 89,* 464–482.

Dickens, W. J., & Perlman, D. (1981). Friendship over the life-cycle. In S. Duck & R. Gilmour (Eds.), *Personal relationships 2: Developing personal relationships* (pp. 91–122). London: Academic Press.

Diehl, M., Elnick, A. B., Bourbeau, L. S., & Labouvie-Vief, G. (1998). Adult attachment styles: Their relations to family context and personality. *Journal of Personality and Social Psychology, 74,* 1656–1669.

Diener, E. (2000). Subjective well-being: The science of happiness and a proposal for a national index. *American Psychologist, 55,* 34–43.

Diener, E., Wolsic, B., & Fujita, F. (1995). Physical attractiveness and subjective well-being. *Journal of Personality and Social Psychology, 69,* 120–129.

Dijkstra, P., & Buunk, B. P. (1998). Jealousy as a function of rival characteristics: An evolutionary perspective. *Personality and Social Psychology Bulletin, 24,* 1158–1166.

Dill, J. C., & Anderson, C. A. (1999). Loneliness, shyness, and depression: The etiology and interrelationships of everyday problems in living. In T. Joiner & J. C. Coyne (Eds.), *The interactional nature of depression* (pp. 93–125). Washington, DC: American Psychological Association.

Dindia, K. (2000a). Relational maintenance. In C. Hendrick & S. S. Hendrick (Eds.), *Close relationships: A sourcebook.* (pp. 287–299). Thousand Oaks, CA: Sage.

Dindia, K. (2000b). Sex differences in self-disclosure, reciprocity of self-disclosure, and self-disclosure and liking: Three meta-analyses reviewed. In S. Petronio (Ed.), *Balancing the secrets of private disclosures* (pp. 21–35). Mahwah, NJ: Erlbaum.

Dindia, K., & Allen, M. (1992). Sex differences in self-disclosure: A meta-analysis. *Psychological Bulletin, 112,* 106–124.

Dindia, K., & Baxter, L. A. (1987). Strategies for maintaining and repairing marital relationships. *Journal of Social and Personal Relationships, 4,* 143–158.

Dindia, K., & Fitzpatrick, M. A. (1985). Marital communication: Three approaches compared. In S. Duck & D. Perlman (Eds.), *Understanding personal relationships: An interdisciplinary approach* (pp. 137–157). London: Sage.

Dindia, K., Fitzpatrick, M. A., & Kenny, D. A. (1997). Self-disclosure in spouse and stranger interaction: A social relations analysis. *Human Communication Research, 23,* 388–412.

Dion, K. K., & Dion, K. L. (1996). Cultural perspectives on romantic love. *Personal Relationships, 3,* 5–17.

Dion, K. K., Berscheid, E., & Walster, E. (1972). What is beautiful is good. *Journal of Personality and Social Psychology, 24,* 285–290.

DiTommaso, E., & Spinner, B. (1995). Social and emotional loneliness: A re-examination of Weiss' Typology of loneliness. *Personality and Individual Differences, 22,* 417–427.

Dobash, R. P., Dobash, R. E., Wilson, M., & Daly, M. (1992). The myth of sexual symmetry in marital violence. *Social Problems, 39,* 71–91.

Doherty, W. J., & Walker, B. J. (1982). Marriage encounter casualties: A preliminary investigation. *American Journal of Family Therapy, 10,* 15–25.

Dolgin, K. G., & Minowa, N. (1997). Gender differences in self-presentation: A comparison of the roles of flatteringness and intimacy in self-disclosure to friends. *Sex Roles, 36,* 371–380.

Dovidio, J. F., Ellyson, S. L., Keating, C. F., Heltman, K., & Brown, C. E. (1988). The relationship of social power to visual displays of dominance between men and women. *Journal of Personality and Social Psychology, 54,* 233–242.

Downey, G., & Feldman, S. I. (1996). Implications of rejection sensitivity for intimate relationships. *Journal of Personality and Social Psychology, 70,* 1327–1343.

Downey, G., Feldman, S. I., & Ayduk, O. (2000). Rejection sensitivity and male violence in romantic relationships. *Personal Relationships, 7,* 45–61.

Downey, G., Freitas, A. L., Michaelis, B., & Khouri, H. (1998). The self-fulfilling prophecy in close relationships: Rejection sensitivity and rejection by romantic partners. *Journal of Personality and Social Psychology, 75,* 545–560.

Downs, A. C., & Lyons, P. M. (1991). Natural observations of the links between attractiveness and initial legal judgments. *Personality and Social Psychology Bulletin, 17,* 541–547.

Drigotas, S. M., & Rusbult, C. E. (1992). Should I stay or should I go?: A dependence model of breakups. *Journal of Personality and Social Psychology, 62,* 62–87.

Drigotas, S. M., Rusbult, C. E., & Verette, J. (1999). Level of commitment, mutuality of commitment, and couple well-being. *Personal Relationships, 6,* 389–409.

Drigotas, S. M., Rusbult, C. E., Wieselquist, J., & Whitton, S. W. (1999). Close partner as sculptor of the ideal self: Behavioral affirmation and the Michelangelo phenomenon. *Journal of Personality and Social Psychology, 77,* 293–323.

Drigotas, S. M., Safstrom, C. A., & Gentilia, T. (1999). An investment model of dating infidelity. *Journal of Personality and Social Psychology, 77,* 509–524.

Driscoll, R., Davis, K. W., & Lipetz, M. E. (1972). Parental interference and romantic love. *Journal of Personality and Social Psychology, 24,* 1–10.

Dryer, D. C., & Horowitz, L. M. (1997). When do opposites attract? Interpersonal complementarity versus similarity. *Journal of Personality and Social Psychology, 72,* 592–603.

Duck, S. (1982). A typography of relationship disengagement and dissolution. In S. Duck (Ed.), *Personal relationships. 4: Dissolving personal relationships* (1–30). London: Academic Press.

Duck, S. (Ed.). (1997). *Handbook of personal relationships: Theory, research and interventions* (2nd ed.). Chichester, England: Wiley.

Dunphy, D. C. (1963). The social structures of urban adolescent peer groups. *Sociometry, 26,* 230–246.

Duran-Aydintug, C. (1998). Emotional support during separation: Its sources and determinants. *Journal of Divorce and Remarriage, 29,* 121–141.

Dutton, D. G. (1987). Wife assault: Social psychological contributions to criminal justice policy. In S. Oskamp (Ed.), *Applied social psychology annual: Vol. 7. Family process and problems: Social psychological aspects* (pp. 238–261). Newbury Park, CA: Sage.

Dutton, D. G., & Aron, A. P. (1974). Some evidence for heightened sexual attraction under conditions of high anxiety. *Journal of Personality and Social Psychology, 30,* 510–517.

Dweck, S., & Ivey, M. (1998). *Baby, all those curves and me with no brakes: Over 500 new no-fail pickup lines for men and women.* New York: Hyperion.

Dykstra, P. A. (1995). Loneliness among the never and formerly married: The importance of supportive friendships and a desire for independence. *Journal of Gerontology: Social Sciences, 50B,* S321–S329.

Eagly, A. H. (1997). Sex differences in social behavior: Comparing social role theory and evolutionary psychology. *American Psychologist, 52,* 1380–1383.

Eagly, A. H., Ashmore, R. D., Makhijani, M. G., Longo, L. C. (1991). What is beautiful is good, but. . . : A meta-analytic review of research on the physical attractiveness stereotype. *Psychological Bulletin, 110,* 109–128.

Eagly, A. H., & Wood, W. (1999). The origins of sex differences in human behavior: Evolved dispositions versus social roles. *American Psychologist, 54,* 408–423.

Ebbesen, E. B., Kjos, G. L., & Konecni, V. J. (1976). Spatial ecology: Its effects on the choice of friends and enemies. *Journal of Experimental Social Psychology, 12,* 505–518.

Edmonds, V. H. (1967). Marriage conventionalization: Definition and measurement. *Journal of Marriage and the Family, 29,* 681–688.

Edmonds, V. H., Withers, G., & Dibatista, B. (1972). Adjustment, conservatism, and marital conventionalization. *Journal of Marriage and the Family, 34,* 96–103.

Eidelson, R. J. (1980). Interpersonal satisfaction and level of involvement: A curvilinear relationship. *Journal of Personality and Social Psychology, 39,* 460–470.

Eidelson, R. J. (1981). Affiliative rewards and restrictive costs in developing relationships. *British Journal of Social Psychology, 20,* 197–204.

Eidelson, R. J., & Epstein, N. (1982). Cognition and relationship maladjustment: Development of a measure of dysfunctional relationship beliefs. *Journal of Consulting and Clinical Psychology, 50,* 715–720.

Eisenberg, A. R. (1992). Conflicts between mothers and their young children. *Merrill-Palmer Quarterly, 38,* 21–43.

Ekman, P., Friesen, W. V., & O'Sullivan, M. (1988). Smiles when lying. *Journal of Personality and Social Psychology, 54,* 414–420.

Ekman, P., Friesen, W. V., O'Sullivan, M., Chan, A., Diacoyanni-Tarlatzis, I., Heider, K., Krause, R., LeCompte, W. A., Pitcairn, T., Ricci-Bitti, P. E., Scherer, K., Tomita, M., & Tzavaras, A. (1987). Universals and cultural differences in the judgments of facial expressions of emotion. *Journal of Personality and Social Psychology, 53,* 712–717.

Ekman, P., & O'Sullivan, M. (1991). Who can catch a liar? *American Psychologist, 46,* 913–920.

Ekman, P., O'Sullivan, M., & Frank, M. G. (1999). A few can catch a liar. *Psychological Science, 10,* 263–266.

Elder, G. H., Jr. (1969). Appearance of education in marriage mobility. *American Sociological Review, 34,* 519–533.

Ellis, A. (1993). The advantages and disadvantages of self-help therapy materials. *Professional Psychology: Research & Practice, 24,* 335–339.

Ellis, A., & Harper, R. (1961). *Creative marriage.* New York: Lyle Stuart.

Ellyson, S. L., Dovidio, J. F., & Brown, C. E. (1992). The look of power: Gender differences and similarities in visual dominance behavior. In C. Ridgeway (Ed.), *Gender and interaction: The role of microstructures in inequality* (pp. 50–80). New York: Springer-Verlag.

Elwood, R. W., & Jacobson, N. S. (1982). Spouses' agreement in reporting their behavioral interactions: A clinical replication. *Journal of Consulting and Clinical Psychology, 50,* 783–784.

Emerson, R. (1962). Power-dependence relations. *American Sociological Review, 27,* 31–41.

Emery, R. E. (1999a). *Marriage, divorce and children's adjustment* (2nd ed.). Thousand Oaks, CA: Sage.

Emery, R. E. (1999b). Postdivorce family life for children: An overview of research and some implications for policy. In R. A. Thompson & P. R. Amato (Eds.), *The postdivorce family: Children, parenting and society* (pp. 3–27). Thousand Oaks, CA: Sage.

Emmers, T. M., & Dindia, K. (1995). The effect of relational stage and intimacy on touch: An extension of Guerrero and Andersen. *Personal Relationships, 2,* 225–236.

Epley, S. W. (1974). Reduction of the behavioral effects of aversive stimulation by the presence of companions. *Psychological Bulletin, 81,* 271–283.

Epstein, N. (1982). Cognitive therapy with couples. *American Journal of Family Therapy, 10,* 5–16.

Epstein, N., & Eidelson, R. J. (1981). Unrealistic beliefs of clinical couples: Their relationship to expectations, goals, and satisfaction. *American Journal of Family Therapy, 9,* 13–22.

Erikson, E. (1950). *Childhood and society.* New York: Norton.

Ernst, J. M., & Cacioppo, J. T. (1999). Lonely hearts: Psychological perspectives on loneliness. *Applied and Preventive Psychology, 8,* 1–22.

Eskey, K. (1992, December 9). Fewer saying "I do." *Houston Chronicle,* p. 5A.

Etcoff, N. (1999). *Survival of the prettiest: The science of beauty.* New York: Doubleday.

Evans, M. A. (1993). Communicative competence as a dimension of shyness. In K. H. Rubin & J. B. Asendorpf (Eds.), *Social withdrawal, inhibition, and shyness in childhood* (pp. 189–212). Hillsdale, NJ: Erlbaum.

Falato, W. L., Meyer, C. R., Weiner, J. L., Afifi, W. A., & Riggs, N. (1999, June). *Now what? The influence of discovery method on relationship progress.* Paper presented at the meeting of the International Network on Close Relationships, Louisville, KY.

Falbo, T., & Peplau, L. A. (1980). Power strategies in intimate relationships. *Journal of Personality and Social Psychology, 38,* 618–628.

Falbo, T., Hazen, M. D., & Linimon, D. (1982). The costs of selecting power bases associated with the opposite sex. *Sex Roles, 8,* 147–158.

Farber, B. (1987). The future of the American family: A dialectical account. *Journal of Family Issues, 8,* 431–433.

Feeney, J. A. (1994). Attachment style, communication patterns, and satisfaction across the life cycle of marriage. *Personal Relationships, 1,* 333–348.

Feeney, J. A. (1998). Adult attachment and relationship-centered anxiety: Responses to physical and emotional distancing. In J. A. Simpson & W. S. Rholes (Eds.), *Attachment theory and close relationships* (pp. 189–218). New York: Guilford Press.

Feeney, J. A. (1999). Adult romantic attachment and couple relationships. In J. Cassidy & P. R. Shaver (Eds.), *Handbook of attachment: Theory, research and clinical applications* (pp. 355–377). New York: Guilford Press.

Feeney, J. A., & Noller, P. (1990). Attachment style as a predictor of adult romantic relationships. *Journal of Personality and Social Psychology, 58,* 281–291.

Feeney, J., Peterson, C., & Noller, P. (1994). Equity and marital satisfaction over the family life cycle. *Personal Relationships, 1,* 83–99.

Fehr, B. (1994). Prototype-based assessment of laypeople's views of love. *Personal Relationships, 1,* 309–331.

Fehr, B. (1996). *Friendship processes.* Thousand Oaks, CA: Sage.

Fehr, B. (1999a). Laypeople's conceptions of commitment. *Journal of Personality and Social Psychology, 76,* 90–103.

Fehr, B. (1999b). Stability and commitment in friendships. In J. M. Adams & W. H. Jones (Eds.), *Handbook of interpersonal commitment and stability* (pp. 259–280) New York: Kluwer Academic/Plenum.

Fehr, B., & Russell, J. A. (1991). The concept of love viewed from a prototype perspective. *Journal of Personality and Social Psychology, 60,* 425–438.

Feingold, A. (1988). Matching for attractiveness in romantic partners and same-sex friends: A meta-analysis and theoretical critique. *Psychological Bulletin, 104,* 226–235.

Feingold, A. (1990). Gender differences in effects of physical attractiveness on romantic attraction: A comparison across five research paradigms. *Journal of Personality and Social Psychology, 59,* 981–993.

Feingold, A. (1992a). Gender differences in mate selection preferences: A test of the Parental Investment Model. *Psychological Bulletin, 112,* 125–139.

Feingold, A. (1992b). Good-looking people are not what we think. *Psychological Bulletin, 111,* 304–341.

Felmlee, D. H. (1995). Fatal attractions: Affection and disaffection in intimate relationships. *Journal of Social and Personal Relationships, 12,* 295–311.

Felmlee, D. H. (1998). "Be careful what you wish for. . . .": A quantitative and qualitative investigation of "fatal attractions." *Personal Relationships, 5,* 235–253.

Felmlee, D. H., & Sprecher, S. (2000). Close relationships and social psychology: Intersections and future paths. *Social Psychology Quarterly, 63,* pp. 365–376.

Ferguson-Isaac, C., Ralston, T. K., & Couch, L. L. (1999, June). *Testing assumptions about coping with interpersonal betrayal.* Paper presented at the meeting of the International Network on Personal Relationships, Louisville, KY.

Fergusson, D. M., Horwood, L. J., Kershaw, K. L., & Shannon, F. T. (1986). Factors associated with reports of wife assault in New Zealand. *Journal of Marriage and the Family, 48,* 407–412.

Festinger, L., Schachter, S., & Back, K. W. (1950). *Social pressures in informal groups: A study of human factors in housing.* New York: Harper & Brothers.

Filsinger, E. E., & Thoma, S. J. (1988). Behavioral antecedents of relationship stability and adjustment: A five-year longitudinal study. *Journal of Marriage and the Family, 50,* 785–795.

Fincham, F. D. (2000). The kiss of porcupines: From attributing responsibility to forgiving. *Personal Relationships, 7,* 1–23.

Fincham, F. D., & Beach, S. R. H. (1999). Conflict in marriage: Implications for working with couples. *Annual Review of Psychology, 50,* 47–77.

Fincham, F. D., & Bradbury, T. N. (1993). Marital satisfaction, depression, and attributions: A longitudinal analysis. *Journal of Personality and Social Psychology, 64,* 442–452.

Fincham, F. D., Bradbury, T. N., & Beach, S. R. H. (1990). To arrive where we began: A reappraisal of cognition in marriage and in marital therapy. *Journal of Family Psychology, 4,* 167–184.

Fincham, F. D., Bradbury, T. N., & Grych, J. H. (1990). Conflict in close relationships: The role of interpersonal phenomena. In S. Graham & V. S. Folkes (Eds.), *Attribution theory: Applications to achievement, mental health, and interpersonal conflict* (pp. 161–184). Hillsdale, NJ: Erlbaum.

Fincham, F. D., Harold, G. T., & Gano-Phillips, S. (2000). The longitudinal association between attributions and marital satisfaction. Direction of effects and role of efficacy expectations. *Journal of Family Psychology, 14,* 267–285.

Finkenauer, C., & Hazam, H. (2000). Disclosure and secrecy in marriage: Do both contribute to marital satisfaction? *Journal of Social and Personal Relationships, 17,* 245–263.

Firestone, R. W., & Catlett, J. (1999). *Fear of intimacy.* Washington, DC: American Psychological Association.

Fischer, C. S., & Oliker, J. (1983). A research note on friendship, gender, and the life cycle. *Social Forces, 62,* 124–133.

Fischer, C. S., & Phillips, S. L. (1982). Who is alone? Social characteristics of people with small networks. In L. A. Peplau & D. Perlman (Eds.), *Loneliness: A sourcebook of current theory, research, and therapy* (pp. 21–39). New York: Wiley Interscience.

Fisher, H. (1995). The nature and evolution of romantic love. In W. Jankowiak (Ed.), *Romantic passion: A universal experience?* (pp. 23–41). New York: Columbia University Press.

Fisher, W. A. (1986). A psychological approach to human sexuality: The sexual behavior sequence. In D. Byrne & K. Kelley (Eds.), *Alternative approaches to the study of sexual behavior* (pp. 131–171). Hillsdale, NJ: Erlbaum.

Fisher, W. A., Miller, C. T., Byrne, D., & White, L. A. (1980). Talking dirty: Responses to communicating a sexual message as a function of situational and personality factors. *Basic and Applied Psychology, 1,* 111–115.

Fitness, J. (2001). Betrayal, rejection, revenge, and forgiveness. In M. R. Leary (Ed.), *Interpersonal rejection* (pp. 73–103). New York: Oxford University Press.

Fitzpatrick, J., & Sollie, D. L. (1999a). Influence of individual and interpersonal factors on satisfaction and stability in romantic relationships. *Personal Relationships, 6,* 337–350.

Fitzpatrick, J., & Sollie, D. L. (1999b). Unrealistic gendered and relationship-specific beliefs: Contributions to investments and commitment in dating relationships. *Journal of Social and Personal Relationships, 16,* 852–867.

Fletcher, G. J. O., Simpson, J. A., & Thomas, G. (2000a). Ideals, perceptions, and evaluations in early relationship development. *Journal of Personality and Social Psychology, 80,* 933–940.

Fletcher, G. J. O., Simpson, J. A., & Thomas, G. (2000b). The measurement of perceived relationship quality components: A confirmatory factor analytic approach. *Personality and Social Psychology Bulletin, 26,* 340–354.

Fletcher, G. J. O., Simpson, J. A., Thomas, G., & Giles, L. (1999). Ideals in intimate relationships. *Journal of Personality and Social Psychology, 76,* 72–89.

Fletcher, M. A. (1999, July 3). Fewer Americans marrying than ever before, study shows. *Houston Chronicle,* p. 8A.

Foa, E. B., & Foa, U. G. (1980). Resource theory: Interpersonal behavior as exchange. In K. J. Gergen, M. S. Greenberg, & R. H. Willis (Eds.), *Social exchange: Advances in theory and research* (pp. 77–94). New York: Plenum.

Foa, U. G. (1971). Interpersonal and economic resources. *Science, 171,* 345–351.

Folkes, V. S. (1982a). Communicating the reasons for social rejection. *Journal of Experiemental Social Psychology, 18,* 235–252.

Folkes, V. S. (1982b). Forming relationships and the matching hypothesis. *Personality and Social Psychology Bulletin, 8,* 631–636.

Fonagy, P., Steele, H., & Steele, M. (1991). Maternal representations of attachment during pregnancy predict the organization of infant–mother attachment at one year of age. *Child Development, 62,* 891–905.

Forgas, J. P., Levinger, G., & Moylan, S. J. (1994). Feeling good and feeling close: Affective influences on the perception of intimate relationships. *Personal Relationships, 1,* 165–184.

Forste, R., & Tanfer, K. (1996). Sexual exclusivity among dating, cohabiting, and married women. *Journal of Marriage and the Family, 58,* 33–47.

Forsyth, D. R., & Schlenker, B. R. (1977). Attributional egocentrism following performance of a competitive task. *Journal of Social Psychology, 102,* 215–222.

Foster, C. A., Witcher, B. S., Campbell, W. K., & Green, J. D. (1998). Arousal and attraction: Evidence for automatic and controlled processes. *Journal of Personality and Social Psychology, 74,* 86–101.

Fraley, R. C., & Davis, K. E. (1997). Attachment formation and transfer in young adults' close friendships and romantic relationships. *Personal Relationships, 4,* 131–144.

Fraley, R. C., & Waller, N. G. (1998). Adult attachment patterns: A test of the typological model. In J. A. Simpson & W. S. Rholes (Eds.), *Attachment theory and close relationships* (pp. 77–114). New York: Guilford Press.

Frazier, P. A., Byer, A. L., Fischer, A. R., Wright, D. M., & DeBord, K. A. (1996). Adult attachment style and partner choice: Correlational and experimental findings. *Personal Relationships, 3,* 117–136.

French, J. R. P., Jr., & Raven, B. H. (1959). The bases of social power. In D. Cartwright (Ed.), *Studies in social power* (pp. 150–167). Ann Arbor: University of Michigan Press.

Friedman, H. S., DiMatteo, M. R., & Mertz, T. J. (1980). Nonverbal communication on television news: The facial expressions of broadcasters during coverage of a presidential election campaign. *Personality and Social Psychology Bulletin, 6,* 427–435.

Frieze, I. H., Olson, J. E., & Russell, J. (1991). Attractiveness and income for men and women in management. *Journal of Applied Social Psychology, 21,* 1039–1057.

Frieze, I. H., Parsons, J. E., Johnson, P. B., Ruble, D. N., & Zellman, G. L. (1978). *Women and sex roles: A social psychological perspective.* New York: W. W. Norton.

Frost, D. E., & Stahelski, A. J. (1988). The systematic measurement of French and Raven's bases of social power in workgroups. *Journal of Applied Social Psychology, 18,* 375–389.

Fuendeling, J. M. (1998). Affect regulation as a stylistic process within adult attachment. *Journal of Social and Personal Relationships, 15,* 291–322.

Fuller T. L., & Fincham, F. D. (1995). Attachment style in married couples: Relation to current marital functioning, stability over time, and method of assessment. *Personal Relationships, 2,* 17–34.

Funder, D. C., Kolar, D. C., & Blackman, M. C. (1995). Agreement among judges of personality: Interpersonal relations, similarity, and acquaintanceship. *Journal of Personality and Social Psychology, 69,* 656–672.

Furnham, A., Dias, M., & McClelland, A. (1998). The role of body weight, waist-to-hip ratio, and breast size in judgments of female attractiveness. *Sex Roles, 39,* 311–326.

Furr, R. M., & Funder, D. C. (1998). A multimodal analysis of personal negativity. *Journal of Personality and Social Psychology, 74,* 1580–1591.

Fyfe, B. (1983). "Homophobia" or homosexual bias reconsidered. *Archives of Sexual Behavior, 12*, 549–554.

Gaelick, L., Bodenhausen, G. V., & Wyer, R. S., Jr. (1985). Emotional communication in close relationships. *Journal of Personality and Social Psychology, 49*, 1246–1265.

Gaertner, L., & Foshee, V. (1999). Commitment and the perpetration of relationship violence. *Personal Relationships, 6*, 227–239.

Gagné, F. M., & Lydon, J. E. (2000, June). *When are we (in)accurate at predicting relationship survival?* Paper presented at the meeting of the International Society for the Study of Personal Relationships, Brisbane.

Gaines, S. O., Jr., & Brennan, K. (2001). Establishing and maintaining satisfaction in multicultural relationships. In J. H. Harvey & A. E. Wenzel (Eds.), *Close romantic relationships: Maintenance and enhancement,* (pp. 237–253). Mahwah, NJ: Erlbaum.

Galati, D., Scherer, K. R., & Ricci-Bitti, P. E. (1997). Voluntary facial expression of emotion: Comparing congenitally blind with normally sighted encoders. *Journal of Personality and Social Psychology, 73*, 1363–1379.

Gambrill, E., Florian, V., & Thomas, K. (1999). *Rules people use in making and keeping friends.* Unpublished manuscript, University of California, Berkeley.

Gangestad, S. W., & Buss, D. M. (1993). Pathogen prevalence and human mate preference. *Ethology and Sociobiology, 14*, 89–96.

Gangestad, S. W., & Simpson, J. A. (1993). Toward an evolutionary history of female sociosexual variation. *Journal of Personality, 58*, 69–96.

Gangestad, S. W., & Snyder, M. (2000). Self-monitoring: Appraisal and reappraisal. *Psychological Bulletin, 126*, 530–555.

Garcia, S., Stinson, L., Ickes, W., Bissonnette, V., & Briggs, S. R. (1991). Shyness and physical attractiveness in mixed-sex dyads. *Journal of Personality and Social Psychology, 61*, 35–49.

Garland, D. S. R. (1983). *Working with couples for marriage enrichment: A guide to developing, conducting, and evaluating programs.* San Francisco: Jossey-Bass.

Garrity, T. F., & Stallones, L. (1998). Effects of pet contact on human well-being: Review of recent research. In C. C. Wilson & D. C. Turner (Eds.), *Companion animals in human health* (pp. 3–22).Thousand Oaks, CA: Sage.

Gaulin, S. J. C., & McBurney, D. H. (2001). *Psychology: An evolutionary approach.* Upper Saddle River, NJ: Prentice-Hall.

Geary, D. C. (1998). *Male, female: The evolution of human sex differences.* Washington, DC: American Psychological Association.

Geary, D. C. (2000). Evolution and proximate expression of human paternal investment. *Psychological Bulletin, 126*, 55–77.

Geis, B. D., & Gerrard, M. (1984). Predicting male and female contraceptive behavior: A discriminant analysis of groups high, moderate, and low in contraceptive effectiveness. *Journal of Personality and Social Psychology, 46*, 669–680.

Geiss, S. K., & O'Leary, K. D. (1981). Therapist ratings of frequency and severity of marital problems: Implications for research. *Journal of Marital and Family Therapy, 7*, 515–520.

Gelles, R. J. (1976). Abused wives: Why do they stay? *Journal of Marriage and the Family, 38*, 659–668.

Gelles, R. J., & Straus, M. A. (1988). *Intimate violence.* New York: Simon & Schuster.

Gentry, M. (1998). The sexual double standard: The influence of number of relationships and level of sexual activity on judgments of women and men. *Psychology of Women Quarterly, 22*, 505–511.

Gephart, J. M., & Agnew, C. R. (1997, August). *Power strategies in romantic relationships.* Paper presented at the meeting of the American Psychological Association, Chicago, IL.

Gerrard, M. (1987). Emotional and cognitive barriers to effective contraception: Are males and females really different? In K. Kelley (Ed.), *Females, males, and sexuality: Theories and research* (pp. 213–242). Albany: State University of New York Press.

Giblin, P., Sprenkle, D., & Sheehan, R. (1985). Enrichment outcome research: A meta-analysis of premarital, marital and family interventions. *Journal of Marriage and Family Therapy, 11,* 257–271.

Gifford, R., & Gallagher, T. M. B. (1985). Sociability: Personality, social context, and physical setting. *Journal of Personality and Social Psychology, 48,* 1015–1023.

Gilbert, D. T., Krull, D. S., & Pelham, B. W. (1988). Of thoughts unspoken: Social inference and the self-regulation of behavior. *Journal of Personality and Social Psychology, 55,* 685–694.

Gilbert, D. T., & Osborne, R. E. (1989). Thinking backward: Some curable and incurable consequences of cognitive busyness. *Journal of Personality and Social Psychology, 57,* 940–949.

Gilbertson, J., Dindia, K., & Allen, M. (1998). Relational continuity constructional units and the maintenance of relationships. *Journal of Social and Personal Relationships, 15,* 774–790.

Gillespie, D. L. (1976). Who has the power? The marital struggle. In S. Cox (Ed.), *Female psychology: The emerging self* (pp. 192–211). Chicago: Science Research Associates.

Gilovich, T., Savitsky, K., & Medvec, V. H. (1998). The illusion of transparency: Biased assessments of others' ability to read one's emotional states. *Journal of Personality and Social Psychology, 75,* 332–346.

Ginsberg, B. G., & Vogelsong, F. (1977). Premarital relationship improvement by maximizing empathy and self-disclosure. The PRIMES program. In B. Guerney (Ed.), *Relationship enhancement* (pp. 268–288). San Francisco: Jossey-Bass.

Gladue, B. A., & Delaney, H. J. (1990). Gender differences in perception of attractiveness of men and women in bars. *Personality and Social Psychology Bulletin, 16,* 378–391.

Glass, C. R., & Shea, C. A. (1986). Cognitive therapy for shyness and social anxiety. In W. H. Jones, J. M. Cheek, & S. R. Briggs (Eds.), *Shyness: Perspectives on research and treatment* (pp. 315–327). New York: Plenum.

Glass, S. P., & Wright, T. L. (1985). Sex differences in type of extramarital involvement and marital dissatisfaction. *Sex Roles, 12,* 1101–1120.

Glass, S. P., & Wright, T. L. (1992). Justifications for extramarital relationships: The association between attitudes, behaviors, and gender. *Journal of Sex Research, 29,* 361–387.

Glazer-Malbin, N. (1975). Man and woman: Interpersonal relationships in the marital pair. In N. Glazer-Malbin (Ed.), *Old family/new family* (pp. 27–66). New York: Van Nostrand.

Glenn, N. D. (1996). Values, attitudes, and the state of the American marriage. In D. Popenoe, J. B. Elshtain, & D. Blankenhorn (Eds.), *Promises to keep: Decline and renewal of marriage in America* (pp. 15–33). Lanham, MD: Rowman & Littlefield.

Glenn, N. D., & Kramer, K. B. (1987). The marriages and divorces of the children of divorce. *Journal of Marriage and the Family, 49,* 811–825.

Glenn, N. D., & Weaver, C. N. (1988). The changing relationship of marital status to reported happiness. *Journal of Marriage and the Family, 50,* 317–324.

Gold, J. A., Ryckman, R. M., & Mosley, N. R. (1984). Romantic mood induction and attraction to a dissimilar other: Is love blind? *Personality and Social Psychology Bulletin, 10,* 358–368.

Goldfarb, L., Gerrard, M., Gibbons, F. X., & Plante, T. (1988). Attitudes toward sex, arousal, and the retention of contraceptive information. *Journal of Personality and Social Psychology, 55,* 634–641.

Gonzalez, R., & Griffin, D. (2000). On the statistics of interdependence. Treating dyadic data with respect. In W. Ickes & S. Duck (Eds.), *The social psychology of personal relationships* (pp. 181–213). Chichester, England: Wiley.

Goode, E. (1996). Gender and courtship entitlement: Responses to personal ads. *Sex Roles, 34,* 141–169.

Goodwin, S. A., Fiske, S. T., Rosen, L. D., & Rosenthal, A. M. (1997). *Romantic outcome dependency and the (in)accuracy of impression formation: A case of clouded judgment.* Unpublished manuscript, Boston College.

Gordon, A. K., & Miller, A. G. (2000). Perspective differences in the construal of lies: Is deception in the eye of the beholder? *Personality and Social Psychology Bulletin, 26,* 46–55.

Gordon, R. A. (1996). Impact of ingratiation on judgments and evaluations: A meta-analytic investigation. *Journal of Personality and Social Psychology, 71,* 54–70.

Gordon, S. (1976). *Lonely in America.* New York: Simon & Schuster.

Gotlib, I. H., & Whiffen, V. E. (1991). The interpersonal context of depression: Implications for theory and research. In W. H. Jones & D. Perlman (Eds.), *Advances in personal relationships: A research annual* (Vol. 3, pp. 177–206). London: Jessica Kingsley.

Gottman, J. M., Notarius, C., Markman, H., Bank, S., Yoppi, B., & Rubin, M. E. (1976). Behavior exchange theory and marital decision making. *Journal of Personality and Social Psychology, 34,* 14–23.

Gottman, J. M. (1993). The roles of conflict engagement, escalation, and avoidance in marital interaction: A longitudinal view of five types of couples. *Journal of Consulting and Clinical Psychology, 61,* 6–15.

Gottman, J. M. (1994a). *What predicts divorce? The relationship between marital processes and marital outcomes.* Hillsdale, NJ: Erlbaum.

Gottman, J. M. (1994b). *Why marriages succeed or fail.* New York: Simon & Schuster.

Gottman, J. M. (1999). *The marriage clinic: A scientifically-based marital therapy.* New York: W. W. Norton.

Gottman, J. M., & Carrère, S. (1994). Why can't men and women get along? Developmental roots and marital inequities. In D. J. Canary & L. Stafford (Eds.), *Communication and relational maintenance* (pp. 203–229). San Diego: Academic Press.

Gottman, J. M., Carrère, S., Swanson, C., & Coan, J. (2000). Reply to "From Basic Research to Interventions." *Journal of Marriage and the Family, 62,* 265–273.

Gottman, J. M., Coan, J., Carrère, S., & Swanson, C. (1998). Predicting marital happiness and stability from newlywed interactions. *Journal of Marriage and the Family, 60,* 5–22.

Gottman, J. M., & Krokoff, L. J. (1989). Marital interaction and satisfaction: A longitudinal view. *Journal of Consulting and Clinical Psychology, 57,* 47–52.

Gottman, J. M., & Levenson, R. W. (1992). Marital processes predictive of later dissolution: Behavior, physiology, and health. *Journal of Personality and Social Psychology, 63,* 221–233.

Gottman, J. M., Notarius, C., Gonso, J., & Markman, H. (1976). *A couple's guide to communication.* Champaign, IL: Research Press.

Gottman, J. M., & Porterfield, A. L. (1981). Communication dysfunction in the nonverbal behavior of marital couples. *Journal of Marriage and the Family, 43,* 817–827.

Gottman, J. M., & Silver, N. (1999). *The seven principles for making marriage work.* New York: Crown.

Graham, T., & Ickes, W. (1997). When women's intuition isn't greater than men's. In W. Ickes (Ed.), *Empathic accuracy* (pp. 117–143). New York: Guilford Press.

Grammer, K., & Thornhill, R. (1994). Human (Homo sapiens) facial attractiveness and sexual selection: The role of symmetry and averageness. *Journal of Comparative Psychology, 108,* 233–242.

Gray, J. (1992). *Men are from Mars, women are from Venus.* New York: HarperCollins.

Gray-Little, B., & Burks, N. (1983). Power and satisfaction in marriage: A review and critique. *Psychological Bulletin, 93,* 513–538.

Greeley, A. M. (1991). *Faithful attraction: Discovering intimacy, love, and fidelity in American marriage.* New York: Doherty.

Green, B. L., & Kenrick, D. T. (1994). The attractiveness of gender-typed traits at different relationship levels: Androgynous characteristics may be desirable after all. *Personality and Social Psychology Bulletin, 20,* 244–253.

Green, S. K., Buchanan, D. R., & Heuer, S. K. (1984). Winners, losers, and choosers: A field investigation of dating initiation. *Personality and Social Psychology Bulletin, 10,* 501–511.

Greenfield, S., & Thelen, M. (1997). Validation of the Fear of Intimacy Scale with a lesbian and gay male population. *Journal of Social and Personal Relationships, 14,* 707–716.

Green-Hennessy, S., & Reis, H. T. (1998). Openness in processing social information among attachment types. *Personal Relationships, 5,* 449–466.

Greenstein, T. N. (1990). Marital disruption and the employment of married women. *Journal of Marriage and the Family, 52,* 657–676.

Greer, A. E., & Buss, D. M. (1994). Tactics for promoting sexual encounters. *Journal of Sex Research, 31,* 185–201.

Grice, J. W., & Seely, E. (2000). The evolution of sex differences in jealousy: Failure to replicate previous results. *Journal of Research in Personality, 34,* 348–356.

Griffitt, W., & Veitch, R. (1974). Preacquaintance attitude similarity and attraction revisited: Ten days in a fall-out shelter. *Sociometry, 37,* 163–173.

Griggs, L. (1990, July 2). A losing battle with AIDS. *Time,* pp. 41–43.

Grimm, L. G., & Yarnold, P. R. (Eds.). (1995). *Reading and understanding multivariate statistics.* Washington, DC: American Psychological Association.

Gronlund, N. E., & Holmlund, W. S. (1958). The value of elementary school sociometric status scores for predicting pupils' adjustment in high school. *Education Administration and Supervision, 44,* 255–260.

Grote, N. K., & Frieze, I. H. (1994). The measurement of friendship-based love in intimate relationships. *Personal Relationships, 1,* 275–300.

Grote, N. K., & Frieze, I. H. (1998). "Remembrance of things past": Perceptions of marital love from its beginnings to the present. *Journal of Social and Personal Relationships, 15,* 91–109.

Grote, N. K., Frieze, I. H., & Stone, C. A. (1996). Children, traditionalism in the division of family work, and marital satisfaction: "What's love got to do with it?" *Personal Relationships, 3,* 211–228.

Gruber, K. J., & White, J. W. (1986). Gender differences in the perceptions of self's and others' use of power strategies. *Sex Roles, 15,* 109–118.

Guerney, B., Jr., Brock, G., & Coufal, J. (1986). Integrating marital therapy and enrichment: The relationship enhancement approach. In N. S. Jacobson & A. S. Gurman (Eds.), *Clinical handbook of marital therapy* (pp. 151–172). New York: Guilford.

Guerney, B., Jr., & Maxson, P. (1990). Marital and family enrichment research: A decade review and look ahead. *Journal of Marriage and Family Therapy, 52,* 1127–1135.

Guerney, B. G. (1977). *Relationship enhancement.* San Francisco: Jossey-Bass.

Guerrero L. K. (1997). Nonverbal involvement across interactions with same-sex friends, opposite-sex friends and romantic partners: Consistency or change? *Journal of Social and Personal Relationships, 14,* 31–58.

Guerrero, L. K. (1998). Attachment-style differences in the experience and expression of romantic jealousy. *Personal Relationships, 5,* 273–291.

Guerrero, L. K., & Andersen, P. A. (1998a). The dark side of jealousy and envy: Desire, delusion, desperation, and destructive communication. In B. H. Spitzberg & W. R. Cupach (Eds.), *The dark side of close relationships* (pp. 33–70). Mahwah, NJ: Erlbaum.

Guerrero, L. K., & Andersen, P. A. (1998b). Jealousy experience and expression in romantic relationships. In P. A. Andersen & L. K. Guerrero (Eds.), *Handbook of communication and emotion* (pp. 155–188). San Diego: Academic Press.

Guerrero, L. K., Andersen, P. A., Jorgensen, P. F., Spitzberg, B. H., & Eloy, S. V. (1995). Coping with the green-eyed monster: Conceptualizing and measuring communicative responses to romantic jealousy. *Western Journal of Communication, 59,* 270–304.

Guerrero, L. K., & Reiter, R. L. (1998). Expressing emotion: Sex differences in social skills and communicative responses to anger, sadness, and jealousy. In D. J. Canary & K. Dindia (Eds.), *Sex differences and similarities in communication: Critical essays and empirical investigations of sex and gender in interaction* (pp. 321–350). Mahwah, NJ: Erlbaum.

Gupta, U., & Singh, P. (1982). Exploratory study of love and liking and type of marriages. *Indian Journal of Applied Psychology, 19,* 92–97.

Gurman, A. S., & Kniskern, D. P. (Eds.). (1981). *Handbook of family therapy.* New York: Brunner/Mazel.

Gurtman, M. B. (1986). Depression and the response of others: Reevaluating the reevaluation. *Journal of Abnormal Psychology, 95,* 99–101.

Gurtman, M. B., Martin, K. M., & Hintzman, N. M. (1990). Interpersonal reactions to displays of depression and anxiety. *Journal of Social and Clinical Psychology, 9,* 256–267.

Guttentag, M., & Secord, P. F. (1983). *Too many women? The sex ratio question.* Beverly Hills, CA: Sage.

Haas, A. (1979). Male and female spoken language differences: Stereotypes and evidence. *Psychological Bulletin, 86,* 616–626.

Haas, S. M., & Stafford, L. (1998). An initial examination of maintenance behaviors in gay and lesbian relationships. *Journal of Social and Personal Relationships, 15,* 846–855.

Haavio-Mannila, E., & Kontula, O. (1997). Correlates of increased sexual satisfaction. *Archives of Sexual Behavior, 26,* 399–419.

Hadley, T., & Jacob, T. (1976). The measurement of family power. *Sociometry, 39,* 384–395.

Hall, E. T. (1966). *The hidden dimension.* Garden City, NY: Doubleday.

Hall, J. A. (1998). How big are nonverbal sex differences? The case of smiling and sensitivity to nonverbal cues. In D. J. Canary & K. Dindia (Eds.), *Sex differences and similarities in communication: Critical essays and empirical investigations of sex and gender in interaction* (pp. 155–177). Mahwah, NJ: Erlbaum.

Hall, J. A., & Veccia, E. M. (1990). More "touching" observations: New insights in men, women, and interpersonal touch. *Journal of Personality and Social Psychology, 59,* 1155–1162.

Halliday, G. (1991). Psychological self-help books: How dangerous are they? *Psychotherapy, 28,* 678–680.

Hamermesh, D. S., & Biddle, J. E. (1994). Beauty and the labor market. *American Economic Review, 84,* 1174–1195.

Hammen, C. L., & Peters, S. D. (1978). Interpersonal consequences of depression: Responses to men and women enacting a depressed role. *Journal of Abnormal Psychology, 87,* 322–332.

Hammock, G., Rosen, S., Richardson, D., & Bernstein, S. (1989). Aggression as equity restoration. *Journal of Research in Personality, 23*, 398–409.

Hampton, R. L., Gelles, R. J., & Harrop, J. W. (1989). Is violence in black families increasing? A comparison of 1975 and 1985 national survey rates. *Journal of Marriage and the Family, 51*, 969–980.

Hancock, M., & Ickes, W. (1996). Empathic accuracy: When does the perceiver-target relationship make a difference? *Journal of Social and Personal Relationships, 13*, 179–199.

Hanley-Dunn, P., Maxwell, S. E., & Santos, J. P. (1985). Interpretation of interpersonal interactions: The influence of loneliness. *Personality and Social Psychology Bulletin, 11*, 445–456.

Hansen, G. L. (1985a). Dating jealousy among college students. *Sex Roles, 12*, 713–721.

Hansen, G. L. (1985b). Perceived threats and marital jealousy. *Social Psychology Quarterly, 48*, 262–268.

Hanson, T. L., McLanahan, S. S., & Thomson, E. (1998). Windows on divorce: Before and after. *Social Science Research, 27*, 329–349.

Hansson, R. O., & Jones, W. H. (1981). Loneliness, cooperation, and conformity among American undergraduates. *Journal of Social Psychology, 115*, 103–108.

Harrell, J., & Guerney, B. (1976). Training married couples in conflict negotiation skills. In D. H. Olson (Ed.), *Treating relationships* (pp. 151–165). Lake Mills, IA: Graphic Publishing.

Harris, C. R. (2000). Psychophysiological responses to imagined infidelity: The specific innate modular view of jealousy reconsidered. *Journal of Personality and Social Psychology, 78*, 1082–1091.

Harris, C. R., & Christenfeld, N. (1996). Gender, jealousy, and reason. *Psychological Science, 7*, 364–366.

Harris, M. J., & Rosenthal, R. (1985). Mediation of interpersonal expectancy effects: 31 meta-analyses. *Psychological Bulletin, 97*, 363–386.

Hartup, W. W. (1993). Adolescents and their friends. In B. Laursen (Ed.), *Close friendships in adolescence: No. 60. New directions for child development* (pp. 3–22). San Francisco: Jossey-Bass.

Harvey, J. H., Hendrick, S. S., & Tucker, K. (1988). Self-report methods in studying personal relationships. In S. Duck (Ed.), *Handbook of personal relationships: Theory, research, and interventions* (pp. 99–113). New York: Wiley.

Harvey, J. H., Wells, G. L., & Alvarez, M. D. (1978). Attribution in the context of conflict and separation in close relationships. In J. H. Harvey, W. J. Ickes, & R. F. Kidd (Eds.), *New directions in attributional research* (Vol. 2, pp. 235–260). Hillsdale, NJ: Erlbaum.

Haselton, M. G., & Buss, D. M. (2000). Error Management Theory: A new perspective on biases in cross-sex mind reading. *Journal of Personality and Social Psychology, 78*, 81–91.

Haslam, N., & Fiske, A. P. (1999). Relational models theory: A confirmatory factor analysis. *Personal Relationships, 6*, 241–250.

Hatala, M. N., Baack, D. W., & Parmenter, R. (1998). Dating with HIV: A content analysis of gay male HIV-positive and HIV-negative personal advertisements. *Journal of Social and Personal Relationships, 15*, 268–276.

Hatfield, E. (1983). Equity theory and research: An overview. In H. H. Blumberg, A. P. Hare, V. Kent, & M. Davies (Eds.), *Small groups and social interaction* (Vol. 2, pp. 401–412). Chichester, England: Wiley.

Hatfield, E. (1984). The dangers of intimacy. In V. J. Derlega (Ed.), *Communication, intimacy, and close relationships* (pp. 207–220). Orlando: Academic Press.

Hatfield, E., Greenberger, D., Traupmann, J., & Lambert, P. (1982). Equity and sexual satisfaction in recently married couples. *Journal of Sex Research, 17,* 18–32.

Hatfield, E., & Rapson, R. L. (1987). Passionate love: New directions in research. In W. H. Jones & D. Perlman (Eds.), *Advances in personal relationships* (Vol. 1, pp. 109–139). Greenwich, CT: JAI Press.

Hatfield, E., & Sprecher, S. (1986). Measuring passionate love in intimate relationships. *Journal of Adolescence, 9,* 383–410.

Havighurst, R. J. (1961). Successful aging. *Gerontologist, 1,* 8–13.

Haynes, J. M. (1981). *Divorce mediation.* New York: Springer.

Hays, R. B. (1985). A longitudinal study of friendship development. *Journal of Personality and Social Psychology, 48,* 909–924.

Hazan, C., & Shaver, P. (1987). Romantic love conceptualized as an attachment process. *Journal of Personality and Social Psychology, 52,* 511–524.

Hazan, C., & Zeifman, D. (1994). Sex and the psychological tether. In K. Bartholomew & D. Perlman (Eds.), *Attachment processes in adulthood* (pp. 151–178). London: Jessica Kingsley.

Heaton, T. B., & Albrecht, S. L. (1991). Stable unhappy marriages. *Journal of Marriage and the Family , 53,* 747–758.

Heavey, C. L., Christensen, A., & Malamuth, N. M. (1995). The longitudinal impact of demand and withdrawal during marital conflict. *Journal of Consulting and Clinical Psychology, 63,* 797–801.

Heavy, C. L., Layne, C., & Christensen, A. (1993). Gender and conflict structure in marital interaction: A replication and extension. *Journal of Consulting and Clinical Psychology, 61,* 16–27.

Hebl, M. R., Foster, J. M., Mannix, L. M., & Dovidio, J. F. (2000). *Formal and interpersonal discrimination: A field study examination of applicant bias.* Manuscript submitted for publication.

Hebl, M. R., & Heatherton, T. F. (1998). The stigma of obesity in women: The difference is black and white. *Personality and Social Psychology Bulletin, 24,* 417–426.

Hecht, M. A., & LaFrance, M. (1998). License or obligation to smile: The effect of power and sex on amount and type of smiling. *Personality and Social Psychology Bulletin, 24,* 1332–1342.

Hecht, M. L., Marston, P. J., & Larkey, L. K. (1994). Love ways and relationship quality in heterosexual relationships. *Journal of Social and Personal Relationships, 11,* 25–43.

Heider, F. (1958). *The psychology of interpersonal relations.* New York: Wiley.

Heiman, J. R., LoPiccolo, L., & LoPiccolo, J. (1981). The treatment of sexual dysfunction. In A. S. Gurman & D. P. Kniskern (Eds.), *Handbook of family therapy* (pp. 631–661). New York: Brunner/Mazel.

Heiman, J. R., & Verhulst, J. (1990). Sexual dysfunction and marriage. In F. D. Fincham & T. N. Bradbury (Eds.), *The psychology of marriage: Basic issues and applications* (pp. 299–322). New York: Guilford Press.

Helgeson, V. S., & Fritz, H. L. (1999). Unmitigated agency and unmitigated communion: Distinctions from agency and communion. *Journal of Research in Personality, 33,* 131–158.

Henderson, L., & Zimbardo, P. (1998). Shyness. In H. S. Friedman (Ed.), *Encyclopedia of mental health* (Vol. 3, pp. 497–509). San Diego, CA: Academic Press.

Henderson-King, D. H., & Veroff, J. (1994). Sexual satisfaction and marital well-being in the first years of marriages. *Journal of Social and Personal Relationships, 11,* 509–534.

Hendrick, C., Hendrick, S. S., & Dicke, A. (1998). The Love Attitudes Scale: Short Form. *Journal of Social and Personal Relationships, 15,* 147–159.

Hendrick, S. S. (1981). Self-disclosure and marital satisfaction. *Journal of Personality and Social Psychology, 40,* 1150–1159.

Hendrick, S. S., & Hendrick, C. (1987). Love and sex attitudes: A close relationship. In W. H. Jones & D. Perlman (Eds.), *Advances in personal relationships* (Vol. 1, pp. 141–169). Greenwich, CT: JAI Press.

Hendrick, S. S., & Hendrick, C. (1993). Lovers as friends. *Journal of Social and Personal Relationships, 10,* 459–466.

Hendrick, S. S., & Hendrick, C. (1995). Gender differences and similarities in sex and love. *Personal Relationships, 2,* 55–65.

Henley, N. M. (1977). *Body politics: Power, sex, and nonverbal communication.* Englewood Cliffs, NJ: Prentice-Hall.

Herek, G. M., & Capitanio, J. P. (1996). "Some of my best friends": Intergroup contact, concealable stigma, and heterosexuals' attitudes toward gay men and lesbians. *Personality and Social Psychology Bulletin, 22,* 412–424.

Herek, G. M., & Glunt, E. K. (1993). Interpersonal contact and heterosexuals' attitudes toward gay men: Results from a national survey. *Journal of Sex Research, 30,* 239–244.

Hetherington, E. M., Bridges, M., & Insabella, G. M. (1998). What matters? What does not? Five perspectives on the association between marital transitions and children's adjustment. *American Psychologist, 53,* 167–184.

Hickman, S. E., & Muehlenhard, C. L. (1999). "By the semi-mystical appearance of a condom": How young women and men communicate sexual consent in heterosexual situations. *Journal of Sex Research, 36,* 258–272.

Hieger, L. J., & Troll, L. A. (1973). A three-generation study of attitudes concerning the importance of romantic love in mate selection. *Gerontologist, 13* (3, Part 2), 86.

Hill, C. A., Blakemore, J. E. O., & Drumm, P. (1997). Mutual and unrequited love in adolescence and young adulthood. *Personal Relationships, 4,* 15–23.

Hill, C. A., & Preston, L. K. (1996). Individual differences in the experience of sexual motivation: Theory and measurement of dispositional sexual motives. *Journal of Sex Research, 33,* 27–45.

Hill, C. T., Rubin, Z., Peplau, L. A., & Willard, S. G. (1979). The volunteer couple: Sex differences, couple commitment, and participation in research on interpersonal relationships. *Social Psychology Quarterly, 41,* 415–420.

Hinkin, T. R., & Schreischeim, C. A. (1990). Relationships between subordinate perceptions of supervisor influence tactics and attributed bases of supervisory power. *Human Relations, 43,* 221–237.

Hoffman, L. (1981). *Foundation of family life.* New York: Basic Books.

Hokanson, J. E., Loewenstein, D. A., Hedeen, C., & Howes, M. J. (1986). Dysphoric college students and roommates: A study of social behaviors over a three month period. *Personality and Social Psychology Bulletin, 12,* 311–324.

Holman, T. B., & Jarvis, M. O. (2000). *Replicating and validating Gottman's couple conflict types using survey data.* Unpublished manuscript, Brigham Young University, Provo, UT.

Holmes, D. S. (1991). *Abnormal psychology.* New York: Harper & Row.

Holmes, J. G. (1991). Trust and the appraisal process in close relationships. In W. H. Jones & D. Perlman (Eds.), *Advances in personal relationships* (Vol. 2, pp. 57–106). London: Jessica Kingsley.

Holmes, J. G., & Boon, S. D. (1990). Developments in the field of close relationships: Creating foundations for intervention strategies. *Personality and Social Psychology Bulletin, 16,* 23–41.

Holmes, J. G., & Levinger, G. (1994). Paradoxical effects of closeness in relationships on perceptions of justice: An interdependence-theory perspective. In M. J. Lerner & G. Mikula (Eds.), *Entitlement and the affectional bond: Justice in close relationships* (pp. 149–173). New York: Plenum.

Holtzworth-Munroe, A., & Jacobson, N. S. (1985). Causal attributions of marital couples: When do they search for causes? What do they conclude when they do? *Journal of Personality and Social Psychology, 48,* 1398–1412.

Holtzworth-Munroe, A., & Jacobson, N. S. (1988). Toward a methodology for coding spontaneous causal attributions: Preliminary results with married couples. *Journal of Social and Clinical Psychology, 7,* 101–112.

Homans, G. C. (1961). *Social behavior.* New York: Hartcourt, Brace & World.

Honeycutt, J. M. (1996). How "helpful" are self–help relational books? Common sense or counterintuitive information. *Personal Relationship Issues, 3,* 1–3.

Honeycutt, J. M., Cantrill, J. G., Kelly, P., & Lambkin, D. (1998). How do I love thee? Let me consider my options: Cognition, verbal strategies, and the escalation of intimacy. *Human Communication Research, 25,* 39–63.

Hoobler, G. D. (1999, June). *Ten years of personal relationships research: Where have we been and where are we going?* Paper presented at the meeting of the International Network on Personal Relationships, Louisville, KY.

Hopper, J. (1993). The rhetoric of motives in divorce. *Journal of Marriage and the Family, 55,* 801–813.

Horneffer, K. J., & Fincham, F. D. (1996). Attributional models of depression and marital distress. *Personality and Social Psychology Bulletin, 22,* 678–689.

Hornstein, G. A., & Truesdell, S. E. (1988). Development of intimate conversation in close relationships. *Journal of Social and Clinical Psychology, 7,* 49–64.

Horowitz, L. M. (1979). On the cognitive structure of interpersonal problems treated in psychotherapy. *Journal of Consulting and Clinical Psychology, 47,* 5–15.

Horwitz, A. V. (1982). Sex-role expectations, power, and psychological distress. *Sex Roles, 8,* 607–624.

Houston, J. P. (1981). *The pursuit of happiness.* Glenview, IL: Scott, Foresman.

Houts, A. C., Cook, T. D., & Shadish, W. R., Jr. (1986). The person-situation debate: A critical multiplist perspective. *Journal of Personality, 54,* 52–105.

Howard, J. A., Blumstein, P., & Schwartz, P. (1986). Sex, power, and influence tactics in intimate relationships. *Journal of Personality and Social Psychology, 51,* 102–109.

Howard, J. W., & Dawes, R. M. (1976). Linear prediction of marital happiness. *Personality and Social Psychology Bulletin, 2,* 478–480.

Howes, C. (1996). The earliest friendships. In W. M. Bukowski, A. F. Newcomb, & W. W. Hartup (Eds.), *The company they keep: Friendship in childhood and adolescence* (pp. 66–86). New York: Cambridge University Press.

Hughes, D. K., & Surra, C. A. (2000). The reported influence of research participation on premarital relationships. *Journal of Marriage and the Family, 62,* 822–832.

Humphrey, F. G. (1983). *Marital therapy.* Englewood Cliffs, NJ: Prentice-Hall.

Hunt, M. (1974). *Sexual behavior in the 1970s.* Chicago: Playboy Press.

Hunt, M. M. (1959). *The natural history of love.* New York: Knopf.

Hupka, R. B., & Bank, A. L. (1996). Sex differences in jealousy: Evolution or social construction? *Cross-Cultural Research, 30,* 24–59.

Hupka, R. B., Buunk, B., Falus, G., Fulgosi, A., Ortega, E., Swain, R., & Tarabrina, N. V. (1985). Romantic jealousy and romantic envy: A seven-nation study. *Journal of Cross-Cultural Psychology, 16,* 423–446.

Huppe, M., & Cyr, M. (1997). Division of household labor and marital satisfaction of dual income couples according to family life cycle. *Canadian Journal of Counseling, 31*, 145–162.

Hurlbert, D. F., & Apt, C. (1995). The coital alignment technique and directed masturbation: A comparative study on female orgasm. *Journal of Sex and Marital Therapy, 21*, 21–29.

Hurvitz, N. (1970). Interaction hypotheses in marriage counseling. *Family Coordinator, 19*, 64–75.

Huston, T. L. (1973). Ambiguity of acceptance, social desirability, and dating choice. *Journal of Experimental Social Psychology, 9*, 32–42.

Huston, T. L. (1983). Power. In H. H. Kelley, E. Berscheid, A. Christensen et al. (Eds.), *Close relationships* (pp. 169–219). New York: Freeman.

Huston, T. L. (1999). *The connubial crucible: Newlywed years as predictors of marital delight, distress, and divorce.* Paper presented at the meeting of the American Psychological Association, Boston.

Huston, T. L. (2000). The social ecology of marriage and other intimate unions. *Journal of Marriage and the Family, 62*, 298–320.

Huston, T. L., & Chorost, A. F. (1994). Behavioral buffers on the effect of negativity on marital satisfaction: A longitudinal study. *Personal Relationships, 1*, 223–239.

Huston, T. L., & Houts, R. M. (1998). The psychological infrastructure of courtship and marriage: The role of personality and compatibility in romantic relationships. In T. N. Bradbury (Ed.), *The developmental course of marital dysfunction* (pp. 114–151). New York: Cambridge University Press.

Hyde, J. S., & DeLamater, J. (2000). *Understanding human sexuality* (7th ed.) New York: McGraw-Hill.

Hymel, S., Tarulli, D., Hayden Thompson, L., & Terrell-Deutsch, B. (1999). Loneliness through the eyes of children. In K. J. Rotenberg & S. Hymel (Eds.), *Loneliness in childhood and adolescence* (pp. 80–106). New York: Cambridge University Press.

Ickes, W. (1985). Sex-role influences on compatibility in relationships. In W. Ickes (Ed.), *Compatible and incompatible relationships* (pp. 187–208). New York: Springer-Verlag.

Ickes, W. (2000). Methods of studying close relationships. In W. Ickes & S. Duck (Eds.), *The social psychology of personal relationships* (pp. 159–180). Chichester, England: Wiley.

Ickes, W., & Barnes, R. D. (1978). Boys and girls together—and alienated: On enacting stereotyped sex roles in mixed-sex dyads. *Journal of Personality and Social Psychology, 36*, 669–683.

Ickes, W., & Simpson, J. A. (1997). Managing empathic accuracy in close relationships. In W. J. Ickes (Ed.), *Empathic accuracy* (pp. 218–250). New York: Guilford Press.

Ickes, W. J. (Ed.). (1997). *Empathic accuracy.* New York: Guilford Press.

Ijsendoorn, M. H., & Sagi, A. (1999). Cross–cultural patterns of attachment: Universal and contextual dimensions. In J. Cassidy & P. R. Shaver (Eds.), *Handbook of attachment: Theory, research and clinical applications* (pp. 713–734). New York: Guilford Press.

Isabella, R. A. (1998). Origins of attachment: The role of context, duration, frequency of observation, and infant age in measuring maternal behavior. *Journal of Social and Personal Relationships, 15*, 538–554.

Jackson, T., Towson, S., & Narduzzi, K. (1997). Predictors of shyness: A test of variables associated with self-presentational models. *Social Behavior and Personality, 25*, 149–154.

Jacobson, N. S., & Christensen, A. (1996). *Integrative couple therapy: Promoting acceptance and change.* New York: W. W. Norton.

Jacobson, N. S., Follette, W. C., & McDonald, D. W. (1982). Reactivity to positive and negative behavior in distressed and nondistressed married couples. *Journal of Consulting and Clinical Psychology, 50,* 706–714.

Jacobson, N. S., & Gurman, A. S. (Eds.). (1986). *Clinical handbook of marital therapy.* New York: Guilford Press.

Jacobson, N. S., & Margolin, G. (1979). *Marital therapy: Strategies based on social learning and behavior exchange principles.* New York: Brunner/Mazel.

Jacoby, A. P., & Williams, J. D. (1985). Effects of premarital sexual standards and behavior on dating and marriage desirability. *Journal of Marriage and the Family, 47,* 1059–1065.

Jamieson, D. W., & Thomas, K. W. (1974). Power and conflict in the student-teacher relationship. *Journal of Applied Behavioral Science, 10,* 321–336.

Jankowiak, W., & Fischer, E. (1992). A cross-cultural perspective on romantic love. *Ethnology, 31,* 149–155.

Jensen-Campbell, L. A., Graziano, W. G., & West, S. G. (1995). Dominance, prosocial orientation, and female preferences: Do nice guys really finish last? *Journal of Personality and Social Psychology, 68,* 427–440.

Jessor, R., Costa, F., Jessor, L., & Donovan, J. E. (1983). Time of first intercourse: A prospective study. *Journal of Personality and Social Psychology, 44,* 608–626.

Johnson, C. L. (1975). Authority and power in Japanese-American marriage. In R. E. Cromwell & D. H. Olson (Eds.), *Power in families* (pp. 182–196). New York: Wiley.

Johnson, C. L., & Troll, L. E. (1994). Constraints and facilitators to friendships in late life. *Gerontologist, 34,* 79–87.

Johnson, M. P. (1995). Patriarchal terrorism and common couple violence: Two forms of violence against women. *Journal of Marriage and the Family, 57,* 283–294.

Johnson, M. P. (1999). Personal, moral, and structural commitment to relationships: Experiences of choice and constraint. In J. M. Adams & W. H. Jones (Eds.), *Handbook on interpersonal commitment and relationship stability* (pp. 73–87). New York: Kluwer Academic/Plenum.

Johnson, M. P. (2000). *Domestic violence is not a unitary phenomenon: A major flaw in the domestic violence literature.* Unpublished manuscript, Pennsylvania State University, University Park, PA.

Johnson, M. P. (in press). Conflict and control: Images of symmetry and asymmetry in domestic violence. In A. Booth, A. C. Crouter, & M. Clements (Eds.), *Couples in conflict.* Hillsdale, NJ: Erlbaum.

Johnson, M. P., Caughlin, J. P., & Huston, T. L. (1999). The tripartite nature of marital commitment: Personal, moral, and structural reasons to stay married. *Journal of Marriage and the Family, 61,* 160–177.

Johnson, M. P., & Ferraro, K. J. (2000). Research on domestic violence in the 1990s: Making distinctions. *Journal of Marriage and the Family, 62,* 948–963.

Johnson, M. P., & Leone, J. M. (2000, July). *The differential effects of patriarchal terrorism and common couple violence: Findings from the National Violence Against Women Survey.* Paper presented at the 10th International Conference on Personal Relationships, Brisbane, Australia.

Johnson, P. (1976). Women and power: Toward a theory of effectiveness. *Journal of Social Issues, 33,* 99–110.

Johnson, P. (1978). Women and interpersonal power. In I. H. Frieze, J. Parsons, P. B. Johnson, D. Ruble, & G. Zellman (Eds.), *Women and sex roles: A social psychological perspective* (pp. 301–320). New York: Norton.

Johnson, S. M., & Greenberg, L. (1995). The emotionally focused approach to problems in adult attachment. In N. S. Jacobson & A. S. Gurman (Eds.), *Clinical handbook of couple therapy* (pp. 121–141). New York: Guilford.

Johnson, S. M., Hunsley, J., Greenberg, L., & Schindler, D. (1999). Emotionally focused couples therapy: Status and challenges. *Clinical Psychology: Science and Practice, 6,* 67–79.

Joiner, T. E., Jr., & Metalsky, G. I. (1995). A prospective test of an integrative interpersonal theory of depression: A naturalistic study of college roommates. *Journal of Personality and Social Psychology, 69,* 778–788.

Joiner, T. E., Jr., Metalsky, G. I., Katz, J., & Beach, S. R. H. (1999). Depression and excessive reassurance-seeking. *Psychological Inquiry, 10,* 269–278.

Jones, D. (1995). Sexual selection, physical attractiveness, and facial neotony: Cross-cultural evidence and implications. *Current Anthropology, 36,* 723–748.

Jones, E. E., & Pittman, T. (1982). Toward a general theory of strategic self-presentation. In J. Suls (Ed.), *Psychological perspectives on the self* (pp. 231–262). Hillsdale, NJ: Erlbaum.

Jones, J. T., & Cunningham, J. D. (1996). Attachment styles and other predictors of relationship satisfaction in dating couples. *Personal Relationships, 3,* 387–399.

Jones, W. H. (1990). Loneliness and social exclusion. *Journal of Social and Clinical Psychology, 9,* 214–220.

Jones, W. H. (2000, June). *Loneliness and relationship dynamics: Betrayal, apology, and forgiveness.* Paper presented at the meeting of the International Society for the Study of Personal Relationships, Brisbane.

Jones, W. H., & Burdette, M. P. (1994). Betrayal in relationships. In A. L. Weber & J. H. Harvey (Eds.), *Perspectives on close relationships* (pp. 243–262). Boston: Allyn & Bacon.

Jones, W. H., & Carpenter, B. N. (1986). Shyness, social behavior, and relationships. In W. H. Jones, J. M. Cheek, & S. R. Briggs (Eds.), *Shyness: Perspectives on research and treatment* (pp. 227–238). New York: Plenum.

Jones, W. H., & Carver, M. D. (1991). Adjustment and coping implications of loneliness. In C. R. Snyder & D. R. Forsyth (Eds.), *Handbook of social and clinical psychology: The health perspective* (pp. 395–415). New York: Pergamon Press.

Jones, W. H., Cavert, C. W., Snider, R. L., & Bruce, T. (1985). Relational stress: An analysis of situations and events associated with loneliness. In S. Duck & D. Perlman (Eds.), *Understanding personal relationships: An interdisciplinary approach* (pp. 221–242). London: Sage.

Jones, W. H., Cheek, J. M., & Briggs, S. R. (Eds.). (1986). *Shyness: Perspectives on research and treatment.* New York: Plenum.

Jones, W. H., Crouch, L. L., & Scott, S. (1997). Trust and betrayal: The psychology of trust violations. In R. Hogan, J. Johnson, & S. R. Briggs (Eds.), *Handbook of personality psychology* (pp. 466–482). New York: Academic Press.

Jones, W. H., Freemon, J. E., & Goswick, R. A. (1981). The persistence of loneliness: Self and other determinants. *Journal of Personality, 49,* 27–48.

Jones, W. H., Hobbs, S. A., & Hackenbury, D. (1982). Loneliness and social skills deficits. *Journal of Personality and Social Psychology, 42,* 682–689.

Jones, W. H., Sansome, C., & Helm, B. (1983). Loneliness and interpersonal judgments. *Personality and Social Psychology Bulletin, 9,* 437–442.

Kahneman, D., & Tversky, A. (1982). The psychology of preferences. *Scientific American, 246,* 160–173.

Kalb, C. (1999, August 9). Our quest to be perfect. *Newsweek, 134,* 52–59.

Kalick, S. M., & Hamilton, T. E. (1986). The matching hypothesis reexamined. *Journal of Personality and Social Psychology, 51,* 673–682.

Kalick, S. M., Zebrowitz, L. A., Langlois, J. H., & Johnson, R. M. (1998). Does human facial physical attractiveness honestly advertise health? Longitudinal data on an evolutionary question. *Psychological Science, 9,* 8–13.

Kandel, D. B. (1978). Similarity in real-life adolescent friendship pairs. *Journal of Personality and Social Psychology, 36,* 306–312.

Kantor, G. K., & Jasinski, J. L. (1998). Dynamics and risk factors in partner violence. In J. L. Jasinski & L. M. Williams (Eds.), *Partner violence: A comprehensive review of 20 years of research* (pp. 1–43). Thousand Oaks, CA: Sage.

Karney, B. R., & Bradbury, T. N. (1995). The longitudinal course of marital quality and stability: A review of theory, methods, and research. *Psychological Bulletin, 118,* 3–34.

Karney, B. R., & Bradbury, T. N. (1997). Neuroticism, marital interaction, and the trajectory of marital satisfaction. *Journal of Personality and Social Psychology, 72,* 1075–1092.

Karney, B. R., & Bradbury, T. N. (2000). Attributions in marriage: State or trait? A growth curve analysis. *Journal of Personality and Social Psychology, 78,* 295–309.

Karney, B. R., & Coombs, R. H. (2000). Memory bias in long-term close relationships: Consistency or improvement? *Personality and Social Psychology Bulletin, 26,* 959–970.

Karney, B. R., Davila, J., Cohan, C. L., Sullivan, K. T., Johnson, M. D., Bradbury, T. N. (1995). An empirical investigation of sampling strategies in marital research. *Journal of Marriage and the Family, 57 ,* 909–920.

Karney, B. R., McNulty, J. K., & Fry, N. E. (2001). A social-cognitive perspective on the maintenance and deterioraion of relationship satisfaction. In J. H. Harvey & A. E. Wenzel (Eds.), *Close romantic relationships: Maintenance and enhancement* (pp. 195–214). Mahwah, NJ: Erlbaum.

Kashy, D. A., & DePaulo, B. M. (1996). Who lies? *Journal of Personality and Social Psychology, 70,* 1037–1051.

Katvez, A. R., Warner, R. L., & Acock, A. C. (1994). Girls or boys? The relationship of child gender to marital instability. *Journal of Marriage and the Family, 56,* 89–100.

Katz, J., Anderson, P., & Beach, S. R. H. (1997). Dating relationship quality: Effects of global self-verification and self-enhancement. *Journal of Social and Personal Relationships, 14,* 829–842.

Kellerman, J., Lewis, J., & Laird, J. D. (1989). Looking and loving: The effects of mutual gaze on feelings of love. *Journal of Research in Personality, 23,* 145–161.

Kelley, H. H. (1979). *Personal relationships: Their structures and processes.* Hillsdale, NJ: Erlbaum.

Kelley, H. H. (1983). Love and commitment. In H. H. Kelley, E. Berscheid, A. Christensen et al. (Eds.), *Close relationships* (pp. 265–314). New York: Freeman.

Kelley, H. H., & Thibaut, J. W. (1978). *Interpersonal relations: A theory of interdependence.* New York: Wiley.

Kelley, K., & Rolker-Dolinsky, B. (1987). The psychosexology of female initiation and dominance. In D. Perlman & S. Duck (Eds.), *Intimate relationships: Development, dynamics, and deterioration* (pp. 63–87). Newbury Park, CA: Sage.

Kelly, E. L., & Conley, J. J. (1987). Personality and compatibility: A prospective analysis of marital stability and marital satisfaction. *Journal of Personality and Social Psychology, 52,* 27–40.

Kelly, J. B. (1995). A decade of divorce mediation research: Some answers and questions. *Family and Conciliation Courts Review, 34,* 373–385.

Keltner, D. (1995). Signs of appeasement: Evidence for the distinct displays of embarrassment, amusement, and shame. *Journal of Personality and Social Psychology, 68,* 441–454.

Kenny, D. A. (1994). *Interpersonal perception: A social relations analysis.* New York: Guilford Press.

Kenrick, D. T., & Cialdini, R. B. (1977). Romantic attraction: Misattribution versus reinforcement explanations. *Journal of Personality and Social Psychology, 35,* 381–391.

Kenrick, D. T., & Gutierres, S. E. (1989). Influence of popular erotica on judgments of strangers and mates. *Journal of Experimental Social Psychology, 25,* 159–167.

Kenrick, D. T., & Keefe, R. C. (1992). Age preferences in mates reflect sex differences in reproductive strategies. *Behavioral and Brain Sciences, 15,* 75–133.

Kenrick, D. T., Keefe, R. C., Bryan, A., Barr, A., & Brown, S. (1995). Age preferences and mate choice among homosexuals and heterosexuals: A case for modular psychological mechanisms. *Journal of Personality and Social Psychology, 69,* 1166–1172.

Kenrick, D. T., Montello, D. R., Gutierres, S. E., & Trost, M. R. (1993). Effects of physical attractiveness on affect and perceptual judgments: When social comparison overrides social reinforcement. *Personality and Social Psychology Bulletin, 19,* 195–199.

Kenrick, D. T., Sadalla, E. K., Groth, G., & Trost, M. R. (1990). Evolution, traits, and the stages of human courtship: Qualifying the parental investment model. *Journal of Personality, 58,* 97–116.

Kenrick, D. T., & Trost, M. R. (2000). An evolutionary perspective on human relationships. In W. Ickes & S. Duck (Eds.), *The social psychology of personal relationships* (pp. 9–35). Chichester, England: Wiley.

Kephart, W. (1967). Some correlates of romantic love. *Journal of Marriage and the Family, 29,* 470–479.

Kiecolt-Glaser, J. K. (1999) Stress, personal relationships, and immune function: Health implications. *Brain, Behavior and Immunity, 13 ,* 61–72.

Kiecolt-Glaser, J. K., Fisher, L. D., Ogrocki, P., Stout, J. C., Speicher, C. E., & Glaser, R. (1987). Marital quality, marital disruption, and immune function. *Psychosomatic Medicine, 49,* 13–34.

Kiecolt-Glaser, J. K., Garner, W., Speicher, C., Penn, G. M., Holliday, J., & Glaser, R. (1984). Psychosocial modifiers of immunocompetence in medical students. *Psychosomatic Medicine, 46,* 7–14.

Kiecolt-Glaser, J. K., Malarkey, W. B., Chee, M., Newton, T., Cacioppo, J. T., Hsiao-Yin, M., & Glaser, R. (1993). Negative behavior during marital conflict is associated with immunological down–regulation. *Psychosomatic Medicine, 55,* 395–409.

Kiesler, S. B., & Baral, R. L. (1970). The secret for a romantic partner: The effects of self-esteem and physical attractiveness on romantic behavior. In K. J. Gergen & D. Marlowe (Eds.), *Personality and social behavior* (pp. 155–166). Reading, MA: Addison-Wesley.

Kirkpatrick, L. A. (1999). Attachment and religious representations and behavior. In J. Cassidy & P. R. Shaver (Eds.), *Handbook of attachment: Theory, research and clinical applications* (pp. 803–822). New York: Guilford.

Kirkpatrick, L. A., & Hazan, C. (1994). Attachment styles and close relationships: A four-year prospective study. *Personal Relationships, 1,* 123–142.

Kitson, G. C., Barbi, K. B., & Roach, M. J. (1985). Who divorces and why?: A review. *Journal of Family Issues, 6,* 255–293.

Kitson, G. C., & Morgan, L. A. (1990). The multiple consequences of divorce: A decade review. *Journal of Marriage and the Family, 44,* 924–973.

Klein, R. C. A. (1998). Conflict and violence in the family: Cross-disciplinary issues. In R. C. A. Klein (Ed.), *Multidisciplinary perspectives on family violence* (pp. 1–13). New York: Routledge.

Kleinke, C. L. (1986). Gaze and eye contact: A research review. *Psychological Bulletin, 100,* 78–100.

Kleinke, C. L., & Dean, G. O. (1990). Evaluation of men and women receiving positive and negative responses with various acquaintance strategies. *Journal of Social Behavior and Personality, 5,* 369–377.

Klohnen, E. C., & Bera, S. (1998). Behavioral and experiential patterns of avoidantly and securely attached women across adulthood: A 31-year longitudinal perspective. *Journal of Personality and Social Psychology, 74,* 211–223.

Kluwer, E. S., Heesink, J. A. M., & Van De Vliert, E. (1997). The marital dynamics of conflict over the division of labor. *Journal of Marriage and the Family, 59,* 635–653.

Knee, C. R. (1998). Implicit theories of relationships: Assessment and prediction of romantic relationship initiation, coping, and longevity. *Journal of Personality and Social Psychology, 74,* 360–370.

Knox, D., Jr. (1970). Conceptions of love at three developmental levels. . *Family Coordinator, 19,* 151–156.

Kobak, R. R., & Sceery, A. (1988). Attachment in late adolescence: Working models, affect regulation, and representations of self and others. *Child Development, 59,* 135–146.

Koestner, R., & Wheeler, L. (1988). Self-presentation in personal advertisements: The influence of implicit notions of attraction and role expectations. *Journal of Social and Personal Relationships, 5,* 149–160.

Kollock, P., Blumstein, P., & Schwartz, P. (1985). Sex and power in interaction: Conversational privileges and duties. *American Sociological Review, 50,* 34–46.

Koski, L. R., & Shaver, P. R. (1997). Attachment and relationship satisfaction across the lifespan. In R. J. Sternberg & M. Hojjat (Eds.), *Satisfaction in close relationships* (pp. 26–55). New York: Guilford Press.

Kotlar, S. L. (1965). Middle-class role perceptions and marital adjustments. *Sociology and Social Research, 49,* 283–293.

Kouri, K. M., & Lasswell, M. (1993). Black-White marriages: Social change and intergenerational mobility. *Marriage and Family Review, 19,* 241–255.

Kowalski, R. M. (2000). "I was only kidding!": Victims' and perpetrators' perceptions of teasing. *Personality and Social Psychology Bulletin, 26,* 231–241.

Kowalski, R. M. (Ed.). (1997). *Aversive interpersonal behaviors.* New York: Plenum.

Kowalski, R. M. (Ed.). (2000). *Behaving badly: Aversive behaviors in interpersonal relationships.* Washington, DC: American Psychological Association.

Kraut, R. E., & Poe, D. B. (1980). Behavioral roots of person perception: The deception judgments of customs inspectors and laymen. *Journal of Personality and Social Psychology, 39,* 784–798.

Kraut, R., Patterson, M., Lundmark, V., Kiesler, S., Mukophadhyay, T., & Scherlis, W. (1998). Internet paradox: A social technology that reduces social involvement and psychological well-being? *American Psychologist, 53,* 1017–1031.

Krishnan, V. (1998). Premarital cohabitation and marital disruption. *Journal of Divorce and Remarriage, 28,* 157–170.

Kropp, J. P., & Haynes, O. M. (1987). Abusive and nonabusive mothers' ability to identify general and specific emotion signals of infants. *Child Development, 58,* 187–190.

Krueger, J., Ham, J. J., & Linford, K. M. (1996). Perceptions of behavioral consistency: Are people aware of the actor-observer effect? *Psychological Science, 7,* 259–264.

Kruger, J., & Gilovich, T. (1999). "Naïve cynicism" in everyday theories of responsibility assessment: On biased assumption of bias. *Journal of Personality and Social Psychology, 76,* 743–753.

Kruglanski, A. W. (1996). Motivated social cognition: Principles of the interface. In E. T. Higgins & A. W. Kruglanski (Eds.), *Social psychology: Handbook of basic principles* (pp. 493–520). New York: Guilford Press.

Kuczmarski, R. J., Flegal, K. M., Campbell, S. M., & Johnson, C. L. (1994). Increasing prevalence of overweight among US adults: The national health and nutrition examination surveys, 1960 to 1991. *Journal of the American Medical Association, 272,* 205–211.

Kunda, Z. (1999). *Social cognition: Making sense of people.* Cambridge, MA: MIT Press.

Kupersmidt, J. B., Coie, J. D., & Dodge, K. A. (1990). The role of poor peer relationships in the development of disorder. In S. R. Asher & J. D. Coie (Eds.), *Peer rejection in childhood* (pp. 274–305). New York: Cambridge University Press.

Kurdek, L. A. (1991). Sexuality in homosexual and heterosexual couples. In K. McKinney & S. Sprecher, *Sexuality in close relationships* (pp. 177–191). Hillsdale, NJ: Erlbaum.

Kurdek, L. A. (1992). Relationship stability and relationship satisfaction in cohabiting gay and lesbian couples: A prospective longitudinal test of the contextual and interdependence models. *Journal of Social and Personal Relationships, 9,* 125–142.

Kurdek, L. A. (1993). Nature and prediction of changes in marital quality for first-time parent and nonparent husbands and wives. *Journal of Family Psychology, 6,* 255–265.

Kurdek, L. A. (1994a). Areas of conflict for gay, lesbian, and heterosexual couples: What couples argue about influences relationship satisfaction. *Journal of Marriage and the Family, 56,* 923–934.

Kurdek, L. A. (1994b). The nature and correlates of relationship quality in gay, lesbian, and heterosexual cohabiting couples: A test of the individual difference, interdependence, and discrepancy models. In B. Greene & G. M. Herek (Eds.), *Lesbian and gay psychology: Theory, research, and clinical applications* (pp. 133–155). Thousand Oaks, CA: Sage.

Kurdek, L. A. (1998a). Developmental changes in marital satisfaction: A 6-year prospective longitudinal study of newlywed couples. In T. N. Bradbury (Ed.), *The developmental course of marital dysfunction* (pp. 180–204). Cambridge: Cambridge University Press.

Kurdek, L. A. (1998b). Relationship outcomes and their predictors: Longitudinal evidence from heterosexual married, gay cohabiting, and lesbian cohabiting couples. *Journal of Marriage and the Family, 60,* 553–568.

Kurdek, L. A., & Schmitt, J. P. (1986a). Interaction of sex role self-concept with relationship quality and relationship beliefs in married, heterosexual cohabiting, gay, and lesbian couples. *Journal of Personality and Social Psychology, 51,* 365–370.

Kurdek, L. A., & Schmitt, J. P. (1986b). Relationship quality in heterosexual married, heterosexual cohabitating, and gay and lesbian relationships. *Journal of Personality and Social Psychology, 51,* 711–720.

Kyes, K. B. (1990). The effect of a "safer sex" film as mediated by erotophobia and gender on attitudes toward condoms. *Journal of Sex Research, 27,* 297–303.

Kyes, K. B., Brown, I. S., & Pollack, R. H. (1991). The effect of exposure to a condom script on attitudes toward condoms. *Journal of Psychology and Human Sexuality, 4,* 21–36.

LaFrance, M. (1992). Gender and interruptions: Individual infraction or violation of the social order? *Psychology of Women Quarterly, 16,* 497–512.

Lakoff, R. (1975). *Language and woman's place.* New York: Harper & Row.

Lamm, H., & Wiesmann, U. (1997). Subjective attributes of attraction: How people characterize their liking, their love, and their being in love. *Personal Relationships, 4,* 271–284.

Landers, A. (1982). *Love or sex . . . and how to tell the difference.* Chicago: Field Enterprises.

Landers, A. (1997, March 22). Nurse offers article to help families, friends of bereaved parents. *The Bryan-College Station Eagle,* p. C7.

Lane, J. D., & Wegner, D. M. (1994). Secret relationships: The back alley to love. In R. Erber & R. Gilmour (Eds.), *Theoretical frameworks for personal relationships* (pp. 67–85). Hillsdale, NJ: Erlbaum.

Lane, J. D., & Wegner, D. M. (1995). The cognitive consequences of secrecy. *Journal of Personality and Social Psychology, 69,* 237–253.

Lang, F. R., & Carstensen, L. L. (1994). Close emotional relationships in late life: Further support for proactive aging in the social domain. *Psychology and Aging, 9,* 315–324.

Langlois, J. H., Kalakanis, L., Rubenstein, A. J., Larson, A., Hallam, M., & Smoot, M. (2000). Maxims or myths of beauty? A meta-analytic and theoretical review. *Psychological Bulletin, 126,* 390–423.

Langlois, J. H., Ritter, J. M., Roggman, L. A., & Vaughn, L. S. (1991). Facial diversity and infant preferences for attractive faces. *Developmental Psychology, 27,* 79–84.

Langlois, J. H., & Roggman, L. A. (1990). Attractive faces are only average. *Psychological Science, 1,* 115–121.

Langston, C. A., & Cantor, N. (1989). Anxiety and social constraint: When making friends is hard. *Journal of Personality and Social Psychology, 56,* 649–661.

Lansford, J. E., Sherman, A. M., & Antonucci, T. C. (1998). Satisfaction with social networks: An examination of socioemotional selectivity theory across cohorts. *Psychology and Aging, 13,* 544–552.

Larson, R. (1990). The solitary side of life: An examination of the time people spend alone from childhood to old age. *Developmental Review, 10,* 155–183.

Larson, R., & Richards, M. H. (1991). Daily companionship in late childhood and early adolescence: Changing developmental contexts. *Child Development, 62,* 284–300.

Larson, R., Richards, M. H., Moneta, G., Holmbeck, G., & Duckett. E. (1996). Changes in adolescents' daily interactions with their families from ages 10 to 18: Disengagement and transformation. *Developmental Psychology, 32,* 744–754.

Lauer, J., & Lauer, R. (1985, June). Marriages made to last. *Psychology Today,* pp. 22–26.

Laumann, E. O., Gagnon, J. H., Michael, R. T., & Michaels, S. (1994). *The social organization of sexuality: Sexual practices in the United States.* Chicago: University of Chicago Press.

Laurenceau, J., Barrett, L. F., & Pietromonaco, P. R. (1998). Intimacy as an interpersonal process: The importance of self-disclosure, partner disclosure, and perceived partner responsiveness in interpersonal exchanges. *Journal of Personality and Social Psychology, 74,* 1238–1251.

Laursen, B., & Collins, W. A. (1994). Interpersonal conflict during adolescence. *Psychological Bulletin, 115,* 197–209.

Laursen, B., Coy, K. C., & Collins, W. A. (1998). Reconsidering changes in parent-child conflict across adolescence: A meta-analysis. *Child Development, 69,* 817–832.

Lawrance, K., & Byers, E. S. (1995). Sexual satisfaction in long-term heterosexual relationships: The interpersonal exchange model of sexual satisfaction. *Personal Relationships, 2,* 267–285.

Laws, J. (1971). A feminist review of marital adjustment literature: The rape of the Locke. *Journal of Marriage and the Family, 33,* 483–516.

Leaper, C., & Holliday, H. (1995). Gossip in same-gender and cross-gender friends' conversations. *Personal Relationships, 2,* 237–246.

Leary, M. R. (1983). *Understanding social anxiety: Social, personality, and clinical perspectives.* Beverly Hills, CA: Sage.

Leary, M. R. (1986). The impact of interactional impediments on social anxiety and self-presentation. *Journal of Experimental Social Psychology, 22,* 122–135.

Leary, M. R. (1987). A self-presentation model for the treatment of social anxieties. In J. E. Maddux, C. D. Stoltenberg, & R. Rosenweig (Eds.), *Social processes in clinical and counseling psychology* (pp. 126–138). New York: Springer-Verlag.

Leary, M. R. (1995). *Self-presentation: Impression management and interpersonal behavior.* Madison, WI: Brown & Benchmark.

Leary, M. R. (2001a). Social anxiety as an early warning system: A refinement and extension of the self-presentational theory of social anxiety. In S. G. Hofmann & P. M. DiBartolo (Eds.), *Social phobia and social anxiety: An integration* (pp. 321–334). New York: Allyn & Bacon.

Leary, M. R. (2001b). Toward a conceptualization of interpersonal rejection. In M. R. Leary (Ed.), *Interpersonal rejection* (pp. 3–20). New York: Oxford University Press.

Leary, M. R., & Baumeister, R. F. (2000). The nature and function of self-esteem: Sociometer theory. In M. Zanna (Ed.), *Advances in experimental social psychology* (Vol. 32, pp. 1–62). San Diego: Academic Press.

Leary, M. R., & Kowalski, R. M. (1995). *Social anxiety.* New York: Guilford Press.

Leary, M. R., & Miller, R. S. (2000). Self-presentational perspectives on personal relationships. In W. Ickes & S. Duck (Eds.), *The social psychology of personal relationships* (pp. 129–155). Chichester, England: Wiley.

Leary, M. R., Nezlek, J. B., Downs, D. L., Radford-Davenport, J., Martin, J., & McMullen, A. (1994). Self-presentation in everyday interactions. *Journal of Personality and Social Psychology, 67,* 664–673.

Leary, M. R., Springer, C., Negel, L., Ansell, E., & Evans, K. (1998). The causes, phenomenology, and consequences of hurt feelings. *Journal of Personality and Social Psychology, 74,* 1225–1237.

Lebow, J. L, & Gurman, A. S. (1995). Research assessing couple and family therapy. *Annual Review of Psychology, 46,* 27–57.

Leck, K., & Simpson, J. A. (1999). Feigning romantic interest: The role of self-monitoring. *Journal of Research in Personality, 33,* 69–91.

Lee, J. A. (1977). A typology of styles of loving. *Personality and Social Psychology Bulletin, 3,* 173–182.

Lee, J. A. (1988). Love-styles. In R. J. Sternberg & M. L. Barnes (Eds.), *The psychology of love* (pp. 38–67). New Haven, CT: Yale University Press.

Lee, L. (1984). Sequences in separation: A framework for investigating endings of the personal (romantic) relationship. *Journal of Social and Personal Relationships, 1,* 49–73.

Leffler, A., Gillespie, D. L., & Conaty, J. C. (1982). The effects of status differentiation on nonverbal behavior. *Social Psychology Quarterly, 45,* 153–161.

Lehman, D. R., Ellard, J. H., & Wortman, C. B. (1986). Social support for the bereaved: Recipients' and providers' perspectives on what is helpful. *Journal of Consulting and Clinical Psychology, 54,* 438–446.

Lehman, D. R., & Taylor, S. E. (1987). Date with an earthquake: Coping with a probable unpredictable disaster. *Personality and Social Psychology Bulletin, 13,* 546–555.

Lehrer, E. L., & Chiswick, C. U. (1993). Religion as a determinant of marital stability. *Demography, 30,* 385–404.

Leigh, B. C., & Stall, R. (1993). Substance use and risky sexual behavior for exposure to HIV: Issues in methodology, interpretation, and prevention. *American Psychologist, 48,* 1035–1045.

Lemp, G., Hirozawa, A., et al. (1994). Seroprevalence of HIV and risk behaviors among young homosexual and bisexual men. *Journal of the American Medical Association, 272,* 449–454.

Leonard, K. E., & Roberts, L. J. (1997). Marital aggression, quality, and stability in the first year of marriage: Findings from the Buffalo Newlywed Study. In T. N. Bradbury (Ed.), *The developmental course of marital dysfunction* (pp. 44–73). Cambridge: Cambridge University Press.

Leridon, H. (1990). Cohabitation, marriage, separation: An analysis of life histories of French cohorts from 1968 to 1985. *Populations Studies, 44,* 127–144.

Leslie, L. A., Huston, T. L., & Johnson, M. P. (1986). Parental reactions to dating relationships: Do they make a difference? *Journal of Marriage and the Family, 48,* 57–66.

Lester, M. E., & Doherty, W. J. (1983). Couples' long-term evaluations of their Marriage Encounter experience. *Journal of Marital and Family Therapy, 9,* 183–188.

Levenson, R. W., Carstensen, L. L., & Gottman, J. M. (1993). Long-term marriage: Age, gender, and satisfaction. *Psychology and Aging, 8,* 301–313.

Levenson, R. W., Carstensen, L. L., & Gottman, R. M. (1994). Influence of age and gender on affect, physiology, and their interrelations: A study of long-term marriages. *Journal of Personality and Social Psychology, 67,* 56–68.

Lever, J. (1994, August 23). Sexual revelations. *The Advocate,* 17–24.

Levin, J. (2000). A prolegomenon to an epidemiology of love: Theory, measurement, and health outcomes. *Journal of Social and Clinical Psychology, 19,* 117–136.

Levine, T. R., & McCornack, S. A. (1992). Linking love and lies: A formal test of the McCornack and Parks model of deception detection. *Journal of Social and Personal Relationships, 9,* 143–154.

Levinger, G. (1976). A social psychological perspective on marital dissolution. *Journal of Social Issues, 32*(1), 21–47.

Levinger, G. (1979). A social exchange view on the dissolution of pair relationships. In R. L. Burgess & T. L. Huston (Eds.), *Social exchange in developing relationships* (pp. 169–193). New York: Academic Press.

Levinger, G. (1999). Duty toward whom? Reconsidering attractions and barriers as determinants of commitment in a relationship. In J. M. Adams & W. H. Jones (Eds.), *Handbook on interpersonal commitment and relationship stability* (pp. 37–52). New York: Kluwer Academic/Plenum.

Levinger, G., & Breedlove, J. (1966). Interpersonal attraction and agreement: A study of marriage partners. *Journal of Personality and Social Psychology, 3,* 367–372.

Levinger, G., & Snoek, J. D. (1972). *Attraction in relationships: A new look at interpersonal attraction.* Morristown, NJ: General Learning Press.

Levitt, M. J., Silver, M. E., & Franco, N. (1996). Troublesome relationships: A part of human experience. *Journal of Social and Personal Relationships, 13,* 523–536.

Levy, M. B., & Davis, K. E. (1988). Love styles and attachment styles compared: Their relations to each other and to various relationship characteristics. *Journal of Social and Personal Relationships, 5,* 439–471.

Lewis, R., Jr., Yancey, G., & Bletzer, S. S. (1997). Racial and nonracial factors that influence spouse choice in Black/White marriages. *Journal of Black Studies, 28,* 60–78.

Liberman, R. P., Wheeler, E. C., deVisser, L. A. K. M., Kuehnel, J., & Kuehnel, T. (1980). *Handbook of marital therapy.* New York: Plenum.

Liebowitz, M. R. (1983). *The chemistry of love.* Boston: Little, Brown.

Lin, Y. W., & Rusbult, C. E. (1995). Commitment to dating relationships and cross-sex friendships in America and China. *Journal of Social and Personal Relationships, 12,* 7–26.

Lippa, R., & Hershberger, S. (1999). Genetic and environmental influences on individual differences in masculinity, femininity, and gender diagnosticity: Analyzing data from a classic twin study. *Journal of Personality, 67,* 127–155.

Lipton, D., McDonel, E. C., & McFall, R. M. (1987). Heterosocial perception in rapists. *Journal of Consulting and Clinical Psychology, 55,* 17–21.

Lloyd, S. A. (1987). Conflict in premarital relationships: Differential perceptions of males and females. *Family Relations, 36,* 290–294.

Lloyd, S. A., & Emery, B. C. (1994). Physically aggressive conflict in romantic relationships. In D. D. Cahn (Ed.), *Conflict in personal relationships* (pp. 27–46). Hillsdale, NJ: Erlbaum.

Lloyd, S. A., & Emery, B. C. (2000). *The dark side of courtship: Physical and sexual aggression.* Thousand Oaks, CA: Sage.

Locke, K. D., & Horowitz, L. M. (1990). Satisfaction in interpersonal interactions as a function of similarity in level of dysphoria. *Journal of Personality and Social Psychology, 58,* 823–831.

Lockhart, L. L. (1987). A reexamination of the effects of race and social class on the incidence of marital violence: A search for reliable differences. *Journal of Marriage and the Family, 49,* 603–610.

Lokey, W. D., & Schmidt, G. W. (2000, February). *Association between adult attachment style and extramarital affairs in men.* Paper presented at the meeting of the Society for Personality and Social Psychology, Nashville, TN.

London, K. A., & Wilson, B. F. (1988, October). Divorce. *American Demographics,* pp. 22–26.

Long, C. J., & Andrews, D. W. (1990). Perspective taking as a predictor of marital adjustment. *Journal of Personality and Social Psychology, 59,* 126–131.

Long, E. C. J., Angera, J. J., Carter, S. J., Nakamoto, M., & Kalso, M. (1999). Understanding the one you love: A longitudinal assessment of an empathy training program for couples in romantic relationships. *Family Relations, 48,* 235–242.

Lopata, H. Z. (1969). Loneliness, forms and components. *Social Problems, 17,* 248–261.

Lott, A. J., & Lott, B. E. (1974). The role of reward in the formation of positive interpersonal attitudes. In T. Huston (Ed.), *Foundations of interpersonal attraction* (pp. 171–189). New York: Academic Press.

Lydon, J., Pierce, T., & O'Regan, S. (1997). Coping with moral commitment to long-distance dating relationships. *Journal of Personality and Social Psychology, 73,* 104–113.

Lykken, D. T., & Tellegen, A. (1993). Is human mating adventitious or the result of lawful choice? A twin study of mate selection. *Journal of Personality and Social Psychology, 65,* 56–68.

Lynn, M., & Bolig, R. (1985). Personal advertisements: Sources of data about relationships. *Journal of Social and Personal Relationships, 2,* 377–383.

MacDonald, G., Zanna, M. P., & Holmes, J. G. (2000). An experimental test of the role of alcohol in relationship conflict. *Journal of Experimental Social Psychology, 36,* 182–193.

MacDonald, T. K., MacDonald, G., Zanna, M. P., & Fong, G. T. (2000). Alcohol, sexual arousal, and intentions to use condoms in young males: Applying alcohol myopia theory to risky sexual behavior. *Health Psychology, 19,* 290–298.

MacDonald, T. K., & Ross, M. (1999). Assessing the accuracy of predictions about dating relationships: How and why do lovers' predictions differ from those made by observers? *Personality and Social Psychology Bulletin, 25,* 1417–1429.

MacDonald, T. K., Zanna, M. P., & Fong, G. T. (1996). Why common sense goes out the window: Effects of alcohol on intentions to use condoms. *Personality and Social Psychology Bulletin, 22,* 763–775.

MacDonald, T. K., Zanna, M. P., & Fong, G. T. (1998). Alcohol and intentions to engage in risky health-related behaviors: Experimental evidence for a causal relationship. In J. G. Adair & D. Belanger (Eds.), *Advances in psychological science, vol. 1: Social, personal, and cultural aspects,* (407–428). Hove, England: Psychology Press/Erlbaum.

Mace, D., & Mace, V. (1976). Marriage enrichment—A preventative group approach for couples. In D. H. Olson (Ed.), *Treating relationships* (pp. 321–336). Lake Mills, IA: Graphic Publishing.

Madden, M. F. (1987). Perceived control and power in marriage: A study of marital decision making and task performance. *Personality and Social Psychology Bulletin, 13,* 73–82.

Maddux, J. E., Norton, L. W., & Leary, M. R. (1988). Cognitive components of social anxiety: An investigation of the integration of self-presentation theory and self-efficacy theory. *Journal of Social and Clinical Psychology, 6,* 180–190.

Madey, S. F., Simo, M., Dillworth, D., Kemper, D., Toczynski, A., & Perella, A. (1996). They do get more attractive at closing time, but only when you are not in a relationship. *Basic and Applied Social Psychology, 18,* 387–393.

Mahoney, A., Pargament, K. I., Tarakeshwar, N., & Swank, A. B. (in press). Religion in the home in the 1980s and 90s: Meta-analyses and conceptual analyses of links between religion, marriage and parenting. *Journal of Family Psychology.*

Major, B., Carrington, P. I., & Carnevale, P. J. D. (1984). Physical attractiveness and self-esteem: Attributions for praise from an other-sex evalutator. *Personality and Social Psychology Bulletin, 10,* 43–50.

Major, B., & Heslin, R. (1982). Perceptions of same-sex and cross-sex nonreciprocal touch: It's better to give than to receive. *Journal of Nonverbal Behavior, 6,* 148–162.

Major, B., Schmidlin, A. M., & Williams, L. (1990). Gender patterns in social touch: The impact of setting and age. *Journal of Personality and Social Psychology, 58,* 634–643.

Marcus, D. K., & Miller, R. S. (2001). *Sex differences in judgments of physical attractiveness: A social relations analysis.* Manuscript submitted for publication.

Marecek, J. (1987). Counseling adolescents with problem pregnancies. *American Psychologist, 42,* 89–93.

Margolin, G. (1983). Behavioral marital therapy: Is there a place for passion, play, and other non-negotiable dimensions? *The Behavior Therapist, 6,* 65–68.

Margolin, G. (1987). Marital therapy: A cognitive-behavioral-affective approach. In N. S. Jacobson (Ed.), *Psychotherapists in clinical practice: Cognitive and behavioral perspectives* (pp. 232–285). New York: Guilford Press.

Margolin, L., & White, L. (1987). The continuing role of physical attractiveness in marriage. *Journal of Marriage and the Family, 49,* 21–28.

Markman, H. J. (1981). Prediction of marital distress: A 5-year follow-up. *Journal of Consulting and Clinical Psychology, 49,* 760–762.

Markman, H., Stanley, S., & Blumberg, S. L. (1994). *Fighting for your marriage: Positive steps for preventing divorce and preserving a lasting love.* San Francisco: Jossey-Bass.

Marks, G., & Miller, N. (1982). Target attractiveness as a mediator of assumed attitude similarity. *Personality and Social Psychology Bulletin, 8,* 728–735.

Marshall, G. D., & Zimbardo, P. G. (1979). Affective consequences of inadequately explained physiological arousal. *Journal of Personality and Social Psychology, 37,* 970–988.

Marston, P. J., Hecht, M. L., Manke, M. L., McDaniel, S., & Reeder, H. (1998). The subjective experience of intimacy, passion, and commitment in heterosexual loving relationships. *Personal Relationships, 5,* 15–30.

Martin, D. J., Garske, J. P., & Davis, M. K. (2000). Relation of the therapeutic alliance with outcome and other variables: A meta-analytic review. *Journal of Consulting and Clinical Psychology, 68,* 438–450.

Martin, J. (1997, October 21). Bereaved may face insensitivity. *Houston Chronicle,* p. 10F.

Martin, R. (1997). "Girls don't talk about garages!": Perceptions of conversation in same- and cross-sex friendships. *Personal Relationships, 4,* 115–130.

Martin, T. C., & Bumpass, L. (1989). Recent trends in martial disruption. *Demography, 26,* 37–51.

Masciuch, S., & Kienapple, K. (1993). The emergence of jealousy in children 4 months to 7 years of age. *Journal of Social and Personal Relationships, 10,* 421–435.

Mason, A., & Blankenship, V. (1987). Power and affiliation motivation, stress, and abuse in intimate relationships. *Journal of Personality and Social Psychology, 52,* 203–210.

Masters, W. H., & Johnson, V. F. (1970). *Human sexual inadequacy.* Boston: Little, Brown.

Mathes, E. W., Adams, H. E., & Davies, R. M. (1985). Jealousy: Loss of relationship rewards, loss of self-esteem, depression, anxiety, and anger. *Journal of Personality and Social Psychology, 48,* 1552–1561.

Maticka-Tyndale, E., Herold, E. S., & Mewhinney, D. (1998). Casual sex on spring break: Intentions and behaviors of Canadian students. *Journal of Sex Research, 35,* 254–264.

Matthews, K. A., & Rodin, J. (1989). Women's changing work roles: Impact on health, family, and public policy. *American Psychologist, 44,* 1389–1393.

Matthews, L. S., Wickrama, K. A. S., & Conger, R. D. (1996). Predicting marital instability from spouse and observer reports of marital interaction. *Journal of Marriage and the Family , 58,* 641–655.

Mayseless, O., Sharabany, R., & Sagi, A. (1997). Attachment concerns of mothers as manifested in parental, spousal, and friendship relationships. *Personal Relationships, 4,* 255–269.

McAdams, D. P. (1985). Motivation and friendship. In S. Duck & D. Perlman (Eds.), *Understanding personal relationships: An interdisciplinary approach* (pp. 85–105). London: Sage.

McAdams, D. P., & Bryant, F. B. (1987). Intimacy motivation and subjective mental health in a nationwide sample. *Journal of Personality, 55,* 395–414.

McAdams, D. P., Healy, S., & Krause, S. (1984). Social motives and friendship patterns. *Journal of Personality and Social Psychology, 47,* 828–838.

McAdams, D. P., & Vaillant, G. E. (1982). Intimacy motivation and psychosocial adjustment: A longitudinal study. *Journal of Personality Assessment, 46,* 586–593.

McCornack, S. A. (1997). The generation of deceptive messages: Laying the groundwork for a viable theory of interpersonal deception. In J. O. Greene (Ed.), *Message production: Advances in communication theory* (pp. 91–126). Mahwah, NJ: Erlbaum.

McCornack, S. A, & Levine, T. R. (1990a). When lies are uncovered: Emotional and relational outcomes of discovered deception. *Communication Monographs, 57,* 119–138.

McCornack, S. A, & Levine, T. R. (1990b). When lovers become leery: The relationship between suspicion and accuracy in detecting deception. *Communication Monographs, 57,* 219–230.

McCornack, S. A, & Parks, M. R. (1990). What women know that men don't: Sex differences in determining the truth behind deceptive messages. *Journal of Social and Personal Relationships, 7,* 107–118.

McCown, J. A. (2000, August). *Internet relationships: People who meet people.* Paper presented at the meeting of the American Psychological Association, Washington, DC.

McCrae, R. R., & Costa, P. T., Jr. (1997). Personality trait structure as a human universal. *American Psychologist, 52,* 509–516.

McCullough, M. E. (2000). Forgiveness as human strength: Theory, measurement, and links to well-being. *Journal of Social and Clinical Psychology, 19,* 43–55.

McCullough, M. E., Rachal, K. C., Sandage, S. J., Worthington, E. L., Jr., Brown, S. W., & Hight, T. L. (1998). Interpersonal forgiving in close relationships: II. Theoretical elaboration and measurement. *Journal of Personality and Social Psychology, 75,* 1586–1603.

McDonald, G. W. (1980). Family power: The assessment of a decade of theory and research. *Journal of Marriage and the Family, 42,* 841–854.

McDonald, G. W. (1981). Structural exchange and marital interaction. *Journal of Marriage and the Family, 43,* 825–839.

McFarland, C., & Ross, M. (1987). The relation between current impression and memories of self and dating partners. *Personality and Social Psychology Bulletin, 13,* 228–238.

McGonagle, K. A., Kessler, R. C., & Schilling, E. A. (1992). The frequency and determinants of marital disagreements in a community sample. *Journal of Social and Personal Relationships, 9,* 507–524.

McGregor, I., & Holmes, J. G. (1999). How storytelling shapes memory and impressions of relationship events over time. *Journal of Personality and Social Psychology, 76,* 403–419.

McKenna, K. Y. A., & Bargh, J. A. (2000). Plan 9 from cyberspace: The implications of the Internet for personality and social psychology. *Personality and Social Psychology Review, 4,* 57–75.

McMurray, L. (1970). Emotional stress and driving performance: The effect of divorce. *Behavioral Research in Highway Safety, 1,* 100–114.

McWhirter, B. T. (1997). Loneliness, learned resourcefulness, and self-esteem in college students. *Journal of Counseling and Development, 75,* 460–469.

Mealey, L., Bridgstock, R., & Townsend, G. C. (1999). Symmetry and perceived facial attractiveness: A monozygotic co-twin comparison. *Journal of Personality and Social Psychology, 76,* 151–158.

Meeks, B. S., Hendrick, S. S., & Hendrick, C. (1998). Communication, love and relationship satisfaction. *Journal of Social and Personal Relationships, 15,* 755–773.

Mendes de Leon, C. F., Glass, T. A., Beckett, L. A., Seeman, T. E., Evans, D. A., & Berkman, L. F. (1999). Social networks and disability transitions across eight intervals of yearly data in the New Haven EPESE. *Journals of Gerontology: Series B: Psychological Sciences and Social Sciences, 54B*(3), S162–S172.

Merkle, E. R., & Richardson, R. A. (2000). Digital dating and virtual relating: Conceptualizing computer mediated romantic relationships. *Family Relations, 49,* 187–192.

Messman, S. J., Canary, D. J., & Hause, K. S. (2000). Motives to remain platonic, equity, and the use of maintenance strategies in opposite-sex friendships. *Journal of Social and Personal Relationships, 17,* 67–94.

Metts, S. (1989). An exploratory investigation of deception in close relationships. *Journal of Social and Personal Relationships, 6,* 159–179.

Metts, S. (1994). Relational transgressions. In W. R. Cupach & B. H. Spitzberg (Eds.), *The dark side of interpersonal communication* (pp. 217–239). Hillsdale, NJ: Erlbaum.

Metts, S., & Cupach, W. R. (1990). The influence of romantic beliefs and problem-solving responses on satisfaction in romantic relationships. *Human Communication Research, 17,* 170–185.

Metts, S., Sprecher, S., & Regan, P. C. (2000). Communication and sexual desire. In P. A. Andersen and L. K. Guerrero (Eds.), *Communication and emotion.* Orlando, FL: Academic Press.

Meyer, D. R. (1999). Compliance with child support orders in paternity and divorce cases. In R. A. Thompson & P. R. Amato (Eds.), *The postdivorce family: Children, parenting and society* (pp. 127–157). Thousand Oaks, CA: Sage.

Michael, R. T., Gagnon, J. H., Laumann, E. O., & Kolata, G. (1994). *Sex in America: A definitive survey.* Boston: Little, Brown.

Michaels, S. (1996). The prevalence of homosexuality in the United States. In R. P. Cabaj & T. S. Stein (Eds.), *Textbook of homosexuality and mental health* (pp. 43–63). Washington, DC: American Psychiatric Press.

Michela, J. L., Peplau, L. A., & Weeks, D. G. (1982). Perceived dimensions of attributions for loneliness. *Journal of Personality and Social Psychology, 43*, 929–936.

Mickelson, K. D., Kessler, R. C., & Shaver, P. R. (1997). Adult attachment in a nationally representative sample. *Journal of Personality and Social Psychology, 73*, 1092–1106.

Mikula, G., Athenstaedt, U., Heschgl, S., & Heimgartner, A. (1998). Does it only depend on the point of view? Perspective-related differences in justice evaluations of negative incidents in personal relationships. *European Journal of Social Psychology, 28*, 931–962.

Mikulincer, M. (1997). Adult attachment style and information processing: Individual differences in curiosity and cognitive closure. *Journal of Personality and Social Psychology, 72*, 1217–1230.

Mikulincer, M. (1998). Attachment working models and the sense of trust: An exploration of interaction goals and affect regulation. *Journal of Personality and Social Psychology, 74*, 1209–1224.

Mikulincer, M., Orbach, I., & Iavnieli, D. (1998). Adult attachment style and affect regulation: Strategic variations in subjective self-other similarity. *Journal of Personality and Social Psychology, 75*, 436–448.

Milardo, R. M., Johnson, M. P., & Huston, T. L. (1983). Developing close relationships: Changing patterns of interaction between pair members and social networks. *Journal of Personality and Social Psychology, 44*, 964–976.

Milhausen, R. R. & Herold, E. S. (1999). Does the sexual double standard still exist? Perceptions of university women. *Journal of Sex Research, 36*, 361–368.

Miller, B. C., & Bingham, C. R. (1989). Family configuration in relation to the sexual behavior of female adolescents. *Journal of Marriage and the Family, 51*, 499–506.

Miller, J. B. (1976). *Toward a new psychology of women.* Boston: Beacon Press.

Miller, J. B., & Noirot, M. (1999). Attachment memories, models and information processing. *Journal of Social and Personal Relationships, 16*, 147–173.

Miller, L. C. (1990). Intimacy and liking: Mutual influence and the role of unique relationships. *Journal of Personality and Social Psychology, 59*, 50–60.

Miller, L. C., Berg, J. H., & Archer, R. L. (1983). Openers: Individuals who elicit intimate self-disclosure. *Journal of Personality and Social Psychology, 44*, 1234–1244.

Miller, M. A., & Rahe, R. H. (1997). Life changes scaling for the 1990s. *Journal of Psychomatic Research, 43*, 279–292.

Miller, P. J., Huston, T. L., & Caughlin, J. P. (2000, July). *Psychological femininity and the developmental course of marital satisfaction.* Paper presented at the meeting of the International Society for the Study of Personal Relationships, Brisbane.

Miller, R. S. (1996). *Embarrassment: Poise and peril in everyday life.* New York: Guilford Press.

Miller, R. S. (1997a). Inattentive and contented: Relationship commitment and attention to alternatives. *Journal of Personality and Social Psychology, 73*, 758–766.

Miller, R. S. (1997b). We always hurt the ones we love: Aversive interactions in close relationships. In R. Kowalski (Ed.), *Aversive interpersonal interactions* (pp. 11–29). New York: Plenum.

Miller, R. S. (2001). Breaches of propriety. In R. M. Kowalski (Ed.), *Behaving badly: Aversive behaviors in interpersonal relationships* (pp. 29–58). Washington, DC: American Psychological Association.

Miller, R. S. (in press). Shyness and embarrassment compared: Siblings in the service of social evaluation. In W. R. Crozier & L. E. Alden (Eds.), *International handbook of social anxiety: Research and interventions relating to the self and shyness.* Chichester, England: Wiley.

Miller, R. S., & Schlenker, B. R. (1985). Egotism in group members: Public and private attributions of responsibility for group performance. *Social Psychology Quarterly, 48,* 85–89.

Miller, S. L., Miller, P. A., Nunnally, E. W., & Wackman, D. B. (1991). *Talking and listening together: Couple communication, I.* Littleton, CO: Interpersonal Communication Programs.

Miller, S. L., Nunnally, E. W., & Wackman, D. B. (1976). Minnesota Couples Communication Program (MCCP): Premarital and marital groups. In D. H. Olson (Ed.), *Treating relationships* (pp. 21–40). Lake Mills, IA: Graphic Publishing.

Mondloch, C. J., Lewis, T. L., Budreau, D. R., Maurer, D., Dannemiller, J. L., Stephens, B. R., & Kleiner-Gathercoal, K. A. (1999). Face perception during early infancy. *Psychological Science, 10,* 419–422.

Monroe, W. S. (1898). Discussion and reports. Social consciousness in children. *Psychological Review, 5 ,* 68–70.

Monsour, M. (1992). Meanings of intimacy in cross- and same-sex friendships. *Journal of Social and Personal Relationships, 9,* 277–295.

Montepare, J. M., & Vega, C. (1988). Women's vocal reactions to intimate and casual male friends. *Personality and Social Psychology Bulletin, 14,* 103–113.

Moreland, R. L., & Beach, S. R. (1992). Exposure effects in the classroom: The development of affinity among students. *Journal of Experimental Social Psychology, 28,* 255–276.

Moreno, J. L. (1934). *Who shall survive? A new approach to the problem of human interrelationships.* Washington, DC: Nervous and Mental Disease Publishing.

Morier, D., & Seroy, C. (1994). The effect of interpersonal expectancies on men's self-presentation of gender role attitudes to women. *Sex Roles, 31,* 493–504.

Morrow, G. D., Clark, E. M., & Brock, K. F. (1995). Individual and partner love styles: Implications for the quality of romantic involvements. *Journal of Social and Personal Relationships, 12,* 363–387.

Moustakas, C. (1972). *Loneliness and love.* New York: Prentice-Hall.

Muehlenhard, C. L., & Hollabaugh, L. C. (1988). Do women sometimes say no when they mean yes? The prevalence and correlates of women's token resistance to sex. *Journal of Personality and Social Psychology, 54,* 872–879.

Muehlenhard, C. L., & Miller, E. N. (1988). Traditional and nontraditional men's responses to women's dating initiation. *Behavior Modification, 12,* 385–403.

Mulac, A. (1998). The gender-linked language effect: Do language differences really make a difference? In D. J. Canary & K. Dindia (Eds.), *Sex differences and similarities in communication: Critical essays and empirical investigations of sex and gender in interaction* (pp. 127–153). Mahwah, NJ: Erlbaum.

Mullen, B., Futrell, D., Stairs, D., Tice, D. M., Baumeister, R. F., Dawson, K. E., Riordan, C. A., Radloff, C. E., Goethals, G. R., Kennedy, J. G., & Rosenfeld, P. (1986). Newscasters' facial expressions and voting behavior of viewers: Can a smile elect a president? *Journal of Personality and Social Psychology, 51,* 291–295.

Munger, K., & Harris, S. J. (1989). Effects of an observer on handwashing in a public restroom. *Perceptual and Motor Skills, 69,* 733–734.

Munro, B., & Adams, G. R. (1978) Love American style: A test of role structure theory on changes in attitudes toward love. *Human Relations, 31,* 215–228.

Murray, S. L. (1999). The quest for conviction: Motivated cognition in romantic relationships. *Psychological Inquiry, 10,* 23–34.

Murray, S. L., & Holmes, J. G. (1997). A leap of faith? Positive illusions in romantic relationships. *Personality and Social Psychology Bulletin, 23,* 586–604.

Murray, S. L., & Holmes, J. G. (1999). The (mental) ties that bind: Cognitive structures that predict relationship resilience. *Journal of Personality and Social Psychology, 77,* 1228–1244.

Murray, S. L., Holmes, J. G., Bellavia, G., Griffin, D. W., & Dolderman, D. (2000, June). *Kindred spirits? The benefits of egocentrism in close relationships.* Paper presented at the meeting of the International Society for the Study of Personal Relationships, Brisbane.

Murray, S. L., Holmes, J. G., & Griffin, D. W. (1996a). The benefits of positive illusions: Idealization and the construction of satisfaction in close relationships. *Journal of Personality and Social Psychology, 70,* 79–98.

Murray, S. L., Holmes, J. G., & Griffin, D. W. (1996b). The self-fulfilling nature of positive illusions in romantic relationships: Love is not blind, but prescient. *Journal of Personality and Social Psychology, 71,* 1155–1180.

Murray, S. L., Holmes, J. G., & Griffin, D. W. (2000). Self-esteem and the quest for felt security: How perceived regard regulates attachment processes. *Journal of Personality and Social Psychology, 78,* 478–498.

Murray, S. L., Holmes, J. G., MacDonald, G., & Ellsworth, P. C. (1998). Through the looking glass darkly? When self-doubts turn into relationship insecurities. *Journal of Personality and Social Psychology, 75,* 1459–1480.

Murstein, B. I. (1972). Person perception and courtship progress among premarital couples. *Journal of Marriage and the Family, 34,* 621–626.

Murstein, B. I. (1976). *Who will marry whom? Theories and research in marital choice.* New York: Springer.

Murstein, B. I. (1987). A clarification and extension of the SVR theory of dyadic pairing. *Journal of Marriage and the Family, 49,* 929–933.

Murstein, B. I., & Beck, C. D. (1972). Personal perception, marriage adjustment and social desirability. *Journal of Consulting and Clinical Psychology, 29,* 396–403.

Myers, D. G. (2000). *The American paradox: Spiritual hunger in an age of plenty.* New Haven: Yale University Press.

Myers, D. G., & Diener, E. (1995). Who is happy? *Psychological Science, 6,* 10–19.

Myers, S. A., & Berscheid, E. (1997). The language of love: The difference a preposition makes. *Personality and Social Psychology Bulletin, 23,* 347–362.

National Center for Health Statistics. (2000). Births, marriages, divorces and deaths: Provisional data for September, 1999. *National Vital Statistics Reports, 48 (13),* 1–2.

Neimeyer, G. J. (1984). Cognitive complexity and marital satisfaction. *Journal of Social and Clinical Psychology, 2,* 258–263.

Newcomb, M. D., Huba, G. J., & Bentler, P. M. (1986). Determinants of sexual and dating behaviors among adolescents. *Journal of Personality and Social Psychology, 50,* 428–438.

Newcomb, T. M. (1961). *The acquaintance process.* New York: Holt, Rinehart & Winston.

Newcomer, S., & Udry, J. R. (1987). Parental marital status effects on adolescent sexual behavior. *Journal of Marriage and the Family, 49,* 235–240.

Neyer, F. J. (1997). Free recall or recognition in collecting egocentered networks: The role of survey techniques. *Journal of Social and Personal Relationships, 14,* 305–316.

Noller, P. (1980). Misunderstandings in marital communication: A study of couples' nonverbal communications. *Journal of Personality and Social Psychology, 39,* 1135–1148.

Noller, P. (1981). Gender and marital adjustment level differences in decoding messages from spouses and strangers. *Journal of Personality and Social Psychology, 41,* 272–278.

Noller, P. (1987). Nonverbal communication in marriage. In D. Perlman & S. Duck (Eds.), *Intimate relationships: Development, dynamics, and deterioration* (pp. 149–175). Newbury Park, CA: Sage.

Noller, P. (1996). What is this thing called love? Defining the love that supports marriage and family. *Personal Relationships, 3,* 97–115.

Noller, P., Feeney, J. A., Bonnell, D., & Callan, V. J. (1994). A longitudinal study of conflict in early marriage. *Journal of Social and Personal Relationships, 11,* 233–252.

Noller, P., & Vernardos, C. (1986). Communication awareness in married couples. *Journal of Social and Personal Relationships, 3,* 31–42.

Offermann, L. R., & Schrier, P. E. (1985). Social influence strategies: The impact of sex, roles, and attitudes toward power. *Personality and Social Psychology Bulletin, 11,* 286–300.

Oggins, J., Loeber, D., & Veroff, J. (1993). Race and gender differences in black and white newlyweds' perceptions of sexual and marital relationships. *Journal of Sex Research, 30,* 152–160.

O'Keefe, M. (1997). Predictors of dating violence among high school students. *Journal of Interpersonal Violence, 12,* 546–568.

Okonski, B. (1996, May 6). Just say something. *Newsweek, 131,* 14.

O'Leary, K. D. (2000). Are women really more aggressive than men in intimate relationships: Comment on Archer (2000). *Psychological Bulletin, 126,* 685–689.

O'Leary, K. D., & Turkewitz, H. (1978). Marital therapy from a behavioral perspective. In T. J. Paolino & B. McCrady (Eds.), *Marriage and marital therapy: Psychoanalytic, behavioral and systems theory perspectives* (pp. 240–297). New York: Brunner/Mazel.

O'Leary, K. D., & Vivian, D. (1990). Physical aggression in marriage. In F. D. Fincham & T. N. Bradbury (Eds.), *The psychology of marriage: Basic issues and applications* (pp. 323–348). New York: Guilford Press.

Oliver, M. B., & Hyde, J. S. (1993). Gender differences in sexuality: A meta-analysis. *Psychological Bulletin, 114,* 29–51.

Oliver, M. B., & Sedikides, C. (1992). Effects of sexual permissiveness on desirability of partner as a function of low and high commitment to relationship. *Social Psychology Quarterly, 55,* 321–333.

Olsen, R. B., Olsen, J., Gunner-Svensson, F., & Waldstrom, B. (1991). Social networks and longevity: A 14-year follow-up study among elderly in Denmark. *Social Science and Medicine, 33,* 1189–1195.

Olson, D. H. (1977). Insiders' and outsiders' views of relationships: Research strategies. In C. Levinger & H. L. Raush (Eds.), *Close relationships* (pp. 115–135). Amherst: University of Massachusetts Press.

Olson, D. H., & Cromwell, R. E. (1975). Methodological issues in family power. In R. E. Cromwell & D. H. Olson (Eds.), *Power in families* (pp. 131–150). New York: Wiley.

Olson, D. H., Russell, C., & Sprenkle, J. (1980). Marriage and family therapy: A decade review. *Journal of Marriage and the Family, 42,* 973–994.

Omarzu, J., Whalen, J., & Harvey, J. H. (2001). How well do you mind your relationship? A preliminary scale to test the minding theory of relating. In J. H. Harvey & A. E. Wenzel (Eds.), *Close romantic relationships: Maintenance and enhancement* (pp. 345–356). Mahwah, NJ: Erlbaum.

O'Rourke, J. F. (1963). Field and laboratory: The decision making behavior of family groups in two experimental conditions. *Sociometry, 26,* 422–435.

Orvis, B. R., Kelley, H. H., & Butler, D. (1976). Attributional conflict in young couples. In J. H. Harvey, W. J. Ickes, & R. E. Kidd (Eds.), *New directions in attribution research* (Vol. 1, pp. 353–386). Hillsdale, NJ: Erlbaum.

Osborne, R. E., & Gilbert, D. T. (1992). The preoccupational hazards of social life. *Journal of Personality and Social Psychology, 62,* 219–228.

O'Sullivan, L. F., & Gaines, M. E. (1998). Decision-making in college students' heterosexual dating relationships: Ambivalence about engaging in sexual activity. *Journal of Social and Personal Relationships, 15,* 347–363.

Page, R. M., & Cole, G. E. (1991). Demographic predictors of self-reported loneliness in adults. *Psychological Reports, 68,* 939–945.

Pakaluk, M. (Ed.). (1991). *Other selves: Philosophers on friendship.* Indianapolis, IN: Hackett.

Papero, D. V. (1995). Bowen family systems and marriage. In N. S. Jacobson & A. S. Gurman (Eds.), *Clinical handbook of couple therapy* (pp. 11–30). New York: Guilford.

Park, B., Kraus, S., & Ryan, C. S. (1997). Longitudinal changes in consensus as a function of acquaintance and agreement in liking. *Journal of Personality and Social Psychology, 72,* 604–616.

Parker, J. G., & Asher, S. R. (1987). Peer relations and later personal adjustment: Are low-accepted children at risk? *Psychological Bulletin, 102,* 357–389.

Parks, M. R., & Floyd, K. (1996a). Making friends in cyberspace. *Journal of Communication, 46,* 80–97.

Parks, M. R., & Floyd, K. (1996b). Meanings for closeness and intimacy in friendship. *Journal of Social and Personal Relationships, 13,* 85–107.

Parrott, W. G. (1991). The emotional experiences of envy and jealousy. In P. Salovey (Ed.), *The psychology of jealousy and envy* (pp. 3–30). New York: Guilford Press.

Parrott, W. G., & Smith, R. H. (1993). Distinguishing the experiences of envy and jealousy. *Journal of Personality and Social Psychology, 64,* 906–920.

Pasch, L. A., & Bradbury, T. N. (1998). Social support, conflict, and the development of marital dysfunction. *Journal of Consulting and Clinical Psychology, 66,* 219–230.

Patterson, M. L. (1988). Functions of nonverbal behavior in close relationships. In S. Duck (Ed.), *Handbook of personal relationships: Theory, research, and interventions* (pp. 41–56). New York: Wiley.

Patterson, M. L. (1990). Functions of non-verbal behavior in social interaction. In H. Giles & W. P. Robinson (Eds.), *Handbook of language and social psychology* (pp. 101–120). Chichester, England: Wiley.

Paul, E. L., McManus, B., & Hayes, A. (2000). "Hookups": Characteristics and correlates of college students' spontaneous and anonymous sexual experiences. *Journal of Sex Research, 37,* 76–88.

Paul, L., Foss, M. A., & Galloway, J. (1993). Sexual jealousy in young men and women: Aggressive responsiveness to partner and rival. *Aggressive Behavior, 19,* 401–420.

Paulhus, D. L., & Morgan, K. L. (1997). Perceptions of intelligence in leaderless groups: The dynamic effects of shyness and acquaintance. *Journal of Personality and Social Psychology, 72,* 581–591.

Pedersen, F. A. (1991). Secular trends in human sex ratios: Their influence on individual and family behavior. *Human Nature, 2,* 271–291.

Pegalis, L. J., Shaffer, D. R., Bazzini, D. G., & Greenier, K. (1994). On the ability to elicit self-disclosure: Are there gender-based and contextual limitations on the opener effect? *Personality and Social Psychology Bulletin, 20,* 412–420.

Pennebaker, J. W. (1997). Writing about emotional experiences as a therapeutic process. *Psychological Science, 8,* 162–166.

Pennebaker, J. W., Dyer, M. A., Caulkins, R. J., Litowitz, D. L., Ackerman, P. L., Anderson, D. B., & McGraw, K. M. (1979). Don't the girls get prettier at closing time: A country and western application to psychology. *Personality and Social Psychology Bulletin, 5,* 122–125.

Penton-Voak, I. S., Perrett, D. I., Castles, D. L., Kobayashi, T., Burt, D. M., Murray, L. K., & Minamisawa, R. (1999). Menstrual cycle alters face preference. *Nature, 399,* 741–742.

Peplau, L. A., Bikson, T. K., Rook, K. S., & Goodchilds, J. D. (1982). Being old and living alone. In L. A. Peplau & D. Perlman (Eds.), *Loneliness: A sourcebook of current theory, research, and therapy* (pp. 327–347). New York: Wiley Interscience.

Peplau, L. A., & Campbell, S. M. (1989). Power in dating and marriage. In J. Freeman (Ed.), *Women: A feminist perspecitve* (4th ed. pp. 121–137). Mountain View, CA: Mayfield Publishing.

Peplau, L. A., Russell, D., & Heim, M. (1979). The experience of loneliness. In I. Frieze, D. Bar-Tal, & J. Carroll (Eds.), *New approaches to social problems: Applications of attribution theory* (pp. 53–78). San Francisco: Jossey-Bass.

Peplau, L. A., & Spalding, L. R. (2000). The close relationships of lesbians, gay men and bisexuals. In C. Hendrick & S. S. Hendrick (Eds.), *Close relationships: A sourcebook* (pp. 111–123). Thousand Oaks, CA: Sage.

Peplau, L. A., Veniegas, R. C., & Campbell, S. M. (1996). Gay and lesbian relationships. In R. C. Savin-Williams & K. M. Cohen (Eds.), *The lives of lesbians, gays and bisexuals: Children to adults* (pp. 250–273). Orlando: Harcourt Brace.

Perlman, D. (1988). Loneliness: A life span, developmental perspective. In R. M. Milardo (Ed.), *Families and social networks* (pp. 190–220). Newbury Park, CA: Sage.

Perlman, D. (1989, August). *You bug me: A preliminary report on hassles in relationships.* Paper presented at the meeting of the American Psychological Association, New Orleans.

Perlman, D. (1991). *Age differences in loneliness: A meta analysis.* Vancouver, Canada: University of British Columbia. (ERIC Document Reproduction Service No. ED 326767).

Perlman, D. (1999). Tendencias actuales en el estudio de las relaciones cercanas. Un vistazo hacia el pasado para predecir el futuro [Current trends in the study of close relationships: Glancing backward to forecast the future]. *Revista de Psicologia Social y Personalidad, 15,* 157–178.

Perlman, D., & Fehr, B. (1987). The development of intimate relationships. In D. Perlman & S. Duck (Eds.), *Intimate relationships: Development, dynamics, and deterioration* (pp. 13–42). Newbury Park, CA: Sage.

Perlman, D., & Landolt, M. A. (1999). Examination of loneliness in children/adolescents and in adults: Two solitudes or unified enterprise? In K. J. Rotenberg & S. Hymel (Eds.), *Loneliness in childhood and adolescence* (pp. 325–347). New York: Cambridge University Press.

Perlman, D., & Peplau, L. A. (1981). Toward a social psychology of loneliness. In S. Duck & R. Gilmour (Eds.), *Personal relationships. 3: Personal relationships in disorder* (pp. 31–56). New York: Academic Press.

Perlman, D., & Peplau, L. A. (1998). Loneliness. In H. Friedman (Ed.), *Encyclopedia of mental health* (Vol. 2, pp. 571–581). San Diego, CA: Academic Press.

Perloff, L. S. (1987). Social comparison and illusion of invulnerability to negative life events. In C. R. Snyder & C. E. Ford (Eds.), *Coping with negative life events: Clinical and social psychological perspectives* (pp. 217–242). New York: Plenum.

Perrett, D. I., Lee, K. J., Penton-Voak, I., Rowland, D., Yoshikawa, S., Burt, D. M., Henzi, S. P., Castles, D. L., & Akamatsu, S., (1998). Effects of sexual dimorphism on facial attractiveness. *Nature, 394,* 884–887.

Perrett, D. I., May, K. A., & Yoshikawa, S. (1994). Facial shape and judgments of female attractiveness. *Nature, 368,* 239–242.

Peterson, D. R. (1983). Conflict. In H. H. Kelley, E. Berscheid, A. Christensen, J. H. Harvey, T. L. Huston, G. Levinger, E. McClintock, L. A. Peplau, & D. R. Peterson, *Close relationships* (pp. 360–396). New York: W. H. Freeman.

Petronio, S., Olson, C., & Dollar, N. (1989). Privacy issues in relational embarrassment: Impact on relational quality and communication satisfaction. *Communication Research Reports, 6,* 21–27.

Philliber, W. W., & Vannoy-Hiller, D. (1990). The effect of husband's occupational attainment on wife's achievement. *Journal of Marriage and the Family, 52,* 323–329.

Phillips, R. (1988). *Putting asunder: A history of divorce in Western society*. Cambridge: Cambridge University Press.

Pietromonaco, P. R., & Rook, K. S. (1987). Decision style in depression: The contribution of perceived risk versus benefits. *Journal of Personality and Social Psychology, 52*, 399–408.

Pines, A., & Aronson, E. (1983). Antecedents, correlates, and consequences of sexual jealousy. *Journal of Personality, 51*, 108–136.

Pines, A. M. (1998). *Romantic jealousy: Causes, symptoms, cures*. New York: Routledge.

Planalp, S., & Benson, A. (1992). Friends' and acquaintances' conversations I: Perceived differences. *Journal of Social and Personal Relationships, 9*, 483–506.

Pleck, J. H., Sonenstein, F. L., & Ku, L. C. (1991). Adolescent males' condom use: Relationships between perceived cost-benefits and consistency. *Journal of Marriage and the Family, 53*, 733–745.

Pliner, P., & Chaiken, S. (1990). Eating, social motives, and self-presentation in men and women. *Journal of Experimental Social Psychology, 26*, 240–254.

Podsakoff, P. M., & Schriesheim, C. A. (1985). Field studies of French and Raven's bases of power: Critique, reanalysis, and suggestions for future research. *Psychological Bulletin, 97*, 387–411.

Pollard, J. S. (1995). Attractiveness of composite faces: A comparative study. *International Journal of Comparative Psychology, 8*, 77–83.

Popenoe, D., & Whitehead, B. D. (1999). *The state of our unions: The social health of marriage in America*. New Brunswick, NJ: Rutgers University, The National Marriage Project. Retrieved July 1999 from the World Wide Web: http://marriage.rutgers.edu/State.html.

Poppen, P. J., & Segal, N. J. (1988). The influence of sex and sex role orientation on sexual coercion. *Sex Roles, 19*, 689–701.

Porter, S., & Yuille, J. C. (1996). The language of deceit: An investigation of the verbal clues to deception in the interrogation context. *Law and Human Behavior, 20*, 443–458.

Porterfield, E. (1982). Black-American intermarriage in the United States. *Marriage and Family Review, 5*, 17–34.

Prager, K. J. (1995). *The psychology of intimacy*. New York: Guilford Press.

Prentice, D., & Carranza, E. (2000, February). *He should be mature, and she should be bubbly; but really, he's ruthless and she's moody: Prescriptive and descriptive gender stereotypes*. Paper presented at the meeting of the Society for Personality and Social Psychology, Nashville.

Price, R. A., & Vandenberg, S. S. (1979). Matching for physical attractiveness. *Personality and Social Psychology Bulletin, 5*, 398–400.

Prins, K. S., Buunk, B. P., & VanYperen, N. W. (1993). Equity, normative disapproval and extramarital relationships. *Journal of Social and Personal Relationships, 10*, 39–53.

Prochaska, J., & Prochaska, J. (1978). Twentieth century trends in marriage and family therapy. In T. J. Paolino & B. McCrady (Eds.), *Marriage and marital therapy: Psychoanalytic, behavioral and systems theory perspectives* (pp. 1–24). New York: Brunner/Mazel.

Purnine, D., & Carey, M. (1997). Interpersonal communication and sexual adjustment: The roles of understanding and agreement. *Journal of Consulting and Clinical Psychology, 65*, 1017–1025.

Purvis, J. A., Dabbs, J. M., Jr., & Hopper, C. H. (1984). The "opener": Skilled user of facial expression and speech pattern. *Personality and Social Psychology Bulletin, 10*, 61–66.

Putnam, R. D. (2000). *Bowling alone: The collapse and revival of American community*. New York: Simon & Schuster.

Pyke, K. D. (1994). Women's employment as a gift or burden? Marital power across marriage, divorce, and remarriage. *Gender and Society, 8*, 73–91.

Raina, P., Waltner-Toews, D., Bonnett, B., Woodward, C., & Abernathy, T. (1999). Influence of companion animals on the physical and psychological health of older people: An analysis of a one-year longitudinal study. *Journal of the American Geriatrics Society, 47,* 323–329.

Rands, M. (1988). Changes in social networks following marital separation and divorce. In R. M. Milardo (Ed.), *Families and social networks* (pp. 127–146). Newbury Park, CA: Sage.

Rauscher, F. H., Krauss, R. M., & Chen, Y. (1996). Gesture, speech, and lexical access: The role of lexical movements in speech production. *Psychological Science, 7,* 226–231.

Raven, B. H. (1988). Social power and compliance in health care. In S. Maes, C. D. Spielberger, P. B. Defares, & I. G. Sarason (Eds.), *Topics in health psychology* (pp. 229–244). London/New York: Wiley.

Raven, B. H., Centers, R., & Rodrigues, A. (1975). The bases of conjugal power. In R. E. Cromwell & D. H. Olson (Eds.), *Power in families* (pp. 217–232). New York: Wiley.

Regan, P. C. (1998). Of lust and love: Beliefs about the role of sexual desire in romantic relationships. *Personal Relationships, 5,* 139–157.

Regan, P. C., Kocan, E. R., & Whitlock, T. (1998). Ain't love grand! A prototype analysis of the concept of romantic love. *Journal of Social and Personal Relationships, 15,* 411–420.

Regan, P. C., & Sprecher, S. (1995). Gender differences in the value of contributions to intimate relationships: Egalitarian relationships are not always perceived to be equitable. *Sex Roles, 33,* 221–238.

Reis, H. T. (1986). Gender effects in social participation: Intimacy, loneliness, and the conduct of social interaction. In R. Gilmour & S. Duck (Eds.), *The emerging field of personal relationships* (pp. 91–105). London: Academic Press.

Reis, H. T. (1998). Gender differences in intimacy and related behaviors: Context and process. In D. J. Canary & K. Dindia (Eds.), *Sex differences and similarities in communication: Critical essays and empirical investigations of sex and gender in interaction* (pp. 203–234). Mahwah, NJ: Erlbaum.

Reis, H. T., Lin, Y., Bennett, M. E., & Nezlek, J. B. (1993). Change and consistency in social participation during early adulthood. *Developmental Psychology, 29,* 633–645.

Reis, H. T., Nezlek, J., & Wheeler, L. (1980). Physical attractiveness in social interaction. *Journal of Personality and Social Psychology, 38,* 604–617.

Reis, H. T., & Patrick, B. C. (1996). Attachment and intimacy: Component processes. In E. T. Higgins & A. W. Kruglanski (Eds.), *Social psychology: Handbook of basic principles* (pp. 523–563). New York: Guilford Press.

Reis, H. T., Senchak, M., & Solomon, B. (1985). Sex differences in the intimacy of social interaction: Further examination of potential explanations. *Journal of Personality and Social Psychology, 48,* 1204–1217.

Reis, H. T., Sheldon, R. M., Gable, S. L., Roscoe, J., & Ryan, R. M. (2000). Daily well-being: The role of autonomy, competence, and relatedness. *Personality and Social Psychology Bulletin, 26,* 419–435.

Reis, H. T., Wheeler, L., Spiegel, N., Kernis, M. H., Nezlek, J., & Perri, M. (1982). Physical attractiveness in social interaction: II. Why does appearance affect social experience? *Journal of Personality and Social Psychology, 43,* 979–996.

Reisenzein, R., (1983). The Schachter theory of emotion: Two decades later. *Psychological Bulletin, 94,* 239–264.

Reiss, I. (1967). *The social context of premarital sex permissiveness.* New York: Holt.

Revenson, T. A. (1981). Coping with loneliness: The impact of causal attributions. *Personality and Social Psychology Bulletin, 7,* 565–571.

Rhodes, G., & Tremewan, T. (1996). Averageness, exaggeration, and facial attractiveness. *Psychological Science, 7,* 105–110.

Rhodes, G., Sumich, A., & Byatt, G. (1999). Are average facial configurations attractive only because of their symmetry? *Psychological Science, 10*, 52–58.

Richard, L. S., Wakefield, J. A., & Lewak, R. (1990). Similarity of personality variables as predictors of marital satisfaction: A Minnesota Multiphasic Personality Inventory (MMPI) item analysis. *Personality and Individual Differences, 11*, 39–43.

Ridge, S. R., & Feeney, J. A. (1998). Relationship history and relationship attitudes in gay males and lesbians: Attachment style and gender differences. *Australian and New Zealand Journal of Psychiatry, 32*, 848–859.

Ridley, C., Busboom, A., Collins, D., Gilson, M., Almeida, D., Feldman, C., & Cate, R. (2000, June). *Lusting after one's partner: Changing patterns within the relational context.* Presented at the meeting of the International Society for the Study of Personal Relationships, Brisbane.

Riesch, S. K., Bush, L., Nelson, C. J., Ohm, B. J., Portz, P. A., Abell, B., Wightman, M. R., & Jenkins, P. (2000). Topics of conflict between parents and young adolescents. *Journal of the Society of Pediatric Nurses, 5*, 27–40.

Rindfuss, R. R., & Stephen, E. H. (1990). Marital noncohabitation: Separation does not make the heart grow fonder. *Journal of Marriage and the Family, 52*, 259–270.

Riordan, C. A., & Tedeschi, J. T. (1983). Attraction in aversive environments: Some evidence for classical conditioning and negative reinforcement. *Journal of Personality and Social Psychology, 44*, 683–692.

Robbins, C., Kaplan, H. B., & Martin, S. S. (1985). Antecedents of pregnancy among unmarried adolescents. *Journal of Marriage and the Family, 47*, 567–583.

Robin, A. L., & Foster, S. L. (1989). *Negotiating parent-adolescent conflict: A behavioral family systems approach.* New York: Guilford.

Robins, L. N., Helzer, J. E., Weissman, M. M., Orvaschel, H., Gruenberg, E., Burke, J. D., & Reigier, D. A. (1984). Lifetime prevalence of specific psychiatric disorders in three sites. *Archives of General Psychiatry, 41*, 949–958.

Robins, R. W., Caspi, A., & Moffitt, T. E. (2000). Two personalities, one relationship: Both partners' personality traits shape the quality of their relationship. *Journal of Personality and Social Psychology, 79*, 251–259.

Rodgers, J. L., Nakonezny, P. A., & Shull, R. D. (1999). Did no-fault divorce legislation matter? Definitely yes and sometimes no. *Journal of Marriage and the Family, 61*, 803–809.

Rodman, H. (1972). Marital power and the theory of resources in cultural context. *Journal of Comparative Family Studies, 3*, 50–69.

Rogers, S. J., & Amato, P. R. (1997). Is marital quality declining? The evidence from two generations. *Social Forces, 75*, 1089–1100.

Rogler, L. H., & Procidano, M. F. (1989). Egalitarian spouse relations and wives' marital satisfaction in intergenerationally linked Puerto Rican families. *Journal of Marriage and the Family, 51*, 37–39.

Roloff, M., & Cloven, D. H. (1990). The chilling effect in interpersonal relationships: The reluctance to speak one's mind. In D. D. Cahn (Ed.), *Intimates in conflict: A communication perspective* (pp. 49–76). Hillsdale, NJ: Erlbaum.

Roloff, M. E., & Ifert, D. (1998). Antecedents and consequences of explicit agreements to declare a taboo topic in dating relationships. *Personal Relationships, 5*, 191–205.

Rook, K. S. (1984a). Promoting social bonding: Strategies for helping the lonely and socially isolated. *American Psychologist, 39*, 1389–1407.

Rook, K. S. (1984b). The negative side of social interaction: Impact on psychological well-being. *Journal of Personality and Social Psychology, 46*, 1097–1108.

Rook, K. S. (1988). Toward a more differentiated view of loneliness. In S. Duck (Ed.), *Handbook of personal relationships: Theory, research, and interventions* (pp. 571–589). New York: Wiley.

Rook, K. S. (1998). Investigating the positive and negative sides of personal relation-ships: Through a lens darkly? In B. H. Spitzberg & W. R. Cupach (Eds.), *The dark side of close relationships* (pp. 369–393). Mahwah, NJ: Erlbaum.

Rook, K. S., & Peplau, L. A. (1982). Perspectives on helping the lonely. In L. A. Peplau & D. Perlman (Eds.), *Loneliness: A sourcebook of current theory, research, and therapy* (pp. 351–378). New York: Wiley Interscience.

Rosenbaum, M. E. (1986). The repulsion hypothesis: On the nondevelopment of rela-tionships. *Journal of Personality and Social Psychology, 51,* 1156–1166.

Rosenthal, D. A., Smith, A. M. A., & de Visser, R. (1999). Personal and social factors influencing age at first sexual intercourse. *Archives of Sexual Behavior, 28,* 319–333.

Rosenthal, R. (1994). Interpersonal expectancy effects: A 30-year perspective. *Current Di-rections in Psychological Science, 3,* 176–179.

Rosenthal, R., & DePaulo, B. M. (1979). Sex differences in eavesdropping on nonverbal cues. *Journal of Personality and Social Psychology, 37,* 273–285.

Ross, E. A. (1921). *Principles of sociology.* New York: Century.

Ross, M., & Sicoly, F. (1979). Egocentric biases in availability and attribution. *Journal of Personality and Social Psychology, 37,* 322–336.

Rotenberg, K. J., & Hymel, S. (Eds.). (1999). *Loneliness in childhood and adolescence.* New York: Cambridge University Press.

Rotenberg, K. J., & Morrison, J. (1993). Loneliness and college achievement: Do Loneli-ness Scale scores predict college drop-out? *Psychological Reports, 73,* 1283–1288.

Rowatt, W. C., Cunningham, M. R., & Druen, P. B. (1999). Lying to get a date: The effect of facial physical attractiveness on the willingness to deceive prospective dating partners. *Journal of Social and Personal Relationships, 16,* 209–223.

Ruane, M. E. (1999, December 26). FWIW, Internet slang is running wild on ur kids' e-mail, etc. etc. *Houston Chronicle,* p. 2A.

Rubenstein, C. M., & Shaver, P. (1980). Loneliness in two northeastern cities. In J. Hartog, J. R. Audy, & Y. A. Cohen (Eds.), *The anatomy of loneliness* (pp. 319–337). New York: International Universities Press.

Rubenstein, C. M., & Shaver, P. (1982). *In search of intimacy.* New York: Delacorte Press.

Rubenstein, C. M., Shaver, P., & Peplau, L. A. (1979). Loneliness. *Human Nature, 2,* 58–65.

Rubin, C. M., & Rubin, J. Z. (1993). Dynamics of conflict escalation in families: The role of threat, promises, guilt induction and passive manipulation. In D. Perlman & W. H. Jones (Eds.), *Advances in personal relationships* (Vol. 4, pp. 165–191). London: Jessica Kingsley.

Rubin, J. Z., Pruitt, D. G., & Kim, S. H. (1994). *Social conflict: Escalation, stalemate, and set-tlement* (2nd ed.). New York: McGraw-Hill.

Rubin, Z. (1973). *Liking and loving.* New York: Holt, Rinehart & Winston.

Rubin, Z. (1980). *Children's friendships.* Cambridge, MA: Harvard University Press.

Rubin, Z., & Mitchell, C. (1976). Couples research as couples counseling: Some unin-tended effects of studying close relationships. *American Psychologist, 31,* 17–25.

Rudman, L. A. (1998). Self–promotion as a risk factor for women: The costs and benefits of counterstereotypical impression management. *Journal of Personality and Social Psychology, 74,* 629–645.

Rudman, L. A., & Glick, P. (1999). Feminized management and backlash toward agentic women: The hidden costs to women of a kinder, gentler image of middle managers. *Journal of Personality and Social Psychology, 77,* 1004–1010.

Ruggles, S. (1997). The rise of divorce and separation in the United States: 1880–1990. *Demography, 34,* 455–466.

Rusbult, C. E., & Arriaga, X. B. (1997). Interdependence theory. In S. Duck (Ed.), *Handbook of personal relationships: Theory, research, and intervention* (2nd ed., pp. 221–250). Chichester, England: Wiley.

Rusbult, C. E., & Martz, J. M. (1995). Remaining in abusive relationships: An investment model analysis of nonvoluntary dependence. *Personality and Social Psychology Bulletin, 21,* 558–571.

Rusbult, C. E., Bissonnette, V. L., Arriaga, X. B., & Cox, C. L. (1998). Accommodation processes during the early years of marriage. In T. N. Bradbury (Ed.), *The developmental course of marital dysfunction* (pp. 74–113). New York: Cambridge University Press.

Rusbult, C. E., Drigotas, S. M., & Verette, J. (1994). The investment model: An interdependence analysis of commitment processes and relationship maintenance phenomena. In D. J. Canary & L. Stafford (Eds.), *Communication and relational maintenance* (pp. 115–139). San Diego: Academic Press.

Rusbult, C. E., Olsen, N., Davis, J. L., & Hannon, M. A. (2001). Commitment and relationship maintenance mechanisms. In J. H. Harvey & A. E. Wenzel (Eds.), *Close romantic relationships: Maintenance and enhancement* (pp. 87–113). Mahwah, NJ: Erlbaum.

Rusbult, C. E., Verette, J., Whitney, G. A., Slovik, L. F., & Lipkus, I. (1991). Accommodation processes in close relationships: Theory and preliminary empirical evidence. *Journal of Personality and Social Psychology, 60,* 53–78.

Rusbult, C. E., Wieselquist, J., Foster, C. A., & Witcher, B. S. (1999). Commitment and trust in close relationships: An interdependence analysis. In J. M. Adams & W. H. Jones (Eds.), *Handbook on interpersonal commitment and relationship stability* (pp. 427–449). New York: Kluwer Academic/Plenum.

Russell, D., Cutrona, C. E., Rose, J., & Yurko, K. (1984). Social and emotional loneliness: An examination of Weiss's typology of loneliness. *Journal of Personality and Social Psychology, 46,* 1313–1321.

Russell, D., Peplau, L. A., & Cutrona, C. E. (1980). The revised UCLA Loneliness Scale: Concurrent and discriminant validity evidence. *Journal of Personality and Social Psychology, 39,* 472–480.

Russell, D. W. (1996). The UCLA Loneliness Scale (Version 3): Reliability, validity and factorial structure. *Journal of Personality Assessment, 66,* 20–40.

Ruvolo, A. P. (1998). Marital well-being and general happiness of newlywed couples: Relationships across time. *Journal of Social and Personal Relationships, 15,* 470–489.

Ruvolo, A. P., & Veroff, J. (1997). For better or for worse: Real-ideal discrepancies and the marital well-being of newlyweds. *Journal of Social and Personal Relationships, 14,* 223–242.

Ryff, C. D., & Singer, B. (2000). Interpersonal flourishing: A positive health agenda for the new millenium. *Personality and Social Psychology Review, 4,* 30–44.

Sabatelli, R. M., Buck, R., & Dreyer, A. (1980). Communication via facial cues in intimate dyads. *Personality and Social Psychology Bulletin, 6,* 242–247.

Sabatelli, R. M., Buck, R., & Dreyer, A. (1982). Nonverbal communication accuracy in married couples: Relationship with marital complaints. *Journal of Personality and Social Psychology, 43,* 1088–1097.

Sabin, E. P. (1993). Social relationships and mortality among the elderly. *Journal of Applied Gerontology, 12,* 44–60.

Sadalla, E. K., Kenrick, D. T., & Vershure, B. (1987). Dominance and heterosexual attraction. *Journal of Personality and Social Psychology, 52,* 730–738.

Sadava, S. W., & Matejcic, C. (1987). Generalized and specific loneliness in early marriage. *Canadian Journal of Behavioural Science, 19,* 56–65.

Safilios-Rothschild, C. (1970). The study of family power structure: A review, 1960–1969. *Journal of Marriage and the Family, 32,* 535–552.

Safilios-Rothschild, C. (1976a). The dimensions of power distribution in the family. In H. Grunebaum & J. Christ (Eds.), *Contemporary marriage: Structure, dynamics and therapy* (pp. 275–292). Boston: Little, Brown.

Safilios-Rothschild, C. (1976b). A macro- and micro-examination of family power and love: An exchange model. *Journal of Marriage and the Family, 38,* 355–362.

Safilios-Rothschild, C. (1981). Toward a social psychology of relationships. *Psychology of Women Quarterly, 5,* 377–384.

Sagarin, B. J., Becker, V., Guadagno, R. E., Nicastle, L. D., & Millevoi, A. (2000, August). *Beyond forced-choice: Evolutionary responses to sexual and emotional infidelities.* Paper presented at the meeting of the American Psychological Association, Washington, DC.

Sagarin, B. J., Rhoads, K. V. L., & Cialdini, R. B. (1998). Deceiver's distrust: Denigration as a consequence of undiscovered deception. *Personality and Social Psychology Bulletin, 24,* 1167–1176.

Sagrestano, L. M. (1992). Power strategies in interpersonal relationships: The effects of expertise and gender. *Psychology of Women Quarterly, 16,* 481–495.

Salovey, P. (Ed.). (1991). *The psychology of jealousy and envy.* New York: Guilford Press.

Salovey, P., & Rodin, J. (1988). Coping with envy and jealousy. *Journal of Social and Clinical Psychology, 7,* 15–33.

Saluter, A. F. (1996, February). Marital status and living arrangements: March, 1994. *Current population reports: Population characteristics (P20-484).* Washington, DC: U.S. Bureau of the Census.

Sandnabba, N. K., & Ahlberg, C. (1999). Parents' attitudes and expectations about children's cross-gender behavior. *Sex Roles, 40,* 249–263.

Sanford, K. (1997). Two dimensions of adult attachment: Further validation. *Journal of Social and Personal Relationships, 14,* 133–143.

Sapadin, L. A. (1988). Friendship and gender: Perspectives of professional men and women. *Journal of Social and Personal Relationships, 5,* 387–403.

Satir, V. (1967). *Conjoint family therapy.* Palo Alto, CA: Science and Behavior Books.

Satterfield, A. T., & Muehlenhard, C. L. (1997). Shaken confidence: The effects of an authority figure's flirtatiousness on women's and men's self-rated creativity. *Psychology of Women Quarterly, 21,* 395–416.

Schachter, S. (1959). *The psychology of affiliation: Experimental studies of the sources of gregariousness.* Stanford, CA: Stanford University Press.

Schachter, S. (1964). The interaction of cognitive and physiological determinants of emotional state. In L. Berkowitz (Ed.), *Advances in experimental social psychology* (Vol. 1, pp. 49–80). New York: Academic Press.

Scharfe, E., & Bartholomew, K. (1994). Reliability and stability of adult attachment patterns. *Personal Relationships, 1,* 23–43.

Scharfe, E., & Bartholomew, K. (1995). Accommodation and attachment representations in young couples. *Journal of Social and Personal Relationships, 12,* 389–401.

Scharfe, E., & Bartholomew, K. (1998). Do you remember?: Recollections of adult attachment patterns. *Personal Relationships, 5,* 219–234.

Scharff, J. (1995). Psychoanalytic marital therapy. In N. S. Jacobson & A. S. Gurman (Eds.), *Clinical handbook of couple therapy* (pp. 164–193). New York: Guilford Press.

Schlenker, B. R., & Britt, T. W. (1999). Beneficial impression management: Strategically controlling information to help friends. *Journal of Personality and Social Psychology, 76,* 559–573.

Schlenker, B. R., & Leary, M. R. (1982). Social anxiety and self-presentation: A conceptualization and model. *Psychological Bulletin, 92,* 641–669.

Schlenker, B. R., & Pontari, B. A. (2000). The strategic control of information: Impression management and self-presentation in daily life. In A. Tesser, R. B. Felson, & J. M. Suls (Eds.), *Psychological perspectives on self and identity* (pp. 199–232). Washington, DC: American Psychological Association.

Schmid, D. E. (1996, March 13). Americans are slower to get married, Census Bureau says. *The Bryan-College Station Eagle*, p. A14.

Schmidt, N., & Sermat, V. (1983). Measuring loneliness in different relationships. *Journal of Personality and Social Psychology, 44*, 1038–1047.

Schmitt, J. P., & Kurdek, L. A. (1985). Age and gender differences in and personality correlates of loneliness in different relationships. *Journal of Personality Assessment, 49*, 485–496.

Schultz, N. R., Jr., & Moore, D. (1986). The loneliness experience of college students: Sex differences. *Personality and Social Psychology Bulletin, 12*, 111–119.

Schultz, N. R., Jr., & Moore, D. (1988). Loneliness: Differences across three age levels. *Journal of Social and Personal Relationships, 5*, 275–284.

Schutz, A. (1999). It was your fault! Self-serving biases in autobiographical accounts of conflicts in married couples. *Journal of Social and Personal Relationships, 16*, 193–208.

Schwab, S. H., Scalise, J. J., Ginter, E. J., & Whipple, G. (1998). Self-disclosure, loneliness and four interpersonal targets: Friend, group of friends, stranger, and group of strangers. *Psychological Reports, 82*, 1264–1266.

Schwartz, P., & Rutter, V. (1998). *The gender of sexuality*. Thousand Oaks, CA: Pine Forge Press.

Seal, S. W., Agostinelli, G., & Hannett, C. A. (1994). Extradyadic romantic involvement: Moderating effects of sociosexuality and gender. *Sex Roles, 3*, 1–22.

Sears, D. O. (1986). College sophomores in the laboratory: Influences of a narrow data base on social psychology's view of human nature. *Journal of Personality and Social Psychology, 51*, 515–530.

Secord, P. F. (1983). Imbalanced sex ratios: The social consequences. *Personality and Social Psychology Bulletin, 9*, 525–543.

Sedikides, C., Campbell, W. K., Reeder, G. D., & Elliot, A. J. (1998). The self-serving bias in relational context. *Journal of Personality and Social Psychology, 74*, 378–386.

Sedikides, C., Oliver, M. B., & Campbell, W. K. (1994). Perceived benefits and costs of romantic relationships for women and men: Implications for exchange theory. *Personal Relationships, 1*, 5–21.

Sedikides, C., & Strube, M. J. (1997). Self-evaluation: To thine own self be good, to thine own self be true, and to thine own self be better. In M. Zanna (Ed.), *Advances in experimental social psychology* (Vol. 29, pp. 209–269). San Diego: Academic Press.

Segal, M. W. (1974). Alphabet and attraction: An unobtrusive measure of the effect of propinquity in a field setting. *Journal of Personality and Social Psychology, 30*, 654–657.

Segrin, C. (1998). Disrupted interpersonal relationships and mental health problems. In B. H. Spitzberg & W. R. Cupach (Eds.), *The dark side of close relationships* (pp. 327–365). Mahwah, NJ: Erlbaum.

Seiffge-Krenke, I. (1997). Imaginary companions in adolescence: Sign of a deficient or positive development? *Journal of Adolescence, 20*, 137–154.

Seligman, M. E. P. (1995). The effectiveness of psychotherapy: The Consumer Reports study. *American Psychologist, 50*, 965–974.

Selman, R. L. (1981). The child as a friendship philosopher. In S. R. Asher & J. M. Gottman (Eds.), *The development of children's friendships* (pp. 242–272). New York: Cambridge University Press.

Selman, R. L., & Jaquette, D. (1977). Stability and oscillation in interpersonal awareness: A clinical-developmental analysis. In C. B. Keasey (Ed.), *Nebraska Symposium on Motivation: Vol. 25. Social cognitive development* (pp. 261–304). Lincoln: University of Nebraska Press.

Sermat, V. (1980). Some situational and personality correlates of loneliness. In J. Hartog, J. R. Audy, & Y. A. Cohen (Eds.), *The anatomy of loneliness* (pp. 305–318). New York: International Universities Press.

Shackelford, T. K., & Buss, D. M. (1997). Cues to infidelity. *Personality and Social Psychology Bulletin, 23,* 1034–1045.

Shackelford, T. K., & Larsen, R. J. (1997). Facial asymmetry as an indicator of psychological, emotional, and physiological distress. *Journal of Personality and Social Psychology, 72,* 456–466.

Shadish, W. R., Ragsdale, K., Glaser, R. R., & Montgomery, L. M. (1995). The efficacy and effectiveness of marital and family therapy: A perspective from meta-analysis. *Journal of Marital and Family Therapy, 21,* 345–360.

Shaffer, D. R., & Bazzini, D. G. (1997). What do you look for in a prospective date? Reexamining the preferences of men and women who differ in self-monitoring propensities. *Personality and Social Psychology Bulletin, 23,* 605–616.

Shaffer, D. R., Pegalis, L. J., & Bazzini, D. G. (1996). When boy meets girl (revisited): Gender, gender-role orientation, and prospect of future interaction as determinants of self-disclosure among same- and opposite-sex acquaintants. *Personality and Social Psychology Bulletin, 22,* 495–506.

Shaffer, D. R., Ruammake, C., & Pegalis, L. J. (1990). The "opener": Highly skilled as interviewer or interviewee. *Personality and Social Psychology Bulletin, 16,* 511–520.

Shanteau, J., & Nagy, G. F. (1979). Probability of acceptance in dating choice. *Journal of Personality and Social Psychology, 37,* 522–533.

Sharp, E. A., & Ganong, L. H. (2000). Raising awareness about marital expectations: Are unrealistic beliefs changed by integrative teaching? *Family Relations, 49,* 71–76.

Sharpsteen, D. J. (1993). Romantic jealousy as an emotion concept: A prototype analysis. *Journal of Social and Personal Relationships, 10,* 69–82.

Sharpsteen, D. J., & Kirkpatrick, L. A. (1997). Romantic jealousy and adult romantic attachment. *Journal of Personality and Social Psychology, 72,* 627–640.

Shaver, P., & Brennan, K. A. (1990). Measures of depression and loneliness. In J. P. Robinson, P. R. Shaver, & L. S. Wrightsman (Eds.), *Measures of personality and social psychological attitudes* (pp. 195–289). Orlando, FL: Academic Press.

Shaver, P., Furman, W., & Buhrmester, D. (1985). Transition to college: Network changes, social skills, and loneliness. In S. Duck & D. Perlman (Eds.), *Understanding personal relationships: An interdisciplinary approach* (pp. 193–219). London: Sage.

Shaver, P. R., & Hazan, C. (1988). A biased overview of the study of love. *Journal of Social and Personal Relationships, 5,* 573–501.

Shaver, P. R., Hazan, C., & Bradshaw, D. (1988). Love as attachment: The integration of three behavioral systems. In R. J. Sternberg & M. L. Barnes (Eds.), *The psychology of love* (pp. 68–99). New Haven, CT: Yale University Press.

Shaver, P. R., Morgan, H. J., & Wu, S. (1996). Is love a "basic" emotion? *Personal Relationships, 3,* 81–96.

Shaver, P., & Rubenstein, C. (1980) Childhood attachment experience and adult loneliness. In L. Wheeler (Ed.), *Review of personality and social psychology* (Vol. 1, pp. 42–73). Beverly Hills, CA: Sage.

Shepperd, J. A., & Strathman, A. J. (1989). Attractiveness and height: The role of stature in dating preference, frequency of dating, and perceptions of attractiveness. *Personality and Social Psychology Bulletin, 15,* 617–627.

Shettel-Neuber, J., Bryson, J. B., & Young, L. E. (1978). Physical attractiveness of the "other person" and jealousy. *Personality and Social Psychology Bulletin, 4*, 612–615.

Shibazaki, K., & Brennan, K. A. (1998). When birds of different feathers flock together: A preliminary comparison of intra-ethnic and inter-ethnic dating relationships. *Journal of Social and Personal Relationships, 15*, 248–256.

Shotland, R. L. (1989). A model of the causes of date rape in developing and close relationships. In C. Hendrick (Ed.), *Review of personality and social psychology: Vol. 10. Close relationships* (pp. 247–270). Newbury Park, CA: Sage.

Shotland, R. L., & Craig, J. M. (1988). Can men and women differentiate between friendly and sexually-interested behavior? *Social Psychology Quarterly, 51*, 66–73.

Sicoly, F., & Ross, M. (1978). *Interpersonal perceptions of division of labor and marital satisfaction.* Unpublished paper. University of Waterloo, Toronto, Ontario.

Sillars, A. L. (1985). Interpersonal perception in relationships. In W. Ickes (Ed.), *Compatible and incompatible relationships* (pp. 277–305). New York: Springer-Verlag.

Sillars, A. L. (1998). (Mis)understanding. In B. H. Spitzberg & W. R. Cupach (Eds.), *The dark side of close relationships* (pp. 73–102). Mahwah, NJ: Erlbaum.

Sillars, A. L., Folwell, A. L., Hill, K. C., Maki, B. K., Hurst, A. P., & Casano, R. A. (1994). Marital communication and the persistence of understanding. *Journal of Social and Personal Relationships, 11*, 611–617.

Simpson, J. A. (1990). Influence of attachment styles on romantic relationships. *Journal of Personality and Social Psychology, 59*, 971–980.

Simpson, J. A., Campbell, B., & Berscheid, E. (1986). The association between romantic love and marriage: Kephart (1967) twice revisited. *Personality and Social Psychology Bulletin, 12*, 363–372.

Simpson, J. A., & Gangestad, S. W. (1991). Individual differences in sociosexuality: Evidence for convergent and discriminant validity. *Journal of Personality and Social Psychology, 60*, 870–883.

Simpson, J. A., Ickes, W., & Blackstone, T. (1995). When the head protects the heart: Empathic accuracy in dating relationships. *Journal of Personality and Social Psychology, 69*, 629–641.

Simpson, J. A., Ickes, W., & Grich, J. (1999). When accuracy hurts: Reactions of anxious-ambivalent dating partners to a relationship-threatening situation. *Journal of Personality and Social Psychology, 76*, 754–769.

Simpson, J. A., Ickes, W., & Orina, M. (2001). Empathic accuracy and preemptive relationship maintenance. In J. H. Harvey & A. E. Wenzel (Eds.), *Close romantic relationships: Maintenance and enhancement,* (pp. 27–46). Mahwah, NJ: Erlbaum.

Simpson, J. A., Rholes, W. S., & Nelligan, J. S. (1992). Support seeking and support giving within couples in an anxiety-provoking situation: The role of attachment styles. *Journal of Personality and Social Psychology, 62*, 434–446.

Singh, D. (1993). Adaptive significance of waist-to-hip ratio and female physical attractiveness. *Journal of Personality and Social Psychology, 65*, 293–307.

Singh, D. (1994). Is thin really beautiful and good? Relationship between waist-to-hip ratio (WHR) and female attractiveness. *Personality and Individual Differences, 16*, 123–132.

Singh, D. (1995). Female judgment of male attractiveness and desirability for relationships: Role of waist-to-hip ratio and financial status. *Journal of Personality and Social Psychology, 69*, 1089–1101.

Singh, D. & Luis, S. (1995). Ethnic and gender consensus for the effect of waist-to-hip ratio on judgments of women's attractiveness. *Human Nature, 6*, 51–65.

Slater, P. E. (1968). Some social consequences of temporary systems. In W. G. Bennes & P. E. Slater (Eds.), *The temporary society* (pp.77–96). New York: Harper & Row.

Sluzki, C. E. (1978). Marital therapy from a systems theory perspective. In T. J. Paolino, Jr., & B. McCrady (Eds.), *Marriage and marital therapy: Psychoanalytic, behavioral and systems theory perspectives* (pp. 366–394). New York: Brunner/Mazel.

Smith, A. E., Jussim, L., & Eccles, J. (1999). Do self-fulfilling prophecies accumulate, dissipate, or remain stable over time? *Journal of Personality and Social Psychology, 77,* 548–565.

Smith, T. W. (1994). *The demography of sexual behavior.* Menlo Park, CA: Kaiser Family Foundation.

Snodgrass, S. E. (1985). Women's intuition: The effect of subordinate role on interpersonal sensitivity. *Journal of Personality and Social Psychology, 49,* 146–155.

Snodgrass, S. E. (1992). Further effects of role versus gender on interpersonal sensitivity. *Journal of Personality and Social Psychology, 62,* 154–158.

Snyder, C. R., Higgins, R. L., & Stucky, R. J. (1983). *Excuses: Masquerades in search of grace.* New York: Wiley.

Snyder, M. (1974). The self-monitoring of expressive behavior. *Journal of Personality and Social Psychology, 30,* 526–537.

Snyder, M. (1981). Seek, and ye shall find: Testing hypotheses about other people. In E. T. Higgins, C. P. Herman, & M. P. Zanna (Eds.), *Social cognition: The Ontario symposium* (Vol. 1, pp. 277–303). Hillsdale, NJ: Erlbaum.

Snyder, M. (1987). *Public appearances, private realities: The psychology of self-monitoring.* New York: W. H. Freeman.

Snyder, M., Berscheid, E., & Glick, P. (1985). Focusing on the exterior and the interior: Two investigations of the initiation of personal relationships. *Journal of Personality and Social Psychology, 48,* 1427–1439.

Snyder, M., Berscheid, E., & Matwychuk, A. (1988). Orientations toward personnel selection: Differential reliance on appearance and personality. *Journal of Personality and Social Psychology, 54,* 972–979.

Snyder, M., & DeBono, K. G. (1985). Appeals to image and claims about quality: Understanding the psychology of advertising. *Journal of Personality and Social Psychology, 49,* 586–597.

Snyder, M., & Gangestad, S. (1986). On the nature of self-monitoring: Matters of assessment, matters of validity. *Journal of Personality and Social Psychology, 51,* 125–139.

Snyder, M., Gangestad, S., & Simpson, J. A. (1983). Choosing friends as activity partners: The role of self-monitoring. *Journal of Personality and Social Psychology, 45,* 1061–1072.

Snyder, M., & Simpson, J. A. (1984). Self-monitoring and dating relationships. *Journal of Personality and Social Psychology, 47,* 1281–1291.

Snyder, M., & Simpson, J. A. (1987). Orientations toward romantic relationships. In D. Perlman & S. Duck (Eds.), *Intimate relationships: Development, dynamics, and deterioration* (pp. 45–62). Newbury Park, CA: Sage.

Snyder, M., Simpson, J. A., & Gangestad, S. (1986). Personality and sexual relations. *Journal of Personality and Social Psychology, 51,* 181–190.

Snyder, M., & Swann, W. B., Jr. (1978a). Behavioral confirmation in social interaction: From social perception to social reality. *Journal of Experimental Social Psychology, 14,* 148–163.

Snyder, M., & Swann, W. B., Jr. (1978b). Hypothesis-testing processes in social interaction. *Journal of Personality and Social Psychology, 36,* 1202–1212.

Snyder, M., Tanke, E. D., & Berscheid, E. (1977). Social perception and interpersonal behavior: On the self-fulfilling nature of social stereotypes. *Journal of Personality and Social Psychology, 35,* 656–666.

Solano, C. H., Batten, P. G., & Parish, E. A. (1982). Loneliness and patterns of self-disclosure. *Journal of Personality and Social Psychology, 43,* 524–531.

Solano, C. H., & Koester, N. H. (1989). Loneliness and communication problems: Subjective anxiety or objective skills? *Personality and Social Psychology Bulletin, 15,* 126–133.

Soldz, S., & Vaillant, G. E. (1999). The Big Five personality traits and the life course: A 45-year longitudinal study. *Journal of Research in Personality, 33,* 208–232.

South, S. J. (1988). Sex ratios, economic power, and women's roles: A theoretical extension and empirical test. *Journal of Marriage and the Family, 50,* 19–31.

South, S. J., & Lloyd, K. M. (1995). Spousal alternatives and marital dissolution. *American Sociological Review, 60,* 21–35.

Spanier, G. B., & Margolis, R. L. (1983). Marital separation and extramarital sexual behavior. *Journal of Sex Research, 19,* 23–48.

Spence, J. T., & Helmreich, R. (1981). Androgyny vs. gender schema: A comment on Bem's gender schema theory. *Psychological Review, 88,* 365–368.

Spencer, S. (1980). *Endless love.* New York: Avon Books.

Spitzberg, B. H. (1999). An analysis of empirical estimates of sexual aggression victimization and perpetration. *Violence and Victims, 14,* 241–260.

Spitzberg, B. H., & Canery, D. J. (1985). Loneliness and relationally competent communication. *Journal of Social and Personal Relationships, 2,* 387–402.

Spitzberg, B. H., & Cupach, W. R. (Eds.). (1998). *The dark side of close relationships.* Mahwah, NJ: Erlbaum.

Spitzer, B. L., Henderson, K. A., & Zivian, M. T. (1999). Gender differences in population versus media body sizes: A comparison over four decades. *Sex Roles, 40,* 545–565.

Sprecher, S. (1985). Sex differences in bases of power in dating relationships. *Sex Roles, 12,* 449–462.

Sprecher, S. (1986). The relation between inequity and emotions in close relationships. *Social Psychology Quarterly, 49,* 309–321.

Sprecher, S. (1987). The effects of self-disclosure given and received on affection for an intimate partner and stability of the relationship. *Journal of Social and Personal Relationships, 4,* 115–127.

Sprecher, S. (1989). The importance to males and females of physical attractiveness, earning potential, and expressiveness in initial attraction. *Sex Roles, 21,* 591–607.

Sprecher, S. (1992). How men and women expect to feel and behave in response to inequity in close relationships. *Social Psychology Quarterly, 55,* 57–69.

Sprecher, S. (1998a). The effect of exchange orientation on close relationships. *Social Psychology Quarterly, 61,* 220–231.

Sprecher, S. (1998b). Insiders' perspectives on reasons for attraction to a close other. *Social Psychology Quarterly, 61,* 287–300.

Sprecher, S. (1998c). Social exchange theories and sexuality. *Journal of Sex Research, 35,* 32–44.

Sprecher, S. (1999, June). *Equity and other social exchange variables in close, heterosexual relationships: Associations with satisfaction, commitment, and stability.* Paper presented at the meeting of the American Sociological Association, Chicago.

Sprecher, S., Aron, A., Hatfield, E., Cortese, A., Potapova, E., & Levitskaya, A. (1994). Love: American style, Russian style, and Japanese style. *Personal Relationships, 1,* 349–369.

Sprecher, S., & Duck, S. (1994). Sweet talk: The importance of perceived communication for romantic and friendship attraction experienced during a get-acquainted date. *Personality and Social Psychology Bulletin, 20,* 391–400.

Sprecher, S., & Felmlee, D. (1997). The balance of power in romantic heterosexual couples over time from "his" and "her" perspectives. *Sex Roles, 37,* 361–380.

Sprecher, S., & McKinney, K. (1993). *Sexuality.* Newbury Park, CA: Sage.

Sprecher, S., McKinney, K., & Orbuch, T. L. (1987). Has the double standard disappeared? An experimental test. *Social Psychology Quarterly, 50,* 24–31.

Sprecher, S., & Metts, S. (1989). Development of the "Romantic Beliefs Scale" and examination of the effects of gender and gender-role orientation. *Journal of Social and Personal Relationships, 6,* 387–411.

Sprecher, S., & Metts, S. (1999). Romantic beliefs: Their influence on relationships and patterns of change over time. *Journal of Social and Personal Relationships, 16,* 834–851.

Sprecher, S., Metts, S., Burleson, B., Hatfield, E., & Thompson, A. (1995). Domains of expressive interaction in intimate relationships: Associations with satisfaction and commitment. *Family Relations, 44,* 203–210.

Sprecher, S., & Regan, P. C. (1996). College virgins: How men and women perceive their sexual status. *Journal of Sex Research, 33,* 3–15.

Sprecher, S., & Regan, P. C. (1998). Passionate and companionate love in courting and young married couples. *Sociological Inquiry, 68,* 163–185.

Sprecher, S., Regan, P. C., & McKinney, K. (1998). Beliefs about the outcomes of extramarital sexual relationships as a function of the gender of the "cheating spouse." *Sex Roles, 38,* 301–311.

Sprecher, S., Regan, P. C., McKinney, K., Maxwell, K., & Wazienski, R. (1997). Preferred level of sexual experience in a date or mate: The merger of two methodologies. *Journal of Sex Research, 34,* 327–337.

Sprecher, S., & Schwartz, P. (1994). Equity and balance in the exchange of contributions in close relationships. In M. J. Lerner & G. Mikula (Eds.), *Entitlement and the affectional bond: Justice in close relationships* (pp. 11–41). New York: Plenum.

Sprecher, S., & Sedikides, C. (1993). Gender differences in perceptions of emotionality: The case of close heterosexual relationships. *Sex Roles, 28,* 511–530.

Sprey, J. (1975). Family power and process: Toward a conceptual integration. In R. E. Cromwell & D. H. Olson (Eds.), *Power in families* (pp. 61–79). New York: Wiley.

Stack, S. (1995). *Gender, marriage and loneliness: A cross-national study.* Unpublished manuscript, Wayne State University.

Stack, S. (1998). Marriage, family and loneliness: A cross–national study. *Sociological Perspectives, 41,* 415–432.

Stafford, L., & Canary, D. J. (1991). Maintenance strategies and romantic relationship type, gender and relational characteristics. *Journal of Social and Personal Relationships, 8,* 217–242.

Stafford, L., & Dainton, M. (1994). The dark side of "normal" family interaction. In W. R. Cupach & B. H. Spitzberg (Eds.), *The dark side of interpersonal communication* (pp. 259–280). Hillsdale, NJ: Erlbaum.

Stall, R. D., Coates, T. J., & Hoff, C. (1988). Behavioral risk reduction for HIV infection among gay and bisexual men. *American Psychologist, 43,* 878–885.

Stanfield, J. R., & Stanfield, J. B. (1997). Where has love gone? Reciprocity, redistribution, and the Nurturance Gap. *Journal of Socio-Economics, 26,* 111–126.

Stanley, S. M., Blumberg, S. L., & Markman, H. J. (1999). Helping couples fight for their marriages: The PREP approach. In R. Berger & M. Hannah (Eds.), *Handbook of preventive approaches in couple therapy* (pp. 279–303). New York, NY: Brunner/Mazel.

Stanley, S. M., Bradbury, T. N., & Markman, H. J. (2000). Structural flaws in the bridge from basic research on marriage to interventions. *Journal of Marriage and the Family, 62,* 256–264.

Stanovich, K. (1998). *How to think straight about psychology* (5th ed.). New York: Longman.

Steele, C. M., & Josephs, R. A. (1990). Alcohol myopia: Its prized and dangerous effects. *American Psychologist, 45,* 921–933.

Steele, C. M., Critchlow, B., & Liu, T. J. (1985). Alcohol and social behavior: II. The helpful drunkard. *Journal of Personality and Social Psychology, 48,* 35–46.

Steil, J. M., & Hillman, J. L. (1993). The perceived value of direct and indirect influence strategies: A cross-cultural comparison. *Psychology of Women Quarterly, 17,* 457–462.

Steinglass, P. (1978). The conceptualization of marriage from a systems theory perspective. In T. J. Paolino, Jr., & B. McCrady (Eds.), *Marriage and marital therapy: Psychoanalytic, behavioral and systems theory perspectives* (pp. 298–365). New York: Brunner/Mazel.

Steinglass, P., (1987). A systems view of family interaction and psychopathology. In T. Jacobs (Ed.), *Family interaction and psychopathology* (pp. 25–65). New York: Plenum.

Steinmetz, S. K. (1978). Violence between family members. *Marriage and Family Review, 1,* 1–16.

Steinmetz, S. K. (1987). Family violence: Past, present, and future. In M. B. Sussman & S. K. Steinmetz (Eds.), *Handbook of marriage and the family* (pp. 725–765). New York: Plenum.

Steinmetz, S. K., & Lucca, J. S. (1988). Husband battering. In V. B. Van Hasselt, R. L. Morrison, A. S. Bellack, & M. Hersen (Eds.), *Handbook of family violence* (pp. 233–246). New York: Plenum.

Stephan, W., Berscheid, E., & Walster, E. (1971). Sexual arousal and heterosexual perception. *Journal of Personality and Social Psychology, 20,* 93–101.

Sternberg, R. J. (1986). A triangular theory of love. *Psychological Review, 93,* 119–135.

Sternberg, R. J. (1987). *The triangle of love: Intimacy, passion, commitment.* New York: Basic Books.

Sternberg, R. J. (1998). *Cupid's arrow: The course of love through time.* New York: Cambridge University Press.

Stets, J. E. (1990). Verbal and physical aggression in marriage. *Journal of Marriage and the Family, 52,* 501–514.

Stevens, C. K., & Kristof, A. L. (1995). Making the right impression: A field study of applicant impression management during job interviews. *Journal of Applied Psychology, 80,* 587–606.

Stevens, J., Kumanyika, S. K., & Keil, J. E. (1994). Attitudes towards body size and dieting: Differences between elderly Black and White women. *American Journal of Public Health, 84,* 1322–1325.

Stewart, A. J., & Chester, N. L. (1982). Sex differences in human social motives: Achievement, affiliation, and power. In A. J. Stewart (Ed.), *Motivation and society* (pp. 172–218). San Francisco: Jossey-Bass.

Stewart, A. J., Copeland, A. P., Chester, N. L., Malley, J. E., & Barenbaum, N. B. (1997). *Separating together: How divorce transforms families.* New York: Guilford Press.

Stewart, A. J., & Rubin, Z. (1976). The power motive in the dating couple. *Journal of Personality and Social Psychology, 34,* 305–309.

Stier, D. S., & Hall, J. A. (1984). Gender differences in touch: An empirical and theoretical review. *Journal of Personality and Social Psychology, 47,* 440–459.

Stiles, W. B., Walz, N. C., Schroeder, M. A. B., Williams, L. L., & Ickes, W. (1996). Attractiveness and disclosure in initial encounters of mixed-sex dyads. *Journal of Social and Personal Relationships, 13,* 303–312.

Stillwell, A. M., & Baumeister, R. F. (1997). The construction of victim and perpetrator memories: Accuracy and distortion in role-based accounts. *Personality and Social Psychology Bulletin, 23,* 1157–1172.

Stinson, L., & Ickes, W. (1992). Empathic accuracy in the interactions of male friends versus male strangers. *Journal of Personality and Social Psychology, 62,* 787–797.

Stokes, J., & Levin, I. (1986). Gender differences in predicting loneliness from social network characteristics. *Journal of Personality and Social Psychology, 51,* 1069–1074.

Stone, L. (1988). Passionate attachments in the West in historical perspective. In W. Gaylin & E. Person (Eds.), *Passionate attachments: Thinking about love* (pp. 15–26). New York: Free Press.

Stone, M. R., & Brown, B. B. (1999). Identity claims and projections: Descriptions of self and crowds in secondary school. In J. A. McLellan & M. J. V. Pugh (Eds.), *The role of peer groups in adolescent social identity: Exploring the importance of stability and change* (pp. 7–20). San Francisco: Jossey-Bass.

Storms, M. D. (1980). Theories of sexual orientation. *Journal of Personality and Social Psychology, 38*, 783–792.

Storrs, D., & Kleinke, C. L. (1990). Evaluation of high and equal status male and female touchers. *Journal of Nonverbal Behavior, 14*, 87–95.

Strack, S., & Coyne, J. C. (1983). Social confirmation of dysphoria: Shared and private reactions to depression. *Journal of Personality and Social Psychology, 44*, 798–806.

Straus, M. A. (1995). Trends in cultural norms and rates of partner violence: An update to 1992. In S. M. Stith & M. A. Straus (Eds.), *Understanding partner violence: Prevalence, causes, consequences, and solutions* (pp. 30–33). Minneapolis, MN: National Council on Family Relations.

Straus, M. A., Gelles, R. J., & Steinmetz, S. K. (1980). *Behind closed doors.* Garden City, NY: Anchor Books.

Stroup, A. L., & Pollock, G. E. (1994). Economic consequences of marital dissolution. *Journal of Divorce and Remarriage, 22*, 37–54.

Strube, M. J. (1988). The decision to leave an abusive relationship: Empirical evidence and theoretical issues. *Psychological Bulletin, 104*, 236–250.

Strube, M. J., & Barbour, L. S. (1983). The decision to leave an abusive relationship: Economic dependence and psychological commitment. *Journal of Marriage and the Family, 45*, 785–794.

Stuart, R. B. (1969). Operant interpersonal treatment for marital discord. *Journal of Consulting and Clinical Psychology, 33*, 675–682.

Stuart, R. B. (1980). *Helping couples change: A social learning appeal to marital therapy.* New York: Guilford.

Stuckert, R. P. (1963). Role perception and marital satisfaction—A configurational approach. *Marriage and Family Living, 25*, 415–419.

Stueve, C. A., & Gerson, K. (1977). Personal relations across the life cycle. In C. S. Fischer, R. M. Jackson, C. A. Stueve, K. Gerson, & L. M. Jones, *Networks and places: Social relations in the urban setting* (pp. 79–98). New York: Free Press.

Surra, C. A., & Longstreth, M. (1990). Similarity of outcomes, interdependence, and conflict in dating relationships. *Journal of Personality and Social Psychology, 59*, 501–516.

Swann, W. B., Jr. (1996). *Self-traps: The elusive quest for higher self-esteem.* New York: W. H. Freeman.

Swann, W. B., Jr. (1997). The trouble with change: Self-verification and allegiance to the self. *Psychological Science, 8*, 177–180.

Swann, W. B., Jr., De La Ronde, C., & Hixon, J. G. (1994). Authenticity and positivity strivings in marriage and courtship. *Journal of Personality and Social Psychology, 66*, 857–869.

Swann, W. B., Jr., & Ely, R. J. (1984). A battle of wills: Self-verification versus behavioral confirmation. *Journal of Personality and Social Psychology, 46*, 1287–1302.

Swann, W. B., Jr., & Gill, M. J. (1997). Confidence and accuracy in person perception: Do we know what we think we know about our relationship partners? *Journal of Personality and Social Psychology, 73*, 747–757.

Swann, W. B., Jr., Hixon, J. G., Stein-Seroussi, A., & Gilbert, D. T. (1990). The fleeting gleam of praise: Cognitive processes underlying behavioral reactions to self-relevant feedback. *Journal of Personality and Social Psychology, 59*, 17–26.

Swann, W. B., Jr., & Pelham, B. (1999). *Who wants out when the going gets good? Psychological investment and preference for self-verifying college roommates.* Manuscript submitted for publication.

Swann, W. B., Jr., Silvera, D. H., & Proske, C. U. (1995). On "knowing your partner": Dangerous illusions in the age of AIDS? *Personal Relationships, 2,* 173–186.

Sweeney, P. D., Anderson, K., & Bailey, S. (1986). Attributional style in depression: A meta-analytic review. *Journal of Personality and Social Psychology, 50,* 974–991.

Szinovacz, M. E. (1981). Relationship among marital power measures. A critical review and an empirical test. *Journal of Comparative Family Studies, 12,* 151–169.

Tan, D. T. Y., & Singh, R. (1995). Attitudes and attraction: A developmental study of the similarity-attraction and dissimilarity–repulsion hypotheses. *Personality and Social Psychology Bulletin, 21,* 975–986.

Tanner, W. M., & Pollack, R. H. (1988). The effect of condom use and erotic instructions on attitudes toward condoms. *Journal of Sex Research, 25,* 537–541.

Tavris, C. (1989). *Anger: The misunderstood emotion.* New York: Touchstone.

Taylor, A. E. (1967). Role perception, empathy, and marriage adjustment. *Sociology and Social Research, 52,* 22–34.

Taylor, J. (1999). *Falling: The story of one marriage.* New York: Random House.

Taylor, M. (1999). *Imaginary companions and the children who create them.* New York: Oxford University Press.

Terman, L. M., Buttenweiser, P., Ferguson, L. W., Johnson, W. B., & Wilson, D. P. (1938). *Psychological factors in marital happiness.* New York: McGraw-Hill.

Terrell-Deutsch, B. (1999). The conceptualization and measurement of childhood loneliness. In K. J. Rotenberg & S. Hymel (Eds.), *Loneliness in childhood and adolescence* (pp. 11–33). New York: Cambridge University Press.

Tesser, A., Beach, S. R. H., Mendolia, M., Crepaz, N., Davies, B., & Pennebaker, J. (1998). Similarity and uniqueness focus: A paper tiger and a surprise. *Personality and Social Psychology Bulletin, 24,* 1190–1204.

Tesser, A., & Paulus, D. L. (1976). Toward a causal model of love. *Journal of Personality and Social Psychology, 34,* 1095–1105.

Testa, R. J., Kinder, B. N., & Ironson, G. (1987). Heterosexual bias in the perception of loving relationships of gay males and lesbians. *Journal of Sex Research, 23,* 163–172.

Thayer, S. (1988, March). Close encounters. *Psychology Today, 52,* 30–36.

Thibaut, J. W., & Kelley, H. H. (1959). *The social psychology of groups.* New York: Wiley.

Thomas, G. (2000, June). *Empathic accuracy in intimate relationships.* Paper presented at the meeting of the International Society for the Study of Personal Relationships, Brisbane.

Thomas, G., & Fletcher, G. J. O. (1997). Empathic accuracy in close relationships. In W. Ickes (Ed.), *Empathic accuracy* (pp. 194–217). New York: Guilford Press.

Thomas, G., Fletcher, G. J. O., & Lange, C. (1997). On-line empathic accuracy in marital interaction. *Journal of Personality and Social Psychology, 72,* 839–850.

Thompson, A. P. (1984). Emotional and sexual components of extramarital relations. *Journal of Marriage and the Family, 46,* 35–42.

Thompson, S. C., & Kelley, H. H. (1981). Judgments of responsibility for activities in close relationships. *Journal of Personality and Social Psychology, 41,* 469–477.

Thornton, A. (1989). Changing attitudes toward family issues in the United States. *Journal of Marriage and the Family, 51,* 873–893.

Thornton, B., & Moore, S. (1993). Physical attractiveness contrast effect: Implications for self-esteem and evaluations of the social self. *Personality and Social Psychology Bulletin, 19,* 474–480.

Tice, D. M., Butler, J. L., Muraven, M. B., & Stillwell, A. M. (1995). When modesty prevails: Differential favorability of self-presentation to friends and strangers. *Journal of Personality and Social Psychology, 69,* 1120–1138.

Tichenor, V. J. (1999). Status and income as gendered resources: The case of marital power. *Journal of Marriage and the Family, 61,* 638–650.

Tjaden, P., & Thoennes, N. (1999). *Extent, nature, and consequences of intimate partner violence: Findings from the National Violence Against Women Survey.* Washington, DC: National Institute of Justice/Centers for Disease Control and Prevention.

Todd, T. C. (1986). Structural-strategic marital therapy. In N. S. Jacobson & A. S. Gurman (Eds.), *Clinical handbook of marital therapy* (pp. 71–105). New York: Guilford.

Tolstedt, B. E., & Stokes, J. P. (1984). Self-disclosure, intimacy, and the de-penetration process. *Journal of Personality and Social Psychology, 46,* 84–90.

Tornstam, L. (1992). Loneliness in marriage. *Journal of Social and Personal Relationships, 9,* 197–217.

Townsend, P. (1968). Isolation, desolation and loneliness. In E. Shanas, P. Townsend, D. Wedderburn, H. Friis, P. Milhoj, & J. Stehouwer (Eds.), *Old people in three industrial societies* (pp. 258–287). New York: Atherton Press.

Traupmann, J., Hatfield, E., & Wexler, P. (1983). Equity and sexual satisfaction in dating couples. *British Journal of Social Psychology, 22,* 33–40.

Treas, J., & Giesen, D. (2000). Sexual infidelity among married and cohabiting Americans. *Journal of Marriage and the Family, 62,* 48–60.

Trent, K., & South, S. J. (1989). Structural determinants of the divorce rate: A cross-societal analysis. *Journal of Marriage and the Family, 51,* 391–404.

Triandis, H. C., McCusker, C., & Hui, C. H. (1990). Multimethod probe of individualism and collectivism. *Journal of Personality and Social Psychology, 59,* 1006–1020.

Trinke, S. J., & Bartholomew, K. (1997). Hierarchies of attachment relationships in young adulthood. *Journal of Social and Personal Relationships, 14,* 603–625.

Tucker, J. S., & Anders, S. L. (1999). Attachment style, interpersonal perception accuracy, and relationship satisfaction in dating couples. *Personality and Social Psychology Bulletin, 25,* 403–412.

Tucker, P., & Aron, A. (1993). Passionate love and marital satisfaction at key transition points in the family life cycle. *Journal of Social and Clinical Psychology, 12,* 135–147.

Turk, J. L., & Bell, N. W. (1972). Measuring power in families. *Journal of Marriage and the Family, 34,* 215–227.

Turque, B. (1992, September 14). Gays under fire. *Newsweek,* 35–40.

Twaite, J. A., Keiser, S., & Luchow, A. K. (1998). Divorce mediation: Promises, criticisms, achievements and current challenges. *Journal of Psychiatry and Law, 26,* 353–381.

Twenge, J. M. (1997). Changes in masculine and feminine traits over time: A meta-analysis. *Sex Roles, 36,* 305–325.

U.S. Bureau of the Census. (1976). *The statistical history of the United States: From colonial times to the present.* New York: Basic Books.

U.S. Bureau of the Census. (1995). Child support for custodial mothers and fathers: 1989. *Current Population Reports,* Series P-60, no. 187.

U.S. Bureau of the Census. (1998a). Marital status and living arrangements: March, 1998 (Update). *Current Population Reports,* Series P20-514.

U.S. Bureau of the Census. (1998b). *Statistical abstract of the United States: 1998. The national data book* (118th ed.). Washington, DC: Government Printing Office. Retrieved from the World Wide Web: http://www.census.gov:80/prod/3/98pubs/98statab/cc98stab.htm.

U.S. National Center for Health Statistics. (1995, March 22). Advance Report of Final Divorce Statistics, 1989 and 1990. *Monthly Vital Statistics Report, 43*(9).

United Nations Department of Economic and Social Affairs. (1999). *Demographic yearbook: 1997* (49th ed.). New York: Author.

van der Molen, H. T. (1990). A definition of shyness and its implications for clinical practice. In W. R. Crozier (Ed.), *Shyness and embarrassment: Perspectives from social psychology* (pp. 255–285). Cambridge: Cambridge University Press.

Vangelisti, A. L., & Young, S. L. (2000). When words hurt: The effects of perceived intentionality on interpersonal relationships. *Journal of Social and Personal Relationships, 17,* 393–424.

Van Horn, K. R., Arnone, A., Nesbitt, K., Desilets, L., Sears, T., Giffin, M., & Brudi, R. (1997). Physical distance and interpersonal characteristics in college students' romantic relationships. *Personal Relationships, 4,* 25–34.

Van Lange, P. A. M., & Rusbult, C. E. (1995). My relationship is better than—and not as bad as—yours is: The perception of superiority in close relationships. *Personality and Social Psychology Bulletin, 21,* 32–44.

Van Lange, P. A. M., Rusbult, C. E., Drigotas, S. M., Arriaga, X. B., Witcher, B. S., & Cox, C. L. (1997). Willingness to sacrifice in close relationships. *Journal of Personality and Social Psychology, 72,* 1373–1395.

Van Lange, P. A. M., Rusbult, C. E., Semin-Goossens, A., Görts, C. A., & Stalpers, M. (1999). Being better than others but otherwise perfectly normal: Perceptions of uniqueness and similarity in close relationships. *Personal Relationships, 6,* 269–289.

van Tilburg, T., de Jong Gierveld, J., Lecchini, L., & Marsiglia, D. (1998). Social integration and loneliness: A comparative study among older adults in the Netherlands and Tuscany, Italy. *Journal of Social and Personal Relationships, 15,* 740–754.

Vaughn, B. E., & Bost, K. K. (1999). Attachment and temperament: Redundant, independent, or interacting influences on interpersonal adaptation and personality development? In J. Cassidy & P. R. Shaver (Eds.), *Handbook of attachment: Theory, research, and clinical applications* (pp. 198–225). New York: Guilford Press.

Vaux, A. (1988a). Social and emotional loneliness: The role of social and personal characteristics. *Personality and Social Psychology Bulletin, 14,* 722–734.

Vaux, A. (1988b). Social and personal factors in loneliness. *Journal of Social and Clinical Psychology, 6,* 462–471.

Veniegas, R. C., & Peplau, L. A. (1997). Power and the quality of same-sex friendships. *Psychology of Women Quarterly, 21,* 279–297.

Veroff, J., & Feld, S. (1971). *Marriage and work in America: A study of motives and roles.* New York: Van Nostrand Reinhold.

Veroff, J., Hatchett, S. & Douvan, E. (1992). Consequences of participating in a longitudinal study of marriage. *Public Opinion Quarterly, 56 ,* 315–327.

Veroff, J., & Veroff, J. B. (1972). Reconsideration of a measure of power motivation. *Psychological Bulletin, 78,* 279–291.

Vincent, J. P., Weiss, R. L., & Birchler, G. R. (1975). Dyadic problem solving behavior as a function of marital distress and spousal vs. stranger interactions. *Behavior Therapy, 6,* 475–487.

Vittengl, J. R., & Holt, C. S. (1998). A time-series diary study of mood and social interaction. *Motivation and Emotion, 22,* 255–275.

Vittengl, J. R., & Holt, C. S. (2000). Getting acquainted: The relationship of self-disclosure and social attraction to positive affect. *Journal of Social and Personal Relationships, 17,* 53–66.

Vogel, D. L., Wester, S. R., & Heesacker, M. (1999). Dating relationships and the demand/withdraw pattern of communication. *Sex Roles, 41,* 297–306.

Vonk, R. (1998). The slime effect: Suspicion and dislike of likeable behavior toward superiors. *Journal of Personality and Social Psychology, 74,* 849–864.

Vorauer, J. D., & Ratner, R. K. (1996). Who's going to make the first move? Pluralistic ignorance as an impediment to relationship formation. *Journal of Social and Personal Relationships, 13,* 483–506.

Vuchinich, S. (1987). Starting and stopping spontaneous family conflicts. *Journal of Marriage and the Family, 49,* 591–601.

Waas, G. A., & Graczyk, P. A. (1998). Group interventions for the peer-rejected child. In K. C. Stoiber & T. R. Kratochwill (Eds.), *Handbook of group intervention for children and families* (pp. 141–158). Needham Heights, MA: Allyn & Bacon.

Waite, L. J., & Lillard, L. A. (1991). Children and marital disruption. *American Journal of Sociology, 96,* 930–953.

Walker, A. J. (1996). Couples watching television: Gender, power, and the remote control. *Journal of Marriage and the Family, 58,* 813–823.

Walker, L. E. A., & Browne, A. (1985). Gender and victimization by intimates. *Journal of Personality, 53,* 179–195.

Wall, S. M., Pickert, S. M., & Paradise, L. V. (1984). American men's friendships: Self-reports on meaning and changes. *Journal of Psychology, 116,* 179–186.

Waller, N. G., & Shaver, P. R. (1994). The importance of nongenetic influences on romantic love styles: A twin-family study. *Psychological Science, 5,* 268–274.

Waller, W. (1937). The rating and dating complex. *American Sociological Review, 2,* 727–734.

Waller, W. W., & Hill, R. (1951). *The family, a dynamic interpretation.* New York: Dryden Press.

Walster, E., Aronson, V., Abrahams, D., & Rottman, L. (1966). The importance of physical attractiveness in dating behavior. *Journal of Personality and Social Psychology, 4,* 508–516.

Walster, E., Traupmann, J., & Walster, G. W. (1978). Equity and extramarital sexuality. *Archives of Sexual Behavior, 7,* 127–141.

Walster, E., & Walster, G. W. (1978). *A new look at love.* Reading, MA: Addison-Wesley.

Walster, E., Walster, G. W., & Berscheid, E. (1978). *Equity: Theory and research.* Boston: Allyn & Bacon.

Walster, E., Walster, G. W., & Traupmann, J. (1978). Equity and premarital sex. *Journal of Personality, 36,* 82–92.

Warren, B. L. (1966). A multiple variable approach to the assortive mating phenomenon. *Eugenics Quarterly, 13,* 285–298.

Watson, D. (2000, February). *Personality similarity and relationship satisfaction.* Paper presented at the meeting of the Society for Personality and Social Psychology, Nashville.

Watson, D., Hubbard, B., & Wiese, D. (2000a). General traits of personality and affectivity as predictors of satisfaction in intimate relationships: Evidence from self- and partner-ratings. *Journal of Personality, 68,* 413–449.

Watson, D., Hubbard, B., & Wiese, D. (2000b). Self-other agreement in personality and affectivity: The role of acquaintanceship, trait visibility, and assumed similarity. *Journal of Personality and Social Psychology, 78,* 546–558.

Way, N., Cowal, K., Gingold, R., Pahl, K., & Bissessar, N. (2001). Friendship patterns among African American, Asian American, and Latino adolescents from low-income families. *Journal of Social and Personal Relationships, 18,* 29–53.

Webb, E. J., Campbell, D. T., Schwartz, R. D., Sechrest, L., & Grove, J. B. (1981). *Nonreactive measures in the social sciences* (2nd ed.). Boston: Houghton Mifflin.

Weber, A. L. (1992). The account-making process: A phenomenological approach. In T. L. Orbuch (Ed.), *Close relationship loss: Theoretical approaches* (pp. 174–191). New York: Springer-Verlag.

Weber, A. L., & Harvey, J. H. (1994). Accounts in coping with relationship loss. In A. L. Weber & J. H. Harvey (Eds.), *Perspectives on close relationships* (pp. 285–306). Boston: Allyn & Bacon.

Weeks, D. G., Michela, J. L., Peplau, L. A., & Bragg, M. E. (1980). The relation between loneliness and depression: A structural equation analysis. *Journal of Personality and Social Psychology 39*, 1238–1244.

Wegner, D. M., Erber, R., & Raymond, P. (1991). Transactive memory in close relationships. *Journal of Personality and Social Psychology, 61*, 923–929.

Wegner, D. M., & Gold, D. B. (1995). Fanning old flames: Emotional and cognitive effects of suppressing thoughts of a past relationship. *Journal of Personality and Social Psychology, 68*, 782–792.

Wegner, D. M., & Lane, J. D. (1995). From secrecy to psychopathology. In J. W. Pennebaker (Ed.), *Emotion, disclosure, & health* (pp. 25–46). Washington, DC: American Psychological Association.

Wegner, D. M., Lane, J. D., & Dimitri, S. (1994). The allure of secret relationships. *Journal of Personality and Social Psychology, 66*, 287–300.

Weiss, R. L. (1978). The conceptualization of marriage from a behavioral perspective. In T. J. Paolino, Jr., & B. McCrady (Eds.), *Marriage and marital therapy: Psychoanalytic, behavioral and systems theory perspectives* (pp. 165–239). New York: Brunner/Mazel.

Weiss, R. L., Birchler, G. R., & Vincent, J. P. (1974). Contractual models for negotiating training in marital dyads. *Journal of Marriage and the Family, 36*, 321–330.

Weiss, R. L., & Dehle, C. (1994). Cognitive behavioral perspectives on marital conflict. In D. D. Cahn (Ed.), *Conflict in personal relationships* (pp. 95–115). Hillsdale, NJ: Erlbaum.

Weiss, R. L., Hops, H., & Patterson, G. R. (1973). A framework for conceptualizing marital conflict, a technology for altering it, some data for evaluating it. In L. A. Hamerlynck, L. C. Handy, & E. J. Mash (Eds.), *Behavior change: Methodology, concepts and practice* (pp. 309–342). Champaign, IL: Research Press.

Weiss, R. S. (1973). *Loneliness.* Cambridge, MA: MIT Press.

Weiss, R. S. (1979). The emotional impact of marital separation. In G. Levinger & O. C. Moles (Eds.), *Divorce and separation: Context, causes, and consequences* (pp. 201–210). New York: Basic Books.

Wentzel, K. R., & Erdley, C. A. (1993). Strategies for making friends: Relations to social behavior and peer acceptance in early adolescence. *Developmental Psychology, 29*, 819–826.

West, C., & Zimmerman, D. H. (1983). Small insults: A study of interruptions in cross-sex conversations between unacquainted persons. In B. Thorne, C. Kramarge, & N. Henley (Eds.), *Language, gender and society* (pp. 102–117). Rowley, MA: Newbury House.

Wheeler, L., & Kim, Y. (1997). What is beautiful is culturally good: The physical attractiveness stereotype has different content in collectivistic cultures. *Personality and Social Psychology Bulletin, 23*, 795–800.

Wheeler, L., Reis, H., & Nezlek, J. (1983). Loneliness, social interaction, and sex roles. *Journal of Personality and Social Psychology, 45*, 943–953.

Whisman, M. A., & Allan, L. E. (1996). Attachment and social cognition theories of romantic relationships: Convergent or complementary perspectives? *Journal of Social and Personal Relationships, 13*, 263–278.

Whitaker, C. A. (1975). A family therapist looks at marital therapy. In A. S. Gurman & D. G. Rice (Eds.), *Couples in conflict* (pp. 165–174). New York: Jason Aronson.

Whitcher, S. J., & Fisher, J. D. (1979). Multidimensional reaction to therapeutic touch in a hospital setting. *Journal of Personality and Social Psychology, 37*, 87–96.

White, G. L. (1980a). Inducing jealousy: A power perspective. *Personality and Social Psychology Bullein, 6*, 222–227.

White, G. L. (1980b). Physical attractiveness and courtship progress. *Journal of Personality and Social Psychology, 39*, 660–668.

White, G. L. (1981a). A model of romantic jealousy. *Motivation and Emotion, 5*, 295–310.

White, G. L. (1981b). Some correlates of romantic jealousy. *Journal of Personality, 49*, 129–147.

White, G. L., Fishbein, S., & Rutstin, J. (1981). Passionate love: The misattribution of arousal. *Journal of Personality and Social Psychology, 41*, 56–62.

White, G. L., & Kight, T. D. (1984). Misattribution of arousal and attraction: Effects of salience of explanation of arousal. *Journal of Experimental Social Psychology, 20*, 55–64.

White, G. L., & Mullen, P. E. (1989). *Jealousy: Theory, research, and clinical strategies.* New York: Guilford Press.

White, J. W., & Koss, M. P. (1991). Courtship violence: Incidence in a national sample of higher education students. *Violence and Victims, 6*, 247–256.

White, L. K. (1990). Determinants of divorce: A review of research in the eighties. *Journal of Marriage and the Family, 52*, 904–912.

White, L. K., & Booth, A. (1991). Divorce over the life course: The role of marital happiness. *Journal of Family Issues, 12*, 5–21.

Whitley, B. E. (1988). The relation of gender-role orientation to sexual experience among college students. *Sex Roles, 19*, 619–638.

Whitley, B. E., Jr. (1993). Reliability and aspects of the construct validity of Sternberg's Triangular Love Scale. *Journal of Social and Personal Relationships, 10*, 475–480.

Whyte, W. F. (1955). *Street corner society: The social structure of an Italian slum.* Chicago: University of Chicago Press.

Widmer, E. D., Treas, J., & Newcomb, R. (1998). Attitudes toward nonmarital sex in 24 countries. *Journal of Sex Research, 35*, 349–358.

Wiederman, M. W. (1997). Extramarital sex: Prevalence and correlates in a national survey. *Journal of Sex Research, 34*, 167–174.

Wiederman, M. W. (1999). Volunteer bias in sexuality research using college student participants. *Journal of Sex Research, 36* , 59–66.

Wiederman, M. W., & Hurd, C. (1999). Extradyadic involvement during dating. *Journal of Social and Personal Relationships, 16*, 265–274.

Wiederman, M. W., & Kendall, E. (1999). Evolution, sex, and jealousy: Investigation with a sample from Sweden. *Evolution and Human Behavior, 20*, 121–128.

Wiggins, J. S. (Ed.). (1996). *The five-factor model of personality: Theoretical perspectives.* New York: Guilford Press.

Wile, D. B. (1995). *After the fight: Using your disagreements to build a stronger relationship.* New York: Guilford Press.

Wilkie, J. R., Ferree, M., & Ratcliff, K. S. (1998). Gender and fairness: Marital satisfaction in two-earner couples. *Journal of Marriage and the Family, 60*, 577–594.

Williams, J. C., & Solano, C. H. (1983). The social reality of feeling lonely: Friendship and reciprocation. *Personality and Social Psychology Bulletin, 9*, 237–242.

Williams, J. E., & Best, D. L. (1990). *Measuring sex stereotypes: A multination study* (Rev. ed.). Newbury Park, CA: Sage.

Williamson, G. M., & Clark, M. S. (1989). Providing help and desired relationship type as determinants of changes in moods and self-evaluations. *Journal of Personality and Social Psychology, 56*, 722–734.

Williamson, G. M., Clark, M. S., Pegalis, L. J., & Behan, A. (1996). Affective consequences of refusing to help in communal and exchange relationships. *Personality and Social Psychology Bulletin, 22,* 34–47.

Wills, T. A., Weiss, R. L., & Patterson, G. R. (1974). A behavioral analysis of the determinants of marital satisfaction. *Journal of Consulting and Clinical Psychology, 42,* 802–811.

Winstead, B. A., Derlega, V. J., & Rose, S. (1997). *Gender and close relationships.* Thousand Oaks, CA: Sage.

Winter, D. G. (1973). *The power motive.* New York: Free Press.

Winter, D. G. (1988). The power motive in women—and men. *Journal of Personality and Social Psychology, 54,* 510–519.

Winter, D. G., & Barenbaum, N. B. (1985). Responsibility and the power motive in women and men. *Journal of Personality, 53,* 335–355.

Winter, D. G., Stewart, A. J., & McClelland. D. C. (1977). Husband's motives and wife's career level. *Journal of Personality and Social Psychology, 35,* 159–166.

Wiseman, J., & Duck, S. (1995). Having and managing enemies: A very challenging relationship. In S. Duck & J. T. Wood (Eds.), *Confronting relationship challenges,* (pp. 43–72). Thousand Oaks, CA: Sage.

Wittenberg, M. T., & Reis, H. T. (1986). Loneliness, social skills, and social perception. *Personality and Social Psychology Bulletin, 12,* 121–130.

Wolfinger, N. H. (1999). Trends in the intergenerational transmission of divorce. *Demography, 36,* 425–420.

Woll, S. B. (1989). Personality and relationship correlates of loving styles. *Journal of Research in Personality, 23,* 480–505.

Woll, S. B., & Crosby, P. C. (1987). Videodating and other alternatives to traditional methods of relationship initiation. In W. H. Jones & D. Perlman (Eds.), *Advances in personal relationships* (Vol. 1, pp. 69–108). Greenwich, CT: JAI Press.

Wood, J. T., & Dindia, K. (1998). What's the difference? A dialogue about differences and similarities between men and women. In D. J. Canary & K. Dindia (Eds.), *Sex differences and similarities in communication: Critical essays and empirical investigations of sex and gender in interaction* (pp. 19–39). Mahwah, NJ: Erlbaum.

Wright, P. H. (1982). Men's friendships, women's friendships and the alleged inferiority of the latter. *Sex Roles, 8,* 1–20.

Wright, P. H. (1998). Toward an expanded orientation to the study of sex differences in friendship. In D. J. Canary and K. Dindia (Eds.), *Sex differences and similarities in communication: Critical essays and empirical investigations of sex and gender in interaction* (pp. 41–63). Mahwah, NJ: Erlbaum.

Wright, T. L., Ingraham, L. J., & Blackmer, D. R. (1985). Simultaneous study of individual differences and relationship effects in attraction. *Journal of Personality and Social Psychology, 47,* 1059–1062.

Wu, Z., & Balakrishnan, T. R. (1995). Dissolution of premarital cohabitation in Canada. *Demography, 32,* 521–532.

Xiaohe, X., & Whyte, M. K. (1990). Love matches and arranged marriages: A Chinese replication. *Journal of Marriage and the Family, 52,* 709–722.

Yarab, P. E., Allgeier, E. R., & Sensibaugh, C. C. (1999). Looking deeper: Extradyadic behaviors, jealousy, and perceived unfaithfulness in hypothetical dating relationships. *Personal Relationships, 6,* 305–316.

Zadro, L., & Williams, K. D. (2000, June). *The silent treatment: Ostracism in intimate relationships.* Paper presented at the meeting of the International Society for the Study of Personal Relationships, Brisbane.

Zammichieli, M. E., Gilroy, F. D., & Sherman, M. F. (1988). Relation between sex-role orientation and marital satisfaction. *Personality and Social Psychology Bulletin, 14,* 747–754.

Zanna, M. P., & Pack, S. J. (1975). On the self–fulfilling nature of apparent sex differences in behavior. *Journal of Experimental Social Psychology, 11,* 583–591.

Zillman, D. (1978). Attribution and misattribution of excitatory reactions. In J. H. Harvey, W. Ickes, & R. F. Kidd (Eds.), *New directions in attribution research* (Vol. 2, pp. 335–368). Hillsdale, NJ: Erlbaum.

Zillmann, D. (1984). *Connections between sex and aggression.* Hillsdale, NJ: Erlbaum.

Zillman, D. (1993). Mental control of angry aggression. In D. M. Wegner & J. W. Pennebaker (Eds.), *Handbook of mental control* (pp. 370–392). Englewood Cliffs, NJ: Prentice Hall.

Zillmann, D., Weaver, J. B., Mundorf, N., & Aust, C. F. (1986). Effects of an opposite-gender companion's affect to horror on distress, delight, and attraction. *Journal of Personality and Social Psychology, 51,* 586–594.

Zimbardo, P. G. (1977). *Shyness.* New York: Jove.

Zimmer-Gembeck, M. J. (1999). Stability, change and individual differences in involvement with friends and romantic partners among adolescent females. *Journal of Youth and Adolescence, 28,* 419–438.

Zimmerman, D. H., & West, C. (1975). Sex roles, interruptions and silences in conversations. In B. Thorne & N. Henley (Eds.), *Language and sex: Difference and dominance* (pp. 105–129). Rowley, MA: Newbury House.

Zuckerman, M., DePaulo, B. M., & Rosenthal, R. (1981). Verbal and nonverbal communication of deception. In L. Berkowitz (Ed.), *Advances in experimental social psychology* (Vol. 14, pp. 1–59). New York: Academic Press.

Zuckerman, M., Driver, R., & Koestner, R. (1982). Discrepancy as a cue to actual and perceived deception. *Journal of Nonverbal Behavior, 7,* 95–100.

Zuckerman, M., Koestner, R., & Alton, A. O. (1984). Learning to detect deception. *Journal of Personality and Social Psychology, 46,* 519–528.

Credits

Photo Credits: **page 8:** © Ariel Skelley/Stock Market; **page 43:** © Chuck Savage/Stock Market; **page 48:** © AP/Wide World Photos; **page 84:** © PhotoDisc; **page 97:** © Jean-Claude Lejeune/Stock Boston; **page 151:** © Bruce Ayres/Stone; **page 196:** © Suzanne Hanover/Everett Collection; **page 223:** © Areil Skelly/Stock Market; **page 263:** © Edwin Remsberg/Liaison Agency; **page 266:** © Joel Larson/Stone; **page 287:** © Bob Daemmerich/Stock Boston; **page 326:** © Ilene Perlman/Stock Boston; **page 358:** © Rhoda Sidney/Photo Edit; **page 360:** © Tom & Dee Ann McCarthy/Stock Market; **page 388:** © Bob Daemmerich/Stock Boston/PictureQuest; **page 418:** © David Young Wolf/Stone; **page 439:** © Zigy Kaluzny/Stone.

Chapter 1: **Figure 1.1:** Data from U.S. Census Bureau, 1998. **Figure 1.2:** Data from 1960–2000 Census Bureau. **Figure 1.3:** From F. A. Pedersen, "Secular Trends in Human Sex Ratios: Their Influence on Individual and Family Behavior," Human Nature, 2, No. 3, 271–291, 1991. **Table 1.1:** From P. Shaver, C. Hazan, and D. Bradshaw, "Love as Attachment: The Integration of Three Behavior Systems," in *The Psychology of Love,* by R. Sternberg and M. L. Barnes (eds), 1998, Yale University Press. Copyright © 1998 Yale. University Press. Reprinted with permission.

Chapter 2: **Figure 2.1:** Courtesy of William Ickes. **Table 2.3:** From V. H. Edmonds, "Marriage Conventionalization: Definition and Measurement," *Journal of Marriage and the Family, 26,* 681–688. National Council on Family Relationships, 3989 Central Avenue NE, #550, Minneapolis, MN 55421. Reprinted with permission.

Chapter 3: **Figure 3.1:** From David Myers, Social Psychology, 5th edition, Copyright © The McGraw-Hill Companies. Reproduced with permission of The McGraw- Hill Companies, Inc. **Table 3-2:** Findings from K. K. Dion, E. Berscheid, and E. Walster, 1972. "What Is Beautiful is Good," *Journal of Personality and Social Psychology, 24,* 285–290. **Figure 3.2:** From D. M. Buss and D. P. Schmitt, "Sexual Strategies Theory: An Evolutionary Perspective on Human Mating," *Psychological Review, 100,* 204–232, 1993. Copyright © 1993 by the American Psychological Association. Reprinted with permission. **Figure 3.3:** From Franzoi, *Social Psychology,* 2nd edition, Copyright © 2000 The McGraw-Hill Companies, Inc. Reproduced with permission of The McGraw-Hill Companies, Inc. **Figure 3.4:** From D. M. Buss and D. P. Schmitt, "Sexual Strategies Theory: An Evolutionary Perspective on Human Mating," *Psychological Review, 100,* 204–232, 1993. Copyright © 1993 by the American Psychological Association. Reprinted with permission.

Chapter 4: **Figure 4.1:** From W. B. Swann, Jr. and M. J. Gill, 1997. "Confidence and Accuracy in Person Perception: Do We Know What We Think We Know About Our Relationship Partners?" *Journal of Personality and Social Psychology, 73,* 747–757. **Figure 4.2:** Sharon S. Brehm and Saul Kassin, *Social Psychology.* Copyright © 1990 by Houghton Mifflin Company. Used with permission. **Table 4.1:** Reprinted by permission of Sage Publications Ltd from S. Sprecher and S. Metts, "Development of the 'Romantic Beliefs Scale' and Examination of the Effects of Gender and Gender-Role Orientation," *Journal of Social and Personal Relationships, 6*, 387–411. Copyright © 1989 Sage Publications Ltd. **Figure 4.3:** From M. R. Leary and R. S. Miller, *Social Psychology and Dysfunctional Behavior: Origins, Diagnosis, and Treatment*, 1986. Springer-Verlag. **Table 4.2:** From M. Snyder and S. Gangestad, "On the Nature of Self-Monitoring: Matters of Assessment, Matters of Validity," *Journal of Personality and Social Psychology, 51*, 125–139, 1986. Copyright © 1986 by the American Psychological Association. Reprinted with permission

Chapter 5:   **Figure 5.1:** Adapted from J. M. Gottman, C. Notarius, J. Gonson & H. Markman (1976) *A Couples Guide to Communication*, Research Press. **Table 5.1:** From M. L. Patterson "Functions of Nonverbal Behaviors in Intimate Relationships" In S. Duck (ed), *Handbook of Personal Relationships: Theory, Research, and Interventions*. © 1988. John Wiley and Sons. **Figure 5.2:** Adapted from I. H. Frieze, J. E. Parsons, P .B. Johnson, D. N. Ruble and G. L. Zellman, 1978. *Women and Sex Roles: A Social Psychological Perspective*. W. W. Norton, p. 330.

Chapter 6:   **Figure 6.2:** From J. M. Gottman and R. W. Levenson, "Marital Processes Predictive of Later Dissolution: Behavior, Physiology and Health," *Journal of Personality and Social Psychology, 63*, 221–233, 1992. Copyright © 1992 by the American Psychological Association. Reprinted with permission. **Figure 6.3:** From R. J. Eidelson, "Affiliative Rewards and Restrictive Costs in Developing Relationships," *British Journal of Social Psychology, 20*, 197–204, 1981. Reproduced with permission from *The British Journal of Social Psychology*, Copyright © The British Psychological Society. **Figure 6.4:** Adapted from R. J. Eidelson, "Interpersonal Satisfaction and Level of Involvement: A Curvilinear Relationship," *Journal of Personality and Social Psychology, 39*, 460–470, 1980. **Figure 6.5:** From B. R. Karney and T. N. Bradbury, "Neuroticism, Marital Interaction, and the Personal and Social Psychology," 72, 1075–1092, 1997. **Figure 6.6:** Figure from "The Investment Model: An Interdependence Analysis of Commitment Processes and Relationship Maintenance Phenomena," in *Communication and Relational Maintenance*, edited by D. J. Canary and L. Stafford, copyright © 1994 by Academic Press, reproduced by permission of the publisher.

Chapter 7:   **Table 7.2:** Adapted from R. L. Selman and D. Jaguette, "Stability and Oscillation in Interpersonal Awareness: A Clinical-Developmental Analysis." In C. B. Keasey (ed) *Nebraska Symposium on Motivation: Vol. 25. Social Cognitive Development*, pp. 261–304, 1977. University of Nebraska Press. **Box 7.2:** From R. L. Selman, "The Child as a Friendship Philosopher," in *The Development of Children's Friendships*, S. R. Asher and J. M. Gottman, eds, 1981, p. 242. Reprinted with the permission of Cambridge University Press. **Table 7.3:** From D. Buhrmester and W. Furman, "The Changing Functions of Friends in Childhood: A Neo-Sullivnian Perspective" in *Friendship and Social Interaction*, by V. J. Derlega and B. A. Winstead, eds., pp. 41–52. 1986. Reprinted with permission of Springer-Verlag. **Table 7.4:** Reprinted from *Social Forces, 62*. "A Research Note on Friendship, Gender, and Life Cycle," by C .S. Fischer and Stacey J. Oliker. Copyright © The University of North Carolina Press.

Chapter 8:   **Table 8.1:** Brehm, Sharon S., and Saul Kassin, *Social Psychology*. Copyright © 1990 by Houghton Mifflin Company. Used with permission. **Table 8.2:** E. Hatfield and R. L. Rapson, "Passionate Love: New Directions in Research," in *Advances in Personal Relationships*, W. L. Jones and D. Perlman, eds. Vol. 1, pp. 109–139, 1987. Copyright © Jessica Kingsley Publishers. **Table 8.4:** Brehm, Sharon S., and Saul Kassin, *Social Psychology*. Copyright © 1990 by Houghton Mifflin Company. Used with permission. **Figure 8.2:** Adapted from K. Bartholomew and P. R. Shaver,

"Methods of assessing adult attachment: Do they converge?" In J. A. Simpson and W. S. Rholes (eds.), *Attachment Theory and Close Relationships*, pp. 25–45, 1989. New York: Guilford Press and K. A. Brennan, C. L. Clark and "Adult Attachment: An Integrative Overview." J. A. Simpson and W. S. Rholes (eds.), *Attachment Theory and Close Relationships*, pp. 46–76, 1998. New York: Guilford Press. **Figure 8.3:** From David Myers, *Social Psychology*, 5th edition, Copyright © The McGraw-Hill Companies. Reproduced with permission of The McGraw-Hill Companies, Inc. **Figure 8.4:** From V. Call, S. Sprecher, and P. Schwartz, "The Incidence and Frequency of Marital Sex in a National Sample," *Journal of Marriage and the Family, 57, 639–652, 1995.*

Chapter 9:   **Table 9.1:** Adapted from E. D. Widmer, J. Tres and R. Newcomb, "Attitudes Toward Nonmarital Sex in 24 Countries." *Journal of Sex Research 35, 349–358, 1998.* **Figure 9.1:** Figure from *American Couples* by Philip B. Blumstein and Pepper S. Schwartz. Copyright © 1983 by Philip B. Blumstein and Pepper S. Schwartz. Reprinted by permission of HarperCollins Publishers, Inc. **Figure 9.2:** Figure from *American Couples* by Philip B. Blumstein and Pepper S. Schwartz. Copyright © 1983 by Philip B. Blumstein and Pepper S. Schwartz. Reprinted by permission of Harper-Collins Publishers, Inc. **Box 9.2:** From J. A. Simpson and S. W. Gangestad, "Individual Differences in Socio-Sexuality: Evidence for Convergent and Discriminant Validity," *Journal of Personality and Social Psychology, 60,* p. 883, 1991. Copyright © by the American Psychological Association. Reprinted with permission.

Chapter 10:   **Table 10.3:** From W. H. Jones & M. P. Burdette, in A. L. Weber & J. H. Harvey, Eds, "Betrayal in Relationships" in *Perspectives on Close Relationships.* Copyright © 1994 by Allyn & Bacon. Reprinted by permission. **Cartoon:** ZIGGY © 1974 ZIGGY AND FRIENDS, INC. Reprinted with permission of UNIVERSAL PRESS SYNDICATE. All rights reserved.

Chapter 12:   **Figure 12.1:** From Close Relationships by H. H. Kelley, E. Bershceid, A. Christensen, J. H. Harvey, T. L. Huston, G. Levinger, E. McClintock, L. A. Peplau, and D. R. Peterson © 1983 by W. H. Freeman and Company. Used with permission. **Table 12.1:** From S. K. Riesch, et al., "Topics of Conflict Between Parents and Young Adolescents," *Journal of the Society of Pediatric Nurses, 5,* 27–40, 2000. Reprinted with permission of Nurse Com, Inc. **Table 12.2:** From A. Christensen and C. L. Heavey, "Gender Differences in Marital Conflict: The Demand/Withdraw Interaction Pattern," in *Gender Issues in Contemporary Society,* by S. Oskamp and M. Costanzo, Eds., pp. 113–141. Copyright © 1993 by Sage Publications. Reprinted by permission of Sage Publications, Inc. **Figure 12.2:** From C. E. Rusbult, J. Verette, G. A. Whitney, L. F. Slovik, and I. Lipkus, "Accommodation Processes in Close Relationships: Theory and Preliminary Empirical Evidence," *Journal* p. 69, 1991. Copyright © 1991 by the American Psychological Corporation. Reprinted with permission. **Box 12.2:** From T. B. Holman and M. O. Jarvis, "Replicating and Validating Gottman's Couple Conflict Types Using Survey Data," unpublished manuscript, Brigham Young University, 2000. Reprinted with permission of Thomas B. Holman. **Excerpt:** From J. M. Gottman, "The Roles of Conflict Engagement: Escalation and Avoidance in Marital Interaction: A Longitudinal View of Five Types of Couples," *Journal of Consulting and Clinical Psychology, 61,* p. 10, 1993. Copyright © 1993 by the American Psychological Association. Reprinted with permission. **Table 12.3:** Adapted from G. R. Bach and P. Wyden, The Intimate Enemy. NY: Morrow. 1968. **Figure 12.3:** From M.A. Straus, "Measuring Intrafamily Conflict and Violence: The Conflict Tactics (CT) Scales," *Journal of Marriage and the Family, 41,* 75–88. Copyright © 1979 by Murray A. Straus. Reprinted with permission of Murray A. Straus. **Figure 12.4:** From M.A.

Straus, "Trends in Cultural Norms and Rates of Partner Violence: An Update to 1992." In S. M. Smith and M. A. Straus (eds.), *Understanding Partner Violence: Prevalence, Causes, Consequences and Solutions,* pp. 30–33. Reprinted with permission of Murray A. Straus. **Figure 12.5:** From E. Pence and M. Paymar, *Education Groups for Men Who Batter: The Duluth Model,* 1993. Reprinted with permission of Springer Publishing Company. **Table 12.4:** From B. H. Spitzberg, "An Analysis of Empirical Estimates of Sexual Aggression, Victimization and Perpetration," *Violence of Victims, 14,* 241–260, 1999. Reprinted with permission of Springer Publishing Company.

Chapter 13:   **Box 13.2:** From A. L. Weber & J. H. Harvey, Eds., *Perspectives on Close Relationships.* Copyright © 1994 by Allyn & Bacon. Reprinted by permission.

Chapter 14:   **Excerpt:** From S. Borys and D. Perlman, "Gender Differences in Loneliness," *Personality and Social Psychology Bulletin, 11,* 63–76. Copyright © 1985 by Sage Publications. Reprinted by permission of Sage Publications, Inc. **Table 14.1:** Reprinted with permission of Daniel W. Russell. **Table 14.2:** From C. Rubenstein, P. Shaver, and L.A. Peplau, "Loneliness," *Human Nature,* February 1979. **Figure 14.2:** From D. W. Russell, C. E. Cutrona, A. de la Mora, and R. B. Wallace, "Loneliness and Nursing Home Admission Among Rural Older Adults," *Psychology and Aging, 12,* 574–589, 1997. Copyright © 1997 by the American Psychological Association. Reprinted with permission. **Table 14.3:** From "Gender, Marriage and Loneliness: A Cross-National Study," by Steven J. Stack, Jr., Unpublished manuscript, Wayne State University. Reprinted with permission of Steven J. Stack, Jr. **Figure 14.3:** From C. Rubenstein, P. Shaver, and L.A. Peplan, "Loneliness," *Human Nature,* February 1979. **Table 14.4:** Brehm, Sharon S., and Saul Kassin, *Social Psychology.* Copyright © 1990 by Houghton Mifflin Company. Used with permission. **Table 14.5:** From *In Search of Intimacy* by Carin Rubenstein and Phillip Shaver, copyright © 1982 by Carin Rubenstein and Phillip Shaver. Used by permission of Dell Publishing, a division of Random House, Inc. **Table 14.6:** From K. S. Rook and L. A. Peplau, "Helping the Lonely" in *Loneliness: A Current Theory, Research & Therapy,* L. A. Peplau and D. Perlman, (eds.). Copyright © 1982. Reprinted by permission of John Wiley & Sons, Inc. **Table 14.7:** From K. S. Rook and L. A. Peplau, "Helping the Lonely" in *Loneliness: A Current Theory, Research & Therapy,* L. A. Peplau and D. Perlman, (eds.). Copyright © 1982. Reprinted by permission of John Wiley & Sons, Inc.

Chapter 15:   **Table 15.1:** From R. Wentzel and C. A. Erdley, "Strategies for Making Friends: Relations to Social Behavior and Peer Acceptance in Early Adolescence," *Developmental Psychology, 29,* 819–826, 1993. Copyright © 1993 by the American Psychological Association. Reprinted with permission. **Table 15.2:** "Equity in the Preservation of Personal Relationships" In *Close Romantic Relationships: Maintenance and Enhancement,* J. M. Harvey and A. E. Wenzel (Eds.), in press. **Table 15.3:** From N. S. Jacobson and G. Margolin, *Marital Therapy: Strategies Based on Social Learning and Behavior Exchange Principles,* 1979. Reprinted with permission of the authors. **Figure 15.1:** Caryl Rusbult, Nils Olsen, Judy L. Davis, and Margaret A. Hannon, "Commitment and Relationship Maintenance Mechanisms" in *Close Romantic Relationships: Maintenance and Enhancement,* J. M. Harvey and A. E. Wenzel (Eds.), in press.

Name Index

Abbey, A., 271, 273
Abernathy, T., 197
Ables, B. S., 442
Abrahams, D., 74
Abrahams, M. F., 319
Acitelli, A. K., 36, 44, 118, 432
Acker, M., 224, 241, 243
Acock, A. C., 379
Adams, G. R., 239
Adams, H. E., 284
Adams, J. M., 183
Adams, M., 327
Adams, R. G., 189, 205, 206, 209, 210, 211
Afifi, W., 297
Afifi, W. A., 299, 302
Agnew, C. R., 4, 183, 311
Agostinelli, G., 256
Agostinelli, J., 180
Aguinis, H., 317
Ahlberg, C., 23
Ahrons, C., 387–388, 392
Aida, Y., 319, 320
Ainsworth, M. D. S., 14
Akerlind, I., 400
Albrecht, S. L., 160, 161
Allan, L. E., 111
Allen, J., 233
Allen, J. B., 320
Allen, K., 83
Allen, M., 70, 144
Allgeier, E. R., 285
Altman, I., 138, 139, 140, 141, 142
Alton, A. O., 297
Altrocchi, I., 324
Alvarez, M. D., 103
Amato, P. R., 167, 302, 374, 380, 388, 389, 390
Ambady, N., 118, 130, 131
Anders, S. L., 118

Andersen, P. A., 129
Anderson, C. A., 281, 413
Anderson, D. E., 298
Anderson, J. L., 75
Anderson, P., 25
Anderson, P. A., 283, 284, 286, 287, 291
Andres, D., 262
Andrews, D. W., 330
Angleitner, A., 291
Ansell, E., 300
Ansfield, M. E., 279
Antill, J. K., 22
Antonucci, T. C., 209
Apt, C., 437, 452
Archer, J., 357
Archer, R., 143
Archibald, F. S., 408
Argyle, M., 191–192, 207
Arias, H., 330
Aristotle, 36, 210
Aron, A., 138, 143, 224, 232, 233, 241, 243, 244, 432
Aron, A. P., 226
Aron, E. N., 138, 232, 233, 243, 432
Aronson, E., 82, 286
Aronson, V., 74
Arriaga, X. B., 103, 158, 184, 345
Asch, S. E., 96
Asendorpf, J. B., 23, 280, 281
Asher, S. R., 201, 405
Ashmore, R. D., 72
Assh, S. D., 6
Athenstaedt, U., 296
Attridge, M., 10, 164, 173
Aube, J., 23, 145
Auerback, A., 269
Ault, L. K., 114
Auslander, N., 399

Aust, C. F., 225
Avrill, J. R., 166
Axtell, R. E., 130
Ayduk, O., 31
Aylmer, R. C., 443

Baack, D. W., 86
Babad, E., 131
Bach, G. R., 351
Back, K. W., 38, 69
Baeccman, C., 27
Bakeman, R., 56
Balakrishnan, T. R., 373
Baldwin, M. W., 16, 105, 110
Bank, A. L., 290
Bank, B. J., 213
Bannester, E. M., 308
Baral, R. L., 160
Barbee, A. P., 73, 74, 173
Barber, N., 12, 76
Barbi, K. B., 376
Barbour, L. S., 361
Barbre, A. R., 399
Barenbaum, N. B., 326, 383
Barenhoim, C., 195
Bargh, J. A., 147
Barling, J., 359
Barnes, K. E., 193
Barnes, M., 91
Barnes, R. D., 22
Barnett, O. W., 357, 359
Barrett, L. F., 138
Bart, P. B., 273
Bartholomew, K., 16, 111, 236–237, 238, 239, 346, 359, 408
Bator, R. J., 138
Batten, P. G., 410
Baucom, D. H., 446
Bauman, L. J., 262

535

Subject Index